Lecture Notes in Computer Science 12875

More information about this subseries at http://www.springer.com/series/7409

Artem Polyvyanyy · Moe Thandar Wynn ·
Amy Van Looy · Manfred Reichert (Eds.)

Business Process Management

19th International Conference, BPM 2021
Rome, Italy, September 06–10, 2021
Proceedings

 Springer

Editors
Artem Polyvyanyy [iD]
The University of Melbourne
Carlton, VIC, Australia

Amy Van Looy [iD]
Ghent University
Ghent, Belgium

Moe Thandar Wynn [iD]
NICTA Queensland Research Lab
Queensland University of Technology
Brisbane, QLD, Australia

Manfred Reichert [iD]
Institut fur Datenbanken, Info System
Universitat Ulm
Ulm, Germany

ISSN 0302-9743   ISSN 1611-3349 (electronic)
Lecture Notes in Computer Science
ISBN 978-3-030-85468-3   ISBN 978-3-030-85469-0 (eBook)
https://doi.org/10.1007/978-3-030-85469-0

LNCS Sublibrary: SL3 – Information Systems and Applications, incl. Internet/Web, and HCI

This Springer imprint is published by the registered company Springer Nature Switzerland AG
The registered company address is: Gewerbestrasse 11, 6330 Cham, Switzerland

Preface

This volume contains the papers presented at the 19th International Conference on Business Process Management (BPM 2021), held during September 6–10, 2021, in Rome, Italy. Like the 2020 edition, BPM 2021 faced the international COVID-19 pandemic, and we had to tackle many uncertainties about how to practically organize this conference. In addition, the series of lockdown situations forced many of us to change our way of working and take on additional duties (such as online teaching and lecture recording) in order to continuously support our students at all levels. Despite this increasing workload, we could only observe how flexible the BPM community is, without losing sight of conducting and completing research in this domain. We are proud to share an excellent conference program, which we put together thanks to such a resilient BPM community.

While last year's edition was fully online, BPM 2021 was able to connect its members in a hybrid setting. Thanks to the latest technological advancements, conference participants could attend talks and discussions in a mixed setting, allowing for physical and online presence. This hybrid mode also reflects the desire of many researchers to re-connect after almost one and a half years of mandatory telework. In this context, the conference received 123 submissions. The committee decided to accept 23 papers, which reflects an acceptance rate of 18.7%. The program also included three invited keynote talks.

BPM 2021 was organized with full respect to BPM's philosophy, containing three research tracks that correspond to the different communities of the conference series. First, the "Foundations" track reflects the computer science tradition in BPM. Track II, "Engineering," is focused on information systems engineering. Finally, the "Management" track covers the approach represented by information systems management. All 123 papers were first screened based on their fit to the conference call (in terms of topic and template use) as well as the completeness of the manuscript, leading to 92 submissions that reached the single-blind review round (24 in the "Foundations" track, 41 in the "Engineering" track, and 27 in the "Management" track). In the remainder of this preface, we would like to thank the many people for helping us to realize the BPM 2021 conference.

To account for the different research topics and methods per track, a dedicated track chair and Program Committee were responsible for coordinating each track. The respective track chairs of BPM 2021 were: Artem Polyvyanyy (Track I, "Foundations"), Moe Thandar Wynn (Track II, "Engineering"), and Amy Van Looy (Track III, "Management"). Manfred Reichert acted as the Consolidation Chair. Three to four Program Committee members reviewed each paper, and a Senior Program Committee member was responsible for moderating the discussion and summarizing a meta-review, assuring a thorough quality check. Besides the 23 accepted papers in this volume (i.e., 5 in Track I, 12 in Track II, and 6 in Track III), our in-depth screening also resulted in 16 submissions appearing in the BPM Forum, published in a separate volume of the Springer LNBIP series.

The studies accepted in this volume show the wide variety of topics and research methods that characterize the BPM community. For instance, we can report on diverse insights obtained via behavioral-science thinking (e.g., case studies) and design-science research (e.g., method development). Topics range from process modeling and mining, over conformance checking, to stakeholder engagement and digital process innovation. Similar to last year, we highly embraced the principles of "Open Science," including reproducibility and replicability. As a result, we asked authors to add a link in their papers to one or more repositories, where the reviewers could find additional information (e.g., prototypes, interview protocols, questionnaires). This volume also reflects the "Open Science" principle by including a large number of chapters with permanent links to such artifacts.

Besides the accepted research papers, BPM 2021 was enriched by three renowned keynote speakers. Firstly, Hajo Reijers, from Utrecht University, provided us with a historical perspective on BPM by reflecting on how the ancient Romans organized their work processes and linking modern and past process management practices. Secondly, Stefanie Rinderle-Ma, from the Technical University of Munich, inspired us to think about sensor-aware process analysis and interactive process automation. By offering real-world use cases, she shared her experience with the EU project ADVENTURE for adopting process technology at a factory site. Thirdly, Giuseppe De Giacomo, from Sapienza Università di Roma, spoke about artificial intelligence-based process synthesis for BPM, while making a specific link to declarative BPM. In addition, this volume features four short papers that complement the accepted BPM 2021 tutorials.

This volume and the research behind it would not have been possible without the exceptional support of different BPM committees. More specifically, besides the main conference and the BPM Forum, BPM 2021 was also the venue of multiple gatherings within committees (each with dedicated chairs), responsible for workshops, demonstrations and resources, tutorials and panels, a doctoral consortium, an industry forum, a Robotic Process Automation forum, a Blockchain forum, as well as for publicity.

We wish to extend a special thanks to the track's Program Committees and Senior Program Committees. We greatly appreciate their assistance in keeping an intensive review procedure running and guaranteeing that only relevant and rigorous studies be included in this volume. We also acknowledge our sponsors for their support in making this conference happen: Signavio, Celonis, DCR Solutions, P4I – Partners4Innovation, Springer, Sapienza Università di Roma, and the organizing agency Consulta Umbria. Finally, we also appreciate the use of EasyChair for streamlining an intensive reviewing period.

To conclude, special acknowledgment goes to Massimo Mecella, the general chair of BPM 2021. We are especially thankful for his efforts in facilitating the conference, arranging all practical details, and replying to hundreds of emails. We also wish to show our appreciation of the Organizing Committee, including Simone Agostinelli, Dario Benvenuti, Eleonora Bernasconi, Francesca de Luzi, Lauren Stacey Ferro, Francesco Leotta, Andrea Marrella, Francesco Sapio, and Silvestro Veneruso. We are grateful for all of their efforts to concretize this conference, dealing with the complicated COVID-19 pandemic challenges, and offering a hybrid mode with a physical and online organization. Their motivation and inspiration have acted as a great incentive to glue our BPM community, even in challenging times.

Finally, we wish all the readers a nice reading experience.

September 2021

Artem Polyvyanyy
Moe Thandar Wynn
Amy Van Looy
Manfred Reichert

Organization

The 19th International Conference on Business Process Management (BPM 2021) was organized by the research group on Data Management, Service-Oriented Computing, and Process Management of the Dipartimento di Ingegneria informatica automatica e gestionale Antonio Ruberti, Sapienza Università di Roma, Italy. The conference was conducted in a hybrid mode due to the ongoing travel restrictions in many countries imposed by the global COVID-19 pandemic. Therefore, the participants could choose to attend the event in Rome or connect and participate in the talks and discussions virtually via the Internet.

Steering Committee

Mathias Weske (Chair)	University of Potsdam, Germany
Boualem Benatallah	University of New South Wales, Australia
Jörg Desel	FernUniversität in Hagen, Germany
Marlon Dumas	Tartu Ülikool, Estonia
Jan Mendling	Humboldt University Berlin, Germany
Manfred Reichert	Ulm University, Germany
Hajo A. Reijers	Utrecht University, The Netherlands
Stefanie Rinderle-Ma	Technical University of Munich, Germany
Michael Rosemann	Queensland University of Technology, Australia
Shazia Sadiq	The University of Queensland, Australia
Wil van der Aalst	RWTH, Aachen University, Germany
Barbara Weber	University of St. Gallen, Switzerland

Executive Committee

General Chair

Massimo Mecella	Sapienza Università di Roma, Italy

Main Conference PC Chairs

Artem Polyvyanyy (Track Chair, Track I)	The University of Melbourne, Australia
Moe Thandar Wynn (Track Chair, Track II)	Queensland University of Technology, Australia
Amy Van Looy (Track Chair, Track III)	Ghent University, Belgium
Manfred Reichert (Consolidation Chair)	Ulm University, Germany

Workshop Chairs

Andrea Marrella   Sapienza Università di Roma, Italy
Barbara Weber   University of St. Gallen, Switzerland

Demonstrations and Resources Chairs

Francesco Leotta   Sapienza Università di Roma, Italy
Arik Senderovich   University of Toronto, Canada
Marcos Sepúlveda   Pontificia Universidad Católica de Chile, Chile

Tutorial and Panel Chairs

Claudio Di Ciccio   Sapienza Università di Roma, Italy
Avigdor Gal   Technion – Israel Institute of Technology, Israel
Shazia Sadiq   The University of Queensland, Australia

Publicity Chairs

Adriano Augusto   The University of Melbourne, Australia
Chiara Di Francescomarino   Fondazione Bruno Kessler, Italy
Flavia Santoro   University of the State of Rio de Janeiro, Brazil

Doctoral Consortium Chairs

Estefania Serral Asensio   KU Leuven, Belgium
Remco Dijkman   Eindhoven University of Technology, The Netherlands
Fabrizio Maria Maggi   University of Bolzano, Italy

Industry Forum Chairs

Massimiliano de Leoni   University of Padua, Italy
Minseok Song   Pohang University of Science and Technology,
                                     South Korea
Maximilian Röglinger   University of Bayreuth, Germany

RPA Forum Chairs

José González Enríquez   University of Seville, Spain
Peter Fettke   German Research Center for Artificial Intelligence
                                     (DFKI) and Saarland University, Germany
Inge van de Weerd   Utrecht University, The Netherlands

Blockchain Forum Chairs

Søren Debois   IT University of Copenhagen, Denmark
Pierluigi Plebani   Politecnico di Milano, Italy
Ingo Weber   TU Berlin, Germany

Organizing Committee Chair

Massimo Mecella   Sapienza Università di Roma, Italy

Organizing Committee Members

Simone Agostinelli	Sapienza Università di Roma, Italy
Dario Benvenuti	Sapienza Università di Roma, Italy
Eleonora Bernasconi	Sapienza Università di Roma, Italy
Francesca de Luzi	Sapienza Università di Roma, Italy
Lauren Stacey Ferro	Sapienza Università di Roma, Italy
Francesco Sapio	Sapienza Università di Roma, Italy
Silvestro Veneruso	Sapienza Università di Roma, Italy

Organizing Agency

Consulta Umbria, Italy

Track I: Foundation

Senior Program Committee

Jörg Desel	FernUniversität in Hagen, Germany
Claudio Di Ciccio	Sapienza Università di Roma, Italy
Chiara Di Francescomarino	Fondazione Bruno Kessler, Italy
Dirk Fahland	Eindhoven University of Technology, The Netherlands
Luciano García Bañuelos	Tecnológico de Monterrey, Mexico
Thomas Hildebrandt	IT University of Copenhagen, Denmark
Fabrizio Maria Maggi	Free University of Bozen-Bolzano, Italy
Marco Montali	Free University of Bozen-Bolzano, Italy
Oscar Pastor Lopez	Universidad Politécnica de Valencia, Spain
Arthur ter Hofstede	Queensland University of Technology, Australia
Wil van der Aalst	RWTH, Aachen University, Germany
Jan Martijn van der Werf	Utrecht University, The Netherlands
Hagen Voelzer	IBM Research – Europe, Germany
Matthias Weidlich	Humboldt-Universität zu Berlin, Germany
Mathias Weske	University of Potsdam, Germany

Program Committee

Lars Ackermann	University of Bayreuth, Germany
Adriano Augusto	The University of Melbourne, Australia
Ahmed Awad	Tartu Ülikool, Estonia
Diego Calvanese	Free University of Bozen-Bolzano, Italy
Johannes De Smedt	KU Leuven, Belgium
Søren Debois	IT University of Copenhagen, Denmark
Rik Eshuis	Eindhoven University of Technology, The Netherlands
Peter Fettke	DFKI and Saarland University, Germany
Hans-Georg Fill	University of Fribourg, Switzerland
Maria Teresa Gómez López	Universidad de Sevilla, Spain
Guido Governatori	Data61, Australia
Gianluigi Greco	Università della Calabria, Italy

Richard Hull	New York University, USA
Akhil Kumar	Penn State University, USA
Sander J. J. Leemans	Queensland University of Technology, Australia
Irina Lomazova	HSE University, Russia
Xixi Lu	Utrecht University, The Netherlands
Felix Mannhardt	Eindhoven University of Technology, The Netherlands
Andrea Marrella	Sapienza Università di Roma, Italy
Werner Nutt	Free University of Bozen-Bolzano, Italy
Chun Ouyang	Queensland University of Technology, Australia
Daniel Ritter	SAP, Germany
Andrey Rivkin	Free University of Bozen-Bolzano, Italy
Arik Senderovich	University of Toronto, Canada
Tijs Slaats	University of Copenhagen, Denmark
Farbod Taymouri	The University of Melbourne, Australia
Ernest Teniente	Universitat Politècnica de Catalunya, Spain
Sebastiaan J. van Zelst	RWTH Aachen University, Germany
Eric Verbeek	Eindhoven University of Technology, The Netherlands
Karsten Wolf	University of Rostock, Germany
Francesca Zerbato	University of St. Gallen, Switzerland

Track II: Engineering

Senior Program Committee

Boualem Benatallah	University of New South Wales, Australia
Andrea Burattin	Technical University of Denmark, Denmark
Josep Carmona	Universitat Politècnica de Catalunya, Spain
Remco Dijkman	Eindhoven University of Technology, The Netherlands
Jochen De Weerdt	KU Leuven, Belgium
Marlon Dumas	Tartu Ülikool, Estonia
Avigdor Gal	Technion – Israel Institute of Technology, Israel
Chiara Ghidini	Fondazione Bruno Kessler, Italy
Jorge Munoz-Gama	Pontificia Universidad Católica de Chile, Chile
Luise Pufahl	Hasso-Plattner-Institut, Germany
Hajo A. Reijers	Utrecht University, The Netherlands
Stefanie Rinderle-Ma	Technical University of Munich, Germany
Shazia Sadiq	The University of Queensland, Australia
Pnina Soffer	University of Haifa, Israel
Boudewijn Van Dongen	Eindhoven University of Technology, The Netherlands
Barbara Weber	University of St. Gallen, Switzerland
Ingo Weber	Technische Universität Berlin, Germany

Program Committee

Marco Aiello	University of Stuttgart, Germany
Robert Andrews	Queensland University of Technology, Australia
Abel Armas-Cervantes	The University of Melbourne, Australia

Cristina Cabanillas	Universidad de Sevilla, Spain
Fabio Casati	University of Trento, Italy
Massimiliano de Leoni	Università degli Studi di Padova, Italy
Joerg Evermann	Memorial University of Newfoundland, Canada
Walid Gaaloul	Télécom SudParis, France
Daniela Grigori	LAMSADE – Université Paris-Dauphine, France
Georg Grossmann	University of South Australia, Australia
Gert Janssenswilen	UHasselt – Universiteit van vandaag, Belgium
Mieke Jans	UHasselt – Universiteit van vandaag, Belgium
Anna Kalenkova	The University of Melbourne, Australia
Dimka Karastoyanova	University of Groningen, The Netherlands
Agnes Koschmider	Christian-Albrechts-Universität zu Kiel, Germany
Henrik Leopold	Kühne Logistics University, Germany
Elisa Marengo	Free University of Bozen-Bolzano, Italy
Rabeb Mizouni	Khalifa University, United Arab Emirates
Helen Paik	University of New South Wales, Australia
Cesare Pautasso	University of Lugano, Switzerland
Pierluigi Plebani	Politecnico di Milano, Italy
Pascal Poizat	Université Paris Nanterre, France
Barbara Re	Università di Camerino, Italy
Manuel Resinas	Universidad de Sevilla, Spain
Renuka Sindhgatta	Queensland University of Technology, Australia
Marcos Sepúlveda	Pontificia Universidad Católica de Chile, Chile
Natalia Sidorova	Eindhoven University of Technology, The Netherlands
Minseok Song	POSTECH, South Korea
Seppe Vanden Broucke	KU Leuven, Belgium
Stefan Schönig	Universität Regensburg, Germany
Nick van Beest	Data61, Australia
Han van der Aa	Universität Mannheim, Germany
Nicola Zannone	Eindhoven University of Technology, The Netherlands

Track III: Management

Senior Program Committee

Wasana Bandara	Queensland University of Technology, Australia
Jörg Becker	University of Muenster (ERCIS), Germany
Daniel Beverungen	Paderborn University, Germany
Adela Del Río Ortega	Universidad de Sevilla, Spain
Paul Grefen	Eindhoven University of Technology, The Netherlands
Mojca Indihar Štemberger	University of Ljubljana, Slovenia
Marta Indulska	The University of Queensland, Australia
Peter Loos	Saarland University, Germany
Jan Mendling	Humboldt University Berlin, Germany
Juergen Moormann	Frankfurt School of Finance & Management, Germany
Maximilian Roeglinger	FIM Research Center, Germany

Michael Rosemann	Queensland University of Technology, Australia
Flavia Santoro	University of the State of Rio de Janeiro (UERJ), Brazil
Peter Trkman	University of Ljubljana, Slovenia
Jan vom Brocke	University of Liechtenstein, Liechtenstein

Program Committee

Tahir Ahmad	Ghent University, Belgium
Alessio Maria Braccini	Università degli Studi della Tuscia, Italy
Ann-Kristin Cordes	University of Münster, Germany
Dries Couckuyt	Ghent University, Belgium
Patrick Delfmann	University of Koblenz-Landau, Germany
Michael Fellmann	University of Rostock, Germany
Renata Gabryelczyk	University of Warsaw, Poland
Andreas Gadatsch	Hochschule Bonn-Rhein-Sieg, Germany
Thomas Grisold	University of Liechtenstein, Liechtenstein
Tomislav Hernaus	University of Zagreb, Croatia
Christian Janiesch	TU Dresden, Germany
Ralf Knackstedt	University of Hildesheim, Germany
Andrea Kö	Corvinus University of Budapest, Hungary
John Krogstie	Norwegian University of Science and Technology, Norway
Michael Leyer	University of Rostock, Germany
Alexander Mädche	Karlsruhe Institute of Technology, Germany
Paul Mathiesen	Queensland University of Technology, Australia
Martin Matzner	Friedrich-Alexander-Universität Erlangen-Nürnberg, Germany
Sven Overhage	University of Bamberg, Germany
Ralf Plattfaut	Fachhochschule Südwestfalen, Germany
Geert Poels	Ghent University, Belgium
Jens Poeppelbuss	Ruhr-Universität Bochum, Germany
Dennis Riehle	University of Muenster, Germany
Stefan Sackmann	University of Halle-Wittenberg, Germany
Alexander Schiller	University of Regensburg, Germany
Werner Schmidt	Technische Hochschule Ingolstadt Business School, Germany
Oktay Turetken	Eindhoven University of Technology, The Netherlands
Irene Vanderfeesten	Open University of the Netherlands, The Netherlands
Axel Winkelmann	University of Wuerzburg, Germany

Additional Reviewers

Ebaa Alnazer
Nour Assy
Vladimir Bashkin
Sebastian Bräuer
Adam Burke
Silvano Colombo Tosatto
Carl Corea
Sebastian Dunzer
Jasper Feine
Laura Genga
Ilche Georgievski
Ulrich Gnewuch
Marie Godefroid
Torsten Gollhardt
Lukas-Valentin Herm
Ambrose Hill
Felix Holz
Felix Härer
Georgi Kerpedzhiev
Krzysztof Kluza
Julian Koch

Ingo Kregel
Yulia Litvinova
Niels Martin
Alexey A. Mitsyuk
Sabine Nagel
Maximilian Raab
Henning Dirk Richter
Tim Rietz
Johannes Schneider
Thorsten Schoormann
Anja Seiffer
Brian Setz
Tobias Seyffarth
Syed Wajid Ali Shah
John Shepherd
Johannes Tenschert
Frank Vanhoenshoven
Julian Weidinger
Sven Weinzierl
Bastian Wurm
Sandra Zilker

Keynote Abstracts

What Have the Romans Ever Done for Us? The Ancient Antecedents of Business Process Management

Hajo A. Reijers[1,2] (iD)

[1] Utrecht University, Princetonplein 5, 3584 CC, Utrecht, The Netherlands
h.a.reijers@uu.nl
[2] Eindhoven University of Technology, Groene Loper 3, 3508 TC, Eindhoven,
The Netherlands

Abstract. The origins of Business Process Management (BPM) are often traced back to the Business Process Reengineering wave in the 1990s (e.g. [1, 3]), as well as to the Total Quality Management movement of the 1980s (e.g. [2, 4]). However, at the start of the 20th century, Frederick Taylor already concerned himself with analyzing activities to find the "one best way" to perform work [7]. Still earlier, in the 18th century, Adam Smith and others identified the *division of labor* principle [6], which is still important for the design of modern business processes.

Undoubtedly, it is possible to identify earlier precursors to the concepts that have to come to underpin BPM. After all, people have been manufacturing products, as well as administering their activities since the dawn of history.

On the occasion of the 19th edition of the BPM conference series, BPM 2021, I like to focus on a special episode of human history. Sine this edition is organized in the eternal city of Rome, I find it both appropriate and exciting to reflect on how the ancient Romans thought about work. I like to to show the principles they applied in organizing and innovating their work processes. To demonstrate the links between ancient and modern practices, I will use as as a backbone for my keynote a set of redesign heuristics, which I compiled more than 15 years ago [5].

The message of my talk is that there are striking parallels between how the ancient Romans thought about organizing and improving work processes and how we do so in our day. At the same time, there are important differences, notably due to the advent of digital information and communication technologies in our modern time.

If I manage to let my audience marvel about the accomplishments of the ancient Romans, then I will be quite pleased. I will try and link the contents of my presentation with the archaeological and historic evidence still available to us today. These pointers hopefully inspire people to visit the sites of the ancient Roman world and learn more about its history.

If my audience also realizes that BPM is an evolving discipline that is tightly interwoven with the history of humankind, then I will be delighted. I hope that my keynote stimulates researchers to reflect on the concepts and technologies that underpin BPM, inspires them to expand to expand its knowledge basis, and encourages them to present their work at future editions of the BPM conference series –sss weherever they take place. In the end, all roads lead to Rome.

References

1. Davenport, T.H.: Process innovation: reengineering work through information technology. Harvard Business Press (1993)
2. Feigenbaum, A.V.: Total quality control. McGraw-Hill (1991)
3. Hammer, M., Champy, J.: Reengineering the Corporation: A Manifesto for Business Revolution. Collins (1993)
4. Ishikawa, K.: What is total quality control? The Japanese way. Prentice Hall (1985)
5. Reijers, H.A., Mansar, S.L.: Best practices in business process redesign: an overview and qualitative evaluation of successful redesign heuristics. Omega **33**(4), 283–306 (2005)
6. Smith, A.: An inquiry into the nature and causes of the wealth of nations: Volume One. Strahan and Cadell (1776)
7. Taylor, F.W.: The Principles of Scientific Management. Harper and Brothers (1911)

Artificial Intelligence-based Declarative Process Synthesis for BPM

Giuseppe De Giacomo ⓘ

Dipartimento di Ingegneria Informatica, Automatica e Gestionale, Università
degli Studi di Roma "La Sapienza", Roma, Italy
degiacomo@diag.uniroma1.it

Abstract. Artificial intelligence is recently studying processes that autonomously take decisions and re-program themselves to act strategically in reaction to unexpected outcomes in a nondeterministic partially controllable environment. These studies are developing synergies among reactive process synthesis and verification in Formal Methods, AI planning, MDPs with non-Markovian rewards and dynamics, model learning, i.e., learning environment dynamics from trace, and reinforcement learning. The talk will look into these studies and discuss their special relevance for BPM, building on the already established connections in declarative process management.

Keywords: Declarative business processes · Artificial intelligence · Formal methods · Automated process synthesis

Supported by ERC Advanced Grant WhiteMech (No. 834228).

Contents

Keynote Paper

Process Automation and Process Mining in Manufacturing

Stefanie Rinderle-Ma$^{(\boxtimes)}$ and Juergen Mangler

Department of Informatics, Technical University of Munich, Boltzmannstrasse 3,
85748 Garching, Germany
{stefanie.rinderle-ma,juergen.mangler}@tum.de

Abstract. Process automation and process mining are (interconnected)
key technologies with respect to digital transformation. Hence, expectations are high, in particular, in challenging application domains such
as manufacturing that combine systems, machines, sensors, and users.
Moreover, manufacturing processes operate at a high level of collaboration, e.g. in inter-factory or cross-organizational settings. This paper
investigates the following questions: 1) How to automate manufacturing
processes? 2) What are the specifics with respect to the involvements
of humans? 3) How do the automation strategies impact process mining
options and vice versa? For 1), we discuss two starting positions in practice, i.e., legacy automation and greenfield automation. For 2), we discuss the range of automation options with respect to human involvement,
i.e., non-interactive automation, robotic process automation, supportive
process automation, and interactive process automation. For 3), the different automation settings and strategies are examined with respect to
data collection and integration capabilities. Conversely, process mining
is discussed as technology to further process automation in manufacturing. The paper builds on more than a decade of experience with process
automation in manufacturing. We built an orchestration engine based on
which 16 real-world manufacturing processes have been realized so far,
resulting in various benefits for the companies such as traceability, flexibility, and sustainability. The investigation of the manufacturing domain
also sheds light on other challenging scenarios with similar requirements
such as health care and logistics.

Keywords: Process automation · Process mining · Manufacturing ·
Human aspect · Data collection and preparation

1 Introduction

Process automation and process mining are regarded as key technologies for
digital transformation [6]. Process mining provides the required transparency
for digital transformation and can complement process automation [13]. In this
work, we discuss these prospects for a challenging domain, i.e., manufacturing. Manufacturing is challenging–and one of the most interesting domains for

© Springer Nature Switzerland AG 2021
A. Polyvyanyy et al. (Eds.): BPM 2021, LNCS 12875, pp. 3–14, 2021.
https://doi.org/10.1007/978-3-030-85469-0_1

Business Process Management–as it *"combines high demands on process transparency and digital transformation and it combines the physical world (e.g., sensors, machines), human work, and manufacturing systems"* [17]. As such the manufacturing domain, poses high demands on *integration*, i.e., vertical integration across the automation pyramid [11] and horizontal integration of multiple entities and partners, e.g., inter-factory or cross-organizational settings [15].

This paper investigates the following questions:

1. *How to automate manufacturing processes?* We discuss two starting positions that are prevalent in practice, i.e., legacy automation–starting with existing hardware and software–and greenfield automation, i.e., at least for the software part being able to start from scratch. For both starting positions, guidelines based on experience from different automation projects are provided.
2. *What are the specifics of process automation with respect to the inclusion of (human) users?* This point is crucial as *"smart data, insights, and transparency will be useless if the process experts or process owners do not appreciate and support the approach"* [13]. A range of automation options exist that have different impact on the involvement of humans, i.e., non-interactive automation, robotic process automation [1], supportive process automation, and interactive process automation [8]. We illustrate the different options with real-world scenarios.
3. *How do process automation strategies impact process mining options and vice versa?* Process automation and process mining are perceived as being intertwined. The different automation settings and strategies are examined with respect to data collection and integration capabilities. Conversely, process mining is discussed as technology to further process automation in manufacturing. We will report on our experiences from process mining projects in manufacturing where the expectations are high, but especially for small and medium sized enterprises the infrastructure poses a critical challenge [18]. Manufacturing offers opportunities for process mining as an abundance of data is available, for example, process event data[1] plus sensor data in form of time series [19] and engineering drawings [14].

The paper builds on more than a decade of experience with process automation and mining in manufacturing. We built the manufacturing orchestration engine `centurio.work` [11]. It is based on open source process execution engine CPEE[2] [10] which is employed worldwide and has been downloaded 500.000 times[3] by today plus an additional 23.000 downloads[3] for manufacturing specific add-ons, e.g., for connecting machines using standard format OPC-UA[4]. 16 process scenarios at 7 manufacturing companies run or are currently in various stages of

---

[1] stored in process event logs (*logs* for short in the following.).
[2] https://cpee.org.
[3] https://rubygems.org/profiles/eTM, last accessed on 2021-07-02.
[4] https://opcfoundation.org/about/opc-technologies/opc-ua/.

realization based on centurio.work. This results in various benefits for the companies such as traceability, flexibility, and sustainability. The investigation of the manufacturing domain also sheds light on other challenging scenarios with similar requirements such as health care and logistics.

The remainder of the paper is structured as follows: Sect. 2 starts with legacy process automation and contrasts it with subsequent greenfield process automation ($\mapsto$ Question 1). Section 3 picks up the human aspect as key factor in digital transformation projects and examines different automation settings along their inclusion of humans ($\mapsto$ Question 2). Section 4 sheds light on the intertwining of process mining and automation in manufacturing ($\mapsto$ Question 3). In Sect. 5, we discuss the findings and provide an outlook on future topics.

2 Automating Legacy vs. Automating Greenfield Scenarios in Manufacturing

The automation of legacy and greenfield scenarios constitute two "extremes" on a range of possible starting points in manufacturing and other domains. Starting points in between, i.e., with "mixed" circumstances, are common. Hence, often the techniques and circumstances elaborated below have to be considered.

2.1 Automating Legacy Scenarios

Legacy scenarios suffer from the constraint that pre-existing hardware and software has to be reused, and that environmental constraints potentially limit how the processes are carried out. The proximity of physical machines, for example, might influence the optimal order of tasks or interactions with humans.

We assume that processes exist, although in a non-formalized choreography between humans, software, machines and the environment. These processes

- are not fully understood by individual human actors, i.e., process participants.
- are not fully structured. They include a large amount of leeway regarding the order of steps and exception handling. Common sub-processes shared between different parts of the processes are often not perceived as such.

What we will not find in the real-world are logs alongside the execution of these processes. Consequently, at this point, there is no chance that process mining can be applied to discover the process model for process automation. In fact, machines log data into individual data tanks without any notion of different produced parts, or differentiation of when they produce parts or when they are just idle. Heterogeneous software components of varied age typically also keep their own logs, with no notion of orders, customers, or parts.

So unless the whole factory floor–order management, production, packing and delivery including humans, software, machines, and environmental involvement–has to be mapped into a single big process (which will most probably not yield any useful results), it is imperative that an initial notion of how things work is established. This has to be done by domain experts. Only then can the properties according to which the logs have to be split, be understood and techniques like process mining can yield useful results. A remaining question is whether process elicitation (e.g., by interviewing domain experts) is done beforehand. In any case, corresponding techniques can be used to check the progress in formalizing domain knowledge.

Roughly knowing the processes is a first step. The iterative evolution from passive observation of the scenario to actively controlling the interaction between humans, software, machines and the environment [11] is a much more complex endeavour. The following questions can be used to plan for this evolution:

1. *Hardware read capabilities:* Which event data streams can be read during operation (reading state/configuration is considered a command)? Do we need additional sensors (e.g., temperature, vibration) for meaningful data analysis?
2. *Hardware command capabilities:* What is the granularity of the digital interface, i.e., component level such as individual motor control vs. operation control? How and when are humans involved?
3. *Humans:* What are the observable points in time where it is exactly known that a human starts something, or ends something?
4. *Software:* How to access static data, observe data changes, track operations? Is it possible to observe how humans interact with the software?

1. Hardware read capabilities: Machines should be observable during operation. If a machine cannot provide data about its operational state, and parameter changes during operation, it has to be replaced or updated with suitable capabilities. All future data analysis to improve the process depends on data. In addition, supplementary sensors can be added around or inside the machine with separate interfaces that are not crucial for production, but add context to it.

2. Hardware command capabilities have to be seen strictly separate from the read capabilities. While the readable interface yields data streams, and can be used to passively monitoring the machine, hardware command is about active automation. Machines often expose fine granular commands such as switch on/off individual parts, start individual motors or auxiliary systems, or execute NC (numerical control) programs. Many of these individual steps might be performed by humans in certain sequence all the time. So it is imperative to identify when a human is really required/desirable, and what are sequences that can be bundled together as static sub/processes to be reused over and over again.

3. Humans: Their tasks often represent the **digital gap**. It is important to split their work into individually/automatically observable units. This often requires additional sensors, or additional effort by the humans to tell an information system what they are actually doing right now. It is imperative for the well-being of humans, that tracking is as passive as possible. Being required to do reporting in addition to the actual work can lead to frustration and errors, and humans have a tendency to minimize such tasks, cmp. (health) care [16].

4. Software: Finally integrating legacy software systems is often the most challenging part, because their complexity is often much higher and they are much more of a black box than any involved hardware or human. The following aspects should be analysed in roughly this given order:

– Does the software expose a comprehensive network accessible interface? In this case everything is fine. Even if legacy protocols are used, it is simple wrap the software into a service to provide for full automation capability.
– Does the software expose a local API? In this case again a network accessible wrapper service can solve the automation problem.
– Does the software utilize a database? Is it possible to infer operations or human interactions from data changes? This requires additional analytical steps, e.g., building differential snapshots [7].
– Does the software expose a UI? If none of the above ways of interacting with the software can be utilized, techniques such as Robot Process Automation (RPA) can be employed. Few approaches have considered RPA in manufacturing-related scenarios yet. [20] look at RPA for automotive, but focus on ordering and reporting processes rather than on lower-level production processes. In one of our projects, RPA was used with some hardware, e.g., a rubber finger pressing a button. RPA for manufacturing processes is further discussed from the human perspective in Sect. 3.

If the software does expose logs, they can be utilized to create a (run-time) event stream. Of course it has to be determined what the latency between operation and logging is to judge the usefulness for automation.

Approaches such as RPA, although not circumventable for some legacy scenarios, should be avoid whenever possible as they (1) tend to subtly break with small changes to UIs, (2) can/should never be reused for inevitable replacements of legacy software. Modern software typically encompasses the long-taught principle of software development to separate UI, business logic, and data. Accessing data is typically exposed through well-defined, network-accessible APIs (accompanying UIs–web, mobile, desktop–and custom extensions typically are separated from the core and also access data through these interfaces).

2.2 Automating Greenfield Scenarios

Regarding the utilization of machines and humans, greenfield automation projects are no different from legacy projects.

When selecting or developing software, for integration with process aware information systems, the following guiding principles have proven useful:

– *Always separate the business logic:* Process management/orchestration engines are a means to separate the application/business logic from functions. Individual software include no hard-coded or configured assumptions about the environment or how to interact with peers (e.g., protocol or addressing). Loosely coupled systems are easier to maintain, debug, and evolve for future yet unknown scenarios.

- *Modularization:* Evolving and adapting your system to ever-changing business conditions works best when you have small self-contained services, that expose functionality or data. Changes to the functionality itself should be as localized as possible. It is easier to maintain small and overseeable pieces of software than bit and complex pieces. Localizing errors is easier when functionalities are clearly separated as services.
- *Avoid central databases:* Services should each have their own data storage when possible. Software often breaks when data structures are changed and different functionalities sharing these data structures have to be adapted to realize the change. All data should be passed between services through the service interfaces if possible. This greatly reduces coupling and allows of localized changes. Compatibility can be ensured and made transparent through separated transformation (e.g., additional steps in a process models or service chains).
- *Focus on Observability:* Process automation is about orchestrating services and their interaction. Maximizing the information accompanying each interaction between services makes it easier to conduct the necessary analysis steps for process improvement. Observability includes data streams about system health (e.g., resource utilization), exceptions, metrics (e.g., performance or inner state), and auditing (e.g., information focused on checking sanity/compliance of involvement in business logic).

3   The Human Aspect in Process Automation

Humans have many roles, even in fully automated scenarios. In general, humans are involved in running processes in the following two capacities: they are either *process observers* or *process actors*.

Process observers are monitoring the execution of processes, but they not actively participate in them. They typically do passive tasks such as error detection, compliance checking, quality checking, or safety monitoring. The tasks of process observers are the same, whether a process is fully automated or fully manual. Collecting information and enacting the consequences, of course, may be different in fully automated vs. fully manual scenarios. Process observers typically enact the following consequence action: *"stop the process"* based on observed anomalies or violations. It is then up to process actors to fix things.

Process actors again might exist in fully automated and manual manufacturing scenarios: periodic as well as problem-related maintenance, for example, is always connected to human interaction. Process actors might exist in two roles:

- *Active* process actors hold business logic and exert control over the process by actively directing it, e.g., by selecting the machines that produce something, or selecting the next steps.
- *Passive* process actors which only act within well defined constraints. They are basically not distinguishable from software, as from the point of view

of a process orchestration engine they behave the same: (1) they get a well-defined set of instructions/parameters and (2) they return a well-defined data-structure that represents the computer-readable result of the instructions. Humans involved in a fully automated scenario through a worklist [12] are such an example.

Thus a fully automated scenario is not characterized by the non-involvement of humans, but instead by the formalization and automatic observability of all interactions between humans, machines, software and the environment.

Figure 1 depicts a range of scenarios with focus on the human involvement as well as techniques that are typically used to solve the challenges imposed by the scenario.

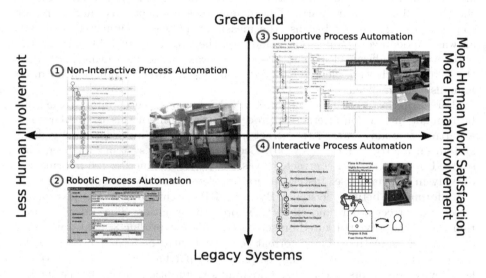

Fig. 1. Manufacturing process scenarios and the involvement of humans

The X axis denotes the requirement for the involvement of process actors. Many scenarios in manufacturing, health care, or any other domain are currently neither feasible nor efficient to be carried out without humans. The Y axis picks up the two starting positions discussed in Sect. 2, i.e., to evolve scenarios which include legacy systems into fully automated scenarios and to design and realize everything from the ground up (greenfield).

Scenario ①, further detailed in [11], describes the automation of a mixture of legacy machines and additional hardware. The purpose of the automation was, to do away with all human interaction and allow for fully automatic production of batches. The following machines are involved: a turning machine, that produces the part, a bar loader that feeds parts to the turning machine, a robot that extracts the parts, puts them into a "close-to-production" measuring machine and then puts them onto an autonomous guided vehicle (AGV). The AGV drives a full load (60 pieces) to a tactile coordinate-measuring machine (CMM), where a robot puts each piece into the CMM, and extracts them again, after the measurement finishes. When a batch is ready the AGV drives the batch to packaging, and then goes back to get new parts. This fairly involves humans purely as process observers, that check quality deviations, and if they are too big, signal production stop. Then human actors change tools (them being blunt–depending on temperature and type of part produced–being a main source of error).

Before the full automation humans were starting the machine manually (a repetitive task), and also taking manual measurements "close-to-production". While starting the machine manually required a skilled worker to be present at all time, after automation the worker could do more useful things like planning the production of future parts. The manual measurement was another major source of errors, mainly because the measurement was documented by hand, an was handed over the person in charge pf the CMM. Predictably enough the notes were not always clear, and lots of time was wasted measuring parts with the CMM which were clearly faulty to start with. After automation no more humans were involved.

For Scenario ②, legacy software, which only has a user interface, has to be brought into a non-interactive process automation. In this particular case, a partner company wanted to extract information from an order management system on an IBM iSeries (AS400). Because the whole system had been outsourced under a certain contract, it was not possible to access the information directly in the database. Instead operators were manually using a UI to copy the information between systems. By using RPA techniques, it was possible to select the correct order, and extract the order information. The order information was differently structured on screen for different products. It also was in a different and sometimes faulty format compared with the format needed in the second system: before introducing RPA that format had been graciously translated by the operators in their head, including assumptions about faulty entries. So besides extracting the information through RPA, even bigger effort went into interpreting to data to be valid input for the second system. From the point-of-view of the process engine utilized in the project, RPA was just one task (extract information). Additional tasks and decisions dealt with transforming data to be valid input for the final task (print production label and QR code). In this scenario, the process actors have been replaced and RPA was a necessity due a legacy system. The inevitable replacement of the legacy system will lead to the replacement of the RPA task, with a simple "read order data" task that gets the information from a database or through a microservice interface.

Scenario ③ is a worker-assistance scenario, which we currently automate together with a company partner. Worker assistance is typically deployed due to the following reasons and properties of a scenario:

- The scenario is complex with lots of variants and special cases. The actual scenario deals with the assembly of highly customizable parts which are a mix of mechanical and electronic parts with a custom firmware. The number of mechanical variations exceeds 20000. This number multiplies when custom firmware flashing and configuration is taken into account.

- Due to the many variants and the tedious assembly process, automation with robots or machines is not feasible.
- Humans involved in the production process have different skill levels, and have to be supported with different levels of information.

In this particular scenario, the goal was to introduce a production line with fine-grained labor division. While before automation, the parts where assembled by two humans, after automation, eight people are to be involved. The production line thus consists of eight working stations. The parts are autonomously transported between the working stations. The purpose of the worker assistance system is to identify the part present in a working station, identify the human present in a working station, and display information tailored for a specific variant AND the skill level of the worker.

While experienced workers can be slowed down by detailed information (individual steps have to be acknowledged to provide insight into assembly timing thus error sources), less skilled workers greatly benefit from looking up information in a multitude of binders, being presented with all relevant information.

Work satisfaction in this scenario greatly increased, as well as overall productiveness. At the same time faulty parts due to faulty assembly could be reduced. Through fine-grained monitoring of human assembly also bottlenecks could be detected, as well as faulty raw-materials could be identified faster due to integrated reporting capabilities. All interactions between humans, the production line, and additional hardware was realized through micro-services [9], and orchestrated with a process engine.

Scenario ④, further detailed in [8], describes how at the beginning or the end of a non-interactive process automation humans might interact with machines, here through a loading station. A loading station enacts a pick-and-place scenario, where humans put tools or raw materials on designated area, in no particular order, position or rotation. A robot then visually detects, selects, orders and consistently places the provided objects (with high precision, no deviations from position) for further processing. Humans are exonerated in that the rules are simplified - they interact just like with fellow humans; they provide parts. From the point of view of automation this is also a simplification. After the loading station deterministic behaviour prevails, that can be solved by simple logic instead of focusing on variations throughout the automation. Loading stations can hence be a simple solution for interfaces between humans and legacy production lines.

4   Process Mining and Automation: Are They Twins?

The discussion of automation scenarios in Sects. 2 and 3 indicates that process automation and mining are intertwined in the following ways:

1. Process mining can support automation. The precondition is the existence of suitable data.
2. Process automation can yield integrated and contextualized data collections [11] and hence lead to increased quality of process mining results and unlock novel ways of analyzing the data [19].

The collection of process event logs as input for process mining is a critical and tedious task. One of the conclusions from the focus group interviews with manufacturing experts presented in [18] is that, particularly for small and medium sized manufacturing enterprises, *"logging is part of the business logic and data-centric. Selected milestones in the production produce a data dump with a timestamp, while most process steps in the manufacturing domain just produce no events at all"*. If there is no (process-oriented) integration across the levels of the automation pyramid already in place, the log data can possibly accessed "per level", i.e., from top to bottom, the Enterprise Resource Planning (ERP) system level, the Plant Management level, the Process Control level, and the Control (PLC) level [11]. The log data possibly accessible at the different levels varies in quality with respect to the L* quality model proposed for process mining [2], ranging from *** (events are automatically recorded, but unsystematically, some correctness guarantees can be assumed) for the ERP level to ** (events are automatically recorded, but unsystematically, no correctness guarantees exist, leading to e.g., missing events) for the other levels. There are (commercial) connectors/adaptors for process mining on ERP data, e.g., for open source platform ProM [4] and Celonis for SAP©[5]. However, in addition to the probably low data quality, there is no interconnection between the systems, resulting in isolated analysis results.

Hence, process automation with its strong integration aspect can immediately lift up the quality level to at least a quality of ****, i.e., the data is recorded in an automatic, systematic, and reliable way, and the contextualization in processes and process instances is automatically provided [2].

If process event logs of suitable quality are available, especially *conformance checking* [3] is perceived as a great instrument to monitor manufacturing processes during runtime [18].

On top of integration and data contextualization, process automation in manufacturing also offers several opportunities with respect to considering data sources in addition to the process event log data that can be analyzed in different phases of the process life cycle A first example for such additional data is time series data as emitted by machines and sensors, e.g., temperature [5]. Process mining has been augmented with dynamic time warping on sensor data for predicting and explaining concept drifts, i.e., upcoming process evolution due to, for example, chips on the parts causing decreasing quality [19]. Another example for additional data relevant to manufacturing are engineering drawings and standards such as ISO norms. Engineering drawings contain the essential information for setting up the manufacturing process and the subsequent quality

---

[5] https://www.celonis.com/solutions/systems/sap/.

control, i.e., the dimensions of the produced parts and tolerances, together with links to the underlying standards [14]. DigiEDraw [14], for example, provides conceptual and tool support to automatically extract this information from the drawings such that they can be included in the process models, but also in process analysis. Approaches such as [21] provide NLP-based concepts and tools to check the *compliance* of (manufacturing) processes with regulatory documents.

5   Discussion and Outlook

We refer back to the questions set out in the introduction: 1) How to automate manufacturing processes? It depends on the starting point (legacy vs. greenfield, and in between) and raises many (technical) challenges, e.g., how to connect machines to the process. 2) What are the specifics with respect to the involvements of humans? Humans are always involved, either active or passive. If active, the involvement ranges from working on tasks (interface: worklist), over being supported (interface: UI), to interactively working on and designing the process (interface: loading station). As a lesson learned, physical devices can serve as interfaces between process and human, as well. 3) How do the automation strategies impact process mining options and vice versa? Process mining quality heavily depends on data collection and quality which an be provided by process automation. Process mining can go new ways by integration of process event logs with additional data such as time series. These findings for manufacturing are likely to be relevant for other domains with similar requirements such as health care or logistics, as well.

References

1. van der Aalst, W.M.P., Bichler, M., Heinzl, A.: Robotic process automation. Bus. Inf. Syst. Eng. **60**(4), 269–272 (2018). https://doi.org/10.1007/s12599-018-0542-4
2. van der Aalst, W.M.P., et al.: Process mining manifesto. In: Business Process Management Workshops, pp. 169–194 (2011). https://doi.org/10.1007/978-3-642-28108-2_19
3. Carmona, J., van Dongen, B.F., Solti, A., Weidlich, M.: Conformance Checking - Relating Processes and Models. Springer, Heidelberg (2018). https://doi.org/10.1007/978-3-319-99414-7
4. Günther, C.W., van der Aalst, W.M.P.: A generic import framework for process event logs. In: Eder, J., Dustdar, S. (eds.) BPM 2006. LNCS, vol. 4103, pp. 81–92. Springer, Heidelberg (2006). https://doi.org/10.1007/11837862_10
5. Kammerer, K., Pryss, R., Hoppenstedt, B., Sommer, K., Reichert, M.: Process-driven and flow-based processing of industrial sensor data. Sensors **20**(18), 5245 (2020). https://doi.org/10.3390/s20185245
6. Kerremans, M., Searle, S., Srivastava, T., Iijima, K.: Market guide for process mining (2020). www.gartner.com
7. Labio, W., Garcia-Molina, H.: Efficient snapshot differential algorithms for data warehousing. In: Vijayaraman, T.M., Buchmann, A.P., Mohan, C., Sarda, N.L. (eds.) Very Large Data Bases, pp. 63–74 (1996)

8. Mangat, A.S., Mangler, J., Rinderle-Ma, S.: Interactive process automation based on lightweight object detection in manufacturing processes. Comput. Ind. **130** (2021). https://doi.org/10.1016/j.compind.2021.103482

9. Mangler, J., Beran, P.P., Schikuta, E.: On the origin of services using RIDDL for description, evolution and composition of restful services. In: Cluster, Cloud and Grid Computing, pp. 505–508 (2010). https://doi.org/10.1109/CCGRID.2010.126

10. Mangler, J., Rinderle-Ma, S.: CPEE - cloud process execution engine. In: BPM Demo Sessions, p. 51 (2014). http://ceur-ws.org/Vol-1295/paper22.pdf

11. Mangler, J., Pauker, F., Rinderle-Ma, S., Ehrendorfer, M.: centurio.work - industry 4.0 integration assessment and evolution. In: BPM Industry Forum, 17th International Conference on Business Process Management, pp. 106–117 (2019). http://ceur-ws.org/Vol-2428/paper10.pdf

12. Reichert, M., Dadam, P., Rinderle-Ma, S., Jurisch, M., Kreher, U., Goeser, K.: Architecural principles and components of adaptive process management technology. In: Process Innovation for Enterprise Software, pp. 81–97 (2009). No. P-151

13. Reinkemeyer, L.: Process Mining in Action - Principles, Use Cases and Outlook. Springer, Heidelberg (2020). https://doi.org/10.1007/978-3-030-40172-6

14. Scheibel, B., Mangler, J., Rinderle-Ma, S.: Extraction of dimension requirements from engineering drawings for supporting quality control in production processes. Comput. Ind. **129** (2021). https://doi.org/10.1016/j.compind.2021.103442

15. Schulte, S., Schuller, D., Steinmetz, R., Abels, S.: Plug-and-play virtual factories. IEEE Internet Comput. **16**(5), 78–82 (2012). https://doi.org/10.1109/MIC.2012.114

16. Stertz, F., Mangler, J., Rinderle-Ma, S.: Balancing patient care and paperwork automatic task enactment and comprehensive documentation in treatment processes. Enterp. Model. Inf. Syst. Archit. Int. J. Concept Model. **15**, 11:1–11:28 (2020). https://doi.org/10.18417/emisa.15.11

17. Stertz, F., Mangler, J., Rinderle-Ma, S.: The Role of Time and Data: Online Conformance Checking in the Manufacturing Domain (2021). arXiv:2105.01454

18. Stertz, F., Mangler, J., Scheibel, B., Rinderle-Ma, S.: Expectations vs. experiences - process mining in small and medium sized manufacturing companies. In: Business Process Management (Forum) (2021). (accepted for publication)

19. Stertz, F., Rinderle-Ma, S., Mangler, J.: Analyzing process concept drifts based on sensor event streams during runtime. In: Business Process Management, pp. 202–219 (2020). https://doi.org/10.1007/978-3-030-58666-9_12

20. Wewerka, J., Reichert, M.: Robotic process automation in the automotive industry - lessons learned from an exploratory case study. Presented at the (2021). https://doi.org/10.1007/978-3-030-75018-3_1

21. Winter, K., van der Aa, H., Rinderle-Ma, S., Weidlich, M.: Assessing the compliance of business process models with regulatory documents. In: Conceptual Modeling, vol. 12400, pp. 189–203 (2020). https://doi.org/10.1007/978-3-030-62522-1_14

Tutorials

Cognitive Effectiveness of Representations for Process Mining

Jan Mendling[1,2]([✉]) [iD], Djordje Djurica[2] [iD], and Monika Malinova[2] [iD]

[1] Humboldt-Universität zu Berlin, Unter den Linden 6, 10099 Berlin, Germany
jan.mendling@hu-berlin.de
[2] Wirtschaftsuniversität Wien, Welthandelsplatz 1, 1020 Vienna, Austria
{jan.mendling,djordje.djurica,monika.malinova}@wu.ac.at

Abstract. This paper raises the issue that visual representations generated by process mining techniques have mostly been evaluated from a precision and recall angle. We observe this to be a problem, because it hardly takes into account how effective these representations are for users and for which analysis tasks they are useful. We aim to rectify this research problem by developing a cognitive perspective for researching process mining. To this end, we build both on the CogniDia framework for effective cognitive processing of diagrams and an initial list of process mining analysis tasks.

Keywords: Process mining · Process diagrams · Visual representation · Cognitive processing · CogniDia

1 Introduction

Process mining is an area of research that is concerned with the development of novel techniques that provide fact-based insights into business processes [1]. A process mining technique typically takes as input an event log and applies an algorithm to produce some visual representation as an output. These visual representations are often diagrams, such as directly-follows graphs, Petri nets, BPMN models, and several other modeling languages [5].

So far, research on process mining has been largely concerned with devising new algorithms for automatic discovery and conformance checking. These algorithms are commonly evaluated for their effectiveness, which is often measured using precision and recall against a gold standard [5]. What is surprising is the fact that hardly any user studies have been conducted on using process mining tools and visual representations generated from event logs. That is a problem, because precision and recall evaluations ignore the representation format of how process mining outputs are presented to a user and the relationship to the user's tasks at hand. Insights from process modeling research such as [10,13] cannot be readily applied for two reasons. First, visual representations generated by process mining algorithms extend beyond the set of languages studied in modeling research and enhance existing languages with additional information. Second,

© Springer Nature Switzerland AG 2021
A. Polyvyanyy et al. (Eds.): BPM 2021, LNCS 12875, pp. 17–22, 2021.
https://doi.org/10.1007/978-3-030-85469-0_2

the tasks considered in modeling research focus on general understanding while process mining users have more specific analytical tasks with a selective focus on parts of the process.

In this paper, we address this research problem by developing a cognitive perspective for researching process mining. To this end, we build on the CogniDia framework for effective cognitive processing of diagrams. This framework defines criteria for visual, verbal, semantic, and task processing of diagrams [12]. Furthermore, we identify a set of analysis tasks based on classifications in the literature [3,4,7].

The remainder of the paper is structured as follows. Section 2 describes the spectrum of visual representations used in process mining. Section 3 discusses the CogniDia framework and its application to process mining tasks. Section 4 highlights two examples of recent papers that evaluate process mining contributions based on user studies and identifies good practices, before Sect. 5 concludes.

2 Visual Representations for Process Mining

In this section, we describe external representations that are used in process mining. External representations are texts, images, diagrams and other sorts of man-made information objects that extend the human cognitive processing capabilities [19]. A subclass of external representations are visual representations. Their visual nature has been emphasized to be of advantage to several generic problem-solving tasks [18].

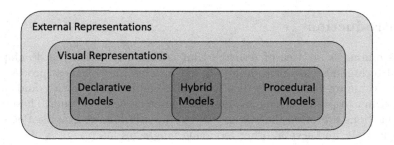

Fig. 1. External representations used for process mining

Process mining research has focused mostly on visual models that adhere to the specification of a particular modeling language. More specifically, Fig. 1 shows three classes of such visual models that have been distinguished: declarative, procedural and hybrid models. Studies that compare the mutual benefits of declarative and procedural models find mutual strengths and weaknesses, with declarative being strong in clarifying the conditions upon which a case unfolds, while procedural providing clarity about how a case proceeds [8,14]. Hybrid (also called mixed-paradigm) models combine these strengths with the ambition to represent behaviour in the most compact and understandable manner [6]. Within these three classes of declarative, procedural and hybrid models, there are several different representations. The review in [5] lists more than a dozen different types of models for process discovery only.

So far, the discussion for and against specific representations in the context of process mining is largely driven by arguments on execution semantics of the generated outputs. For instance, van der Aalst stresses the benefits of process trees for the fact of their soundness by definition [2]. From the same standpoint, limitations of directly-follows graphs are highlighted [16]. The focus on the potential to replay event logs by the help of a model with sound behavioural properties explains the emphasis on evaluation based on precision and recall [15]. This focus is justified in its own right, but comes without an explicit consideration of the analysis tasks for which representations generated by process mining are used by analysts.

3   Cognitive Effectiveness of Process Mining Outputs

Arguably, not much is known about the analyst using process mining techniques for gaining analytical insights into a business process. So far, there has been a limited focus on the tasks of analysts and on the question to which extent representations generated by process mining techniques are cognitively effective. Here, we refer to the CogniDia framework [12] that discusses criteria for effective cognitive processing of diagrams and other visual representations.

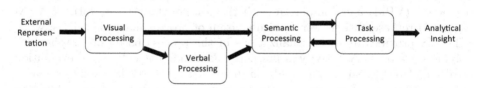

Fig. 2. Effective cognitive processing as described by the CogniDia framework [12]

Figure 2 shows that CogniDia distinguishes four stages of cognitive processing [12]. First, visual processing is concerned with identifying informational entities in visual inputs. Visual processing is effective when a visual representation is aesthetic, simple, consistent, with distinguishable and mnemonic elements. Second, verbal processing focuses on textual information entities. Verbal processing is effective when text elements are short and uniform. Third, semantic processing relates the understanding of both representations and associated modeling languages. Semantic processing is effective when representations are correct and easy to understand, while languages should facilitate an appropriate and faithful representation of the domain. Fourth, task processing proceeds by decomposition along a mentally constructed goal hierarchy. Task processing is effective when representations satisfy user expectations and information needs.

Several use cases and analysis types have been identified for process mining. Notably, these have often been described as technical operations and not from the goals of the analyst. Consider, for example, the use case "Discover Model from Event Data" described in [3]. The description refers to the general interest in extracting knowledge about a process from event logs, but by and large provides a high-level description of a technical operation. Closer to the goals of an analyst is the use case description of "Distribution of cases over paths" [4] (also called variant analysis [7]) that emphasizes the interest to understand this distribution analysis types. Arguably, these uses cases and analysis types focus on means, but pay little attention to the ends in view of the analyst. A lens on the decision-making and problem-solving tasks would foreground the goal to decide what is the issue of the process that offers the greatest return when being fixed, or the goal to understand the root causes of an observed issue. Evaluation with a focus on replay with precision and recall has little to offer for discussing the effectiveness of supporting these goals.

4   Evaluating Process Mining from a Cognitive Angle

Even though precision and recall evaluations are predominant in process mining research, there are some notable examples that recognize the need to make tasks explicit and to conduct empirical user studies. Here, we summarize two examples by Leotta et al. [11] and by Graafmans et al. [9].

The first example we discuss is a comparative user evaluation by Leotta et al. [11] on tools that allow to visualize human habits based on sensor event data. The authors develop a process mining based approach called Visual Process Maps (VPM) and compare it with the state-of-the art tool Situvis. VPM generated representations were a combination of process map and DRGs, while SITUVIS provides its own visualizations of the process based on graphs with polylines where every activity is presented as a different color. The evaluation involved 14 participants and builds on different analysis tasks including search and understanding. Furthermore, the users were asked to rate their confidence for different interpretations of output. Users had to work on the same tasks with both alternative tools. In this way, their assessment offers insights into mutual strengths and weaknesses of usability and graphical expressiveness of both tools.

The second example we discuss is a user study by Graafmans et al. [9] for a process mining tool using realistic analyst tasks. The authors develop guidelines for how six-sigma analysis can be supported by process mining. They involve users at different stages of the design process. Most notably, they conducted a usability study with 12 six sigma and process mining experts for tasks associated with a realistic analysis scenario. For working on the tasks, the participants had to interact with the tool and make use of several of its visual representations. After providing answers to the scenario-related tasks, participants had to answer to standard questionnaire items for technology acceptance [17], including their perceived usefulness, perceived ease of use, and intention to use the proposed guideline and its accompanying tool. The authors also conducted interviews with participants to gain qualitative feedback.

The two papers help us to identify several good practices for evaluating process mining representations based on user studies. First, the paper by Leotta et al. [11] highlights the benefits of a comparative evaluation. Second, both papers underline the need to let users work with the tool on realistic tasks. Graafmans et al. [9] explicitly state that the analyst as a user of a process mining tool typically has the goal to identify improvement opportunities. Any representation generated by process mining techniques has to be judged in this light. Third, the paper by Graafmans et al. [9] exemplifies the reuse of established evaluation frameworks such as usability analysis and items of the technology acceptance model. Fourth, both papers highlight that users have specific goals that are anchored in their work context, such as identifying improvement opportunities. The representations they use are more complex than a specific type of model. They include any information that is visually, but also textually represented as output of a process mining tool. The CogniDia framework allows us to discuss the mutual benefits of different representations in relation to different user tasks.

5   Conclusion

In this paper, we have raised the issue of how visual representations generated by process mining techniques can be evaluated. We emphasize that evaluations in terms of precision and recall only overlook the connection between visual representations and tasks of the analyst. We sketched the merits of establishing a cognitive perspective on the relationship between tasks and representations based on the CogniDia framework. To this end, we revisited two recent papers that conducted user studies for evaluating process mining contributions.

References

1. van der Aalst, W.M.P.: Process Mining - Data Science in Action. Second Edition. Springer (2016). https://doi.org/10.1007/978-3-662-49851-4
2. van der Aalst, W.M.P., Buijs, J.C.A.M., van Dongen, D.F.: Towards improving the representational bias of process mining. In: Aberer, K., Damiani, E., Dillon, T. (eds.) SIMPDA 2011. LNBIP, vol. 116. Springer, Heidelberg (2012). https://doi.org/10.1007/978-3-642-34044-4
3. Van der Aalst, W.M.: Business process management: a comprehensive survey. Int. Scholarly Res. Notices **2013**, 1–37 (2013)
4. Ailenei, I., Rozinat, A., Eckert, A., van der Aalst, W.M.P.: Definition and validation of process mining use cases. In: Daniel, F., Barkaoui, K., Dustdar, S. (eds.) BPM 2011. LNBIP, vol. 99, pp. 75–86. Springer, Heidelberg (2012). https://doi.org/10.1007/978-3-642-28108-2_7
5. Augusto, A., et al.: Automated discovery of process models from event logs: review and benchmark. IEEE Trans. Knowl. Data Eng. **31**(4), 686–705 (2019). https://doi.org/10.1109/TKDE.2018.2841877
6. van Dongen, B.F., De Smedt, J., Di Ciccio, C., Mendling, J.: Conformance checking of mixed-paradigm process models. Information Systems, 101685 (2020)

7. Dumas, M., La Rosa, M., Mendling, J., Reijers, H.A.: Fundamentals of Business Process Management, 2nd edn. Springer, Heidelberg (2018). https://doi.org/10.1007/978-3-662-56509-4

8. Fahland, D., et al.: Declarative versus imperative process modeling languages: the issue of understandability. In: Halpin, T., et al. (eds.) BPMDS/EMMSAD -2009. LNBIP, vol. 29. Springer, Heidelberg (2009). https://doi.org/10.1007/978-3-642-01862-6

9. Graafmans, T., Turetken, O., Poppelaars, H., Fahland, D.: Process mining for six sigma. Bus. Inf. Syst. Eng. **2020**, 1–24 (2020)

10. La Rosa, M., ter Hofstede, A.H., Wohed, P., Reijers, H.A., Mendling, J., van der Aalst, W.M.: Managing process model complexity via concrete syntax modifications. IEEE Trans. Ind. Inf. **7**(2), 255–265 (2011)

11. Leotta, F., Mecella, M., Sora, D.: Visual analysis of sensor logs in smart spaces: activities vs. situations. In: 2018 IEEE Fourth International Conference on Big Data Computing Service and Applications, pp. 105–114. IEEE (2018)

12. Malinova, M., Mendling, J.: Cognitive diagram understanding and task performance in system analysis and design. MIS Quarterly (2022)

13. Mendling, J., Reijers, H.A., van der Aalst, W.M.P.: Seven process modeling guidelines (7PMG). Inf. Softw. Technol. **52**(2), 127–136 (2010)

14. Pichler, P., Weber, B., Zugal, S., Pinggera, J., Mendling, J., Reijers, H.A.: Imperative versus declarative process modeling languages: an empirical investigation. In: Daniel, F., Barkaoui, K., Dustdar, S. (eds.) BPM 2011. LNBIP, vol. 99. Springer, Heidelberg (2012). https://doi.org/10.1007/978-3-642-28108-2

15. Polyvyanyy, A., Solti, A., Weidlich, M., Ciccio, C.D., Mendling, J.: Monotone precision and recall measures for comparing executions and specifications of dynamic systems. ACM Trans. Softw. Eng. Methodol. (TOSEM) **29**(3), 1–41 (2020)

16. van der Aalst, W.M.: A practitioner's guide to process mining: limitations of the directly-follows graph. Procedia Comput. Sci. **164**, 321–328 (2019). https://doi.org/10.1016/j.procs.2019.12.189

17. Venkatesh, V., Bala, H.: Technology acceptance model 3 and a research agenda on interventions. Decis. Sci. **39**(2), 273–315 (2008)

18. Vessey, I.: Cognitive fit: a theory-based analysis of the graphs versus tables literature. Decis. Sci. **22**(2), 219–240 (1991)

19. Zhang, J., Norman, D.A.: Representations in distributed cognitive tasks. Cogn. Sci. **18**(1), 87–122 (1994)

RuM: Declarative Process Mining, Distilled

Anti Alman[1(✉)], Claudio Di Ciccio[2], Fabrizio Maria Maggi[3], Marco Montali[3], and Han van der Aa[4]

[1] University of Tartu, Tartu, Estonia
anti.alman@ut.ee
[2] Sapienza University of Rome, Rome, Italy
claudio.diciccio@uniroma1.it
[3] Free University of Bozen-Bolzano, Bolzano, Italy
{maggi,montali}@inf.unibz.it
[4] University of Mannheim, Mannheim, Germany
han@informatik.uni-mannheim.de

Abstract. Flexibility is a key characteristic of numerous business process management domains. In these domains, the paths to fulfil process goals may not be fully predetermined, but can strongly depend on dynamic decisions made based on the current circumstances of a case. A common example is the adaptation of a standard treatment process to the needs of a specific patient. However, high flexibility does not mean chaos: certain key process rules still delimit the execution space, such as rules that prohibit the joint administration of certain drugs in a treatment, due to dangerous interactions. A renowned means to handle flexibility by design is the declarative approach, which aims to define processes through their core behavioural rules, thus leaving room for dynamic adaptation. This declarative approach to both process modelling and mining involves a paradigm shift in process thinking and, therefore, the support of novel concepts and tools. Complementing our tutorial with the same title, this paper provides a high-level introduction to declarative process mining, including its operationalisation through the RuM toolkit, key conceptual considerations, and an outlook for the future.

Keywords: Declare · Declarative process mining · Rule mining · Process discovery · Conformance checking · Process monitoring · Declarative modelling

1 Introduction

Infusing flexibility in process-aware information systems is widely recognised as a key challenge in business process management (BPM) and information systems engineering [17]. Within the flexibility spectrum, *flexibility by design* advocates that process modelling languages themselves need to offer modelling primitives

© Springer Nature Switzerland AG 2021
A. Polyvyanyy et al. (Eds.): BPM 2021, LNCS 12875, pp. 23–29, 2021.
https://doi.org/10.1007/978-3-030-85469-0_3

that provide freedom to process executors when deciding how to execute the process. The question then becomes how such languages help in finding a suitable trade-off between flexibility and control. Declarative approaches tackle this problem in an extreme way: the model indicates *what* the relevant temporal/dynamic constraints that have to be respected during process execution enforce, leaving the executors free to decide *how* to unfold the concrete executions.

After seminal papers on the topic were published between 1998 and 2003 within BPM and neighboring fields [5,18,19], the community started investigating declarative process modelling more systematically starting from 2006, when Pesic and van der Aalst proposed to apply temporal logic patterns [8] to declaratively capture process constraints [20], eventually leading to the DECLARE language and system [16] and to the definition of a variety of reasoning tasks thanks to different logic-based formalisations [14,15]. This interest was further fueled by the introduction of other declarative approaches, most prominently Dynamic Condition-Response Graphs [11].

A well-known issue with declarative approaches is that while they enjoy flexibility, they typically do not explicitly indicate how the execution has to be controlled. In other words, conforming executions are only implicitly described as those that satisfy all the given constraints. Constraints, in turn, may be quite diverse from each other (e.g., indicating what *is expected* to occur, but also what should *not* happen). At the same time, constraints implicitly and mutually affect each other (a phenomenon referred to as *hidden dependencies* in the cognitive dimension framework used to evaluate the characteristics of notations [6,9,15]). This notoriously challenges understandability and interpretability of declarative process models [10], and calls for toolkits providing continuous support to the end users [9]. One such toolkit is RuM [2], which addresses some of the above-mentioned issues by providing a unified user interface for declarative process mining algorithms.

2   Declarative Process Mining with RuM

RuM [2] is the first software platform natively designed for declarative process modelling and process mining. RuM is based on the well-known modelling language DECLARE [16] and its multi-perspective extension MP-DECLARE [3], that is, DECLARE extended with data and time perspectives.

The following sections give a brief overview of RuM. Further information and the download link can be found in [2] and at https://rulemining.org/. To illustrate RuM's functionality, we use the Sepsis treatment process and event log described in [13].

Automated Process Discovery. RuM includes multiple algorithms for automatically discovering a process model. As usual for DECLARE, the discovered models consist of a set of *constraints* where each constraint describes one specific aspect of the process (i.e., constrains the behaviour of the process in a specific way).

In general, a constraint describes either the cardinality of an activity (i.e., the number of occurrence thereof in a trace) or a relation between two activities (i.e., how the occurrence of an activity requires or disables the occurrence of another one). For example, EXACTLY1(*ER Triage*) means that activity *ER Triage* will occur exactly once in each trace. CHAINRESPONSE(*ER Registration, ER Triage*) means that when activity *ER Registration* occurs then *ER Triage* will occur immediately after.

The discovered model is by default visualised using the standard DECLARE notation (Fig. 1). Alternatively, it is possible to represent the model procedurally as an equivalent deterministic finite state automaton (Fig. 2). Finally, it is possible to represent the entire model as a set of natural language sentences, e.g., "When *ER Registration* occurs, then *ER Triage* occurs immediately afterwards".

Conformance Checking and Monitoring. RuM provides two conformance checking approaches. The first one detects constraint fulfilments and violations (Fig. 3a), which pinpoint both the events that occur as specified in the model and those events that contradict it. The second approach is based on log

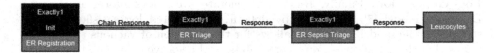

Fig. 1. An example of a DECLARE model represented as a map.

Fig. 2. An automaton representation of the DECLARE model in Fig. 1.

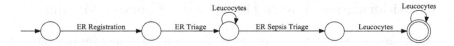

(a) Fulfilments (green) and violations (red)   (b) Log alignment (deletions in yellow)

Fig. 3. Conformance checking approaches

alignments (Fig. 3b), as it identifies the event insertions and/or deletions that would make the event log conforming with the DECLARE model.

The conformance checking results are provided at different levels, i.e., per event log, per trace, and per constraint. The latter is especially useful since it allows for clear insights and overall explainability of the conformance checking results with respect to specific process constraints. Additionally, RuM provides a monitoring functionality, which allows the user to interactively replay the traces one event at a time. During replay, RuM visualises the state of each constraint in the model (possibly/permanently satisfied and possibly/permanently violated) as the events of the trace are occurring.

Model Editing. RuM provides model editing capabilities through a fully MP-Declare compliant model editor, which supports the different representations discussed for process discovery above (cf., Figs. 1 and 2). These representations are updated and the inputs are validated on the fly as the model is being edited. In addition to editing the constraints directly, it is also possible to specify constraints and data conditions by using natural language speech and written text. This functionality is implemented as a simple chatbot named Declo [1].

Log Generation. Finally, RuM can generate event logs based on a given DECLARE model [7]. Although, by default, a generated log satisfies all constraints in the model, RuM also allows for the insertion of vacuous traces, i.e., traces that do not activate some constraints, and negative ones, i.e., traces that violate constraints.

3   Considerations About Declarative Process Mining

The constraint-based nature of the declarative approach has various interesting implications and advantages with respect to the traditional, imperative paradigm. For instance, since declarative constraints establish behavioural rules that delimit the possible execution space for processes, they act like norms with which all process runs have to comply with. This characteristic make declarative models *open*, in that any execution is permitted as long as the expressed rules are not violated, as opposed to the *closed* scope of imperative models (e.g., Workflow nets, BPMN diagrams, event-process chains), which depict the whole execution space, from start to end [12].

From a mining perspective, declarative process mining aims to establish, measure and validate the rules that best *define* the behaviour emerging from the traces recorded in event logs – in the closest etymological sense of "defining", i.e., marking out their boundary. Therefore, exceptional, ad-hoc, or optional variants of process behaviour are fully supported as long as no constraints are expressed that contradict them. By contrast, an imperative model requires an alteration of its structure any time its unfolding does not encompass an alternative path that is evidenced in an event log. Declarative models can be used to represent the distinguishing core rules of event logs exposing high variability as per their stored runs, thereby catering for *flexibility*.

Fig. 4. A DECLARE negative constraint.

Declarative process rules are exerted over whole runs. Such a *global state perspective* differs from the imperative approach in which, given a current state, only the next enabled actions are made explicit (local state perspective). This reflects the difference between functional (declarative) and procedural (imperative) approaches to programming. A declarative rule applies any time a situation that triggers it is reached, regardless of the history of actions that led there. Also, the effect can span the whole execution of the process, i.e., at any moment in the future or the past: for instance, PRECEDENCE(*ER Sepsis Triage, IV Antibiotics*) requires that *ER Sepsis Triage* must occur at any point in time *before* the inoculation of antibiotics. In contrast, imperative models dictate what the possible operations are for the next step given a case's history.

Declarative process models enjoy *compositionality* based on the conjunction of their constraints: the intersection of permitted behaviour from each rule determines the overall specification [4]. Adding rules restricts the range of acceptable runs. In contrast, the addition of new states and transitions to an imperative model enlarges the execution space. We remark two consequences of this difference. Firstly, more flexible processes may create more cluttered imperative models (the so-called spaghetti models) as declarative specifications would represent the core behavioural rules they are subject to rather than all the possible runs that would comply with them [16]. Secondly, declarative models are better suited for the seamless support of *negative* rules, i.e., constraints that impose the disablement of task occurrences given a specified condition. For example, NOTSUCCESSION(*Admission IC, IV Antibiotics*) imposes that after patients are admitted in the intensive care unit, they cannot undergo an inoculation of antibiotics. Adding this constraint to the model depicted in Fig. 1 is straightforward as declarative process models consist of lists of statements dictating the process rules. Graphically, it requires the sole juxtaposition of the constraint illustrated in Fig. 4 to the existing map. Including this constraint in the automaton representation in Fig. 2 requires the addition of numerous states and transitions as illustrated in Fig. 5 though.

To conclude, we remark that as the declarative process specifications dictate the rules that process executions are required to abide by, they can act as a bounding box within which imperative process models need to be defined to represent specific strategies implemented to achieve the goals of the operating organisation, depending on the expertise, resources and context of the latter.

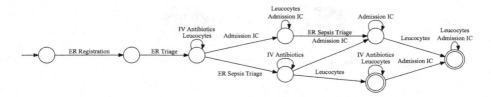

Fig. 5. The automaton representation of the model in Fig. 1 including the constraint in Fig. 4.

4   Research Opportunities

Beyond the current state of the art, we foresee several research opportunities in the context of declarative process modelling and mining. From a modelling perspective, a clear opportunity relates to the graphical notation. The original version of the DECLARE language is known to be difficult to understand [10]. Although some effort has been done in this direction already, an extensive user evaluation to compare the different ways to represent constraints is still missing. Also, an interesting challenge is the analysis of declarative process models mixing crisp and probabilistic constraints, as discovered models often retain constraints that are violated by a set of traces in an event log. Another aspect currently under investigation pertains to the so-called *hybrid process models*, which consist of both imperative and declarative parts. This is important since real processes often contain both structured and unstructured parts. Finally, a highly promising research direction is the development of declarative modelling and mining instruments to deal with object-centric processes. This problem is also closely related to the assessment of the relevance of a constraint in a given process execution, which can depend on the nature of the actions and of the objects involved in the constraint.

Acknowledgements. The work of A. Alman was supported by the Estonian Research Council (project PRG1226) and ERDF via the IT Academy Program. The work of C. Di Ciccio was supported by MIUR under grant "Dipartimenti di eccellenza 2018–2022" of the Department of Computer Science at Sapienza and by the Sapienza research project "SPECTRA".

References

1. Alman, A., Balder, K.J., Maggi, F.M., van der Aa, H.: Declo: a chatbot for user-friendly specification of declarative process models. In: BPM (PhD/Demos), pp. 122–126 (2020)
2. Alman, A., Di Ciccio, C., Haas, D., Maggi, F.M., Nolte, A.: Rule mining with RuM. In: ICPM, pp. 121–128 (2020)
3. Burattin, A., Maggi, F.M., Sperduti, A.: Conformance checking based on multi-perspective declarative process models. Expert Syst. Appl. **65**, 194–211 (2016)

4. Di Ciccio, C., Maggi, F.M., Montali, M., Mendling, J.: Resolving inconsistencies and redundancies in declarative process models. Inf. Syst. **64**, 425–446 (2017)
5. Davulcu, H., Kifer, M., Ramakrishnan, C.R., Ramakrishnan, I.V.: Logic based modeling and analysis of workflows. In: PODS, pp. 25–33. ACM (1998)
6. De Smedt, J., De Weerdt, J., Serral, E., Vanthienen, J.: Discovering hidden dependencies in constraint-based declarative process models for improving understandability. Inf. Syst. **74**(Part 1), 40–52 (2018)
7. Di Ciccio, C., Bernardi, M.L., Cimitile, M., Maggi, F.M.: Generating event logs through the simulation of Declare models. In: EOMAS@CAiSE, pp. 20–36 (2015)
8. Dwyer, M.B., Avrunin, G.S., Corbett, J.C.: Patterns in property specifications for finite-state verification. In: ICSE, pp. 411–420. ACM (1999)
9. Green, T.R.G., Petre, M.: Usability analysis of visual programming environments: a 'cognitive dimensions' framework. Vis. Comp. Lang. **7**(2), 131–174 (1996)
10. Haisjackl, C., et al.: Understanding Declare models: strategies, pitfalls, empirical results. Softw. Syst. Model. **15**(2), 325–352 (2016)
11. Hildebrandt, T.T., Mukkamala, R.R.: Declarative event-based workflow as distributed dynamic condition response graphs. In: PLACES, vol. 69 of EPTCS, pp. 59–73 (2010)
12. Maggi, F.M., Bose, R.P.J.C., van der Aalst, W.M.P.: Efficient discovery of understandable declarative process models from event logs. In: CAiSE, pp. 270–285 (2012)
13. Mannhardt, F., Blinde, D.: Analyzing the trajectories of patients with sepsis using process mining. In: RADAR+EMISA@CAiSE, pp. 72–80 (2017)
14. Montali, M.: Specification and Verification of Declarative Open Interaction Models. LNBIP, vol. 56. Springer, Heidelberg (2010). https://doi.org/10.1007/978-3-642-14538-4
15. Montali, M., Pesic, M., van der Aalst, W.M.P., Chesani, F., Mello, P., Storari, S.: Declarative specification and verification of service choreographies. ACM Trans. Web **4**(1), 3:1–3:62 (2010)
16. Pesic, M., Schonenberg, H., van der Aalst, W.M.P.: DECLARE: full support for loosely-structured processes. In: EDOC, pp. 287–300 (2007)
17. Reichert, M., Weber, B.: Enabling Flexibility in Process-Aware Information Systems - Challenges, Methods, Technologies. Springer, Heidelberg (2012). https://doi.org/10.1007/978-3-642-30409-5
18. Sadiq, S., Sadiq, W., Orlowska, M.: Pockets of flexibility in workflow specification. In: S.Kunii, H., Jajodia, S., Sølvberg, A. (eds.) ER 2001. LNCS, vol. 2224, pp. 513–526. Springer, Heidelberg (2001). https://doi.org/10.1007/3-540-45581-7_38
19. Singh, M.P.: Distributed enactment of multiagent workflows: temporal logic for web service composition. In: AAMAS, pp. 907–914. ACM (2003)
20. van der Aalst, W.M.P., Pesic, M.: DecSerFlow: towards a truly declarative service flow language. In: WS-FM, pp. 1–23 (2006)

Applications of Automated Planning for Business Process Management

Andrea Marrella[1(✉)] and Tathagata Chakraborti[2]

[1] Sapienza Universitá di Roma, Rome, Italy
marrella@diag.uniroma1.it
[2] IBM Research AI, Cambridge, MA, USA
tchakra2@ibm.com

Abstract. This is a brief summary of the applications of automated planning in the field of Business Process Management (BPM); and accompanies a tutorial with the same theme at the 19th International Conference on Business Process Management (BPM 2021). We hope that this report is able to quickly onboard newcomers into this field with a broad overview of the associated challenges and opportunities, as well as provide established practitioners in the field some new food for thought in terms of the state-of-the-art and the evolving nature of these problems.

1 Why Automated Planning for Business Processes?

Automated planning deals with sequential decision-making of autonomous or semi-autonomous systems. Typically, a planning task takes as input a model of how the world works and a description of the task to be solved in that world; and produces as output a sequence of steps (plan) or a mapping from a world state to an action (policy). The representation of the world and task knowledge determines the flavor of planning. In this paper, we will focus on the subcategory "classical planning" or planning compilable to its classical form, where a goal state must be reached from a fully known initial state by applying planning steps having deterministic effects [9].

The discipline of business process management (BPM) deals with the discovery, modeling, analysis, measurement, improvement, optimization, and automation of business processes [19].

While each of these problems within the scope of BPM have a wide range of associated techniques attached to them, the field of automated planning has interesting touch points with every one of them. In the next section, we will describe briefly *how*. But before we get there, we discuss briefly *why*.

– The key advantage of modeling problems in this form is that it is **domain independent**, i.e., we can bring to bear decades of research and tools from the planning community (such as planners, domain-independent heuristics,

A. Polyvyanyy et al. (Eds.): BPM 2021, LNCS 12875, pp. 30–36, 2021.
https://doi.org/10.1007/978-3-030-85469-0_4

editors, visualizers, and so on). The key challenge here is then the interfacing between a BPM practitioner and a representation the planner can understand. We will explore this in various contexts in the next section.

- The representations are **human-interpretable** and hence allows for iterative modeling and refinement with different stakeholders in the process;
- Planning formalisms offer an **exponential scale-up** from the complexity of the representation to the complexity of the process. Though this means that classical planning, i.e., the simplest form of a planning problem, is NP-hard. This theoretical limit is rarely breached when it comes to applications of planning to BPM. Instead, an exponential scale-up means that:
  1. processes of much more sophistication can be composed the same amount of work as manual specification;
  2. much less work is required to specify processes of the same sophistication than manual specification; and
  3. coverage of a wide space of processes from the same domain-independent specification, i.e., a possibility of BPM-practitioners to go past hard-coded solutions to individual problems to domain-independent solutions using compilations to planning formulations.
- Classical planning models constitute implicit **representations of finite state controllers**, and can be thus queried by standard verification techniques, such as Model Checking. In fact, this implicit representation is directly tied to the exponential scale-up since practitioners do not need to specify the control explicitly but rather only its declarative components.

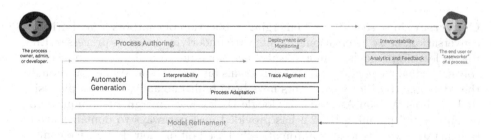

Fig. 1. Different touch points of planning along the life-cycle of a business process.

2 Automated Planning for BPM

We will now reflect on how the advantages described above play out in various applications of planning in world of BPM. Figure 1 conceptualizes the various touch points of planning technologies along the life-cycle of a business process.

2.1 Automated Generation of Process Models

Current BPM technology is generally based on rigid process models making its application difficult in dynamic and possibly evolving domains, where pre-specifying the entire model is not always possible. In this context, the automated generation of process models not starting from an event log (that is often not available) but from the knowledge of the process context and goal is highly desirable. This ability to construct process models automatically from its individual declarative components is the primary application of planning in BPM and is among the many flavors of declarative modeling used in the field [10].

As an example, in [15], the authors applied planning for automated process model synthesis. Specifically, the use of planning enabled to build a plan that led from the world status to the goal status. That plan was the process model. Notice that, typically, a plan is a sequence of steps. Instead, the technique in [15] catered for partial orders allowing to encompass parallelism and (some) choice points. A particularly interesting design of that technique was that a partial knowledge of the world status was sufficient to synthesize the process model. For more examples for this type of application, we refer the reader to [14].

Web Service Composition. One important sub-theme in business process generation is the composition of existing web services to create new ones [20] – this creates complex semi-automated pathways among existing manual processes as well as augments manual paths with automation. Composing web services finds a ready ally in automated planning [2,8]. We refer to [21] for a summary of work done in this area, and [25,29] for a summary of challenges.

Conversational Agents. An emerging application of chatbots is goal-oriented conversation, i.e., conversational agents with underlying business processes. End-to-end learning models cannot specify such bots due to inability to connect the conversational elements to process constrains and execution. While traditionally the "dialogue tree" for such agents have been built manually, for example, using tools such as Watson Assistant or Google Dialogflow, emerging techniques built on automated planning [18,24] has provided new pathways to domain authors to generate these structures automatically based off of their declarative components. This also has synergies with web service composition as well [5].

2.2 Trace Alignment

Within process mining, trace alignment is the problem of verifying if the observed behavior stored in an event log is compliant with the process model that encodes how the process is allowed to be executed to ensure that regulations are not violated. Trace alignment makes it possible to pinpoint the deviations causing nonconformity with a high degree of detail [1]. While there exist manifold explanations why a trace is not conforming, one is interested in finding the most probable explanation, i.e., one of the alignments with the least expensive deviations (i.e., optimal alignments), according to some function assigning costs to deviations. The state-of-the-art techniques to compute optimal alignments against procedural [1] and declarative [7] process models provide ad-hoc implementations of the A* algorithm. The fact is that when process models and event logs are of considerable size the existing approaches do not scale efficiently due to their ad-hoc nature and may be unable to accomplish the alignment task.

Among scalable approaches to solve the alignment task, in [11, 13] the authors have reduced trace alignment (let it be declarative or imperative) to a classical planning problem. This opportunity led to solving a number of additional problems. For example, it became possible to compute alignments in presence of coarse-grained timestamps - such that some events are marked as if they were contemporary, against the typical event log assumption [12].

2.3   Process Adaptation

Process Adaptation is the ability of a process to react to exceptional circumstances and to adapt/modify its structure accordingly [22]. While anticipated exceptions can be foreseen at design-time and incorporated into the process model as exception handlers, unanticipated exceptions refer to situations that emerge at run-time, thus requiring that BPM tools provide real-time monitoring and adaptation features to detect/repair them during process execution.

To overcome the limits of traditional process adaptation, which was based on an ad-hoc definition of exception handlers to build recovery procedures, in [16, 17] the authors presented a planning-based approach to adapt on-the-fly a running process instance requiring no predefined exception handler. Specifically, the SmartPM approach enables to automatically detect unanticipated run-time exceptions and exogenous events by monitoring the discrepancies between the expected reality, i.e., the (idealized) model of reality that reflects the intended outcome of the task execution, and the physical reality, i.e., the real world with the actual values of conditions and outcomes. If the gap between the expected and physical realities is such that the process instance cannot progress, the SmartPM approach resorts to classical planners to build a recovery procedure as a plan, which can thereby reduce the misalignment between the two realities, thus resolving exceptions that were not designed into the original process. In general, this falls under the broader theme of "replanning" in automated planning, and can be adopted to a wide range of problems including the specific case of automated web service composition [4] as discussed before.

2.4   Interpretability and Authoring Tools

The interpretability question for automated composition of process elements using automated planning boils down to *understanding the imperative consequences of declarative design*. These interpretability issues can occur at multiple stages:

Process Definitions. This is meant to reduce the level of expertise required to specify constructs that can interface easily with a planning representation. For example, in the context of web service composition, authors in [3,23] tried out a tag based language that is at once easy to understand from the domain author's point of view and at the same time easily compilable to a representation that an automated planner can consume. Authors in [23,26] also demonstrate how the domain author can make use of not one but multiple compositions to understand how a process will evolve and use that knowledge to constrain their authoring problem. Authors in [18] do the same using a contingent plan instead.

Process Understanding. Once process elements have been defined, it must be ensured that the process author understands how those individual elements get composed into process controllers. Interestingly, the process author here can be the end-user themselves, as well as the usual developer or admin of the process.

In [27], authors introduced a vocabulary for triaging composed processes iteratively through a mixture of foils, landmarks (i.e. necessary steps), and abstractions. In this paradigm, the domain author fixes problems in the most simple abstraction of a process and then tests them in the fully composed process by querying it with "foils" or instantiations of the process that they feel should (or should not) be supported by the automated composition.

In [28], on the other hand, the explanations are for the end-user who wants to explore the inner workings of an "aggregated assistant" composed on the fly – by asking how certain things were done and why. Interestingly, such explanations are sometimes just a feature that is good to have (in terms of increased transparency and establishment of common grounds with the user) but they may also be required by law (e.g. GDPR rules may require establishing provenance and necessity of data flow in certain cases).

3   Conclusions

This concludes a whirlwind overview of the applications of planning for BPM. We encourage the reader to follow-up for more details with related surveys [6,14,30] and our tutorial on this topic at BPM 2021: ibm.biz/bpm-2021-tutorial.

Acknowledgements. The work of Andrea Marrella has been supported by the H2020 project DataCloud and the Sapienza grant BPbots.

References

1. Van der Aalst, W., Adriansyah, A., van Dongen, B.: Replaying History on Process Models for Conformance Checking and Performance Analysis. Data Mining and Knowledge Discovery, Wiley Interdisciplinary Reviews (2012)
2. Araghi, S.S.: Customizing the Composition of Web Services and Beyond. U Toronto (2012). Ph.D. thesis

3. Bouillet, E., Feblowitz, M., Liu, Z., Ranganathan, A., Riabov, A.: A tag-based approach for the design and composition of information processing applications. In: OOPSLA 2008 (2008)
4. Bucchiarone, A., Pistore, M., Raik, H., Kazhamiakin, R.: Adaptation of service-based business processes by context-aware replanning. In: SOCA 2011 (2011)
5. Chakraborti, T., Agarwal, S., Khazaeni, Y., Rizk, Y., Isahagian, V.: D3BA: a tool for optimizing business processes using non-deterministic planning. In: Del Río Ortega, A., Leopold, H., Santoro, F.M. (eds.) BPM 2020. LNBIP, vol. 397, pp. 181–193. Springer, Cham (2020). https://doi.org/10.1007/978-3-030-66498-5_14
6. Chakraborti, T., Ishakian, V., Khalaf, R., Khazaeni, Y., Muthusamy, V., Rizk, Y., Unuvar, M.: From robotic process automation to intelligent process automation: emerging trends. In: BPM RPA Forum (2020)
7. De Leoni, M., Maggi, F.M., van der Aalst, W.M.: Aligning event logs and declarative process models for conformance checking. In: BPM 2012 (2012)
8. Dong, X., Halevy, A., Madhavan, J., Nemes, E., Zhang, J.: Similarity search for web services. In: VLDB (2004)
9. Geffner, H., Bonet, B.: A Concise Introduction to Models and Methods for Automated Planning. Synth, Lectures on AI and Machine Learning (2013)
10. De Giacomo, G.: Artificial Intelligence-based declarative process synthesis for BPM. In: BPM 2021 (Keynote Talk) (2021)
11. De Giacomo, G., Maggi, F.M., Marrella, A., Patrizi, F.: On the disruptive effectiveness of automated planning for LTLf-based trace alignment. In: AAAI 2017 (2017)
12. de Leoni, M., Lanciano, G., Marrella, A.: Aligning partially-ordered process-execution traces and models using automated planning. In: ICAPS 2018 (2018)
13. de Leoni, M., Marrella, A.: Aligning real process executions and prescriptive process models through automated planning. Exp. Syst. with App. **82**, 162–183 (2017)
14. Marrella, A.: Automated planning for business process management. J. Data Semantics **8**(2), 79–98 (2019)
15. Marrella, A., Lespérance, Y.: A planning approach to the automated synthesis of template-based process models. Serv. Oriented Comput. Appl. **11**, 367–392 (2017)
16. Marrella, A., Mecella, M., Sardina, S.: Intelligent process adaptation in the SmartPM system. ACM Trans. Intell. Syst. Technol. **8**(2), 1–43 (2017)
17. Marrella, A., Mecella, M., Sardiña, S.: Supporting adaptiveness of cyber-physical processes through action-based formalisms. AI Commun. 31, 47–74 (2018)
18. Muise, C., et al.: Planning for Goal-Oriented Dialogue Systems. Technical Report (2020)
19. Nathaniel Palmer: What is BPM? https://bpm.com/what-is-bpm
20. Papazoglou, M.P., Georgakopoulos, D.: Service-oriented computing. Commun. ACM **46**(10), 24–28 (2003)
21. Rao, J., Su, X.: A survey of automated web service composition methods. In: Workshop on Semantic Web Services and Web Process Composition (2004)
22. Reichert, M., Weber, B.: Enabling Flexibility in Process-Aware Information Systems. Springer, Heidelberg (2012). https://doi.org/10.1007/978-3-642-30409-5
23. Riabov, A.V., Boillet, E., Feblowitz, M.D., Liu, Z., Ranganathan, A.: Wishful search: interactive composition of data mashups. In: WWW (2008)
24. Rizk, Y., et al.: A unified conversational assistant framework for business process automation. In: AAAI Workshop on IPA (2020)
25. Sohrabi, S.: Customizing the composition of actions, programs, and web services with user preferences. In: ISWC (2010)

26. Sohrabi, S., Riabov, A., Katz, M., Udrea, O.: An AI planning solution to scenario generation for enterprise risk management. In: AAAI 2018 (2018)
27. Sreedharan, S., Chakraborti, T., Muise, C., Khazaeni, Y., Kambhampati, S.: D3WA+ - a case study of XAIP in a model acquisition task for dialogue planning. In: ICAPS 2020 (2020)
28. Sreedharan, S., Chakraborti, T., Rizk, Y., Khazaeni, Y.: Explainable composition of aggregated assistants. In: ICAPS Workshop on Explainable AI Planning (2020)
29. Srivastava, B., Koehler, J.: Web service composition - current solutions and open problems. In: ICAPS Workshop on Planning for Web Services (2003)
30. Vukovic, M., Gerard, S., Hull, R., et al.: Towards automated planning for enterprise services: opportunities and challenges. In: ICSOC 2019 (2019)

Artifact-Driven Process Monitoring: A Viable Solution to Continuously and Autonomously Monitor Business Processes

Giovanni Meroni[(✉)]

Politecnico di Milano, Milan, Italy
`giovanni.meroni@polimi.it`

Abstract. Business process monitoring aims at identifying how well running processes are performing with respect to performance measures and objectives. By observing the execution of a process, process monitoring is also responsible for creating process traces, which can be subsequently used by process mining algorithms to gain further insights on the process.

Among the various monitoring solutions, artifact-driven monitoring has been proposed as a viable solution to continuously and autonomously monitor business processes. By monitoring the changes in the physical and virtual objects (i.e., artifacts) participating in the process, artifact-driven monitoring can autonomously generate traces that include events related to semi-automatic and manual tasks. Also, by relying on a declarative representation of the process to monitor, artifact-driven monitoring can detecting violations in the execution flow as soon as they occur. In addition, artifact-driven monitoring can identify the process elements affected by a violation, and it can continue monitoring the process without human intervention.

This tutorial paper will firstly provide an introduction to process monitoring, and the recent advancements in this field. Then, an overview on how artifact-driven monitoring works will be provided.

Keywords: Business process monitoring · Artifact-driven · Conformance checking

1 Introduction to Process Monitoring

As discussed by Dumas et al. in [2], business process monitoring consists in methods and techniques aiming at collecting and analyzing information on the way business processes are executed. Process monitoring plays a key role in the Business Process Management (BPM) lifecycle, as it allows to verify how well a business process is executed in reality and if the real behavior differs from the one being modeled. The outcome of process monitoring can then be used by the

A. Polyvyanyy et al. (Eds.): BPM 2021, LNCS 12875, pp. 37–43, 2021.
https://doi.org/10.1007/978-3-030-85469-0_5

subsequent phases in the BPM lifecycle to optimize the process or to discover undocumented behaviors.

According to the classification proposed by [7] and [6], process monitoring techniques can be classified in the following groups:

- **Event data logging**. Such techniques identify and record in a so-called execution log events related to a specific process instance being executed. Such events can be related to the activities being executed, the artifacts (i.e., the physical or virtual objects) manipulated by the process, or to the resources (i.e., the human operators or software components responsible for executing activities) participating in the process. Since several other monitoring techniques require event data to work, this technique is often seen as a prerequisite for them.
- **Business Activity Monitoring (BAM)**, also known as "monitoring" [7]. Such techniques analyze real-time information on the activities being executed (e.g., response time and failure rate) in order to measure Key Performance Indicators (KPIs) relevant for the process and to determine how well activities are performed.
- **Runtime Performance Analysis**. Such techniques analyze performance information on the processes being executed and identify bottlenecks or resource allocation problems. Unlike BAM, which focuses on single activities, Runtime performance analysis focuses on process runs, thus accounting for dependencies among activities.
- **Conformance Checking**. Such techniques compare the modeled process behavior with the one evidenced by execution data, in order to detect inconsistencies. To do so, they typically replay events in the execution log and see if they fit the process model.
- **Compliance Checking**. Such techniques verify that constraints representing regulations, guidelines, policies and laws are fulfilled by the process. With respect to conformance checking, compliance constraints focus on specific portions of the process, rather than on the entire model. Also, constraints can predicate both on the structure and on non functional aspects, such as execution time and resource allocation.

1.1 Challenges in Process Monitoring

To cope with the ever changing needs of the market, more and more organizations tend to externalize - either partially or completely - their internal business processes, and to establish short-term collaborations. This causes organizations to no longer have full control on how the process is being executed. Thus, process monitoring plays a critical role in this setting. Nevertheless, being able to monitor processes that span among multiple participants is far from trivial. Most monitoring solutions rely on information coming from Business Process Management Systems (BPMSs) or other corporate information systems, which are typically confined within the premises of an organization. Therefore, to monitor collaborative processes, organizations may have to federate their infrastructure, a complex task that may become problematic especially when the organizations need to collaborate only for a short period of time.

Another relevant challenge in process monitoring consists in ensuring that events related to process executions are accurate, timely, and reliable. When the process is fully automated by a single software component, such as a BPMS, it may be sufficient to collect and analyze the execution logs produced by that component. However, when the process is composed of manual activities, obtaining reliable monitoring information becomes more difficult. Indeed, the human operators responsible for such activities have to input information on how the activity was executed. Thus, the operator may forget to send this information, may make mistakes, or may deliberately introduce misleading information.

Finally, being able to continuously and autonomously determine if the execution differs from the model is a challenging task. Most conformance checking techniques operate off-line with complete event logs, thus can provide monitoring information only after the process ended. Conversely, compliance checking techniques can operate in real-time with partial event logs. However, most of them can only indicate if a constraint was satisfied or violated [3]. Therefore, if the process model is treated as a single constraint, compliance checking techniques can only indicate if the execution adheres to the model or not, but they cannot point out where it differs (e.g., an activity could be skipped). Breaking down the model into multiple constraints may address this issue. However, if constraints modeling all the possible discrepancies that may arise are modeled, the complexity of the compliance checks grows exponentially.

2 Artifact-Driven Monitoring in a Nutshell

Artifact-driven process monitoring [4] is a novel technique aiming at addressing the aforementioned challenges. The key idea behind artifact-driven monitoring is that, by observing the evolution of the artifacts participating in a process, it is possible to infer how the process is being executed. In particular, the Internet of Things (IoT) paradigm is exploited to make the physical artifacts in the process smart. Being equipping with sensors, a computing device (e.g., as a single board computer) and a communication interface, physical artifacts can autonomously collect and exchange with each other information on their conditions and on the environment. In addition, by providing them a representation of the process they participate in, physical artifacts can autonomously keep track of how the process is being executed.

The main advantages of artifact-driven monitoring are thus the following:

- **Manual Activities can be Automatically Monitored.** When executed, a manual activity changes the conditions of one or more artifacts. For example, delivering a package changes the position of that package. Therefore, if the conditions of the artifacts involved in that activity are automatically monitored thank to the IoT, the operator responsible for that activity is no longer required to provide information on when and how that activity was executed.

- **Collaborative Processes Can be Easily Monitored.** Physical artifacts are in close contact with the process they participate in, even when such process spans among multiple organizations. Therefore, they can autonomously collect all the information relevant for the process, without having to be federated with the information systems of the external organizations.
- **Deviations from the Modeled Process can be Immediately and Continuously Identified.** Artifact-driven monitoring relies on an artifact-centric representation of the process to monitor, which treats dependencies among activities as descriptive rather than prescriptive. In this way, it is possible to immediately detect when the execution deviates from the model and which portion of the process is affected. When a deviation is detected, monitoring is not stopped and is capable of detecting subsequent deviations.

2.1 E-GSM Modeling Language

To represent the process to monitor, Artifact-driven Monitoring makes use of Extended-GSM (E-GSM), an extension of the Guard-Stage-Milestone (GSM) notation [1]. In particular, activities and process blocks (e.g., exclusive blocks) are modeled as Stages, which are decorated with Data Flow Guards, Process Flow Guards, Milestones and Fault Loggers.

A Data Flow Guard contains an expression that, when evaluated to true, causes the associated stage to become *opened*, meaning that the process portion represented by that stage was started. Similarly, a Milestone contains an expression that, when evaluated to true, causes the associated stage to become *closed*, meaning that the process portion represented by that stage completed its execution.

A Process Flow Guard defines a prerequisite dependency among other stages (e.g., another stage must be closed). It is evaluated when the associated stage becomes *opened* and, if the dependency is not satisfied, it means that the process portion represented by the associated stage is not compliant with the expected execution flow (e.g. an activity was executed before the previous one was finished). Therefore, the associated stage is marked as *outOfOrder*.

A Fault Logger contains an expression that is evaluated as long as the associated stage is *opened*. If that expression evaluates to true, it means that the process portion represented by the associated stage was incorrectly executed (e.g., an activity failed). Therefore, the associated stage is marked as *faulty*.

Expressions contained in Data Flow Guards, Milestones and Fault Loggers can predicate on the conditions of the artifacts. In this way, when a change in the conditions of an artifact is detected, the corresponding expression is triggered, and the execution of the process can be monitored.

2.2 From BPMN to E-GSM

E-GSM is an expressive but complex modeling language. Also, some of the processes one would like to monitor may already have been modeled in Business Process Model and Notation (BPMN), which is a widely adopted standard in process modeling. To address those issues, a semi-automatic method to transform BPMN collaboration diagrams in E-GSM has been proposed. In this way, process designers do not have to learn E-GSM to monitor a process, and can reuse existing process models and modeling tools.

The first step consists in enriching BPMN collaboration diagrams with information on the artifacts participating in the process and their conditions. This way, it is possible to indicate which artifacts are required for an activity to start, and how such an activity alters the artifacts. To do so, BPMN data objects are used to represent the artifacts, data states to represent the conditions of an artifact, and data associations to represent the artifacts required for activities to start and the ones being produced when it finishes.

The second step consists in transforming the BPMN collaboration diagrams into a BPMN process diagram that represents the view artifacts have on the process. To do so, pools are removed and message flows are transformed in process flows. Indeed, as artifacts can travel along different organizations and participate in activities carried out by different organizations, it no longer makes sense to distinguish activities and dependencies based on the organizations.

The final step consists in transforming the BPMN process diagram in an EGSM model. To do so, translation rules that map BPMN elements and patterns into their corresponding BPMN counterparts. As long as the BPMN process diagram is well-structured, translation rules can be automatically applied with no user interaction required [5].

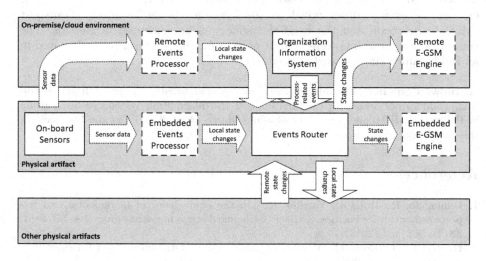

Fig. 1. Reference architecture of our artifact-driven monitoring platform.

2.3   SMARTifact: An Artifact-Driven Monitoring Platform

To implement an artifact-driven monitoring platform, the reference architecture shown in Fig. 1 has been proposed. This architecture is organized along four main modules:

- **On-board Sensors Gateway.** This module runs on each physical artifact, and is responsible for periodically collecting the values coming its sensors.
- **Events Processor.** This module takes as input the data collected by the On-board Sensors Gateway, analyzes them, and determines the state of the artifact. Depending on its complexity and on the computing capabilities of the smart objects, the Events Processor can either run on top of them or remotely in an on-premise or cloud environment.
- **Events Router.** This module runs on each physical artifact, and is responsible for exchanging information with all the physical artifacts, the information systems and the software components involved in the same process execution.
- **E-GSM Engine.** This module contains the E-GSM model of the process to monitor, which is used to determine when activities are executed and if the process deviates from the expected behavior. Whenever the Events Router forwards a new event, the E-GSM Engine examines the event and triggers the expression in the E-GSM model predicating on that event.

This reference architecture was implemented in the SMARTifact platform. In particular, the Events Processor was implemented with the Node-RED flow engine, the events router relied on the Message Queue Telemetry Transport (MQTT) protocol, and the E-GSM engine was implemented in Node.js. The computing requirements were modest enough for the platform to be deployed in an Intel Galileo single board computer.

Acknowledgments. The author would like to acknowledge the input from his colleague and former supervisor Pierluigi Plebani, the Information Systems research group in Politecnico di Milano, and the colleagues Marco Montali and Claudio Di Ciccio in this multi-year research work.

References

1. Damaggio, E., Hull, R., Vaculín, R.: On the equivalence of incremental and fix-point semantics for business artifacts with guard-stage-milestone lifecycles. Inf. Syst. **38**(4), 561–584 (2013)
2. Dumas, M., La Rosa, M., Mendling, J., Reijers, A.: Fundamentals of Business Process Management (2013)
3. Ly, L.T., Maggi, F.M., Montali, M., Rinderle-Ma, S., van der Aalst, W.M.P.: Compliance monitoring in business processes: functionalities, application, and tool-support. Inf. Syst. **54**, 209–234 (2015)
4. Meroni, G.: Assessing and improving process monitorability. In: Artifact-Driven Business Process Monitoring. LNBIP, vol. 368, pp. 93–106. Springer, Cham (2019). https://doi.org/10.1007/978-3-030-32412-4

5. Meroni, G., Baresi, L., Montali, M., Plebani, P.: Multi-party business process compliance monitoring through iot-enabled artifacts. Inf. Syst. **73**, 61–78 (2018)
6. Reichert, M., Weber, B.: Enabling Flexibility in Process-Aware Information Systems - Challenges, Methods, Technologies. Springer (2012)
7. van der Aalst, W.M.P.: Business process management: a comprehensive survey. ISRN Softw. Eng. **2013**(507984), 37 (2013)

Process Discovery

Weighing the Pros and Cons: Process Discovery with Negative Examples

Tijs Slaats[1(✉)], Søren Debois[2,3], and Christoffer Olling Back[1]

[1] Department of Computer Science, University of Copenhagen,
Copenhagen, Denmark
{slaats,back}@di.ku.dk
[2] IT University of Copenhagen, Copenhagen, Denmark
debois@itu.dk
[3] DCR Solutions A/S, Copenhagen, Denmark

Abstract. Contemporary process discovery methods take as inputs only *positive* examples of process executions, and so they are *one-class classification* algorithms. However, we have found *negative* examples to also be available in industry, hence we propose to treat process discovery as a *binary classification* problem. This approach opens the door to many well-established methods and metrics from machine learning, in particular to improve the distinction between what should and should not be allowed by the output model. Concretely, we (1) present a formalisation of process discovery as a binary classification problem; (2) provide cases with negative examples from industry, including real-life logs; (3) propose the Rejection Miner binary classification procedure, applicable to any process notation that has a suitable syntactic composition operator; and (4) apply this miner to the real world logs obtained from our industry partner, showing increased output model quality in terms of accuracy and model size.

Keywords: Process mining · Binary classification · Negative examples · Labelled event logs

1 Introduction

From the perspective of machine learning, process discovery [1] sits uneasily in the gap between unary and binary classification problems [21,31]. Popular contemporary miners, e.g. [5,23], approach process discovery as unary classification: given only positive examples (the input log) they generate a classifier (the output model) which recognizes traces (adhering to the output model) that resemble the training data. However, a process model is really a binary classifier: it classifies traces into those it accepts (desired executions of the process) and those it does not (undesired executions of the process).

Binary classification in machine learning relies on having access to examples of both classes. For process discovery, this means having not only positive examples of desired behaviour to be accepted by the output model, but also negative examples of undesired behaviour that should be rejected.

© Springer Nature Switzerland AG 2021
A. Polyvyanyy et al. (Eds.): BPM 2021, LNCS 12875, pp. 47–64, 2021.
https://doi.org/10.1007/978-3-030-85469-0_6

Negative examples also underpin a substantial part of the mechanics and theory of machine learning, in particular on model evaluation. Output models are evaluated on measures comparing ratios of true and false positives and negatives; however, absent negative examples, it is impossible to apply such measures. Accordingly, in process discovery, we use measures based only on true positive answers, such as *recall*; we are deprived of more fine-grained measures involving true negative or false positive answers such as *accuracy*.

In practical process discovery, negative examples would help distinguish between incidental correlation and actual rules. For instance, suppose that in some log, whenever we see an activity B, that B is preceded by an activity A. Does that mean that we can infer the declarative rule $A \rightarrow\bullet B$, that A is required before B may happen? In general, no: making this distinction requires domain knowledge. E.g., if A is "call taxi" and B is "file minutes from weekly status meeting"; by coincidence, we always call a taxi in the morning the day we file minutes, but clearly there is no rule that we must call a taxi before filing minutes. Conversely, if A is "approve payment" and B is "execute payment", very likely it is a rule that B must be preceded by A.

A mining algorithm does not possess domain knowledge, and so must have help to make such distinctions, to decide whether to add a rule $A \rightarrow\bullet B$ to its output model. Negative examples potentially help here: If BA is in the set of negative examples, adding the rule $A \rightarrow\bullet B$ is justified, as it rejects this trace. Conversely, if a rule rejects no trace from the negative examples, it is not necessary but *discretionary* for the miner to leave out or keep in. In the case of our examples, we would expect to find ample evidence in our negative examples that executing a payment before approving it is bad, whereas we would expect to find little to no evidence that filing minutes before calling a taxi is undesired.

As shown by [28] negative examples *do* exist in practice, some mining algorithms that include negative examples have been proposed, e.g. [22,28], and interestingly recent editions of the process discovery contest[1] have moved towards using labelled test logs (but not training logs) to rank submissions. In this paper we add to these developments with the following contributions:

1. We formalize process discovery as a binary classification problem, and show that not all process notations can express complete solutions to this problem (Sect. 3).
2. We propose the *Rejection Miner*, a notation-agnostic binary mining procedure applicable to *any* process notation with a syntactic composition operator Sect. 4.
3. We describe two cases where negative examples were encountered in industry and provide data sets [34] (Sect. 5).
4. We implement a concrete Rejection Miner and apply it to these data sets, comparing exploratively to contemporary unary miners (Sect. 6). The miner has been integrated in the commercial dcrgraphs.net modelling tool.

---

[1] https://icpmconference.org/2019/process-discovery-contest/
https://icpmconference.org/2020/process-discovery-contest/.

For the latter experiments, do note that the contemporary unary miners with which we compare do not take into account the negative examples. They must guess from the positive examples which traces to reject, whereas the Rejection Miner has the negative examples to guide it. We find that the Rejection Miner achieves noticeably better accuracy, in particular on out-of-sample tests, and produces models that are orders-of-magnitude smaller than the unary miners. We also note that we chose not to compare to other binary miners, as we did not aim to show the merits of the Rejection Miner in particular, but of binary mining in general. We chose the Rejection Miner as representative for binary mining as it allows us to build DCR Graphs, which were requested by the industry partner. The implementation of the Rejection Miner is available on-line [33].

Related Work. There have been several earlier works framing process mining as a binary classification task. [22] formulates constraints as Horn clauses and uses the ICL learning algorithm to successively find constraints which remove negative examples, stopping when there are no negative examples left. They translate these generated clauses to DECLARE. The Rejection Miner generalises this approach in that (a) it replaces the horn clauses with a generic notion of "model" for notations with composition (or synchronous product of models), and thus applies directly to a plethora of languages such as DECLARE and DCR Graphs, (b) the Rejection Miner leaves the choice of which clauses to prune until after a set of constraints ruling out all negative constraints is found, opening the door to non-greedy minimisation, and most importantly (c) we prove correctness for the Rejection Miner. [28] proposes an approach where traces are represented as points in an n-dimensional space (n being the number of unique event classes of the log), each point representing the multiplicity of the event classes in that trace. Finding a model is then reduced to the problem of finding a convex hull for the points such that positive points are included and negative points excluded. Whereas the work only considers the multiplicity of event classes in negative traces, the Rejection Miner is able to also consider the temporal ordering of individual events, while the former works well for the generation of Petri net models, it is less suitable for declarative notations. In [7,18], the authors artificially generate negative labels, but at the level of individual events rather than traces. The authors also defined process mining oriented metrics based on the resulting true positive/negative labels at the level of events. In [29] the development of binary process discovery algorithms was identified as a key open challenge for the field of declarative process discovery. Our work is also closely related to the work on vacuity detection in declarative process mining [15,25] which considers techniques for selecting the most relevant discovered constraints. However, they only consider logs with positive examples. The use of labelled input data is also well-accepted in the field of predictive process monitoring [16,32]. Finally, our test-driven modelling use case presented in Sect. 5.1 is similar to the scenario-based modelling approach introduced in [17], where (potentially negative) scenarios are modelled as small Petri nets which can then be synthesised into a single larger model. Contrary to this approach we input positive and negative scenarios as traces and learn a declarative model from these.

2 Process Notations and Unary Discovery

We recall the traditional definitions of event logs etc. [1].

Definition 1 (Events, traces, logs). *Assume a countably infinite universe $\mathcal{A}$ of all possible activities. As usual, an* alphabet $\Sigma \subseteq \mathcal{A}$ *is a set of activities, and the Kleene-star $\Sigma^\star$ denotes the countably infinite set of finite strings or sequences over Σ; we call such a string a* trace. *A* log L *is a multiset of occurrences of traces $L = \{t_1^{m_1}, \ldots, t_n^{m_n}\}$ where $m_k > 0$ is the multiplicity of the trace $t_k \in \Sigma$. We write $\mathcal{L}_\Sigma$ for the set of all event logs over alphabet Σ.*

When convenient, we treat an event log L also as simply a set of traces by ignoring multiplicities.

When we discuss unary and binary process discovery in the abstract in later sections, we will be interested in applying discovery to a variety of process notations; and we shall propose a miner which can be instantiated to any notation with a suitable composition operator. To make such statements formally, we need a formal notion of process notation. We use $\mathcal{P}(S)$ for the power set of S.

Definition 2 (Process notation). *A* process notation *for an alphabet Σ comprises a set of* models **M** *and an* interpretation function $[\![-]\!] : \mathbf{M} \to \mathcal{P}(\Sigma^\star)$ *assigning to each individual model m the set of traces $[\![m]\!]$ accepted by that model. For a set $S \subseteq \Sigma^\star$, we write $m \models S$ iff $S \subseteq [\![m]\!]$.*

While a process notation comprises the three components Σ, **M**, and $[\![-]\!]$, when no confusion is possible we shall allow ourselves to say "consider a process notation **M**", understanding the remaining two components to be implicit.

Example 3. Here is a toy declarative formalism which allows exactly the condition constraint of DECLARE [2,27] or DCR [12,19] over a countably infinite alphabet $\Sigma = \{A, B, C, \ldots\}$. A "model" is any finite set of pairs $(x, y) \in \Sigma \times \Sigma$, and we interpret each such pair as a condition from x to y. Formally:

$$\mathbf{M}_{\mathsf{cond}} = \{C \subseteq \Sigma \times \Sigma \mid C \text{ finite}\}$$
$$[\![C]\!] = \{t \in \Sigma^\star \mid \forall (x, y) \in C. \text{ each } y \text{ in } t \text{ is preceded by } x\}$$

For instance, $\{(A, B)\} \in \mathbf{M}_{\mathsf{cond}}$ is a model consisting of a single condition from A to B. In DECLARE or DCR, we would write this model "$A \to\bullet B$". Just as in DECLARE or DCR, this model admits all traces in which any occurrence of B is preceded by an occurrence of A. That is, this model admits the trace AB, but not B or $BABA$. Formally, we write

$$AB \in [\![\{(A, B)\}]\!] \qquad \text{or} \qquad \{(A, B)\} \models \{AB\}$$
$$\{B, BABA\} \not\subseteq [\![\{(A, B)\}]\!] \qquad \text{or} \qquad \{(A, B)\} \not\models \{B, BABA\}$$

Any process modelling formalism with trace semantics is a process notation in the above sense; such formalims include DECLARE, DCR, and Workflow Nets [3] (see also [1]).

We conclude this Section by pinning down process discovery: a procedure which given an event log produces a process model which admits that log. Assume a fixed alphabet Σ, and write $\mathcal{L}_\Sigma$ for the set of all valid event logs over Σ.

Definition 4 (Unary process discovery). *A unary process discovery algorithm γ for a process notation $(\mathbf{M}, [\![-]\!])$ over Σ is a function $\gamma : \mathcal{L}_\Sigma \to \mathbf{M}$. We say that γ has* perfect fitness *iff for all $L \in \mathcal{L}_\Sigma$ we have $\gamma(L) \models L$.*

Anticipating our binary miners, we shall refer to "perfect fitness" also as *positive soundness* of the miner.

3   Process Discovery as Binary Classification

We proceed to consider process discovery a binary classification problem. This approach presumes that we have not only positive examples (the set L in Definition 4), which the output model must accept, but also a set of negative examples, which the output model must reject.

Example 5. Consider again the condition models $\mathbf{M}_{\mathsf{cond}}$ of Example 3. Take as positive set of examples the singleton set $\{AB\}$, and take as negative examples the set $\{BA, B\}$. One model which accepts the positive example and rejects the negative ones is the singleton condition $\{(A, B)\}$. This model admits the positive example AB, because B is preceded by A; and it rejects the negative examples, because in both of the traces B and BA, the initial B is *not* preceded by A.

The negative examples here help solve the relevancy problem that plagues unary miners for declarative formalisms: The positive example AB clearly supports the constraint "A is a condition for B", however, as we saw in the introduction, with only positive examples and without domain knowledge, we cannot know whether this is a coincidence or a hard requirement. In the present example, the negative examples tell us that our model must somehow reject the trace BA, encouraging us to include the condition $A \rightarrow\!\bullet\, B$.

Unfortunately, a model accepting a given set P of positive examples and rejecting a given set N of negative ones does not necessarily exists: At the very least, we must have P and N disjoint. To cater to such ambiguous inputs, we allow a binary miner to refuse to produce a model.

Definition 6 (Binary process discovery). *Let $\mathbf{M}$ be a process notation for an alphabet Σ. A binary-classification process discovery algorithm ("binary miner") is a partial function $\eta : \mathcal{L}_\Sigma \times \mathcal{L}_\Sigma \rightharpoonup \mathbf{M}$, taking sets of positive and negative examples P, N to a model $\eta(P, N)$. We require that $\eta(P, N)$ is defined whenever P, N are disjoint.*

In the rest of this paper, unless otherwise stated, we shall implicitly assume that examples P, N are disjoint. We proceed to generalise the notion of fitness from unary mining.

Definition 7 (Soundness, perfection). *Let $P, N \subseteq \mathcal{L}_\Sigma$ be positive and negative examples. We say that a binary miner η is* positively sound *at P, N iff $\eta(P, N) \models P$. Similarly, we say that η is* negatively sound *at P, N iff $N \cap [\![\eta(P, N)]\!] = \emptyset$. We say that η is* perfect *iff for any disjoint P, N it is defined and both positively and negatively sound.*

In other words: A perfect binary miner produces an output whenever its positive and negative examples are not in direct conflict, and that output admits all positive examples and none of the negative examples provided as input.

Over-and Underfitting of Out-of-Sample Data. A perfect binary miner has no choice in how it treats the elements of P and N: it must admit its positive examples P and reject its negative examples N. It is the remaining *undecided* traces where it has a choice. In the limits, we have the overfitting "maximally rejecting miner", whose output always accepts exactly P and nothing else; and the underfitting "maximally accepting miner", whose output rejects exactly N and nothing else.

However, unlike the unary case, where perfect fitness miners are generally quite easy to come by, **perfect binary miners do not necessarily exist**, and helpful ones may in practice be quite hard to come by.

First, let us try to use a unary miner as a binary one. We do so by simply ignoring the negative examples and applying our unary miner to the positive ones. In this case, it is easy to show that for any unary miner (for any notation) which never returns exactly its input log, we can construct a negative example which will be accepted by the output model of that miner for those positive examples:

Proposition 8. *Let γ be a unary miner for a notation* **M** *over alphabet Σ, and assume that for all L we have $[\![\gamma(L)]\!] \neq L$. Then for all $P \in \mathcal{L}_\Sigma$ there exists a $N \in \mathcal{L}_\Sigma$ s.t. N and P are disjoint, yet N is accepted by the output model $\gamma(L)$.*

So in this sense, **non-trivial unary miners *never* generalise to binary ones.** This is perhaps not entirely surprising. Much less obvious, and a core difference between binary and unary mining, we find that some *notations* cannot express distinctions fine enough to distinguish between positive and negative examples. This is in stark contrast to the unary case, where essentially all notations have a model accepting all traces (the "flower model"); moreover, all commonly accepted notations are able to express any finite language, and so for any input log (finite language), a perfectly fitting model must exist.

However, in the binary case, even though our example notation admits the "flower model", it is still too coarse to admit a perfect binary miner.

Lemma 9. *In* $\mathbf{M}_{\mathsf{cond}}$*, take positive examples $P = \{ABC\}$, and negative examples $N = \{AB\}$. Then no model $m \in \mathbf{M}_{\mathsf{cond}}$ exists such that $m \models P$ yet $m \not\models N$.*

Proof. Suppose m is a model with $m \not\models \{AB\}$. Then m requires something preceding either A or B, something which is apparently not there. But then that something is missing also from ABC.

In fact, we prove below that **no perfect binary miner can exist in any notation that has only finitely many possible models.** To understand the ramifications of this Theorem, consider again DCR and DECLARE. For DCR or DECLARE models over a fixed finite alphabet (e.g., the set of tasks present in a given log), DCR has infinitely many such models (with distinct semantics), whereas DECLARE has only finitely many. To see this, note that in DCR, because labels and events are not one-one, we can keep adding events that do affect behaviour, while remaining within a finite set of observable tasks. In DECLARE, if there are n activities to choose from, you can populate only finitely many DECLARE templates with those finitely many tasks. Since the arity of DECLARE templates is bounded, and current DECLARE miners are bounded to a finite set of input templates, you are left with only finitely many models.

Note the following consequence for DECLARE: **any binary miner for DECLARE has inputs P, N for which the output a model has either false positives or false negatives.**

Theorem 10. *No perfect binary miner exists for any process notation that has only finitely many possible models* **M** *over any non-empty finite alphabet Σ.*

Proof. We construct finite positive and negative examples P and N such that no model accepts P and rejects N. First, we construct N. Let I^+ as the subset of models that accepts infinitely many traces, i.e., $I^+ = \{m \in \mathbf{M} \mid [\![m]\!] \text{ infinite}\}$. Since there are only finitely many models, I^+ is finite, and without loss of generality write it $I^+ = \{m_1, \ldots, m_n\}$. For each m_i, choose a $t_i \in [\![m_i]\!]$, and define $N = \{t_1, \ldots, t_n\}$. Next, we construct P. Let $\mathsf{C}([\![m]\!])$ be the complement of the traces generated by a model m and I^- the subset of models which reject infinitely many traces, i.e., $I^- = \{m \in \mathbf{M} \mid \mathsf{C}([\![m]\!]) \text{ infinite}\}$. Again I^- is finite and we write it without loss of generality $I^- = \{p_1, \ldots, p_k\}$. For each of p_j, pick a trace s_j such that $s_j \notin [\![p_j]\!]$ and $s_j \notin N$-this is always possible because $\mathsf{C}[\![m_j]\!]$ is infinite and N finite. Then define $P = \{s_1, \ldots, s_k\}$. Note that by construction P and N are disjoint. Finally, let $m \in \mathbf{M}$ be a model. At least one of $[\![m]\!]$ and $\mathsf{C}[\![m]\!]$ must be infinite; we show that in neither case can m be the output of a perfect binary miner applied to P, N. If $[\![m]\!]$ is infinite, then $m \in I^+$, say $m = m_i$, and it follows that $m \models t_i \in N$; hence m fails to reject all negative examples. If on the other hand $\mathsf{C}([\![m]\!])$ is infinite, then $m \in I^-$, say $m = p_j$ and it follows that $s_j \notin [\![p_j]\!] = [\![m]\!]$; hence m fails to accept the positive example $s_j \in P$.

Alternatively, the above proof can possibly be used to show that there are infinitely many problems P, N with pairwise distinct solutions; the Theorem then follows from the Vapnik-Chervonenkis dimension [4] of the set of interpretations of the finite set of models being necessarily finite, and so unable to shatter this infinite set of distinct solutions.

In unary mining, we may construct a perfect fitness miner like this: As notation, pick simply finite sets of traces, and let the semantics of the notation be that a model (set of traces) T accepts a trace t iff $t \in T$. Then the function $\eta(P) = P$ is a perfect fitness miner. This generalises to any notation strong enough to characterise exactly a given set of T of traces. Obviously, this unary miner has little practical relevance.

It is interesting to note that a similar perfect binary miner exists. Pick as notation pairs of sets of traces T, U, with semantics that T, U accepts t iff $t \in T$ and $t \notin U$. Clearly the function $\eta(P, N) = (P, N)$ is a perfect binary miner, although again, not a particularly helpful one. However, the construction shows that a perfect binary miner exists for any notation strong enough to exactly characterise membership resp. non-membership of finite sets of traces. Notable examples here are Petri-nets and BPMN (through an exclusive choice over the set of positive traces); so it follows that a (trivial) binary miner exists for these notations.

4   Rejection Miners

We proceed to construct a family of binary miners we call "Rejection miners", defined for *any* process notation which has a behaviour-preserving syntactic model composition. Rejection miners are parametric in a "pattern oracle" which selects a set of patterns for consideration; if the patterns selected allow it, the output of the Rejection Miner is perfect. When they do not, the miner does a greedy approximation to optimise for accuracy (i.e., maximising the ratio of true positives and negatives to all inputs).

Definition 11 (Additive process notation). *We say that a process formalism* **M** *over* Σ *is* additive *if it comes equipped with a commutative monoid* $(\oplus, \mathbf{1})$ *on* **M** *such that*

$$\llbracket \mathbf{1} \rrbracket = \Sigma^\star \tag{1}$$

$$\llbracket m \oplus n \rrbracket = \llbracket m \rrbracket \cap \llbracket n \rrbracket \tag{2}$$

We lift the monoid operator to sequences and write $\bigoplus_{i<n} m_i = m_1 \oplus \cdots \oplus m_{n-1}$,

That is, an additive formalism has a flower model $\mathbf{1}$ and a model combination operator $\oplus$. This operator combines two models into a compound one, such that this compound model accepts *exactly* the traces accepted by both of the two original models. DECLARE is an additive formalism: A DECLARE model is a finite set of constraints; the empty such set accepts all traces (1), and the union of two such sets is again such a set, with exactly the desired semantics ($\oplus$). DCR also has a model composition, where the composite model is the union of events, markings, and constraints [11,20]. However, this composition does not preserve semantics in the general case.

In practice, any process notation can be considered additive by forming the synchronous product of models: To check whether a given trace t conforms to a composite model $m \oplus n$, we simply check whether $m \models t$ and $n \models t$. Incidentally, this is a popular implementation mechanism for DECLARE constraints (see, e.g., [10,14]).

The key property of additive process notations used for Rejection Miners is that in such a notation, we can think about models as being the sum of their parts, and the problem of mining can then be reduced to finding suitable such parts. For this approach to be able to generate all models, we would also need to know a subset $\mathbf{S} \subseteq \mathbf{M}$ which generates $\mathbf{M}$ under the model composition operator $-\oplus-$. DECLARE and DCR clearly has such subsets. In keeping with declarative notations and nomenclature, we will refer to such part models as "constraints" in the sequel, however, we emphasise that there is nothing special about them: A constraint m is just another model $m \in \mathbf{M}$.

A rejection miner is parametric in two sub-components: A *pattern oracle*, which given positive and negative examples produces a finite set of (hopefully) relevant constraints; and a *constraint minimiser*, which given a sequence of constraints known to fully reject a set of negative examples selects a subset still fully rejecting those examples.

Definition 12 (Rejection miner components). *Let* $\mathbf{M}$ *be a process notation over an alphabet* Σ. *A pattern oracle is a function* patterns : $\mathcal{L}_\Sigma \times \mathcal{L}_\Sigma \to \mathbf{M}^\star$. *A minimiser is a function* minimise : $\mathbf{M}^\star \times \mathcal{L}_\Sigma \to \mathbf{M}^\star$ *satisfying:*

1. *if* $\sigma \in \mathbf{M}^\star$ *fully rejects* L, *then also* minimise(σ, L) *fully rejects* L; *and*
2. minimise(σ, L) *contains only elements from the input sequence* σ.

An example pattern oracle for DECLARE would be the function that produces all possible instantiations of all templates with activities observed in either of its input logs. An example minimiser is the *greedy minimiser* which, starting from the left of the list of constraints, removes those constraints which reject only traces in N that are already rejected by preceding constraints.

Algorithm 13 (Rejection miner). Let $\mathbf{M}$ be an additive notation over Σ, let patterns be a pattern oracle and let minimise be a minimiser.

```
1:  procedure REJECTIONMINER(P, N)
2:      [m₁,...,mₙ] ← patterns(P, N)
3:      σ ← [mᵢ | mᵢ ⊨ P]                    ▷ remove mⱼ where mⱼ ⊭ P
4:      σ ← ⊕ minimise(σ, N)
5:      if ⟦⊕σ⟧ ∩ N ≠ ∅ then                 ▷ are any negative examples not rejected?
6:          δ ← 1, σ₂ ← []
7:          while δ > 0 and |σ₂| < |σ| do
8:              N' ← {n ∈ N | ⊕σ₂ ⊨ n}       ▷ negative examples not yet rejected
9:              P' ← {p ∈ P | ⊕σ₂ ⊨ n}       ▷ positive examples currently accepted
10:             m, δ ← maxₘⱼ∈σ∖σ₂(|{n ∈ N' | mⱼ ⊭ n}| − |{p ∈ P' | mⱼ ⊭ p}|)
11:             if δ > 0 then
12:                 σ₂ ← σ₂, m
13:             end if
14:         end while
15:     end if
16: end procedure
```

A brief explanation: On line 2, the pattern oracle is invoked to produce a finite list $[m_1, \ldots, m_n]$ of relevant constraints. On Line 3, those constraints *not* modelling the positive examples P are filtered out; only the constraints m_i which *do* model P are retained; we assign the resulting list to σ. We then apply the minimiser in Line 4, which by Definition 12 at most removes constraints. On Line 5, we check whether all negative examples are rejected; if so, we have found a perfect model and return it.

Otherwise, we turn to approximation. In the loop in Line 7 to 13, we repeatedly compute the set N' of negative examples not yet rejected and P' of positive examples currently accepted. In Line 10, we iterate over the constraint m_j of the original pattern oracle and compute for each the difference δ_j between how many additional negative examples m_j rejects (wins) and how many already accepted positive examples m_j rejects (losses); we then pick the m_j with the maximum δ_j. If $\delta > 0$, adding the constraint m_j will improve accuracy, and we add it to the set of output constraints. If $\delta \leq 0$, we cannot improve accuracy by including any more constraints, and the loop terminates.

Recall from the previous section the notions of maximally accepting or maximally rejecting perfect binary miners. The minimiser provides a handle for pushing the Rejection Miner towards either of these extremes. Using the identity function as the minimiser will retain all constraints, and so reject the most undecided traces. Conversely, using a minimiser which finds a least subset of constraints rejecting N will remove more constraints, accepting more undecided traces.

The Rejection Miner is not in general a perfect binary miner: The patterns σ provided to it by the patterns might not, even if all of them were retained, be strong enough to fully reject the set N of negative examples while retaining the positive ones. Moreover, while the Rejection Miner in practice produces decent results, its approximation phase does not find a subset of patterns with optimal accuracy because of its greedy nature.

However, the Rejection Miner will *always* accept all the positive examples; and if the selected patterns σ has any subset σ' which accepts P and rejects N, the Rejection Miner will find such a subset.

Proposition 14. *Let* patterns *be a pattern oracle, let* minimise *be a minimiser, and let P, N be disjoint sets of positive and negative examples. Then the Rejection Miner for this oracle and minimiser has positive soundness at P, N. Moreover if there exists $\sigma \subseteq$ patterns(P, N) such that σ accepts P and fully rejects N, then the Rejection Miner also has negative soundness at P, N.*

Proof (sketch). The former is immediate from line 4; the latter is immediate by the requirements 1 and 2 of Definition 12.

That is: On all inputs where the pattern oracle produces patterns strong enough to make the distinction, the Rejection Miner will exhibit neither false negatives nor positives. Note that this is not in contradiction to Theorem 10: the Rejection Miner is not a perfect miner in general, but if a perfect model exists for a given input and pattern oracle, then it will find such a model.

5   Cases with Negative Examples

The development of the Rejection Miner was not just motivated by academic, but also industrial interest. When pursuing process mining activities in practice we regularly see opportunities to label data and in some cases we have even been asked directly by commercial partners to include counter examples in the construction of models. In this section we discuss the two most developed cases we have encountered, where we both had the opportunity to extract labelled data and publish it in an anonimyzed format. The negative examples in these cases arise from test-driven development and as failures in process engineering.

5.1   DCR Solutions: Test-Driven Modelling

A Danish vendor of adaptive case-management systems, *DCR Solutions*, offers the on-line process modelling portal dcrgraphs.net. In this tool, modellers define *required* (positive) resp. *forbidden* (negative) test cases (traces), expected to be accepted resp. rejected by the model under development. The test cases are also used as input to a process discovery algorithm, which dynamically recommends new constraints to modellers [6]. However, the algorithm used only the positive test-cases, ignoring the negative ones. The extension to consider also those negative ones has been repeatedly requested by the developers of the portal and was implemented as part of this paper. DCR Solutions has kindly allowed us to make the entire data set of test-cases produced in the portal available in an anonymized form [34].

5.2   Dreyer Foundation: Process Engineering

The Danish *Dreyer Foundation* supports budding lawyers and architects, and has previously released an anonymised log of casework [13]. This log documents also testing and early stages of deployment of the system. In a number of cases, process instances that had gone astray were reset to their starting state and partially replayed. The log contains reset markers, and so provides clear negative examples: those prefixes that ended in a reset. We make available here also this partitioning into positive and negative examples [34].

6   Experimental Results

We report on exploratory experiments applying an instantiation of the Rejection Miner to the data sets of Sect. 5, comparing results to current major unary miners.

Data Sets. The DCR Solutions case (Sect. 5.1) comprises 215 logs, each containing at least one negative example, and each produced by users of the portal to codify what a single model should or should not do. The logs contain 7030 events, 1681 unique activities, 589 negative and 705 positive traces. Logs vary enormously in size: the largest log contains 1162 events, 19 activities, 98 negative and 14 positive traces; the smallest log contain but one negative trace of 3 events. Log size distribution is visualised in Fig. 1. The Dreyer case ((Sect. 5.2)) comprises a single log of 10177 events, 33 unique activities, 492 positive and 208 negative traces. The mean trace length is 15 (1–46), and the mean number of activities per trace is 12 (1–24). Both data sets are available on-line [34].

Both data sets were pre-processed to remove any conflicting traces (i.e. that were both marked as positive and negative for the same log). In addition the DCR Solutions data set had a notion of "optional" traces, but what this meant was not well-defined, therefore these were also removed.

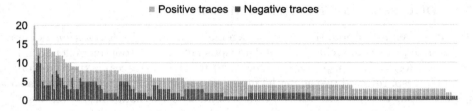

Fig. 1. DCR Solutions data set log size distribution. The largest log of 98 negative and 14 positive traces has been omitted from the diagram.

Metrics. Binary classification mining allows us to rely on traditional machine learning metrics [35] of relative misclassification (true and false positives, TP and FP, and true and false negatives, TN and FN). We use in particular the true positive rate (TPR), true negative rate (TNR), accuracy (ACC), balanced accuracy (BAC), positive predictive value (PPV), and F1-score (F1). We recall their definitions in Table 1. These particular measures demonstrate the difference between what can be measured in the unary and binary settings. In the setting of unary-classification miners, where we do not have negative examples, we can count only TP and FN. In that setting, we can only measure the true positive rate (TPR)-known as "fitness" in the process mining community-but none of the other measures[2]. But in the setting of binary-classification miners, we can measure also how well the output model recognizes negatives (TNR), how reliable a positive classification is (PPV), and generally how accurately both positive and negative traces are classified (ACC, which counts each trace equally and BAC, which balances between positive and negative traces).

Finally, one goal particular to process discovery is to produce output models that are understandable by humans: Output models are not mere devices for classification; they are vehicles for humans to understand the reasons and structure behind that classification. To this end, smaller models are more helpful, so we calculate also the size of the models, dependent on their notation.

---

[2] The name "F1" is used for a metric of unary miners defined like F1 here, except using the escaping-edges notion of precision [8] *en lieu* of the PPV.

For the pattern-based notations such as DECLARE, we use the number of such patterns; for DCR models the number of relations; and for workflow nets the number of edges and places. Of course sizes for models in different notations are not directly comparable, but they give us an insight in the number of elements that need to be processed by the reader and give a rough indication of relative complexity.

Table 1. Confusion matrix for binary mining

Model class.	Log classification			
	Pos.	Neg.	$ACC = \frac{TP+TN}{TP+FP+TN+FN}$
Pos.	TP	FP	$PPV = \frac{TP}{TP+FP}$
Neg.	FN	TN	$BAC = \frac{TPR+TNR}{2}$
	$TPR = \frac{TP}{TP+FN}$	$TNR = \frac{TN}{FP+TN}$	$F1 = 2 \cdot \frac{PPV \cdot TPR}{PPV+TPR}$

Rejection Miner. We provide a JavaScript implementation of the Rejection Miner, available at [33]. We use a pattern oracle which simply instantiates the following list of DECLARE-like patterns at all activities seen in the log: Existence(x), Absence(x), Absence2(x), Absence3(x), Condition(x, y), Response(x, y), NotSuccession(x, y), AlternatePrecedence(x, y), DisjunctiveResponse($x, (y, z)$), and ConjunctiveResponse((x, y), z). The oracle outputs patterns sorted by how many negative examples they exclude. Ties are broken by sorting the disjunctive and conjunctive responses last, to de-emphasise these relatively more complex patterns.

We emphasise the flexibility of the oracle and minimizer selection: if one wants to include more patterns, one simply extends the oracle; if one wants to have a more restrictive model, or a different prioritization of constraints, one simply replaces the minimizer. One can also produce models that sacrifice TPR for accuracy by creating a minimizer that accepts constraints excluding some positive examples, but also excluding many negative examples.

Other Miners. We compare the Rejection Miner (RM) to flagship miners for three major process notations. For DCR graphs [12,19], we use DisCoveR [26]. DisCoveR is used commercially for model recommendation by DCR solutions. We consider DisCoveR with two settings, the default one (intended to emphasise precision, denoted D), and a "light" version intended to emphasise simplicity (DL). For DECLARE [2,27], we use MINERful [9] and consider three settings, (M1) the most restrictive setting where support = 1.0, confidence = 0.0, and interest factor = 0.0; (M2) a less restrictive setting (likely outputting smaller models) with support = 1.0, confidence = 0.5, and interest factor = 0.25; and (M3) with support = 1.0, confidence = 0.75, and interest factor = 0.5. Finally, for Workflow Nets [3], we use the Inductive Miner [1,23], with a noise threshold of 0.0 (IM) and 0.2 (IMf) respectively.

6.1 Results

We performed both in-sample and out-of-sample testing. For the latter we performed 10-fold validation [30] and calculated our measures as the mean values across 10 randomized attempts. The results are shown in Table 2. For the DCR Solutions data set each value is calculated as the mean over all 215 logs. Because of the limited size of most of the logs, we only tested on in-sample data for this case, however, since the primary goal for the company is to find models that accurately fit the training data, in-sample accuracy is highly relevant.

Table 2. Experiment results

Miner	TPR	TNR	ACC	BAC	PPV	F1	Size
DCR Solutions Data set (Sect. 5.1) In-sample							
Rejection (RM)	1.000	1.000	1.000	1.000	1.000	1.000	1.5
DisCoveR (D)	1.000	0.927	0.976	0.964	0.971	0.983	24.8
- light (DL)	1.000	0.921	0.974	0.948	0.967	0.981	19.6
MINERful (M1)	1.000	0.881	0.958	0.941	0.949	0.970	120.5
- 0.5/0.25 (M2)	0.997	0.841	0.942	0.919	0.930	0.957	77.6
- 0.75/0.5 (M3)	0.961	0.657	0.848	0.809	0.850	0.877	37.8
Inductive (IM)	1.000	0.860	0.946	0.930	0.932	0.960	22.1
- 0.2 noise (IMf)	1.000	0.860	0.946	0.930	0.932	0.960	22.1
Dreyer Foundation Data set (Sect. 5.2) In-sample							
Rejection	1.000	0.928	0.979	0.964	0.970	0.985	6.0
DisCoveR	1.000	0.048	0.717	0.524	0.713	0.832	125.0
- light	1.000	0.048	0.717	0.524	0.713	0.832	71.0
MINERful	1.000	0.067	0.723	0.534	0.717	0.835	1124.0
- 0.5/0.25	1.000	0.0288	0.711	0.514	0.709	0.830	174.0
- 0.75/0.5	1.000	0.005	0.704	0.502	0.704	0.826	102.0
Inductive	1.000	0.019	0.709	0.510	0.707	0.828	160.0
- 0.2 noise	1.000	0.019	0.709	0.510	0.707	0.828	160.0
Dreyer Foundation Data set (Sect. 5.2) Out-of-sample							
Rejection	0.985	0.914	0.964	0.950	0.965	0.975	6.2
DisCoveR	0.962	0.362	0.692	0.662	0.706	0.814	127.6
- light	0.968	0.447	0.697	0.707	0.708	0.817	72.9
MINERful	0.906	0.231	0.659	0.569	0.698	0.787	1128.4
- 0.5/0.25	0.962	0.270	0.685	0.616	0.701	0.810	176.4
- 0.75/0.5	0.970	0.081	0.684	0.525	0.698	0.810	104.9
Inductive	0.981	0.339	0.696	0.660	0.703	0.818	158.9
- 0.2 noise	0.983	0.359	0.698	0.671	0.704	0.819	157.8

DCR Solutions. First, on in-sample test data, the Rejection Miner mines perfectly accurate models on every log. This is a small, but meaningful, improvement over the 0.967 accuracy achieved by DisCoveR light, which is currently used for this task. In practice this means that, given a mapping from the Declarative patterns to DCR Graphs, the Rejection Miner will allow the portal to recommend perfectly accurate models for all test cases that have been defined to-date. Secondly, there is an order-of-magnitude gain in simplicity for the Rejection Miner compared to all other miners: the Rejection Miner requires only 1.5 constraints on average per model. We conjecture that this gain is achieved because knowing what behaviour should be forbidden allows the miner to find precisely the constraints we need, instead of having to propose many constraints to forbid all behaviour that was not explicitly seen in the positive samples. This gain in simplicity also directly benefits the business case, as the industry partners have repeatedly voiced a strong preference for fewer, but more relevant, recommended relations. As a result, the Rejection Miner has already been integrated into the portal by the company.

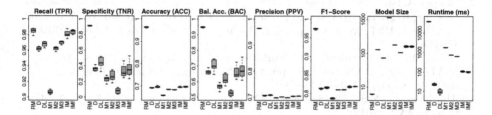

Fig. 2. Boxplots illustrating the distribution of mean performance of various miners across 10 runs of 10-fold cross validation on the Dreyers log.

Dreyers Foundation. The results show that the Rejection Miner once again provides high levels of accuracy while requiring only a small model. Of most interest are the out-of-sample results, shown in more detail in the boxplots of Fig. 2, which indicate that the models found by the Rejection Miner are not only accurate for the training data, but also for unseen test data. In other words, providing the miner with *some* negative examples allows it to accurately predict what *other* negative examples may be seen in the future. In addition there is very little variance in the results of the Rejection Miner, with model size and accuracy scores remaining close to the mean for each randomized run of the 10-fold validation. We also included measures of the run-time performance in Fig. 2, showing that the Rejection Miner is several orders of magnitude slower than the other miners (requiring on average 39.3 s to mine the Dreyers log). We stress however that good run-time performance was never a goal for the current prototype, that there are known methods for improving the run-time performance through a more intelligent initial selection of relevant patterns by the oracle [6,24], and that the results do show that the miner is computationally viable for the experimental data.

7   Conclusion

We propose approaching process discovery as a binary classification problem. We provided a formal account of when binary miners exist; proposed the Rejection Miner; introduced real-world cases of negative examples; and compared the Rejection Miner to contemporary miners for various notations, finding an increase in accuracy and, in particular, output model simplicity.

In future work we will optimize the run-time performance, for example through a more intelligent pattern oracle based on the Declare miner [24] or DisCoveR [6]. We will also pursue additional experiments through labelled real-world logs, such as the PDC datasets and novel use cases from industrial partners.

References

1. Aalst, W.: Process Mining. Springer, Heidelberg (2016). https://doi.org/10.1007/978-3-662-49851-4_1
2. van der Aalst, W.M.P., Pesic, M.: DecSerFlow: towards a truly declarative service flow language. In: Bravetti, M., Núñez, M., Zavattaro, G. (eds.) WS-FM 2006. LNCS, vol. 4184, pp. 1–23. Springer, Heidelberg (2006). https://doi.org/10.1007/11841197_1
3. Aalst, W.M.P.: Verification of workflow nets. In: Azéma, P., Balbo, G. (eds.) ICATPN 1997. LNCS, vol. 1248, pp. 407–426. Springer, Heidelberg (1997). https://doi.org/10.1007/3-540-63139-9_48
4. Abu-Mostafa, Y.S., Magdon-Ismail, M., Lin, H.: Learning from Data: A Short Course. AML (2012)
5. Augusto, A., Conforti, R., Dumas, M., La Rosa, M., Polyvyanyy, A.: Split miner: automated discovery of accurate and simple business process models from event logs. Knowl. Inf. Syst. **59**(2), 251–284 (2019)
6. Back, C.O., Slaats, T., Hildebrandt, T.T., Marquard, M.: DisCoveR: accurate & efficient discovery of declarative process models. Presented at the (2021)
7. Broucke, S.V.: Advances in process mining: artificial negative events and other techniques (2014)
8. Buijs, J.C.A.M., van Dongen, B.F., van der Aalst, W.M.P.: On the role of fitness, precision, generalization and simplicity in process discovery. In: Meersman, R., et al. (eds.) OTM 2012. LNCS, vol. 7565, pp. 305–322. Springer, Heidelberg (2012). https://doi.org/10.1007/978-3-642-33606-5_19
9. Ciccio, C.D., Mecella, M.: A two-step fast algorithm for the automated discovery of declarative workflows. In: CIDM 2013, pp. 135–142, April 2013
10. de Leoni, M., Maggi, F.M., van der Aalst, W.M.P.: An alignment-based framework to check the conformance of declarative process models and to preprocess event-log data. Inf. Sys. **47**, 258–277 (2015). https://doi.org/10.1016/j.is.2013.12.005
11. Debois, S., Hildebrandt, T., Slaats, T.: Hierarchical declarative modelling with refinement and sub-processes. In: Sadiq, S., Soffer, P., Völzer, H. (eds.) BPM 2014. LNCS, vol. 8659, pp. 18–33. Springer, Cham (2014). https://doi.org/10.1007/978-3-319-10172-9_2
12. Debois, S., Hildebrandt, T.T., Slaats, T.: Replication, refinement & reachability: complexity in dynamic condition-response graphs. Acta Informatica **55**(6), 489–520 (2018). https://doi.org/10.1007/s00236-017-0303-8

13. Debois, S., Slaats, T.: The analysis of a real life declarative process. In: SSCI/CIDM 2015, pp. 1374–1382. IEEE (2015)
14. Di Ciccio, C., Bernardi, M.L., Cimitile, M., Maggi, F.M.: Generating event logs through the simulation of declare models. In: Barjis, J., Pergl, R., Babkin, E. (eds.) EOMAS 2015. LNBIP, vol. 231, pp. 20–36. Springer, Cham (2015). https://doi.org/10.1007/978-3-319-24626-0_2
15. Di Ciccio, C., Maggi, F.M., Montali, M., Mendling, J.: On the relevance of a business constraint to an event log. Inf. Syst. **78**, 144–161 (2018)
16. Di Francescomarino, C., Dumas, M., Maggi, F.M., Teinemaa, I.: Clustering-based predictive process monitoring. IEEE Trans. Serv. Comput. **12**(6), 896–909 (2016)
17. Fahland, D.: Oclets – scenario-based modeling with petri nets. In: Franceschinis, G., Wolf, K. (eds.) PETRI NETS 2009. LNCS, vol. 5606, pp. 223–242. Springer, Heidelberg (2009). https://doi.org/10.1007/978-3-642-02424-5_14
18. Goedertier, S., Martens, D., Vanthienen, J., Baesens, B.: Robust process discovery with artificial negative events. J. Mach. Learn. Res. **10**, 1305–1340 (2009)
19. Hildebrandt, T., Mukkamala, R.R.: Declarative event-based workflow as distributed dynamic condition response graphs. In: PLACES 2010. EPTCS, vol. 69, pp. 59–73 (2010). https://doi.org/10.4204/EPTCS.69.5
20. Hildebrandt, T., Mukkamala, R.R., Slaats, T.: Safe distribution of declarative processes. In: Barthe, G., Pardo, A., Schneider, G. (eds.) SEFM 2011. LNCS, vol. 7041, pp. 237–252. Springer, Heidelberg (2011). https://doi.org/10.1007/978-3-642-24690-6_17
21. Khan, S.S., Madden, M.G.: A survey of recent trends in one class classification. In: Coyle, L., Freyne, J. (eds.) AICS 2009. LNCS (LNAI), vol. 6206, pp. 188–197. Springer, Heidelberg (2010). https://doi.org/10.1007/978-3-642-17080-5_21
22. Lamma, E., Mello, P., Montali, M., Riguzzi, F., Storari, S.: Inducing declarative logic-based models from labeled traces. In: Alonso, G., Dadam, P., Rosemann, M. (eds.) BPM 2007. LNCS, vol. 4714, pp. 344–359. Springer, Heidelberg (2007). https://doi.org/10.1007/978-3-540-75183-0_25
23. Leemans, S.J.J., Fahland, D., van der Aalst, W.M.P.: Discovering block-structured process models from event logs - a constructive approach. In: Colom, J.-M., Desel, J. (eds.) PETRI NETS 2013. LNCS, vol. 7927, pp. 311–329. Springer, Heidelberg (2013). https://doi.org/10.1007/978-3-642-38697-8_17
24. Maggi, F.M., Bose, R.P.J.C., van der Aalst, W.M.P.: Efficient discovery of understandable declarative process models from event logs. In: Ralyté, J., Franch, X., Brinkkemper, S., Wrycza, S. (eds.) CAiSE 2012. LNCS, vol. 7328, pp. 270–285. Springer, Heidelberg (2012). https://doi.org/10.1007/978-3-642-31095-9_18
25. Maggi, F.M., Montali, M., Di Ciccio, C., Mendling, J.: Semantic vacuity detection in declarative process mining. In: La Rosa, M., Loos, P., Pastor, O. (eds.) BPM 2016. LNCS, vol. 9850, pp. 158–175. Springer, Cham (2016). https://doi.org/10.1007/978-3-319-45348-4_10
26. Nekrasaite, V., Parli, A.T., Back, C.O., Slaats, T.: Discovering responsibilities with dynamic condition response graphs. In: Giorgini, P., Weber, B. (eds.) CAiSE 2019. LNCS, vol. 11483, pp. 595–610. Springer, Cham (2019). https://doi.org/10.1007/978-3-030-21290-2_37
27. Pesic, M., Schonenberg, H., van der Aalst, W.M.P.: DECLARE: full support for loosely-structured processes. In: EDOC 2007, p. 287 (2007)
28. Ponce de León, H., Nardelli, L., Carmona, J., vanden Broucke, S.K. : Incorporating negative information to process discovery of complex systems. Inf. Sci. **422**, 480–496 (2018)

29. Slaats, T.: Declarative and hybrid process discovery: recent advances and open challenges. J. Data Semant. **9**(1), 3–20 (2020). https://doi.org/10.1007/s13740-020-00112-9

30. Stone, M.: Cross-validatory choice and assessment of statistical predictions. J. R. Stat. Soc. Ser. B (Methodol.) **36**(2), 111–133 (1974)

31. Tax, D.M.J.: One-class classification: Concept learning in the absence of counter-examples (2002)

32. Tax, N., Teinemaa, I., van Zelst, S.J.: An interdisciplinary comparison of sequence modeling methods for next-element prediction. Softw. Syst. Model. **19**(6), 1345–1365 (2020)

33. Slaats, T., Debois, S.: The Rejection Miner, July 2020. https://github.com/tslaats/RejectionMiner

34. Slaats, T., Debois, S., Back, C.O.: Data Sets: DCR Solutions and Dreyers Foundation logs, July 2020. https://github.com/tslaats/EventLogs

35. Witten, I., Frank, E., Hall, M., Pal, C.: Data Mining: Practical Machine Learning Tools and Techniques, 4th edn. Morgan Kaufmann, Burlington (2016)

A Method for Debugging Process Discovery Pipelines to Analyze the Consistency of Model Properties

Christopher Klinkmüller[1]([✉]), Alexander Seeliger[2], Richard Müller[3],
Luise Pufahl[4], and Ingo Weber[4]

[1] CSIRO Data61, Sydney, Australia
`christopher.klinkmueller@data61.csiro.au`
[2] TU Darmstadt, Darmstadt, Germany
`seeliger@tk.tu-darmstadt.de`
[3] Leipzig University, Leipzig, Germany
`rmueller@wifa.uni-leipzig.de`
[4] Chair of Software and Business Engineering, Technische Universitaet Berlin,
Berlin, Germany
`{luise.pufahl,ingo.weber}@tu-berlin.de`

Abstract. Event logs have become a valuable information source for business process management, e.g., when analysts discover process models to inspect the process behavior and to infer actionable insights. To this end, analysts configure discovery pipelines in which logs are filtered, enriched, abstracted, and process models are derived. While pipeline operations are necessary to manage log imperfections and complexity, they might, however, influence the nature of the discovered process model and its properties. Ultimately, not considering this possibility can negatively affect downstream decision making. We hence propose a framework for assessing the consistency of model properties with respect to the pipeline operations and their parameters, and, if inconsistencies are present, for revealing which parameters contribute to them. Following recent literature on software engineering for machine learning, we refer to it as *debugging*. From evaluating our framework in a real-world analysis scenario based on complex event logs and third-party pipeline configurations, we see strong evidence towards it being a valuable addition to the process mining toolbox.

Keywords: Process mining · Discovery · Uncertainty & sensitivity analysis

1 Introduction

Historic process information from *event logs* enables analysts to derive business process insights using *process mining* [1]: *process discovery* [5,19] infers process models from the recorded behavior, *conformance checking* [12,30] relates

© Springer Nature Switzerland AG 2021
A. Polyvyanyy et al. (Eds.): BPM 2021, LNCS 12875, pp. 65–84, 2021.
https://doi.org/10.1007/978-3-030-85469-0_7

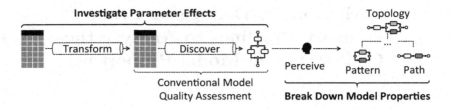

Fig. 1. An extended perspective for the evaluation of process discovery results

observed behavior to an existing process model, process *enhancement* [2,6] repairs models or extends them e.g., with performance and resource information, and *predictive process monitoring* [16,22] forecasts how process instances may unfold during execution.

The maturity of those techniques has led to an increasing adoption of process mining in industry projects, where analysts often find answers to business problems through a divide-and-conquer strategy by breaking down those problems into fine-grain information needs [10]. Here, process discovery plays a crucial role, as analysts interpret the properties of the discovered models to derive insights [32] that then serve as a foundation for understanding related aspects [1,17]. If interpreted carelessly, process discovery insights can hence negatively affect downstream analysis. Thus, *evaluating* insights from mining, particularly discovery, should be a key activity in each project [10,25] to confirm findings and to turn them into reliable and actionable insights [32]. Besides verifying scripts or tool configurations, consulting domain experts, or investigating the process environment, analysts can also perform *data-driven evaluation* [37].

Commonly, discovery results are evaluated by means of model-centric metrics like fitness, precision, generalization, and simplicity [9,15], which are e.g., computed via conformance checking [12,30] with the log that served as input to the discovery algorithm. Those metrics are valuable for assessing the reliability of discovery algorithms, and we want to complement them by expanding the evaluation perspective, as shown in Fig. 1. Analysts typically set up *process discovery pipelines* to transform logs before discovering a model. While necessary to manage log imperfections and complexity, such a pipeline potentially constrains the validity of the behavior covered by the discovered model. Thus, we propose to *examine how pipeline parameters affect properties of the discovered process models* at different granularity levels, because analysts often focus on specific execution paths and patterns to break down the model topology [17].

To this end, we propose a method to investigate the *consistency* of model properties by means of *uncertainty and sensitivity analysis* [36]. Our primary goal is to enable *what-if* analyses in which the reliability of insights is assessed by examining relationships between pipeline parameters and model properties. Yet, the method can also be applied to guide the pipeline definition, or to generate insights from those relationships. In more detail, we present a configurable framework to evaluate, if user-defined model properties are consistent with results from varied configurations of a user-defined pipeline and to quantify the contribution of individual pipeline parameters towards inconsistencies. In doing so, we follow recent work in software engineering [3], which defines a notion of debugging for machine-learning (ML) pipelines. As such, our proposal can be understood as a method for *debugging process discovery pipelines*.

Following, we discuss the problem in Sect. 2, relying on observations from a competitive process analysis challenge and an illustrative analysis of a moderately complex real-world dataset. We then outline the framework and demonstrate its application using the same dataset in Sect. 3. In a separate experiment, we investigate our framework in a realistic analysis setting based on another real-world dataset with high complexity in Sect. 4. Here, we substantiate the utility of our framework by showing that its output is founded in observations by external analysts and theory. The results demonstrate that our debugging framework is a valuable addition to the process mining toolbox: in addition to existing guidelines, patterns, and tools which we discuss in Sect. 5, it enables analysts and their audiences to comprehend the degree to which properties of discovered models are constrained by analytical decisions in a specific context. Finally, we conclude the paper and discuss future directions in Sect. 6.

2   Basic Terminology and Problem Illustration

An *event log L* is a set of traces and each trace is an ordered sequence of events. Event logs also contain features that describe properties of events and traces, such as case identifiers, event timestamps, or activity names. A *process model P* is a directed graph where typed and labeled nodes represent activities, gateways, events, etc., whereas edges depict the control flow. Finally, $\mathcal{L}$ and $\mathcal{P}$ denote the universes of event logs and process models, respectively. Note that for the purposes of this paper this basic understanding is sufficient. We hence omit formal definitions which are e.g., presented in [1, Ch. 3 & 5].

To analyze the process behavior captured in an event log, analysts often define *process discovery pipelines*, either implicitly or explicitly. In this paper, we primarily focus on pipelines that transform a single log into a single model. In the general case, however, a process discovery pipeline can be viewed as a function $\delta : \mathcal{L}^{n_l} \times \mathcal{X}^{n_x} \to \mathcal{P}^{n_p}$ that takes n_l event logs and a set of n_x *parameters* from the universe of parameters $\mathcal{X}$ and returns n_p process models. Pipelines are assembled by combining transformation and discovery operators. Each operator can be configured via its own set of parameters, all of which are included in the set of parameters that serves as input to the discovery pipeline. Pipelines can be implemented as Python or R-scripts based on packages like dplyr[1], bupaR[2], pandas[3], and pm4py[4], or by incrementally executing tools or components, like ProM plugins[5], but they often involve multiple tools and adhoc scripts [17].

---

[1] https://dplyr.tidyverse.org, accessed 2021-05-12.
[2] https://www.bupar.net, accessed 2021-05-12.
[3] https://pandas.pydata.org, accessed 2021-05-12.
[4] https://pm4py.fit.fraunhofer.de, accessed 2021-05-12.
[5] http://www.promtools.org/, accessed 2021-05-12.

Table 1. Complexity of event logs and of discovered models in BPIC 2015

	Logs	1	2	3	4	5
Log Complexity	**# Events**	52,217	44,354	59,681	47,293	59,083
	# Activities	398	410	383	356	389
	# Variants	1,170	828	1,349	1,049	1,153
Model Complexity	**# Activities**					

5   15   25   35   45   55   65   75   85

The reasons for analysts to apply discovery pipelines are twofold. On the one hand, logs might contain *imperfections*, such as missing values or outlier behavior. To eliminate those imperfections, analysts filter traces or events, and manipulate features to improve their quality or to enrich logs with data from other information sources. On the other hand, *log complexity* typically poses a challenge in interpreting the data, when logs contain drifts or describe a diverse range of activities or variants. In addition to filtering cases and events, analysts commonly lift the level of abstraction by defining higher level activities or sub-processes and by aggregating the events in the log accordingly. Note that some operations are directly supported by discovery algorithms, e.g., the inductive miner [19] can filter infrequent behavior, while directly-follows graph mining techniques often allow analysts to filter paths and activities based on their frequencies.

In this work, we postulate that the analytical decisions behind the pipeline configuration ultimately constrain the degree to which the behavior depicted in a discovered process model can be generalized. Consider e.g., the following observations from the *business process intelligence challenge* (BPIC), a competition that invites researchers, students, and experts to submit analysis reports for real-world event logs. Table 1 contrasts the complexity of the five event logs from BPIC 2015[6] with the distribution of complexity of the discovered process models presented in the nine submissions. While the event logs are highly complex with 350+ activities and 800+ variants, the majority of the models contains between 6 and 40 activities. We could not reliably quantify the number of model paths, but observed that the models only allowed for a fraction of the log variants. Moreover, one report in fact included models discovered from the raw logs, to demonstrate that it is impossible to interpret these models. While necessary to manage the cognitive load, the transformations in the underlying pipelines can affect the nature of the discovered model, even if they are less extensive, as illustrated below.

We analyzed the *Sepsis* event log[7] which captures treatments of Sepsis patients in a Dutch hospital [23]. Its complexity is moderate (1,050 cases, 15,214 events, 16 activities), rendering it useful for illustration purposes. We used

---

[6] https://www.win.tue.nl/bpi/doku.php?id=2015:challenge, accessed 2021-05-12.

[7] https://data.4tu.nl/articles/dataset/Sepsis_Cases_-_Event_Log/12707639, accessed 2021-03-12.

the default configuration of the inductive miner [19] (infrequent variant, noise `threshold` = 0.2) to discover a process model. But, we first filtered out short cases with an execution duration smaller than `minDuration` based on a common assumption that short cases represent incomplete or outlier behavior. Next, we abstracted the log by aggregating activities related to the release of patients. That is, if `consolidate` is set to `true`, all release-related events are re-labeled and in each trace all but the last release-related events are removed. Note that these transformations are not presented here as the ideal way to handle the log, but merely for illustration purposes. We chose the transformations, as we observed that they were commonly applied in submissions to different editions of the BPIC.

By varying the two parameters, we yielded the four models shown in Fig. 2. The differences between the models demonstrate that discovery results can strongly depend on a specific pipeline configuration and hence might be inconsistent with models discovered using varied configurations. For instance, model 1 indicates that the registration activities are executed in arbitrary order before all other activities; in model 2 and 3 they are optional and parallel to the treatment activities; and in model 4 the registration activity B requires the completion of the two remaining registration activities A and C. Differences consequently also exist at the level of the model topology. Yet, the models achieve similar fitness values. This shows that model-centric quality metrics may not reflect how pipeline configurations impact properties of the discovered process models.

In summary, we demonstrated that, while configuring a discovery pipeline is necessary to manage log imperfections and complexity, it might constrain the discovered model, when varied pipeline configurations yield inconsistent outputs. This can ultimately affect the certainty with which insights can be inferred from a discovered model. Following the awareness classification from [31] (see Table 2), we argue that insight uncertainties can impact the decision making that is based on the insights. In the presence of uncertainties, the chance of error due to unjustified trust in the insights is high, when analysts are unaware

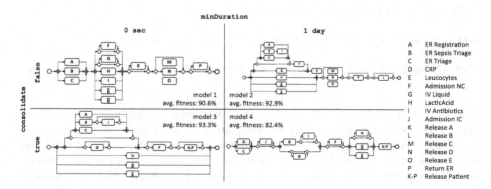

Fig. 2. Sepsis results for different pipeline configurations (fitness calculated with the multi-perspective process explorer in ProM with the transformed event logs).

Table 2. Effects of the analyst's awareness of result uncertainties (adapted from [31])

		Discovery Result	
		No Uncertainties	**Uncertainties**
Analyst	**Aware**	trust in insight: high decision making: unaffected	trust in insight: medium-low decision making: largely unaffected
	Mistaken	trust in insight: medium-low decision making: affected	trust in insight: high decision making: severely affected
	Unaware	trust in insight: medium decision making: unaffected	trust in insight: medium decision making: severely affected

of or mistakenly assume the absence of uncertainties. But also in the absence of uncertainties, decision making might be impaired when analysts unnecessarily question the insight validity due to mistakenly assuming that uncertainties exist. While in the remaining cases the decision making is usually not affected, analysts (and their audiences) should ideally always be aware of the level of uncertainty that is associated with the insights and of its root causes.

3   Debugging of Process Discovery Pipelines

The necessity to address log imperfections and complexity via pipeline operations can result in uncertain insights and impaired decision making (see Sect. 2). Such uncertainty can stem from stochastic operators, but most often is introduced by the pipeline parameters. For example, while there might be a plausible range of threshold values for a filter that removes outlier traces with short durations, the precise value can be uncertain. Diagnosing such uncertainty by manually varying parameters and inspecting the respective outputs is infeasible due to the number of configurations needed to obtain reliable conclusions, especially when model and pipeline complexities, or parameter interactions are present. Moreover, it is not transparent to the model audience. Hence, to assist analysts in debugging their discovery pipelines, we pursue two objectives:

O1: *Assess the consistency of model properties* to unveil potential pipeline constraints.
O2: *Quantify the influence of parameters* to provide explanations for inconsistencies.

While our approach could be used to evaluate steps in pipelines generally, we designed it with the purpose of allowing an analyst to achieve objectives O1 and O2 for a concrete case. As such, the standard situation for applying our framework is: an analyst has created a concrete pipeline with a concrete parameter configuration to generate a *baseline model*. The analyst then investigates how the parameters influence the model properties (i) to substantiate insights inferred from the baseline model, (ii) to iteratively construct a reliable pipeline, or (iii) to generate insights from parameter/property relationships. In all cases, the metrics are calculated relative to the properties of the baseline model.

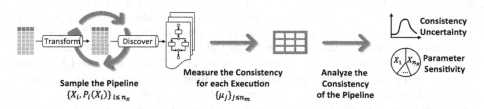

Fig. 3. Framework for investigating property consistency in process discovery pipelines

To this end, one conceivable strategy is to instrument the pipeline and to track the validity of model properties in all steps [45], i.e., in all intermediate logs and the discovered process models. Yet, as this analysis only considers the current configuration, we would not be able to measure the consistency of model properties with it, or to reason about the general influence of parameters. Hence, we adopt *uncertainty and sensitivity analysis* which provides means to quantify effects of varied pipeline configurations. In this regard, a first option are *one-at-a-time* designs [36, pp. 66–69]. In such a design we would examine both objectives by focusing on each parameter individually. Given a parameter, we would repeatedly change its value and for each value execute the pipeline *without* modifying any of the other parameters. Then, we would use the generated outcomes to examine how variations in the parameter change the pipeline outcome. While this is computationally efficient, the analytical results can be skewed in the presence of parameter interactions [34]. *Global sensitivity analysis* overcomes this limitation by studying the effects of simultaneous parameter changes. Here, *variogram analysis of response surfaces* (VARS) [29] aims to reveal the spatial structure and variability of model outputs. Essentially, VARS models the output space as a variogram function that describes the degree to which model outcomes for a specific parameter configuration X depend on outcomes produced by configurations in the vicinity of X. This variogram function is then used to examine properties of input-output relationships. However, VARS does not provide clear indications for the importance of inputs and thus, they should be used to complement *variance-based sensitivity analysis* [28]. We follow this argumentation and build our framework on the scheme for variance-based sensitivity analysis from [35].

As shown in Fig. 3, we first *sample the pipeline* (Sect. 3.1). That is, we execute the user-defined pipeline $\delta : \mathcal{L}^{n_l} \times \mathcal{X}^{n_x} \to \mathcal{P}^{n_p}$ multiple times to generate process models for different parameter configurations. Here, we consider event logs to be constants. This effectively turns discovery pipelines into functions $\delta_X : \mathcal{X}^{n_x} \to \mathcal{P}^{n_p}$ that only take parameters as input. To guide the exploration and the parameter sampling, analysts must specify the *relevant* parameters and their probability measures $\{(X_i, P_i(X_i))\}_{i \leq n_x}$. Next, we *measure the property consistency for each execution* (Sect. 3.2), requiring the analysts to manually determine the model properties for which they want to measure the *consistency*, i.e., the degree to which a (set of) model(s) produced in a single execution satisfies this property. In particular, the analyst must provide a set of n_m *property consistency measurements* $\{\mu_j\}_{j \leq n_m}$ where each function $\mu_j : \mathcal{P}^{n'_{p,j}} \rightarrow [0,1]$ represents a specific property and returns the consistency for this property as observed in a set of $n'_{p,j}$ process models: a value of 0 indicates total inconsistency, a value of 1 perfect consistency, and values in between degrees of consistency. Lastly, we *analyze the property consistency of the pipeline* (Sect. 3.3): an uncertainty analysis assesses the degree to which a model property changes when pipeline parameters vary (O1), whereas sensitivity analysis quantifies the contribution of individual parameters to potential inconsistencies (O2). Below, we describe each step using the Sepsis experiment from Sect. 2 for illustration purposes.

3.1 Sampling the Pipeline

To explore the output of different pipeline configurations, we first create a $k \times n_x$ configuration matrix $\mathbf{A}$ which comprises the configurations for k pipeline executions. Each configuration contains n_x values, one per relevant parameter X_i. We use the configurations in $\mathbf{A}$ to assess whether the pipeline yields inconsistencies (O1, see Sect. 3.3). If there are inconsistencies and it must be analyzed how parameters contribute to them (O2, see Sect. 3.3), then for each parameter X_i we create an additional $k \times n_x$ configuration matrix $\mathbf{AB}_i$ by copying $\mathbf{A}$ and varying the values in the ith column which defines the values for parameter X_i. Comparing the results obtained from the configurations in $\mathbf{A}$ and $\mathbf{AB}_i$ allows us to quantify the influence of parameter X_i. Thus, when desired, O2 requires $k \times n_x$ additional pipeline executions, yielding a total of $k \times (n_x + 1)$ executions.

For a reliable analysis we need configurations that (i) sufficiently sample the entire parameter space and (ii) systematically vary the parameter values. We achieve this based on the procedure that yielded the best results in a comparative evaluation by Saltelli et al. [35]. First, we use a *low-discrepancy* sequence to generate two temporary $k \times n_x$ matrices $\mathbf{A}^t$ and $\mathbf{B}^t$ where each row is a point in the n_x-dimensional unit cube. Low-discrepancy sequences ensure that the parameter space is evenly sampled. We here use the *Sobol' sequence* [39] which, in contrast to sequences like the Latin Hypercube design, has the advantage that we do not necessarily need to fix the sample size, but could in principle dynamically generate new configurations until the analysis results converge. We use the Sobol' sequence to generate a $k \times 2n_x$ matrix that is split in half to obtain the temporary matrices $\mathbf{A}^t$ and $\mathbf{B}^t$ from the left and right half, respectively. While we derive $\mathbf{A}$ directly from $\mathbf{A}^t$, we use $\mathbf{B}^t$ to create the temporary matrices $\{\mathbf{AB}_i^t\}_{i \leq n_x}$ using the *radial sampling* strategy [33]. That is, for each parameter X_i we construct $\mathbf{AB}_i^t$ by copying $\mathbf{A}^t$ and replacing the i-th column with the respective column from $\mathbf{B}^t$. Lastly, we obtain the configuration matrices ($\mathbf{A}$ and $\{\mathbf{AB}_i\}_{i \leq n_x}$) by interpreting the values in the temporary matrices as probabilities: for each parameter we convert each value p in the i-th columns of the temporary matrices to a parameter value x for X_i so that the respective cumulative probability yields the probability p for value x, i.e., $P_i(X_i \leq x) = p$.

The final step is to execute the discovery pipeline for each configuration in $\mathbf{A}$ to discover the process models. The configurations from $\{\mathbf{AB_i}\}_{i \leq n_x}$ are only executed, if inconsistencies exist for which the analyst wishes to inspect the influence of parameters.

In our running example, the Sepsis experiment, we sample the pipeline for the parameters minDuration, consolidate, and threshold, in this order of parameters. We here also consider the threshold parameter, because in Sect. 2 it was set to 0.2 by default and might have influenced the results. For consolidate and threshold we use uniform distributions over their entire domains ($\{$false,true$\}$ and $[0,1]$), whereas for minDuration we use the empirical distribution of case durations in the log for all values $\leq$ 2 days. Setting minDuration to 2 days would exclude about 29% of the cases, and hence we chose this value as an upper bound. Taking a concrete example for a configuration, say the current configuration from $\mathbf{A}^t$ or $\mathbf{AB}_i^t$ is (0.7, 0.6, 0.3); then our approach derives the following parameter values as per the above use of the cumulative probabilities. The 70th percentile of the actual data for minDuration is at 4h 10min, and therefore we get minDuration = 4h 10min. 0.6 > 0.5, hence we get consolidate=true. For threshold, the uniform distribution equals the identity function, hence threshold=0.3. We set the sample size k to 1,000 resulting in 1,000 executions for O1 and $(3 \times 1{,}000) = 3{,}000$ executions for O2.

3.2 Measuring the Property Consistency for a Single Execution

Within our framework, analysts can investigate the consistency of the model topology and of fine-grained model properties like execution patterns and paths by defining property consistency measurements $\mu : \mathcal{P}^{n'_P} \to [0,1]$. While analysts can provide any measurement, we propose two specific measurements for single models ($n'_P = 1$). Both functions rely on the *causal behavioral profile* [42] which captures behavioral relations between a set of activities T as observed in a set of executions E. The *causal behavioral profile* is defined as $C_{T,E} = \{\rightsquigarrow, +, \|, \gg\}$ where activity pairs $(t_1, t_2) \in T \times T$ are

1. in *strict order* ($t_1 \rightsquigarrow t_2$), if in all executions with t_1 and t_2, t_1 occurs before t_2;
2. in *interleaving order* ($t_1 \| t_2$), if they can be executed in arbitrary order;
3. *exclusive* ($t_1 + t_2$), if they are never part of the same execution; and
4. *co-occurring* ($t_1 \gg t_2$), if the presence of t_1 implies the presence of t_2.

We chose behavioral profiles as a foundation for the concrete consistency measurements, as they have been applied for various tasks including process monitoring, complex event processing, conformance checking, and most importantly model consistency assessment [43]. Moreover, they can be computed from heterogeneous inputs. Considering that each trace represents an execution, they can straightforwardly be derived from logs. An efficient computation for *sound* process models [42] derives the profile from a tree representation of the process model. This computation can easily be adopted for discovery algorithms that output process trees such as the inductive miner [19]. For directly-follows graphs with a dedicated start and a dedicated end node, every path from start to end is an execution. Besides these beneficial properties, behavioral profiles might however inaccurately represent behavioral relationships in some cases [27]. Hence, a comparative evaluation of consistency measures is required in future work.

The first type of measurement is the *profile-based consistency* $\mu_C : P \to [0,1]$. It requires the provision of a base profile C_{T_b,E_b}. Then, it applies the *degree of consistency* metric from [41] to compute a consistency score for C_{T_b,E_b} and a profile C_{T_d,E_d} derived from a discovered process model. This metric relies on an *alignment* of the activities from T_b and T_d. It hence allows us to compare profiles at the same and at different levels of granularity. If two profiles are at the same level of granularity, all activities with equal labels are aligned. Otherwise, the pipeline includes a log abstraction step in which fine-grained activities are mapped to higher-level activities e.g., using manually defined hierarchies or automated label comparison [18]. This mapping defines the alignment. Based on the alignment, the first step is to determine the sets of aligned activities T_b^a and T_d^a which contain all activities from T_b and T_d for which the other activity set contains aligned activities. The metric then determines the count γ of activity pairs in $T_b^a \times T_b^a$ and $T_d^a \times T_d^a$ whose relations defined by C_{T_b,E_b} and C_{T_d,E_d} match the relations of the aligned activity pairs from the other profile. The relations of two aligned activity pairs $(t_b', t_b'') \in T_b^a \times T_b^a$ and $(t_d', t_d'') \in T_d^a \times T_d^a$ match, if both pairs are in strict order, interleaving order or exclusive, and they either co-occur or not. If an activity pair (t', t'') is aligned with multiple pairs, then the relations of all these pairs must match the relations of (t', t''). Finally, γ is divided by the number of aligned activity pairs $|T_b^a \times T_b^a| + |T_d^a \times T_d^a|$. In this work, we primarily use the profile from the baseline model discovered with a specific pipeline configuration to track the degree to which behavioral relations change when parameters change. Similar to model-centric quality metrics [9], it is also conceivable to check, if the discovered model accurately reflects the relations in a log, potentially produced during pipeline execution.

A break down of the model topology to investigate more fine-grain aspects can be achieved by removing activities from the base profile to focus on certain activity sets. Additionally, the *rule-based consistency* $\mu_R : P \to \{0,1\}$ enables analysts to specify arbitrary *rules* in terms of boolean expressions which define relations that need to hold between specific activities, e.g., that an activity α must be in strict order with an activity β. The function then returns a value of 1, if the profile derived from the discovered model adheres to the rule and a value of 0 otherwise. Note that this is similar to the use of declarative rules which are defined at the level of events and traces, whereas the rule-based consistency relies on the more abstract level of the behavioral profile.

In the Sepsis example, we observed some inconsistencies at the model and at the activity level. Here, we focus on three properties for which we analyze the pipeline consistency below in Sect. 3.3. First, we use the profile-based consistency to evaluate the model that we obtained, when setting `minDuration` to 2 days, `consolidate` to `true`, and `threshold` to 0.2 (I1), see lower right corner of Fig. 2.

Additionally, we use the rule-based consistency to diagnose specific inconsistencies that we observed when varying the parameters in Fig. 2. In particular, we check if the registration activities A and C occur before all other activities (I2), and if the release activities generally occur at the end of the process (I3). Note that we evaluate all three consistencies based on the same set of configurations and discovered process models, respectively.

3.3   Analyzing the Property Consistency for the Pipeline

The last step conducts the analyses postulated by the two objectives. We first address O1 and examine the uncertainty associated with model properties based on the provided consistency measurements $\{\mu_j\}_{j \leq n_m}$. To this end, we compose the discovery pipeline $\delta_X : \mathcal{X}^{n_x} \to \mathcal{P}^{n_p}$ and each consistency measurement $\mu_j :$ $\mathcal{P}^{n_{p,j}} \to [0,1]$ to functions $f_j = \mu_j \circ \delta_X$ that measure the property consistency for models produced by a given pipeline configuration. This requires that the consistency functions take as many process models as input as discovered by the pipeline in a single execution, i.e., $n_p = n_{p,j}$.

For a measurement μ_j, we first calculate the *mean consistency* $\overline{f_j} = \frac{1}{k}\sum_{l=1}^{k} f_j(\mathbf{A})_l$ over all configurations from the configuration matrix $\mathbf{A}$ (see Sect. 3.1). If the mean consistency is equal or very close to 1 (or 0 respectively), we know that the respective property is (not) free of constrains and hence generally (in-)valid. In all other cases, there is uncertainty regarding the conditions that cause inconsistencies and we next estimate the *consistency variance* $\hat{V}(f_j) = \frac{1}{k}\sum_{l=1}^{k}\left(f_j(\mathbf{A})_l^2 - \overline{\mu_j}^2\right)$. If the variance is close to 0, we can infer that all pipeline configurations yield similar consistency values and that there likely is a systematic difference between the property from the baseline model and the properties of the pipeline output, generally. Such a difference can be explored by comparing the originally discovered model to a few models generated with different configurations. Here, the analyst can also resort to restricting the base profile or defining rule-based consistencies, in order to investigate differences at a more fine-grained level.

Larger variance values indicate that varied pipeline configurations yield process models with different levels of consistency. To analyze the influence of parameters as per O2, we compute the *total effect index* $S_{i,j}$ for each parameter X_i [13]. It measures the contribution of parameter X_i to the variance in the consistency measurement μ_j and considers all variance that is directly caused by X_i and by interactions with other parameters. As suggested in [35], we here use the estimator from [14]: $\hat{S}_{i,j} = \frac{1}{2k \cdot \hat{V}(f_j)}\sum_{l=1}^{k}\left(f_j(\mathbf{A})_l - f_j(\mathbf{AB}_i)_l\right)^2$. This estimator relies on the results of the configuration matrix $\mathbf{AB}_i$. The higher the value of the index for a parameter, the more it contributes to the variance in the consistency measurement. If the sum of the indexes is larger than 1 $\left(\sum_{i=1}^{n_x}(\hat{S}_{i,j}) > 1\right)$ the parameters definitely interact.

We conclude by analyzing the pipeline consistency for the Sepsis experiment considering the sampling configuration and properties from Sect. 3.1 and 3.2.

The mean model consistency (I1) is $\overline{f_1} = .57$ and for the two rule-based measures (I2, I3) we yield mean consistencies of $\overline{f_2} = .08$ and $\overline{f_3} = .21$. These low values are in line with our observations from Fig. 2, because they indicate that the behavioral relations in the baseline model are associated with uncertainty, especially the relations of the registration and release activities. The variances ($\hat{V}(f_1) = .06$, $\hat{V}(f_2) = .07$, $\hat{V}(f_3) = .16$) point to non-systematic differences which are attributed to all parameters. That is because all consistency / parameter combinations yield high total effect indexes on the interval $[.71, .92]$. This implies that the handling of the log is not optimal and should be changed, not least because the indexes reveal that there is significant parameter interaction.

4   Experiment

The primary objective of our experiment is to study whether the framework provides a reliable foundation for investigating the effects of discovery pipeline operations on the discovered model and its properties. In the following, we first outline and justify our experimental design in Sect. 4.1. After that, we discuss our results in Sect. 4.2.

4.1   Experimental Design

Uncertainty and sensitivity analysis are mature techniques that have been studied intensively, e.g., in [13,14,28,29,33,35,36], and hence provide a solid foundation for our work. Software engineering for machine learning [3] is an emerging topic, and has not yet been adopted for process mining (see Sect. 5). Hence, we validate our framework using a *single-case mechanism experiment*, a suitable method for investigating the application of existing technology to a new phenomenon [44, Ch. 18]. To mitigate the effects of a limited *external validity* associated with such a design, i.e., the degree to which the findings can be generalized, we attached great importance to strengthening the *ecological validity*, i.e., the realism with which the setup resembles real-world circumstances, and to minimizing the threat of *experimenter bias*. Moreover, to ensure transparency and reproducibility, we followed open science principles by relying on public data and by publishing our source code[8]. In more detail, we decided to use the BPIC 2015 dataset from Sect. 2. It is a highly complex (see Table 1), publicly available, real-world dataset for which nine independent analysis reports were published. The latter allows us to setup a representative discovery pipeline based on operations commonly applied by external parties on this dataset. We merely use the reports to guide the pipeline setup. It is not our intention to judge the analysts' practices, for which an exact replication of a pipeline would be required (which is neither desired nor feasible with the level of detail in the reports). The dataset contains five event logs from applications for building permits in different Dutch municipalities. Hence, we can reuse the sample pipeline to analyze our framework in (slightly) varied circumstances.

---

[8] https://bitbucket.csiro.au/users/kli039/repos/bpm-2021-debugging-experiments.

Table 3. Pipeline specification for the experiment including the parameters' *emp*-irical or *uni*-form distributions; their *rel*-evance for the variants V1–V5 where a default value is provided for irrelevant parameters (0, 1, f – false, t – true); and the parameter values that were used to generate baseline profiles for different consistency measurements.

Parameter	Probabilities			Variants					Baseline Profile Generation				
	Type	From	To	V1	V2	V3	V4	V5	norm	abst	simp	mod	comp
start date	emp	1/5/13	30/6/13	always relevant					always set to 1/6/13				
end date	emp	1/4/13	31/5/14	always relevant					always set to 30/4/14				
activated	uni	f	t	f	rel	f	f	rel	f	t	f	f	f
activity freq.	uni	0	1	1	1	rel	rel	rel	1	1	.2	.35	.5
variant freq.	uni	0	1	1	1	rel	1	rel	always 1				
threshold	uni	0	1	0	0	0	rel	rel	always 0				

We first categorized the applied transformation operations from the reports and assembled the three most common operations into the pipeline from the last row of Table 3. First, the *log preparation* loads the log and performs computations that ease the analysis. That is, the log specifies an activity code which is the activity identifier, but also contains a sub-process identifier and an order index. As the sub-process identifier is used for log consolidation, we extract it into a separate feature. Because events were logged in batch with overlapping timestamps, we follow advice from the BPIC organizers and establish the execution order based on the order index. After that, we apply a *time window filter* to remove traces that started or completed outside a window defined by pipeline parameters **start** and **end date**. This operation addresses the drifts in the log which impact the discovery, and we here consider a time window from summer 2013 to spring 2014 in which no drift occurred. If parameter **activated** is set to **true**, we perform a *consolidation* in which we define the sub-process identifier as the activity classifier. Further, in each trace we only keep the first and last sub-process event and set the event lifecycle state to **started** for the first event, and retain **completed** for the last. Next, a *frequency filter* can reduce the complexity of the discovered process model by selecting events and traces based on the **activity** and **variant frequency**. Lastly, we apply the infrequent lifecycle variant of the inductive miner [19] where the noise **threshold** also allows for filtering behavior.

To systematically study the effects of combining different operations, we vary the subset of relevant parameters from the above six parameters, and set the remaining parameters to default values. The relevance of parameters for the variants and their probability measures are summarized in Table 3. V1 establishes a baseline in which we only vary the parameters of the time window filter. Here, we expect that the absence of drifts in the considered period (summer 2013 to spring 2014) guarantees a consistent discovery for slightly varied **start** and

end dates. To study the impact of model consolidation, V2 additionally considers the **activated** parameters. Here, we expect that the information loss which is inadvertently linked to abstraction leads to a drop in the consistency, but that the discovered models are largely consistent, as we rely on a clearly defined process hierarchy. In V3 and V4, we add different ways of behavior filtering to V1: while both variants utilize the **activity frequency**, V3 additionally combines it with the **variant frequency** and V4 with the noise **threshold**. We hypothesize that these filters interact with the time window filter, which influences the frequencies in the intermediate log. Finally, in V5 all parameters are relevant.

To investigate the pipeline consistency, we focus on the overall model consistency using the profile-based consistency. In this regard, different baseline models and thus base profiles emulate different degrees of complexity of discovered models (see Table 3). All profiles are derived from the log for the default time window. The *normative* (norm) profile has the highest complexity. It is discovered directly from the default time window log and used for all variants. For V2, we also use an *abstract* (abst) profile obtained by activating the consolidation. Lastly, for V3 and V4 we aimed to replicate different model complexities in line with the model complexities found in the reports (Table 1). We generate the *simple* (simp), *moderate* (mod), and *complex* (comp) profiles by varying the **activity frequency** to obtain models with ≈ 10, ≈ 20 and ≈ 35 of the most frequent activities. We did not use the **variant frequency** or noise **threshold**, as their effects on the model complexity differed across the five logs. Yet, the profile-based consistency still allows us to assess their influence on the discovery results.

4.2   Results

In the analysis, we considered a sample size of $k = 1,000$ for all combinations of pipeline variants and consistency measurements. To ensure that this sample size yields reliable results, we first investigated the convergence of the mean consistencies, variances, and total effect indexes. That is, we computed the values that we obtain for these measures for sample sizes less than 1,000 and observed that for sample sizes larger than 500, all measures yield values that are very close to the respective values obtained for $k = 1,000$ on all five logs for all variant/measurement combinations. While this ensures the reliability of our experiment, it also demonstrates that measuring the convergence of the values is a strategy to control the number of pipeline executions in real-world situations. We did not investigate the run-time performance explicitly, but observed that the inductive miner accounted for a large part of the execution time and that its performance depended (unsurprisingly) on the complexity of the input log. To compute all metrics per variant and dataset, on a customary laptop (Processor: i5-8350U 1.70 GHz; RAM: 16 GB) and using parallel execution we yielded execution times between one and two hours for (V1); but below 5 min for V3–V5, due to complexity reductions in the intermediary logs. Note that this is only a rough indication for the run-time performance, for which we leave deeper investigation and optimization to future work.

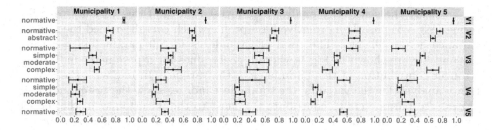

Fig. 4. Mean consistencies (dot) and variances (error bars) for pipeline variants

We first investigate the uncertainty for each variant and consistency combination, see Fig. 4. A first observation is that the consistency of the normative model is very high ($\overline{f_j} > .9$) for V1. This is in line with our expectations, as we knew from the reports that the considered period does not contain drifts. Slight variations in the model can be attributed to a few outlier cases that might occur around the default start and end date. For V2 we also confirm our expectations, as the model consistency drops ($\overline{f_j} > .7$) due to some information loss caused by the consolidation, but is still high. Note that this holds for the abstracted and the normative model, indicating that log abstraction is a reliable means for complexity management. Lastly, the variants that apply filtering (V3–V5) yield very low consistency measures ($\overline{f_j} < .5$). While we expected some interaction with other parameters, we were surprised by the magnitude of the effect of this interaction. However, this observation is in line with guidelines from [11] that postulate to carefully apply random subset selection, as it – in contrast to strategic selection, like the date window filter – can affect the quality of the discovered model. We consider the filter parameters from V3–V5 to fall in this category, as it is hard for analysts to predict the effects of certain value combinations. Moreover, the negative effects pertain all base profiles which shows that the filters affect a large range of the relations and that a broad range of possible behavior can be generated by modifying the respective parameters. Overall, the coherence of our expectations and existing guidelines with the experiment results substantiates the reliability of the consistency measurement.

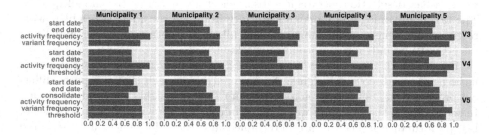

Fig. 5. Total effect indexes for the normative profile and variants V3–V5

To study the sensitivity analysis, we focused on the three variants with filtering (V3–V5) and the normative base profile which overall yielded the largest variance across all logs. The total effect indexes for all parameters per variant and log are shown in Fig. 5 where higher values for a parameter indicate a stronger contribution of this parameter to the variance. In line with the uncertainty analysis for the variants, the total effect indexes show the `frequency` and `threshold` parameters to contribute the most to the uncertainty in the model topology. This provides evidence towards the utility of the sensitivity analysis: an analyst can determine the most influential parameters without manually inspecting possible parameter or pipeline variations. Another interesting finding is that the time window filter and consolidation parameters, which without filtering only impacted the consistency a bit, have a stronger influence in variants V3–V5. This demonstrates that analysts need to carefully assemble discovery pipelines and cannot assume that a 'stable' operation can be straightforwardly reused in other contexts.

5   Related Work

Research has studied issues related to data quality and quantity, in order to ensure that high quality process models can be obtained from event logs. Classifications of data quality issues [8] and data quality patterns for event logs [40] allow for systematic cleaning of event logs to increase process mining result quality. Fitness, precision, generalization, and simplicity have been adopted as metrics to evaluate the quality of a process model based on the event log that served as the input for a process discovery algorithm [1]. Conformance checking allows to obtain further details about if and how an event log deviates from a process model for qualitative evaluation [12,30]. Also, methods have been proposed to balance the behavioral quality of a discovered process model with its complexity, in order to facilitate human inspection. For example, in [20] event attributes are used to generate hierarchical process models that better represent different levels of process granularity. A statistical pre-processing framework for event logs that reduces the amount of data needed to produce high quality process models is presented in [7]. Similarly, the influence of subset selection on the model quality was examined in [11] where it was shown that, in contrast to random-based selection, strategic subset selection increases the model quality. The taxonomy of log and model uncertainty from [26] considers issues like incorrectness, coarseness, and ambiguity, and allows for obtaining upper and lower uncertainty bounds for conformance checking.

Related work also proposed approaches for automatically extracting and evaluating process discovery insights. An automatic approach that compares different process variants with the goal to obtain valuable insights is introduced in [6]. In more detail, the best and worst-performing variants with respect to a set of key performance indicators are determined and their differences are presented to the analyst. ProcessExplorer [38] automatically computes potential subsets of cases and evaluates the interestingness based on statistical differences between insights from the subsets and from the entire event log. Leemans et al. [21] introduce an automatic extraction approach to obtain cohorts from event logs via trace attribute analysis. The authors measure the stochastic distance between trace attribute cohorts to identify their influence to the process model behavior.

Complementary to these techniques, patterns, and guidelines, our consistency framework enables analysts to, in a concrete context, explicate how their decisions, that underlie the configuration of a discovery pipeline including its log transformations and discovery algorithms, affect model properties at different granularity levels.

6   Conclusion

In this work we presented a first framework for debugging of process discovery pipelines. We demonstrated the potential effects of pipeline operations on the discovered models and discussed the implications for downstream decision making. Next, we proposed a debugging framework which relies on uncertainty and sensitivity analysis, in order to assist analysts in assessing the consistency of their insights and to quantify the contribution of pipeline parameters to potential inconsistencies. In an experiment on real-world event logs, we assessed the utility of our framework and found that the uncertainties and explanations delivered by the framework were well-grounded.

As mentioned in Sect. 3.2, comparative evaluations of consistency measures are required to improve the framework's applicability. Beyond that, research opportunities ensue specifically regarding its *usability, computational performance*, and *broader application and evaluation*. Usability topics comprise suitable user interfaces for tools, but also the generalization towards other process mining methods including declarative process mining; support for determining relevant parameters (e.g., via screening [36]) and their probability distributions; and means to diagnose and break down inconsistencies. Moreover, repeatedly executing a pipeline for different configurations can be time-consuming. While screening methods can help to reduce the number of relevant parameters, integrated uncertainty propagation [24] or emulators [36] might speed up the analysis. Lastly, applying the framework to a larger set of real-world scenarios could potentially reveal and confirm (anti-)patterns for process mining pipelines [40].

In general, we believe that applying software engineering practices, as proposed in the context of machine learning [3], is relevant for process mining as well. While traditionally process mining techniques have been made available via visual idioms which combine visual representations and user interaction techniques, packages like BupaR and pm4py have brought process mining to open data processing environments like R, Python, Apache Spark, etc. This enables a paradigm shift towards script-based analysis, where the ability to seamlessly integrate data processing, data mining, and machine learning techniques and tools can ease the definition, execution, documentation, and sharing of process mining pipelines, and reduce their fragmentation. In this regard, challenges from machine learning include testing, experiment management, transparency, and troubleshooting [4]. Empirical studies into the practices of process analysts, such as [17], can help to refine those challenges in the context of process mining.

References

1. van der Aalst, W.: Process Mining: Data Science in Action. Springer, Heidelberg (2016). https://doi.org/10.1007/978-3-662-49851-4
2. Adriansyah, A., Buijs, J.C.A.M.: Mining process performance from event logs. In: BPM Workshops, pp. 217–218 (2013)
3. Amershi, S., et al.: Software engineering for machine learning: a case study. In: ICSE SEIP, pp. 291–300 (2019)
4. Arpteg, A., Brinne, B., Crnkovic-Friis, L., Bosch, J.: Software engineering challenges of deep learning. In: SEAA, pp. 50–59 (2018)
5. Augusto, A., Conforti, R., Dumas, M., La Rosa, M., Polyvyanyy, A.: Split miner: automated discovery of accurate and simple business process models from event logs. Knowl. Inf. Syst. **59**, 251–284 (2019)
6. Ballambettu, N.P., Suresh, M.A., Bose, R.P.J.C.: Analyzing process variants to understand differences in key performance indices. In: CAISE, pp. 298–313 (2017)
7. Bauer, M., Senderovich, A., Gal, A., Grunske, L., Weidlich, M.: How much event data is enough? a statistical framework for process discovery. In: CAISE, pp. 239–256 (2018)
8. Bose, R.P.J.C., Mans, R.S.: Van Der Aalst, W.M.P.: Wanna improve process mining results? In: IEEE SSCI, pp. 127–134 (2013)
9. Buijs, J.C.A.M., van Dongen, B.F., van der Aalst, W.M.P.: Quality dimensions in process discovery: the importance of fitness, precision, generalization and simplicity. Int. J. Coop. Inf. Syst. **23**(01), 1440001 (2014)
10. van Eck, M.L., Lu, X., Leemans, S.J.J., van der Aalst, W.M.P.: PM^2: a process mining project methodology. In: CAISE, pp. 297–313 (2015)
11. Fani Sani, M., van Zelst, S.J., van der Aalst, W.M.P.: The impact of event log subset selection on the performance of process discovery algorithms. In: ADBIS, pp. 391–404 (2019)
12. García-Bañuelos, L., van Beest, N.R.T.P., Dumas, M., Rosa, M.L., Mertens, W.: Complete and interpretable conformance checking of business processes. IEEE Trans. Softw. Eng. **44**(3), 262–290 (2018)
13. Homma, T., Saltelli, A.: Importance measures in global sensitivity analysis of non-linear models. Reliab. Eng. Syst. Saf. **52**(1), 1–17 (1996)
14. Jansen, M.J.W.: Analysis of variance designs for model output. Comput. Phys. Commun. **117**(1), 35–43 (1999)
15. Kalenkova, A., Polyvyanyy, A., La Rosa, M.: A framework for estimating simplicity of automatically discovered process models based on structural and behavioral characteristics. In: BPM, pp. 129–146 (2020)
16. Klinkmüller, C., van Beest, N.R.T.P., Weber, I.: Towards reliable predictive process monitoring. In: CAISE Forum, pp. 163–181 (2018)
17. Klinkmüller, C., Müller, R., Weber, I.: Mining process mining practices: an exploratory characterization of information needs in process analytics. In: BPM, pp. 322–337 (2019)
18. Klinkmüller, C., Weber, I.: Every apprentice needs a master: Feedback-based effectiveness improvements for process model matching. Inf. Syst. **95**, 101612 (2021)

19. Leemans, S.J.J., Fahland, D., van der Aalst, W.M.P.: Discovering block-structured process models from event logs - a constructive approach. In: Petri Nets, pp. 311–329 (2013)
20. Leemans, S.J.J., Goel, K., Van Zelst, S.J.: Using multi-level information in hierarchical process mining: Balancing behavioural quality and model complexity. In: ICPM, pp. 137–144 (2020)
21. Leemans, S.J.J., Shabaninejad, S., Goel, K., Khosravi, H., Sadiq, S., Wynn, M.T.: Identifying cohorts: recommending drill-downs based on differences in behaviour for process mining. In: ER, pp. 92–102 (2020)
22. Maggi, F.M., Di Francescomarino, C., Dumas, M., Ghidini, C.: Predictive monitoring of business processes. In: CAISE, pp. 457–472 (2014)
23. Mannhardt, F., Blinde, D.: Analyzing the trajectories of patients with sepsis using process mining. In: BPMDS, pp. 72–80 (2017)
24. Manousakis, I., Goiri, I.N., Bianchini, R., Rigo, S., Nguyen, T.D.: Uncertainty propagation in data processing systems (2018)
25. Mariscal, G., Marbán, S., Fernández, C.: A survey of data mining and knowledge discovery process models and methodologies. Knowl. Eng. Rev. **25**(2), 137–166 (2010)
26. Pegoraro, M., van der Aalst, W.M.P.: Mining uncertain event data in process mining. In: ICPM, pp. 89–96 (2019)
27. Polyvyanyy, A., Armas-Cervantes, A., Dumas, M., García-Bañuelos, L.: On the expressive power of behavioral profiles. Formal Aspects Comput. **28**(4), 597–613 (2016)
28. Puy, A., Lo Piano, S., Saltelli, A.: Is vars more intuitive and efficient than sobol' indices? Environ. Model Softw. **137**, 104960 (2021)
29. Razavi, S., Gupta, H.V.: A new framework for comprehensive, robust, and efficient global sensitivity analysis: 1. theory. Water Resour. Res. **52**(1), 423–439 (2016)
30. Rozinat, A., van der Aalst, W.M.P.: Conformance checking of processes based on monitoring real behavior. Inf. Syst. **33**(1), 64–95 (2008)
31. Sacha, D., Senaratne, H., Kwon, B.C., Ellis, G., Keim, D.A.: The role of uncertainty, awareness, and trust in visual analytics. IEEE Trans. Vis. Comput. Graph. **22**(1), 240–249 (2016)
32. Sacha, D., Stoffel, A., Stoffel, F., Kwon, B.C., Ellis, G., Keim, D.A.: Knowledge generation model for visual analytics. IEEE Trans. Vis. Comput. Graph. **20**(12), 1604–1613 (2014)
33. Saltelli, A.: Making best use of model evaluations to compute sensitivity indices. Comput. Phys. Commun. **145**(2), 280–297 (2002)
34. Saltelli, A., Aleksankina, K., Becker, W., Fennell, P., Ferretti, F., Holst, N., Li, S., Wu, Q.: Why so many published sensitivity analyses are false: a systematic review of sensitivity analysis practices. Environ. Model Softw. **114**, 29–39 (2019)
35. Saltelli, A., Annoni, P., Azzini, I., Campolongo, F., Ratto, M., Tarantola, S.: Variance based sensitivity analysis of model output design and estimator for the total sensitivity index. Comput. Phys. Commun. **181**(2), 259–270 (2010)
36. Saltelli, A., et al.: Global Sensitivity Analysis. The Primer, Wiley, Hoboken (2008)
37. Sargent, R.G.: Verification and validation of simulation models. J. Simul. **7**, 12–24 (2013)
38. Seeliger, A., Sánchez Guinea, A., Nolle, T., Mühlhäuser, M.: Processexplorer: intelligent process mining guidance. In: BPM (2019)
39. Sobol, I.M.: Uniformly distributed sequences with an additional uniform property. USSR Comput. Math. Math. Phys. **16**(5), 236–242 (1976)

40. Suriadi, S., Andrews, R., ter Hofstede, A.H.M., Wynn, M.T.: Event log imperfection patterns for process mining: Towards a systematic approach to cleaning event logs. Inf. Syst. **64**, 132–150 (2017)
41. Weidlich, M., Mendling, J., Weske, M.: Efficient consistency measurement based on behavioral profiles of process models. IEEE Trans. Softw. Eng. **37**(3), 410–429 (2011)
42. Weidlich, M., Polyvyanyy, A., Mendling, J., Weske, M.: Efficient computation of causal behavioural profiles using structural decomposition. In: Petri Nets, pp. 63–83 (2010)
43. Weidlich, M., Polyvyanyy, A., Mendling, J., Weske, M.: Causal behavioural profiles - efficient computation, applications, and evaluation. Fundam. Inf. **113**(3–4), 399–435 (2011)
44. Wieringa, R.J.: Design Science Methodology for Information Systems and Software Engineering. Springer, Heidelberg (2014). https://doi.org/10.1007/978-3-662-43839-8
45. Yang, K., Huang, B., Stoyanovich, J., Schelter, S.: Fairness-aware instrumentation of preprocessing pipelines for machine learning. In: HILDA (2020)

Extracting Decision Models from Textual Descriptions of Processes

Luis Quishpi[✉], Josep Carmona[✉], and Lluís Padró[✉]

Computer Science Department, Universitat Politècnica de Catalunya, Barcelona, Spain
{quishpi,jcarmona,padro}@cs.upc.edu

Abstract. Decision models are strategic for formalizing how data influences the main decisions in a organization. Due to its importance, standard notations like DMN have appeared in recent years, to serve as a central resource for synchronizing the people and systems with respect to decisions. However, the modeling of DMN specifications can be tedious and error-prone, hampering its adoption in practice. This paper presents a technique to automatically obtain complete DMN models from textual descriptions. The technique, grounded in natural language processing combined with tailored syntactic patterns, allows to extract both the decision requirements and the decision logic described in a text. Our experimental evaluation shows promising results, even for the quite small pattern set used.

1 Introduction

Decision models complement business process models by formalizing the main decision logic that is behind any organization [3]. Back in 2015, the Object Management Group (OMG) proposed the Decision Model and Notation (DMN) language with the aim to standarize and facilitate the interoperability of decisions that affect the processes in organizations [13]. Since then, the adoption of DMN has grown considerably.

DMN specifications consists of two main parts: first, the dependencies between decisions are established. Then, for each dependency, the decision logic between the corresponding data must be determined. Overall, the creation of DMN specifications is a cognitive task that requires a deep understanding of the decision logic. This is why there have been attempts to extract automatically decision models from business process models [1], event logs [2,6], or even textual documents [8].

The present paper tries to continue on our previous work on extracting process information from textual descriptions [15]. Now the focus is on extracting complete DMN specifications from textual documents, i.e., including the two main aforementioned parts: dependencies and decision logic. This represents a clear advantage with respect to the work in [8], where only the dependencies extraction was considered.

We leverage the use of Natural Language Processing (NLP) techniques, combined with hierarchical patterns on top of the dependencies trees arising from the sentences in the text, so that the extraction of dependencies and decision logic is facilitated.

Running Example. Figure 1 shows a text (A) extracted from [8]. The text describes the calculation of a patient' health risk level. The results of our technique for this text are a

© Springer Nature Switzerland AG 2021
A. Polyvyanyy et al. (Eds.): BPM 2021, LNCS 12875, pp. 85–102, 2021.
https://doi.org/10.1007/978-3-030-85469-0_8

complete DMN specification: the Decision Requirement Diagram (B), and the Decision Table (C). The technique presented in this paper is able to automatically extract from a text like the one shown different types of semantic information, such as *decisions*, *input data*, *requirements*, *rules*, *input entries* and *output entries*. Combining this information leads to a Decision Requirement Diagram and a Decision Table.

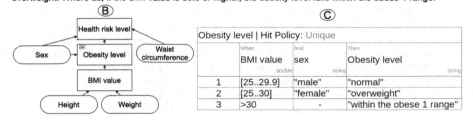

Ⓐ
The health risk level of a patient should be assessed from the obesity level, waist circumference and the sex of the patient. Furthermore, the obesity level should be determined from the BMI value and sex of the patient. Patient's height and weight are considered to calculate his BMI value.
If the patient's sex is male and his BMI value is between 25 and 29.9, then his obesity level is normal. If the patient's sex is female and the BMI value is above 25.0 and less than 30, then the obesity level is overweight. Where as, if the BMI value is 30.0 or higher, the obesity level falls within the obese 1 range.

Ⓑ

Obesity level	Hit Policy: Unique		
	When	And	Then
	BMI value	sex	Obesity level
	double	string	string
1	[25..29.9]	"male"	"normal"
2	[25..30]	"female"	"overweight"
3	>30	-	"within the obese 1 range"

Ⓒ

Fig. 1. Running Example. A: textual description of process with decisions, B: Decision Requirement Diagram (DRD), C: Decision Table

The content of this paper can be summarized as follows: next section describes the existing work related to the extraction of decision models. Section 3 introduces Decision Model and Notation (DMN) and overviews the main technical ingredients used in the techniques of this paper. Section 4 presents the overall framework for automated decision model extraction. Experiments and tool support are reported in Sect. 5, whilst Sect. 6 concludes the paper and provides suggestions for future work.

2   Related Work

Nowadays the dichotomy between process and decision logic is widely accepted [3,7, 11,19,20]. This in turn has triggered different proposals for extracting decision models from structured sources, such as event logs (that record the historical execution of process information) [1,4,6], or even process model specifications such as BPMN or similar [2,10,16].

Assuming the existence of structured information like event logs or process models does not cover all the situations: there are cases where unstructured information is the only information available. Moreover, such structured information may be outdated or simply wrong, and hence, the possibility to analyze alternative sources like textual information complement the aforementioned approaches. Also, one can use textual descriptions to communicate normative (to be) decision logic; notice that this information may be hard to find in event logs, that only represent historical executions.

Recently, one knowledge discovery approach has been proposed for extracting decision model automatically from textual descriptions [8]. To the best of our knowledge, this was the first contribution on this direction.

The work on this paper extends the aforementioned publication in the following perspectives: first, although both techniques are grounded on the NLP analysis initial step, our technique is based on hierarchical analysis of the dependency trees, representing a very robust and flexible alternative, that is adaptable by simply decoupling the extraction logic from the pattern language used for mining the dependencies. Second, our technique mines full DMN models, and not only the decision dependencies part (DRD diagram, see next section). Finally, we have shared the code and experiments so that further extensions can be made.

3   Preliminaries

3.1   Decision Model and Notation (DMN)

DMN is a standard used to represent knowledge regarding decisions made in business processes [13]. Currently DMN has received quite some attention from both commercial users and the scientific community [1,5,10]. DMN has two levels: The first level is about decision requirements, represented by the decision requirement diagram (DRD), which models the decision requirements and the dependencies between the elements involved in the decision. The second level is the decision logic, and is used to specify the detailed logic of each decision. It is generally represented in decision tables. Representing decision logic in tables has been extensively discussed in previous studies [17,18].

In addition, the DMN standard provides a Friendly Enough Expression Language (FEEL) for decision logic notation for the purpose of giving standard executable semantics to many types of expressions in the decision model.

The decision requirements level of a decision model in DMN consists of a Decision Requirements Graph (DRG) depicted in one or more Decision Requirements Diagrams (DRDs). A DRG models a domain of decision-making, showing the most important elements involved in it and the dependencies between them.

Decisions are represented by rectangles, ovals represent data entry, requirements are represented by arrows, and corner-cut rectangles represent business knowledge models.

Decision. A Decision element denotes the act of determining an output from a number of inputs using decision logic.

Input Data. An Input Data element denotes information used by one or more decisions as an input in order to determine the output value.

Requirement. An Information Requirement denotes Input Data or Decision output being used as input to a Decision.

Business Knowledge. A business knowledge model has an abstract part, representing reusable, invocable decision logic, and a concrete part, which mandates that the decision logic must be a single FEEL definition. An important format of business knowledge, specifically supported in DMN, is the Decision Table. Such a business knowledge model may be notated using a Decision Table as shown in Fig. 1(C).

Decision Table. Decision Tables is one of the ways to express the decision logic corresponding to the DRD decision artifact and it is a tabular representation of a set of
related input and output expressions, organized into business rules indicating which
output entry applies to a specific set of input entries.

Business Rule. Business rules are combinations of input values that determine the output value. A rule has one or multiple input entries and one output entry.

In the running example, Fig. 1(C) shows the decision table, where "BMI value" and
"sex" are input columns, "Obesity level" is the output column, the values in the
remaining rows, e.g. "[25..29.9]", "male", etc., are input entries, and the values in
the last columns, e.g. "normal", "overweight", etc. are output entries.

Friendly Enough Expression Language (FEEL). FEEL is the language used by DMN
to formalize decision logic in applicable points of a decision model. The purpose
of FEEL is giving standard executable semantics to many kinds of expressions in
decision model. For instance: the expression *"between 19 and 21"* is represented as
`[19..21]`.

3.2 Natural Language Processing and Annotation

Linguistic analysis tools can be used as a means to structure information contained in
texts for its later processing in applications less related to language itself. This is our
case: we use NLP analyzers to convert a textual description of a process model into
a structured representation. The NLP processing software used in this work is FreeL-
ing[1] [14], an open–source library of language analyzers providing a variety of analysis
modules for a wide range of languages. More specifically, the natural language processing layers used in this work are:

Tokenization & sentence splitting: Given a text, split the basic lexical terms (words,
punctuation signs, numbers, etc.), and group these tokens into sentences.

Morphological analysis: Find out all possible parts-of-speech (PoS) for each token.

PoS-Tagging: Determine the right PoS for each word in a sentence. (e.g. the word *dance*
is a verb in *I dance all Saturdays* but a noun in *I enjoyed our dance together.*)

Named Entity Recognition: Detect named entities in the text, which may be formed
by one or more tokens, and classify them as *person, location, organization, time-
expression, numeric-expression, currency-expression*, etc.

Word sense disambiguation: Determine the sense of each word in a text (e.g. the word
crane may refer to an animal or to a weight-lifting machine). We use WordNet [9]
as the sense catalogue and synset codes as concept identifiers.

Dependency parsing: Given a sentence, get its syntatic structure as a dependency parse
tree (DT). DT are an important element in our approach. The reader can see an
example of a dependency tree in Fig. 4.

Semantic role labeling: Given a sentence, identify its predicates and the main
actors (agent, patient, recipient, etc.) involved in each predicate, regardless of
the surface structure of the sentence (active/passive, main/subordinate, etc.).
E.g. In the sentence *John gave Mary a book written by Peter*, SRL would

---

[1] http://nlp.cs.upc.edu/freeling.

extract two predicates: `give` (with semantic roles `Agent(John,give)`, `Patient(book,give)`, and `Recipient(Mary,give)`), and `write` (with semantic roles: `Agent(Peter,write)` and `Patient(book,write)`).

Coreference resolution: Given a document, group mentions referring to the same entity (e.g. a person can be mentioned as *Mr. Peterson, the director,* or *he*)

The three last steps are of special relevance since they allow the top-level predicate construction, and the identification of actors throughout the whole text: dependency parsing identifies syntactic subjects and objects (which may vary depending, e.g., on whether the sentence is active or passive), while semantic role labeling identifies semantic relations (the *agent* of an action is the same regardless of whether the sentence is active or passive).

3.3   TRegex

In this paper, we use Tregex[2] [12], a query language that allows the definition of regular-expression-like patterns over tree structures. Tregex is designed to match patterns involving the content of tree nodes and the hierarchical relations among them. In our case we will be using Tregex to find substructures within syntactic dependency trees. Applying Tregex patterns on a dependency tree allows us to search for complex labeled tree dominance relations involving different types of information in the nodes. The nodes can contain symbols or a string of characters (e.g. lemmas, word forms, PoS tags) and Tregex patterns may combine those tags with the available dominance operators to specify conditions on the tree. Additionally, as in any regular expression library, subpatterns of interest may be specified and the matching subtree can be retrieved for later use. This is achieved in Tregex using unification variables as shown in pattern (2) in Fig. 2, which also shows the main Tregex operators used in this work to specify pattern queries. Figure 2 (bottom right) shows several example Tregex patterns:

(1) A node E with an ancestor A that has a G descendant.
(2) A node E with an ancestor A, and that is the only child of a B. Node A is captured in variable x and node B in y.
(3) A node K not dominated by any B, but dominated by an ancestor A with a direct child D
(4) A node F not dominated by any A
(5) A node H that is the only child of a D
(6) A node A with a direct child J

The example tree in Fig. 2 (top right) would be a match for patterns (1), (2), and (3), and would not be a match for patterns (4), (5), and (6).

---

[2] https://nlp.stanford.edu/software/tregex.html.

Operator	Meaning
X << Y	X dominates Y
X >> Y	X is dominated by Y
X !>> Y	X is not dominated by Y
X < Y	X immediately dominates Y
X > Y	X is immediately dominated by Y
X >, Y	X is the first child of Y
X >- Y	X is the last child of Y
X >: Y	X is the only child of Y
X $-- Y	X is a right sister of Y

(1) E>> (A<<G)   (4) F!>>A
(2) E>> (A=x) >: (B=y) (5) H>:D
(3) K!>>B>> (A<D)   (6) A<J

Fig. 2. Some operators provided by Tregex (left). The tree on the right would match patterns (1), (2), (3), and would not match patterns (4), (5), (6). Note that unless parenthesized, all operators refer to the first element in the pattern. Pattern (2) captures nodes A and B into variables x and y.

4   Approach

In short, our proposed technique automatically extracts the main DMN elements applying Tregex patterns on the dependency parse tree arising from a textual description of the decisions.

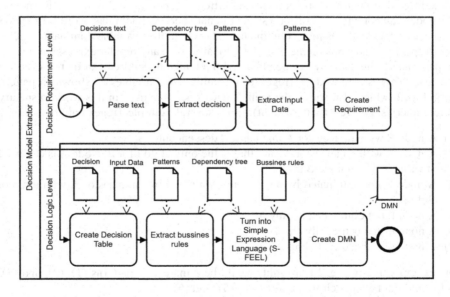

Fig. 3. General framework for automatic Decision Model extraction

The technique follows the steps shown in Fig. 3. As detailed in Sect. 3.1, DMN has 2 levels, therefore we first extract the elements from the decision requirement level and then from the decision logic level.

In order to extract elements from requirements level, the first step consists of performing a NLP analysis pipeline [14] to extract, among other information, verbal predicates, involved actors and objects, syntactic trees of all sentences. The obtained dependency trees (one for each sentence) are transformed to a format suitable for Tregex patterns: A node in the transformed dependency tree is a structured string, containing information about the lemma, PoS tag, and syntactic function of each word. Additionally, nodes marked as predicates by the NLP semantic role labeling step are decorated with an extra <ACTION> label, that identifies them as potential verb that define a decision, input data, input entry, or output entry. Further information about extracting elements based on tree patterns can be found in [15]. Figure 4 shows the transformed tree for the input sentence *"Furthermore, the obesity level should be determined from the BMI value and sex of the patient."*

Next step consists of extracting decisions, input data and requirements as described below in Sect. 4.1. Afterwards, with the decisions and input data extracted in the previous step, we are able to create the decision tables and then relying on an incremental procedure based on Tregex patterns we extract the business rules. See Sect. 4.2 for details on each of these pattern sets. Next, other patterns allow us to convert the input entry and output entry into standard executable semantics (FEEL). Section 4.3 details on each of these pattern sets. Details of these three phases are described next.

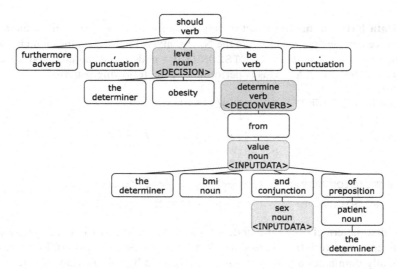

Fig. 4. Dependency tree for the sentence *"Furthermore, the obesity level should be determined from the BMI value and sex of the patient."*

4.1 Decision Requirement Level

Decision Extraction. To identify the decisions, we leverage the results from the NLP analysis and focus on the elements with `Patient` semantic role in some predicate.

To that end, the following Tregex pattern is recursively applied to all dependency trees to select the action verb that matches a predefined list (i.e. `assess`, `consider`, `determine`, `be`) [8] and then, based on the results of the NLP analysis, the `Patient` is extracted, which is the one that defines the `Decision`.

```
PD1  /<ACTION>.*(determine|assess|consider|be)/=result
```

This pattern extract nodes with action verbs contained in the predefined list. For instance: in the sentence *"Furthermore, the obesity level should be determined from the BMI value and sex of the patient."*, the result of the pattern PD1 is locating the verb *determine* and then, based on the results of the NLP analysis, *the obesity level* is extracted as the `Patient` of *determine*, and marked as the <DECISION>. Moreover, the detected verb node is marked as <DECISIONVERB> for later use in further patterns.

For each of extracted elements, the text is simplified to offer a better final representation: The syntactic tree structure is used to purge determiners (*the*, *a*, *some*, etc.) and prepositional phrases (headed by *by*, *of*, *from*, etc.), keeping just the core description of the object. The technique to strip down these text is detailed in [15]. Thus, in the previous example sentence the decision finally extracted is *obesity level*.

Input Data Extraction. To extract the input data, we rely on the result of the pattern PD1 and we leverage the results from the NLP analysis focusing on the elements with a semantic role of `Patient` of <DECISIONVERB> nodes. The captured nodes are then marked as <INPUTDATA>. This is performed by the following patterns:

```
PI1  /<DECISIONVERB>/ < (/noun/=result < /of/)
                       !>> /if/
PI2  /<DECISIONVERB>/ < (/from|by|on/ < /noun/=result)
                       > /verb/
                       !>> /if/
PI3  /<DECISIONVERB>/ < (/from|by/ < /<ACTION>/=result)
PI4  /<DECISIONVERB>/ > (/to/ > /<ACTION>/=result)
```

The first pattern checks for a node with POS tag `noun` that is immediately dominated by an action verb (i.e. marked as <DECISIONVERB> by pattern PD1), and that immediately dominates a prepositional phrase headed by `of`, provided the verb is not dominated by any `if`.

For instance, patterns PI1 can be used to determine that *physical health score* is the input data in the sentence *"Physical health score of a patient determines health evaluation criteria."*. Similarly, pattern PI2 matches the tree in Fig. 4, and extracts the input data *BMI value*.

Patterns PI3 and PI4 capture <ACTION> nodes (predicates detected by the NLP pipeline and marked in the pre-process), and extract the corresponding input data, based on their `Patient` arguments.

For instance, in the sentence "*An IQ of a patient is assessed from testing his verbal level, math level and abstract level.*", applying pattern PI3 we are able to extract *verbal level* as input data. This is because, the `Patient` of *test* verb is *verbal level*.

Patterns PI1-PI4 capture the main input data of the sentence, and apart from extracting it, mark the node as <INPUTDATA> to pass this fact to later patterns. Then, in order to capture the rest of input data of the sentence, we apply the following patterns:

```
PI5  /noun|adjective/=result > (/and/ >> /<INPUTDATA>/)
PI6  /noun/=result $, (/,|also/ >> /<INPUTDATA>/)
PI7  /noun/=result $, (/such/ > /as/) >> /<INPUTDATA>/
```

The strategy to identify the rest of the input data is: if any <INPUTDATA> captured by the patterns PI1-PI4, is inside a list or coordination, then capture in the variable `result` the remaining input data.

For instance, in the sentence "*The health risk level of a patient should be assessed from the obesity level, waist circumference and the sex of the patient.*" with patterns PI5 and PI6 we are able to capture *sex* and *waist circumference* as input data of the sentence. Similarly, pattern PI7 extracts *strength test* as input data from sentence *Physical fitness score is calculated from the sex of a patient and results of various tests such as strength test, coordination test, agility test, stamina test and speed test.*

Requirement Creation. In order to create an information requirement, we start from the list of defined verbs and the previous results of the extraction of decisions and input data, and given the right syntactic patterns are matched, a tuple [input, type → decision] is extracted. The type of a requirement input may be either input data or decision.

For instance, in the sentences "*Furthermore, the obesity level should be determined from the BMI value and sex of the patient. Patient's height and weight are considered to calculate his BMI value.*", the following tuples are extracted:

[*BMI value*, input data → *obesity level*]
[*sex*, input data → *obesity level*]
[*height*, input data → *BMI value*]
[*weight*, input data → *BMI value*]

In the first sentence, the defined verb matches *determine* (extracted by pattern PD1), the decision is *obesity level* , and the input data are *BMI value* and *sex* (patterns PI2, PI5). In the second sentence, the verb is *calculate*, and the input data detected by patterns PI2, PI5 are *height* and *weight*.

After creating all the requirement tuples, a search is carried out to verify whether the input field of any tuple matches the decision field in another. If a match is found, the input type is changed to decision. This would be the case of *BMI value* in the example sentences, producing the final set of requirements:

[*BMI value*, **decision** → *obesity level*]
[*sex*, input data → *obesity level*]
[*height*, input data → *BMI value*]
[*weight*, input data → *BMI value*]

With the requirements obtained a Decision Requirement Diagram (DRD) exactly to Fig. 1(B) can be created.

4.2   Decision Logic Level

Decision Table Extraction A decision table has three basic elements: input (input column), output (output column), and business rules (see Fig. 1C). There may be several input columns and multiple output columns. For our proposal, we assume that the decision table has exactly one output column. Each row in the table will represent a business rule (see Sect. 3.1).

To generate a complete decision table, we first create an empty decision table based on the input data and decision elements extracted from the requirement level. A new table will be created for each decision, and its input columns will be the inputs for that decision encoded in the requirement set.

For instance, the requirements extracted above for the example sentences contain two decisions: *BMI value* and *obesity level*, thus, a table for each will be created. The *BMI value* table will have two input columns (*height* and *weight*) and one output column (*BMI value*). Similarly, the *obesity level* table will have two input columns (*sex* and *BMI value*) and one output column (*obesity level*), obtaining the table shown in running example Fig. 1(C).

Business Rule Extraction. As shown in Fig. 1(C), a business rule is a row in the table, containing one input entry (i.e. a specific value or set of values) for each input column, and one output entry (i.e. a value for the decision). The former are extracted based on the input data and the latter based on the decision.

To extract business rules, we use patterns that find sentences containing two nodes corresponding to a predicate (and thus labeled as <ACTION> by the pattern preprocessing) related via a domination relation involving other nodes containing conditional words such as "*if*", "*in case*", "*whenever*" or "*when*". For those sentences, we detect the two main <ACTION> nodes. One (captured in variable decAction) defines the decision and the other (captured in variable inAction) defines the input data. Then, based on the results of the NLP analysis for each <ACTION>, their Agent and Patient are extracted.

In the decision <ACTION>, the Agent defines the decision name (i.e. output column name), and the Patient defines the value of the corresponding output entry. The name of the decision allows us to know which previously created table (Sect. 4.2) a business rule corresponds to. Similarly, for the input data <ACTION>, the Agent defines the input column name, and the Patient defines the value of the input entry.

Then, the extracted input and output column names are compared with those previously created decision table. If a match is found, a `business rule` is created and added to the decision table, otherwise the extracted information is discarded.

We currently use 23 different patterns to extract business rules. We present a sample below. The whole list can be found in our repository[3].

```
PT1  /<ACTION>/=decAction < (/if/ < /<ACTION>/=inAction)

PT2  /<ACTION>/=decAction < (/if/
                                < (/be|do|have/
                                    < /<ACTION>/=inAction))

PT3  /<ACTION>/=decAction < (/in_case/
                                < /<ACTION>/=inAction)

PT4  /<ACTION>/=decAction < (/in_case/
                                < (/preposition/
                                    < /<ACTION>/=inAction))

PT5  /<ACTION>/=decAction < (/<ACTION>/=inAction < /whenever/)

PT6  /<ACTION>/=decAction < (/<ACTION>/=inAction < /when/)
```

Patterns PT1 and PT2 extract business rules based on the conditional word *if*. Patterns PT3 and PT4 deal with sentences containing *in case*, while PT5 and PT6 handle constructions with *whenever* and *when* respectively.

For instance, in the sentence *"If the patient's sex is male and his BMI value is between 25 and 29.9, then his obesity level is normal."* shown in Fig. 5, with pattern PT1 we are able to extract: `decision` = *obesity level*, `input data` = *sex*, `input entry` = *male* and `output entry` = *normal*.

To extract the other input entries in the sentence, we use the same technique than for the rest of `input data`. Therefore, the complete business rule consists of input entries *male* and *between 25 and 29.9*, and output entry *normal*.

In process textual descriptions, there can be two business rules with decisions in just one sentence. The first business rule is extracted based on some conditional word as explained above and the second is extracted based on words such as *"otherwise"* and *"else"*. The following patterns extract additional business rules from a sentence.

```
PT7  /<ACTION>/=decAction > (/verb/ < (/if/
                                < /<ACTION>/=inAction))
                                    < /otherwise|else/

PT8  /<ACTION>/=decAction > (/be|MD/ < (/in_case/
                                < /<ACTION>/=inAction))
                                    < /otherwise/
```

---

[3] https://github.com/PADS-UPC/DMExtractor.

```
PT9 /<ACTION>/=decAction > (/be/
                    < (/<ACTION>/=inAction < /when/))
                        < /else/
```

For instance, applying the PT1 and PT7 patterns in the sentence "*If the score is 10, the service request is a product change, otherwise the service request is a bug.*", We are able to extract two business rules: One extracted by PT1: input entry "*10*" and output entry "*product change*", and another extracted by PT7: input entry "*not (10)*" and output entry "*bug*". Note that the second business rule the negation (not) in input entry is added because of the word *otherwise*.

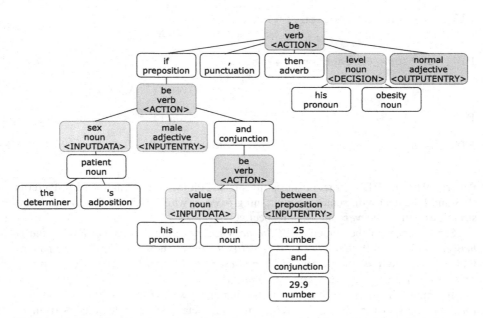

Fig. 5. Dependency tree for the sentence "*If the patient's sex is male and his BMI value is between 25 and 29.9, then his obesity level is normal.*"

4.3 Simple Expression Language

FEEL is a language focusing on the creation of expressions with just enough data types expressions and grammar to describe decisions. This can be used to evaluate expressions in a decision table (see Sect. 3.1).

We use 18 patterns to convert the values extracted from text into actionable Simple Expressions. All patterns can be consulted in our repository. Some example patterns extracting Simple Expressions are:

```
PF1 /number/=number1 >> /between/ < (/and/ << /number/=number2)
```

PF2 /number/=number1 > (/above/ < (/and/
                                    << (/less|fewer|</
                                    << /number/=number2)))

PF3 /number/=number1 << (/or/
                                    << /great|more|high|
                                    above|exceed|begin|>/)

For instance, from the last three sentences of running example Fig. 1(A) with patterns PF1, PF2 and PF3 we are able to extract: *[25..29.9]*, *[25..30]*, and *>30*.

4.4 Decision Model Extraction Without Requirement Level

Not all textual process descriptions contain an explicit definition of the requirement level. However, they may contain the logical level. In these cases, in order to extract the decision requirements we take advantage of the patterns used for the rules extraction in Sect. 4.2, where in order to extract the input entry and the output entry, decision and input data are first extracted.

For instance, in the running example Fig. 1(A), the first three sentences clearly correspond to the requirement level and the last three are logical level. However, the same decision table can be inferred even without the requirement level definitions, since a sentence such as *"if the patient's sex is male and his BMI value is between 25 and 29.9, then his obesity level is normal"* is implicitly stating that *obesity level* is computed using *sex* and *BMI value*.

Thus, if we apply pattern PT1 to the last three sentences in the running example Fig. 1(A), we are still able to extract that *obesity level* is a decision dependent on *BMI value* and *sex* input data, and to create the appropriate requirements:

- [*BMI value*, input data → *obesity level*]
- [*sex*, input data → *obesity level*]

After this process, the elements of the logical level can be extracted as explained in Sect. 4.2 to create –at least partially– the DRD and decision table. Our approach automatically recognises the decision requirements before extracting the elements at the logical level. Currently we assume both elements to be present in the textual description.

4.5 Discussion

The approach presented in this paper to extract DMN models is an extension of the same idea applied to the extraction of Bussines Process Models presented in [15]. However, the variability of language patterns expressing decisions is more reduced than the wide range of possibilities encountered in business process descriptions, which makes this approach more suitable for this case.

Our proposal relies on a classical artificial intelligence (AI) rule-based system, where an expert selects and encodes which are the rules (or patterns in our case) to be applied by the system. Despite the strong current AI trend to use deep neural systems for any task, we believe classical AI approaches still have relevant advantages in applications as ours, where domain is restricted and precision is to be favoured over recall. These advantages are:

– Deep learning systems require huge amounts of annotated training data, which are not always available. The cost of producing such data sets may often be higher than the cost of encoding expert knowledge into rules.
– Deep learning systems operate as black boxes, and it is difficult to tune their behaviour to improve their output when they produce wrong answers. A rule-based system is a white box, its output is explainable, and the rules can be fixed or extended to improve the system behaviour.

From a more specific perspective, our approach differs from previous ones in the kind of information used in the rules: We leverage the whole power of a NLP pipeline, and take advantage of the syntactic structure of the sentences. This is a qualitative step compared to systems based on flat regular expressions, which rely only on word order, so they may fail to capture relations between distant words in the sentence, or lack expressive power to represent specific cases. Moreover, the use of advanced Tregex operators, such as e.g. domination negation, allows the expression of complex syntactic patterns and thus finer control on which sentences are expected to match each rule.

Although our work is in a research stage, and we do not cover all possible decision expressions yet (e.g. we don't handle sentences with multiple outputs), our system is extensible and establishes a good starting point for a more complete implementation.

5   Tool Support and Experiments

The technique of this paper has been implemented in the tool DMExtractor. We evaluated it on a suite of cases based on text examples given in [8] and we report two different results: First, we report extraction performance for requirement level, i.e. input data, decisions, and requirements (see Table 1). Second, we report extraction performance for decision logic level, that is, input entries, output entries, and business rules (Table 2).

The test dataset used in our experiments consists of 12 text-model pairs, each including a textual decision description paired with the corresponding DMN models created by a human. The first 11 models stem from material in the appendix of [8], and the last was created based on a process fragment represented in [1]. The evaluation is performed comparing the elements extracted against gold standard manual annotations. The dataset can be consulted in our repository[4].

---

[4] https://github.com/ProjectTex2Dec/Text2Dec/tree/master/data/collected_data.

Table 1. Results of requirement level. Column *#gold* contains the number of decision, input data and requirement created by a human. Columns *#pred* and *#ok* show the number of elements predicted by the tool, and how many of them were in the gold DMN. Columns *P*, *R*, and *F1* show precision, recall and F-measure respectively. Left hand side columns show results for individual elements, right hand side columns show figures for requirements as a whole.

Source	Decision and InputData						Requirement					
	#gold	#pred	#ok	P	R	F_1	#gold	#pred	#ok	P	R	F_1
1_prepayment	5	5	5	100	100	100	4	4	4	100	100	100
2_health_risk	7	8	7	88	100	93	7	7	7	100	100	100
3_health_evaluation	24	25	23	92	96	94	23	24	20	83	87	85
4_Dataset_1	3	3	3	100	100	100	2	2	2	100	100	100
5_Dataset_2	3	3	2	67	67	67	2	2	1	50	50	50
6_Dataset_3	3	3	2	67	67	67	2	2	1	50	50	50
7_Dataset_4	2	2	2	100	100	100	1	1	1	100	100	100
8_Dataset_5	6	6	6	100	100	100	3	3	3	100	100	100
9_Dataset_6	10	12	10	83	100	91	7	8	6	75	86	80
10_Dataset_7	11	13	10	77	91	83	8	10	7	70	88	78
11_Dataset_8	6	6	5	83	83	83	3	3	2	67	67	67
12_Loyalty_longevity	4	4	3	75	75	75	3	3	2	67	67	67
Total	84	90	78	87	93	**90**	65	69	56	81	86	**84**

Table 1 shows the performance of our tool at the requirement level: The left hand side columns show precision, recall, and F1 score for the extraction of decisions and input data elements, without taking into account whether they are properly combined. The right hand side columns show the performance on requirement extraction, considering that a requirement is properly extracted when all its elements (input data, decision, and their dependency relation) are correctly extracted.

Precision is computed as the percentage of right elements among extracted elements ($P = \#ok/\#pred$). Recall is the percentage of expected elements correctly extracted ($R = \#ok/\#gold$). F_1. F1 score is the harmonic mean of precision and recall ($F_1 = 2PR/(P + R)$). We only count extracted elements as right if they match the gold annotations in words and type (Input data, Decision, Requirement)

Table 2 shows the results obtained by our tool on the decision logic level. Left hand side columns show the results on individual input or output entries, while right hand side columns present the performance of the business rule extraction, considering that a business rule is correct only when all its input and output entries are correctly extracted.

Table 2. Results of decision logic level. Column *#gold* contains the number of input and output entries created by a human. Columns *#pred* and *#ok* show the number of elements predicted by the tool, and how many of them were in the gold DMN. Columns *P*, *R*, and *F1* show precision, recall and F-measure respectively. Left hand side columns show results for individual elements, right hand side columns show figures for business rules as a whole.

Source	Input Entry and Output Entry						Business Rule					
	#gold	#pred	#ok	P	R	F_1	#gold	#pred	#ok	P	R	F_1
1_prepayment	6	5	5	100	83	91	2	2	1	50	50	50
2_health_risk	8	10	8	80	100	89	3	4	3	75	100	86
3_health_evaluation	3	3	3	100	100	100	1	1	1	100	100	100
4_Dataset_1	30	48	30	63	100	77	10	17	8	47	80	59
5_Dataset_2	24	19	17	89	71	79	8	6	5	83	63	71
6_Dataset_3	18	15	15	100	83	91	6	5	4	80	67	73
7_Dataset_4	4	4	3	75	75	75	2	2	1	50	50	50
8_Dataset_5	12	10	10	100	83	91	6	5	5	100	83	91
9_Dataset_6	18	15	15	100	83	91	6	5	5	100	83	91
10_Dataset_7	24	17	17	100	71	83	6	5	4	80	67	73
11_Dataset_8	24	11	11	100	46	63	12	6	4	67	33	44
12_Loyalty_longevity	12	9	9	100	75	86	4	3	3	100	75	86
Total	183	166	143	86	78	**82**	66	61	44	72	67	**69**

6   Conclusions and Future Work

In this paper, we described a technique to automatically obtain complete DMN models from textual descriptions. The technique, grounded in natural language processing combined with tailored syntactic patterns, allows to extract both the decision requirements and the decision logic described in a text. The technique is capable of obtaining DMN models even if the text does not have the explicit requirement level. Furthermore, the evaluations show that the generated DMNs are quite close to the models developed by a human.

In the experiments carried out for this paper, we have considered texts containing only decision descriptions. However, sentences describing decisions are usually embedded in texts describing other process details (activities, work flow, etc.). The combined extraction of both kinds of information, merging the patterns described in [15] with those in this paper, is an interesting research line for future work.

Also as future research, we intend to explore the Case Management Model and Notation (CMMN) and its automatic generation from text, and the use of machine-learning techniques to infer the patterns, provided training data are available.

Acknowledgments. This work has been supported by MINECO and FEDER funds under grant TIN2017-86727-C2-1-R, and by the Ecuadorian National Secretary of Higher Education, Science and Technology (SENESCYT).

References

1. Batoulis, K., Meyer, A., Bazhenova, E., Decker, G., Weske, M.: Extracting decision logic from process models. In: Zdravkovic, J., Kirikova, M., Johannesson, P. (eds.) CAiSE 2015. LNCS, vol. 9097, pp. 349–366. Springer, Cham (2015). https://doi.org/10.1007/978-3-319-19069-3_22

2. Bazhenova, E., Buelow, S., Weske, M.: Discovering decision models from event logs. In: Abramowicz, W., Alt, R., Franczyk, B. (eds.) BIS 2016. LNBIP, vol. 255, pp. 237–251. Springer, Cham (2016). https://doi.org/10.1007/978-3-319-39426-8_19

3. Biard, T., Le Mauff, A., Bigand, M., Bourey, J.P.: Separation of decision modeling from business process modeling using new "decision model and notation" (DMN) for automating operational decision-making. In: Camarinha-Matos, L.M., Bénaben, F., Picard, W. (eds.) 16th IFIP WG 5.5 Working Conference on Virtual Enterprises, vol. 463, pp. 489–496. Springer (2015)

4. Campos, J., Richetti, P., Baião, F.A., Santoro, F.M.: Discovering business rules in knowledge-intensive processes through decision mining: an experimental study. In: Teniente, E., Weidlich, M. (eds.) BPM 2017. LNBIP, vol. 308, pp. 556–567. Springer, Cham (2018). https://doi.org/10.1007/978-3-319-74030-0_44

5. Dangarska, Z., Figl, K., Mendling, J.: An explorative analysis of the notational characteristics of the decision model and notation (DMN). Presented at the (2016)

6. De Smedt, J., Hasić, F., van den Broucke, S.K.L.M., Vanthienen, J.: Holistic discovery of decision models from process execution data. Knowl. Based Syst. **183**, 104866 (2019)

7. Debevoise, T., Taylor, J.: The microguide to process modeling and decision in BPMN/DMN (2014)

8. Etikala, V., Van Veldhoven, Z., Vanthienen, J.: Text2Dec: extracting decision dependencies from natural language text for automated DMN decision modelling. In: Del Río Ortega, A., Leopold, H., Santoro, F.M. (eds.) BPM 2020. LNBIP, vol. 397, pp. 367–379. Springer, Cham (2020). https://doi.org/10.1007/978-3-030-66498-5_27

9. Fellbaum, C.: WordNet: An Electronic Lexical Database. Language, Speech, and Communication. The MIT Press (1998)

10. Janssens, L., Bazhenova, E., De Smedt, J., Vanthienen, J., Denecker, M.: Consistent integration of decision (DMN) and process (BPMN) models. CAiSE Forum **1612**, 121–128 (2016)

11. Kornyshova, E., Deneckère, R.: Decision-making ontology for information system engineering. In: Parsons, J., Saeki, M., Shoval, P., Woo, C., Wand, Y. (eds.) ER 2010. LNCS, vol. 6412, pp. 104–117. Springer, Heidelberg (2010). https://doi.org/10.1007/978-3-642-16373-9_8

12. Levy, R., Andrew, G.: Tregex and tsurgeon: tools for querying and manipulating tree data structures. In: L.R.E.C. (ed.), pp. 2231–2234. Citeseer (2006)

13. OMG: Decision Model and Notation. Version 1.3. DMN. An OMG® Decision Model and Notation TM. Publication (2019)

14. Padró, L., Stanilovsky, E.: Freeling 3.0: Towards wider multilinguality. In: Proceedings of the Eighth International Conference on Language Resources and Evaluation (LREC), pp. 2473–2479 (2012)

15. Quishpi, L., Carmona, J., Padró, L.: Extracting annotations from textual descriptions of processes. In: Fahland, D., Ghidini, C., Becker, J., Dumas, M. (eds.) BPM 2020. LNCS, vol. 12168, pp. 184–201. Springer, Cham (2020). https://doi.org/10.1007/978-3-030-58666-9_11

16. van der Aa, H., Leopold, H., Batoulis, K., Weske, M., Reijers, H.A.: Integrated Process and Decision Modeling for Data-Driven Processes. In: Reichert, M., Reijers, H.A. (eds.) BPM 2015. LNBIP, vol. 256, pp. 405–417. Springer, Cham (2016). https://doi.org/10.1007/978-3-319-42887-1_33

17. Vanthienen, J.: What business rules and tables can do for regulations. Bus. Rules J. **8**(7) (2007)
18. Vanthienen, J., Dries, E.: Illustration of a decision table tool for specifying and implementing knowledge based systems. Int. J. Artif. Intell. Tools **3**(02), 267–288 (1994)
19. Von Halle, B., Goldberg, L.: The Decision Model: A Business Logic Framework Linking Business and Technology. CRC Press (2009)
20. Zarghami, A., Sapkota, B., Eslami, M.Z., van Sinderen, M.: Decision as a service: Separating decision-making from application process logic. Presented at the (2012)

Predictive Process Monitoring

Robust and Generalizable Predictive Models for Business Processes

Praveen Venkateswaran[1]([✉]), Vinod Muthusamy[2], Vatche Isahagian[3],
and Nalini Venkatasubramanian[1]

[1] University of California Irvine, Irvine, USA
{praveenv,nalini}@uci.edu
[2] IBM Research, Yorktown, USA
vmuthus@us.ibm.com
[3] IBM Research, Cambridge, USA
vatchei@ibm.com

Abstract. Machine Learning models, and more recently Deep Learning models have gained popularity for predictive process monitoring. Predicting the process outcome, remaining time to completion, or the next activity of a running process can be crucial to provide decision information and enable timely intervention by case managers. These models fundamentally assume that the process logs used for training and inference follow the same data distribution and patterns. However, many real-world processes can have gradual or sudden changes, and logs themselves may be associated with different versions of process models modified over time, or customized by different departments with different policies. These can introduce spurious biases and correlations in the data, which can influence predictive models during training and adversely impact their accuracy. In this work, we present RoGen, an approach to train robust predictive models that can identify these spurious correlations and generalize to data with differing distributions. We show that our approach can also be adopted by existing predictive models to improve their robustness and generalizability. We evaluate our approach using real-world event logs and show that even in the presence of spurious data correlations, our models remain robust and outperform existing predictive models.

1 Introduction

There has been an increase in the incorporation of machine learning models in numerous application domains, including business processes. They can be used to predict process outcomes, remaining time to completion or even the next activity of running processes which are important for case managers. The goal of any machine learning model is to learn complex prediction rules using the various features or attributes in a given training dataset for future predictions. This could be either a classification task for discrete predictions, or a regression task for predicting continuous variables. Predictive models learn from features or attributes in the training data that have a significant correlation or causal

© Springer Nature Switzerland AG 2021
A. Polyvyanyy et al. (Eds.): BPM 2021, LNCS 12875, pp. 105–122, 2021.
https://doi.org/10.1007/978-3-030-85469-0_9

relationship with the target variable. Such *invariant* features are those whose correlations with the target are strong in any new test data, thus enabling accurate predictions.

However, there are numerous recent examples highlighting the brittleness of models that are trained using traditional approaches [7,13,20,23,26]. This can be attributed to the fact that real-world data used for training often have inherent data biases due to information or sampling bias, confounding factors, etc. These can introduce *spurious* correlations in features that do not have a causal relationship with the target to be predicted. Moreover, since model training involves minimizing the training error, this leads to models absorbing all correlations (both invariant and spurious) found in the training data. This influence of spurious correlations cause models to perform poorly in test data where these spurious biases no longer hold. Moreover, when these models are trained on data with a specific distribution, and have to generalize to data with slightly different distributions, they can often fail.

A classic example on the need for robust and generalizable ML models was highlighted by [3] where a model, trained to classify images of cows in pastures and camels in the desert, failed when the backgrounds were switched because it was influenced by the spurious correlation of the background (i.e., green pastures with cows and sandy deserts with camels) rather than relying on the invariant features (i.e., the cows and camels themselves).

Even in business processes, real-world process models can have gradual or sudden changes, such as concept drift [5]. In addition, the logs used to train models could be associated with different versions of process models modified over time, or even be customized by different departments with differing policies. These factors, among others, can result in the presence of spurious correlations while training predictive models for business processes and adversely impact their robustness and generalizability, resulting in poor performance.

To illustrate this with an example, Table 1 shows the four most common case variants from sample event logs of the servicing departments of a hypothetical car dealership with two locations A and B. The dealership provides periodic servicing reminders to its customers who either purchased the car from the dealer (in-house), or purchased elsewhere but use the dealer for servicing (external). In order to retain their in-house customers, the dealership also provides many of them special offers in the form of discounts, extended warranties, etc. Moreover, at location A, these offers are also provided to customers who sign up for their loyalty program.

The dealership wants a predictive model that, given customer information, can predict whether or not they should be sent special offers. From the table we can see that the model would require all features, and not just the activity sequence, in order to generate accurate predictions. However, a model trained on a consolidated log from both locations composed primarily of these four case-variants, would erroneously correlate the car brand X with giving special offers, and brand Y with not providing special offers. This is a spurious correlation, as opposed to the invariant correlation of determining special offers based on the customer type and loyalty program information. The influence of this spurious correlation might lead the model to incorrectly predict that an in-house customer with a brand Y car should not be given a special offer. Similarly, it might also incorrectly predict that an external customer with a brand X car who is not a loyalty member should be given a special offer.

Table 1. Four most common case variants of the event logs of a car dealership service system from two locations: A (top) and B (bottom)

Case: id (Loc. A)	Timestamp	Activity	Case: cust. type	Case: loyalty member	Case: car brand
1	2/1/21 10:05	Obtain car info.	External	True	X
1	2/1/21 10:30	Email reminder	External	True	X
1	2/1/21 10:35	Special offer	External	True	X
2	10/2/21 13:45	Obtain car info.	In-house	False	X
2	10/2/21 14:10	Email reminder	In-house	False	X
2	10/2/21 14:15	Special offer	In-house	False	X
Case: id (Loc. B)	Timestamp	Activity	Case: cust. type	Case: loyalty member	Case: car brand
3	12/2/21 16:00	Obtain car info.	External	True	Y
3	12/2/21 16:30	Email reminder	External	True	Y
4	15/1/21 10:00	Obtain car info.	external	False	Y
4	15/1/21 10:25	Email reminder	External	False	Y

There have been increasing efforts to develop machine learning models that are robust to spurious correlations and which can generalize to Out-Of-Distribution (OOD) datasets [2, 4, 19]. However, there has not been much existing work in the context of training robust predictive models for business processes.

In this paper, we present our approach, named RoGen, which uses the concept of Invariant Risk Minimization (IRM) [2] to train robust predictive models. IRM has been commonly applied to computer vision tasks, but it has not been used for sequential data like business process event logs. Furthermore, to the best of our knowledge, this is the first paper to develop an approach to train robust and generalizable predictive models for process mining logs that can identify and handle spurious data correlations.

We also show how our approach can work even for training existing predictive models, using a model by [6], and demonstrate the improvement in robustness. We evaluate the performance of the models trained with our approach on real-life event logs against several baselines.

The following section provides background on predictive monitoring, machine learning, and IRM. Section 3 discusses related work in predictive monitoring for business processes. We present our approach in Sect. 4 and evaluate its effectiveness in Sect. 5. Section 6 concludes the paper and discusses opportunities for future work.

2 Background

In this section, we define several elements of process mining and different predictive monitoring tasks. We also provide background on the concept of Invariant Risk Minimization (IRM) that we use to train machine learning models like RNNs and LSTMs that are suited for sequence predictions.

2.1 Event Logs, Traces, and Sequences

Let $\mathcal{A}$ be the set of process activities, $\mathcal{C}$ be the set of case identifiers, $\mathcal{T}$ be the set of timestamps, and $\mathcal{D}_j$ be the set of attributes or features, $1 \leq j \leq m$, where each attribute $d_j \in \mathcal{D}_j$ can be either categorical or numerical. We also define $U = \mathcal{A} \times \mathcal{C} \times \mathcal{T} \times \mathcal{D}_j$ as the event universe.

Definition 1 (Event). *An event $\epsilon_i \in U$ is a tuple $\epsilon_i = (a_i, c_i, t_i, d_{i1}, ..., d_{im})$, where $a_i \in \mathcal{A}$ is the process activity, $c_i \in \mathcal{C}$ is the case identifier, $t_i \in \mathcal{T}$ is its timestamp, and $d_{ij} \in \mathcal{D}_j$, $1 \leq j \leq m$, are the event attributes. Given an event ϵ_i, we define the projection functions $\pi = \{\pi_{\mathcal{A}}, \pi_{\mathcal{C}}, \pi_{\mathcal{T}}, \pi_{\mathcal{D}_j}\}$ where $\pi_{\mathcal{A}} : \epsilon_i \rightarrow a_i$, $\pi_{\mathcal{C}} : \epsilon_i \rightarrow c_i$, $\pi_{\mathcal{T}} : \epsilon_i \rightarrow t_i$, and $\pi_{\mathcal{D}_j} : \epsilon_i \rightarrow d_{ij}$.*

Definition 2 (Trace). *A trace is a non-empty sequence of events $\sigma = \langle \epsilon_1, ..., \epsilon_n \rangle$, $\forall \epsilon_i \in U$ and $n = |\sigma|$, such that for all pairs of events ϵ_i, ϵ_j in a given case, where $1 \leq i < j \leq |\sigma|$, $\pi_{\mathcal{T}}(\epsilon_i) \leq \pi_{\mathcal{T}}(\epsilon_j)$ and $\pi_{\mathcal{C}}(\epsilon_i) = \pi_{\mathcal{C}}(\epsilon_j)$.*

Definition 3 (Trace prefix and suffix). *Given a trace $\sigma = \langle \epsilon_1, \epsilon_2, ..., \epsilon_n \rangle$, the prefix of length k is $\sigma_p^k = \langle \epsilon_1, \epsilon_2, ..., \epsilon_k \rangle$, and the suffix of length k is $\sigma_s^k = \langle \epsilon_{k+1}, ..., \epsilon_n \rangle$, where $n = |\sigma|$ and $1 \leq k < n$.*

Definition 4 (Event log). *An event log is a set of traces $\mathcal{L} = \{\sigma_1, ..., \sigma_l\}$ such that each event appears at most once in $\mathcal{L}$.*

2.2 Predictive Monitoring Tasks

Predictive models, given a prefix σ_p^k of a running case, aim to predict a future event ϵ_{k+1}, or a suffix σ_s^k of future events. Existing work has looked at four kinds of predictive monitoring tasks - (1) Next activity prediction, (2) Next timestamp prediction, (3) Activity suffix prediction, and (4) Remaining time prediction. To define these, let Ω be a predictive model, σ_p^k be a trace prefix as defined above, ϵ' be a future predicted event, and $\oplus$ be the concatenation operator between two sequences.

Definition 5 (Next activity). *Given a trace prefix, the model predicts the next activity of the trace, defined as $\Omega_{\mathcal{A}}(\sigma_p^k) = \pi_{\mathcal{A}}(\epsilon'_{k+1})$.*

Definition 6 (Next timestamp). *Given a trace prefix, the model determines the timestamp of the next activity of the trace by predicting its duration as $\Omega_{\mathcal{T}}(\sigma_p^k) = \pi_{\mathcal{T}}(\epsilon'_{k+1}) - \pi_{\mathcal{T}}(\epsilon_k)$.*

Definition 7 (Activity suffix). *The model predicts the activity suffix of a running case by recursively predicting the next activity for multiple future activities. This can be denoted as* $\Omega_{AS} = \langle \Omega_{\mathcal{A}}(\sigma') = \pi_{\mathcal{A}}(\epsilon'_i) | \sigma' = \sigma_p^k \oplus \langle \epsilon'_{k+1}, ..., \epsilon'_{i-1} \rangle \rangle$.

Definition 8 (Remaining time). *The model predicts the remaining time duration of a running case, by recursively predicting the duration of each future predicted activity. Let* θ *be the sequence of predicted future timestamps where* $\theta = \langle \Omega_{\mathcal{T}}(\sigma') = \pi_{\mathcal{T}}(\epsilon'_i) - \pi_{\mathcal{T}}(\epsilon'_{i-1}) | \sigma' = \sigma_p^k \oplus \langle \epsilon'_{k+1}, ..., \epsilon'_{i-1} \rangle \rangle$. *Then the remaining time can be computed as* $\Omega_{RT}(\sigma_p^k) = \sum_{i=k}^n \theta_i$.

2.3   Neural Networks and Invariant Risk Minimization

A typical neural network model consists of a layer of inputs $\mathbf{X}$, a layer of outputs $\mathbf{Y}$, and multiple layers in between that are referred to as *hidden* layers. The model optimizes the parameters of its hidden layers θ, while learning a mapping $\mathbf{Y} = f(\mathbf{X}; \theta)$ from the input to output space. In order to train these networks, a loss or risk function $\mathcal{L}(\theta) : \mathbb{R}^n \to \mathbb{R}$ is used, which maps the model parameters θ to the expected loss on $X \times Y$ for a given function ℓ:

$$\mathcal{L}(\theta) = \mathbb{E}_{(x,y)} \ell(f_\theta(x), y) \tag{1}$$

where $x \in X$, $y \in Y$, and ℓ is a function like cross-entropy loss for classification. The standard Empirical Risk Minimization (ERM) methodology used by existing predictive monitoring approaches tries to minimize the average loss over all training examples. ERM fundamentally assumes that the data is independent and identically distributed (i.i.d) and that the training and test distributions are similar. However, as described in Sect. 1, this may not hold in real-world datasets and it has been shown that in these situations, ERM is not robust and does not achieve good Out-of-Distribution (OOD) generalization. This has motivated the need for alternative approaches to train predictive models, that can identify and handle spurious correlations.

In this paper, to create robust and generalizable predictive models for business processes, we leverage the concept of Invariant Risk Minimization (IRM) [2]. To use IRM, we consider the event logs to consist of $\mathcal{E} = \{e_1, ..., e_n\}$ *environments*, where $1 \leq |\mathcal{E}| < \infty$. Each environment refers to a potential source of spurious correlations, such as logs from multiple departments, different process model versions, etc. We denote X^e, Y^e as the input and output data collected from each environment $e \in \mathcal{E}$. We can then similarly define the loss for each environment $\mathcal{L}_e(\theta)$ as:

$$\mathcal{L}_e(\theta) = \mathbb{E}_{(x^e \in X^e, y^e \in Y^e)} \ell(f_\theta(x^e), y^e), \ \forall e \in \mathcal{E} \tag{2}$$

Invariant Risk Minimization searches for the invariant set of input attributes across the different environments. As explained in Sect. 1, invariant features have a strong causal relationship with the target variable for any given data, while spurious features may have strong correlations with the target for some data environments, but not in others. Formally, the set of invariant attributes X^I is defined as one where the target prediction probability is consistent across all environments (i.e.) $p(Y|X_i \in X^I, \mathcal{E})$ is approximately constant. Conversely, the set of spurious attributes X^S consists of features whose prediction probabilities vary across environments due to the presence of spurious correlations. It follows that $X^I \cup X^S = X$, and $X^I \cap X^S = \emptyset$, (i.e.) a feature cannot be both invariant and spurious.

The IRM principle finds an invariant data representation $\Phi : X \to H$ such that the optimal predictive model with parameters $\theta : H \to Y$, is the same across all environments $e_i \in \mathcal{E}$ (i.e.) it is not influenced by variations from spurious correlations. Hence, to find a model that optimizes the loss in each environment, while simultaneously identifying invariant feature attributes across environments requires solving the following bi-level optimization problem:

$$\min_{\substack{\Phi:X\to H \\ \theta:H\to Y}} \sum_{e\in\mathcal{E}} \mathcal{L}_e(\theta^\top \Phi(X^e)) \tag{3}$$

$$\text{s.t. } \theta \in \operatorname*{argmin}_{\bar{\theta}} \; \mathcal{L}_e(\bar{\theta}^\top \Phi(X^e)), \;\; \forall e \in \mathcal{E} \tag{4}$$

However, since this optimization is highly intractable, particularly when Φ is non-linear, the authors in [2] propose a tractable variant:

$$\min_{\Phi:X\to Y} \sum_{e\in\mathcal{E}} \underbrace{\mathcal{L}_e(\Phi(X^e))}_{\text{IRM Loss}} + \underbrace{\lambda\|\nabla_\theta \mathcal{L}_e(\theta^\top \Phi(X^e))\|_2^2}_{\text{IRM Penalty}} \tag{5}$$

While training a predictive model using Eq. 5, the IRM Loss term minimizes the training loss in each environment, while the IRM Penalty term balances between the predictive performance of the model within each environment and its invariance across environments using a regularizer $\lambda \in [0, \infty)$. This ensures that a model does not get influenced by spurious correlations which may lead to it performing well for some environments, but not in others. It is trained to balance its performance across environments by identifying the invariant representation, thus leading to robust and generalizable predictive models.

2.4 Sequence Prediction Neural Networks

Recurrent Neural Networks (RNN) and Long Short-Term Memory (LSTM) networks are popular predictive models for the sequential data in business process event logs since they persist information across sequences unlike traditional neural networks. RNNs have a cyclic structure and can be unfolded as shown in Fig. 1. At each step of the sequence, referred to as timestep t, $\mathbf{x}_t$ is the input and the $\mathbf{h}_t$ is the hidden state which contains information extracted from all the timesteps up to t. RNNs perform well for sequential data by sharing parameters across different parts of the model. In an RNN, the hidden state $\mathbf{h}_t$ is updated using the previous hidden state and the current input at each timestep:

$$\mathbf{h}_t = f(U\mathbf{x}_t + W\mathbf{h}_{t-1} + b)$$

Then the output $\mathbf{o}_t$ at time t is computed as:

$$\mathbf{o}_t = f(V\mathbf{h}_t + c)$$

where f is a non-linear activation function (e.g.) tanh or sigmoid, and U, W, V are the weight parameters and b, c the biases of the new input and hidden state. However, RNNs have been shown to perform poorly for long sequences and retaining long-term dependencies, a phenomenon called *catastrophic forgetting*.

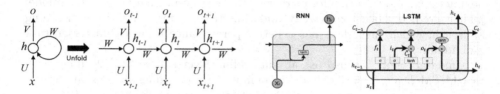

Fig. 1. Unfolding an RNN   **Fig. 2.** LSTM vs RNN

Long Short-Term Memory (LSTM) architectures are a special kind of RNN that solve this issue and can learn long-term dependencies. Unlike the single layer of RNNs, LSTMs have four interacting layers as shown in Fig. 2. The LSTM model can be described by the following equations where the $\odot$ operator denotes the Hadamard element-wise product:

$$\mathbf{f}_t = \text{sigmoid}(W_f\mathbf{x}_t + V_f\mathbf{h}_{t-1} + b_f)$$
$$\mathbf{i}_t = \text{sigmoid}(W_i\mathbf{x}_t + V_i\mathbf{h}_{t-1} + b_i)$$
$$\mathbf{o}_t = \text{sigmoid}(W_o\mathbf{x}_t + V_o\mathbf{h}_{t-1} + b_o)$$
$$\mathbf{C}_t = \mathbf{f}_t \odot \mathbf{C}_{t-1} + \mathbf{i}_t \odot \tanh(W_c\mathbf{x}_t + V_c\mathbf{h}_{t-1} + b_c)$$
$$\mathbf{h}_t = \mathbf{o}_t \odot \tanh(\mathbf{C}_t)$$

The LSTM first decides the information to remove from the cell state using the sigmoid layer $\mathbf{f}_t$ also known as the *forget gate*. It uses $\mathbf{h}_{t-1}$ and $\mathbf{x}_t$ to output a value between 0 and 1, where 0 denotes completely forgetting information, while 1 denotes completely retaining it. This is followed by the *input gate* $\mathbf{i}_t$ which decides which values to update and a tanh layer generates a vector of new candidate values to be added to the state. The new cell state $\mathbf{C}_t$ is obtained by forgetting some and adding new information. The *output gate* $\mathbf{o}_t$ decides the output of the cell state and also updates the hidden state $\mathbf{h}_t$.

3   Related Work

In this section we first discuss existing work on predictive models for business processes. We then present related work on approaches for generalization of machine learning models used in other domains.

3.1   Predictive Models for Business Processes

The work by Evermann et al. [12] looks at next activity prediction using LSTMs combined with an embedding layer to reduce the dimensionality of the input data and include attributes like the resource associated with each event. Their architecture comprises of the embedding layer with an embedding dimension of 125, followed by two LSTM layers.

Tax et al. [24] use an LSTM based architecture consisting of a shared LSTM layer that feeds two independent LSTM layers, one specialized for predicting the next activity, and the other for predicting the next event timestamp. Their model jointly predicts both the activity and timestamp using a multi-task learning approach, which they show has a better performance than learning each task individually.

Camargo et al. [6] also use an embedding layer similar to [12] along with two LSTM layers. They define the number of embedding dimensions as the fourth root of the number of unique activities. Moreover, like [24] they also use specialized layers for the activity and resource attributes and propose three variants of the baseline architecture which concatenate information at different points in the network and use a similar multi-task learning approach.

Mauro et al. [10] and Pasquadibisceglie et al. [18] use Convolutional Neural Networks (CNNs) for the next activity prediction task. In CNNs, a convolutional layer applies a set of filters that are replicated along the whole input to process small local parts. These filters identify specific patterns or signals and the authors propose schema to represent the running case as two-dimensional images.

Taymouri et al. [25] use Generative Adversarial Networks (GANs) for the next activity and next timestamp prediction tasks. GANs are useful when the amount of available training data is insufficient for effective training of LSTM networks.

3.2   Generalization Approaches

There are various approaches to improving out-of-distribution generalization of deep learning models. Data augmentation techniques aim to make the model more robust by training using instances obtained from neighbouring domains hallucinated from the training domains, and thus make the network ready for these neighbouring domains. Shankar et al. [22] augment data using instances perturbed along directions of domain change and use a second classifier to capture this. Carlucci et al. [7] apply augmentation to images during training by simultaneously solving an auxiliary unsupervised jigsaw puzzle alongside.

Decomposition based approaches represent the parameters of the network as the sum of a common parameter and domain-specific parameters during training. Khosla et al. [14] applied decomposition to domain generalization by retaining only the common parameter for inference. Li et al. [16] extended this work to CNNs where each layer of the network was decomposed into common and specific low-rank components.

Another approach is to pose the generalization problem as a meta-learning task, whereby we update parameters using meta-train loss but simultaneously minimizing meta-test loss. Santoro et al. [21] trained models that adapt using small amounts of labeled data from the new domain, while Dou et al. [11] considered distribution shifts in only test data.

4   Our Approach

4.1   Data Preprocessing

In this section we describe our approach to preprocessing the event log to prepare k-prefixes for the training and test data. For the predictive monitoring tasks described in Sect. 2.2, the model has to learn a function that, given a k-prefix $\sigma_p^k = \langle \epsilon_1, ..., \epsilon_k \rangle$, predicts the next activity a_{k+1} and the next timestamp t_{k+1} in addition to the other attributes d_{jk+1}, $1 \leq j \leq m$. This process is then performed recursively to obtain the activity suffix as well as to predict the future timestamps to compute the remaining time of the case. For the timestamp attribute, we use the relative time between activities, calculated as the time elapsed between the timestamps of the current event and its previous event.

The attributes in the prefixes can be categorical or continuous variables. Continuous attributes are typically normalized between 0 and 1 before they are passed as input to the neural network. There are several approaches in the literature to encode a representation of categorical variables e.g. one-hot encoding, label encoding, using embedding dimensions, etc. Authors in [6,12,17] used label encoding followed by embedding dimensions to reduce the dimensions of the input data, while authors in [9,24] use one-hot encoding. The choice of embedding dimensions can impact accuracy, where a small number may not capture feature relations, and a large number may cause model over-fitting. One-hot encoding for features with many unique values, can result in high dimensional input matrices, which can adversely impact model performance.

Since our focus in this work is on feature identification and distinguishing between invariant and spurious features, we represent the categorical features using label encoding which has been shown to perform well on ordinal data such as those found in business process logs. This also ensures that we can handle multiple attributes without a large increase in model complexity or the number of parameters. We note that our approach can easily integrate other encoding approaches as well.

In order to generate the k-prefixes, we use the popular prefix padding approach also used by [6,9,10,18,24], where every possible set of prefixes σ_p^k is considered, where $1 < k \leq n$. The prefixes are padded with zeroes in case they are shorter than the specified vector length. Depending on the size of the dataset, we either set n to be the length of the longest trace or use the n most recent events. We also maintain a vector of lengths of each case which allows us to stop predictions when the case is finished. Table 2 shows an example of the preprocessed inputs, target features and timestamps for a given 4-prefix input. The ϕ symbol denotes the end of the case.

Table 2. Preprocessing of input k-prefix

Input 4-prefix	Input features	Input timestamp	Target features	Target timestamp
$\langle(a_1, 13/1/2021\ 00{:}15\text{AM}, d_{11}, d_{12}, d_{13})$,	$(1, 1, 1, 1)$	0	$(2, 1, 2, 1)$	1500
$(a_2, 13/1/2021\ 00{:}40\text{AM}, d_{11}, d_{22}, d_{13})$,	$(2, 1, 2, 1)$	1500	$(3, 1, 5, 4)$	2280
$(a_3, 13/1/2021\ 01{:}18\text{AM}, d_{11}, d_{52}, d_{43})$,	$(3, 1, 5, 4)$	2280	$(4, 2, 3, 1)$	2700
$(a_4, 13/1/2021\ 02{:}03\text{AM}, d_{21}, d_{32}, d_{13})\rangle$	$(4, 2, 3, 1)$	2700	ϕ	ϕ

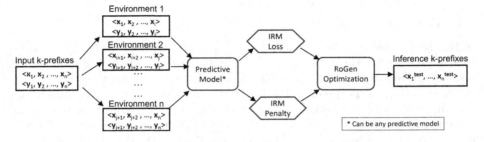

Fig. 3. RoGen training workflow

4.2   RoGen Model Architecture and Training Workflow

In this section, we describe RoGen's model architecture and training workflow. The model architecture consists of an input layer for the k-prefixes from event logs. This is followed by two stacked LSTM layers as described in Sect. 2.4 and a dense output layer. The output layer consists of outputs for predicting both the next activity as well as the next timestamp. RoGen simultaneously optimizes both tasks during training, also known as multi-task or multi-output learning, similar to the approach of [6,24]. This allows RoGen to exploit commonalities and differences across both tasks, which is often present in process trace logs (e.g. activities and their time duration are typically correlated). This multi-task optimization can result in improved training efficiency and prediction accuracy, when compared to training models separately for each task as shown by [6,24].

Figure 3 shows the training workflow of our approach that uses Invariant Risk Minimization (IRM) to train robust and generalizable models as described in Sect. 2.3. The input k-prefixes from the event log are first split into the different environments, which are further divided into training and test environments. The input prefixes and target outputs for the different prediction tasks from each training environment are then passed to the RoGen predictive model. The training algorithm used by the model is detailed in Algorithm 1, where it uses Eq. 5 to compute the training loss (IRM Loss) and penalty (IRM Penalty) for each environment $e \in \mathcal{E}$. The average loss and penalty over all environments are used to optimize the RoGen model using the Adam optimization algorithm. The trained model can then be used for inference on new k-prefixes for robust predictions of future activities and their timestamps. Figure 3 also highlights that the RoGen model can be easily replaced by any existing predictive model, showing the extensibility of our approach.

Algorithm 1. RoGen Training Algorithm

Require: Distribution over inputs X and targets Y;
Require: s: Total learning steps; f_θ: function to learn
Require: w: Warm up steps; $\mathcal{L}$: Loss function for the prediction error
Require: γ: Learning rate; r: Regularization weight; p: IRM Penalty weight
Require: θ: Model parameters ; μ: Mean function
1: **for** $i = 1 \to s$ **do**
2: Sample env e k-prefixes $X^e, Y^e = \langle \mathbf{x}_i, ..., \mathbf{x}_j \rangle, \langle \mathbf{y}_i, ..., \mathbf{y}_j \rangle$, $\forall e \in \mathcal{E}$
3: $l_e = \mathcal{L}_e(f(X^e), Y^e)$, $\forall e \in \mathcal{E}$ ▷ IRM Loss for each environment
4: $L2 = \|\theta\|_2$ ▷ L2 regularization
5: $l_e^{pen} = \text{IRMPenalty}(X^e, Y^e)$, $\forall e \in \mathcal{E}$ ▷ Equation 5
6: **if** $i > w$ **then**
7:      $l_{final} = \mu(l_e) + rL2 + p(\mu(l_e^{pen}))$,$\forall e \in \mathcal{E}$ ▷ Total loss
8: **else**
9:      $l_{final} = \mu(l_e) + rL2$,$\forall e \in \mathcal{E}$
10: **end if**
11: $\theta = \theta - \gamma \nabla \theta l_{final}$ ▷ Optimization
12: **end for**

---

5 Evaluation

We implemented RoGen in Python using PyTorch 1.7.0 and evaluated its performance using five real-life event logs. We experiment using two versions of each event log - first with the original data and attributes, and then augmenting it with an additional spurious attribute to test the robustness and generalizability of the approaches. Our code and data are available[1].

We compared RoGen's performance against four baselines [6,10,12,24] based on their publicly available implementation. Furthermore, to highlight the extensibility of our approach and evaluate its performance when applied to an existing predictive model, we also incorporated the model by Camargo et al. [6] into our training workflow in Fig. 3, which we named RoGen-C in the experiments. We modified the baseline approaches to use the same set of log attributes to perform a fair evaluation.

5.1 Experimental Setup

Datasets: We used five publicly available real-life event logs. Table 3 highlights the characteristics of these logs and we describe them below.

---

[1] https://github.com/praveenv/RoGenBPM.

Table 3. Event logs description

Event Log	Num. traces	Num. events	Num. activities	Avg. activities per trace	Max. activities per trace	Mean duration	Max. duration
Helpdesk	4579	21344	14	4.66	15	40.9 days	59.9 days
BPI 2013	1487	6660	7	4.47	35	178.9 days	2254.8 days
BPI 2015	5647	262628	356	46.50	154	101.4 days	1512.0 days
BPI 2018	43809	2514266	41	57.39	2973	335.3 days	1011.3 days
BPI 2019	251734	1595923	42	6.34	990	71.5 days	25670.5 days

- **Helpdesk:**[2] Contains traces from a ticketing management process of the helpdesk of an Italian software company.
- **BPI 2013:**[3] Contains traces from an incident and problem management system at Volvo IT Belgium.
- **BPI 2015:**[4] Consists of five event-logs containing traces from building permit applications provided by five Dutch municipalities during a period of four years.
- **BPI 2018:**[5] Contains traces of payments for German farmers from the European Agricultural Guarantee Fund over a period of three years. Over the years, there are changes in the process model due to changes in EU regulations. The traces are from four different departments and each of them may have implemented their processes differently.
- **BPI 2019:**[6] Contains traces from an MNC in The Netherlands depicting purchase order handling processes for paints and coatings with different flows in the data. Since the BPI 2018 and BPI 2019 datasets are extremely large, we use a random 10% sampling of data for our experiments.

Spurious Attribute and IRM Environments: To specifically evaluate the robustness of all approaches, we augment every event log with an additional numeric spurious attribute which is a common evaluation methodology [1,8,15]. We also divide the logs into environments for the IRM-based approaches. For the Helpdesk, BPI 2013, and BPI 2019 event logs, we divide them into three environments, two for training with 35% of data each, and the third as test with the remaining 30%. For BPI 2015, we treat logs from each of the five municipalities as an environment, and use four for training and one as test. Similarly, for BPI 2018, logs from the four departments are used as environments, and we use three for training and one as test. This results in BPI 2015 and BPI 2018 having unequal sizes of each environment unlike the other logs, allowing us to demonstrate the effectiveness of RoGen even with unbalanced data distributions.

---

[2] https://doi.org/10.4121/uuid:0c60edf1-6f83-4e75-9367-4c63b3e9d5bb.
[3] https://doi.org/10.4121/uuid:c2c3b154-ab26-4b31-a0e8-8f2350ddac11.
[4] https://doi.org/10.4121/uuid:31a308ef-c844-48da-948c-305d167a0ec1.
[5] https://doi.org/10.4121/uuid:3301445f-95e8-4ff0-98a4-901f1f204972.
[6] https://doi.org/10.4121/uuid:d06aff4b-79f0-45e6-8ec8-e19730c248f1.

In each of the above logs, we identify three common case variants (denoted as A, B, C) that have the highest occurrence rates in the event log. For each environment $e \in \mathcal{E}$, we define the spurious correlation between each variant and a specific value V_i of the spurious feature (i.e.) $p(A|V_1, e) = p(B|V_2, e) = p(C|V_3, e) = \alpha_e$, where V_1, V_2, V_3 are values of the spurious attribute and α_e is the strength of the spurious correlation in environment e. For every other case variant, V_i is set to a random number. We set $\alpha_e = 0.9$ as the highest spurious correlation in one of the training environments, and reduce it by 0.05 for every subsequent training environment. We then set $\alpha_e = 0.1$ for the test environment. We note that approaches that do not require explicit environment definitions can also be used similarly [27].

In the training environments, we set a high value of α_e to build a strong spurious correlation between the common case variants and the spurious attribute. However, in the test environment, for the spurious correlation to no longer hold, we set a low value of α_e to mimic a change in data distribution. As described in Sect. 2.3, the varying values of α_e for the spurious attribute in the training environments is detected by IRM to identify the spurious correlation, and ensure that the model does not get influenced by the spurious attribute. Models that incorrectly get influenced by the strong spurious correlation in the training environments, will fail to generalize to the test environment and hence demonstrate low robustness. For training the baseline approaches, the training environments are consolidated into a single input log.

Evaluation Metrics: We use the same evaluation metrics adopted in the baseline comparison approaches [6,10,12,24]. For the next activity prediction task, we use the percentage of correct predictions over the total number of predictions. For the next timestamp prediction, we report the Mean Absolute Error (MAE) which is the average of the absolute value difference between the predicted timestamps and the ground truth timestamps. For the activity suffix prediction, the Damerau-Levenshtein (DL) edit distance metric is commonly used, which measures the edit distance between two given activity traces without penalizing too harshly any transpositions of activities. This value is then normalized by the lengths of the two traces, obtaining a similarity value between 0 and 1. For the remaining time prediction of a case, we use the average of the MAE obtained for all the recursive next timestamp predictions.

5.2   Results

Table 4. Next activity prediction accuracy (%)

Method	Helpdesk		BPI 2013		BPI 2015		BPI 2018		BPI 2019	
	Orig.	Gen.	Orig.	Gen.	Orig.	Gen.	Orig.	Gen.	Orig.	Gen.
Tax et al. [24]	78.94	65.07	58.99	46.27	38.66	9.85	68.63	35.04	56.75	35.15
Evermann et al. [12]	78.52	61.48	55.67	44.57	38.18	10.29	62.50	34.89	57.43	38.19
Mauro et al. [10]	79.30	61.70	51.29	41.35	35.02	6.43	64.32	34.33	63.43	39.70
Camargo et al. [6]	**80.57**	66.14	**62.23**	51.54	43.90	10.41	73.41	35.65	73.39	41.47
RoGen	80.37	71.06	61.18	**56.75**	47.48	**33.37**	74.20	56.25	**74.07**	**66.43**
RoGen-C	79.78	**72.07**	61.75	56.23	**52.10**	29.84	**76.74**	**57.27**	73.94	63.30

Next Activity and Timestamp Prediction: Table 4 shows the accuracy percentages achieved by all the approaches in predicting the next activity for both the original event logs (Orig.) as well as the logs with the additional spurious feature (Gen.). For the original logs, we see that RoGen and RoGen-C achieve comparable accuracies to [6] and outperform the other baselines across all the event logs. We also observe that for BPI 2015 and BPI 2018, where the logs were collected from multiple sources, treating them as separate environments using IRM results in an increase in accuracy even when the underlying predictive model is the same (RoGen-C and [6]).

For the logs with the spurious feature, our IRM based approaches outperform all the baselines. We observe that the models of the baseline approaches are influenced by the spurious correlations and have a significant drop in accuracy ranging from an average of 19% for the Helpdesk dataset, to an average of 76% for the BPI 2015 dataset. On the other hand, RoGen and RoGen-C are more robust to the spurious correlation and do not have a large drop in accuracy.

Similarly, Table 5 compares the Mean Absolute Error (MAE) values of all the approaches for the next timestamp prediction task. The MAE values are reported in days and lower error values signify better performance. We only use [6,24] as the baselines since [10,12] do not handle this task. We observe that for a majority of both kinds of event logs – original and with the spurious feature, our approaches outperform the baselines. In particular, RoGen-C achieved

Table 5. Next timestamp prediction Mean Absolute Error (MAE)

Method	Helpdesk		BPI 2013		BPI 2015		BPI 2018		BPI 2019	
	Orig.	Gen.	Orig.	Gen.	Orig.	Gen.	Orig.	Gen.	Orig.	Gen.
Tax et al. [24]	5.18	7.56	**14.11**	15.13	1.96	1.98	6.12	6.82	6.60	12.01
Camargo et al. [6]	4.99	7.35	16.35	14.50	1.92	2.03	5.31	**6.78**	6.36	11.20
RoGen	5.06	7.40	14.74	14.11	**1.74**	1.95	**3.38**	7.51	6.48	10.09
RoGen-C	**4.95**	**7.19**	15.37	**11.87**	1.92	**1.94**	4.90	7.48	**5.88**	**9.63**

consistently lower MAE than the other approaches for both kinds of logs. From Tables 4 and 5, we can see that models using IRM do not degrade in accuracy even if the logs do not have any spurious data correlations. In addition, when spurious correlations exist in event logs, the IRM based models significantly outperform traditional predictive models.

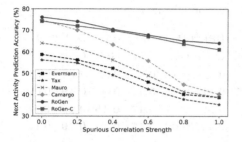
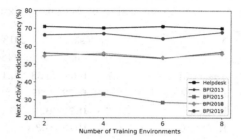

Fig. 4. Comparison of next activity prediction accuracy for varying strengths of spurious correlation

Fig. 5. RoGen next activity prediction accuracy for varying number of environments

Impact of Strength of Spurious Correlations: To understand the impact of the strength of spurious correlations in an event log on model performance, we evaluate the approaches for varying strengths of spurious correlations α_e in each of the two training environments for the BPI 2019 event log. Figure 4 shows the next activity prediction accuracy achieved by all the approaches where the spurious correlation strength refers to the average spurious correlation $\mu(\alpha_e)$ across the two training environments. We see that when there is no spurious correlation (i.e.) $\mu(\alpha_e) = 0.0$, all the approaches have accuracies similar to their performance on the original event log as observed in Table 4. However, when $\mu(\alpha_e)$ is increased, the baseline approaches are influenced by the spurious feature and their test accuracy degrades. We observe for high levels of spurious correlation, the baseline approaches have low accuracy values. On the other hand, RoGen and RoGen-C show good robustness to the increasing levels of spurious correlations and continue to perform well.

Impact of Number of Environments: We evaluate the scalability and robustness of RoGen to multiple sources of spurious correlations, by varying the number of training environments in Fig. 5. For each event log, we use the same strengths of spurious correlation, but vary the number of environments from {2, 4, 6, 8}. We observe that the accuracy achieved by RoGen does not have much variance even with a larger number of environments. This shows that our approach can handle large and diverse event logs with multiple sources of spurious correlations.

Suffix Prediction: Tables 6 and 7 show the results of the activity suffix prediction and remaining time prediction tasks respectively. RoGen and RoGen-C continue to outperform the baselines, particularly in logs with the spurious feature. For some of the logs, all the approaches achieve similar results since we limited the number of future predictions due to the size of the log.

Table 6. Activity suffix prediction DL similarity

Method	Helpdesk		BPI 2013		BPI 2015		BPI 2018		BPI 2019	
	Orig.	Gen.	Orig.	Gen.	Orig.	Gen.	Orig.	Gen.	Orig.	Gen.
Tax et al. [24]	0.75	0.68	0.33	0.19	0.14	0.03	0.15	0.06	0.18	0.07
Camargo et al. [6]	**0.76**	**0.72**	0.37	0.27	0.10	0.02	**0.17**	0.06	**0.19**	0.09
RoGen	**0.76**	**0.72**	**0.38**	**0.32**	0.14	**0.09**	**0.17**	**0.13**	**0.19**	**0.16**
RoGen-C	0.75	**0.72**	**0.38**	0.27	**0.15**	**0.09**	**0.17**	**0.13**	**0.19**	0.14

Table 7. Remaining time prediction MAE

Method	Helpdesk		BPI 2013		BPI 2015		BPI 2018		BPI 2019	
	Orig.	Gen.	Orig.	Gen.	Orig.	Gen.	Orig.	Gen.	Orig.	Gen.
Tax et al. [24]	17.85	8.84	**22.32**	20.79	61.21	**60.97**	53.46	53.04	38.82	29.92
Camargo et al. [6]	18.35	9.21	23.92	20.94	**60.93**	**60.97**	53.40	52.51	38.53	28.69
RoGen	17.85	8.35	23.44	20.49	**60.93**	**60.97**	**50.74**	52.43	38.55	27.96
RoGen-C	**17.40**	**8.03**	23.09	**20.05**	**60.93**	**60.97**	51.29	**52.00**	**38.48**	**27.76**

6   Conclusion and Future Work

In this paper, we present a novel approach to train predictive models for business processes that are robust and generalizable in the presence of spurious data correlations. Existing work on predictive business process monitoring have not accounted for the presence of spurious correlations in event logs which can arise due to various factors. Since predictive monitoring tasks are often used by case managers, deploying robust models is critical for many real-world business processes.

Our approach uses the concept of Invariant Risk Minimization and we also demonstrate how existing predictive models can utilize IRM to improve their robustness. Our experiments highlight the importance of our approach, where our robust predictive models outperform several existing baselines on real-life logs, especially when they also have varying levels of spurious correlations. We also show that our implementation can easily be used to improve the robustness of any predictive model and our logs with spurious correlations can be used to evaluate robustness.

We intend to extend our work to incorporate and compare other techniques to achieve robustness like meta-learning, data augmentation, adversarial learning, etc. We also plan to improve our approach to handle logs where the sources of spurious correlations may be hard to identify. We also intend to evaluate different kinds of predictive models in this context and also extend our approach to handle other prediction tasks.

References

1. Ahuja, K., Shanmugam, K., Varshney, K., Dhurandhar, A.: In: In: ICML (ed.) Invariant Risk Minimization Games, pp. 145–155. PMLR (2020)
2. Arjovsky, M., Bottou, L., Gulrajani, I., Lopez-Paz, D.: Invariant risk minimization. Stat **1050**, 27 (2020)
3. Beery, S., Van Horn, G., Perona, P.: Recognition in terra incognita. In: Proceedings of the European Conference on Computer Vision (ECCV), pp. 456–473 (2018)
4. Bengio, Y., Deleu, T., Rahaman, N., et al.: A meta-transfer objective for learning to disentangle causal mechanisms. In: ICLR (2019)
5. Bose, R.J.C., Van Der Aalst, W.M., et al.: Dealing with concept drifts in process mining. IEEE Trans. Neural Networks Learn. Syst. **25**(1), (2013)
6. Camargo, M., Dumas, M., González-Rojas, O.: Learning accurate lstm models of business processes. In: International Conference on Business Process Management, pp. 286–302. Springer (2019)
7. Carlucci, F.M., et al.: Domain generalization by solving jigsaw puzzles. In: CVPR, pp. 2229–2238 (2019)
8. Choe, Y.J., Ham, J., Park, K.: An empirical study of invariant risk minimization. arXiv preprint arXiv:2004.05007 (2020)
9. Di Francescomarino, C., Ghidini, C., Maggi, F.M., Petrucci, G., Yeshchenko, A.: An eye into the future: leveraging a-priori knowledge in predictive business process monitoring. In: Carmona, J., Engels, G., Kumar, A. (eds.) BPM 2017. LNCS, vol. 10445, pp. 252–268. Springer, Cham (2017). https://doi.org/10.1007/978-3-319-65000-5_15
10. Di Mauro, N., Appice, A., Basile, T.M.A.: Activity prediction of business process instances with inception CNN models. In: Alviano, M., Greco, G., Scarcello, F. (eds.) AI*IA 2019. LNCS (LNAI), vol. 11946, pp. 348–361. Springer, Cham (2019). https://doi.org/10.1007/978-3-030-35166-3_25
11. Dou, Q., de Castro, D.C., Kamnitsas, K., Glocker, B.: Domain generalization via model-agnostic learning of semantic features. In: Advances in Neural Information Processing Systems, pp. 6450–6461 (2019)
12. Evermann, J., Rehse, J.R., Fettke, P.: Predicting process behaviour using deep learning. Decis. Support Syst. **100**, 129–140 (2017)
13. de Haan, P., Jayaraman, D., Levine, S.: Causal confusion in imitation learning. arXiv preprint arXiv:1905.11979 (2019)
14. Khosla, A., Zhou, T., Malisiewicz, T., Efros, A.A., Torralba, A.: Undoing the damage of dataset bias. In: European Conference on Computer Vision, pp. 158–171. Springer (2012)
15. Krueger, D., Caballero, E., Jacobsen, J.H., et al.: Out-of-distribution generalization via risk extrapolation (rex). arXiv preprint arXiv:2003.00688 (2020)
16. Li, D., Yang, Y., Song, Y.Z., Hospedales, T.M.: Deeper, broader and artier domain generalization. In: Proceedings of the IEEE International Conference on Computer Vision, pp. 5542–5550 (2017)

17. Lin, L., Wen, L., Wang, J.: Mm-pred: A deep predictive model for multi-attribute event sequence. In: Proceedings of SDM, pp. 118–126. SIAM (2019)
18. Pasquadibisceglie, V., Appice, A., Castellano, G., Malerba, D.: Using convolutional neural networks for predictive process analytics. In: ICPM, pp. 129–136 (2019)
19. Piratla, V., Netrapalli, P., Sarawagi, S.: In: ICML (ed.) Efficient Domain Generalization via Common-Specific Low-Rank Decomposition, pp. 7728–7738. PMLR (2020)
20. Recht, B., Roelofs, R., Schmidt, L., Shankar, V.: Do imagenet classifiers generalize to imagenet? In: ICML, pp. 5389–5400. PMLR (2019)
21. Santoro, A., Bartunov, S., Botvinick, M., Wierstra, D., Lillicrap, T.: Meta-learning with memory-augmented neural networks. In: International Conference on Machine Learning, pp. 1842–1850 (2016)
22. Shankar, S., Piratla, V., Chakrabarti, S., Chaudhuri, S., Jyothi, P., Sarawagi, S.: Generalizing across domains via cross-gradient training. arXiv preprint arXiv:1804.10745 (2018)
23. Srivastava, M., Hashimoto, T., Liang, P.: In: In: ICML. (ed.) Robustness to Spurious Correlations via Human Annotations, pp. 9109–9119. PMLR (2020)
24. Tax, N., Verenich, I., La Rosa, M., Dumas, M.: Predictive business process monitoring with LSTM neural networks. In: Dubois, E., Pohl, K. (eds.) CAiSE 2017. LNCS, vol. 10253, pp. 477–492. Springer, Cham (2017). https://doi.org/10.1007/978-3-319-59536-8_30
25. Taymouri, F., Rosa, M.L., Erfani, S., Bozorgi, Z.D., Verenich, I.: Predictive business process monitoring via generative adversarial nets: the case of next event prediction. In: Fahland, D., Ghidini, C., Becker, J., Dumas, M. (eds.) BPM 2020. LNCS, vol. 12168, pp. 237–256. Springer, Cham (2020). https://doi.org/10.1007/978-3-030-58666-9_14
26. Tzeng, E., Hoffman, J., Saenko, K., Darrell, T.: Adversarial discriminative domain adaptation. IEEE CVPR (2017)
27. Venkateswaran, P., Muthusamy, V., Isahagian, V., Venkatasubramanian, N.: Environment agnostic invariant risk minimization for classification of sequential datasets. In: Proceedings of the 27th ACM SIGKDD International Conference on Knowledge Discovery & Data Mining, p. To appear (2021)

Incremental Predictive Process Monitoring: The Next Activity Case

Stephen Pauwels$^{(\boxtimes)}$ (ID) and Toon Calders (ID)

University of Antwerp, Antwerp, Belgium
{stephen.pauwels,toon.calders}@uantwerpen.be

Abstract. Next-activity prediction methods for business processes are always introduced in a static setting, implying a single training phase followed by the application of the learned model during the test phase. Real-life processes, however, are often dynamic and prone to changes over time. Therefore, all state-of-the-art methods need regular retraining on new data to be kept up to date. It is, however, not straightforward to determine when to retrain nor what data to use; for instance, should all historic data be included or only new data? Updating models that still perform at an acceptable level wastes a potentially large amount of computational resources while postponing an update too much will deteriorate model performance. In this paper, we present incremental learning strategies for updating these existing models that do not require fully retraining them, hence reducing the number of computational resources needed while still maintaining a more consistent and correct view of the process in its current form. We introduce a basic neural network method consisting of a single dense layer. This architecture makes it easier to perform fast updates to the model and enables us to perform more experiments. We investigate the differences between our proposed incremental approaches. Experiments performed with a prototype on real-life data show that these update strategies are a promising way forward to further increase the power and usability of state-of-the-art methods.

Keywords: Business process · Event prediction · Incremental learning · Neural networks · Dynamic Bayesian Network

1 Introduction

Predictive process monitoring uses historical data to predict several aspects of ongoing business processes, such as remaining time prediction, outcome prediction, and next-activity prediction. Recently proposed next-activity prediction methods always assume a static setting, where we divide the datasets into fixed training and test parts. One important aspect of Business Processes, however, is that they are inherently dynamic and that different time periods in the log can have different characteristics. Although some authors propose to retrain the model regularly to incorporate the changes in the data, this might not be the

© Springer Nature Switzerland AG 2021
A. Polyvyanyy et al. (Eds.): BPM 2021, LNCS 12875, pp. 123–140, 2021.
https://doi.org/10.1007/978-3-030-85469-0_10

most efficient way of updating a model in terms of both runtime and accuracy. Furthermore, no method describes which events to use to retrain the model. It can be beneficial not to use all available historical events as they are no longer relevant for future activities, due to drifts in the processes [4]. No state-of-the-art method proposes how to perform these updates or has been evaluated under these dynamic circumstances.

In this paper, we explore different strategies that can be used for incremental learning of next-activity prediction models. Ranging from completely retraining the models for every new batch of data to only using the newly arrived data to update the existing model. These update strategies can shed new light on the performance of the different methods, as not all methods are equally well suited to be adapted for a dynamic environment.

It is important to note that the strategies proposed in this paper apply to a variety of existing methods, especially neural networks. We aim at showing that the update strategies have significant benefits in a dynamic environment without specifying which of the described models is better.

To visualize the performance over time (with more or less data used for training/updating) we propose a graphical representation of the average accuracy on a given time within a given window. This sliding window technique gives an accurate view of how the predictive performance of the models changes over time.

We show that some incremental methods outperform the completely retrained models despite the *catastrophic forgetting* [26] property of neural networks. Which is the phenomenon when a neural network forgets and ignores the original input when retraining the model with new data. This phenomenon is often a potential risk when updating neural networks. However, we can leverage catastrophic forgetting to gradually forget older, less relevant, events in the presence of concept drift.

Because we needed a lightweight neural network for our initial experiments, we created a basic neural network architecture that consists of a single dense layer. During the experiments, we show that this new architecture (which requires only a limited amount of computational resources) performs on par or outperforms the selected more complex state-of-the-art architectures.

The contributions of our paper are the following:

1. We introduce a simple, but accurate, neural network architecture for next-activity prediction.
2. We compare different update strategies in terms of accuracy and runtime.

The next section gives an overview of related work on incremental learning, concept drift and predictive process monitoring and positions our paper within the field of incremental predictive process monitoring. Section 3 explains the different strategies that can be used for updating. In Sect. 4 we introduce our basic neural network architecture. Experiments on all possible update strategies are performed in Sect. 5.

2   Related Work

2.1   Predictive Process Monitoring

Predictive Process Monitoring aims at correctly predicting various aspects of running business processes. Existing methods deal with predicting the remaining time [1], the outcome [30] or the next activity [27,33] of a running case. In this paper, we focus on predicting the next activity in a running case.

In recent years different types of models are proposed to predict the next activity in a business process. With neural networks becoming extremely popular, lots of new methods are proposed every year.

The first type of network uses a Long-Short-Term-Memory (LSTM) architecture. This type of model is capable of learning the behavior of a sequence of events (hence the memory). Recent methods using this technique are proposed by Evermann et al. [15], Tax et al. [28], Lin et al. [18] and Camargo et al. [7].

The LSTM architecture has also been used in combination with Generative Adversarial Networks by Taymouri et al. [29]. In this type of model, the network exists out of two parts: the first part tries to predict the best activity as well as possible, while the other tries to divide the real activities that happened from the predicted ones. Both parts of the model are trying to outperform the other. In this way, the predictive model gets more accurate feedback about its performance.

LSTM models, however, require significant training time. To address this performance issue posed by the LSTM models, Convolutional Neural Networks (CNNs) were proposed. They also can incorporate the sequential nature of a business process but can train more efficiently. Methods using the CNN architecture have been proposed by Di Mauro et al. [8] and Pasquadibisceglie et al. [22,23].

Pauwels et al. [24] propose to build models using Dynamic Bayesian Networks (DBN). This method is based on techniques in which the data is preprocessed so that it incorporates the time aspect of an event log. The DBN model learns different dependencies between attributes (from both the control-flow and data perspective) that are present in the data and depict the conditional probability of a certain activity happening, given a certain history of events. The activity in the current timestep can depend on every attribute in a previous time step in the k-context log.

2.2   Concept Drift Detection

Concept drift in process mining is well described by Bose et al. [4]. Bose et al. show that concept drift can occur in all perspectives (control-flow, data, resource) and that different types of drift exist, each of which may require a different approach to deal with it. In their paper, Bose et al. focus on detecting the drift points. A disadvantage of this technique is, however, that drifts are only detected after they occurred, leading to a delay in the ability to update existing models.

To detect drifts, Bose et al. propose a sliding window approach. This window is divided into two sub-windows which we want to compare to each other to determine if drift has occurred between the two windows. The characterization of changes between windows is done using a statistical test, such as the Kolmogorov-Smirnov test, the Mann-Whitney U test, or the Hotelling T^2 test.

2.3   Incremental Learning Algorithms

Different applications exist that make use of the dynamic nature of business processes. Some of these applications which are adapted for use in an online setting are: business process discovery [6], conformance checking [5] and concept drift detection [21].

Learning in a setting in which data changes its nature and characteristics over time is a known and well-studied problem within machine learning [17,25]. A popular solution is to use a sliding window to move over the data that indicates which data to use for building a model at a particular moment. One of the downsides of such a sliding window is that they are often of a fixed size, which is determined a priori by the user. This can lead to window sizes that are too big, and thus too insensitive for changes, or too small, in which case too many changes are detected. The correct window size depends on the data itself, and can also vary over time. Therefore, Bifet and Gavalda proposed a learning technique that uses an adaptive window size (ADWIN) [3]. On the one hand, when the data is stationary the window size grows, and on the other, the window size shrinks when changes are detected. In contrast to other proposed adaptive methods, Bifet and Gavalda show that the performance of their adaptive window is guaranteed by providing bounds on the false positive and false negative rates.

Another application of incremental learning algorithms is when the data arrives in the form of a data stream in which the compute resources are not able to keep all the arrived data in memory. Hoeffding trees, as proposed by Domingos and Hulten [11], are incremental decision trees that are learned from a massive data stream. This method does, however, assume that the distribution generating the arriving samples does not change over time. Hoeffding trees can be learned in a constant time proportional to the number of attributes.

Gama et al. [16] consider concept drift as described by Bose et al. but propose the use of different incremental algorithms to deal with these changes. This incremental learning overcomes, by constantly updating the learned models, the issue of concept drift often being unexpected and unpredictable. Incremental learning is thus able to update the model in a timely manner, well ahead of models using a concept drift detection method. We continue some of the ideas presented in this work and further elevate them for use with neural networks and next-activity prediction. Gama et al. indicate that besides the types proposed by Bose et al., also outliers may occur in the data. These outliers do not follow the general behavior and should be ignored, rather than incorporated in the model.

Also for neural networks, the task of incrementally learning has already been studied [20,26]. These studies show a typical behavior that occurs when updating existing neural networks called *catastrophic forgetting*. Catastrophic forgetting occurs when a neural network loses the information it learned in previous iterations after new data was used to update the model. Often this forgetting poses significant challenges when updating an existing model, as knowledge learned during the first training phases needs to be remembered. When looking at the dynamic nature of Business Processes, however, we can employ this catastrophic forgetting to our benefit as a natural way of updating the model, while gradually forgetting details of the obsolete distribution.

2.4   Incremental Predictive Process Monitoring

Maisenbacher et al. [19] and Di Francescomarino et al. [9] use the above-mentioned incremental learning algorithms to create incremental models that can predict the outcome of a running case. The main focus of their work is using incremental classifiers that can classify ongoing traces based on their predicted outcome. Maisenbacher et al. look at different existing approaches, like the ones described above, and explore the performances of these approaches when applied to business processes. Di Francescomarino et al. focus on a clustered-based and index-based technique to predict the outcome for an ongoing trace. One of the disadvantages of their work is that they do not show if existing methods could be adapted to incorporate the incremental learning aspect. Their work does indicate the potential benefit of incremental learning in predictive process monitoring.

Berti et al. [2] propose a method for remaining time prediction that can deal with concept drift in the data, by only training on the relevant part of the data that correctly behaves according to the current business process. One disadvantage of their approach is that they need existing concept drift detection methods (like the one proposed by Bose et al.). Knowing which intervals behave in a static way they propose to use distance functions between an ongoing trace and the traces present in the current static interval. Using this distance function they calculate the reliability of a trace in the context of predicting the remaining time for an ongoing trace. In contrast to the approach proposed by Maisenbacher et al., Berti et al. require some a priori knowledge about the different drifts present in the data, making it less suitable for online use.

3   Update Strategies

Different strategies exist that deal with the presence of drifts in the data. We divide them into two main categories; the first category trains a new model (*reset*), the second category updates the existing model (*update*). In the remainder of this paper, we use *learning* to either indicate reset or update. Next, we take a look at how we can select the data used for learning the model.

3.1   Data Selection

Relearning a model after every event is both infeasible and unnecessary. Therefore we divide the event log into windows of a certain size. These windows can be divided by specifying the number of events per window, or by specifying a time interval for every window (days, weeks, months, ...). A log consists of an ordered list of windows $w_0, w_1, \ldots, w_n$ where w_t is the window arrived at time t and n the latest time present in the log. We have for w_i and w_j with $i < j$ that all events in window w_i occurred before all event in window w_j.

Using these windows we can define three different strategies to determine which data to use for learning a model. The first strategy uses all historical data to learn the model (w_0, w_1, ..., w_{t-1}). The next strategy only takes a limited, fixed amount of the immediate history (windows) into account ($w_{t-\ell}$, $w_{t-\ell+1}$, ..., w_{t-1} with ℓ the number of windows to consider). The last method retrains its model when a drift occurred and updates the model after every window with all windows starting from the last drift point up to the current window (w_{d_t}, w_{d_t+1}, ..., w_{t-1} with d_t the time of the latest detected drift).

We can combine all strategies with both the reset and update methods. This leads to six different options for incremental predictive models. The options using the reset strategy can be used straightforwardly with existing methods. When using the update options, existing approaches possibly need extra adaptation.

In this paper, we consider both neural net methods and Dynamic Bayesian Networks. Both these types of methods are already learned in an iterative process, and can thus easily be extended to our incremental approach. Every iteration during training results in a (slightly) adapted model. When, according to a selected loss function, this model performs better than the previous one, we keep this model to start the next iteration with. Updating these models thus only implies that we have to perform extra iterations on the existing model using our updated data.

3.2   Update Existing Methods

In this section, we describe in more detail how the incremental aspect can be added to both neural networks and dynamic bayesian networks based on how these models are learned from data.

Drift-Based Predictions. We use the method proposed by [4] to detect drifts present in the data. To update the model, we retrain the model after every batch using all available data starting from the last seen drift until the most recent used batch of events.

Incremental Neural Networks. Training a neural network is an iterative procedure that tries to optimize a certain model score. This score indicates how accurate the current model is for predicting events (validates the model). Neural network learners use a subset of events from the training data for this validation and the remaining events for actually updating the parameters of the model.

Using new data for updating the model causes the model to diverge from what it originally learned, as it is now validating using new data. Therefore, the model can potentially be less optimal for the original data that was used for the initial training. This is the typical catastrophic forgetting phenomenon that occurs when updating a neural network. For a dataset that contains drift, this is, however, a positive feature rather than a weakness.

As all considered neural network methods train their model in the same way, we can use this incremental method on every proposed neural network model such as the Single Dense Layer (SDL), LSTM, and CNN based methods.

Incremental Dynamic Bayesian Networks. Dynamic Bayesian Networks consist of a model structure and model parameters. Both the structure and parameters are learned from data, and can thus both be updated separately.

The structure of a DBN describes the conditional dependencies between attributes in the data. We learn the model using a hill-climbing algorithm, where we perform iterations of adding or removing dependencies as long as these actions improve the model score. To update the structure we run this algorithm on the existing model. While improvements can be made to the structure, the algorithm will continue to perform iterations.

The parameters of the DBN describe the conditional probabilities for all attributes, and can be calculated as follows:

$$P(A|Pa(A)) = \frac{P(A \cap Pa(A))}{P(Pa(A))} \tag{1}$$

Where $Pa(A)$ are the attributes on which A depends.

To easily being able to compute these probabilities, we create an inverted index for every attribute. Instead of keeping track of the different values that occur in a single row, we keep track of the rows in which a certain value occurs. Due to this inverted index, the DBN method is very suitable for an incremental setting.

Example 1. Consider the event log as shown in Table 1a. We can create an inverted index for the attributes Activity, Role, and Department by listing for every value of the attributes in which event they occur using the event ID. The inverted indexes are shown in Tables 1b, c, and d.

For calculating a conditional probability we can use set operations when dealing with categorical values only:

$$P(Act = A|Role = r_1, Dept = d_0) = \frac{P(Act = A, Role = r_1, Dept = d_0)}{P(Role = r_1, Dept = d_0)} \tag{2}$$

$$= \frac{\#(\{0\} \cap \{0,1\} \cap \{0,1,3\})}{\#(\{0,1\} \cap \{0,1,3\})} = \frac{1}{2} \tag{3}$$

To further improve our implementation we can only keep track of the counts we need in Eq. 3. To update the model, we increment the values that correspond with the combinations of the nominator and denominator.

Table 1. Example log with extra attributes Role and Department (a) and the inverted indexes for Activity (b), Role (c) and Department (d).

eventID	Activity	Role	Department
0	A	r_1	d_0
1	B	r_1	d_0
2	C	r_2	d_1
3	B	r_2	d_0

(a)

Value	IDs
A	{0}
B	{1,3}
C	{2}

(b)

Value	IDs
r_1	{0,1}
r_2	{2,3}

(c)

Value	IDs
d_0	{0,1,3}
d_1	{2}

(d)

4   Reference Model: Single Dense Layer (SDL)

Incrementally updating existing models adds a level of complexity and cost. To reduce the overall cost of learning and updating the models we propose a neural network with a single dense layer for predicting the next event. We did not find any paper exploring the use of simple NNs with only dense layers, without the need of using Petri Nets as intermediate structure [31]. As we show in Sect. 5, such a shallow fully-connected network benefits from low runtimes and high accuracy both in an incremental and non-incremental situation.

We use a prefix-based approach, as this kind of approach captures the sequential nature of the event logs, while at the same time giving an easy, flattened data structure. The SDL network consists of a layer of input cells, corresponding to the number of history steps and the number of attributes used. The selection of these attributes depends on the data used and can vary significantly between datasets. We encode the data using an encoding layer, which encodes the data using one-hot encoding. In the case of numeric attributes, we do not have to encode the values and can use them as-is. These cells are then concatenated before they are linked with a dense layer with as many cells as there are activities and a dropout of 0.2, as proposed by other methods. As the output layer, we use a softmax layer, ensuring that the network returns a probability distribution over all possible events. All input cells $i_0, i_1, \ldots, i_n$ represent the activities and extra attributes present in the entire prefix. We thus have $n = |\mathcal{A}| * k$ input cells in the network, with $\mathcal{A}$ the set of all considered attributes (from both activity and data perspective), and k the size of the history taken into account. The cells $e_0, e_1, \ldots, e_n$ create a integer encoding of the attributes.

Example 2. Suppose we have an event log containing both the activity and resource executing the activity. If we want to create a model with prefix size

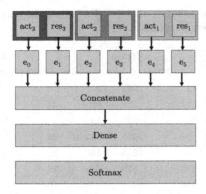

Fig. 1. Example SDL network that takes 3 previous time steps into account from both the activity and resource attribute.

$k = 3$, we have the following input cells: $i_0, i_1, i_2, i_3, i_4, i_5$. Where i_0, i_2, i_4 represent the activities and i_1, i_3, i_5 the resources for the 3 time steps in the prefix. A visual overview of the resulting network can be found in Fig. 1.

5   Experiments

To test the different update strategies we selected 4 methods, each using a different type of model. These methods were selected based on their diversity to cover a wide variety of state-of-the-art methods with shown performance [24]. For this study we use the following methods:

- **Dynamic Bayesian Networks (DBN)**: Pauwels et al. [24]
- **Single Dense Layer NN (SDL)**
- **Long-Short-Term-Memory NN (LSTM)**: Tax et al. [28]
- **Convolutional Neural Network (CNN)**: Di Mauro et al. [10]

In the first place, we are interested in how the accuracy of the different methods changes over time. We define accuracy as the portion of correctly predicted activities. For this purpose, we use a sliding window of fixed size for which we calculate the accuracy obtained within this window. We then use a graphical representation with the event index (in chronological order) on the X-axis and the window accuracy on the Y-axis. This *accuracy-plot* gives us an easy tool to compare different methods and see how the accuracy changes over time. We can use these graphs to see if the tested model does suffer from drifts in the data and if it can recover from changes.

As described in Sect. 3, first a batch size has to be determined that indicates the frequency of performing an update to the model. In our study we tested three different ways of dividing the data into batches; by day, week, or month. Preliminary tests show only minor differences between these batch sizes. Therefore, we decided to use monthly batches for our experiments.

Table 2. Overview of the different datasets. Including the number of days, weeks and month in the train and test parts used.

Dataset	#cases	#events	#activities	Train			Test		
				#days	#weeks	#months	#days	#weeks	#months
Helpdesk	4,580	21,348	14	623	97	23	683	112	27
BPIC11	1,143	150,291	624	622	90	21	550	79	19
BPIC12	13,087	262,200	36	87	14	3	80	12	4
BPIC15_1	1,199	52,217	398	562	112	26	595	122	30
BPIC15_2	832	44,354	410	555	116	28	550	117	28
BPIC15_3	1,409	59,681	383	678	117	29	604	117	28
BPIC15_4	1,053	47,293	356	621	126	30	516	107	26
BPIC15_5	1,156	59,083	389	566	112	27	569	121	29

During our experiments, we are interested in the difference between all update strategies and how a model that uses updates, performs in contrast to a static one. We are thus less interested in determining the single best model to use when incorporating updates in our next-activity predictor.

When evaluating the performance of the update strategies we use an *interleaved-test-then-train* approach. Each batch of data is first used to test the model before we use it for updating the model. All code used for the experiments can be found in our Github Repository[1].

5.1   Dataset Selection

To best test the update capabilities of the models, we need datasets where some drifts occur in the activity perspective. We start with looking at the following datasets which are often used in the literature and have different characteristics:

- **Helpdesk** [32]: a log containing ticket requests of the helpdesk from an Italian software company
- **BPIC11** [14]: a log of a Dutch academic hospital. It shows the different activities and phases the patients go through.
- **BPIC12** [12]: a log containing applications for personal loans. The log contains three intertwined processes.
- **BPIC15** [13]: a log containing building permit applications from five different Dutch municipalities. The log is splitted into five sublogs, one for every municipality (**BPIC15_1** to **BPIC15_5**).

The events in the datasets were first sorted according to timestamp and then split 50/50 in train and test set in chronological order. The details of the different datasets can be found in Table 2. The train set is used to train the initial model and the test set is used to test the method and incrementally update the initial models. To best answer our research questions, we use datasets that do contain

---

[1] https://github.com/StephenPauwels/edbn.

variation over time in the activity perspective. To look if any drifts occur in the datasets we train a model on the first half of the data. We then test the remaining half using this static model. Using our accuracy-plot, which uses a sliding window to calculate the accuracy, we can then look for changes in accuracy over time.

Figure 2 shows some (small) changes in accuracy over time for the Helpdesk, BPIC11, and BPIC15 datasets when not using any update strategy. The BPIC15 datasets suffer the highest loss of accuracy. This experiment also shows the constant performance of the BPIC12 data. This dataset is useful to see the performance of our incremental learners when no drifts are present. Ideally, the incremental algorithms should perform similarly to the non-incremental ones.

5.2 Baseline Comparison

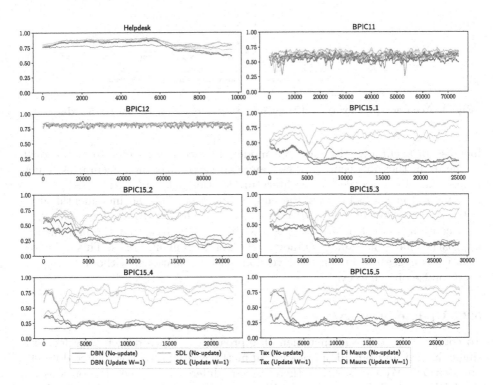

Fig. 2. Accuracy-plot for both a static model and an incremental model using a window size of 1.

A first question that needs to be answered is how much accuracy gain there is when using an incremental algorithm in contrast to the non-incremental ones. Figure 2 shows the average accuracies for the four methods on all datasets. This experiment shows the need for an incremental approach when utilizing prediction models in a real-life setting. The results from the BPIC15 datasets show a large

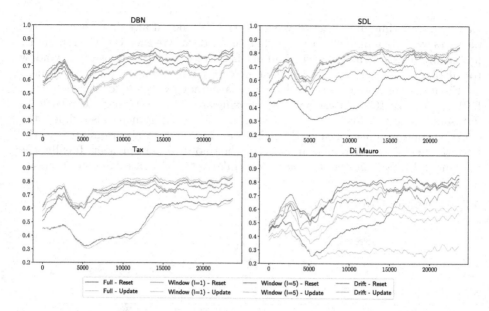

Fig. 3. Accuracy-plot for the different update strategies for the BPIC15_1 dataset.

increase in accuracy. Although the models first seem to suffer from the drift in the data, they all recuperate fast and can keep fairly high accuracies, much higher than the ones seen in the literature for this dataset.

This graph also shows another important aspect of the incremental algorithms; as we do not know in advance if and when a drift occurs, the data may contain no drift at all. Our results on BPIC12 show that the incremental approaches have the same accuracy as the non-incremental ones. This indicates that we can use the incremental versions in all situations, without having to compromise on accuracy.

5.3   Update Strategy

To compare the different incremental approaches we introduced, we selected a single dataset and ran all options for all methods. Figure 3 shows three different observations. We can see that there is little difference between the options for the DBN method. This can be explained by the fact that the DBN model has no way to forget older events.

The SDL and LSTM (Tax et al.) methods show similar behavior. Using all data to update the model, consistently shows the worst performance, as using the full dataset ensures that the model is unable to forget the older events that became irrelevant. We see that using an update strategy using a window scores the best for both methods, thus making use of the catastrophic forgetting to gradually replace the older with newer knowledge. The use of drift detection

Table 3. Runtime (average *(stdev)*) for the update iterations for the BPIC15_1 dataset (in seconds)

Strategy	Batch	DBN	SDL	Tax	Di Mauro
Initial training		48	78	433	188
Reset	Full	106 *(25)*	73 *(18)*	985 *(394)*	450 *(132)*
	Window (size 1)	17 *(4)*	5 *(1)*	37 *(10)*	20 *(9)*
	Window (size 5)	26 *(6)*	14 *(1)*	175 *(39)*	68 *(14)*
	Drift	28 *(15)*	14 *(10)*	187 *(178)*	98 *(87)*
Update	Full	60 *(12)*	56 *(12)*	505 *(101)*	132 *(27)*
	Window (size 1)	1 *(0.5)*	1 *(0.5)*	11 *(4)*	3 *(1)*
	Window (size 5)	7 *(0.8)*	6 *(1)*	59 *(7)*	15 *(2)*
	Drift	3 *(5)*	2 *(1)*	13 *(6)*	6 *(7)*

also gives good results, but this involves running an extra algorithm for every batch to decide whether a drift has occurred.

The architecture using convolutional neural networks (Di Mauro et al.) shows different behavior, in the graph we see that retraining completely achieves the highest accuracy. This can be due to the difference in nature of the convolution layers used in this model.

5.4 Runtime Results

Table 3 shows the average time for each update using the different strategies. Overall we see that SDL is the fastest algorithm to learn, followed by DBN, Di Mauro, and the LSTM architecture of Tax show to be the slowest.

5.5 Overall Results

Table 4 shows an overview of the accuracy obtained by all methods, using the different update strategies on all datasets. This table confirms the behavior that we saw in the previous experiments. We see consistent results for all different methods.

These results also show the performance of our SDL method in comparison to existing methods (both with and without the incremental aspect). We see that our new architecture performs at par with existing methods. On top of that, as the complexity of our model is fairly low, training this model takes considerably less time than training the existing methods.

Table 4. Average accuracy for all methods on all different update settings. Batches grouped using months.

Dataset	Update strategy	Batch	DBN	SDL	LSTM	CNN
Helpdesk	No-update		0.78	0.77	0.77	0.78
	Reset	Full	0.82	0.80	0.78	0.81
		Window (size 1)	0.82	0.83	0.83	0.82
		Window (size 5)	0.84	0.84	0.82	0.83
		Drift	0.83	0.82	0.81	0.82
	Update	Full	0.81	0.80	0.77	0.80
		Window (size 1)	0.81	0.85	0.84	0.84
		Window (size 5)	0.81	0.84	0.83	0.84
		Drift	0.83	0.85	0.84	0.84
BPIC11	No-update		0.54	0.56	0.60	0.57
	Reset	Full	0.58	0.62	0.66	0.63
		Window (size 1)	0.51	0.56	0.58	0.55
		Window (size 5)	0.58	0.63	0.66	0.62
		Drift	0.56	0.60	0.64	0.60
	Update	Full	0.60	0.62	0.60	0.64
		Window (size 1)	0.58	0.62	0.67	0.59
		Window (size 5)	0.58	0.63	0.68	0.60
		Drift	0.57	0.60	0.62	0.58
BPIC12	No-update		0.80	0.81	0.79	0.83
	Reset	Full	0.81	0.81	0.79	0.83
		Window (size 1)	0.79	0.79	0.80	0.82
		Window (size 5)	0.81	0.81	0.80	0.83
		Drift	0.81	0.81	0.79	0.83
	Update	Full	0.81	0.81	0.79	0.83
		Window (size 1)	0.81	0.80	0.80	0.83
		Window (size 5)	0.81	0.81	0.80	0.83
		Drift	0.81	0.80	0.79	0.83
BPIC15_1	No-update		0.20	0.24	0.25	0.21
	Reset	Full	0.68	0.50	0.52	0.55
		Window (size 1)	0.71	0.64	0.68	0.65
		Window (size 5)	0.74	0.75	0.75	0.71
		Drift	0.73	0.69	0.70	0.71
	Update	Full	0.61	0.74	0.50	0.32
		Window (size 1)	0.62	0.76	0.76	0.56
		Window (size 5)	0.61	0.76	0.77	0.50
		Drift	0.72	0.73	0.73	0.69

(continued)

Table 4. (*continued*)

Dataset	Update strategy	Batch	DBN	SDL	LSTM	CNN
BPIC15_2	No-update		0.27	0.26	0.30	0.34
	Reset	Full	0.68	0.48	0.51	0.74
		Window (size 1)	0.71	0.60	0.66	0.61
		Window (size 5)	0.73	0.73	0.74	0.74
		Drift	0.73	0.67	0.69	0.71
	Update	Full	0.67	0.73	0.49	0.42
		Window (size 1)	0.67	0.76	0.75	0.65
		Window (size 5)	0.66	0.76	0.76	0.65
		Drift	0.73	0.72	0.71	0.66
BPIC15_3	No-update		0.30	0.30	0.28	0.28
	Reset	Full	0.71	0.50	0.53	0.51
		Window (size 1)	0.74	0.69	0.71	0.71
		Window (size 5)	0.76	0.77	0.78	0.72
		Drift	0.76	0.72	0.72	0.74
	Update	Full	0.70	0.76	0.51	0.40
		Window (size 1)	0.70	0.79	0.78	0.63
		Window (size 5)	0.70	0.79	0.79	0.58
		Drift	0.76	0.77	0.76	0.75
BPIC15_4	No-update		0.25	0.25	0.21	0.21
	Reset	Full	0.74	0.52	0.54	0.60
		Window (size 1)	0.73	0.68	0.71	0.69
		Window (size 5)	0.79	0.79	0.79	0.74
		Drift	0.75	0.58	0.58	0.61
	Update	Full	0.74	0.79	0.52	0.40
		Window (size 1)	0.74	0.81	0.79	0.60
		Window (size 5)	0.73	0.81	0.81	0.54
		Drift	0.75	0.79	0.79	0.65
BPIC15_5	No-update		0.27	0.23	0.26	0.24
	Reset	Full	0.68	0.50	0.52	0.58
		Window (size 1)	0.74	0.68	0.71	0.71
		Window (size 5)	0.75	0.76	0.77	0.71
		Drift	0.76	0.71	0.72	0.74
	Update	Full	0.67	0.75	0.50	0.37
		Window (size 1)	0.69	0.79	0.78	0.55
		Window (size 5)	0.68	0.78	0.78	0.50
		Drift	0.76	0.77	0.76	0.72

6   Conclusion

In this paper, we looked at the situation in which we want to predict the next activity in a business process in a situation where the underlying process can be subject to change. We changed the standard way of evaluating the performance of the methods from using a static training and testing part of the data to a way that we can use all previous events to help predict the next event.

We looked at different options on how to select the data to use for updating the models. We can use the full data, a sliding window technique, or the data after the last detected drift. Updating the models with only a limited number of events reduces the computational resources needed for learning. Furthermore, we looked at the difference in performance when strictly updating an existing model, or by completely retraining models.

We showed that neural network methods can take advantage of the catastrophic forgetting phenomenon that occurs when updating these networks. As the event logs can have dynamic underlying processes, it is logical to give more importance to more recent events. The proposed methods for updating existing models did improve the overall accuracy greatly, without suffering from performance loss when no drift or variation is present in the data.

The DBN method also improved when using an incremental learning approach, but often this improvement was less than the improvement observed for neural network methods. One reason for this is that the current update method for DBNs has no mechanism that forgets older events and/or gives more priority to newer events. In future research, we would like to take a closer look at how to incorporate this in the DBN method to improve the results and make it more flexible when used with changing processes.

Our new architecture showed to perform at par or even outperform some state-of-the-art methods but at a substantially lower computational complexity. In the light of incremental learners, this lower complexity comes at an extra advantage, as updating can be done faster or more often. But, as shown in the experiments, the use of the SDL method should not be limited to incremental settings.

As we only use four different methods in this paper, we cannot make strong conclusions about the best way of solving the incremental next-activity prediction problem. This is often highly dependent on the characteristics of the considered process. We showed that we can leverage existing state-of-the-art methods to cope with variation and drifts in the data by adding a basic incremental framework. Some of the datasets used in our experiments often get ignored in the literature due to their dynamic nature. We showed that, when using a suitable update strategy, most methods are ready to be used in a more challenging environment than the test settings and datasets used most of the time in literature.

References

1. Van der Aalst, W.M., Schonenberg, M.H., Song, M.: Time prediction based on process mining. Inf. Syst. **36**(2), 450–475 (2011)
2. Berti, A.: Improving process mining prediction results in processes that change over time. Data Anal. **2016**, 49 (2016)
3. Bifet, A., Gavalda, R.: SIAM: learning from time-changing data with adaptive windowing. In: Proceedings of the 2007 SIAM International Conference on Data Mining (SDM), pp. 443–448. SIAM (2007)
4. Bose, R.J.C., Van Der Aalst, W.M., Žliobaitė, I., Pechenizkiy, M.: Dealing with concept drifts in process mining. IEEE Trans. Neural Netw. Learn. Syst. **25**(1), 154–171 (2013)
5. Burattin, A., Carmona, J.: A framework for online conformance checking. In: Teniente, E., Weidlich, M. (eds.) BPM 2017. LNBIP, vol. 308, pp. 165–177. Springer, Cham (2018). https://doi.org/10.1007/978-3-319-74030-0_12
6. Burattin, A., Cimitile, M., Maggi, F.M., Sperduti, A.: Online discovery of declarative process models from event streams. IEEE Trans. Serv. Comput. **8**(6), 833–846 (2015). https://doi.org/10.1109/TSC.2015.2459703
7. Camargo, M., Dumas, M., González-Rojas, O.: Learning accurate LSTM models of business processes. In: Hildebrandt, T., van Dongen, B.F., Röglinger, M., Mendling, J. (eds.) BPM 2019. LNCS, vol. 11675, pp. 286–302. Springer, Cham (2019). https://doi.org/10.1007/978-3-030-26619-6_19
8. Di Francescomarino, C., Ghidini, C., Maggi, F.M., Milani, F.: Predictive process monitoring methods: which one suits me best? In: Weske, M., Montali, M., Weber, I., vom Brocke, J. (eds.) BPM 2018. LNCS, vol. 11080, pp. 462–479. Springer, Cham (2018). https://doi.org/10.1007/978-3-319-98648-7_27
9. Di Francescomarino, C., Ghidini, C., Maggi, F.M., Rizzi, W., Persia, C.D.: Incremental predictive process monitoring: How to deal with the variability of real environments. arXiv preprint arXiv:1804.03967 (2018)
10. Di Mauro, N., Appice, A., Basile, T.M.A.: Activity prediction of business process instances with inception CNN models. In: Alviano, M., Greco, G., Scarcello, F. (eds.) AI*IA 2019. LNCS (LNAI), vol. 11946, pp. 348–361. Springer, Cham (2019). https://doi.org/10.1007/978-3-030-35166-3_25
11. Domingos, P., Hulten, G.: Mining high-speed data streams. In: Proceedings of the Sixth ACM SIGKDD International Conference on Knowledge Discovery and Data Mining, pp. 71–80 (2000)
12. van Dongen, B.: BPI challenge (2012). https://doi.org/10.4121/uuid:3926db30-f712-4394-aebc-75976070e91f
13. van Dongen, B.: BPI challenge (2015). https://doi.org/10.4121/uuid:31a308ef-c844-48da-948c-305d167a0ec1
14. van Dongen, B.: Real-life event logs - hospital log, March 2011. https://doi.org/10.4121/uuid:d9769f3d-0ab0-4fb8-803b-0d1120ffcf54
15. Evermann, J., Rehse, J.R., Fettke, P.: Predicting process behaviour using deep learning. Decis. Support Syst. **100**, 129–140 (2017)
16. Gama, J., Žliobaitė, I., Bifet, A., Pechenizkiy, M., Bouchachia, A.: A survey on concept drift adaptation. ACM Comput. Surv. (CSUR) **46**(4), 1–37 (2014)
17. Gepperth, A., Hammer, B.: Incremental learning algorithms and applications. In: European Symposium on Artificial Neural Networks (ESANN) (2016)
18. Lin, L., Wen, L., Wang, J.: MM-PRED: a deep predictive model for multi-attribute event sequence. In: Proceedings of the 2019 SIAM International Conference on Data Mining, pp. 118–126. SIAM (2019)

19. Maisenbacher, M., Weidlich, M.: Handling concept drift in predictive process monitoring. SCC **17**, 1–8 (2017)
20. McCloskey, M., Cohen, N.J.: Catastrophic interference in connectionist networks: the sequential learning problem. In: Psychology of Learning and Motivation, vol. 24, pp. 109–165. Elsevier (1989)
21. Ostovar, A., Maaradji, A., La Rosa, M., ter Hofstede, A.H.M., van Dongen, B.F.V.: Detecting drift from event streams of unpredictable business processes. In: Comyn-Wattiau, I., Tanaka, K., Song, I.-Y., Yamamoto, S., Saeki, M. (eds.) ER 2016. LNCS, vol. 9974, pp. 330–346. Springer, Cham (2016). https://doi.org/10.1007/978-3-319-46397-1_26
22. Pasquadibisceglie, V., Appice, A., Castellano, G., Malerba, D.: Using convolutional neural networks for predictive process analytics. In: 2019 International Conference on Process Mining (ICPM), pp. 129–136. IEEE (2019)
23. Pasquadibisceglie, V., Appice, A., Castellano, G., Malerba, D.: Predictive process mining meets computer vision. In: Fahland, D., Ghidini, C., Becker, J., Dumas, M. (eds.) BPM 2020. LNBIP, vol. 392, pp. 176–192. Springer, Cham (2020). https://doi.org/10.1007/978-3-030-58638-6_11
24. Pauwels, S., Calders, T.: Bayesian network based predictions of business processes. In: Fahland, D., Ghidini, C., Becker, J., Dumas, M. (eds.) BPM 2020. LNBIP, vol. 392, pp. 159–175. Springer, Cham (2020). https://doi.org/10.1007/978-3-030-58638-6_10
25. Rokach, L., Maimon, O.: Clustering methods. In: Maimon, O., Rokach, L. (eds.) Data Mining and Knowledge Discovery Handbook. Springer, Boston (2005). https://doi.org/10.1007/0-387-25465-X_15
26. Serrà Julià, J., Surís, D., Miron, M., Karatzoglou, A.: Overcoming catastrophic forgetting with hard attention to the task. In: Dy, J., Krause, A., (eds.) Proceedings of the 35th International Conference on Machine Learning (ICML 2018), 10–15 July 2018, Stockholmsmässan, Sweden [Massachusetts: PMLR; 2018], pp. 4548–4557. Proceedings of Machine Learning Research (2018)
27. Tax, N., Teinemaa, I., van Zelst, S.J.: An interdisciplinary comparison of sequence modeling methods for next-element prediction. Softw. Syst. Model. **19**(6), 1345–1365 (2020)
28. Tax, N., Verenich, I., La Rosa, M., Dumas, M.: Predictive business process monitoring with LSTM neural networks. In: Dubois, E., Pohl, K. (eds.) CAiSE 2017. LNCS, vol. 10253, pp. 477–492. Springer, Cham (2017). https://doi.org/10.1007/978-3-319-59536-8_30
29. Taymouri, F., Rosa, M.L., Erfani, S., Bozorgi, Z.D., Verenich, I.: Predictive business process monitoring via generative adversarial nets: the case of next event prediction. In: Fahland, D., Ghidini, C., Becker, J., Dumas, M. (eds.) BPM 2020. LNCS, vol. 12168, pp. 237–256. Springer, Cham (2020). https://doi.org/10.1007/978-3-030-58666-9_14
30. Teinemaa, I., Dumas, M., Rosa, M.L., Maggi, F.M.: Outcome-oriented predictive process monitoring: review and benchmark. ACM Trans. Knowl. Discov Data (TKDD) **13**(2), 1–57 (2019)
31. Theis, J., Darabi, H.: Decay replay mining to predict next process events. IEEE Access **7**, 119787–119803 (2019)
32. Verenich, I.: Helpdesk, mendeley data, v1 (2016). https://doi.org/10.17632/39bp3vv62t.1
33. Weinzierl, S., et al.: An empirical comparison of deep-neural-network architectures for next activity prediction using context-enriched process event logs. arXiv preprint arXiv:2005.01194 (2020)

Learning Uncertainty with Artificial Neural Networks for Improved Remaining Time Prediction of Business Processes

Hans Weytjens[✉] and Jochen De Weerdt

Research Centre for Information Systems Engineering (LIRIS),
KU Leuven, Leuven, Belgium
{hans.weytjens,jochen.deweerdt}@kuleuven.be

Abstract. Artificial neural networks will always make a prediction, even when completely uncertain and regardless of the consequences. This obliviousness of uncertainty is a major obstacle towards their adoption in practice. Techniques exist, however, to estimate the two major types of uncertainty: model uncertainty and observation noise in the data. Bayesian neural networks are theoretically well-founded models that can learn the model uncertainty of their predictions. Minor modifications to these models and their loss functions allow learning the observation noise for individual samples as well. This paper is the first to apply these techniques to predictive process monitoring. We found that they contribute towards more accurate predictions and work quickly. However, their main benefit resides with the uncertainty estimates themselves that allow the separation of higher-quality from lower-quality predictions and the building of confidence intervals. This leads to many interesting applications, enables an earlier adoption of prediction systems with smaller datasets and fosters a better cooperation with humans.

Keywords: Process mining · Remaining time prediction · Bayesian neural networks · Concrete dropout · Uncertainty · Heteroscedasticity · Convolutional neural networks · Long short-term memory models

1 Introduction

Modern information systems and data availability led to the acceleration of process mining research and deployment of its algorithms in industry in recent years. Process mining analyzes event data generated by such information systems with the goal of process discovery, process conformance checking and process enhancement. Predictive process monitoring is an important sub-field of process mining and concerns predicting next events, process outcomes and remaining execution times. Recent advances in machine learning propelled predictive process monitoring to the next level and many researchers intensified the use of artificial neural networks (NNs) for their predictions.

However, the adoption of these powerful and versatile NNs has not followed suit in practice. Practitioners are reluctant to use NNs that cannot explain their

© Springer Nature Switzerland AG 2021
A. Polyvyanyy et al. (Eds.): BPM 2021, LNCS 12875, pp. 141–157, 2021.
https://doi.org/10.1007/978-3-030-85469-0_11

predictions. A related, consequential problem is that NNs are unaware of the uncertainty of their predictions. They will always make a prediction, even when confronted with inputs they were never trained on. This can lead to potentially expensive or even catastrophic mistakes. Uncertainty awareness would therefore be a tremendous asset.

The uncertainty of predictions is the subject of this paper. Our core contribution is the introduction of NN-based uncertainty estimation techniques including heteroscedasticity learning and loss attenuation, concrete dropout and Bayesian neural networks (BNNs) to predictive process monitoring. We test their impact on overall prediction quality, uncertainty estimation quality, and computational time in a carefully designed experimental assessment using three public real-life datasets. Furthermore, we shed light on the practical applications. We consider the problem of remaining execution time prediction of ongoing processes which is highly relevant in practice, as it allows management to stop or alter running processes or initiate other actions. For example, an organization can inform its customers about the expected feedback/fulfillment time for their requests/orders and divert cases with long expected remaining times to a special track to speed them up.

We define our learning problem and position this paper relative to other work in Sect. 2. Section 3 explains two types of uncertainty before introducing techniques adapting plain-vanilla NNs to learn them. We then derive the precise questions we seek to address with our experiments. Section 4 describes the setup of these experiments, whose results are presented in Sect. 5. We subsequently present applications enabled by the uncertainty estimates in Sect. 6 before summarizing our findings and formulating paths for future research in the final Sect. 7.

2   Remaining Time Prediction: Definition and Related Work

In predictive process monitoring, datasets are event logs describing processes, often called *cases*. These cases consist of *events*. A number of attributes, also called *features* or variables, describe these cases and events. In remaining time prediction problems, every event is associated with a *target* feature describing the remaining time until completion of the case. A *prefix* is an ongoing, incomplete case, with the *prefix length* its number of completed events. Our learning problem is to train a learner using a training dataset containing events, described by their features and organized in prefixes that are labeled with targets, with the goal of predicting the targets of unseen prefixes.

In 2008, the first published research on process remaining time prediction [1] used non-parametric regressions, followed a few years later by [2] proposing to build an annotated transition system. Later, increasingly sophisticated approaches [3] deployed classic machine learning techniques such as support vector regression and naive Bayes and included the events' attributes other than activity name and time into their calculations. Recently, long short-term memory models (LSTMs) entered the scene [4,5]. Such deep learning techniques permit the substitution of automatic feature engineering for the error-prone, domain-knowledge-based manual feature engineering of the classic machine learning techniques. The authors of [6] provide an overview of papers until 2017. Our paper further extends this line of research by complementing the point estimates of these NN with predictions of the respective uncertainty. As such, we realize our goal of not only improving the overall quality of these point estimates, but also of unlocking many applications based on the knowledge of the predictions' uncertainty.

3   Estimating Uncertainty

In the context of predicting with models, we can distinguish two kinds of uncertainty [7]. The first, the *epistemic* (a.k.a. reducible) uncertainty expresses the model's uncertainty and finds its origin in the paucity of training data. Adding more samples to the training dataset will reduce the epistemic uncertainty. The first two graphs in Fig. 1 visualize two examples. The second type of uncertainty, the *aleatoric uncertainty* is a measure for the observation noise of the underlying distribution that generated the samples. It is often expressed as σ and will not decrease by observing more data. Many models in practice assume the aleatoric noise to be constant or homoscedastic (as in the third graph in Fig. 1). In reality, heteroscedasticity (fourth graph in Fig. 1) is probably much more common: the aleatoric noise varies across the domain.

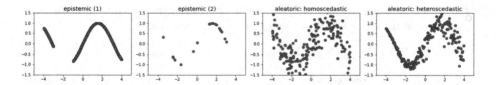

Fig. 1. Examples of uncertainty types

3.1   Estimating Epistemic Uncertainty with Bayesian Neural Networks

In regular, *deterministic* neural networks, the maximum likelihood estimate (MLE) of a model $\mathcal{H}$'s weights ω maximizes the probability $p(\boldsymbol{Y}|\boldsymbol{X}, \omega, \mathcal{H})$ of the observed outcomes $\boldsymbol{Y}$ given corresponding inputs $\boldsymbol{X}$. Prediction leads to a point estimate $y^* = \mathcal{H}(\boldsymbol{x}^*, \omega)$. Whilst good function approximators, (unregularized) deterministic NNs are prone to overfitting, especially when dealing with small training sets, and therefore struggle dealing with points $\boldsymbol{x}^*$ far away from the training data $\boldsymbol{X}$. Deterministic models have no knowledge of their point predictions' uncertainty.

The Bayesian approach is *stochastic* by nature: we look for the maximum a posteriori (MAP) distribution of the weights $\boldsymbol{\omega}$ given the training set $[\boldsymbol{X}, \boldsymbol{Y}]$, that can be expressed using the Bayesian rule:

$$p(\boldsymbol{\omega}|\boldsymbol{X}, \boldsymbol{Y}, \mathcal{H}) = \frac{p(\boldsymbol{Y}|\boldsymbol{X}, \boldsymbol{w}, \mathcal{H}).p(\boldsymbol{\omega}|\mathcal{H})}{p(\boldsymbol{Y}, \boldsymbol{X})} \quad \text{or} \quad \text{posterior} = \frac{\text{likelihood x prior}}{\text{evidence}}$$

Note that the likelihood equals the MLE problem above. To predict the outcome for a given $\boldsymbol{x}^*$, we marginalize the likelihood over $\boldsymbol{\omega}$, a process called *inference* ($\mathcal{H}$ dropped to simplify notation):

$$p(y^*|\boldsymbol{x}^*, \boldsymbol{X}, \boldsymbol{Y}) = \int p(y^*|\boldsymbol{x}^*, \boldsymbol{\omega}).p(\boldsymbol{\omega}|\boldsymbol{X}, \boldsymbol{Y}).d\boldsymbol{\omega} \quad (1)$$

This is no longer a point estimate, but rather a distribution from which moments (mean, variance, etc.) can be derived. These statistics provide both a point estimate (mean) and a measure of the uncertainty of that estimate (variance), opening a range of possibilities that will be the subject of this paper. Under certain assumptions, there is an analytical solution to compute the posterior $p(\boldsymbol{\omega}|\boldsymbol{X}, \boldsymbol{Y})$ [8] but it is prohibitively computationally-expensive, as would be Markov Chain Monte Carlo sampling. Consequently, we resort to seeking a closed, approximate function $q_\theta(\boldsymbol{\omega})$ over the same domain $\boldsymbol{\omega}$ and parameterized by θ. This can be achieved by minimizing the Kullback-Leibler (KL) divergence between the two distributions:

$$\min KL\left(q_\theta(\boldsymbol{\omega})||p(\boldsymbol{\omega}|\boldsymbol{X}, \boldsymbol{Y})\right) = \int q_\theta(\boldsymbol{\omega}).\log\frac{q_\theta(\boldsymbol{\omega})}{p(\boldsymbol{\omega}|\boldsymbol{X}, \boldsymbol{Y})}$$

After some mathematical manipulations, the minimization problem above is equivalent to maximizing the *evidence lower bound* (ELBO):

$$\text{ELBO} = \mathbf{E}_{q_\theta(\boldsymbol{\omega})}\log p(\boldsymbol{X}, \boldsymbol{Y}|\boldsymbol{\omega}) - KL\left(q_\theta(\boldsymbol{\omega})||p(\boldsymbol{\omega})\right) = \boxed{1} - \boxed{2} \quad (2)$$

Maximizing $\boxed{1}$ is the standard MLE approach with $\boxed{2}$ acting as a regularizer keeping the approximative posterior $q_\theta(\boldsymbol{\omega})$ as closely as possible to the prior $p(\boldsymbol{\omega})$. Unlike $\boxed{2}$, the (derivative of) $\boxed{1}$ cannot be computed in closed form. Since the density function $q_\theta(\boldsymbol{\omega})$ in $\frac{\partial}{\partial\theta}\int q_\theta(\boldsymbol{\omega})\log p(\boldsymbol{X}, \boldsymbol{Y}|\boldsymbol{\omega}).d\boldsymbol{\omega}$ itself depends on θ, regular Monte Carlo (MC) integration is not feasible either. [9] proposes to use the so called *reparameterization trick* [10] to solve $\frac{\partial}{\partial\theta}\int q_\theta(\boldsymbol{\omega})\log p(\boldsymbol{X}, \boldsymbol{Y}|\boldsymbol{\omega}).d\boldsymbol{\omega}$. It involves expressing $\boldsymbol{\omega}$ as a deterministic function $g(\epsilon, \theta)$ in which ϵ is an unconditional parameter, allowing to sample ϵ from $\mathcal{N}(0, I)$ rather than sampling $\boldsymbol{\omega}$ from $q_\theta(\boldsymbol{\omega})$. The above approach is called *stochastic variational inference*. Often, a Gaussian distribution is placed over every weight $\boldsymbol{\omega}$ in the network with $\boldsymbol{\omega} = g(\epsilon, \theta) = \mu + \sigma.\epsilon$. This method has two serious drawbacks: it doubles the number of parameters to be estimated (μ and σ instead of a single $\boldsymbol{\omega}$ for every node) and requires relatively complex coding.

Dropout [11] is a popular regularization technique to prevent NNs from overfitting. It resembles training a large number of networks in parallel by dropping out, or randomly ignoring the outputs of nodes (including the network's inputs) during training by multiplying each one by a parameter ϵ sampled from a Bernoulli distribution with probability p. By simply transforming this stochasticity from the feature space in the NNs' dropout scenario to the weight space in BNNs, maximizing ELBO equals minimizing the NNs' dropout loss function with an additional L2 regularizer [12]. We are, thus, able to use standard NNs with easy-to-implement dropout regularization as BNNs, overcoming the drawbacks aforementioned. *Concrete dropout* [13] eliminates the need for tuning the dropout parameters p_i (for each layer i) by automatically optimizing p_i, replacing the discrete Bernoulli distribution with a continuous relaxation (concrete distribution relaxation [14]). In the traditional approach, dropout layers are placed between the convolutional layers in CNNs and only after the inputs and the last LSTM layer in LSTMs. This traditional approach leads to unsatisfying results. In our BNNs (we used both LSTMs and CNNs, see Subsect. 3.3), we therefore applied dropout to the inner-product layers (kernels) [15] in CNNs and to all eight weight matrices within the LSTM cells [16] which reduces overfitting problems more successfully.

After training the model as described above, we proceed to inference or prediction by using MC sampling again, performing T stochastic forward passes of our trained model. The predictive mean of Eq. 1 is estimated by the predictive mean of the MC samples:

$$\mathbf{E}_{p(y^*|x^*,X,Y)}[y^*] \approx \frac{1}{T}\sum_t \mathcal{H}(x^*,\hat{\omega}) \tag{3}$$

with $\hat{\omega}$ indirectly sampled from $q_\theta(\omega)$ by sampling ϵ from $\mathcal{N}(0,I)$. The variance is given by:

$$\mathrm{Var}_{p(y^*|x^*,X,Y)}[y^*] \approx \sigma^2 + \frac{1}{T}\sum_t \mathcal{H}(x^*,\hat{\omega})^2 - \left(\frac{1}{T}\sum_t \mathcal{H}(x^*,\hat{\omega})\right)^2 = \sigma^2 + \boxed{3} \tag{4}$$

$\boxed{3}$ is the sample variance of the T stochastic forward passes and can be interpreted as the model's or epistemic uncertainty. Adding more samples to the training dataset will reduce it. Hence, BNNs enable the ability to gauge the model's uncertainty for every prediction made.

3.2 Estimating Heteroscedastic Aleatoric Uncertainty

The σ in the above Eq. 4 is the aleatoric uncertainty. As most models assume σ to be constant, or homoscedastic, over the entire domain, they do not include it in their loss functions (the last term in Eq. 5 is simply dropped). However, learning an individual σ_n for each sample n would be valuable to better assess the variance of our predictions in Eq. 4. This is achieved by doubling the last dense layer in the model (unsupervised learning) [7]. By re-completing the loss function (ignoring the regulation term) to include the learned σ_n:

$$L = \min \frac{1}{N}\sum \frac{1}{2\sigma_n^2}(y_n - \mathcal{H}(x_n))^2 + \frac{1}{2}\log\sigma_n^2 \tag{5}$$

it becomes less sensitive to noisy data, as it will predict high uncertainty for poor predictions and vice versa. This process is called *loss attenuation* and should lead to better overall predictions. The second term in Eq. 5 ensures that the model does not simply predict high uncertainty for every sample.

3.3 LSTM Vs. CNN

The techniques described above all depend on the underlying NNs. LSTMs [17] have been the intuitive instrument of choice in predictive process monitoring problems. An LSTM processes every sequence of events it is presented one time step at a time. At any given time step, it will pass a vector containing information about the current and previous time steps to the next time step, until reaching the last one whose output is propagated to the next layer. In contrast, convolutional neural networks (CNN) [18] work with fixed-sized, spatially-organized data. A series of alternating convolution layers applying weight-sharing filters and dimension-reducing pooling layers enables the models to automatically recognize patterns and extract features from the input data. These features are then passed to a series of dense layers for the final regression. Interpreting time as a spatial dimension, one-dimensional CNNs can be successfully applied to sequence processing as well, as a growing body of research (e.g. [19]) points out. This thesis is supported by [20] for the related case of process outcome prediction. We, therefore, ran our experiments using both CNNs and LSTMs to gain further insight into the applicability of both models.

3.4 Objectives

Equipped with this understanding, we can now translate our research goal of investigating uncertainty for remaining time prediction into more detailed objectives. First, we assess the effect on the overall quality of point estimates of the following techniques (Subsect. 5.1):

1. **Heteroscedasticity**: Estimating the observation loss for individual samples (σ_n) permits loss attenuation. Can it improve point estimates?
2. **Dropout**: BNNs resemble NNs with dropout regularization. What are the merits of isolated dropout in a non-Bayesian context?
3. **Concrete dropout**: allows in-model estimating the dropout parameters p_i. How does it affect results?
4. **BNN**: Using the heteroscedastic NNs with concrete dropout, we apply MC sampling (T stochastic forward passes) and average to calculate point estimates (Eq. 3). Do we get better predictions?
5. **CNN/LSTM/base case**: We compare CNNs to LSTMs, as well as to a baseline to get an intuition for the absolute performances.

From the theory, we expect each of the first four techniques to contribute to better point estimates. CNNs should produce results at least at par with LSTMs.

Second, we investigate whether the uncertainty estimates' succeed in separating good from bad predictions and in building reliable confidence intervals based on these uncertainty estimates (Subsect. 5.2) as is theoretically expected. Third (Subsect. 5.3), we wish to gain insights in the computation time for training and inference respectively. Finally, our fourth objective (Sect. 6) is to explore and assess applications stemming from the knowledge of predictions' uncertainties.

4 Experimental Setup

4.1 Datasets

We used three publicly available datasets from the BPI Challenges[1]. BPIC_2017[2] is a rich and large dataset containing logs of a loan application process at a Dutch bank. BPIC_2019[3], while comparable in size, has much shorter cases and concerns a purchase order handling process. BPIC_2020[4] is a collection of five smaller datasets related to travel administration at a university. The five subsets are records of processes covering international declaration documents (Intl. Declarations), expense claims (Travel Costs), travel permits (Permits), pre-paid travel costs and requests for payment (Payments) and domestic declaration documents (Domestic Declarations). Our target for all these datasets was defined as the fractional number of days until case completion.

4.2 Preprocessing

To maintain a realistic setting, we refrained from filtering. Other than adding a few synthetic features based on the event time stamps (e.g. event number, elapsed time since previous event, day of the week, ...), we did not apply any domain knowledge whatsoever to our approach. The chronologically 15% last starting cases (10% for BPIC_2020) were withheld as a test dataset. Since the duration of a case is only known at its end (when the process is finished), we deleted all cases from the remaining training set that ended after the start of the first test dataset case[5]. This left us with approximately two thirds of the original cases for BPIC_2017 and BPIC_2019. Given the shorter recording time frame for BPIC_2020, this approach drastically reduced the number of samples for training, especially where cases take longer (Intl. Declarations is only left with 57 events from five cases in the training set). With longer cases (with more deviations) and more levels for the categorical variables, BPIC_2017 differs significantly from BPIC_2019. To add further variety, we worked with more features in BPIC_2017 (10) than in BPIC_2019 (5). To observe how results depend on the training set size, we performed our experiments on different shares of the available training

---

[1] https://data.4tu.nl (4TU Centre for Research Data).

[2] https://data.4tu.nl/articles/dataset/BPI_Challenge_2017/12696884.

[3] https://data.4tu.nl/articles/dataset/BPI_Challenge_2019/12715853.

[4] https://data.4tu.nl/collections/BPI_Challenge_2020/5065541.

[5] A theoretical possibility of data leakage remains. In reality, some case variables such as "Amount" are possibly unknown at the beginning of the case, even though every event log has a value for them.

samples for both large datasets (keeping the same test sets), ranging from 0.1% to 100%. Table 1 shows the respective datasets' key statistics and illustrates their differences.

Table 1. Statistics of the used datasets.

Dataset	Avg. case length	Share of events used	Training events	Validation events	Test events	Range features	Categorical features	Levels
BPIC_2017	38.5	.001	629	220	181, 189	5	5	113
		.002	1,286	363				
		...	...	...				
		.5	327,959	79,190				
		1	655,271	159,306				
BPIC_2019	5.2	.001	625	192	162, 753	3	2	18
		.002	1,263	341				
		...	...	...				
		.5	328,994	85,622				
		1	657,187	171,724				
Intl. declarations	29.6	1	57	20	4, 416	3	3	18
Travel costs	7.7	1	1,706	412	1, 652	5	9	74
Permits	10.0	1	8,030	2,132	6, 537	5	9	94
Payments	5.3	1	21,049	5,743	3, 746	4	8	107
Domestic declarations	8.1	1	23,434	6,216	3, 533	4	6	66

Range features were standardized. The number of levels of categorical variables was not clipped (non-frequent labels may be a reason for uncertain estimates). The labels were mapped to integers that were then passed to an embedding layer in the neural networks. All possible prefixes were derived from the cases and then standardized to a pre-determined *sequence length* by padding the shorter and truncating the longer ones. All experiments were coded in Python/Pytorch and ran on a desktop with a 3.50 Ghz CPU, 64 Gb of RAM and GeForce 1080 GPU. Our code is published on GitHub[6] for reproducibility. The metric used was the mean absolute error (MAE).

4.3   Estimating the Epistemic, Aleatoric and Total Uncertainty

In the case of BNNs, we performed $T = 50$ stochastic forward passes (MC sampling) for every prefix in the test set, each time with a different mask over the weights, by sampling a different ϵ for every ω at every run (as per Eq. 3). The final predictions are the averages over these 50 samples, discussed in Sect. 5. Using their variance, we calculated the model's uncertainty, i.e. the epistemic uncertainty, for every prediction in the test set using $\boxed{3}$ in Eq. 4. Moreover, we computed the per-point aleatoric uncertainty in an additional final dense layer in the models and included it in the loss function as in Eq. 5. We added together both types of uncertainty to calculate the total uncertainties used in Subsect. 5.2 and Sect. 6. All predictions in the following are averages of 20 runs of the respective models.

---

[6] https://github.com/hansweytjens/uncertainty-remaining_time.

4.4   Base Case

Despite the widespread use of public datasets in predictive process monitoring, assessing the quality of different methods remains hard as the filtering of the datasets, other preprocessing steps, model architectures, etc. are far from uniform across papers. Furthermore, the metrics used allow for comparisons of the methods within a paper but fail to convey an intuition about their absolute merits. To remedy the latter, we included the transition system-based method [2] as a baseline in our experiments.

5   Results

5.1   Overall Performance

We investigated whether the techniques in Subsect. 3.4 contribute to achieving more accurate point estimates. The results are summarized in Fig. 2 in which every row pertains to a dataset (BPIC_2017, BPIC_2019, BPIC_2020 respectively). Every column compares two or more techniques and will be discussed in the five following subsections. The horizontal axis in the graphs for BPIC_2017 and BPIC_2019 represents the share of the available training set that was used for training, ranked from small to large. In the last row, however, it is the five sub-datasets that are ranked from small to large. The vertical axis represents the models' MAE, with the scale being shared throughout the respective rows. Note that we normalized the MAE in the last row, with the respective base cases equal to one.

Loss Attenuation Inconclusive (Fig. 2: Column 1). We found no evidence in our experiments for the theoretically-derived hypothesis that learning the heteroscedastic uncertainty and using it by introducing loss attenuation (Eq. 5) in the loss functions leads to more accurate predictions. The black lines in Fig. 2 represent the plain-vanilla NNs, whereas the cyan lines stand for models including the technique. Results on BPIC_2017 and BPIC_2020 significantly worsened. Only in the case of BPIC_2019 did the technique lower MAE. Two effects could explain that. First, the added complexity may require larger datasets. Second, for datasets with rather homoscedastic aleatoric noise, or datasets with a rather randomly distributed heteroscedastic aleatoric noise, one cannot expect superior results from introducing loss attenuation. We did not further investigate this matter. Nevertheless, learning heteroscedastic uncertainty is indispensable for judging the quality of predictions. We will treat this in Subsect. 5.2.

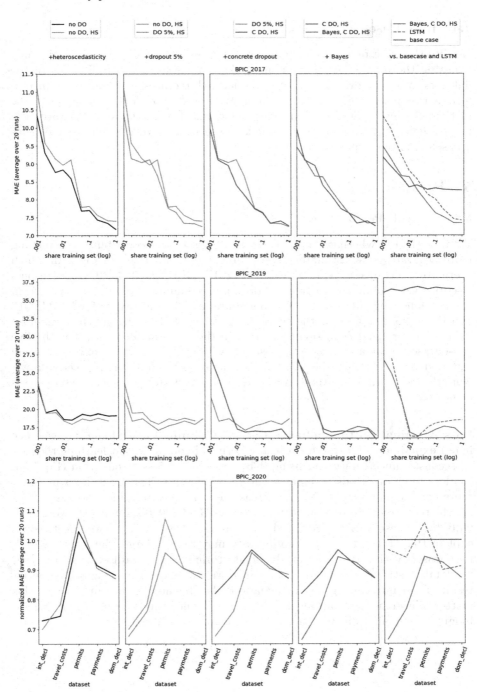

Fig. 2. Overall results on complete test sets. no DO: no dropout = plain-vanilla NN, HS: heteroscedastic, DO 5%: 5% dropout probability, C DO: concrete dropout, Bayes: BNN. Rows show three datasets, stepwise different techniques in columns. BPIC_2020 results normalized with base case = 1.

Dropout Effectively Combats Overfitting (Fig. 2: Column 2). The heteroscedastic models are again represented by the cyan lines in column 2. They already included an early-stopping mechanism. But, since the validation sets were in certain cases very small, and some concept drift may exist in the datasets, some overfitting still happened. In line with expectations, the dropout mechanism (orange lines) successfully further reduced overfitting on practically all datasets and training set sizes.

Concrete Dropout Works for Medium to Large Datasets (Fig. 2: Column 3). When comparing classic dropout with a fixed dropout parameter (orange lines) to concrete dropout (blue lines), our experiments suggest that, for some very small to small datasets (BPIC_2019 < 1%, BPIC_2020), concrete dropout negatively affects the overall quality of the predictions. For all other datasets, concrete dropout appeared to work or even improve results as expected. The use of concrete dropout also eliminates the need for the expensive optimization of the dropout parameter(s) $p_{(i)}$ that requires part of the training set to be set aside as a validation set.

Bayesian Learning Improves Results for Very Small Datasets (Fig. 2: Column 4). Until now, we used deterministic NNs to arrive at such models using concrete dropout (blue lines). In column 4, we introduce stochastic NNs in the form of BNNs (green lines), that predict distributions of which the arithmetic averages yield point estimates. BPIC_2017 and especially BPIC_2020 support the claim that BNNs produce superior results for smaller datasets. For larger datasets, the effect is negligible, possibly slightly negative. As explained in Sect. 3, the variance of the produced distributions can be interpreted as a measure for the models' (epistemic) uncertainty, a property we use below. As mentioned in Sect. 3, BNNs by default add L2 regularization to the dropout models. Since the combination of these regularization techniques (in our case even with early-stopping on top) makes these models so robust to overfitting, it is recommended to build models with large capacity to avoid underspecification and train them sufficiently long.

CNNs Outperform LSTMs, BNNs Outperform the Base Cases (Fig. 2: Column 5). The models in columns 1–4 were all CNNs. When comparing the last one (BNN, full green line) with an otherwise identical LSTM model (dotted green line), it becomes apparent that the CNNs nearly always outperformed the LSTMs. Of course, the chosen architectures (number of layers, nodes, etc.) influenced these outcomes, but the results support similar findings in [19,20]. Unless otherwise mentioned, we will use these heteroscedastic Bayesian CNNs with concrete dropout in the remainder of this paper and simply refer to them as BNN. With the exception of shares of less than 2% of the BPIC_2017 dataset and of the BPIC_2019 Permits dataset, the BNNs outperformed the base cases.

5.2   Uncertainty Estimates

We analyze the quality of the total uncertainty estimates, focusing on their correlation with the quality of the predictions and on the reliability of confidence intervals based on them.

Certainty of Predictions Correlates Strongly with Accuracy. We ranked the predictions in the test set and then retained different shares of the predictions while rejecting the others for different uncertainty thresholds (100%, 75%, 50%, 25%, 10%, 5% best). Figure 3 shows how well this worked for all datasets and dataset sizes: higher uncertainty led to worse predictions, without fail. Unfortunately, the quality of the uncertainty estimates suffered together with the quality of the predictions when datasets became too small, thus also reducing the possibility to separate good from bad predictions as can be witnessed at the left end of the graphs in Fig. 3.

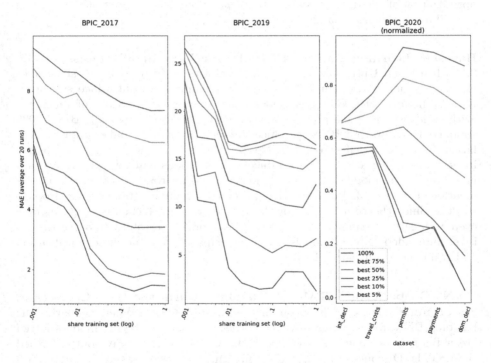

Fig. 3. We ranked the samples in the test sets based on the sum of the predicted epistemic and aleatoric uncertainties. In all three datasets, we observe lower MAE (better predictions) for lower levels of uncertainty. We used BNNs with concrete dropout and heteroscedasticity.

Predictions with Confidence Intervals. To build a confidence interval around a point estimate, the product of a so called *critical value* (z^* in statistics) and the uncertainty is added/subtracted to/from that point estimate to determine the upper/lower bound of the confidence interval. For each desired confidence level (50%, 75%, 90%, 95%, 99%) we computed the required critical value based on the last 5,000 samples in the training set. Since the BPIC_2017 dataset exhibits drift (changes over time), it did not suffice to determine these critical values only once: they had to be calculated online, as can be seen in the left part of Fig. 4. In the right part of Fig. 4, the real shares of true values in the respective confidence intervals are shown. They oscillate around their ideal values (horizontal lines), proving their reliability.

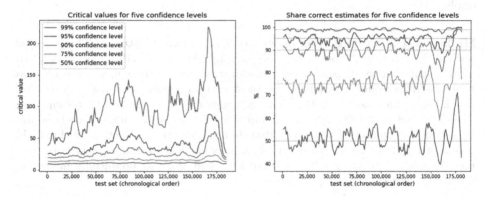

Fig. 4. Left: critical values for confidence levels of 50%, 75%, 90%, 95% and 99% computed on 5,000 preceding samples every 1,000th sample in the test set. Right: Corresponding share of true values in following 5,000 samples within the confidence interval. Dataset is BPIC_2017 (complete).

5.3   Computation Time

BNNs Train and Predict Relatively Fast. To gain an insight in the computation time of BNNs, we disabled the early stopping mechanism and trained the models for 20 epochs on the complete BPIC_2017 training set. Training the BNNs took around 335 s, approximately 38% more than the corresponding plain-vanilla deterministic models' 242 s. As inference requires MC sampling (we performed 50 MC forward passes), BNN predictions took longer (32 vs 0.65 s for all 181,189 test set points). Whilst in most settings the inference time is low enough to ignore, this may not be the case in certain online environments requiring near-instantaneous decisions.

Compared to plain-vanilla, deterministic models, the BNNs' hyperparameter space is definitely of a lower dimensionality. There is no need to determine values for the dropout parameter(s) p_i (assuming concrete dropout), model size (we can safely use large-capacity BNNs), number of epochs trained, etc. This may turn their small speed disadvantage into a considerable advantage.

CNNs Outspeed LSTMs. As already observed in previous work [20], CNNs train nearly an order of magnitude faster than LSTMs requiring non-parallelizable sequential calculations. The custom coding to implement dropout within the LSTM cells prevented us from using the very efficient standard PyTorch neural network libraries we used for the CNNs. As a result, our LSTM models slowed down even further and kept us from publishing a fair speed comparison in our specific setting.

6   Applications of Uncertainty

The knowledge of a prediction's quality opens the door to useful practical applications:

Higher Accuracy and Acceptance of Prediction Systems. The previous section demonstrated how the techniques we introduced will generally lead to more accurate overall predictions. However, a yet much higher accuracy can be reached by concentrating on the most certain predictions. An organization requiring a given accuracy threshold can now deploy a prediction system that does not reach that threshold overall but that is aware which of its predictions are expected to surpass it. Predictions that do not reach the (un)certainty threshold can be ignored or passed to humans or another system. In summary, not only can models produce better predictions, but they will also flag potentially incorrect, absurd or even dangerous predictions.

Improved Human-Machine Symbiosis. The ability to isolate inaccurate predictions permits two-track systems. Cases with good predictions remain on the automated track. Cases with predictions below an uncertainty threshold are passed to the human track. These latter cases will generally be the hardest to solve, more irregular, more interesting ones which could lead to more satisfying work for the involved humans and a better leverage of their cognitive faculties.

Working with Smaller Datasets: Earlier Adoption of Prediction Systems. As Figs. 2 and 3 show, the lack of data often leads to underperforming predictions systems. Organizations will not deploy them or delay their adoption until they feel their dataset is large enough. This may lead to a competitive disadvantage in this digital era requiring rapid innovations, speedy implementation and constant learning where waiting for perfection is no longer an option. The ability to identify predictions that meet a pre-set uncertainty threshold allows for a much faster adoption of prediction systems. Originally, only a relatively small share of the best predictions is actually used. But as the dataset grows, that share continually increases. During this phase-in period, the organization will gain invaluable information to further improve its systems and data collection otherwise lost when remaining on the sidelines.

Uncertainty-Based Analysis. The estimates of the predictions' uncertainty enables further analysis. For example, as in Fig. 5, we can plot the test set uncertainty in function of the prefix length and the real number of remaining days (unknown to the model). Given their high aleatoric uncertainty, the model is rightfully very uncertain about the prefixes of length one (first column). The model clearly gains in confidence when prefixes get longer, at least for the most common remaining time lengths (lower than 4 days, lowest four rows). When prefixes start getting longer than six events, the model becomes increasingly wary of its predictions again. Indeed, parts of the domain with fewer samples (e.g. prefix length > six events, real remaining time > 50 days) should have a higher epistemic, and hence total uncertainty. Outliers, such as the confident predictions of prefixes with length five or those in the second row (10–19 days) of prefix length one, deserve closer attention and may lead to interesting insights. Of course, the uncertainty can be plotted against any other feature as well. A detailed analysis falls outside this paper's scope.

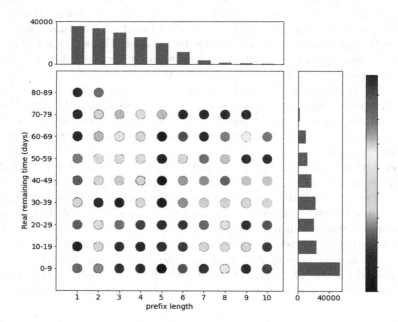

Fig. 5. BPIC_2019, 20% of training set: Uncertainty (blue = low, red = high) in function of prefix length and real number of remaining days. Grey bars indicate frequency of occurence. Prefix length cut of at 10, corresponding to >99% of samples in test set. (Color figure online)

7   Conclusion and Future Work

The stochastic Bayesian approach leads neural networks to predict distributions rather than point estimates. These distributions can be used both to derive more precise point estimates (mean) and to estimate the model's epistemic uncertainty (variance). It can be proven that BNNs are nearly identical to deterministic NNs with dropout, which makes them easy to implement. Concrete dropout renders optimizing the dropout parameters p_i obsolete. A dataset's heteroscedastic aleatoric noise can be learned in-model by means of a simple modification to the model and its loss function (loss attenuation). Whilst inconclusive on the benefits of loss attenuation, this paper shows how dropout, concrete dropout and BNNs generally contribute to more accurate remaining time predictions. CNNs prove to work better and faster than LSTMs. Not all of these techniques work well on all datasets: small datasets pose problems for concrete dropout while they benefit from the Bayesian models that themselves add no value with larger datasets. The presented techniques require little extra coding, learn nearly as fast and are less data-hungry than corresponding regular neural networks. Rather than improving overall accuracy, however, the main benefits of learning uncertainty reside with the new options this knowledge enables. Users can set thresholds to retain those predictions that meet any required accuracy, build confidence intervals around predictions, divide cases between computers and humans in a clever way, adopt prediction models earlier before huge datasets are collected, gain additional insights e.g. in the search for anomalies, etc. We hope that the techniques we proposed help remove some of the barriers that slow down or prevent the adoption of neural networks and could help to extract more value from information systems.

This new field of research can be extended in a variety of ways. First, the validity of our results should be tested on a diverse range of datasets to reach more general conclusions. Also other predictive process monitoring regression and classification problems are logical extensions. Dropout is not the only option to implement variational inference, other methods could be tested as well and may have other characteristics. We also believe that the knowledge of uncertainties can lead to more applications than the ones here presented. As we only concentrated on the total uncertainty, evaluating the respective merits of epistemic and aleatoric uncertainty constitutes another path for future research.

References

1. van Dongen, B.F., Crooy, R.A., van der Aalst, W.M.P.: Cycle time prediction: when will this case finally be finished? In: Meersman, R., Tari, Z. (eds.) OTM 2008. LNCS, vol. 5331, pp. 319–336. Springer, Heidelberg (2008). https://doi.org/10.1007/978-3-540-88871-0_22
2. Van der Aalst, W.M.P., Schonenberg, M.H., Song, M.: Time prediction based on process mining. Inf. Syst. **36**, 450–475 (2011)
3. Polato, M., Sperduti, A., Burattin, A., de Leoni, M.: Data-aware remaining time prediction of business process Instances. Presented at the (2014)

4. Tax, N., Verenich, I., La Rosa, M., Dumas, M.: Predictive business process monitoring with LSTM neural networks. Lecture Notes Computer Science, vol. 10253, pp. 477–492 (2017)
5. Navarin, N., Vincenzi, B., Polato, M., Sperduti, A.: LSTM networks for data-aware remaining time prediction of business process instances. arXiv:1711.03822v1 (2017)
6. Verenich, I., Dumas, M., La Rosa, M., Maggi, F.M., Teinemaa, I.: Survey and cross-benchmark comparison of remaining time prediction methods in business process monitoring. ACM Trans. Intell. Syst. Technol. (TIST) **10**(4), 1–34 (2019)
7. Kendall, A., Gal, Y.: What uncertainties do we need in Bayesian deep learning for computer vision? Presented at the (2017)
8. MacKay, D.: Bayesian methods for neural networks: theory and applications. In: Neural Networks Summer School. University of Cambridge (1995)
9. Gal, Y.: Uncertainty in deep learning: PhD thesis. University of Cambridge (2016). http://mlg.eng.cam.ac.uk/yarin/thesis/thesis.pdf
10. Kingma, D.P., Welling, M.: Auto-encoding variational Bayes. arXiv:1312.6114 (2014)
11. Srivastava, N., Hinton, G., Krizhevsky, A., Sutskever, I., Salakhutdinov, R.: Dropout: a simple way to prevent neural networks from overfitting. J. Mach. Learn. Res. **15**, 1929–1958 (2014)
12. Gal, Y., Ghahramani, Z.: Dropout as a Bayesian approximation: representing model uncertainty in deep learning. In: Proceedings of the 33rd International Conference on Machine Learning, vol. 48 (2016)
13. Gal, Y., Hron, J., Kendall, A.: Concrete dropout. Presented at the (2017)
14. Maddison, C.J., Mnih, A., Teh, Y.W.: The concrete distribution: a continuous relaxation of discrete random variables arXiv:1611.00712v3 (2017)
15. Gal, Y., Ghahramani, Z.: Bayesian convolutional neural networks with Bernoulli approximate variational inference. arXiv:1506.02158v1 (2015)
16. Gal, Y., Ghahramani, Z.: A theoretically grounded application of dropout in recurrent neural networks. Presented at the (2016)
17. Hochreiter, S., Schmidhuber, J.: Long short-term memory. Neural Comput. **9**(8), 1735–1780 (1997)
18. LeCun, Y., Bottou, L., Bengio, Y., Haffner, P.: Gradient-based learning applied to document recognition. Presented at the (1998)
19. Bai, S.J., Kolter, J.Z., Koltun, V.: An empirical evaluation of generic convolutional and recurrent networks for sequence modeling. arXiv:1803.01271v2 (2018)
20. Weytjens, H., De Weerdt, J.: Process outcome prediction: CNN vs. LSTM (with attention). Presented at the (2020)

Data- and Time-awareness in BPM

Zoom and Enhance: Action Refinement via Subprocesses in Timed Declarative Processes

Håkon Normann[1,2], Søren Debois[1,3(✉)], Tijs Slaats[2], and Thomas T. Hildebrandt[2]

[1] DCR Solutions, Copenhagen, Denmark
{normann,debois}@dcrsolutions.net
[2] Department of Computer Science, University of Copenhagen, Copenhagen, Denmark
{normann,slaats,hilde}@di.ku.dk
[3] Department of Computer Science, IT University of Copenhagen, Copenhagen, Denmark
debois@itu.dk

Abstract. This paper addresses the open technical problems of *evolving* executable, event-based process models by refinement, that is, by iteratively expanding a model until it has the required level of detail. Such iterative development is helpful because of the expectation that the next-step model is semantically compatible with the previous one, only with more detail. We provide in this paper a formal notion of refinement of single atomic actions (events) into entire subprocesses, and a theoretical framework for providing guarantees that such a next-step model is formally a refinement of the previous one. Our work is set within the declarative, event-based process modelling language of timed Dynamic Condition Response (DCR) graphs, which can express timed constraints (conditions with delay and obligations with deadlines) between events, liveness, safety, and concurrency. Concretely, we extend DCR graph syntax and semantics with a notion of subprocess, provide examples of its use, and give sound approximations of situations where replacing an event with a subprocess formally is a refinement of the original process.

Keywords: DCR graphs · Subprocesses · Action refinement · Decomposition

1 Introduction

Step-wise refinement [35] is a classical method in software development where systems and processes are defined in steps by iteratively refining their descriptions. This approach works particularly well when combined with decomposition, where one is able to maintain different levels of abstractions in a single program or model of a program. For example, one may start with a high-level view of the

© Springer Nature Switzerland AG 2021
A. Polyvyanyy et al. (Eds.): BPM 2021, LNCS 12875, pp. 161–178, 2021.
https://doi.org/10.1007/978-3-030-85469-0_12

system, describing only key activities, then refine this by replacing some activities with more detailed subprocesses, resulting in a hierarchical description.

To facilitate formal reasoning about the behaviour of software systems, a tight semantic connection between the system before refinement, and the one after is needed. Some notion of state machine refinement between (models of) the systems behaviour is a commonly used approach, for which a substantial literature exists for various modelling notations.

The present paper achieves step-wise refinement in the setting of timed declarative process models via the mechanism of (iteratively) expanding atomic events into entire subprocesses. From a modelling perspective, this approach is very natural: Refining a single event "approve expense reimbursement" is naturally refined into a subprocess involving a local manager, the accounting department, and an employee requesting a reimbursement. From a technical perspective, we show when such expansions can be formally guaranteed to uphold previous semantics via the theory of DCR graph refinement introduced in earlier work. This is a key advance of the present work: The majority of work on subprocesses in the declarative space is on their effect on understandability, e.g., [30,31,41,42]. Moreover, work on defining subprocesses in this space did not explain how to refine single actions into subprocesses *in a semantics preserving fashion*. E.g., [26,42] does discuss decomposition, but does not provide any formal refinement guarantees; conversely work on step-wise refinement of declarative models [11,12] did not provide clear tools for decomposition.

It is important to note that despite the similarity in name, the "process refinement" introduced in [11] and the "action refinement" introduced in the present paper are not the same concepts. Process refinement adds additional activities and constraints to a model, whereas action refinement replaces atomic actions (events) with (single instance) sub processes.

While the new notion of subprocess seemingly does not expand the expressiveness of DCR graphs, we show later that it does improve *conciseness*. Subprocesses as introduced in this paper have been implemented in the commercially available dcrgraphs.net DCR modelling tool suite used e.g. for case management systems in the public sector, and is a reasonably popular modelling construct: since July 2020, it was used in 564 models, representing ca. 9% of newly created models in that period[1].

In summary, we make the following contributions: 1. We define a new notion of compositional subprocess for DCR models, 2. We define a notion of semantics preserving *refinement* allowing the replacement of an atomic activity (event) with an entire subprocess, 3. We provide an efficiently decidable sufficient condition for such a replacement to be a refinement.

2 Timed DCR Graphs

DCR graphs were originally introduced [18] as a declarative workflow process model. The work was motivated by providing a formal foundation for case

---

[1] This number should be seen in light of the fact that subprocesses only become relevant in larger graphs, where compositionality matters.

management systems developed by our industrial partners, and the DCR notation is now supported by both commercial and academic modelling and simulation tools [8,22] and DCR variants have been embedded in commercial systems used by thousands of users in Denmark by both central government institutions such as universities and local government institutions such as municipalities [9,12].

Since their inception the DCR Graph modelling language has been extended in several ways, including modelling of time dependencies [19], inferring independence between events [10] resulting in a so-called true concurrent semantics, dynamically spawned multi-instance subprocesses and a theory of process refinement [11]. Presently, we extend timed DCR graphs from [19] with single-instance subprocesses and prove that it fits well with the theory of refinement [11]. We begin by recalling timed DCR Graphs:

Definition 1 ([19, Def. 3.2]). *A timed DCR Graph G is given by a tuple $(E, M, \rightarrow\!\bullet, \bullet\!\rightarrow, \rightarrow\!\diamond, \rightarrow\!+, \rightarrow\!\%, L, l)$ where*

(i) E is a finite set of events,
(ii) $M = (Ex, Re, In) \in ((E \rightarrow \omega) \times (E \rightarrow \infty) \times E)$ is the timed marking,
(iii) $\rightarrow\!\bullet\; \subseteq E \times \omega \times E$, is the timed condition relation,
(iv) $\bullet\!\rightarrow\; \subseteq E \times \infty \times E$, is the timed response relation,
(v) $\rightarrow\!\diamond, \rightarrow\!+, \rightarrow\!\% \subseteq E \times E$ are the milestone, include and exclude relations respectively,
(vi) L is the set of labels,
(vii) l is the labelling function between events and labels.

Technically, this definition slightly generalises the original one in allowing a pair of events to have multiple responses between them (with different deadlines), whereas the original definition allowed only one. The difference is immaterial, since we will later define that the most urgent deadline wins, however, the generalisation streamlines the presentation significantly.

We explain the definition by introducing our running example of a timed DCR graph in Fig. 1, representing a simple process for handling an expense report, from submission to potential payout. The nodes of a DCR graph is a set of labelled events E and the edges are relations determining the possible executions of events. This graph has four events $E = \{e_1, e_2, e_3, e_4\}$ labelled respec-

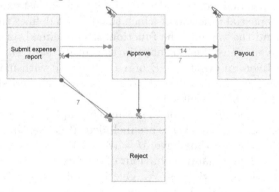

Fig. 1. Expense report

tively Submit expense report, Approve, Payout, and Reject and depicted as boxes with the label in the middle (the graphical notation does not show the identities e_i of the events). The relations $\rightarrow\!\bullet$ and $\bullet\!\rightarrow$ are the timed condition and response relations. We write $e \xrightarrow{k}\!\bullet e'$ for $(e, k, e') \in \rightarrow\!\bullet$, representing that e is a condition for e' with delay $k \in \omega$ meaning that the target event e' can not happen before k time steps[2] after the last execution of the source event e. We write $e \rightarrow\bullet e'$ for $e \overset{0}{\rightarrow}\bullet e'$, i.e. the delay is zero. Similarly write $e \overset{k}{\bullet\rightarrow} e'$ for $(e, k, e') \in\bullet\rightarrow$, representing that e' is a response to e with deadline k. Deadlines can be in the range $\infty = \omega \cup \{\omega\}$, i.e. a finite number or infinite ω, the latter meaning that the target event should happen eventually after the source event happens (or be excluded), allowing the specification of liveness properties, and write $e \bullet\rightarrow e'$ for $e \overset{\omega}{\bullet\rightarrow} e'$. The relation $\rightarrow\%$ is the exclude relation and the relation $\rightarrow+$ is the include relation. An exclusion (resp. inclusion) relation means that the targeted events is excluded (resp. included) from the graph when the source event happens. While excluded, an event cannot be executed, and any deadline on it and conditions from it are ignored. Finally, $\rightarrow\diamond$ is the milestone relation. The event pointed to by a milestone relation can not be executed if the source is included and pending.

We have a condition relation (with no delay) in the example from Submit expense report to Reject and Approve; these mean that the expense report can not be approved or rejected before it has been submitted. We have a timed condition relation from Approve to Payout with delay 7, meaning that Payout can happen at least 7 time steps after Approve. We have a response relation from Submit expense report to Reject with a deadline of 7; meaning that (Reject) must happen or be excluded within at most 7 time steps after the last execution of Submit expense report. Similarly, we have a response relation from Approve to Payout with a deadline of 14. Both Approve and Payout have an exclusion to themselves, so that each event can only happen once. Approve also has exclude relations to Submit expense report and Reject, which means that after approval the expense report can not be resubmitted or rejected anymore.

The marking M captures the current state of the DCR graph. A marking comprises three elements (Ex, Re, In) where $Ex : E \rightharpoonup \omega$ is partial function of which the domain defines the set of executed events and the value of the function, when defined, provides the time since the last execution of the event, $Re : E \rightharpoonup \infty$ is partial function of which the domain defines the set of pending response events and the value of the function, when defined, provides the deadline for when the event must be executed in the future, and $In \subseteq E$ the set of included events. Given an event $e \in E$ of a DCR graph with marking $M = (Ex, Re, In)$, we let $e \in Ex$ be short for $Ex(e)$ being defined and similarly let $e \in Re$ be short for $Re(e)$ being defined.

The marking of the example graph has no executed events and no pending events and all events are included. Representing the functions Ex and Re as sets of pairs we thus have $M = (\emptyset, \emptyset, E)$.

The dynamic behaviour of a DCR graph is defined by advancing time or execution of activities. We give in Table 1 below an example of a run of the DCR Graph in Fig. 1 and define the formal semantics in Definition 5 in the following section. Each row defines a marking, with the top row being the initial marking

---

[2] A time step is a discrete duration of time orthogonal to the execution of events. A time step can represent any duration, examples being a computers clock cycle, a day or a year. For the examples in this paper a time step is a day.

where all four events are included and no event has been executed or is pending. The left-most column indicates the steps between markings. Whenever an activity is executed, the marking is changed according to the include/exclude and pending relations from that activity (changes are indicated by a dark grey box).

For instance, the first step is the execution of Submit, setting the time since execution of Submit to 0 and the response deadline for Reject to 7. The next step advances time by 3, increasing the time since execution for Submit and decreasing the deadline for Reject correspondingly. Time can not advance past a deadline of an included event. The time since execution is used together with the delays on condition relations to determine when events become enabled and only increased to the maximum possible delay, which in the example is 7. E.g., in the second last step where the time is advanced by 8, the time since execution of the previously executed events is set to 7 regardless of when they were executed. An important consequence is that timed DCR graphs are finite state systems [19].

Table 1. Example evolution of the marking of the process of Fig. 1.

	Submit			Approve			Reject			Payout		
	Ex	Re	In	Ex	Re	In	Ex	Re	In	Ex	Re	In
(initial marking)	$\bot$	$\bot$	$\top$	$\bot$	$\bot$	$\top$	$\bot$	$\bot$	$\top$	$\bot$	$\bot$	$\top$
Submit	0	$\bot$	$\top$	$\bot$	$\bot$	$\top$	$\bot$	7	$\top$	$\bot$	$\bot$	$\top$
Advance(3)	3	$\bot$	$\top$	$\bot$	$\bot$	$\top$	$\bot$	4	$\top$	$\bot$	$\bot$	$\top$
Reject	3	$\bot$	$\top$	$\bot$	$\bot$	$\top$	0	$\bot$	$\top$	$\bot$	$\bot$	$\top$
Advance(1)	4	$\bot$	$\top$	$\bot$	$\bot$	$\top$	1	$\bot$	$\top$	$\bot$	$\bot$	$\top$
Submit	0	$\bot$	$\top$	$\bot$	$\bot$	$\top$	1	7	$\top$	$\bot$	$\bot$	$\top$
Advance(4)	4	$\bot$	$\top$	$\bot$	$\bot$	$\top$	5	3	$\top$	$\bot$	$\bot$	$\top$
Approve	4	$\bot$	$\bot$	0	$\bot$	$\bot$	5	3	$\bot$	$\bot$	14	$\top$
Advance(8)	7	$\bot$	$\bot$	7	$\bot$	$\bot$	7	0	$\bot$	$\bot$	6	$\top$
Payout	7	$\bot$	$\bot$	7	$\bot$	$\bot$	7	0	$\bot$	0	$\bot$	$\bot$

3   Timed DCR Graphs with Subprocesses

We now formally extend the syntax and semantics of timed DCR graphs to encompass also subprocesses. Definitions in this section are all new and generalise timed DCR graphs without subprocesses [19], except in the few cases where definitions can be carried over unchanged; these definitions are marked out as such. Subprocesses are represented by a partial function sp which tells us what the *subprocess parent*, if any, of a given activity is.

Definition 2. *A timed DCR Graph with subprocesses G is given by a tuple $(E, M, \rightarrow\bullet, \bullet\rightarrow, \rightarrow\diamond, \rightarrow+, \rightarrow\%, L, l, sp)$ where*

(i) $(E, M, \rightarrow\bullet, \bullet\rightarrow, \rightarrow\diamond, \rightarrow+, \rightarrow\%, L, l)$ is a timed DCR Graph and
(ii) $sp \in E \rightharpoonup E$ is a partial function for which sp^+ is irreflexive.

We define the set of atomic events E_a *as those that do not have children, and dually the set of* subprocess events E_s *as those that do have children, formally* $E_a = \{e \mid sp^{-1}(e) = \emptyset\}$ *and* $E_s = \{e \mid sp^{-1}(e) \neq \emptyset\}$. *Finally, the* top-level events E_t *are those with no parents, i.e.,* $E_t = \{e \mid sp(e) = \bot\}$.

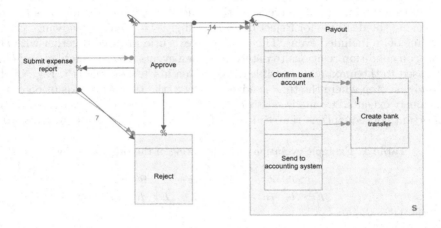

Fig. 2. Expense report where Payout has been expanded through refinement

To give an example, we add in Fig. 2 a subprocess to the Fig. 1. Here, we have expanded the event e_3 labelled Payout in the example of Fig. 1 to be a subprocess containing three events labelled Confirm bank account, Send to accounting system and Create bank transfer. Technically, the three new events have been added to the graph and $sp(-)$ is undefined except at those new events, where it is defined to be e_3. In Sect. 4 we will see that this is an example of a refinement: In a formal sense, the possible behaviours of the refined model correspond exactly to the possible behaviours of the old.

To get to that point, we must first account for what is the behaviour of a timed DCR graph with subprocesses. The intuition is that a subprocess adds detail: it shows the actual (sub-)process necessary to perform to executed what was previously abstracted into a single step. In that sense, it is natural that both those steps commencing and completing must obey the constraints on the subprocess event itself: the internal events of the subprocess can take steps iff the event the subprocess replaces is allowed to.

We formalize this in the definition of enabledness of an event contained in a subprocess depends on the enabledness of the subprocess. That is, in Fig. 2, the Payout subprocess event cannot execute before Approve has, because of the condition between the two. We define that the events *inside* a subprocess (Payout) may not execute unless the subprocess itself can. From Fig. 2 we can see that until a Payout has been approved, it makes no sense to send the expense report to the accounting system.

Definition 3 (Ancestors). *Let G be a timed DCR graph with subprocesses with events E. The set of ancestors of an event $e \in E$ is defined as* ancestors$(e) = \{e' \mid \exists k \geq 0.sp^k(e) = e'\}$*, i.e. the reflexive transitive closure of e under sp.*

Moreover, we need to define when a subprocess has completed, e.g., when do we consider Payout complete. For this, we use *acceptance* of DCR graphs: no included event is pending (required). When an activity in a sub process is executed and the marking of the events in the subprocess is accepting, the subprocess itself executes. Next we define that an event is *effectively included* if it is included and all its ancestors are included, and similarly, it is *effectively pending* if it is pending and all its ancestors are pending. In the example graph in Fig. 2, Create bank transfer is effectively included and pending, but not effectively pending. This means that the overall graph is accepting. But if an expense report is submitted and approved, Payout becomes pending (and effectively pending), and therefore Create bank transfer becomes effectively pending.

Definition 4 (Effectively included and pending events). *Let G be a timed DCR graph with subprocesses and marking (Ex, Re, In). Define the set of effectively included events as $In^\star = \{e \mid$ ancestors$(e) \subseteq In\}$. Define the set of effectively pending events as $Re^\star = \{e \mid$ ancestors$(e) \subseteq Re\}$*

We can now define when events and time steps in a timed DCR graph with subprocesses are *enabled*, i.e. when they can be executed.

Definition 5 (Event and time step enabling). *Let $G = (E, M, \rightarrow\bullet, \bullet\rightarrow, \rightarrow\diamond, \rightarrow+, \rightarrow\%, L, l, sp)$ be a timed DCR graph with subprocessses. An event $e \in E$ is* enabled *for the marking M, writing* enabled(M, e) *if and only if:*

1. $e \in In^\star$
2. $\forall e' \in In^\star. e' \xrightarrow{k}\bullet e \implies (e' \in Ex \wedge k \leq Ex(e'))$
3. $\forall e' \in In^\star. e' \rightarrow\diamond e \implies Re(e') = \bot$
4. $sp(e) \neq \bot \implies$ enabled$(M, sp(e))$

For $n \in \omega$ we say that the time step n is enabled, *written* enabled(M, n)*, if $miner_G \geq n$, where $miner_G = min\{Re(e) \mid \exists e \in Re^\star \cap In^\star\}$ is the minimal response deadline on an effectively included and effectively pending event.*

The conditions state that for an event e to be enabled, (1) it and all its ancestors must be included. (2) Whenever e is conditional upon an effectively included event e' with delay k, then this e' was executed at least k time steps ago. (3) No effectively included milestone e' for e is pending. (4) If e is contained in a subprocess then that subprocess must be enabled. A time step n denotes that time advances n steps and can only happen if there are no effectively included pending events with deadline less than n.

The definition of enabledness conservatively extends the definition of enabledness in timed DCR graphs without subprocesses. I.e., for DCR graphs that have no subprocesses, enabledness in the present sense is identical to the one of original timed DCR graphs:

Lemma 6. *Given a graph G with no subprocesses ($sp(e) = \bot$ for all e), and event e is enabled according to Definition 5 iff it is enabled under the definition of enabledness for timed DCR graphs [19, Def. 3.3].*

In Fig. 2, only the event Submit expense report is enabled, the other events are blocked by conditions or are blocked because they are a part of the Payout subprocess which is not itself enabled. We can take timesteps of any length. However, if we were to execute Submit expense report, then the maximum allowed timestep would be 7, as there would be a timed pending response on Reject.

Below we define the immediate effect of executing an event e for a given marking M. First we introduce some notation for updating markings.

Notation. *When $f : X \to Y$ is a (possibly partial) function, we write $f[x \mapsto y]$ for the function $f' : X \to Y$ which is identical to f, except $f'(x) = y$. We apply this notation also to sets, taking $f[x \mapsto y \mid P(x,y)]$ to be the function f' which is identical to f except that $f'(x) = y$ for all x, y satisfying the given predicate $P(x,y)$.*

We now define the effect of executing an event. The definition is morally equivalent to the original [19, Def. 3.3]]; however, since we allow multiple responses between a single pair events (see comments before Definition 1), we generalise the original definition to specify that one always chooses the most urgent deadline if there are more than one.

Definition 7 ([19, Def. 3.3]). *For a timed DCR graph G with marking $M = (Ex, Re, In)$ define the immediate effect of executing an enabled event e to be the marking $\text{effect}_G(M, e) = (Ex', Re', In')$ where*

$$Re' = Re[e \mapsto \bot][e' \mapsto k \mid \exists k'. \ e \overset{k'}{\bullet\!\!\to} e' \wedge k = min\{k' \mid e \overset{k'}{\bullet\!\!\to} e'\}]$$
$$Ex' = Ex[e \mapsto 0]$$
$$In' = (In \setminus (e \to\!\!\%)) \cup (e \to\!\!+)$$

The result is a new marking where the time since the last execution of the event e is set to 0, the event e is added to the set of executed events, the event e is first set to be non pending, and afterwards all new responses are added with their respective deadlines, and the set of included events is updated such that any excluded events are removed and any newly included events are added.

The immediate effect of executing Submit expense report in Fig. 2 would be to set Submit expense report as executed with timestamp 0 and Reject as pending with timestamp 7.

Compared to classical DCR graphs, the execution of an event e in a DCR graph with subprocesses can give rise to a cascading execution of subprocess events in the same atomic step. This is because the subprocess $sp(e)$ executes when e executes, if the graph contained in $sp(e)$ enters an accepting state by the execution of e.

We will need a notion of a subprocess being *accepting*. An accepting subprocess (or DCR graph) is ready to terminate, but can choose to take additional steps. To generalise the notion of acceptance to both subprocesses and DCR graphs, we will use the following definitions.

Definition 8 (Accepting graph). *A timed DCR graph with subprocesses G is accepting in marking $M = (Ex, Re, In)$, written $\mathsf{accept}(M, G)$, when $e \in E_t \cap In \implies e \notin Re$, i.e. no included top-level event is pending.*

We then define projection of graphs.

Definition 9 (Projection graph). *Let G be a DCR graph with events E, and let $X \subseteq E$ be a set of events. The projection of G to X, written $G|_X$ is defined as $G|_X = (E \cap X, R|_X, (Ex \cap X \times \omega, Re \cap X \times \infty, In \cap X), sp \cap X \times X)$ where a relation $r \in R$ is projected pointwise, that is, $r|_X = r \cap X \times X$.*

Definition 10 (Acceptance). *A subprocess event e is accepting in a marking M for a graph G written $\mathsf{accept}_G(e, M)$ when $G|_{e\downarrow}$ is accepting, where $e\downarrow = \{e' \in E \mid e \in \mathsf{ancestors}(e')\}$.*

While, in Fig. 2, the subprocess Payout is not accepting because of the pending response on Create bank transfer, the whole graph is accepting because Payout is not itself pending. After executing Submit expense report the graph will no longer be accepting as Reject will be pending.

We can now define the full effect of executing an event in a DCR graph with subprocesses, including potential ancestor subprocess executions.

Notation. *We let $\tilde{e}$ denote a finite, nonempty sequence $\tilde{e} = e_1, \ldots, e_n$ of events, and write $\mathsf{hd}(\tilde{e})$ for e_1, the head of the sequence, and $\tilde{f} \cdot \tilde{e}$ for concatenation.*

Definition 11. *We define the recursive event application function $\mathsf{apply}(M, e)$ as follows*

$$\mathsf{apply}(M, \tilde{e}) = \begin{cases} \mathsf{apply}(M', e' \cdot \tilde{e}) & \text{when } sp(e_1) = e' \wedge \mathsf{enabled}(e', M') \wedge \mathsf{accept}(e', M') \\ (M', \tilde{e}) & otherwise \end{cases}$$

for $e_1 = \mathsf{hd}(\tilde{e})$ and $M' = \mathsf{effect}_G(M, e_1)$

The $\mathsf{apply}(M, \tilde{e})$ function executes the head event $e_1 = \mathsf{hd}(\tilde{e})$ of the sequence $\tilde{e}$ in the marking M. If e_1 belongs to a parent subprocess event $e' = sp(e_1)$, which is enabled and accepting after executing the event e_1, then e' is added to the sequence of executed events $\tilde{e}$ and the apply function is applied recursively.

In our example graph, if we have previously executed Submit expense report and Approve, then Payout becomes enabled. We can now execute Confirm bank account and Send to Accounting System, followed by Create bank transfer, after which Payout will execute automatically as the subprocess enters an accepting state by satisfying the pending response.

Finally from parts of Definition 3.3 in [19] we recall the definition of how time advances.

Definition 12 (Time step, [19, Def. 3.3]). *We define the result of advancing time with n for some marking $M_t = (Ex, Re, In)$ by* $\text{effect}_G(M_t, n) = (Ex \oplus n, Re \ominus n, In)$ *where* $(Ex \oplus n)(e) = min\{Ex(e) + n, maxc_G\}$ *and* $(Re \ominus n)(e) = max\{Re(e) - n, 0\}$.

Here, for a time step of length n, the time since the last execution of all events is increased by n up-to the maximum delay on any condition in the graph, the deadline on responses is decreased by n or set to 0, if the deadline is less than n. As also explained in Sect. 2, the limits on these operations ensure that there is a finite number of reachable markings for any graph, meaning that also the transition system has a finite state space. Also note that time can only advance if the time step is enabled.

Lemma 13. *The LTS for any finite timed DCR Graph G has a finite number of reachable states.*

Proof. Consider the set of possible markings of a finite timed DCR graph. For each event, the marking records last executed time, current deadline, and inclusion state. The latter is boolean and so obviously finite. The current deadline is an integer value limited by the largest deadline on any response relation in the graph, and so bounded by some integer d. (see Definition 12.) The executed time is bounded by the largest delay found on any condition relation in the graph, and so bounded by some integer c. (see again Definition 12.) Altogether, all three components of the marking are finite, hence the set of states of the LTS is finite.

We are now ready to define the transition semantics of DCR Graphs. Transitions are labelled by either a time step n or a lists of events $\tilde{e} = e_1 \ldots e_n$, where e_n is an atomic event, potentially preceded by ancestors.

Definition 14 (Transitions). *Let $G = (E, M, \rightarrow\bullet, \bullet\rightarrow, \rightarrow\diamond, \rightarrow+, \rightarrow\%, L, l, sp)$ and $G' = (E, M', \rightarrow\bullet, \bullet\rightarrow, \rightarrow\diamond, \rightarrow+, \rightarrow\%, L, l, sp)$ be timed DCR graphs with subprocesses. For e an atomic event $e \in E_a$ there is an event transition $G \xrightarrow{\tilde{e}} G'$ iff* $\text{enabled}(M, e)$ *and* $\text{apply}(M, e) = (M', \tilde{e})$. *There is a time step transition $G \xrightarrow{n} G'$ iff* $\text{enabled}(M, n)$ *and* $\text{effect}_G(M, n) = M'$. *Let α range over $E^+ \cup \omega$, i.e. event transitions and time steps.*

The runs of a timed DCR graph with subprocesses is then defined as follows.

Definition 15 (Runs). *A run of a timed DCR graph with subprocesses G is a finite or infinite sequence of transitions $G_0 \xrightarrow{\alpha_1} G_1 \xrightarrow{\alpha_2} G_2 \xrightarrow{\alpha_3} \cdots$ We write $Runs(G)$ for the set of all possible runs for a graph G.*

An example run of the graph EX of Fig. 2 is:

$$EX \xrightarrow{\text{Submit...}} EX_1 \xrightarrow{\text{Approve}} EX_2 \xrightarrow{\text{Confirm...}} EX_3 \xrightarrow{\text{Send...}} EX_4 \xrightarrow{\text{Payout, Create...}} EX_5$$

We then define the accepting runs of a DCR graph as follows.

Definition 16 (Accepting runs). *Let $\bar{\alpha}$ be a finite or infinite run $G_0 \xrightarrow{\alpha_1} G_1 \xrightarrow{\alpha_2} \cdots$ of length $k \in \infty$ with $M_i = (Ex_i, Re_i, In_i)$ the marking of G_i. We say that $\bar{\alpha}$ is accepting and write $\text{accept}_t(\bar{\alpha})$ iff*

(i) For all $i \leq k$ and all $e \in E_t$, if $e \in Re_i \cap In_i$, then for some $j > i$ we have $\alpha_j = e \cdot \tilde{e}$ or $e \notin Re_j \cap In_j$

(ii) If $\bar{\alpha}$ is infinite, it contains infinitely many time steps.

Here (i) captures that if a root element ever is pending and included it will eventually be executed or no longer pending and included. (ii) captures that an accepting run is non-zeno, i.e. only finitely many event transitions can happen between each time step transition. The example run shown above is accepting.

Definition 17 (Trace). *A trace t of a graph G is a sequence $\alpha_1, \alpha_2, \alpha_3, \cdots$ such that there exists an accepting run $G \xrightarrow{\alpha_1} G_1 \xrightarrow{\alpha_2} G_2 \xrightarrow{\alpha_3} \cdots$. We write $\text{Traces}(G)$ for the set of all possible traces in the graph G.*

Definition 18. *We say that a graph G with marking $M = (Ex, Re, In)$ is insertable if and only if 1) $Re(e) = k$ implies $k = \infty$, 2) $(e, k, e') \in \rightarrow\bullet$ implies $k = 0$, 3) forall markings M' reachable from M there exists a marking M'' reachable in one or more event steps from M' with $\text{accept}(M'', G)$.*

Condition 1) ensures that the insertable graph does not have any deadlines on pending events that may force the graph to enter an accepting state. Condition 2) on the other hand ensures, that the insertable graph does not force delays that may hinder the graph to enter an accepting state at the right time. Finally, condition 3) ensures that the insertable graph can always eventually make a step and enter an accepting state. In Fig. 2, the graph internal to subprocess Payout is insertable.

4   Refinement via Subprocess Expansion

In this section we show how we can formally extend a DCR Graph with new elements and how the expansion of an event into a more complex subprocess is one particular such extension. We then show how such an expansion is a form of action refinement and has the desirable property that it does not materially affect the language of the outer graph.

From the graph in Fig. 1 we obtain the graph in Fig. 2 by inserting the graph in Fig. 3. We shall see in this section why this is a "safe refinement".

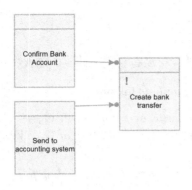

Fig. 3. Process of doing a bank transfer and ensuring it is accounted

A safe refinement means that we can take the set of traces from the new refined graph, project this trace to only the events in the original graph, and recover the set of traces possible in the original graph.

We immediately identify three preconditions for a refinement to be safe. First, the graph inserted by the refinement has to be able to reach an accepting state at some point in the future. Otherwise, the parent subprocess will never be executed, and no trace containing this event in the original graph can be simulated in the refined graph. Second, no conditions have delays. Otherwise, a delay inside the refined subprocess may make it take *longer* before the subprocess is executed than possible in the original graph, making any trace with the shorter time not possible in the refined graph. Third, there can not be any initial deadlines in the graph inserted. This is because it would potentially force the subprocess to execute earlier than it had to in the original graph.

We now generalise the notion of *composing* two DCR-graphs, orginally introduced in [13], to encompass also the present graphs with subprocesses.

Definition 19. *Let G, G' be DCR graphs with subprocesses and let u be a function on $E \cup E' \to E \cup E'$ such that $sp \cup sp' \subseteq u$ and u is acyclic when considered as a relation. Then the composition $G \mid_u G'$ of DCR-graphs G and G' under u is defined by pointwise union of all components:*

$$G \mid_u G' = (E \cup E', R \cup R', (Ex \cup Ex', Re \cup Re', In \cup In'), u)$$

We use composition to define expansion of an event into a subprocess:

Definition 20 (Insertion). *Let G_0 and G_1 be DCR graphs with subprocesses. Suppose $e \in G_0$ and $E_0 \cap E_1 = \emptyset$. We define the DCR-graph $G = \mathsf{insert}(G_0, e, G_1)$ to be the graph $G_0 \mid_u G_1$ where $u = sp_0 \cup sp_1 \cup \{(e', e) \mid e' \in E_{t_1}\}$.*

Note that when E, E' are disjoint, sp'' is clearly a function. In addition to the standard composition of graphs we set the event e to have all the root events of G' as its direct children.

Notation. *Given a string x, write $x\mid_Y$ for the string x with all elements $y \notin Y \cup \omega$ removed.*

We lift the notion of projection to apply to entire traces, by applying it pointwise on each label; and similarly for languages.

Definition 21 (Projection, language). *Let $t \in Traces(G)$ be a trace of G; write $t = (t_i)_{i \le n}$. The projection of t onto X is the sequence $t\mid_X = (t_i\mid_X)_{i \le n}$. The projection of the language $Traces(G)$ onto X is the set of so projected traces:*

$$Traces(G)\mid_X = \{t\mid_X \mid t \in Traces(G)\} .$$

Lemma 22. *Let G_1 be a DCR graph, let $e \in E_0$ be an atomic event of G_0, let G_1 be a DCR graph with $E_0 \cap E_1 = \emptyset$, and let $G = \mathsf{insert}(G_0, e, G_1)$. Suppose $G_1 \xrightarrow{t} G_1'$ with G_1' not accepting. If $G \xrightarrow{t} G'$ and t is not a timestep, we have that $G'|_{E_0} = G|_{E_0} = G_0$.*

Proof (sketch). Note that the marking of the events in the parent graph is not affected by an event execution inside the subprocess that leaves the subprocess in a not accepting state.

Lemma 23. *Let G_0 be a DCR graph, let $e \in E_0$ be an atomic event of G_0, let G_1 be an insertable DCR graph with $E_0 \cap E_1 = \emptyset$, and finally let $G = \mathsf{insert}(G_0, e, G_1)$. Then forall traces $t_0 \in Traces(G_0)$ there exists a trace $t \in Traces(G)$ such that $t|_{E_0} = t_0$.*

Proof (sketch). We can from Lemma 22 ignore all steps $s \in t$ where $s \cap E_1 = \emptyset$. Lemma 22 also allows us to insert any steps s' into t, $s' \cap E_1 = \emptyset$ without affecting the statement.

Lemma 24. *Let G_0 be a DCR graph, let $e \in E_0$ be an atomic event of G_0, let G_1 be an insert able DCR graph with $E_0 \cap E_1 = \emptyset$, and finally let $G = \mathsf{insert}(G_0, e, G_1)$. Then for all traces $t \in Traces(G)$, we have $t|_{E_0} \in Traces(G_0)$.*

Proof (sketch). This is true for the same reasons that Lemma 23 is, and because any transition inside G_1 is not visible in the projection.

This brings us to the main theorem of the paper: Insertion guaranteees refinement. If we expand an event to be a subprocess that is always finitely accepting, then we know for certain that the language of the top-level process does not change: if we project away subprocess events then any run that was previously allowed is still allowed, and no new runs will be introduced. The proof is immediate from Lemmas 23 and 24.

Theorem 25. *Let G_0 be a DCR graph, let $e \in E_0$ be an atomic event of G_0, let G_1 be an insertable DCR graph with $E_0 \cap E_1 = \emptyset$, and finally let $G = \mathsf{insert}(G_0, e, G_1)$. Then $Traces(G_0) = Traces(G)|_{E_0}$.*

Proof. By Lemma 23 $Traces(G_0) \subseteq Traces(G0)|_{E_0}$; from Lemma 24 it then follows that $Traces(G)|_{E_0} \subseteq Traces(G_0)$. But then $Traces(G_0) = Traces(G)|_{E_0}$

Because of this theorem, DCR graphs with subprocesses realises the modular design of processes: we can first model the process at a high level of granularity and then safely refine the model by expanding events into subprocesses, while being sure that desired properties at the high level will be maintained.

Corollary 26. *Let G_0 be a DCR graph, let $e \in E_0$ be an atomic event of G_0, and let G_1 be an insertable DCR graph with $E_0 \cap E_1 = \emptyset$. Then $G = \mathsf{insert}(G_0, e, G_1)$ is a refinement of G_0 in the sense of [11].*

Note that Theorem 25 is *stronger* than refinement as defined in [11]. To be a refinement, it is sufficient that all behaviour of the new model as allowed already in the old (new events not withstanding). However, Theorem 25 guarantees *also* that all old behaviour is *still* admitted by the new model.

In Fig. 1 Payout was a single event, which we expanded to a subprocess in Fig. 2. Let us examine more closely this expansion. Consider the subprocess of Fig. 3. This graph is clearly always insertable: we can do the bank transfer once we have confirmed the bank account and sent the necessary information to the accounting system. We can after we created a bank transfer the first time, do any event and the process will end in an accepting state. We also have that it does not contain any references to time initially so the requirement on delays and initial pending events holds. It follows that the graph in Fig. 3 satisfies in Definition 20. The graph in Fig. 2 is the result of this expansion. If we decide that instead of paying out with a bank transfer, we want to have the payout done with cash wire transfer, we can just replace the graph inside payout with a graph who models either of these ways of doing a payment. This kind of modularity has so far been missing in DCR graphs.

Finally, note that it is possible to introduce subprocesses as a refactoring of a process which is not a refinement, as exemplified in Fig. 4.

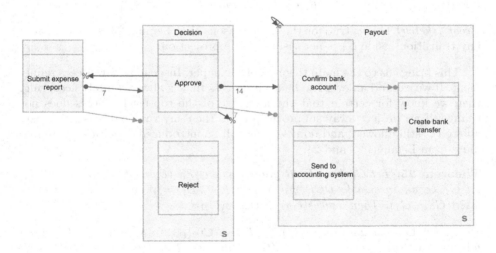

Fig. 4. Expense reimbursement with Decision refactored

5   Conclusions, Related and Future Work

We have in this paper introduced and demonstrated compositional, single instance subprocesses for timed DCR models that fits with a formal notion of action refinement. We provided an efficiently decidable sufficient condition for replacement of an event with a single-instance subprocess to be a refinement.

Related Work. The notion of hierarchical decomposition has been studied extensively for imperative process models, in particular Petri nets and Workflow nets [1,5,21,34,37]. Similarly, most work on refinement has focussed on imperative notations such as BPMN [2,14,20,24,36] and Petri nets [15,29,32]. While the underlying goal of achieving step-wise refinement in imperative and declarative notations is similar (to replace an high-level abstract activity by a more complex subprocess in a safe way), the foundational differences between the imperative and declarative paradigms manifest as different practical challenges to achieving this goal. In imperative notations one analyses flow to ensure that a subprocess behaves similarly and/or has similar entry and exit points as the original activity, but such a notion of flow does not exist for declarative notations. Instead we need to reason about constraints between activities, which may be internal and external to the subprocess and want to guarantee that the constraints after a change are a refinement of the constraints before the change.

Work on subprocesses and step-wise refinement for declarative notations include test-driven modelling [38,39], the introduction of subprocesses to declarative models [26,42] and empirical investigations into the understandability of such models [40,42]. However none of these works provide any formal refinement guarantees. Most closely related is HiDec [7], a hierarchical variant of Declare, which does support refinement, however, the authors show thatno straightforward restrictions on HiDec refinements guarantee safety.

Within the study of DCR graphs and processes, a notion of refinement was formally proposed in [12] and further studied in [11]. This notion has informed lots of subsequent work, e.g., it formed an important part of the theory of abstract tests in [27]. The notation of subprocesses here is similar to that of structured data in Reseda [6], which employs a language- instead of graph-based syntax and a different transition semantics.

Outside business process management, Glabbeek and Goltz have done seminal work on action refinement of true concurrency models [16,17,33] initiated the work on providing a semantic foundation for step-wise refinement by decomposition. We morally appropriate the concepts of action refinement and moves them from the setting of concurrency theory to declarative process modelling. Specifically, we extend the previously introduced declarative modelling language of timed Dynamic Condition Response (DCR) graphs [19] with a notion of subprocesses, which is shown to allow a formal definition of action refinement.

In this way we also advance upon earlier work on adding time perspectives to declarative process notations [3,4,19,25] and Petri nets, e.g. [23,28], which has not yet provided a unified semantics supporting both time constraints and a notion of sub processes supporting action refinement. Because of their marking-based semantics, DCR graphs are quite different from more logic-based approaches such as Declare, which operationalize their semantics through an encoding in other formalisms such as fLTL and regular expressions [3,4,25], and lack the dynamic aspect that the inclusion and exclusion relations bring. The notion of time used in timed DCR graphs, MP-Declare [4] and Time Petri Net [23] is similar, as both employ a point-based monotonic integer-time semantics. Still there are differences, e.g. delays and deadlines are specified on constraints in timed DCR graphs, while they are specified on transitions and relative to the enabling of the transition for Time Petri Nets. We conjecture, that while the results in this paper are not immediately applicable to Time Petri Nets, MP-Declare and other logic-based notations, they are likely to provide insights into how similar timed refinement results could be achieved.

Future Work. An expansion of the current work will be extend the formalisation to allow for interface events. This will potentially allow for both action refinement and fragmentation of more general graphs than what is possible now. More specifically it may allow for graphs with relations going in and out of a subprocess while still providing some form of refinement guarantees.

References

1. Van der Aalst, W.M.: Decomposing petri nets for process mining: a generic approach. Distributed Parallel Databases **31**(4), 471–507 (2013)
2. Ayari, S., Ben Dali Hlaoui, Y., Jemni Ben Ayed, L.: A new approach for the verification of BPMN models using refinement patterns (2018)
3. Barba, I., Lanz, A., Weber, B., Reichert, M., Del Valle, C.: Optimized time management for declarative workflows (2012)
4. Burattin, A., Maggi, F.M., Sperduti, A.: Conformance checking based on multi-perspective declarative process models. Expert Syst. Appl. **65**(C), 194–211 (2016)
5. Choi, Y., Zhao, J.L.: Decomposition-based verification of cyclic workflows (2005)
6. Costa Seco, J., Debois, S., Hildebrandt, T., Slaats, T.: Reseda: Declaring live event-driven computations as reactive semi-structured data (Oct 2018)
7. De Masellis, R., Di Francescomarino, C., Ghidini, C., Maggi, F.M.: Declarative process models: Different ways to be hierarchical (2016)
8. Debois, S., Hildebrandt, T.: The DCR workbench: declarative choreographies for collaborative processes. In: Gay, S., Ravara, A. (eds.) Behavioural Types: From Theory to Tools, pp. 99–124. River Publishers, June 2017
9. Debois, S., Hildebrandt, T., Marquard, M., Slaats, T.: Hybrid process technologies in the financial sector: the case of BRFkredit. In: Business Process Management Cases, pp. 397–412. Management for Professionals, Springer, Cham (2017)
10. Debois, S., Hildebrandt, T., Slaats, T.: Concurrency and asynchrony in declarative workflows. In: Motahari-Nezhad, H.R., Recker, J., Weidlich, M. (eds.) BPM 2015. LNCS, vol. 9253, pp. 72–89. Springer, Cham (2015). https://doi.org/10.1007/978-3-319-23063-4_5
11. Debois, S., Hildebrandt, T.T., Slaats, T.: Replication, refinement & reachability: complexity in dynamic condition-response graphs. Acta Informatica **55**(6), 489–520 (2018)
12. Debois, S., Slaats, T.: The analysis of a real life declarative process. In: SSCI 2015, pp. 1374–1382. IEEE (2015)
13. Debois, S., Hildebrandt, T.T., Slaats, T.: Hierarchical declarative modelling with refinement and sub-processes (2014)
14. Decker, G., Kopp, O., Leymann, F., Pfitzner, K., Weske, M.: Modeling service choreographies using BPMN and bpel4chor (2008)

15. Ding, Z., Jiang, C., Zhou, M.: Design, analysis and verification of real-time systems based on time petri net refinement. ACM Trans. Embed. Comp. Syst. **12**(1), 1–18 (2013)
16. van Glabbeek, R., Goltz, U.: Equivalence notions for concurrent systems and refinement of actions (1989)
17. van Glabbeek, R., Goltz, U.: Refinement of actions in causality based models (1989)
18. Hildebrandt, T., Mukkamala, R.R.: Declarative event-based workflow as distributed dynamic condition response graphs. In: Post-Proceedings of PLACES 2010. EPTCS, vol. 69, pp. 59–73 (2010)
19. Hildebrandt, T.T., Mukkamala, R.R., Slaats, T., Zanitti, F.: Contracts for cross-organizational workflows as timed dynamic condition response graphs. J. Log. Algebr. Program. **82**(5–7), 164–185 (2013)
20. Horita, H., Honda, K., Sei, Y., Nakagawa, H., Tahara, Y., Ohsuga, A.: Transformation approach from kaos goal models to BPMN models using refinement patterns (2014)
21. Lee, K., Favrel, J.: Hierarchical reduction method for analysis and decomposition of petri nets. IEEE Trans. Syst. Man Cybern. **SMC-15(2)**, 272–280 (1985)
22. Marquard, M., Shahzad, M., Slaats, T.: Web-based modelling and collaborative simulation of declarative processes (2015)
23. Merlin, P., Farber, D.: Recoverability of communication protocols - implications of a theoretical study. IEEE Trans. Commun. **24**(9), 1036–1043 (1976)
24. Polyvyanyy, A., Weidlich, M., Weske, M.: Isotactics as a foundation for alignment and abstraction of behavioral models (2012)
25. Schönig, S., Zeising, M.: The DPIL framework: tool support for agile and resource-aware business processes. BPM (Demos) **1418**, 125–129 (2015)
26. Slaats, T., Schunselaar, D.M., Maggi, F.M., Reijers, H.A.: The semantics of hybrid process models (2016)
27. Slaats, T., Debois, S., Hildebrandt, T. T.: Open to Change: A Theory for Iterative Test-Driven Modelling (2018)
28. Srba, J.: Comparing the expressiveness of timed automata and timed extensions of petri nets. In: Cassez, F., Jard, C. (eds.) FORMATS 2008. LNCS, vol. 5215, pp. 15–32. Springer, Heidelberg (2008). https://doi.org/10.1007/978-3-540-85778-5_3
29. Suzuki, I., Murata, T.: A method for stepwise refinement and abstraction of petri nets. J. Comput. Syst. Sci. **27**(1), 51–76 (1983)
30. Turetken, O., Dikici, A., Vanderfeesten, I., Rompen, T., Demirors, O.: The influence of using collapsed sub-processes and groups on the understandability of business process models. Bus. Inf. Sys. Eng., 1–21 (2019)
31. Turetken, O., Rompen, T., Vanderfeesten, I., Dikici, A., van Moll, J.: The effect of modularity representation and presentation medium on the understandability of business process models in BPMN (2016)
32. Valette, R.: Analysis of petri nets by stepwise refinements. J. Comput. Syst. Sci. **18**(1), 35–46 (1979)
33. Van Glabbeek, R., Goltz, U.: Refinement of actions and equivalence notions for concurrent systems. Acta Informatica **37**(4–5), 229–327 (2001)
34. Weidlich, M., Polyvyanyy, A., Mendling, J., Weske, M.: Efficient computation of causal behavioural profiles using structural decomposition (2010)
35. Wirth, N.: Prog. development by stepwise refinement. CACM **14**(4), 221–227 (1971)
36. Wong, P.Y., Gibbons, J.: Formalisations and applications of BPMN. Sci. Comput. Programm. **76**(8), 633–650 (2011), special issue on the 7th Int'l Workshop on the Foundations of Coordination Lang. and Soft. Arch. (FOCLASA'08)

37. Zerguini, L.: A novel hierarchical method for decomposition and design of workflow models. J. Integr. Des. Process. Sci. **8**(2), 65–74 (2004)
38. Zugal, S., Pinggera, J., Weber, B.: Creating declarative process models using test driven modeling suite. In: Nurcan, S. (ed.) CAiSE Forum 2011. LNBIP, vol. 107, pp. 16–32. Springer, Heidelberg (2012). https://doi.org/10.1007/978-3-642-29749-6_2
39. Zugal, S., Pinggera, J., Weber, B.: The impact of testcases on the maintainability of declarative process models. Ent., Bus.-Proc. and Inf. Sys. Modelling, 163–177 (2011)
40. Zugal, S., Pinggera, J., Weber, B., Mendling, J., Reijers, H.A.: Assessing the impact of hierarchy on model - a cognitive perspective. In: EESSMod (2011)
41. Zugal, S., Soffer, P., Haisjackl, C., Pinggera, J., Reichert, M., Weber, B.: Investigating expressiveness and understandability of hierarchy in declarative business process models. Softw. Syst. Modeling **14**(3), 1081–1103 (2015)
42. Zugal, S., Soffer, P., Pinggera, J., Weber, B.: Expressiveness and understandability considerations of hierarchy in declarative business process models. In: Bider, I., Halpin, T., Krogstie, J., Nurcan, S., Proper, E., Schmidt, R., Soffer, P., Wrycza, S. (eds.) BPMDS/EMMSAD -2012. LNBIP, vol. 113, pp. 167–181. Springer, Heidelberg (2012). https://doi.org/10.1007/978-3-642-31072-0_12

Delta-BPMN: A Concrete Language and Verifier for Data-Aware BPMN

Silvio Ghilardi[1], Alessandro Gianola[2], Marco Montali[2], and Andrey Rivkin[2(✉)]

[1] Dipartimento di Matematica, Università degli Studi di Milano, Milan, Italy
silvio.ghilardi@unimi.it
[2] Free University of Bozen-Bolzano, Bolzano, Italy
{gianola,montali,rivkin}@inf.unibz.it

Abstract. The increasing recognition of the need for integrating data and processes, both at conceptual and system levels, raises a new demand in standard-friendly, verifiable data-aware process modelling languages. So far, a few proposals in the area have been largely focusing on either uncharted approaches or conceptual proposals that would lack in tool support. In this work, we propose delta-BPMN – a verifiable operational framework for data-aware processes that employs (block-structured) BPMN to capture the process backbone, and a SQL-based language for representing and manipulating volatile and persistent data. We also propose a proof-of-concept implementation of delta-BPMN by realising the front-end part in Camunda and the back-end in a framework that translates language specifications into the executable code of a state-of-the-art SMT-based model checker.

Keywords: Data-aware processes · BPMN · Model checking

1 Introduction

The integration between data and processes is a long-standing challenge in information systems engineering [14,19,21]. This comes with a number of difficulties. On the one hand, the model should be expressive enough to represent complex processes where data influence how the process control-flow routes cases, while the process tasks inspect and manipulate data. On the other hand, such expressiveness has to be suitably controlled towards enabling verification, execution, monitoring, and mining of such multi-perspective models. A third, orthogonal dimension concerns the choice of modeling constructs, which often depart from those offered by process and data modeling standards such as BPMN and SQL, in turn hampering the adoption of the resulting frameworks.

These three dimensions can be recognized in their full complexity when it comes to the *verification* of the resulting integrated models [5,10]. Verification is of particular importance in this spectrum, as even data and process models that appear correct when analyzed in isolation may lead to errors once integrated [18]. "Verifiability" of models is thus typically obtained by using abstract languages that do not adhere to well-established standards when it comes to the data and/or process component: either

© Springer Nature Switzerland AG 2021
A. Polyvyanyy et al. (Eds.): BPM 2021, LNCS 12875, pp. 179–196, 2021.
https://doi.org/10.1007/978-3-030-85469-0_13

the control-flow backbone of the process is captured using Petri nets or other mathematical formalisms for dynamic systems that cannot be directly understood using front-end notations such as BPMN, or the data manipulation part relies on abstract, logical operations that cannot be straightforwardly represented in concrete data manipulation languages such as SQL. At the same time, the repertoire of constructs used to model data-aware processes cannot cover these languages in their full generality, as verification becomes immediately undecidable if they are not suitably controlled [5]. A last crucial issue is that the vast majority of the literature in this spectrum mainly provides foundational results that do not directly translate into effective verification tools.

In this work, we tackle these limitations and propose delta-BPMN, an operational framework at once supporting modeling and verification of BPMN enriched with data management capabilities. delta-BPMN comes with a threefold contribution. First, we introduce the front-end data modeling and manipulation language PDMML, supported by delta-BPMN, which instantiates the data-related aspects of the abstract modeling language studied in [1] by using a SQL-based dialect to represent as well as manipulate volatile and persistent data, and show how it can be embedded into a (block-structured) fragment of BPMN that captures the process backbone. The features of PDMML are based on requirements for concrete, verifiable data-aware process modeling languages distilled from the literature. Second, we show how the delta-BPMN front-end can be realized in actual business process management systems, considering in particular Camunda[1], one of the most popular BPMN environments. Third, we report on the implementation of a translator that, building on the encoding rules abstractly defined in [1], takes a delta-BPMN model created in Camunda and transforms it into the syntax of MCMT[2], a state-of-the-art SMT-based model checker for infinite-state systems that can then be used for verification.

2   Requirement Analysis and Related Work

The integration of data and processes is a long-standing line of research at the intersection of BPM, data management, process mining, and formal methods. Since our focus is on verification, we circumscribe the relevant works to those dealing with the formal analysis of data-aware processes. As pointed out in the introduction, this is also crucial because the choice of language constructs is affected by the task one needs to solve - in particular, verifying such sophisticated models requires to suitably control the data and control-flow components as well as their interaction [5, 10].

A second important point is that the vast majority of the contributions in this line of research provide foundational results, but do not come with corresponding operational tools for verification. Hence, all in all, *we consider in this research only those approaches for the integration of data and processes that come with verification tool support*: VERIFAS [16], BAUML [11], ISML [18], dapSL [4], and the delta-BPMN approach considered here, which relies on the DAB formal model [1] as its foundational basis.

---

[1] https://camunda.com.

[2] http://users.mat.unimi.it/users/ghilardi/mcmt/.

We use these approaches to distill a series of important requirements on languages for verifiable data-aware processes, indicating which provide full (+), partial (+/−), or no support (−) for that requirement. The first two requirements concern verifiability, respectively capturing foundational and practical aspects.

RQ 1. The language should be operationally verifiable with a tool.   ◁

While the approaches above all come with an operational counterpart for verification, there are huge differences in how this support is provided. VERIFAS comes with an embedded, ad-hoc verification tool (+) that supports the model checking of properties expressed in a *fragment of first-order LTL*. BAUML encodes verification into a form of first-order satisfiability checking over the flow of time (+), defining a fixed set of *test cases* expressing properties to be checked as derived predicates. ISML relies on state-space construction techniques for Colored Petri nets, but in doing so it assumes that the data domains are all bounded (+/−); no specific verification language is defined, leaving to the user the decision on how to explore the state space. dapSL relies instead on an ad-hoc state-space construction that, under suitable restrictions, is guaranteed to faithfully represent in a finite-state way the infinite state space induced by the data-aware process; however, no additional techniques are defined to explore the state space or check temporal properties of interest (+/−). Finally, delta-BPMN encodes verification of *(data-aware) safety properties* (expressed in the language defined in [1]) into the state-of-the-art MCMT model checker (+).

Table 1. Requirements coverage (covered +, partially (+/−), not −)

Framework	RQ 1	RQ 2	RQ 3	RQ 4	RQ 5	RQ6	Verification logic
VERIFAS [16]	+	+	−	+	+	y	Fragment of LTL-FO
BAUML [11]	+	+/−	+	+	+	n	Fixed test cases
ISML [18]	+/−	−	+/−	+	+/−	n	State-space exploration
dapSL [4]	+/−	−	+/−	+	+/−	n	State-space exploration
delta-BPMN	+	+	+/−	+	+	y	Data-aware safety

The second requirement concerns the analysis of key properties (such as soundness, completeness, and termination) of the algorithmic techniques used for verification. This is crucial since, in general, verifying data-aware processes is highly undecidable [5,10].

RQ 2. The verification techniques come with an analysis of key properties such as soundness, completeness, termination.   ◁

Since ISML and dapSL do not come with specific algorithmic techniques for verification, no such analysis is provided there (−). BAUML relies on first-order satisfiability techniques that come with semi-decidability guarantees. In [11], it is claimed that for a certain class of state-bounded artifact systems, verification terminates; however, this is not guaranteed, as for that class only decidability of verification is known, not that the specifically employed satisfiability algorithm terminates $(+/-)$. VERIFAS comes with a deep, foundational study on the boundaries of decidability of verification [9]; the study identifies classes of data-aware processes for which finite-state abstractions can be constructed, guaranteeing termination of the verifier when analyzing such classes $(+)$. Finally, delta-BPMN relies on the foundational DAB framework [1], where soundness, completeness, termination of the algorithmic technique implemented in MCMT are extensively studied $(+)$.

The third crucial requirement is about the type of language adopted, and whether it adheres to accepted standards or is instead rather ad-hoc.

RQ 3. The language relies on well-assessed standards for processes and data.   ◁

Recall that, to carry out verification, the features supported by the language need to be carefully controlled. So we do not assess approaches based on their coverage of constructs, but rather focus on which notations they employ. On the one hand, approaches like VERIFAS adopt a language inspired by artifact-centric models but defined in an abstract, mathematical syntax $(-)$. At the other end of the spectrum, BAUML comes with a combination of UML/OCL-based models to specify the various process components $(+)$. In between we find the other proposals $(+/-)$: ISML relies on Petri nets and employs data definition and manipulation languages defined in an ad-hoc way; dapSL instead defines the control-flow implicitly via condition-action rules, and uses a language grounded in the SQL standard for querying and updating the data. delta-BPMN relies on a combination of (block-structured) BPMN and SQL for data manipulation; while standard SQL is employed for data queries and updates, the language has to be extended with some ad-hoc constructs when it comes to actions and (user) inputs $(+/-)$.

In data-aware processes, it is essential to capture the fact that while the process is executed, new data can be acquired.

RQ 4. The language supports the injection of data into the process by the external environment.   ◁

All of the listed approaches agree on the need of equipping the language with mechanisms to inject data from the external environment. VERIFAS and BAUML allow one to nondeterministically assign values from value domains to (special) variables, ISML extends this functionality with an ability to guarantee that assigned values are globally fresh (but then it works by assuming a fixed finite domain for such fresh input), whereas dapSL supports all such functionalities using a language of service calls. In delta-BPMN we adopt a data injection approach similar to the one used in VERIFAS.

When executing process cases, one typically distinguishes at least two types of data: volatile data attached to the case itself, and persistent data that may be accessed and updated by different cases at once. This leads to our last requirement.

RQ 5. The language distinguishes volatile and persistent data elements.   ◁

While BAUML, VERIFAS, and DAB natively provide distinct notions for case variables and underlying persistent data $(+)$, ISML models conceptually account for token data and separate facts, but such facts are not stored in a persistent storage $(+/-)$, while dapSL models all data as tuples of a relational database $(-)$.

At last, a very important aspect that puts the approaches into two distinct groups, is whether persistent data are managed under a unique access policy, or instead there is a fine-grained distinction based on how the process can access them. This impacts the type of verification conducted, as discussed below. Since supporting or not read-only data simply separates the different approaches, but does not correspond to a qualitative difference, we simply put *'yes'* (y) when it is supported and *'no'* (n) when it is not.

RQ 6. The language separates read-only persistent data from persistent data that are updated during the execution.   ◁

This is an important distinction because it heavily affects the type of verification that must be considered [5, 10]. On the one hand, approaches like BAUML, dapSL, and ISML that do not distinguish read-only from updatable persistent data (n) require to fully fix their initial configuration, and provide verification verdicts by considering all possible evolutions of the process starting from this initial configuration. Contrariwise, approaches like VERIFAS and delta-BPMN that do this distinction (y) in turn focus on forms of parameterized verification where the properties of interest are studied for every possible configuration of the read-only data, certifying whether the process correctly works regardless of which specific read-only data are picked.

Table 1 summarizes the different requirements and support provided by the analyzed literature. We take this as a basis to compare the delta-BPMN language and verification infrastructure with the other existing approaches. For completeness, we also indicate in the table which verification properties are considered in each approach.

It is also worth noting that there is a plethora of other approaches falling into the artifact-/data-/object-centric spectrum. For example, Guard-Stage-Milestone (GSM) language [8], the object-aware business process management framework of PHILharmonic Flows [15], the declarative data-centric process language RESEDA based on term rewriting systems [20]. In a nutshell, these approaches combine data and processes dimensions, but largely focus on modeling, with few exceptions offering runtime verification of specific properties (e.g., RESEDA allows for a specific form of liveness checking) supported by a tool.

Other relevant works investigate the integration of data and processes with a system engineering approach [7, 12, 17] tailored to modeling and enactment. Of particular relevance is ADEPT [7], which is similar in spirit to delta-BPMN, as it allows to combine a block-structured process modeling language with SQL statements to interact with an underlying relational storage, with the goal of providing execution and analytic services. The main difference with delta-BPMN is that our PDMML language focuses on conservative extensions of (block-structured) BPMN and SQL to obtain a verifiable, integrated model.

3 The PDMML Language

To realize the modeling requirements introduced in Sect. 2, we start from the approach in [1]. The main issue there is that while the process backbone relies on (block-structured) BPMN, the definition and manipulation of data is done with an abstract, mathematical language that does not come with a concrete, user-oriented syntax.

To define a delta-BPMN model, we then revisit the data component of the process, introducing a Process Data Modeling and Manipulation Language (PDMML). We do so in two steps: first, we start from BPMN and isolate the main data abstractions that must be represented in our framework, introducing suitable *data definition* operations in PDMML; second, we start from the abstract, logical language studied in [1], and introduce a concrete counterpart for *data manipulation* statements in PDMML, using SQL as main inspiration. In this way, we achieve compliance with **RQ** 3. We then integrate PDMML language for data inspection and manipulation within BPMN blocks, so as to comply with **RQ** 3 for both the data and the control-flow aspects.

Notice that, deliberately, PDMML does not come with explicit mechanisms to refer to other process instances from a given instance. This is due to technical reasons related to verification, which will be highlighted in Sect. 4.2.

3.1 Sources of Data and Their Definition

While BPMN does not introduce any specific language to manipulate and query data, it introduces two main abstractions to account for them: *data objects*, representing *volatile data* manipulated by each case in isolation; and *persistent stores*, representing persistent units of information that are accessed and updated possibly by multiple cases.

Persistent Data. To account for **RQ** 6, PDMML allows to define two types of persistent storages with different access policies. More specifically, we use a so-called *repository* $\mathcal{R}$ to store data that can be both queried and updated, and a *catalog store* $\mathcal{C}$ with a read access only. The declaration of these two stores is done with a set of statements, each accounting for a relation schema (or *table*) therein. Each table comes with *typed attributes* defining the *names* of the table columns with the respective *(value) types*.

An attribute is declared in PDMML as A : **T**, where A is an attribute name and **T** is its type. Each type is of one of the following three different forms: *(i)* a *primitive*, system-reserved *type* (such as strings and integers); *(ii)* a dedicated *id type* $\mathbf{T}_R$ accounting for the identifiers of table R (like ISBNs for the *Book* table - if they are used as primary key to identify books); *(iii)* a *data type* accounting for a semantic domain (like person names or addresses). For every catalog table, say, with name R, PDMML also requires to define an attribute with name id and a distinguished id type $\mathbf{T}_R$, so as to account for the primary key of that table in an unambiguous way.

Based on these notions, a *catalog* is a set of *catalog tables*, each defined with a statement of the form $R(\mathrm{id} : \mathbf{T}_R, \mathsf{A}_1 : \mathbf{T}_1, \ldots, \mathsf{A}_n : \mathbf{T}_n)$, where: *(i)* R is the *table name*; *(ii)* id : $\mathbf{T}_R$ is the explicit table identifier of R with a dedicated (identifier) type $\mathbf{T}_R$; *(iii)* $n+1$ is the *table arity*; *(iv)* for every $i \in \{1, \ldots, n\}$, $\mathbf{T}_i$ is a primitive type, an identifier type of some relation in the catalog or a data type. Each catalog table is equipped with a *table id attribute* of the form id : $\mathbf{T}_R$, always assumed to appear in the first position. According to the definition, the other attributes may have, as type, the identifier type of another catalog table. This mechanism is used to define, in a compact way, the presence of a *foreign key* dependency relating two catalog tables.

Similarly to the case of a catalog, a *repository* is a set of *repository tables*, each defined with a similar statement to that of catalog tables, with the only difference that now there is no explicit table identifier. This means that, while repository tables can reference catalog tables, they cannot reference other repository tables, and thus behave like *free relations*. Conceptually, this is not a limitation, since the idea behind the use of the repository is not to support a full-fledged database (as it is done for the catalog), but to provide a working memory where data taken from the catalog, case variables and external sources are accumulated and manipulated. This approach to model the repository is in line with foundational frameworks studied before [1,3,16]. In addition, it enjoys the key properties of the most sophisticated scenarios known in the literature to guarantee verifiability [1,3,9] – hence we have to stick with it in the light of **RQ** 1.

As customary, when defining tables, PDMML requires that each table name is used only once overall (at the catalog *and* repository level). Hence we can use the table name to unambiguously refer to the table as a whole. To disambiguate attributes from different tables, we sometimes use a dot notation, where $R.A$ indicates attribute A within table R. In addition, table aliases can be used within queries towards expressing self-joins.[3]

Volatile Data. For modeling volatile, case data in a way that makes them compatible with persistent data, we use typed variables whose declaration signature is similar to the one of attributes. Specifically, a *case variable* with name v and type T is then simply defined in PDMML as a statement $\#v : \mathbf{T}$. The definition of the volatile data of a process then just consists of a set of case variable statements.

The collective set of declarations for case variables, catalog relations, and repository relations is called *data model*.

Example 1. Consider a mortgage approval process followed by the Customer Service Representatives (CSR) department of a bank.[4] To manage information about available mortgage types, customers' bank accounts, submitted applications, status of their records and possible mortgage approval results, the process relies on multiple sources of data.

Each mortgage application is created by a CSR employee and can be managed throughout the process execution by using process variables. At the same time, certain data values have to be moved from volatile case variables to a persistent repository, and vice-versa. In this process, for example, we use variables $\#cid : \mathbf{CID}$, $\#bid :$ **BaID**, $\#bankAmount : \mathbf{Num}$ to store information about a customer as well as their eligible bank account, and variables $\#tid : \mathbf{MTID}$, $\#duration : \mathbf{Num}$, $\#amount :$ **Num** to collect data for the mortgage contract.

The information static to the process (i.e., it shall never be updated) is stored in the CSR's read-only database. For example, table $BankAccount(\mathsf{BAid} :$ **BankAccountID**, CBA : **CID**, Deposit : **int**, StatusBank : **String**) contains information about possibly multiple bank accounts owned by the customers together with the account status information retained in StatusBank : **String**), whereas $MortgageType(\mathsf{Mid} : \mathbf{MTID}, \mathsf{Name} : \mathbf{String}, \mathsf{Amount} : \mathbf{Num}, \mathsf{Duration} : \mathbf{Num}, \mathsf{Interest} : \mathbf{Num})$ contains details regarding various mortgage offers, including information on mortgage duration and the amount of interests to be paid.   ◁

---

[3] This latter feature is currently not supported by the implementation, but it will be supported soon. The page https://tinyurl.com/y6npo4kz provides a continuously updated list of the most recent, newly added features.

[4] The example builds on a model from Business Process Incubator (see https://tinyurl.com/8au7xfmw) enriched with data by analogy with a similar model from the benchmark in [16].

3.2   The Process Component of delta-BPMN

The control-flow backbone of a delta-BPMN process relies on the recursive composition of block-structured BPMN patterns that adhere to the standard BPMN 2.0 syntax. We focus on block-structured BPMN since this allows us to define a direct execution semantics also for advanced constructs like interrupting exceptions and cancelations, and to exploit this upon verifying the resulting models (see [1] for the technical details). However, our approach would seamlessly carry over to the case where the control-flow backbone of the process is captured using a Petri net, as in [13].

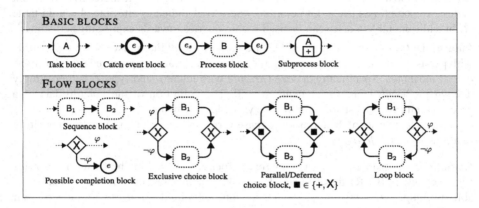

Fig. 1. Supported BPMN blocks

Although, conceptually, delta-BPMN supports the same set of blocks as DAB [1], its current implementation covers the fundamental blocks shown in Figure 1. As usual, blocks are classified into leaf blocks (in our case, tasks and events) and non-leaf blocks that combine sub-blocks in a specific control-flow structure.

Implicitly, each block has a lifecycle. Initially, the block is inactive and its state is idle. When a process instance, throughout its execution, reaches an idle block, it becomes enabled. This means that the enabled element may be then nondeterministically executed depending on the choice of the process executor(s). When the process instance has completed traversing the block, the block lifecycle state changes from enabled to compl. The compl element then advances the progression of the process instance following what is dictated by the parent block. In the exact same moment, the block changes its state back to idle. The execution rules used for regulating the evolution of each block depending on its type faithfully reconstruct what prescribed by the BPMN standard. Consider, for example, a deferred choice block S with two sub-blocks B_1 and B_2. Its lifecycle starts in state enabled, that can be nondeterministically progressed to state active. This progression simultaneously forces the change of state of B_1 and B_2 from idle to enabled. As soon as one of the two sub-blocks, say, B_1 is selected, it moves to active whereas its sibling block B_2 goes back to idle. As soon as B_1 finishes by reaching state compl, it switches to idle and triggers a simultaneous transition of the parent block S from active to compl. Following this logic, one can analogously and exhaustively define the lifecycle model for each type of block.

Example 2. Figure 2 shows the control-flow backbone of the mortgage approval process (Example 1), represented in delta-BPMN by following the same block decomposition.   ◁

The main, open question is how data enter into the definition of blocks. Following the BPMN standard, this is handled in two distinct points: leaf blocks (capturing tasks and events), and (data-driven) choices. Such blocks are annotated with suitable PDMML statements to capture data inspection and manipulation. This is handled next.

3.3   Inspecting and Manipulating Data with PDMML

To express how a task/event inspects and manipulates data, we decorate it with three distinct PDMML expressions, respectively defining: *(i) newly declared variables*, to account for external data input; *(ii)* a *precondition*, providing possible bindings for the input variables of the task/event considering the catalog, the repository, as well as the case and newly defined variables; *(iii)* an *effect* that, once a binding for the newly declared variables and for the input variables is picked, determines how the task/event manipulates the case variables and the repository.

An obvious choice to inspect relational data as those present in our catalog and repository is to resort to relational query languages such as SQL. This choice would be in line with **RQ** 3. However, our setting requires to consider two crucial aspects. On the one hand, it is important to coherently employ a single query language to account for different querying needs, such as expressing the precondition of a task or the conditions determining which route to take in a choice. On the other hand, differently from pure SQL, our queries have to consider the presence of case variables, addressing the possibility of simultaneously working over persistent and volatile data, as well as the possibility of injecting data from the external environment. For example, think of a job category that has been chosen by an applicant during the application process (and thus suitably stored in a dedicated case variable) and for which the process should provide all open positions. In this case one would need to use the job category value in the WHERE clause of a dedicated SELECT query accessing the catalog that already contains information about all the positions for the previously selected category. At the same time, one might also want to query only the current state of the case variables, or to ask the user to provide their credit card number when paying a fee.

Newly Declared Variables. The ability of injecting a data object of type T form the external environment (cf. **RQ** 4) is handled through a *newly declared variable* with the following PDMML statement $decl :: = (\text{var } v : \textbf{T})^*$, where v is the name of the newly declared variable. Upon execution, v is bound to *any* value from T. When attached to a task, newly declared variables can be seen as an abstract representation of a user form or a web service result. When attached to an event, they represent the event payload.

Preconditions. Preconditions indicate under which circumstances a task can be executed or an event triggered. They also retrieve data from the catalog, repository, case variables and newly defined variables attached to the same leaf block. To account for these different aspects, PDMML incorporates a hybrid SQL-based query language that can retrieve volatile and persistent data at once. Consistently with the execution semantics given in [1] that is, in turn, in line with the customary "variable binding" abstraction employed in formalisms such as Colored Petri nets, the typical usage of queries in our framework is to return a set of answers from which one is (nondeterministically) picked to induce a progression step within the process. Notice that this way of managing query results is customary in the artifact-centric literature [3,5,9,16].

To define preconditions, we first need to introduce PDMML conditions, defined as:

$$cond ::= x_1 \odot x_2 \mid cond_1 \text{ } \textbf{AND} \text{ } cond_2 \mid cond_1 \text{ } \textbf{OR} \text{ } cond_2$$

Essentially, a PDMML condition is a boolean expression (with negation pushed inwards) over atomic conditions of the form $x_1 \odot x_2$, where x_1 and x_2 are expression terms (whose specific shape is determined by the context in which the condition is used), and $\odot \in \{=, \neq, >, <, \leq, \geq\}$) is a comparison operator. In atomic conditions, we assume component-wise type compatibility of terms (e.g., the two operands in $x_1 \odot x_2$ must have the same type). Notice that, as customary, the atomic condition TRUE (capturing the condition that always succeeds) can be defined as an abbreviation (similarly for FALSE).

Using conditions as atomic building blocks, a PDMML precondition is defined as:

$$pre ::= cond \mid query$$
$$query ::= \textbf{SELECT } A_1, \ldots, A_s \textbf{ FROM } R_1, \ldots, R_m \textbf{ WHERE } filter$$
$$filter ::= cond \mid \textbf{TUPLE } (x) \textbf{ IN } R \mid \textbf{TUPLE } (x) \textbf{ NOT IN } R$$
$$\mid filter_1 \textbf{ AND } filter_2 \mid filter_1 \textbf{ OR } filter_2$$

Here, each R_i from the SQL-like *query* can be a repository or a catalog relation, whereas R from *filter* can only be a catalog relation. This is in line with theoretical results reported in [1,3]. Terms in *cond* of *pre* can be case variables, constants, or newly defined variables declared in the same leaf block. Instead, terms used in *cond* of *filter* coincide with those from above, but can also use attributes that appear in the **FROM** statement of the contingent *query* expression (i.e., $A_1, \ldots, A_s$). When writing queries, notation $R.A$ can be used to more explicitly refer to attribute A of table R.

Example 3. In the mortgage approval process scenario touched in Examples 1 and 4, the following query can be used to list bank accounts of the customers who have completed the mortgage application procedure:

> **SELECT** BAid, CBA, StatusBank **FROM** *BankAccount*
> **WHERE** CBA $= \#cid$ **AND** $\#status =$ CompletedApplication

Here, $\#status$: **String** indicates the current status of the process.

Effects. Task/event effects consist of data manipulation PDMML statements operating over case variables and repository tables. In the following, we use term *input variable* to refer to newly defined variables or attributes of the precondition attached to the same leaf block of the effect under scrutiny.

Each case variable $\#v$ can be *updated* using a trivial assignment statement $\#v = u$, where u is either a constant or an input variable. It is assumed that, for each case variable, at most one case variable assignment statement can be written within one update.

One can also model insertion and deletion of tuples into the persistent storage. Since the catalog is read-only, these updates can be performed only on the repository relations.

An *insertion* (statement) on some repository relation R is defined as **INSERT** $v_1, \ldots, v_n$ **INTO** R, where each v_i is either a constant, a case variable or an input variable. This INSERT statement is similar to the corresponding classical DML (data manipulation language) statement in SQL. However, we deliberately avoid using the VALUES clause since we insert one tuple at a time, and so we can rely on the more compact notation where the elements to be inserted are directly indicated close to R.

A *deletion* (statement) is defined as **DELETE** $v_1, \ldots, v_n$ **FROM** R. Here, similarly to the insertion, each v_i is either a constant, a (case) variable, or an input variable, whose type coincides with the type of the i-th attribute in R.

We also allow to perform *conditional updates*. For that, we employ a modified SQL CASE statement directly embedded into the update logic. This statement logically resembles an *if-then-else* expression with multiple *else-if* branches, and in which each condition in the *if*-part is a query. To ensure verifiability [1,3] (cf. **RQ** 1), it is necessary for the statement to obey to one limitation: it cannot access any other repository table beyond the one that is being updated. The conditional update statement has the form:

> **UPDATE** R **SET** $R.\mathsf{a}_1$=@v_1, ..., $R.\mathsf{a}_m$=@v_m **WHERE**
> **CASE WHEN** F_1 **THEN** @v_1=u_1^1, ..., @v_m=u_m^1
>   ...
> **WHEN** F_k **THEN** @v_1=u_1^k, ..., @v_m=u_m^k
> **ELSE** @v_1=u_1^e, ..., @v_m=u_m^e

This statement is the most sophisticated one in the offered language as it requires the modeler to take care of the following two aspects. First, similarly to the SQL's UPDATE statement, which can modify multiple tuples in a table, ours performs a (conditional) *bulk edit* of elements in *each* tuple of R, and the SET clause specifies (using names of the attributes of R with the R's name in the prefix)[5] what are exactly those elements. The SET clause also uses placeholder variables @v_j that support the conditional update logic: whenever a tuple in R satisfies one of the F_i filters, the corresponding THEN clause will assign concrete values u_j^i to all the placeholder variables mentioned in SET. Second, the modeler has to carefully control the variables and attributes used both in the WHEN and THEN clauses. As we have already mentioned above, each F_i cannot access repository relations but R itself. At the same time, it can reuse elements from the precondition query such as variables and attributes. This, in turn, allows to use F_i for filtering results returned by the precondition query, and thus allowing to carefully select the data that are going to be used in the final update of every single tuple of R. As for the elements appearing in THEN clauses, their values can be constants as well

---

[5] This disambiguates the situation where the same relation R is used in the update precondition with some of its attributes both appearing in the SELECT and some of the WHEN clauses.

as elements taken from results returned by the precondition query. In the following we provide a few examples demonstrating correct and illegal update statements.

Example 4. Continuing with our running example, we now give the example of a legal conditional update handling the assessment of the eligibility of a mortgage application. To manage key information about the applications submitted for the mortgage approval, the bank employs a repository that consists of one relation schema:

$$Info(\text{Bank}: \textbf{BaID}, \text{StatusB}: \textbf{String}, \text{Reliability}: \textbf{String})$$

◁

Here, for each application, CSR performs an assessment procedure, during which all customer's bank accounts are checked for reliability. All the accounts with histories that did not include any fraudulent charges, are then marked accordingly in relation *Info*. Technically, we formalize this situation with a conditional update of the form:

```
UPDATE Info SET Info.Reliability=@v WHERE
CASE WHEN Info.StatusB!=fraud THEN @v=Yes
     ELSE @v= No
```

Note that the *when-then-else* clause allows us to perform a bulk update over the repository relation *Info* by changing the reliability status of its entries.

Consider the repository relation *Rejected*(Bank : **BaID**), storing bank accounts that have been already rejected before in the process by another department. The following update statement, that additionally checks if the bank account has already been rejected, is illegal, since the condition of the first case involves the repo-relation *Rejected*:

```
UPDATE Info SET Info.Reliability=@v WHERE
CASE WHEN Info.StatusB!=fraud AND TUPLE (Info.Bank) NOT IN Rejected
THEN @v=Yes ELSE @v=No
```

The overall execution semantics of leaf blocks is defined as follows. Once the leaf block is `enabled`, a binding for its newly defined attributes can be provided. If, under this binding, the precondition of the leaf block evaluates to true for at least one binding of its attributes, then the leaf block may nondeterministically fire, depending on the choice of the process executors. Upon firing, the binding of precondition attributes and of newly defined variables provide a grounding the for effect attached to the leaf block. Once the effect has been performed, the block completes its execution, and the state of its lifecycle becomes `compl`, as described above. The only additional requirement is that, in the case of a task having both a precondition and an effect, we assume that the task is atomic at the level of data updates. This is not for a technical reason, but for a conceptual one: it is essential to ensure that insertions/deletions/updates are applied on the same data snapshot that was used for checking the task precondition, in accordance with the standard *transactional semantics* of relational updates. Breaking simultaneity would lead to race conditions with other update specifications potentially operating over the same case variables or repository tables. Notice that race conditions can still occur at the level of the process, when parallel blocks and sequences of tasks/events are employed. Consequently, requiring atomicity for leaf blocks with preconditions and effects does not lead to a loss of generality.

3.4 Guards for Conditional Flows

The last place where PDMML statements are needed is in the context of blocks employ-ing choice splits as a way to conditionally route process instances. Specifically, each conditional flow is linked to a PDMML condition whose terms are case variables or constants. Notice that using only case variables is not a limitation, since, as we have seen before, case variables can be filled with data extracted from the catalog/repository, or injected from the external environment.

As shown in Fig. 1, we assume that each choice split foresees two outputs with complementary guards. This means that the user has to specify only one guard φ, while the other guard (indicated as $\neg\varphi$ in the figure) is automatically constructed via syntactic manipulation of φ as follows: De Morgan laws are applied until negation appears just in front of atomic conditions, and then the negated atomic conditions are replaced by their corresponding, complementary conditions (e.g., $\leq$ is substituted by $>$).

We have now completed the definition of PDMML. In the next section we show how PDMML is practically realised in delta-BPMN.

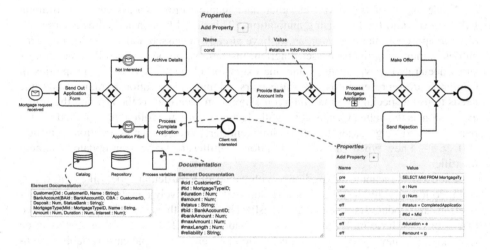

Fig. 2. A delta-BPMN model with a few examples of Camunda-based annotations (taken as screenshots from the tool)

4 delta-BPMN in Action

We now put delta-BPMN in action, considering both modeling and verification.

4.1 Modeling delta-BPMN Processes with Camunda

We discuss how Camunda, one of the most widely employed (open-source) platforms for process modeling and automation, can be directly adapted to model delta-BPMN processes. We in particular employ the Camunda Modeler environment (camunda.com) to create the process control-flow, and its extension part to incorporate PDMML statements. At this stage, it is not essential to recognize the process blocks (and check whether the process control-flow is block-structured): we just annotate the overall process model with the data definitions, the tasks/events with the corresponding PDMML preconditions and effects, and the choice branches with PDMML boolean queries.

An alternative possibility would have been to require the modeler to explicitly insert data object and data store icons in the process model, and annotate those. However, this would clutter the visual representation of the process, creating unreadable diagrams.

More specifically, to declare repository (resp., catalog) relations we use a dedicated persistent store symbol called `Repository` (resp., `Catalog`). The declarations themselves, separated by the semicolon from one another, are put into the documentation box of the element's documentation. For example, Fig. 2 demonstrates a snapshot of a catalog declaration containing definitions of two relations *Customer* and *MortgageType* from Example 1. We deal similarly with case variables: a single data object called `Process variables` is used, whose documentation box contains all case variable declarations with the semicolon being used as a separator (cf. Fig. 2).

Modelling queries as well as other data manipulation expressions in traditional BPMN 2.0 could be done using annotations. This could be considered as a more traditional approach that, however, as we have already discussed above, can lead to difficulties in managing the processes diagram. Instead, we propose to handle such expressions declaratively within the Camunda extension elements. Given that properties in Camunda are represented as key-value pairs, adding a declaration is rather easy: one needs to use a special data manipulation expression identifier as the key and the actual expression as the value. Consistently with Sect. 3, we use the following reserved identifiers: *(i)* `cond` – a gateway/flow condition identifier; *(ii)* `pre` – a precondition identifier; *(iii)* `var` – a new typed variable declaration identifier; *(iv)* `eff` – an update statement identifier.

Each key is meant to be used only with values of a particular type. Like that, `cond` and `pre` identify queries, whereas `var` and `eff` respectively denote new variable declarations and update statements. All the BPMN elements that admit the aforementioned extensions can have multiple `var` and `eff` identifiers. This is useful as there can be more than one new typed variable declaration as well as multiple case variable assignment statements.

Example 5. Task Process Complete Application in Fig. 2 selects a mortgage type in case a customer has agreed to apply for it. This is done by adding a `pre`-identified property to extension elements of the task with the following query that nondeterministically selects one mortgage type from the *MortgageType* relation:

SELECT Mid **FROM** *MortgageType* **WHERE** $\#status = $ FillApp **AND** $e > 0$ **AND** $g > 0$

As an effect, this task is supposed to move a chosen mortgage type ID to a dedicated case variable, and decide on the amount of money asked as well as the interest to be paid in case the mortgage offer gets accepted. The latter is done with two newly declared variables e and g, and three `eff`-identified properties with the following case variable assignments: $\#tid = $ Mid, $\#duration = e$ and $\#amount = g$. Note that the last two essentially model a user input and thus realize the data injection mentioned in **RQ** 4. ◁

All the queries identified with cond can be used only in blocks containing choice splits (i.e., blocks from Fig. 1 with φ annotations on the arcs). In Fig. 2, we show a screenshot of a simple condition assigned to one of the XOR gateways of the loop block.

4.2   Encoding delta-BPMN Camunda Processes in MCMT

To make delta-BPMN processes modeled in Camunda verifiable (cf. **RQ** 1) we have implemented a translator that takes as input a .bpmn file produced by Camunda following the modeling guidelines of the previous section, and transforms it into the syntax of a state-of-the-art model checker that can verify data-aware processes parametrically to the read-only relations, namely the latest version of MCMT [1–3].

The translation first checks whether the input model is block-structured, isolating the various blocks. This is done through traversal algorithm that is of independent interest. Each block is then separately converted into a corresponding set of MCMT instructions by implementing, rule by rule, the encoding mechanism proposed in [1]. This works since the concrete PDMML syntax introduced here for data definition and manipulation faithfully mirrors the abstract, logical language employed there.

For verification, we obviously need also to express which properties we want to check. Every property is defined as a condition that specifies a "bad", undesired state of the model. To add a property, we employ the same mechanism as above that uses Camunda extension elements. More specifically, we add another reserved identifier verify which can be used to add property key-value pairs directly to the process. For example, one can write the PDMML condition ($\#status$=Archived **AND** $lifecycleMortgage$=Completed) to verify the safety of the model in Fig. 2, in particular ascertaining whether the mortgage approval process has been finalized with the customer not being interested in the related offer (see the related End event Client not interested in Fig. 2), thus resulting in her application being archived. Notice that here we use a special variable $lifecycleMortgage$ to access the process lifecycle state. In general, one may query the process lifecyle by using a special internal variable $lifecycleModelName$, where $ModelName$ is the actual process model name. Verification of lifecycle properties for single blocks can be tackled by introducing dedicated case variables, manipulating them in effects according to the lifecycle evolution of the block.

It is important to mention that, although this feature is not explicitly reflected in the PDMML language, delta-BPMN provides support for modeling and verification of multi-instance scenarios in which process instances can access and manipulate the same catalog and repository. Formal details are given in [1]. In summary, [1] indicates that unboundedly many simultaneously active process instances can be verified for safety if they do not explicitly refer to each other (i.e., they do not expose their own case identifiers to other instances). Explicit mutual references can instead be handled if the maximum number of simultaneously active process instances is known a-priori.

Figure 3 shows the overall toolchain employed for verification. First, a modeler has to produce a delta-BPMN process by enriching a regular block-structured BPMN 2.0 process with a PDMML specification via Camunda extensions using the technique from above. Camunda Modeler then allows to export the delta-BPMN process as an XML-formatted .bpmn file. This file can be then processed by our Java-based tool, called

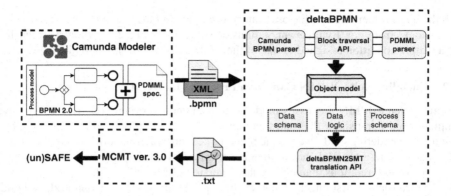

Fig. 3. Conceptual architecture of the delta-BPMN framework

deltaBPMN, that employs the following APIs for generating the process specification that can be readily verified by MCMT (http://users.mat.unimi.it/users/ghilardi/mcmt/). In the nutshell, the tool takes two major steps to process the delta-BPMN model. First, it uses the Camunda's BPMN model API to access process components from the input .bpmn file and uses our block traversal API as well as PDMML parser to recognize blocks as well as PDMML statements/declarations and consecutively generate delta-BPMN objects. The latter are specified according to the object model that has been mainly distilled from the formalism studied in [1] and that consists of three major parts: a data schema storing all case variable and relation declarations (from both $\mathcal{R}$ and $\mathcal{C}$), a process schema storing nested supported process block definitions, and a data logic containing update declarations and conditions assigned to blocks. The block traversal API uses a newly developed algorithm for detecting nested blocks that comply to the object model structure. Via the *deltaBPMN2SMT* translation API that internally follows the translation in [1], the tool then processes the extracted object model and generates a text file containing the delta-BPMN process specification rewritten in the MCMT syntax.

Finally, the derived specification can be directly checked in the MCMT tool that, in turn, will detect whether the specification is safe or unsafe with respect to the *"bad"* property specified in the initial model. MCMT can be executed in the command line using the following command: **[time] mcmt <filename>**. Here, argument **[time]** is not mandatory, but can be used if one wants to display the MCMT execution time. More information on the model checker installation process, the language for specifying safety properties of delta-BPMN models, advanced execution options and additional details, together with the actual delta-BPMN implementation, can be found on the tool website here: https://tinyurl.com/y6npo4kz.

5   Conclusions

We have introduced a SQL-based language for modeling and manipulating volatile and persistent data, and demonstrated how it can be incorporated into the existing BPMN standard, resulting in a language for modeling data-aware BPMN that we called delta-BPMN. We showed how this delta-BPMN processes can be modeled with Camunda using its native extension capabilities. We also reported on an implementation of a prototype that takes delta-BPMN models produced in Camunda and automatically translates them into the syntax of MCMT that, in turn, allows for their immediate verification. Given that Camunda also allows to extend its user interface with additional third-party functionalities, we intend to develop a fully integrated environment for modelling and verification of delta-BPMN processes. We also plan to investigate in more detail usability aspects of our proposal and set up a concrete benchmark that could be then fully adopted (including process- and data-specific metrics) within the RePRoSitory platform [6].

Acknowledgments. This research has been partially supported by the UNIBZ projects *REKAP*, *VERBA* and *DUB*. We would like to thank Davide Cremonini for contributing to the initial phase of the delta-BPMN implementation.

References

1. Calvanese, D., Ghilardi, S., Gianola, A., Montali, M., Rivkin, A.: Formal modeling and SMT-based parameterized verification of data-aware BPMN. In: Hildebrandt, T., van Dongen, B., Röglinger, M., Mendling, J. (eds.) BPM 2019. LNCS, vol. 11675, pp. 157–175. Springer, Cham (2019). https://doi.org/10.1007/978-3-030-26619-6_12
2. Calvanese, D., Ghilardi, S., Gianola, A., Montali, M., Rivkin, A.: From model completeness to verification of data aware processes. In: Lutz, C., Sattler, U., Tinelli, C., Turhan, A.-Y., Wolter, F. (eds.) Description Logic, Theory Combination, and All That. LNCS, vol. 11560, pp. 212–239. Springer, Cham (2019). https://doi.org/10.1007/978-3-030-22102-7_10
3. Calvanese, D., Ghilardi, S., Gianola, A., Montali, M., Rivkin, A.: SMT-based verification of data-aware processes: a model-theoretic approach. Math. Struct. Comput. Sci. **30**(3), 271–313 (2020)
4. Calvanese, D., Montali, M., Patrizi, F., Rivkin, A.: Modeling and in-database management of relational, data-aware processes. In: Giorgini, P., Weber, B. (eds.) CAiSE 2019. LNCS, vol. 11483, pp. 328–345. Springer, Cham (2019). https://doi.org/10.1007/978-3-030-21290-2_21
5. Calvanese, D., De Giacomo, G., Montali, M.: Foundations of data-aware process analysis: a database theory perspective. In: Proceedings of PODS 2013, pp. 1–12. ACM (2013)
6. Corradini, F., Fornari, F., Polini, A., Re, B., Tiezzi, F.: Reprository: a repository platform for sharing business process models. In: Proceedings of BPM (PhD/Demos). CEUR Workshop Proceedings, vol. 2420, pp. 149–153. CEUR-WS.org (2019)
7. Dadam, P.: From ADEPT to AristaFlow BPM suite: a research vision has become reality. In: Rinderle-Ma, S., Sadiq, S., Leymann, F. (eds.) BPM 2009. LNBIP, vol. 43, pp. 529–531. Springer, Heidelberg (2010). https://doi.org/10.1007/978-3-642-12186-9_50
8. Damaggio, E., Hull, R., Vaculín, R.: On the equivalence of incremental and fixpoint semantics for business artifacts with Guard-Stage-Milestone lifecycles. In: Rinderle-Ma, S., Toumani, F., Wolf, K. (eds.) BPM 2011. LNCS, vol. 6896, pp. 396–412. Springer, Heidelberg (2011). https://doi.org/10.1007/978-3-642-23059-2_29
9. Deutsch, A., Li, Y., Vianu, V.: Verification of hierarchical artifact systems. In: Proceedings of PODS 2016, pp. 179–194. ACM (2016)

10. Deutsch, A., Hull, R., Li, Y., Vianu, V.: Automatic verification of database-centric systems. ACM SIGLOG News **5**(2), 37–56 (2018)
11. Estañol, M., Sancho, M., Teniente, E.: Ensuring the semantic correctness of a BAUML artifact-centric BPM. Inf. Softw. Technol. **93**, 147–162 (2018)
12. Fahland, D., Meyer, A., Pufahl, L., Batoulis, K., Weske, M.: Automating data exchange in process choreographies (extended abstract). In: Proceedings of EMISA 2016. CEUR Workshop Proceedings, vol. 1701, pp. 13–16. CEUR-WS.org (2016)
13. Ghilardi, S., Gianola, A., Montali, M., Rivkin, A.: Petri nets with parameterised data - modelling and verification. In: Fahland, D., Ghidini, C., Becker, J., Dumas, M. (eds.) BPM 2020. LNCS, vol. 12168, pp. 55–74. Springer, Cham (2020). https://doi.org/10.1007/978-3-030-58666-9_4
14. Hull, R.: Artifact-centric business process models: brief survey of research results and challenges. In: Meersman, R., Tari, Z. (eds.) OTM 2008. LNCS, vol. 5332, pp. 1152–1163. Springer, Heidelberg (2008). https://doi.org/10.1007/978-3-540-88873-4_17
15. Künzle, V., Weber, B., Reichert, M.: Object-aware business processes: fundamental requirements and their support in existing approaches. Int. J. Inf. Syst. Model. Des. **2**(2), 19–46 (2011)
16. Li, Y., Deutsch, A., Vianu, V.: VERIFAS: A practical verifier for artifact systems. PVLDB **11**(3), (2017)
17. Meyer, A., Pufahl, L., Fahland, D., Weske, M.: Modeling and enacting complex data dependencies in business processes. In: Daniel, F., Wang, J., Weber, B. (eds.) BPM 2013. LNCS, vol. 8094, pp. 171–186. Springer, Heidelberg (2013). https://doi.org/10.1007/978-3-642-40176-3_14
18. Polyvyanyy, A., van der Werf, J.M.E.M., Overbeek, S., Brouwers, R.: Information systems modeling: language, verification, and tool support. In: Giorgini, P., Weber, B. (eds.) CAiSE 2019. LNCS, vol. 11483, pp. 194–212. Springer, Cham (2019). https://doi.org/10.1007/978-3-030-21290-2_13
19. Reichert, M.: Process and data: two sides of the same coin? In: Meersman, R., Panetto, H., Dillon, T., Rinderle-Ma, S., Dadam, P., Zhou, X., Pearson, S., Ferscha, A., Bergamaschi, S., Cruz, I.F. (eds.) OTM 2012. LNCS, vol. 7565, pp. 2–19. Springer, Heidelberg (2012). https://doi.org/10.1007/978-3-642-33606-5_2
20. Seco, J.C., Debois, S., Hildebrandt, T.T., Slaats, T.: RESEDA: declaring live event-driven computations as reactive semi-structured data. In: Proceedings of EDOC 2018, pp. 75–84. IEEE (2018)
21. Steinau, S., Marrella, A., Andrews, K., Leotta, F., Mecella, M., Reichert, M.: DALEC: a framework for the systematic evaluation of data-centric approaches to process management software. Softw. Syst. Model. **18**(4), 2679–2716 (2019)

A Real-Time Method for Detecting Temporary Process Variants in Event Log Data

Sudhanshu Chouhan[1]([envelope]) [ID], Anna Wilbik[2] [ID], and Remco Dijkman[1] [ID]

[1] Eindhoven University of Technology, Eindhoven 5612 AZ, The Netherlands
{s.g.r.chouhan,r.m.dijkman}@tue.nl
[2] Maastricht University, Maastricht 6229 GT, The Netherlands
a.wilbik@maastrichtuniversity.nl

Abstract. During the execution of a business process, organizations or individual employees may introduce mistakes, as well as temporary or permanent changes to the process. Such mistakes and changes in the process can introduce anomalies and deviations in the event logs, which in turn introduce temporary and periodic process variants. Early identification of such deviations from the most common types of cases can help an organization to act on them. Keeping this problem in focus, we developed a method that can discover temporary and periodic changes to processes in event log data in real-time. The method classifies cases into common, periodic, temporary, and anomalous cases. The proposed method is evaluated using synthetic and real-world data with promising results.

Keywords: Process discovery · Fuzzy clustering · Process variant

1 Introduction

In flexible business processes, such as in hospitals and administrative offices, the executions of the activities are not always according to the defined process. In such processes, it is possible that the workplace employees deviate from the defined process and follow a different process per case. It is also possible that for a certain period of time they deviate from the defined process for most cases. For example, the employees may temporarily skip some process steps when there is a high workload. When the workload goes back to normal, they follow the normal process again. This temporary deviation from the defined process may cause temporal deviations in the event log data. Another example is that the rules and regulations pertaining to the processes may change with time, which can lead to a permanent shift in the way in which the process is normally executed. This permanent shift may induce a persistent deviation in the event log data. It may be interesting to remark that what is "normal" is usually not exactly clear, because there may be frequent deviations from the defined process flow as

© Springer Nature Switzerland AG 2021
A. Polyvyanyy et al. (Eds.): BPM 2021, LNCS 12875, pp. 197–214, 2021.
https://doi.org/10.1007/978-3-030-85469-0_14

well. There may even be deviations from the process flow that are anomalous, but are not considered deviations because there is no temporal aspect to them. Identification of temporary and periodic process variants introduced by such temporal and permanent deviations from the most common type of cases followed in the process can help a business get better understanding of their actual process as it changes periodically or over time. It also enables them to take appropriate actions, if necessary.

While there exist methods for detecting anomalous cases in business processes, these methods will not detect different variants of the process, as we will also show in the evaluation section of the paper. Nonetheless, the detection of such temporary process variants caused by temporal deviations is important. For example, because they may point to some problem that must be solved, some policy that employees use that should be made explicit in the process, or cases that must be filtered from the log before doing an analysis of the performance of the business process.

To fill this gap, this paper proposes a method to discover, in real time, temporary and permanent changes to the process from event log data, in addition to anomalies. The method classifies cases in an event log into four categories: (i) common cases (type of cases which are most followed in the process), (ii) temporary cases (type of cases which are followed temporarily in the process), (iii) periodic cases (type of cases which are followed at certain times in the process), and (iv) anomalous cases (type of cases which are anomalous). At the core of this method lies a clustering approach using Non-Euclidean Relational Fuzzy c-Means (NERFCM) supported by Correlation Cluster Validity (CCV). CCV is used to determine possible number of clusters existing in the event log data and NERFCM is used to form those clusters. In addition, the proposed method also includes a feature to forget a cluster when no new case falls in it for a defined period of time.

Against this background, the remainder of the paper is organized as follows: Sect. 2 presents a review of the literature related to this topic. Section 3 briefly discusses theoretical concepts involved in working of the proposed method. Section 4 details the proposed method. The evaluation of the proposed method is presented in Sect. 5. Section 6 provides conclusions and suggestions for future work.

2   Related Work

The roots of process mining can be traced back to about half a century ago [17,28,32] but it emerged only in the last decade [42,43]. Even after this rapid emergence, in the last decade, the topic of anomaly detection was not frequently researched [2,3]. In context of event logs, it is interesting to observe that after years of research, the literature still has not settled on a unified definition of anomaly. Despite not having a formal definition, the literature has developed an intuition and suggests on what can be considered anomalous; an anomaly is "some kind of unlikely or infrequently occurring behaviour" [7]. It is well known that the analysis of the event logs is influenced by noise and irregular behaviour of a process [27], which can also be considered anomalous. The research done on the topic of anomaly detection in event logs in the last decade proposed using process discovery algorithms in order to mine a reference process model from business process event logs, and then use the discovered model for conformance checking to detect presence of anomalous behaviour.

Compared to the previous decade, there is a noticeable boom in the research outputs on this topic. The authors of [11] and [5] presented a frequency-based algorithm which finds less occurring and never occurring process executions and considers them anomalous. The authors of [12] presented a similar approach by using integer linear programming for detection and removal of infrequent behaviour observed in an event log. In [26] another approach is proposed using frequent pattern outlier factor which intends to use empirical rule of statistics to differentiate between normal and anomalous instances of a process. Moving forward from frequency-based algorithms, [6] presented a multi-perspective anomaly detection method which is based on likelihood of occurrence of execution events. [22] presented a similar approach of filtering out infrequent events based on expectation of occurrence of an activity.

Clustering algorithms from the domain of data science have also been applied and tested in the domain of process mining [19], for example, k-nearest neighbour [21,40], and use of density based clustering [41]. Use of neural networks has recently caught attention of researchers in process mining which has resulted in some of the best anomaly detection algorithms [29]). Other approaches for anomaly detection in event logs are as follows: dynamic threshold algorithm based on conformance threshold [4], based on Bayesian network [31,34], based on Markov model [1,18,24], based on association rule mining [8,35], based on correlation analysis [30], and based on Needleman–Wunsch algorithm [9].

The anomaly detection methods found in the related work can be distinguished into two types: (i) online methods (to detect anomaly in a running case) [29,41], and (ii) offline methods (to detect anomaly in historic event log) [5,6,31]. Moreover, in both the approaches, anomalies are detected as infrequent cases, or some kind of improbable combination of event attributes. We found that these methods do not give any indication of changes in the process overtime. In literature we also found research done on real-time detection of concept drift [25], process discovery [44], and conformance checking [45], but these methods try to discover the process and changes in the process overtime while not considering anomalous executions of the process. The method we propose can work both online and offline and is able to categorize the cases as common, periodic, temporary, and anomalous.

3   Background

The proposed method employs NERFCM clustering algorithm and CCV index, therefore in the next sub-sections we introduce them briefly.

3.1 Non-Euclidean Relational Fuzzy C-Means (NERFCM)

NERFCM is a clustering algorithm, an adaptation of k-means algorithm that generate fuzzy clusters (i.e. a cluster member can belong to more than one cluster) based on a dissimilarity matrix D between the data points. [20]. The dissimilarity matrix D expresses the pairwise distinction between two traces. In context of event logs, a trace is nothing but a concatenated sequence of activities occurred in a case. For example, in a case if three activities Activity_A, Activity_B, and Activity_C were performed one after another, then their respective trace could be 'abc'. If we consider other traces 'abcd' and 'acde', then computing distances among all the three traces we could obtain a dissimilarity matrix of order 3×3.

Typical distance types used to measure non-euclidean distances between two data points are Jaccard and Levenshtein distances [13]. NERFCM can handle such distances.

In addition to D, the NERFCM algorithm requires three other parameters as input: fuzzifier m, convergence criteria *epsilon*, and number of clusters c. For a specified number of clusters c and fuzzifier $m \in (1, \infty)$ the output of NERFCM is a fuzzy c-partition U which is an approximate local minimizer of a global squared-error type criterion, similar to k-means method. For more elaborate description of NERFCM algorithm please refer to [20].

Number of clusters c sets the number of clusters the input set of traces will be clustered into. This c is computed using a correlation cluster validity index as discussed in the following sub-section.

3.2 Correlation Cluster Validity (CCV)

NERFCM requires from a user a parameter, that is the number of clusters to be created, c. In order to determine number of clusters we are using Cluster Correlation Validity (CCV) [33]. CCV is an universal cluster validity measure that can be applied to partitions obtained by any relational or object data clustering algorithm (NERFCM in our case). The reason of choosing CCV over other validity indices such as Davies-Bouldin index, Xi-Beni Index [46] or Relational Xi-Beni [36] is that CCV is better at finding number of clusters in a dataset compared to all other validity indices [33].

The CCV index adopted in this method is Spearman CCV Index (v_{ccvs}); based on Spearman's Correlation Coefficient (CC), which quantifies the linear relationship between the $n(n-1)/2$ dissimilarity pairs with $i \neq j$ after ordering the elements of D and D(U) as vectors in $\Re^{n(n-1)/2}$. This is accomplished without actually ordering the elements using Eq. 1 [23,33].

$$v_{\mathrm{ccvs}}(\mathrm{D}, \mathrm{D}(\mathrm{U})) = 1 - \left(\frac{6 \cdot \sum_{i=1}^{n} \sum_{j=1}^{n} (\mathrm{D}_{ij} - [\mathrm{D}(\mathrm{U})]_{ij})^2}{n^3 - n} \right) \tag{1}$$

where D is the input dissimilarity matrix (or reference matrix), and D(U) is the dissimilarity matrix between the partition matrix rows. CCV index can be used to evaluate and compare different partitions. A partition with a highest value of the index represents the best clustering. One can generate partitions for different number of clusters $c = 2, 3, \ldots$ and select one with the highest value of CCV index.

4 Proposed Method

This section presents our proposed method for finding periodic and temporary process variants in the event log data while simultaneously detecting anomalies. First we list the input parameters and then we provide a brief overview of the proposed method followed by an in depth step-by-step explanation on how the proposed method works.

4.1 Input Parameters

The proposed method takes the following parameters as inputs: *event_log* - the event log dataset, *distance_type* - for now Jaccard Distance only, *initial_cases* - number of cases for initial clustering, *merging_criteria* - if any two clusters have this much similarity then they will merge (range 100% similarity to 0% similarity), *forgetting_type* - Yes, if clusters are to be forgotten. No, if clusters are not to be forgotten, *forget_after* - number of days after which a cluster is to be forgotten or anomalies are to be saved. Two other input parameters are for NERFCM, *m* - fuzzifier (default value 2) and *epsilon* - convergence criteria (default value 0.0001) [20].

4.2 Overview of Proposed Method

This subsection provides a brief overview of the steps elicited in Algorithm 1. First, the user defines the number of initial cases (*initial_cases*) to be used to form initial clusters. A distance matrix D is computed for the *initial_cases* using the selected *distance_type*. Then CCV algorithm is applied on the selected number of cases. The result of CCV algorithm is the probable number of clusters c that exist in *initial_cases*. Next, the NERFCM algorithm is applied on the selected number of cases, and initial clustering is performed using D and c as input. The formed clusters are saved in *cluster_list*. At this stage the *cut_off_size_for_new_cluster* is also computed - it tells us how large a new cluster should be to qualify as a cluster (explained in *initialize_clusters()*). Once the initial clustering is done, when a new case arrives and it falls under the radius of any of the existing clusters then is added to that cluster, otherwise it is stored in *anomaly_list* (explained in *update_clusters()*). Simultaneously, it is checked if there are new clusters forming inside the *anomaly_list*. If at any point a cluster in *anomaly_list* becomes larger than the *cut_off_size_for_new_cluster*, then it is removed from the *anomaly_list* and added to the main *cluster_list* (explained in *form_new_clusters()*). Next, if at any point in time the similarity between any two or more clusters in the *cluster_list* becomes greater than the *merging_criteria* then those clusters are merged (explained in *merge_clusters()*). If no new case is added to a cluster in *cluster_list* for *forget_after* days, then that cluster is removed from the *cluster_list* and is added to *cluster_list_forgotten* (explained in *forget_clusters()*). At last, if no new case is added to the *anomaly_list* for *forget_after* days, then all the cases are removed from the *anomaly_list* and are saved in *anomaly_list_saved* (explained in *save_anomalies()*). Then the algorithm waits for a new case to arrive and implements all the functions from *update_clusters()* to *save_anomalies()*. A detailed explanation of each step is provided in subsection 4.3.

4.3   Steps

The steps detailed inside the While loop in Algorithm 1 produce the following output: *cluster_list* - a list of all the formed clusters, *cluster_list_forgotten* - a list of all the clusters that were forgotten after *forget_after* days, *anomaly_list* - a list of all the cases that were detected anomalous, *anomaly_list_saved* - a list of all the cases that were saved as anomalies after *forget_after* days. Cases in these clusters are then categorized as common, periodic, temporary, and anomalous in the post analysis step.

Brief overview of the steps of the proposed method is presented in Algorithm 1, followed by detailed textual description of each step.

Algorithm 1: Steps included in the proposed method

---

initialize_clusters()
while *True* **do**
    update_clusters()
    if *len_current_anomaly_list > len_last_anomaly_list* **then**
       | *form_new_clusters()*
    if *similarity between any two clusters >= merging_criteria* **then**
       | *merge_clusters()*
    if *no new case added to an existing cluster in forget_after day* **then**
       | *forget_clusters()*
    if *no new case added to the anomaly_list in forget_after day* **then**
       | *save_anomalies()*
end
post analysis

---

initialize_clusters(): In order to form initial clusters, a number of initial cases need to be picked, i.e. the parameter *initial_cases*. The value of parameter *initial_cases* is dependent on the user and the dataset. For example *initial_cases* can be number of all the cases completed within one week from beginning of the process. Then the distance matrix D is computed for the *initial_cases*, and using CCV initial number of clusters c is determined. After finding c, the value of parameter *cut_off_size_for_new_cluster* is computed as *initial_cases*/c; value is useful in implementing function *form_new_clusters()*. It is to be noted that the proposed method assumes that all the incoming cases are completed and contain an end-timestamp. It is important that the cases are complete because unless a case is completed, it cannot be assigned to any cluster. The end-timestamps are important to know the order of arrival of the cases.

Next, NERFCM algorithm is implemented using D and c to obtain a partition matrix U. It is to be noted that initialization of prototypes in NERFCM is not random which makes this method deterministic. Next, using D and U, c initial clusters are formed among the *initial_cases*. Since in a partition matrix each data point belongs to each partition with a certain degree of membership, therefore each trace is only kept in the cluster with which it has the highest degree of membership. After the creation of initial clusters, their respective *cluster_center* and *cluster_radius* are determined. For each cluster, the cluster member with the highest degree of membership to a cluster is selected as its *cluster_center*. For each cluster, the weighted average distance between the cluster center and each cluster member is computed; longest of all these distances is selected as *cluster_radius*. Finally, all the traces falling outside their respective cluster radius are added to *anomaly_list*.

update_clusters(): When a new completed case arrives, its activities are combined to form a trace (*newTrace*), and its similarity with all existing clusters is checked. If *newTrace* falls in any of the existing clusters then it is added to that cluster, else it is added to the *anomaly_list*.

form_new_clusters(): In this step, existing anomaly list is explored to find if there exist any clusters in the *anomaly_list*. For this purpose, similar process as *initialize_clusters()* is carried out but on the traces in *anomaly_list*. A distance matrix D_a is computed for all the traces in *anomaly_list* and using CCV initial number of clusters c_a is determined. After finding c_a, NERFCM algorithm is implemented using D_a and c_a to obtain a partition matrix U_a. Using D_a and U_a, c_a clusters are formed and saved in a temporary list of clusters *cluster_list_temp*. Similar to *initialize_clusters()*, each trace is only kept in the cluster with which it has the highest degree of membership. Next, cluster center and cluster radius are determined, and all the traces falling outside their respective cluster radius are added to a temporary list of anomaly *anomaly_list_temp*. Once all the temporary clusters are formed then the temporary clusters which are larger or equal in size to *cut_off_size_for_new_cluster* are added to the main *cluster_list* and the contents of these clusters are deleted from the main *anomaly_list*. The idea behind computation of *cut_off_size_for_new_cluster* is that if c clusters exist in *initial_cases*, then on average each cluster has *initial_cases*/c traces; so, when a cluster formed in *anomaly_list* has equal or more traces than that average, then it can be considered as a valid cluster.

merge_clusters(): Any two clusters are merged on satisfaction of either of the two following conditions: *(i)* if distance between the two clusters is less than or equal to the parameter *merging_criteria*, or *(ii)* if the overall percentage of number of common elements in the two clusters exceed *1−merging_criteria*. In case two clusters are merged, then cluster center and radius is computed for the merged cluster. Also, the traces which do not fall under the new cluster radius are added to the *anomaly_list*.

forget_clusters(): If value of parameter *forgetting_type* is set to 'Yes' and if no *newTrace* is added to any existing cluster for *forget_after* days, then that cluster is removed from the main *cluster_list* and added to the *cluster_list_forgotten*.

save_anomalies(): If value of parameter *forgetting_type* is set to 'Yes' and if no *newTrace* is added to *anomaly_list* for *forget_after* days, then the cases existing in *anomaly_list* are removed from the *anomaly_list* and added to the *anomaly_list_saved*.

Once all the steps are completed, the algorithm wait for arrival of a new case. As soon as a new case arrives, it calls *update_clusters()* function and continues the while loop. When all the cases are processed, the user must go through post analysis of the output.

Post Analysis: Based on the performed clustering, the completed cases of an event log are categorized into the following four categories:

1. **Common Cases**: cases in main *cluster_list* are considered common since they were never forgotten or saved as anomalies.
2. **Periodic Cases**: cases in *cluster_list_forgotten* are considered periodic if they reappear again in main *cluster_list* or in *cluster_list_forgotten*.
3. **Temporary Cases**: cases in *cluster_list_forgotten* are considered temporary if they do not reappear in the main *cluster_list* or in *cluster_list_forgotten*; they were probably used for some special cases.
4. **Anomalous Cases**: at any given time, cases in *anomaly_list_saved* and *anomaly_list* are considered anomalous since they never belong to any cluster (whether forgotten or not forgotten).

5   Method Evaluation

In this section, first we discuss the event logs used to evaluate the method and the anomalies that are introduced to those event logs. Next we discuss the parameters selected to evaluate the method, followed by the results obtained from applying the proposed method on the selected event logs.

5.1   Event Logs

To assess the performance of an anomaly detection algorithm, it is necessary to know which traces in a process are anomalous and which traces are not anomalous. For this purpose we require synthetic event logs where we already know the process. We used PLG [10] to create six process models and their event logs with varying complexity of number of activities, breadth, and width. These event logs are the same as used in [29]. In addition to the synthetic event logs, we also used 9 real-life event logs from the Business Process Intelligence Challenge (BPIC) - BPIC12 [16], BPIC13 [37–39], and BPIC15 [15]. In the remaining of this paper, the event logs are referred by their names as defined in Table 1.

Table 1. Overview of event Logs

Name	Number of Logs	Number of Activities	Number of Cases	Number of Events
Small	1	41	5k	45.2k
Medium	1	65	5k	29.8k
Large	1	85	5k	55.6k
Huge	1	109	5k	40.6k
Gigantic	1	154–157	5k	31.5k
Wide	1	68–69	5k	30.4k
BPIC12	1	24	13k	262.8k
BPIC13	3	11–27	0.8k–7.5k	4k–81k
BPIC15	5	422–486	0.8k–1.4k	46k–62k
Alpha	1	78	3.5k	32k

To test the effectiveness of the proposed method, we needed to use an event log in which we know where common, periodic, and temporary cases occur. For this reason we created another synthetic event log which was created using combination of three event logs from Table 1, namely Large, Gigantic, and Huge. We named this synthetic event log 'Alpha'. The Alpha event log contains total 3500 cases: 2000 cases from Large, 1000 cases from Gigantic, and 500 cases from Huge. To induce periodicity in the Alpha event log, 500 cases from Gigantic are added at 14 days from the beginning of the event log, and the remaining 500 cases are added 14 days after that. Whereas, to introduce temporal nature in the event log, all of the 500 cases from Huge are added at 4 weeks from the completion of first case in the event log.

Moreover, random anomalies of type Rework, Skip, Early, Late, and Insert were introduced to the datasets, using the approach proposed by Nolle et al. [29] to make the event log dataset more realistic. The introduction of anomalies is done for the purpose of completeness.

5.2   Experiment Setup

To test the working of the proposed method, a set of values for the input parameters (Sect. 4.1) needed to be defined. For the first input parameter, *distance_type*, we selected Jaccard Distance because it is computationally more efficient than Levenshtein Distance (linear versus quadratic time complexity) [14]. For *initial_cases*, we propose three variants - *small*, *medium*, and *large*. Variant *small* selects all the cases ending within one week from the starting date of the first case; for *medium* variant this range is till two weeks from the starting date of the first case; and for *large* variant it is four weeks. The values of fuzzifier *m* and converging criteria *epsilon* were set to their default values. For *merging_criteria*, we use three distinct values - 90%, 80% and 70% similarity. Both 'Yes' and 'No' values are tested for parameter *forgetting_type*. The value of *forget_after* is set to 7 days.

It is to be noted that the evaluation of the method is done mainly by varying values of the parameters *initial_cases*, *merging_criteria*, and *forget_type*. Considering the values of these parameters to be set as mentioned in the previous paragraph, we obtain 18 distinct combinations. Since it would be impractical to discuss results from all 18 combinations for each of 16 event logs ($18 \times 16 = 288$ combinations), therefore, for brevity, we only present in-depth results for the Alpha event log.

5.3 Results

Using the selected parameters, we receive a set of results for Alpha event log as shown in Fig. 1 and Table 2. Figure 1 shows a visual comparison between results obtained by setting the parameter *forgetting_type* as 'No' and 'Yes'. In the Fig. 1 each row represents a cluster, where cluster C_n represents common cases, cluster PC_n represents periodic cases, cluster TC_n represents temporary cases; where n is the number of cluster. For instance, C_1 shows the first cluster in the main *cluster_list*. The last row in both Fig. 1a and Fig. 1b shows the *anomaly_list_saved* (ALS). The horizontal axis represents the arrival of cases in the order of their time of completion. Each vertical bar in a cluster shows the assignment of case to that cluster. The legend in each cluster shows the number of cases that were added to that cluster. For instance, Fig. 1a shows that 812 cases were added to the first cluster, and 583 cases were added to the anomaly list.

In Fig. 1b, PC_1-PC_5 and TC_1 are the clusters which were forgotten from the main cluster list at some point in time since no new case was added to them. In the post analysis of the results, it is found that a similar cluster to PC_1 reappeared again in PC_2, PC_3 and part of PC_4. Also, part of PC_4 reappeared in PC_5. Since, all these reappearing clusters are similar to each other and they were forgotten after some time, therefore, by definition of Periodic Cases (in Subsect. 4.3) they are categorized as periodic cases. On the other hand, TC_1 is a cluster of cases which was forgotten after some time but no similar cluster ever reappeared in main clusters or forgotten clusters. For this reason, the cases in TC_1 are categorized as temporary cases. Furthermore, in Fig. 1a, all the periodic and temporary cases are included in the main cluster. Cases falling in these clusters makes up of periodic and temporary process variants.

In Table 2, the first thing we observe is that when value of parameter *initial_cases* is kept constant (e.g. small), the number of clusters formed at the

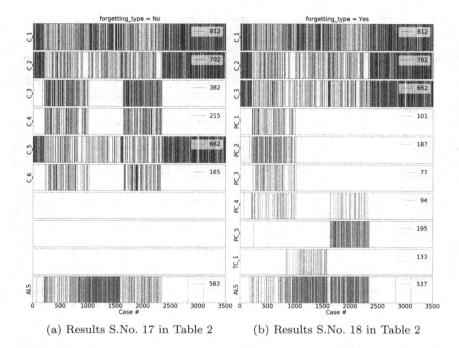

(a) Results S.No. 17 in Table 2   (b) Results S.No. 18 in Table 2

Fig. 1. Comparison of *forgetting_type* = No versus *forgetting_type* = Yes. Blue bars are common cases, Green bars are periodic case, Orange bars are temporary cases, and Red bars are cases marked anomalous. (Color figure online)

start of the run is always the same. For example, in S.No. 1 to S.No. 6, the number of clusters at start is always 9. This is always true even if other parameters are changed. The reason behind this consistency is that the initial clusters are formed using *initial_cases* (in *initialize_clusters()*); so as long as the value of *initial_cases* is unchanged, the number of clusters formed at the beginning will always be same.

Additionally, in comparison to using *forgetting_type* as 'Yes', the number of clusters formed in the end is always more when using *forgetting_type* as 'No'. This gives us a hint that in the entire duration of the event log generation, the process being followed is not always the same. Moreover, it indicates that there may exist periodic and temporary cases in the event log data. The presence of periodic and temporary cases is confirmed when exploring the results further. It can be observed that when the method is not set to forget clusters, it does not detect any periodic and temporary cases. To be noted that *forgetting_type* 'Yes' may not always detect periodic and temporary cases unless the data suggests so.

In Table 2, P, R, and F1 refer to Precision, Recall, and F1-Score calculated for detection of periodic, temporary and anomalous cases. It can be observed that precision for detecting periodic and temporary cases is high. Also, compared to small and medium variant of *initial_cases*, the recall for the large variant is

Table 2. Evaluation of the proposed method on Alpha event log with varying parameters

S. No.	init. cases	merge crit.	forget type	c		Periodic cases			Temporary cases			Anomaly cases		
				Start	End	P	R	F1	P	R	F1	P	R	F1
1	Small	90%	No	9	20	–	–	–	–	–	–	1.00	0.01	0.02
2	Small	90%	Yes	9	4	1.00	0.94	0.97	1.00	0.76	0.86	0.26	0.02	0.04
3	Small	80%	No	9	19	–	–	–	–	–	–	1.00	0.01	0.02
4	Small	80%	Yes	9	3	1.00	0.94	0.97	1.00	0.76	0.86	0.55	0.01	0.02
5	Small	70%	No	9	18	–	–	–	–	–	–	1.00	0.01	0.02
6	Small	70%	Yes	9	3	1.00	0.94	0.97	1.00	0.76	0.86	1.00	0.01	0.03
7	Med	90%	No	9	23	–	–	–	–	–	–	1.00	0.03	0.06
8	Med	90%	Yes	9	9	1.00	0.94	0.97	1.00	0.77	0.87	1.00	0.02	0.04
9	Med	80%	No	9	16	–	–	–	–	–	–	1.00	0.04	0.08
10	Med	80%	Yes	9	7	1.00	0.91	0.96	1.00	0.75	0.86	0.47	0.07	0.12
11	Med	70%	No	9	16	–	–	–	–	–	–	1.00	0.04	0.08
12	Med	70%	Yes	9	3	1.00	0.93	0.96	1.00	0.77	0.87	0.96	0.04	0.08
13	Large	90%	No	5	6	–	–	–	–	–	–	0.16	0.19	0.18
14	Large	90%	Yes	5	3	1.00	0.65	0.79	1.00	0.27	0.42	0.15	0.16	0.15
15	Large	80%	No	5	6	–	–	–	–	–	–	0.16	0.19	0.18
16	Large	80%	Yes	5	3	1.00	0.65	0.79	1.00	0.27	0.42	0.15	0.16	0.15
17	Large	70%	No	5	6	–	–	–	–	–	–	0.16	0.19	0.18
18	Large	70%	Yes	5	3	1.00	0.65	0.79	1.00	0.27	0.42	0.15	0.16	0.15

significantly small. Moreover, precision for anomalous cases is high for small and medium variants, and very small for the large variant. The reason for this that for the large variant the radii are larger since initial clustering was done on a large number of cases. So, the arriving anomalous cases may be considered not different enough and hence fall in the cluster.

The results also show that the anomalous cases introduced by us are not well detected by our method. The reason we found is that since they are too similar to an existing cluster center, thus they are added to an existing cluster. Please note that we used Jaccard distance, in which order of activities performed is ignored. For example, for our method, traces 'abcde' and 'bdcea' are same since Jaccard Distance between them is zero.

Similar results can be observed when the method was tested with other event logs considered in the study (Table 3).

Table 3 shows the results of the clustering performed on other event logs, including BPIC event logs. Since we do not know if periodic and temporary cases are present in these event logs, we cannot comment on precision, recall and F1-scores for these event log. For this reason we present how many cases were categorized as common, periodic, temporary, and anomalous (also in how many clusters). We take this opportunity to present the utility of this clustering method. For instance, considering BPIC12 event log: we form 5 clusters which consist of 12881 common cases. This tells us that there are 5 types of most common processes followed during the generation of this event log. These 5 types of processes are nothing but the cluster centers of those 5 clusters (as shown in Table 4). Other cases that lie in these 5 clusters have $(1 - cluster\_radius)\%$ of

Table 3. Evaluation of the proposed method on other event logs with parameters *initial_cases* = small, *merging_criteria* = 70%, *forgetting_type* = Yes, *forget_after* = 7 days

Name	c		Common cases (clusters)	Periodic cases (clusters)	Temporary cases (clusters)	Anomalous cases
	Start	End				
Small	2	2	4832 (2)	0 (0)	0 (0)	49
Medium	3	6	4814 (6)	0 (0)	0 (0)	48
Large	3	5	4946 (5)	0 (0)	0 (0)	36
Huge	3	10	4948 (10)	0 (0)	0 (0)	24
Gigantic	2	7	4867 (7)	83 (1)	0 (0)	51
Wide	4	4	4924 (4)	46 (1)	0 (0)	48
BPIC12	2	5	12869 (1)	0 (0)	0 (0)	217
BPIC13_1	7	1	1394 (1)	0 (0)	0 (0)	27
BPIC13_2	6	1	7373 (1)	0 (0)	0 (0)	175
BPIC13_3	5	1	668 (1)	40 (2)	0 (0)	142
BPIC15_1	4	0	0 (0)	138 (31)	863 (48)	183
BPIC15_2	4	4	77 (4)	105 (21)	589 (124)	63
BPIC15_3	2	3	199 (3)	0 (0)	933 (12)	277
BPIC15_4	4	5	96 (5)	137 (23)	774 (131)	49
BPIC15_5	3	3	202 (3)	197 (9)	588 (27)	172

similarity to their respective cluster centers. For example, trace 'abuucddddsd' only lies in the first cluster (with 66.67% similarity), whereas trace 'abuucuddsd' lies in both first and third cluster because its distance to both cluster centers is less than their cluster radius (0.33 and 0.42 respectively). We observed similar results while testing the method on all the other event logs but for brevity they are not discussed in this paper.

Table 4. Cluster centers for BPIC12 event log showing the most common type of cases followed in the process

Cluster	Trace	Case	Cluster radius
1	abuuuusu	173856	0.50
2	abcdddddegfhijdjkljlwlwwwww wwlwlllomnpl	176596	0.12
3	abcddabtd	178167	0.50
4	addefghijdjqtj	175976	0.50
5	abuucduddddefghijdjjjkljlwlwwww wwwwwlwlsvl	174261	0.12

Overall, the proposed method is able to discover common, periodic, and temporary process variants in the event log data with a high precision by categorizing the cases as common, periodic, and temporary, while simultaneously marking infrequent cases as anomalous.

6   Conclusions

In this paper we presented a real-time method of discovering different process variants in the event log data which categorizes cases into four categories: common, periodic, temporary, anomalous. The method is able to produce at run-time an update on which type of cases are being executed at present by assigning cases to clusters. After testing on an artificially generated event log, it was found that the proposed method is able to categorize the event log data into the four categories with high precision.

Detecting different process variants in an event log data is an easy task if the entire event log data is known beforehand. It becomes challenging when the event log data is unknown. This is why we designed this method to work in real-time as soon as any new case is completed. Another reason to make the method process cases in real-time is that we wanted to capture the periodic and temporal nature in the event log data. Also, we wanted to capture the evolution of the clusters with time. Note that this method can also be used offline. A possible application of this method could be to use the obtained clusters in real-time process discovery and solving problem of spaghetti like models. This can be done by discovering the process model by using only the cluster representatives. Each cluster representative may also indicate a sub-process. Furthermore, we have information on periodic cases which can be used to discover periodic (sub-) process models.

As good as the method is in categorizing cases into the first three categories, we found out that it is not very efficient at detecting anomalies. Since many non-anomalous cases are categorized as anomalous, we suggest that the detected anomalies need to be further analysed by experts. This further analysis is necessary because the method only categorizes a case as anomalous if it is significantly different from rest of the cases executed prior to its completion. We realise that it is difficult to qualitatively assess the amount of the required expert input, and therefore we have identified a need for explanation of anomalies.

Moreover, all the forgotten clusters also need to be validated with the help of experts to understand whether that is how those cases were supposed to processed. This validation by experts is important because it is possible that the organisation recently made some changes to the process on purpose and they want to standardize those sub-processes. In this case, the process expert may mark a forgotten cluster as a main cluster. The same validation is also important for the detected anomalies.

Since the method proposed in this paper is able to cluster any new kind of case in real-time, it also provides a basis for providing explanation about when certain type of cases are used in a process. Our future work will be mainly focused on the explanation of anomalies.

One may argue that temporary cases can also be considered anomalous since they only happens once in a series and never again. We think it is a valid argument, but we believe the domain expert should have the freedom to make this decision.

A limitation of the proposed method is that it includes a uni-perspective anomaly detection method. As discussed earlier, the method discovers the structure in the event log data and also detects some anomalies as its byproduct. However, this is not a multi-perspective anomaly detection method since it only uses activities performed in each case. In future we want to include a multi-perspective view to the proposed method by providing weights to resources and other attributes associated with the activities.

Another limitation of this method is that when using Jaccard Distance, the method is good at finding the structure but detects less anomalies. In future work we would like to modify the method to work with Levenshtein Distance. In this work Levenshtein Distance is not used as it introduces two challenges: (i) It is difficult to decide on *merging_criteria* as, unlike Jaccard Distance, the Levenshtein Distance does not lie in the range [0, 1], which makes it difficult to define a global value of *merging_criteria*. (ii) As mentioned earlier in this paper, for larger data sets, using Levenshtein Distance increases computation time.

To overcome these challenges, we plan to use the study by Dolev et al. [14] to find a relation between Jaccard and Levenshtein distances and use that relation instead of computing Levenshtein distance every time a new case arrives.

As part of our future work we identify a need to make the parameter *forget_after* adapt to change in the frequency of arrival cases. The reasoning behind this need is explained in the following example. Let us assume value of the parameter *forget_after* is set to 7 days, and *cut_off_size_for_new_cluster* is 40. If we assume that generally we have an average of 50 cases arriving per day, but in summer time, because it is holiday period, we have an average of 5 cases arriving per day. It may be the situation that the cases completed in the summer time were added to the *anomaly_list* because they were different from the most common cases. As a result, all 25 cases execute in the last week were added to the *anomaly_list* and in the following 7 days they were saved as anomalies. Now even if the method detected a new cluster of 25 cases in the *anomaly_list*, it would not have qualified to be added to the main *cluster_list* because 25 is less than the *cut_off_size_for_new_cluster*, i.e. 40. For such situations, in a period of low frequency of arrival of cases, we think it is important that the method adapts to the situation and extends the window of *forget_after* days. This extension will give more chance to formation of a new cluster in such periods of low frequency of cases.

References

1. Armentano, M.G., Amandi, A.A.: Detection of sequences with anomalous behavior in a workflow process. In: Chen, Q., Hameurlain, A., Toumani, F., Wagner, R., Decker, H. (eds.) DEXA 2015. LNCS, vol. 9261, pp. 111–118. Springer, Cham (2015). https://doi.org/10.1007/978-3-319-22849-5_8

2. Bezerra, F., et al: Anomaly detection algorithms in business process logs. In: 10th International Conference on Enterprise Information Systems (2008)

3. Bezerra, F., Wainer, J., van der Aalst, W.M.P.: Anomaly detection using process mining. In: Halpin, T., et al. (eds.) BPMDS/EMMSAD -2009. LNBIP, vol. 29, pp. 149–161. Springer, Heidelberg (2009). https://doi.org/10.1007/978-3-642-01862-6_13

4. Bezerra, F.L., et al.: A dynamic threshold algorithm for anomaly detection in logs of process aware systems (2012)

5. Bezerra, F., et al.: Algorithms for anomaly detection of traces in logs of process aware information systems. Inf. Syst. **38**(1), 33–44 (2013)

6. Böhmer, K., Rinderle-Ma, S.: Multi-perspective anomaly detection in business process execution events. In: Debruyne, C., et al. (eds.) OTM 2016. LNCS, vol. 10033, pp. 80–98. Springer, Cham (2016). https://doi.org/10.1007/978-3-319-48472-3_5

7. Böhmer, K., et al.: Anomaly detection in business process runtime behavior-challenges and limitations. arXiv:1705.06659 (2017)

8. Böhmer, K., Rinderle-Ma, S.: Association rules for anomaly detection and root cause analysis in process executions. In: Krogstie, J., Reijers, H.A. (eds.) CAiSE 2018. LNCS, vol. 10816, pp. 3–18. Springer, Cham (2018). https://doi.org/10.1007/978-3-319-91563-0_1

9. Bouarfa, L., et al.: Workflow mining and outlier detection from clinical activity D logs. J. Biomed. Inf. **45**(6), 1185–1190 (2012)

10. Burattin, A.: Plg2: multiperspective processes randomization and simulation for online and offline settings. arXiv preprint arXiv:1506.08415 (2015)

11. Chuang, Y.-C., Hsu, P.Y., Wang, M.T., Chen, S.-C.: A frequency-based algorithm for workflow outlier mining. In: Kim, T., Lee, Y., Kang, B.-H., Ślęzak, D. (eds.) FGIT 2010. LNCS, vol. 6485, pp. 191–207. Springer, Heidelberg (2010). https://doi.org/10.1007/978-3-642-17569-5_21

12. Conforti, R., et al.: Filtering out infrequent behavior from business process event logs. IEEE Trans. Knowl. Data Eng. **29**(2), 300–314 (2016)

13. Dijkman, R., et al.: Linguistic summarization of event logs-a practical approach. Inf. Syst. **67**, 114–125 (2017)

14. Dolev, S., et al.: Relationship of jaccard and edit distance in malware clustering and online identification. In: 2017 IEEE 16th International Symposium on Network Computing and Applications (NCA), pp. 1–5. IEEE (2017)

15. van Dongen, B.B.: Bpi challenge 2015 (May 2015). https://doi.org/10.4121/uuid:31a308ef-c844-48da-948c-305d167a0ec1, https://data.4tu.nl/collections/BPI_Challenge_2015/5065424/1

16. van Dongen, B.: Bpi challenge 2012 (April 2012). https://doi.org/10.4121/uuid:3926db30-f712-4394-aebc-75976070e91f, https://data.4tu.nl/articles/dataset/BPI_Challenge_2012/12689204/1

17. Gold, E.M.: Language identification in the limit. Inf. Control **10**(5), 447–474 (1967)

18. Gupta, N., Anand, K., Sureka, A.: Pariket: mining business process logs for root cause analysis of anomalous incidents. In: Chu, W., Kikuchi, S., Bhalla, S. (eds.) DNIS 2015. LNCS, vol. 8999, pp. 244–263. Springer, Cham (2015). https://doi.org/10.1007/978-3-319-16313-0_19

19. Han, H., et al.: Abnormal process instances identification method in healthcare environment. In: International Conference on Trust, Security and Privacy in Computing and Communications, pp. 1387–1392. IEEE (2011)

20. Hathaway, R.J., et al.: Nerf c-means: Non-euclidean relational fuzzy clustering. Pattern Recogn. **27**(3), 429–437 (1994)

21. Hsu, P.Y., et al.: Using contextualized activity-level duration to discover irregular process instances in business operations. Inf. Sci. **391**, 80–98 (2017)
22. Huang, Y., et al.: Filtering out infrequent events by expectation from business process event logs. In: 2018 14th International Conference on CIS, pp. 374–377. IEEE (2018)
23. Kendall, M.: Rank correlation methods (1948)
24. Linn, C., Werth, D.: Sequential anomaly detection techniques in business processes. In: Abramowicz, W., Alt, R., Franczyk, B. (eds.) BIS 2016. LNBIP, vol. 263, pp. 196–208. Springer, Cham (2017). https://doi.org/10.1007/978-3-319-52464-1_18
25. Maggi, F.M., Burattin, A., Cimitile, M., Sperduti, A.: Online process discovery to detect concept drifts in LTL-based declarative process models. In: Meersman, R., et al. (eds.) OTM 2013. LNCS, vol. 8185, pp. 94–111. Springer, Heidelberg (2013). https://doi.org/10.1007/978-3-642-41030-7_7
26. Mardani, S., et al.: Fraud detection in process aware information systems using mapreduce. In: 2014 6th Conference on Information and Knowledge Technology (IKT), pp. 88–91. IEEE (2014)
27. Mărușter, et al.: A rule-based approach for process discovery: dealing with noise and imbalance in process logs. Data Min. Knowl. Disc. **13**(1), 67–87 (2006)
28. Nerode, A.: Linear automaton transformations. Proc. Am. Math. Soc. **9**(4), 541–544 (1958)
29. Nolle, T., et al.: Binet: Multi-perspective business process anomaly classification. Inf. Syst. (2019). https://doi.org/10.1016/j.is.2019.101458
30. Park, C.G., et al.: Temporal outlier detection and correlation analysis of business process executions. IEICE Trans. Inf. Syst. **102**(7), 1412–1416 (2019)
31. Pauwels, S., et al.: An anomaly detection technique for business processes based on extended dynamic bayesian networks. In: Proceedings of the 34th ACM/SIGAPP Symposium on Applied Computing, pp. 494–501 (2019)
32. Petri, C.: Kommunikation mit automaten (phd thesis). Institut für Instrumentelle Mathematik, Bonn, Germany (1962)
33. Popescu, M., et al.: Correlation cluster validity. In: 2011 IEEE International Conference on Systems, Man, and Cybernetics, pp. 2531–2536 (2011)
34. Rogge-Solti, A., Kasneci, G.: Temporal anomaly detection in business processes. In: Sadiq, S., Soffer, P., Völzer, H. (eds.) BPM 2014. LNCS, vol. 8659, pp. 234–249. Springer, Cham (2014). https://doi.org/10.1007/978-3-319-10172-9_15
35. Sarno, R., et al.: Business process anomaly detection using ontology-based process modelling and multi-level class association rule learning. In: 2015 International Conference on Computer, Control, Informatics and its Applications (IC3INA), pp. 12–17. IEEE (2015)
36. Sledge, I.J., et al.: Relational generalizations of cluster validity indices. IEEE Trans. Fuzzy Syst. **18**(4), 771–786 (2010)
37. Steeman, W.: Bpi challenge 2013, closed problems (April 2013). https://doi.org/10.4121/uuid:c2c3b154-ab26-4b31-a0e8-8f2350ddac11, https://data.4tu.nl/articles/dataset/BPI_Challenge_2013_closed_problems/12714476/1
38. Steeman, W.: Bpi challenge 2013, incidents (April 2013). https://doi.org/10.4121/uuid:500573e6-accc-4b0c-9576-aa5468b10cee, https://data.4tu.nl/articles/dataset/BPI_Challenge_2013_incidents/12693914/1
39. Steeman, W.: Bpi challenge 2013, open problems (April 2013). https://doi.org/10.4121/uuid:3537c19d-6c64-4b1d-815d-915ab0e479da, https://data.4tu.nl/articles/dataset/BPI_Challenge_2013_open_problems/12688556/1
40. Sureka, A.: Kernel based sequential data anomaly detection in business process event logs. arXiv preprint arXiv:1507.01168 (2015)

41. Tavares, G.M., et al.: Anomaly detection in business process based on data stream mining. In: Brazilian Symposium on Information Systems, pp. 1–8 (2018)
42. Der Aalst, V., et al.: Workflow mining: a survey of issues and approaches. Data Knowl. Eng. **47**(2), 237–267 (2003)
43. Der Aalst, V., et al.: Business process mining: an industrial application. Inf. Syst. **32**(5), 713–732 (2007)
44. van Zelst, S.J., van Dongen, B.F., van der Aalst, W.M.P.: Online discovery of cooperative structures in business processes. In: Debruyne, C., et al. (eds.) OTM 2016. LNCS, vol. 10033, pp. 210–228. Springer, Cham (2016). https://doi.org/10.1007/978-3-319-48472-3_12
45. van Zelst, S.J., Bolt, A., Hassani, M., van Dongen, B.F., van der Aalst, W.M.P.: Online conformance checking: relating event streams to process models using prefix-alignments. Int. J. Data Sci. Anal. **8**(3), 269–284 (2017). https://doi.org/10.1007/s41060-017-0078-6
46. Wang, W., et al.: On fuzzy cluster validity indices. Fuzzy Sets Syst. **158**(19), 2095–2117 (2007)

Conformance Checking

CoCoMoT: Conformance Checking of Multi-perspective Processes via SMT

Paolo Felli, Alessandro Gianola, Marco Montali, Andrey Rivkin,
and Sarah Winkler[✉]

Free University of Bozen-Bolzano, Bolzano, Italy
{pfelli,gianola,montali,rivkin,winkler}@inf.unibz.it

Abstract. Conformance checking is a key process mining task for comparing the expected behavior captured in a process model and the actual behavior recorded in a log. While this problem has been extensively studied for pure control-flow processes, conformance checking with multi-perspective processes is still at its infancy. In this paper, we attack this challenging problem by considering processes that combine the data and control-flow dimensions. In particular, we adopt data Petri nets (DPNs) as the underlying reference formalism, and show how solid, well-established automated reasoning techniques can be effectively employed for computing conformance metrics and data-aware alignments. We do so by introducing the CoCoMoT (Computing Conformance Modulo Theories) framework, with a fourfold contribution. First, we show how SAT-based encodings studied in the pure control-flow setting can be lifted to our data-aware case, using SMT as the underlying formal and algorithmic framework. Second, we introduce a novel preprocessing technique based on a notion of property-preserving clustering, to speed up the computation of conformance checking outputs. Third, we provide a proof-of-concept implementation that uses a state-of-the-art SMT solver and report on preliminary experiments. Finally, we discuss how CoCoMoT directly lends itself to a number of further tasks, like multi- and anti-alignments, log analysis by clustering, and model repair.

1 Introduction

In process mining, the task of conformance checking is crucial to test the expected behavior described by a process model against the actual action sequences documented in a log [10]. While the problem has been thoroughly studied for pure control-flow processes such as classical Petri nets [10,28], the situation changes for process models equipped with additional perspectives beyond the control-flow, such as for example the data perspective. Notice that, while there are various works that primarily focus on the formalization and analysis of data or object-aware extensions of Petri nets (e.g., [17,20,24,26]), attacking the conformance checking problem in the non-classical setting is a very challenging task. This problem indeed requires to simultaneously consider, in a combined way, both the control-flow of the process and the data that the process manipulates.

© Springer Nature Switzerland AG 2021
A. Polyvyanyy et al. (Eds.): BPM 2021, LNCS 12875, pp. 217–234, 2021.
https://doi.org/10.1007/978-3-030-85469-0_15

Existing approaches almost exclusively focused on control-flow alignments and can therefore not be applied off-the-shelf. To the best of our knowledge, there are in fact very few existing approaches dealing with the aforementioned problem, and they concentrate on declarative [7] and procedural [21,22] multi-perspective process models with rather restrictive assumptions on the data dimension.

In this paper, we provide a new stepping stone in the line of research focused on conformance checking of multi-perspective procedural, Petri net-based process models. Specifically, we introduce a novel general framework, called CoCoMoT, to tackle conformance checking of data Petri nets (DPNs), an extensively studied formalism within BPM [13,14,18] and process mining [21–23]. The main feature of CoCoMoT is that, instead of providing ad-hoc algorithmic techniques for checking conformance, it provides an overarching approach based on the theory and practice of Satisfiability Modulo Theories (SMT) [2]. By relying on an SMT backend, we employ well-established automated reasoning techniques that can support data and operations from a variety of theories, restricting the data dimension as little as possible.

On top of this basis, we provide a fourfold contribution. First, we show that conformance checking of DPNs can be reduced to satisfiability of SMT formulas over the theory of linear integer and rational arithmetic. While our approach is inspired by the use of SAT solvers for a similar purpose [5,12], the use of SMT not only allows us to support data, but also capture unbounded nets. Our CoCoMoT approach results in a conformance checking procedure running in NP, which is optimal for the problem, in contrast to earlier approaches running in exponential time [21,22].

Second, we show how to simplify and optimize conformance checking by introducing a preprocessing, trace clustering technique for DPNs that groups together traces that have the same minimal alignment cost. Clustering allows one to compute conformance metrics by just computing alignments of one representative per cluster, and to obtain alignments for other members of the same cluster from a simple adjustment of the alignment computed for the representative trace. Besides the general notion of clustering, we then propose a concrete clustering strategy grounded in data abstraction for variable-to-constant constraints, and show how this strategy leads to a significant speedup in our experiments.

Third, we report on a proof-of-concept implementation of CoCoMoT, discussing optimization techniques and showing the feasibility of the approach with an experimental evaluation on three different benchmark sets.

Finally, we discuss how our approach, due to its modularity, directly lends itself to a number of further process analysis tasks such as computing *multi-* and *anti-alignments*, using CoCoMoT as a *log clustering* method in the spirit of earlier work for Petri nets without data [4,12], doing *model repair*, and handling more sophisticated data such as persistent, relational data.

The remainder of the paper is structured as follows. In Sect. 2 we recall the relevant basics about data Petri nets and alignments. This paves the way to present our SMT encoding in Sect. 3. Our clustering technique that serves as a preprocessor for conformance checking is the topic of Sect. 4. In Sect. 5 we describe our prototype implementation and the conducted experiments. Afterwards, we discuss perspectives and potential of our approach in Sect. 6.

2 Preliminaries

In this section we provide the required preliminaries. We first recall data Petri nets (DPNs) and their execution semantics, then delve into event logs and conformance checking alignments, and finally discuss the main machinery behind our approach for satisfiability modulo theories (SMT).

2.1 Data Petri Nets

We use Data Petri nets (DPNs) for modelling multi-perspective processes, adopting a formalization as in [21,22].

We start by introducing sorts – data types of variables manipulated by a process. We fix a set of *(process variable) sorts* $\Sigma = \{\texttt{bool}, \texttt{int}, \texttt{rat}, \texttt{string}\}$ with associated domains of booleans $\mathcal{D}(\texttt{bool}) = \mathbb{B}$, integers $\mathcal{D}(\texttt{int}) = \mathbb{Z}$, rationals $\mathcal{D}(\texttt{rat}) = \mathbb{Q}$, and strings $\mathcal{D}(\texttt{string}) = \mathbb{S}$. A set of *process variables* V is *sorted* if there is a function $sort \colon V \to \Sigma$ assigning a sort to each variable in V. For a set of variables V, we consider two disjoint sets of annotated variables $V^r = \{v^r \mid v \in V\}$ and $V^w = \{v^w \mid v \in V\}$ to be respectively read and written by process activities, as explained below, and we assume $sort(v^r) = sort(v^w) = sort(v)$ for every $v \in V$. For a sort $\sigma \in \Sigma$, V_σ denotes the subset of $V^r \cup V^w$ of annotated variables of sort σ. To manipulate sorted variables, we consider expressions c with the following grammar:

$$c = V_{\texttt{bool}} \mid \mathbb{B} \mid n \geq n \mid r \geq r \mid r > r \mid s = s \mid b \wedge b \mid \neg b \qquad s = V_{\texttt{string}} \mid \mathbb{S}$$
$$n = V_{\texttt{int}} \mid \mathbb{Z} \mid n + n \mid -n \qquad\qquad\qquad\qquad\qquad\qquad r = V_{\texttt{rat}} \mid \mathbb{Q} \mid r + r \mid -r$$

Standard equivalences apply, hence disjunction (i.e., $\vee$) and comparisons $\neq$, $<$, $\leq$ can be used as well (`bool` and `string` only support (in)equality). These expressions form the basis for capturing conditions on the values of variables that are read and written during the execution of activities in the process. For this reason, we call them *constraints*. Intuitively, a constraint $(v_1^r > v_2^r)$ dictates that the current value of variable v_1 is greater than the current value of v_2. Similarly, $(v_1^w > v_2^r + 1) \wedge (v_1^w < v_3^r)$ requires that the new value given to v_1 (i.e., assigned to v_1 as a result of the execution of the activity to which this constraint is attached) is greater than the current value of v_2 plus 1, and smaller than v_3. More in general, given a constraint c as above, we refer to the annotated variables in V^r and V^w that appear in c as the *read* and *written variables*, respectively. The set of read and written variables that appear in a constraint c is denoted by $\mathcal{V}ar(c)$, hence $\mathcal{V}ar(c) \subseteq V^w \cup V^r$. We denote the set of all constraints by $\mathcal{C}(V)$.

Definition 1 (DPN). *A Petri net with data (DPN) is given by a tuple $\mathcal{N} = (P, T, F, \ell, A, V, guard)$, where (1) (P, T, F, ℓ) is a Petri net with two non-empty disjoint sets of places P and transitions T, a flow relation $F : (P \times T) \cup (T \times P) \to \mathbb{N}$ and a labeling function $\ell : T \to A \cup \{\tau\}$, where A is a finite set of activity labels and τ is a special symbol denoting silent transitions; (2) V is a sorted set of process variables; and (3) $guard \colon T \to \mathcal{C}(V)$ is a guard assignment.*

As customary, given $x \in P \cup T$, we use $\bullet x := \{y \mid F(y,x) > 0\}$ to denote the *preset* of x and $x^\bullet := \{y \mid F(x,y) > 0\}$ to denote the *postset* of x. In order to refer to the variables read and written by a transition t, we use the notations $read(t) = \{v \mid v^r \in Var(guard(t))\}$ and $write(t) = \{v \mid v^w \in Var(guard(t))\}$. Finally, $G_\mathcal{N}$ is the set of all the guards appearing in $\mathcal{N}$.

To assign values to variables, we use variable assignments. A *state variable assignment* is a total function α that assigns a value to each variable in V, such that $\alpha(v) \in \mathcal{D}(sort(v))$ for all $v \in V$. These assignments are used to specify the current value of all variables. Similarly, a *transition variable assignment* is a partial function β that assigns a value to annotated variables, namely $\beta(x) \in \mathcal{D}(sort(x))$, with $x \in V^r \cup V^w$. These are used to specify how variables change as the result of activity executions (cf. Definition 2).

A *state* in a DPN $\mathcal{N}$ is a pair (M, α) constituted by a marking $M : P \to \mathbb{N}$ for the underlying Petri net (P, T, F, ℓ), plus a state variable assignment α. Therefore, a state simultaneously accounts for the control flow progress and for the current values of all variables in V, as specified by α.

We now define when a Petri net transition may fire from a given state.

Definition 2 (Transition firing). *A transition $t \in T$ is enabled in state (M, α) if a transition variable assignment β exists such that:*

(i) $\beta(v^r) = \alpha(v)$ for every $v \in read(t)$, i.e., β is as α for read variables;
(ii) $\beta \models guard(t)$, i.e., β satisfies the guard; and
(iii) $M(p) > F(p,t)$ for every $p \in \bullet t$;
(iv) $\mathrm{DOM}(\beta) = Var(guard(t))$, where DOM denotes the domain of functions: β is defined for the annotated variables in the guard.

An enabled transition may fire, producing a new state (M', α'), s.t. $M'(p) = M(p) - F(p,t) + F(t,p)$ for every $p \in P$, and $\alpha'(v) = \beta(v^w)$ for every $v \in write(t)$, and $\alpha'(v) = \alpha(v)$ for every $v \notin write(t)$. A pair (t, β) as above is called (valid) transition firing, and we denote its firing by $(M, \alpha) \xrightarrow{(t,\beta)} (M', \alpha')$.

Given $\mathcal{N}$, we fix one state (M_I, α_0) as *initial*, where M_I is the initial marking of the underlying Petri net (P, T, F, ℓ) and α_0 specifies the initial value of all variables in V. Similarly, we denote the final marking as M_F, and call *final* any state of $\mathcal{N}$ of the form (M_F, α_F) for some α_F.

We say that (M', α') is *reachable* in a DPN iff there exists a sequence of transition firings $\mathbf{f} = (t_1, \beta_1), \ldots, (t_n, \beta_n)$, s.t. $(M_I, \alpha_0) \xrightarrow{(t_1,\beta_1)} \ldots \xrightarrow{(t_n,\beta_n)} (M', \alpha')$, denoted as $(M_I, \alpha_0) \xrightarrow{\mathbf{f}} (M_n, \alpha_n)$. Moreover, $\mathbf{f}$ is called a (valid) *process run* of $\mathcal{N}$ if $(M_I, \alpha_0) \xrightarrow{\mathbf{f}} (M_F, \alpha_F)$ for some α_F, that is, if the run leads to a final state from the initial state (M_I, α_0). Similar to [22], we restrict to DPNs that are *relaxed data sound*, that is, where at least one final state is reachable.

We denote the set of valid transition firings of a DPN $\mathcal{N}$ as $\mathcal{F}(\mathcal{N})$, and the set of process runs as $Runs(\mathcal{N})$.

Example 1. Let $\mathcal{N}$ be as shown (with initial marking $[p_0]$ and final marking $[p_3]$):

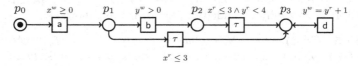

The set $Runs(\mathcal{N})$ contains, e.g., $\langle(\mathsf{a}, \{x^w \mapsto 2\}), (\mathsf{b}, \{y^w \mapsto 1\}), (\tau, \{x^r \mapsto 2, y^r \mapsto 1\})\rangle$ and $\langle(\mathsf{a}, \{x^w \mapsto 1\}), (\tau, \{x^r \mapsto 1\}), (\mathsf{d}, \{y^w \mapsto 1\})\rangle$, for $\alpha_0 = \{x \mapsto 0, y \mapsto 0\}$.

2.2   Event Logs and Alignments

Given an arbitrary set A of activity labels, an *event* is a pair (b, α), where $b \in A$ and α is a so-called *event variable assignment*, that is, a function that associates values to variables in V. Differently from state variable assignments, an event variable assignment can be a partial function.

Definition 3 (Log trace, event log). *Given a set $\mathcal{E}$ of events, a log trace $\mathbf{e} \in \mathcal{E}^*$ is a sequence of events in $\mathcal{E}$ and an* event log $L \in \mathcal{M}(\mathcal{E}^*)$ *is a multiset of log traces from $\mathcal{E}$, where $\mathcal{M}(\mathcal{E}^*)$ denotes the set of multisets over $\mathcal{E}^*$.*

We focus on a conformance checking procedure that aims at constructing an *alignment* of a given log trace $\mathbf{e}$ w.r.t. the process model (i.e., the DPN $\mathcal{N}$), by matching events in the log trace against transitions firings in the process runs of $\mathcal{N}$. However, when constructing an alignment, not every event can always be put in correspondence with a transition firing, and vice versa. Therefore, we introduce a special "skip" symbol $\gg$ and the extended set of events $\mathcal{E}^{\gg} = \mathcal{E} \cup \{\gg\}$ and, given $\mathcal{N}$, the extended set of transition firings $\mathcal{F}^{\gg} = \mathcal{F}(\mathcal{N}) \cup \{\gg\}$.

Given a DPN $\mathcal{N}$ and a set $\mathcal{E}$ of events as above, a pair $(e, f) \in \mathcal{E}^{\gg} \times \mathcal{F}^{\gg} \setminus \{(\gg, \gg)\}$ is called *move*.[1] A move (e, f) is called: (i) *log move* if $e \in \mathcal{E}$ and $f = \gg$; (ii) *model move* if $e = \gg$ and $f \in \mathcal{F}(\mathcal{N})$; (iii) *synchronous move* if $(e, f) \in \mathcal{E} \times \mathcal{F}(\mathcal{N})$. Let $Moves_{\mathcal{N}}$ be the set of all such moves. We now show how moves can be used to define alignments of log traces.

For a sequence of moves $\gamma = (e_1, f_1), \ldots, (e_n, f_n)$, the *log projection* $\gamma|_L$ of γ is the subsequence $e_1', \ldots, e_i'$ of $e_1, \ldots, e_n$ such that $e_1', \ldots, e_i' \in \mathcal{E}^*$ is obtained by projecting away from γ all $\gg$ symbols. Similarly, the *model projection* $\gamma|_M$ of γ is the subsequence $f_1', \ldots, f_j'$ of $f_1, \ldots, f_n$ such that $f_1', \ldots, f_j' \in \mathcal{F}(\mathcal{N})^*$.

Definition 4 (Alignment). *Given $\mathcal{N}$, a sequence of legal moves γ is an alignment of a log trace $\mathbf{e}$ if $\gamma|_L = \mathbf{e}$, and it is complete if $\gamma|_M \in Runs(\mathcal{N})$.*

Example 2. The sequences γ_1, γ_2 and γ_3 below are possible complete alignments of the log trace $\mathbf{e} = \langle(\mathsf{a}, \{x \mapsto 2\}), (\mathsf{b}, \{y \mapsto 1\})\rangle$ w.r.t. the DPN from Example 1:

$$\gamma_1 = \begin{array}{|c|c|c|} \hline \mathsf{a} \quad x \mapsto 2 & \mathsf{b} \quad y \mapsto 1 & \gg \\ \hline \mathsf{a} \quad x^w \mapsto 2 & \mathsf{b} \quad y^w \mapsto 1 & \tau \ldots \\ \hline \end{array} \quad \gamma_2 = \begin{array}{|c|c|c|} \hline \mathsf{a} \quad x \mapsto 2 & \gg & \mathsf{b} \quad y \mapsto 1 \\ \hline \mathsf{a} \quad x^w \mapsto 3 & \tau \ldots & \gg \\ \hline \end{array} \quad \gamma_3 = \begin{array}{|c|c|c|} \hline \mathsf{a} \quad x \mapsto 2 & \mathsf{b} \quad y \mapsto 1 & \gg & \gg \\ \hline \gg & \gg & \mathsf{a} \quad x^w \mapsto 3 & \tau \ldots \\ \hline \end{array}$$

---

[1] In contrast to [22], we do not distinguish between synchronous moves with correct and incorrect write operations, and defer this differentiation to the cost function.

We denote by $Align(\mathcal{N}, \mathbf{e})$ the set of complete alignments for a log trace $\mathbf{e}$ w.r.t. $\mathcal{N}$. A *cost function* is a mapping $\kappa\colon Moves_{\mathcal{N}} \to \mathbb{R}^+$ that assigns a cost to every move. It is naturally extended to alignments as follows.

Definition 5 (Cost). *Given $\mathcal{N}$, $\mathbf{e}$ and $\gamma = (e_1, f_1), \ldots, (e_n, f_n) \in Align(\mathcal{N}, \mathbf{e})$, the* cost *of γ is obtained by summing up the costs of its moves, that is, $\kappa(\gamma) = \sum_{i=1}^{n} \kappa(e_i, f_i)$. Moreover, γ is* optimal *for $\mathbf{e}$ if $\kappa(\gamma)$ is minimal among all complete alignments for $\mathbf{e}$, namely there is no $\gamma' \in Align(\mathcal{N}, \mathbf{e})$ with $\kappa(\gamma') < \kappa(\gamma)$.*

We denote the cost of an optimal alignment for $\mathbf{e}$ with respect to $\mathcal{N}$ by $\kappa_{\mathcal{N}}^{opt}(\mathbf{e})$. Given $\mathcal{N}$, the set of optimal alignments for $\mathbf{e}$ is denoted by $Align^{opt}(\mathcal{N}, \mathbf{e})$.

2.3 Satisfiability Modulo Theories (SMT)

The SAT problem asks, given a propositional formula φ, to either find a satisfying assignment ν under which φ evaluates to true, or detect that φ is unsatisfiable. For instance, given the formula $(p \vee q) \wedge (\neg p \vee r) \wedge (\neg r \vee \neg q)$, a satisfying assignment is $\nu(p) = \nu(r) = \top$, $\nu(q) = \bot$. The Satisfiability Modulo Theories (SMT) problem [2] extends SAT by asking to decide satisfiability of a formula φ whose language extends propositional formulas by constants and operators from one or more theories $\mathcal{T}$ (e.g., arithmetics, bit-vectors, arrays, uninterpreted functions). For this paper, only the theories of linear integer and rational arithmetic ($\mathcal{LIA}$ and $\mathcal{LQA}$) are relevant. For instance, the SMT formula $a > 1 \wedge (a + b = 10 \vee a - b = 20) \wedge p$, where a, b are integer and p is a propositional variable, is satisfiable by the assignment ν such that $\nu(a) = \nu(b) = 5$ and $\nu(p) = \top$. Another important problem studied in the area of SMT and relevant to this paper is the one of Optimization Modulo Theories (OMT) [27]. The OMT problem asks, given a formula φ, to find a satisfying assignment of φ that minimizes or maximizes a given objective expression. SMT-LIB [1] is an international initiative aiming at providing an extensive on-line library of benchmarks and promoting the adoption of common languages and interfaces for SMT solvers. In this paper, we make use of the SMT solvers Yices 2 [16] and Z3 [15].

3   Conformance Checking via SMT

In this section we illustrate our approach. We first describe in Sect. 3.1 a generic distance measure to be used as cost function. Then, in Sect. 3.2 we detail our encoding of the problem of finding optimal alignments in SMT. Notably, this technique works also for nets with arc multiplicities and unbounded nets, beyond the safe case considered in [5]. Finally, in Sect. 3.3 we analyze the computational complexity. Full proofs and details can be found in [19].

3.1   Distance-Based Cost Function

We present here a function used to measure the distance between a log trace and a process run. The recursive definition has the same structure as that of the standard edit distance, which allows us to adopt a similar encoding as used in the literature [3]. However, it generalizes both the standard edit distance and distance functions previously used for multi-perspective conformance checking [21,22], and admits also other measures that are specific to the model and the SMT theory used. Our measure is parameterized by three functions:

$$P_L : \mathcal{E} \to \mathbb{N} \qquad P_M : \mathcal{F}(\mathcal{N}) \to \mathbb{N} \qquad P_= : \mathcal{E} \times \mathcal{F}(\mathcal{N}) \to \mathbb{N}$$

respectively called the *log move penalty*, *model move penalty*, and *synchronous move penalty* functions (cf. Section 2.2). We use these functions to assign penalties to log moves, model moves, or synchronous moves. In what follows, we denote prefixes of length j of a log trace $\mathbf{e} \in \mathcal{E}^*$ of length m as $\mathbf{e}|_j$, provided $0 \le j \le m$, and analogously for a process run $\mathbf{f} \in Runs(\mathcal{N})$ (recall that these are sequences of transition firings in $\mathcal{F}(\mathcal{N})$).

Definition 6 (Edit distance). *Given a DPN $\mathcal{N}$, let $\mathbf{e} = e_1, \dots, e_m$ be a log trace and $\mathbf{f} = f_1, \dots, f_n$ a process run. For all i and j, $0 \le i \le m$ and $0 \le j \le n$, the edit distance $\delta(\mathbf{e}|_i, \mathbf{f}|_j)$ is recursively defined as follows:*

$$\delta(\epsilon, \epsilon) = 0$$
$$\delta(\mathbf{e}|_{i+1}, \epsilon) = P_L(e_{i+1}) + \delta(\mathbf{e}|_i, \epsilon)$$
$$\delta(\epsilon, \mathbf{f}|_{j+1}) = P_M(f_{j+1}) + \delta(\epsilon, \mathbf{f}|_j)$$
$$\delta(\mathbf{e}|_{i+1}, \mathbf{f}|_{j+1}) = \min \begin{cases} \delta(\mathbf{e}|_i, \mathbf{f}|_j) + P_=(e_{i+1}, f_{j+1}) \\ P_L(e_{i+1}) + \delta(\mathbf{e}|_i, \mathbf{f}|_{j+1}) \\ P_M(f_{j+1}) + \delta(\mathbf{e}|_{i+1}, \mathbf{f}|_j) \end{cases}$$

Definition 6 can be used to define a cost function by setting $\kappa(\gamma) = \delta(\gamma|_L, \gamma|_M)$, for any alignment γ. In the sequel, we call such a cost function *distance-based*. Moreover, it is known that for any trace $\mathbf{e}$ and process run $\mathbf{f}$ with $|\mathbf{e}| = m$ and $|\mathbf{f}| = n$, given the $(n+1) \times (m+1)$-matrix D such that $D_{ij} = \delta(\mathbf{e}|_i, \mathbf{f}|_j)$, one can reconstruct an alignment of $\mathbf{e}$ and $\mathbf{f}$ that is optimal with respect to κ [5,25].

Remark 1. By fixing the parameters $P_=$, P_L, and P_M of Definition 6, one obtains concrete, known distance-based cost functions, such as the following:

Standard Cost Function. Definition 6 can be instantiated to the measure in [22, Ex. 2], [21, Def. 4.5]. To that end, we set $P_L(b, \alpha) = 1$; $P_M(t, \beta) = 0$ if t is silent (i.e., $\ell(t) = \tau$) and $P_M(t, \beta) = |write(t)| + 1$ otherwise; and $P_=((b, \alpha), (t, \beta)) = |\{v \in \text{DOM}(\alpha) \mid \alpha(v) \ne \beta(v^w)\}|$ if $b = \ell(t)$ and $P_=((b, \alpha), (t, \beta)) = \infty$ otherwise.

Levenshtein Distance. The standard edit distance is obtained with $P_L(b, \alpha) = P_M(t, \beta) = 1$, and $P_=((b, \alpha), (t, \beta)) = 0$ if $b = \ell(t)$ and $P_=((b, \alpha), (t, \beta)) = \infty$ otherwise. Note that this measure ignores transition variable assignments β.

For instance, for the alignments γ_1, γ_2, and γ_3 from Example 2, the standard cost function yields $\kappa(\gamma_1) = 0$; $\kappa(\gamma_2) = 2$ (because we get penalty 1 for a synchronous move with incorrect write operation, no penalty for the silent model move, and penalty 1 for the log move); and $\kappa(\gamma_3) = 4$ (because we get penalty 1 for each of the log moves, penalty 2 for a non-silent model move that writes one variable, and no penalty for the silent model move).

3.2   Encoding

Our approach relies on the fact that the optimal alignment for a given log trace is upper-bounded in length. To this end, we use the following observation.

Remark 2. Given a DPN $\mathcal{N}$ and a log trace $\mathbf{e} = e_1, \ldots, e_m$, let $\mathbf{f} = f_1, \ldots, f_n$ be a valid process run such that $\sum_{j=1}^{n} P_M(f_j)$ is minimal. Then an optimal alignment γ for $\mathbf{e}$ and $\mathcal{N}$ satisfies $\kappa(\gamma) \leq \kappa(\gamma_{max})$, and hence $|\gamma| \leq |\gamma_{max}|$, where γ_{max} is the alignment $(e_1, \gg), \ldots, (e_m, \gg), (\gg, f_1), \ldots (\gg, f_n)$.

Given a log trace $\mathbf{e} = e_1, \ldots, e_m$ and a DPN $\mathcal{N}$ with initial marking M_I, initial state variable assignment α_0, final marking M_F, we want to construct an optimal alignment $\gamma \in Align^{opt}(\mathcal{N}, \mathbf{e})$. To that end, we assume throughout this section that the number of non-empty model steps in γ is bounded by some fixed number n (cf. Rem. 2). Our approach comprises the following four steps: (1) represent the alignment symbolically by a set of SMT variables, (2) set up constraints Φ that symbolically express optimality of this alignment, (3) solve the constraints Φ to obtain a satisfying assignment ν, and (4) decode an optimal alignment γ from ν. We next elaborate these steps in detail.

(1) Alignment representation. We use the following SMT variables:

(a) transition step variables S_i for $1 \leq i \leq n$ of type integer; if $T = \{t_1, \ldots, t_{|T|}\}$ then it is ensured that $1 \leq S_i \leq |T|$, with the semantics that S_i is assigned j iff the i-th transition in the process run is t_j;

(b) marking variables $M_{i,p}$ of type integer for all i, p with $0 \leq i \leq n$ and $p \in P$, where $M_{i,p}$ is assigned k iff there are k tokens in place p at instant i;

(c) data variables $X_{i,v}$ for all $v \in V$ and i, $0 \leq i \leq n$; the type of these variables depends on v, with the semantics that $X_{i,v}$ is assigned r iff the value of v at instant i is r; we also write X_i for $(X_{i,v_1}, \ldots, X_{i,v_k})$;

(d) distance variables $\delta_{i,j}$ of type integer for $0 \leq i \leq m$ and $0 \leq j \leq n$, where $\delta_{i,j} = d$ if d is the cost of the prefix $\mathbf{e}|_i$ of the log trace $\mathbf{e}$, and the prefix $\mathbf{f}|_j$ of the (yet to be determined) process run $\mathbf{f}$, i.e., $d = \delta(\mathbf{e}|_i, \mathbf{f}_j)$ by Definition 6.

Note that variables (a)–(c) comprise all information required to capture a process run with n steps, which will make up the model projection of the alignment γ, while the distance variables (d) will be used to encode the alignment.

(2) Encoding. To ensure that the values of variables correspond to a valid run, we assert the following constraints:

• The initial marking M_I and the initial assignment α_0 are respected:

$$\bigwedge_{p \in P} M_{0,p} = M_I(p) \wedge \bigwedge_{v \in V} X_{0,v} = \alpha_0(v) \qquad (\varphi_{init})$$

- The final marking M_F is respected:

$$\bigwedge_{p \in P} M_{n,p} = M_F(p) \qquad\qquad (\varphi_{final})$$

- Transitions correspond to transition firings in the DPN:

$$\bigwedge_{1 \le i \le n} 1 \le S_i \le |T| \qquad\qquad (\varphi_{trans})$$

In contrast to [3], no constraints are needed to express that at every instant exactly one transition occurs, since the value of S_i is unique.

- Transitions are enabled when they fire:

$$\bigwedge_{1 \le i \le n} \bigwedge_{1 \le j \le |T|} (S_i = j) \to \bigwedge_{p \in \, {}^\bullet t_j} M_{i-1,p} \ge |{}^\bullet t_j|_p \qquad (\varphi_{enabled})$$

where $|{}^\bullet t_j|_p$ denotes the multiplicity of p in the multiset ${}^\bullet t_j$.

- We encode the token game:

$$\bigwedge_{1 \le i \le n} \bigwedge_{1 \le j \le |T|} (S_i = j) \to \bigwedge_{p \in P} M_{i,p} - M_{i-1,p} = |t_j{}^\bullet|_p - |{}^\bullet t_j|_p \quad (\varphi_{mark})$$

where $|t_j{}^\bullet|_p$ is the multiplicity of p in the multiset $t_j{}^\bullet$.

- The transitions satisfy the constraints on data:

$$\bigwedge_{1 \le i < n} \bigwedge_{1 \le j \le |T|} (S_i = j) \to guard(t_j)\chi \wedge \bigwedge_{v \notin write(t_j)} X_{i-1,v} = X_{i,v} \quad (\varphi_{data})$$

where the substitution χ uniformly replaces V^r by X_{i-1} and V^w by X_i.

- The encoding of the data edit distance depends on the penalty functions $P_=$, P_M, and P_L. We illustrate here the formulae obtained for the standard cost function in Remark 1. Given a log trace $\mathbf{e} = (b_1, \alpha_1), \dots, (b_m, \alpha_m)$, let the expressions $[P_L]$, $[P_M]_j$, and $[P_=]_{i,j}$ be defined as follows, for all i and j:

$$[P_L] = 1$$
$$[P_M]_j = ite(S_j = 1, c_w(t_1), \dots ite(S_j = |T| - 1, c_w(t_{|T|-1}), c_w(t_{|T|})) \dots)$$
$$[P_=]_{i,j} = ite(S_j = b_i, \sum_{v \in write(b_i)} ite(\alpha_i(v) = X_{i,v}, 0, 1), \infty)$$

where the *write cost* $c_w(t)$ of transition $t \in T$ is 0 if $\ell(t) = \tau$, or $|write(t)| + 1$ otherwise, and *ite* is the if-then-else operator. It is then straightforward to encode the data edit distance by combining all equations in Definition 6:

$$\delta_{0,0} = 0 \qquad \delta_{i+1,0} = [P_L] + \delta_{i,0} \qquad \delta_{0,j+1} = [P_M]_{j+1} + \delta_{0,j} \qquad (\varphi_\delta)$$
$$\delta_{i+1,j+1} = \min([P_=]_{i+1,j+1} + \delta_{i,j},\ [P_L] + \delta_{i,j+1},\ [P_M]_{j+1} + \delta_{i+1,j})$$

(3) **Solving.** We use an SMT solver to obtain a satisfying assignment ν for the following constrained optimization problem:

$$\varphi_{init} \wedge \varphi_{final} \wedge \varphi_{trans} \wedge \varphi_{enabled} \wedge \varphi_{mark} \wedge \varphi_{data} \wedge \varphi_\delta \quad \text{minimizing} \quad \delta_{m,n}$$
$$(\Phi)$$

(4) Decoding. We obtain a valid process run $\mathbf{f} = f_1, \dots, f_n$ by decoding with respect to ν the variable sets S_i (to get the transitions taken), $M_{i,p}$ (to get the markings), and $X_{i,v}$ (to get the state variable assignments) for every instant i, as described in Step (1). Moreover, we use the known correspondence between edit distance and alignments [25] to reconstruct an alignment $\gamma = \gamma_{m,n}$ of $\mathbf{e}$ and $\mathbf{f}$. To that end, consider the (partial) alignments $\gamma_{i,j}$ recursively defined as follows:

$$\gamma_{0,0} = \epsilon \qquad \gamma_{i+1,0} = \gamma_{i,0} \cdot (e_{i+1}, \gg) \qquad \gamma_{0,j+1} = \gamma_{0,j} \cdot (\gg, f_{j+1})$$

$$\gamma_{i+1,j+1} = \begin{cases} \gamma_{i,j+1} \cdot (e_{i+1}, \gg) & \text{if } \nu(\delta_{i+1,j+1}) = \nu([P_L] + \delta_{i,j+1}) \\ \gamma_{i+1,j} \cdot (\gg, f_{j+1}) & \text{if otherwise } \nu(\delta_{i+1,j+1}) = \nu([P_M]_{j+1} + \delta_{i+1,j}) \\ \gamma_{i,j} \cdot (e_{i+1}, f_{j+1}) & \text{otherwise} \end{cases}$$

To obtain an optimal alignment, we use the following result:

Theorem 1. *Let $\mathcal{N}$ be a DPN, $\mathbf{e}$ a log trace and ν a solution to (Φ). Then $\gamma_{m,n}$ is an optimal alignment for $\mathbf{e}$, i.e., $\gamma_{m,n} \in Align^{opt}(\mathcal{N}, \mathbf{e})$.*

3.3   Complexity

In this section we briefly comment on the computational complexity of our approach and the (decision problem version of the) optimal alignment problem. To that end, let a cost function κ be *well-behaved* if it is distance-based and its parameter functions $P_=$, P_M, and P_L are effectively computable and can be defined by linear arithmetic expressions and case distinctions. For $c \in \mathbb{N}$ and a well-behaved cost function κ, let ALIGN_c be the problem that, given a relaxed data-sound DPN and a log trace, checks whether an alignment of cost c with respect to κ exists. For any given DPN $\mathcal{N}$, log trace $\mathbf{e}$ and cost c, the encoding presented in Sec. 3.2 is used to construct an SMT problem over linear integer/rational arithmetic that is satisfiable if and only if an alignment of cost c exists. The size of such an encoding is polynomial in the size of the DPN and the length of the log trace. Thus, since satisfiability of the relevant class of SMT problems is in NP [6], our approach to decide ALIGN_c is in NP. In contrast, the approach presented in [21,22] is exponential in the length of the log trace. Moreover, ALIGN_c is NP-hard since it is easy to reduce satisfiability of a boolean formula (SAT) to ALIGN_0. Hence, all in all ALIGN_c is NP-complete. Given a boolean formula φ with variables V, let $\mathcal{N}_\varphi$ be the following DPN:

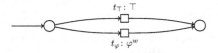

where φ^w is the formula obtained from φ by replacing all variables $v \in V$ by v^w. The DPN $\mathcal{N}_\varphi$ is relaxed data-sound due to the transition $t_\top$. Let $\mathbf{e}$ be the log trace consisting of the single event $(t_\varphi, \emptyset)$, and κ the standard edit distance (cf.

Rem. 1). Note that $Runs(\mathcal{N}_\varphi)$ contains at most two valid process runs: we have $\mathbf{f}_0 = (t_\top, \varnothing) \in Runs(\mathcal{N}_\varphi)$ and $\kappa(\mathbf{e}, \mathbf{f}_0) = \infty$. If φ is satisfiable by some transition variable assignment β, we also have $\mathbf{f}_1 = (t_\varphi, \beta_w) \in Runs(\mathcal{N}_\varphi)$, where β_w is the assignment such that $\alpha(v) = \beta_w(v^w)$ for all $v \in V$, and $\kappa(\mathbf{e}, \mathbf{f}_1) = 0$. Thus, $\mathbf{e}$ admits an alignment of cost 0 if and only if φ is satisfiable.

4   Trace Clustering

Clustering techniques are used to group together multiple traces in a process log so as to simplify and optimize several forms of analysis [29], including conformance checking [4,12]. In this section we introduce a novel form of clustering that is instrumental to simplify our multi-perspective conformance checking technique. The idea is to partition the log into *clusters*, where all traces within the same cluster share the same optimal alignment cost. We do so in two steps. We first introduce a general equivalence relation on the log traces, which thus identifies clusters as equivalence classes. We then provide an instantiation of such a relation that compares traces in the log by considering the satisfaction of guards of the DPN, thus providing a sort of data abstraction-based clustering.

Definition 7 (Cost-based clustering). *Given a DPN $\mathcal{N}$, a log L, and a cost function κ, a cost-based clustering is an equivalence relation $\equiv_{\kappa_\mathcal{N}^{opt}}$ over L, where, for all traces $\mathbf{e}, \mathbf{e}' \in L$ s.t. $\mathbf{e} \equiv_{\kappa_\mathcal{N}^{opt}} \mathbf{e}'$ we have that $\kappa_\mathcal{N}^{opt}(\mathbf{e}) = \kappa_\mathcal{N}^{opt}(\mathbf{e}')$.*

Notice that, according to the definition, different clusters do not necessarily correspond to different optimal alignment costs. We now introduce one specific equivalence relation that focuses on DPN guards performing *variable-to-constant* comparisons, and then show that this equivalence relation is a cost-based clustering. By focusing on such guards, one can improve performance of alignment-based analytic tasks. Indeed, variable-to-constant guards, although simple, are extensively used in practice, and they have been subject to an extensive body of research [13]. Moreover, this class of guards is common in benchmarks from the literature, is the one required to model decisions based on the DMN S-FEEL standard, and is the target of guard discovery techniques based on decision trees [23]. Note, however, that we do not at all restrict the DPNs we consider to use only such guards - richer guards are simply not exploited in the clustering.

Recalling that constraints are used in DPNs as guards associated to transitions, and that a constraint is in general a boolean expression whose atoms are comparisons (cf. Section 2.1), we use $Atoms(c)$ to define the set of all atoms in a guard $c \in G_\mathcal{N}$. Given a DPN $\mathcal{N}$, a *variable-to-constant* atom is an expression of the form $x \odot k$, where $\odot \in \{>, \geq, =\}$, $x \in V^r \cup V^w$ and k is a constant in $\mathbb{Z}$ or $\mathbb{Q}$. We say that a variable $v \in V$ is *restricted to constant comparison* if all atoms in the guards of $\mathcal{N}$ that involve v^r or v^w are variable-to-constant atoms. For such variables, we also introduce the set $ats_v = \{v \odot k \mid x \odot k \in Atoms(c), \text{ for some } c \in G_\mathcal{N}, x \in \{v^r, v^w\}\}$, i.e., the set of comparison atoms $v \odot k$ as above, this time expressed with non-annotated variables. The set ats_v can be seen as a set of predicates with free variable v.

Intuitively, given a cost function as in Remark 1, the optimal alignment of a log trace does not depend on the actual variable values specified in the events in the log trace, but only on whether the atoms in ats_v are satisfied. In this sense, our approach can be considered as a special form of *predicate abstraction*. Based on this idea, trace equivalence is defined as follows.

Definition 8. *For a variable v that is restricted to constant comparison and two values u_1, u_2, let $u_1 \sim_{cc}^v u_2$ if for all $v \odot k \in ats_v$, $u_1 \odot k$ holds iff $u_2 \odot k$ holds. Two event variable assignments α and α' are equivalent up to constant comparison, denoted $\alpha \sim_{cc} \alpha'$, if $\mathrm{DOM}(\alpha) = \mathrm{DOM}(\alpha')$ and for all variables $v \in \mathrm{DOM}(\alpha)$, either (i) $\alpha(v) = \alpha'(v)$, or (ii) v is restricted to constant comparison and $\alpha(v) \sim_{cc}^v \alpha'(v)$.*

This definition intuitively guarantees that α and α' "agree on satisfying" the same atomic constraints in the process. For example, if $\alpha(x) = 4$ and $\alpha'(x) = 5$, then, given two constraints $x > 3$ and $x < 2$, we will get that $\alpha \models x > 3$ and $\alpha' \models x > 3$, whereas $\alpha \not\models x < 2$ as well as $\alpha' \not\models x < 2$.

Definition 9 (Equivalence up to constant comparison). *Two events $e = (b, \alpha)$ and $e' = (b', \alpha')$ are equivalent up to constant comparison, denoted $e \sim_{cc} e'$, if $b = b'$ and $\alpha \sim_{cc} \alpha'$. Two log traces $\mathbf{e}$, $\mathbf{e}'$ are equivalent up to constant comparison, denoted $\mathbf{e} \sim_{cc} \mathbf{e}'$, iff their events are pairwise equivalent up to constant comparison. That is, $\mathbf{e} = e_1, \ldots, e_n$, $\mathbf{e}' = e_1', \ldots, e_n'$, and $e_i \sim_{cc} e_i'$ for all i, $1 \leq i \leq n$.*

Example 3. In Example 1, variable x is restricted to constant comparison, while y is not. Since $ats_x = \{x \geq 0, x \leq 3\}$, the log traces $\mathbf{e}_1 = \langle(\mathsf{a}, \{x \mapsto 2\}), (\mathsf{b}, \{y \mapsto 1\})\rangle$ and $\mathbf{e}_2 = \langle(\mathsf{a}, \{x \mapsto 3\}), (\mathsf{b}, \{y \mapsto 1\})\rangle$, satisfy $\mathbf{e}_1 \sim_{cc} \mathbf{e}_2$, but for $\mathbf{e}_3 = \langle(\mathsf{a}, \{x \mapsto 4\}), (\mathsf{b}, \{y \mapsto 1\})\rangle$ we have $\mathbf{e}_1 \not\sim_{cc} \mathbf{e}_3$ because $3 \not\sim_{cc}^x 4$, and $\mathbf{e}_4 = \langle(\mathsf{a}, \{x \mapsto 3\}), (\mathsf{b}, \{y \mapsto 2\})\rangle$ satisfies $\mathbf{e}_1 \not\sim_{cc} \mathbf{e}_4$ because the values for y differ. The equivalent traces $\mathbf{e}_1$ and $\mathbf{e}_2$ have the same optimal cost with respect to the standard cost function from Remark 1: for the alignments

$$\gamma_1 = \begin{array}{|c|c|c|} \hline \mathsf{a} \quad x \mapsto 2 & \mathsf{b} \quad y \mapsto 1 & \gg \\ \hline \mathsf{a} \quad x^w \mapsto 2 & \mathsf{b} \quad y^w \mapsto 1 & \tau \ldots \\ \hline \end{array} \quad \gamma_2 = \begin{array}{|c|c|c|} \hline \mathsf{a} \quad x \mapsto 3 & \mathsf{b} \quad y \mapsto 1 & \gg \\ \hline \mathsf{a} \quad x^w \mapsto 3 & \mathsf{b} \quad y^w \mapsto 1 & \tau \ldots \\ \hline \end{array} \quad \gamma_3 = \begin{array}{|c|c|c|} \hline \mathsf{a} \quad x \mapsto 4 & \mathsf{b} \quad y \mapsto 1 & \gg \\ \hline \mathsf{a} \quad x^w \mapsto 3 & \mathsf{b} \quad y^w \mapsto 1 & \tau \ldots \\ \hline \end{array}$$

we have $\kappa_{\mathcal{N}}^{opt}(\mathbf{e}_1) = \kappa(\gamma_1) = 0$ and $\kappa_{\mathcal{N}}^{opt}(\mathbf{e}_2) = \kappa(\gamma_2) = 0$. Note, however, that the respective process runs $\gamma_1|_M$ and $\gamma_2|_M$ differ. On the other hand, γ_3 is an optimal alignment for $\mathbf{e}_3$ but $\kappa(\gamma_3) = \kappa_{\mathcal{N}}^{opt}(\mathbf{e}_3) = 1$.

Moreover, $\mathbf{e}_1$ and $\mathbf{e}_3$ show that for trace equivalence it does not suffice to consider model transitions with activity labels that occur in the traces: all events in $\mathbf{e}_1$ and $\mathbf{e}_3$ correctly correspond to transitions with the same labels in $\mathcal{N}$, but for a *later* transition the value of x makes a difference. This motivates the requirement that in equivalent traces (Definition 8 and Definition 9) the values of a variable v that is restricted to constant comparison satisfies the same subset of ats_v.

We next show that equivalence up to constant comparison is a cost-based clustering, provided that the cost function is of a certain format. To that end, we consider a distance-based cost function κ from Definition 6 and call it *comparison-based* when the following conditions hold:

1. $P_L(b, \alpha)$ does not depend on the values assigned by α, and $P_M(t, \beta)$ does not depend on the values assigned by β;
2. the value of $P_=((b, \alpha), (t, \beta))$ depends only on whether conditions $b = \ell(t)$ and $\alpha(v) = \beta(v^w)$ are satisfied or not.

Note that this requirement is satisfied by the distance-based cost function in Remark 1. Indeed, in the standard cost function, $P_L(b, \alpha) = 1$ and thus it does not depend on α. Moreover, the second condition is clearly satisfied, as in $P_=((b, \alpha), (t, \beta)) = |\{v \in \text{DOM}(\alpha) \mid \alpha(v) \neq \beta(v^w)\}|$, for $b = \ell(t)$, we only need to check whether $\alpha(v) \neq \beta(v^w)$.

Theorem 2. *Equivalence up to constant comparison is a cost-based clustering with respect to any comparison-based cost function.*

Proof (sketch). We prove that if $\mathbf{e}_1$ has an alignment γ_1 with cost $\kappa(\gamma_1) = \delta(\mathbf{e}_1, \mathbf{f}_1)$, where $\mathbf{f}_1 = \gamma_1|_M$, then there is a process run $\mathbf{f}_2$ such that $\delta(\mathbf{e}_2, \mathbf{f}_2) = \kappa(\gamma_1)$, and hence there is an alignment γ_2 with $\gamma_2|_L = \mathbf{e}_2$, $\gamma_2|_M = \mathbf{f}_2$ and $\kappa(\gamma_2) = \delta(\mathbf{e}_2, \mathbf{f}_2)$. More precisely, if $|\mathbf{e}_1| = |\mathbf{e}_2| = m$ and $|\mathbf{f}_1| = n$, we show by induction on $m + n$ that there is some $\mathbf{f}_2$ such that $|\mathbf{f}_2| = n$, $\delta(\mathbf{e}_1, \mathbf{f}_1) = \delta(\mathbf{e}_2, \mathbf{f}_2)$, and $\mathbf{f}_1$ and $\mathbf{f}_2$ result in state variable assignments that are equivalent up to $\sim_{cc}$. The inductive step works by a case distinction on the cases in Definition 6, exploiting the properties of a comparison-based cost function. The full proof is in [19]. $\square$

An interesting byproduct of the constructive proof of Theorem 2 (see [19]) is that given $\gamma \in Align^{opt}(\mathcal{N}, \mathbf{e})$, for every trace $\mathbf{e}'$ in the same cluster (i.e. $\mathbf{e} \sim_{cc} \mathbf{e}'$) an optimal alignment is easily computed from γ, $\mathbf{e}$, and $\mathbf{e}'$ in linear time.

All in all, we thus get that our clustering technique allows us to compute faithful conformance metrics on logs by calculating alignment costs only on a single representative trace per cluster.

5   Implementation and Experiments

We now report on the DPN conformance checking tool `cocomot`, a proof-of-concept implementation based on the encoding in Sec. 3.2. We focus on implementation, some optimizations, and experiments on benchmarks from the literature. The source code together with related datasets are publicly available on the tool webpage: https://github.com/bytekid/cocomot.

Implementation. Our `cocomot` prototype is a Python command line script: it takes as input a DPN (as `.pnml` file) and a log (as `.xes`) and computes the optimal alignment distance, using the standard cost function from Remark 1, for every trace in the log. In verbose mode, it additionally prints an optimal alignment. To reduce effort, cocomot first preprocesses the log to a sublog of unique traces, and second applies trace clustering as described in Sec. 4 to further partition the sublog into equivalent traces. The conformance check is then run for one representative from every equivalence class.

cocomot uses pm4py (https://pm4py.fit.fraunhofer.de/) to parse traces, and employs the SMT solver Yices 2 [16] , or alternatively Z3 [15], as backend solver. Instead of writing the formulas to files, we use the bindings provided by the respective Python interfaces. Since Yices 2 has no optimization built-in, we implemented a minimization scheme using multiple satisfiability checks. Every check is run with a timeout, to avoid divergence on large problems.

Encoding Optimizations. To prune the search space, we modified the encoding presented in Sect. 3.2. We report here on the four most effective changes. (1) We perform a reachability analysis in a preprocessing step. This allows us to restrict the range of transition variables S_i in (φ_{trans}), as well as the cases $S_i = j$ in ($\varphi_{enabled}$) and (φ_{mark}) to those that are actually reachable. Moreover, if a data variable $v \in V$ will never be written in some step i, $1 \le i \le n$, because no respective transition is reachable, we set $X_{i,v}$ identical to $X_{i-1,v}$ to reduce the number of variables. (2) If the net is 1-bounded, the marking variables $M_{i,p}$ are typed as boolean rather than integer, similarly to [3]. (3) As $\delta_{m,n}$ is minimized, the equation of the form $\delta_{i+1,j+1} = min(e_1, e_2, e_3)$ in (φ_δ) can be replaced by inequalities $\delta_{i+1,j+1} \ge min(e_1, e_2, e_3)$. The latter is equivalent to $\delta_{i+1,j+1} \ge e_1 \vee \delta_{i+1,j+1} \ge e_2 \vee \delta_{i+1,j+1} \ge e_3$, which is processed by the solver much more efficiently since it avoids an if-then-else construct. (4) Several subexpressions are replaced by fresh variables (in particular when occurring repeatedly) - this is empirically known to positively affect performance.

Some of the data sets described below contain data variables of non-numeric types, namely boolean and string variables. The encoding represents the former by boolean SMT variables; and the latter by integer variables, encoding the string literals in the model as distinct natural numbers (cf. [21, p. 87]).

Experiments. We tested cocomot on three data sets used in earlier work [21,22], which have also been made publicly available on the tool's webpage. All experiments were run single-threaded on a 12-core Intel i7-5930K 3.50GHz machine with 32GB of main memory.

The first data set contains 150370 traces (35681 unique) of *road fines* issued by the Italian police. By trace clustering, the log reduces to 4290 non-equivalent traces. In 268 s, cocomot computes optimal alignments for all traces in this set, spending 13% of the computation time on parsing the log, 1.5% on trace clustering, 13% on the generation of the encoding, and the rest on SMT solving.[2] When omitting the clustering preprocessor, cocomot requires about 30 min to process all 35681 traces. We note some data about the model and log. The maximal length of a trace is 20, and its average alignment cost is 1.5. The average time

---

[2] Notice that in this paper we do not fix the exact algorithm for trace clustering, which in our implementation is achieved by exhaustively comparing log traces.

spent on a trace is 0.1 s. The process model has less than 20 transitions, and at most one token around at any point in time.

The second data set contains 100000 traces (4047 unique) of a *hospital billing* process. Trace clustering slightly reduces the number of non-equivalent traces to 4039. For 3392 traces `cocomot` finds an optimal alignment, while SMT timeouts occur for the remaining, very long traces (the maximal trace length is 217).

The third data set is about *sepsis*, and contains 1050 unique (and non-equivalent) traces. For 1006 traces `cocomot` finds an optimal alignment, while it times out for the remaining, very long traces (the maximal trace length is 185).

For the experiments described above we used Yices (with an SMT timeout of 10 min) as Z3 turned out to be considerably slower: checking conformance of the road fine log using Z3 (with its built-in minimization routine) takes more than two hours. On average, only 1% of the time is spent on generating the encoding, while the vast majority of time is used for SMT solving.

Notice that the trace clustering approach suggested in this paper considerably improves the performance over the presented data sets, as already pointed out for the one of road fines.

6 Discussion

In this section we outline how the CoCoMoT approach, due to its modularity, readily lends itself to further tasks related to the analysis of data-aware processes.

The **multi-alignment** problem asks, given a DPN $\mathcal{N}$ and a set of log traces $\{e_1, \ldots, e_n\}$, to find a process run $f \in \mathcal{P}_{\mathcal{N}}$ such that $\sum_{i=1}^{n} \kappa(\gamma_i)$ is minimal, where γ_i is a minimal-cost alignment of e_i and f for all i, $1 \leq i \leq n$ [12].[3] Our encoding can solve such problems by combining n copies of the distance variables and their defining equations (φ_δ) with (φ_{init})–(φ_{data}), and minimizing the above objective. Generalizing alignments, multi-alignments are of interest for their own sake, but also useful for further tasks, described next.

Anti-alignments were introduced to find model runs that deviate as much as possible from a log, e.g., for precision checking [11]. For a set of traces $\{e_1, \ldots, e_n\}$, the aim is to find $f \in \mathcal{P}_{\mathcal{N}}$ of bounded length such that $\sum_{i=1}^{n} \kappa(\gamma_i)$ is *maximal*, with γ_i as before. Using our encoding, this can be done as in the multi-alignment case, replacing minimization by maximization.

Trace clustering was studied as a method to partition event logs into more homogeneous sub-logs, with the hope that process discovery techniques will perform better on the sub-logs than if applied to the original log [12,28]. Chatain et al. [3,12] propose trace clustering based on multi-alignments. In the same fashion, our approach can be used to partition a log of DPN traces.

Our approach can also be used for **model repair** tasks: given a set of traces, we can use multi-alignments to minimize the sum of the trace distances, while replacing a parameter of the DPN by a variable (e.g., the threshold value in a guard). From the satisfying assignment we obtain the value for this parameter

---

[3] Instead of the sum, also other aggregation functions can be used, e.g., maximum.

that fits the observed behavior best. As constraints (φ_{init})–(φ_{data}) symbolically describe a process run of bounded length, our encoding supports **bounded model checking**. Thus we could also implement *scenario-based* conformance checking, to find for a given trace the best-matching process run that satisfies additional constraints, such as that certain data values are not exceeded.

Finally, but crucially, the **main advantage of SMT** is that it offers a multitude of *background theories* to capture the data manipulated by the DPN, and to express sophisticated cost functions. The approach by Mannhardt *et al.* [21,22] needs to restrict guards of DPNs to linear arithmetic expressions in order to use the MILP backend. In our approach, the language of guards may employ *arbitrary* functions and predicates from first-order theories supported by SMT solvers (e.g., uninterpreted functions, arrays, lists, and sets). For example, the use of (relational) predicates would allow to model structured background information, and possibly even refer to full-fledged relational databases from which data injected in the net are taken, following the SMT-based approaches as in [8,9]. Moreover, the background theory allows to express sophisticated cost functions as in Definition 6 with the following parameters (inspired by [21]): $P_{=}((b,\alpha),(t,\beta)) = |\{v \in write(t) \mid \neg R(\alpha(v)), R(\beta(v^w))\}|$ if $b = \ell(t)$, for some relation R from a database DB: in this way, $P_{=}$ counts the number of written variables whose values in the model run are stored in the relation R from DB whereas their values in the log trace are not.

7   Conclusions

We have introduced CoCoMoT, a foundational framework equipped with a proof-of-concept, feasible implementation for alignment-based conformance checking of multi-perspective processes. Beside the several technical results provided in the paper, the core contribution provided by CoCoMoT is to connect the area of (multi-perspective) conformance checking with that of declarative problem solving via SMT. This comes with a great potential for homogeneously tackling a plethora of related problems in a single framework with a solid theoretical basis and several state-of-the-art algorithmic techniques, as shown in Sect. 6. While in this paper we consider simple linear arithmetics for encoding cost functions in SMT, more complex theories, as well as their combinations, can be considered, thanks to the generality offered by SMT techniques. For example, one can capture more sophisticated cost functions involving background knowledge coming from additional data sources (in line of [8]) or correctly addressing privacy related aspects (when one typically needs to employ uninterpreted functions). All this is left for future work, but motivate once again the use of SMT.

Acknowledgments. This research has been partially supported by the UNIBZ projects *SMART-APP, REKAP, VERBA* and *DUB*.

References

1. Barrett, C., Fontaine, P., Tinelli, C.: The SMT-LIB Standard: Version 2.6. Technical report. http://smtlib.cs.uiowa.edu/language.shtml (2018)
2. Barrett, C., Tinelli, C.: Satisfiability modulo theories. In: Clarke, E., Henzinger, T., Veith, H., Bloem, R. (eds.) Handbook of Model Checking, pp. 305–343. Springer, Cham (2018). https://doi.org/10.1007/978-3-319-10575-8_11
3. Boltenhagen, M., Chatain, T., Carmona, J.: Encoding conformance checking artefacts in SAT. In: Di Francescomarino, C., Dijkman, R., Zdun, U. (eds.) BPM 2019. LNBIP, vol. 362, pp. 160–171. Springer, Cham (2019). https://doi.org/10.1007/978-3-030-37453-2_14
4. Boltenhagen, M., Chatain, T., Carmona, J.: Generalized alignment-based trace clustering of process behavior. In: Donatelli, S., Haar, S. (eds.) PETRI NETS 2019. LNCS, vol. 11522, pp. 237–257. Springer, Cham (2019). https://doi.org/10.1007/978-3-030-21571-2_14
5. Boltenhagen, M., Chatain, T., Carmona, J.: Optimized SAT encoding of conformance checking artefacts. Computing 103, 29–50 (2021)
6. Bradley, A.R., Manna, Z.: The Calculus of Computation – Decision Procedures with Applications to Verification. Springer, New York (2007). https://doi.org/10.1007/978-3-540-74113-8
7. Burattin, A., Maggi, F.M., Sperduti, A.: Conformance checking based on multiperspective declarative process models. Expert Syst. Appl. 65, 194–211 (2016)
8. Calvanese, D., Ghilardi, S., Gianola, A., Montali, M., Rivkin, A.: Formal modeling and SMT-based parameterized verification of data-aware BPMN. In: Hildebrandt, T., van Dongen, B.F., Röglinger, M., Mendling, J. (eds.) BPM 2019. LNCS, vol. 11675, pp. 157–175. Springer, Cham (2019). https://doi.org/10.1007/978-3-030-26619-6_12
9. Calvanese, D., Ghilardi, S., Gianola, A., Montali, M., Rivkin, A.: SMT-based verification of data-aware processes: a model-theoretic approach. Math. Struct. Comput. Sci. 30(3), 271–313 (2020)
10. Carmona, J., van Dongen, B.F., Solti, A., Weidlich, M.: Conformance Checking - Relating Processes and Models, Springer, Cham (2018) https://doi.org/10.1007/978-3-319-99414-7
11. Chatain, T., Carmona, J.: Anti-alignments in conformance checking – the dark side of process models. In: Kordon, F., Moldt, D. (eds.) PETRI NETS 2016. LNCS, vol. 9698, pp. 240–258. Springer, Cham (2016). https://doi.org/10.1007/978-3-319-39086-4_15
12. Chatain, T., Carmona, J., van Dongen, B.: Alignment-based trace clustering. In: Mayr, H.C., Guizzardi, G., Ma, H., Pastor, O. (eds.) ER 2017. LNCS, vol. 10650, pp. 295–308. Springer, Cham (2017). https://doi.org/10.1007/978-3-319-69904-2_24
13. de Leoni, M., Felli, P., Montali, M.: A holistic approach for soundness verification of decision-aware process models. In: Trujillo, J.C., et al. (eds.) ER 2018. LNCS, vol. 11157, pp. 219–235. Springer, Cham (2018). https://doi.org/10.1007/978-3-030-00847-5_17
14. de Leoni, M., Felli, P., Montali, M.: Strategy synthesis for data-aware dynamic systems with multiple actors. In: Proceedings of KR 2020, pp. 315–325 (2020)
15. de Moura, L., Bjørner, N.: Z3: an efficient SMT solver. In: Ramakrishnan, C.R., Rehof, J. (eds.) TACAS 2008. LNCS, vol. 4963, pp. 337–340. Springer, Heidelberg (2008). https://doi.org/10.1007/978-3-540-78800-3_24

16. Dutertre, B.: Yices 2.2. In: Biere, A., Bloem, R. (eds.) CAV 2014. LNCS, vol. 8559, pp. 737–744. Springer, Cham (2014). https://doi.org/10.1007/978-3-319-08867-9_49

17. Fahland, D.: Describing behavior of processes with many-to-many interactions. In: Donatelli, S., Haar, S. (eds.) PETRI NETS 2019. LNCS, vol. 11522, pp. 3–24. Springer, Cham (2019). https://doi.org/10.1007/978-3-030-21571-2_1

18. Felli, P., de Leoni, M., Montali, M.: Soundness verification of decision-aware process models with variable-to-variable conditions. In: Proceedings of ACSD 2019, pp. 82–91. IEEE (2019)

19. Felli, P., Gianola, A., Montali, M., Rivkin, A., Winkler, S.: Cocomot: Conformance checking of multi-perspective processes via SMT (extended version). Technical report. arXiv:2103.10507 (2021)

20. Ghilardi, S., Gianola, A., Montali, M., Rivkin, A.: Petri nets with parameterised data. In: Fahland, D., Ghidini, C., Becker, J., Dumas, M. (eds.) BPM 2020. LNCS, vol. 12168, pp. 55–74. Springer, Cham (2020). https://doi.org/10.1007/978-3-030-58666-9_4

21. Mannhardt, F.: Multi-perspective Process Mining. PhD thesis, Technical University of Eindhoven (2018)

22. Mannhardt, F., de Leoni, M., Reijers, H., van der Aalst, W.: Balanced multi-perspective checking of process conformance. Computing **98**(4), 407–437 (2016)

23. Mannhardt, F., de Leoni, M., Reijers, H.A., van der Aalst, W.M.P.: Decision mining revisited - discovering overlapping rules. In: Nurcan, S., Soffer, P., Bajec, M., Eder, J. (eds.) CAiSE 2016. LNCS, vol. 9694, pp. 377–392. Springer, Cham (2016). https://doi.org/10.1007/978-3-319-39696-5_23

24. Montali, M., Rivkin, A.: Db-nets: On the marriage of colored petri nets and relational databases. Trans. Petri Nets Other Model. Concurr. **12**, 91–118 (2017)

25. Needleman, S.B., Wunsch, C.D.: A general method applicable to the search for similarities in the amino acid sequence of two proteins. J. Mol. Biol. **48**(3), 443–453 (1970)

26. Polyvyanyy, A., van der Werf, J.M.E.M., Overbeek, S., Brouwers, R.: Information systems modeling: language, verification, and tool support. In: Giorgini, P., Weber, B. (eds.) CAiSE 2019. LNCS, vol. 11483, pp. 194–212. Springer, Cham (2019). https://doi.org/10.1007/978-3-030-21290-2_13

27. Sebastiani, R., Tomasi, S.: Optimization modulo theories with linear rational costs. ACM Trans. Comput. Log. **16**(2), 12:1–12:43 (2015)

28. van der Aalst, W.M.P.: Process Mining - Discovery, Conformance and Enhancement of Business Processes. Springer, Heidelberg (2011). https://doi.org/10.1007/978-3-642-19345-3

29. Zandkarimi, F., Rehse, J., Soudmand, P., Hoehle, H.: A generic framework for trace clustering in process mining. In: Proceedings of the ICPM 2020, pp. 177–184. IEEE (2020)

Aligning Data-Aware Declarative Process Models and Event Logs

Giacomo Bergami[1(✉)], Fabrizio Maria Maggi[1], Andrea Marrella[2],
and Marco Montali[1]

[1] Free University of Bozen-Bolzano, Bolzano, Italy
gibergami@unibz.it, {maggi,montali}@inf.unibz.it
[2] Sapienza - University of Rome, Rome, Italy
marrella@diag.uniroma1.it

Abstract. Alignments are a conformance checking strategy quantifying the amount of deviations of a trace with respect to a process model, as well as providing optimal repairs for making the trace conformant to the process model. Data-aware alignment strategies are also gaining momentum, as they provide richer descriptions for deviance detection. Nonetheless, no technique is currently able to provide trace repair solutions in the context of data-aware declarative process models: current approaches either focus on procedural models, or numerically quantify the deviance with no proposed repair strategy. After discussing our working hypotheses, we demonstrate how such a problem can be reduced to a data-agnostic trace alignment problem, while ensuring the correctness of its solution. Finally, we show how to find such a solution leveraging Automated Planning techniques in Artificial Intelligence. Specifically, we discuss how to align traces with data-aware declarative models by adding/deleting events in the trace or by changing the attribute values attached to them.

Keywords: Conformance checking · Alignments · Data-aware declarative models · Multi-perspective process mining · Automated planning

1 Introduction

Conformance checking is a branch of process mining assessing whether a sequence of distinguishable events (i.e., a *trace*) conforms to the expected process behavior represented as a *process model* [21]. When a trace does not conform to the model, we say that the trace is *deviant*. In this case, techniques based on cost-driven alignments additionally provide minimal repair strategies to make the trace conformant to the model [2]. Alignments represent a valuable instrument for business analysts, as the combined provision of alternative repair strategies, ranked by alignment cost, supports the business analyst in choosing among different process improvement strategies. In conformance checking, models can be

© Springer Nature Switzerland AG 2021
A. Polyvyanyy et al. (Eds.): BPM 2021, LNCS 12875, pp. 235–251, 2021.
https://doi.org/10.1007/978-3-030-85469-0_16

described by either procedural or declarative languages; while the former fully enumerate the set of all the possible allowed traces, the latter list the constraints delimiting the expected behavior. Declarative process models like Declare models [19], whose semantics can be expressed in Linear Time Logic on finite traces (LTL_f) [9], can always be transformed into constraint automata. The representation of Declare models as automata can be adopted for aligning traces with this type of models [8,13].

Multi-perspective checking for process conformance is gaining momentum, as conformance checking techniques considering both control flow and data annotations as "first-class citizens" enable to discover more deviations [16]. This reflects the essence of real-world business processes inherently, described by both processes and their different domain objects [20] (e.g., employees, products, etc.), which can be encoded as traces and event data. While alignment-based data-aware conformance has been already investigated in the context of procedural models, most of the conformance checking approaches for data-aware declarative models [7] focus on a numerical approximation of the degree of conformance of a trace against the model and do not provide repair strategies.

To tackle this research gap, we propose a novel approach for aligning event logs and data-aware declarative models based on the reduction of this problem into a data-agnostic alignment problem. This solution exploits the following considerations: a) to represent the process model, we use a sub-set of the data-aware extension of Declare presented in [7]. After representing the data-aware Declare model using a data-agnostic LTL_f semantics, b) we exploit the data predicates in the data-aware Declare clauses to partition the data space. This provides propositions representing data in addition to event labels. Then, c) we combine each event label with the propositions generated in b) and transform the model in a) into its data-aware counterpart. The automata-based representation of such a model is used to align traces (seen as sequences of events with a payload of data attribute-value pairs) with the model. In particular, we show that the alignment problem can be expressed as a planning problem in Artificial Intelligence, which can be efficiently solved by selected state-of-the-art planners [8,17].

Despite the resulting data-agnostic alignment via planning is semantically equivalent to customary cost-based aligners [2], our previous work [8] showed that the former outperforms the latter in terms of computational performance and scalability in the presence of models of considerable size, which is the case of this paper. In fact, as a consequence of the reduction of the data-aware alignment problem into a data-agnostic one, the automata-based process models used as input for our approach have several more transitions and states than in traditional alignment problems. Therefore, as we needed to show the feasibility of our approach, we decided to resort to planning-based alignments for both presenting our framework outline and performing the experiments. Planners generate repair strategies able to align traces and a data-aware declarative model based on changes at the level of control flow (such as adding/deleting events) or at the level of the data flow (such as changing the attribute values attached to them).

The rest of the paper is structured as follows: after providing relevant related work (Sect. 2), we introduce the notion of event log (Sect. 3.1) and the data-aware declarative language used to represent the model (Sect. 3.2); we also provide hints on Automated Planning, as we will later exploit the SymBA*-2 optimal planner [24] to compute the alignments (Sect. 3.3). These preliminary notions guide us into the definition of our working assumptions adhering to the literature of reference (Sect. 4). After deep-diving into the technical details providing the solution to the data-aware declarative alignment problem (Sect. 5), we benchmark SymBA*-2 over a synthetic dataset and discuss its performance in this context (Sect. 6). Last, we draw our final conclusions and propose some future work (Sect. 7).

2   Related Work

Most of the conformance checking techniques reported in the scientific literature are based on procedural models. In [2], for the first time, the authors introduce conformance checking augmented with the notion of alignments. A multi-perspective alignment-based approach has been presented in [16], where the authors propose techniques for conformance checking with respect to data-aware procedural models. This work combines the A* algorithm for alignment-based control-flow conformance checking with Integer Linear Programming for data conformance checking.[1]

The work described in [13] presents a (data-agnostic) conformance checking approach based on the concept of alignment for declarative models. It converts a Declare model into an automaton and performs conformance checking of a log with respect to the generated automaton. As a result of the analysis each trace in the log is converted into the most similar trace that the model accepts. This approach is similar to the procedural one presented in [16]. Our first attempt was, therefore, to extend this data-aware procedural approach to the declarative case. However, procedural models allow for a divide-and-conquer approach where, when searching the alignment space for the optimal alignment computation, the contribution of the control flow and of the data can be separately analyzed at first, then combining the obtained results. This is, in general, possible since removing data conditions from a procedural model leads to a more relaxed resulting model. The situation is completely different for declarative models, since removing data conditions from negative constraints could make them stronger, restricting the number of traces that the model accepts. Therefore, it is not possible to search in the space of traces that the model accepts constructed by only considering the control-flow, and then refine the search considering the contribution of data.

More recently, in [6], the authors have presented an approach where the data perspective for conformance checking with Declare is expressed in terms of conditions on global process variables disconnected from the specific Declare constraints expressing the control flow. In other words, data constraints are not bound to control flow constraints and thus it is not possible to bind the control flow behavior to specific data attributes. The only truly multi-perspective

---

[1] Note that, by design, Integer Linear Programming is not suitable to support the lexicographic order of strings, which is instead supported by our approach.

approach based on declarative models is the one presented in [7], in which the authors present an algorithmic framework to efficiently check the conformance of data-aware Declare constraints with respect to event logs. This approach numerically characterizes the degree of conformance of a log trace against the model without, however, providing repair strategies to the user. To go beyond the numerical evaluation of the conformance and build an alignment of a deviant trace, a boolean answer to the constraint-satisfaction problem is not sufficient since we need to solve an optimization problem with respect to a specific cost function. Therefore, in the current paper, Automated Planning has been chosen as a technique to formalize this optimization problem and translate it into an operational framework.

3   Preliminary Definitions

3.1   Event Logs

(Data) *payloads* are finite functions $p \in V^K$, where K is a finite set of keys and V is a (finite) set of data values. We consider also the case in which the value of a certain key k is missing in a payload. In particular, we denote as ε an element $\varepsilon \notin V$, such that $p(k) = \varepsilon$ for $k \notin \operatorname{dom}(p)$. Given a finite set of activity labels Act, an event σ_j is a pair $\langle A, p \rangle$, where $A \in$ Act is an activity label, and p is a payload; we denote with λ (and ς) the first (and second) projection of such pair, i.e., $\lambda(\sigma_j) = A$ (and $\varsigma(\sigma_j) = p$). A *trace* σ is a temporally-ordered and finite sequence of distinct events $\sigma_1 \cdots \sigma_n$, modeling a process run. We distinguish the trace keys (K_t) from the event keys (K_e), such that $K = K_t \cup K_e$ with $K_t \cap K_e = \emptyset$: all events within the same trace associate the same values to the same trace keys, i.e., $\forall \langle A_i, p_i \rangle, \langle A_j, p_j \rangle \in \sigma. \forall k \in K_t. p_i(k) = p_j(k)$. A log $\mathcal{L}$ is a finite set of traces. This characterization is compliant with the EXTENSIBLE EVENT STREAM (XES) format, which is the *de facto* standard for representing event logs within the Business Process Management community [1].

3.2   Data-Aware Declare

Declare is a declarative process modeling language [19]. A Declare model $\mathcal{M}$ is described as a set of constraints $\{ c_1, \ldots, c_m \}$ that must be simultaneously satisfied throughout a process execution. Such constraints express either positive (or negative) dependencies between two events having labels in Act, or quantify the occurrence of an event. In the first case, one of the two clause labels is called *activation*, and the other *target*; while testing a trace σ for conformance over this clause, the presence of the activation label in σ triggers the clause verification, requiring the (non-)execution of an event containing the target label in the same trace.

Declare has been extended to include conditions over data in the Declare constraints [7]. In this paper, we will consider two types of data predicates ϕ^d (*conditions*) decorating activations (i.e., activation conditions) and targets (i.e.,

Table 1. Semantics for MP-Declare constraints in LTL$_f$.

Template	LTL$_f$ semantics
Existence	$\top \rightarrow \mathbf{F}(\mathbf{A} \wedge \phi^d) \vee \mathbf{O}(\mathbf{A} \wedge \phi^d))$
Responded existence	$\mathbf{G}((\mathbf{A} \wedge \phi^d) \rightarrow (\mathbf{O}(\mathbf{B} \wedge \phi^d) \vee \mathbf{F}(\mathbf{B} \wedge \phi^d)))$
Response	$\mathbf{G}((\mathbf{A} \wedge \phi^d) \rightarrow \mathbf{F}(\mathbf{B} \wedge \phi^d))$
Alternate response	$\mathbf{G}((\mathbf{A} \wedge \phi^d) \rightarrow \mathbf{X}(\neg(\mathbf{A} \wedge \phi^d)\mathbf{U}(\mathbf{B} \wedge \phi^d))$
Chain response	$\mathbf{G}((\mathbf{A} \wedge \phi^d) \rightarrow \mathbf{X}(\mathbf{B} \wedge \phi^d))$
Precedence	$\mathbf{G}((\mathbf{B} \wedge \phi^d) \rightarrow \mathbf{O}(\mathbf{A} \wedge \phi^d))$
Alternate precedence	$\mathbf{G}((\mathbf{B} \wedge \phi^d) \rightarrow \mathbf{Y}(\neg(\mathbf{B} \wedge \phi^d)\mathbf{S}(\mathbf{A} \wedge \phi^d))$
Chain precedence	$\mathbf{G}((\mathbf{B} \wedge \phi^d) \rightarrow \mathbf{Y}(\mathbf{A} \wedge \phi^d))$
Not responded existence	$\mathbf{G}((\mathbf{A} \wedge \phi^d) \rightarrow \neg(\mathbf{O}(\mathbf{B} \wedge \phi^d) \vee \mathbf{F}(\mathbf{B} \wedge \phi^d)))$
Not response	$\mathbf{G}((\mathbf{A} \wedge \phi^d) \rightarrow \neg\mathbf{F}(\mathbf{B} \wedge \phi^d))$
Not precedence	$\mathbf{G}((\mathbf{B} \wedge \phi^d) \rightarrow \neg\mathbf{O}(\mathbf{A} \wedge \phi^d))$
Not chain response	$\mathbf{G}((\mathbf{A} \wedge \phi^d) \rightarrow \neg\mathbf{X}(\mathbf{B} \wedge \phi^d))$
Not chain precedence	$\mathbf{G}((\mathbf{B} \wedge \phi^d) \rightarrow \neg\mathbf{Y}(\mathbf{A} \wedge \phi^d))$

target conditions), respectively. While activation conditions must be valid when an event exhibiting the activation label occurs, target conditions impose value limitations on the payload of events containing the target label.

We use atom $\mathbf{A}$ as a shorthand for $\lambda(\sigma_i) = \mathbf{A}$, for each $\mathbf{A} \in \mathsf{Act}$, given an event σ_i to be assessed, while ϕ^d is a propositional formula containing as atoms either the universal truth ($\top$), or the falsehood ($\bot$), or a binary relation "$\mathbf{A}.k \; \Re \; c$", where c is a constant value representing either a number or a string, $\Re$ is either an equality or a precedence/subsequent relation over values in V or their negation, and $k \in K$ acts as a placeholder for $\varsigma(\sigma_i)(k)$, where $\varsigma(\sigma_i)$ is the payload associated to event σ_i and k is associated to a value $\sigma(\sigma_i)(k)$. E.g., "RP.$quality \leq 3$" is formally represented as $\varsigma(\sigma_i)(k) \leq 3$ for key $k = quality$ and for any event σ_i having $\lambda(\sigma_i) = \mathsf{RP}$. This is a widely adopted assumption, that spans from data-aware procedural models [16] to data-aware declarative models [7]. Furthermore, this assumption can also be adapted to categorical data, as strings are ordered via lexicographical orderings over the single characters. We denote the *compound conditions*, namely the conjunction of label requirements and data conditions, as $\psi = \mathbf{A} \wedge \phi^d$.

The semantics of the Declare constraints we consider here is represented in Table 1. Here, the $\mathbf{F}$, $\mathbf{X}$, $\mathbf{G}$, and $\mathbf{U}$ LTL$_f$ future operators have the following meanings: formula $\mathbf{F}\psi_1$ means that ψ_1 holds sometime in the future, $\mathbf{X}\psi_1$ means that ψ_1 holds in the next position, $\mathbf{G}\psi_1$ says that ψ_1 holds forever in the future, and, lastly, $\psi_1\mathbf{U}\psi_2$ means that sometime in the future ψ_2 will hold and until that moment ψ_1 holds (with ψ_1 and ψ_2 LTL$_f$ formulas). The $\mathbf{O}$, $\mathbf{Y}$ and $\mathbf{S}$ LTL$_f$ past operators have the following meaning: $\mathbf{O}\psi_1$ means that ψ_1 holds sometime in the past, $\mathbf{Y}\psi_1$ means that ψ_1 holds in the previous position, and $\psi_1\mathbf{S}\psi_2$ means that ψ_2 has held sometime in the past and since that moment ψ_1 holds.

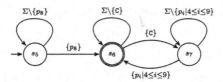

Fig. 1. Representation of the LTL$_f$ formula $\mathbf{G}(\neg c \vee (\mathbf{F}(p_4 \vee p_5 \vee p_6 \vee p_7 \vee p_8 \vee p_9))) \wedge \mathbf{F}p_8$ as a constraint automaton [25], where Σ contains all the non-$\perp$ and non-$\top$ atoms.

3.3   Automated Planning

Planning systems are an Artificial Intelligence technology showing how to reach a prefixed goal configuration given an initial world: the goal is met by exploiting a set of actions that change the initial world to reach the goal configuration [11]. PDDL is the standard Planning Domain Definition Language [10] that can be used to formulate such problems as $\mathcal{P} = (I, G, \mathcal{P_D})$, where I is the description of the initial world, G is the goal configuration, and $\mathcal{P_D}$ is the planning domain. The domain is built upon a set of propositions describing the state of the world (i.e., the set of valid propositions) and a set of actions Ω that can be performed to reach the goal configuration. An action schema $a \in \Omega$ has the form $a = \langle Par_a, Pre_a, Eff_a \rangle$, where Par_a is the list of the input parameters for a, Pre_a defines the preconditions under which a can be performed, and Eff_a specifies the effects of the action on the current world. Both Pre_a and Eff_a are represented as propositions in $\mathcal{P_D}$ via boolean predicates and numeric fluents.

Recently, the planning community has developed several planners implementing scalable search heuristics, which enable the solution of challenging problems in several Computer Science domains [17]. Walking in the footsteps of [8], we focus on planning techniques characterized by fully observable and static domains providing a perfect world description. In these scenarios, a sequence of actions whose execution transforms the initial state into a state satisfying the goal is the desired solution. In order to represent numeric alignment costs, we exploit the former formalization enhanced with the numeric features provided by PDDL 2.1 [10], thus keeping track of the costs of planning actions and synthesizing plans satisfying pre-specified metrics.

4   Working Assumptions

In this section, we outline some working assumptions that can be inferred from the literature of reference. First, we assume that a) compliance requirements of Declare models can be expressed in a formal language such as Linear Time Logic on Finite Traces (LTL$_f$) [9], as business process logs contain only traces of finite length; b) we restrict the possible log trace repairs to the traces generated by the automaton representation of the Declare model [8]; c) differently from [15,16], we can avoid to model reading and writing operations, as the entirety of our analysis will be conducted once traces reach their completion; d) last, each event in a trace must be represented by one single proposition: similarly to the non-data aware scenario [8], each event is associated with just one label.[2] As we will see in the incoming section, the latter consideration will require us to partition the possible data space into distinct atoms.

Given an appropriately chosen set Σ of atoms, it is always possible to represent a trace $\sigma = \sigma_1 \cdots \sigma_n$ as a finite sequence $t_\sigma = t_1 \cdots t_n$, where, for $1 \leq i \leq n$, t_i is a unique atom $t_i \in \Sigma$ such that $\sigma_i \vDash t_i$ [8]. Contextually, any LTL$_f$ formula $\varphi_\mathcal{M}$ representing a Declare model $\mathcal{M}$ can be represented as a deterministic finite-state automaton (DFA) $\mathcal{A}_{\varphi_\mathcal{M}}$ [12] accepting all the sequences t_σ from traces σ satisfying $\varphi_\mathcal{M}$ (see Fig. 1) [25]. A DFA $(\Sigma, Q, q_0, \rho, F)$ is defined over a finite set of states Q reading as input symbols from a finite alphabet Σ that are consumed by traversing the automaton from a starting state $q_0 \in Q$ via a transition function $\rho \colon Q \times \Sigma \to Q$; the input sequence is accepted once the input sequence is completely digested and an accepting state in $F \subseteq Q$ is reached through navigation. Since in the non data-aware Declare scenario the atoms within LTL$_f$ could be either $\top$, or $\bot$, or $\psi = \mathsf{A}$, Σ corresponds to the activity set Act, as each event is associated to one single label. For data-aware Declare we will extend Σ to take into consideration propositional formulas representing data conditions.

We also want to show that our conceptual framework can be translated into an operational framework by taking existing solid techniques and extending them appropriately. Therefore, after reducing the data-aware alignment problem into a data-agnostic one, we choose to operationalize it using Automated Planning, as our previous work [8] already showed that such a strategy outperforms customary cost-based trace aligners in terms of computational performance and scalability.

Last, we freely assume that all the events having the same label will always contain the same set of keys, with possibly differently associated values. This is a common assumption in the relational database field, where all the rows belonging to the same table contain the same number of values.

5   Data-Aware Declarative Conformance Checking as Planning

In this section, we study the problem of aligning log traces $\sigma \in \mathcal{L}$ and a (data-aware) Declare model $\mathcal{M}$ for data-aware declarative conformance checking: to do so, we firstly reduce such a problem to a mere automaton sequence acceptation task via a specific set of atoms Σ (*Cf.* Sect. 4) generated from the compound atoms in $\mathcal{M}$: the finite sequence t_σ generated from the log trace σ is accepted by the automaton $\mathcal{A}_{\varphi_\mathcal{M}}$ iff. σ is conformant to the model $\mathcal{M}$ (Sect. 5.1). Next, we code t_σ and $\mathcal{A}_{\varphi_\mathcal{M}}$ as specific automata (Sect. 5.2) that are exploited by a planner to generate the minimally repaired sequence $\hat{t}_\sigma$ (Sect. 5.3), out of which we generate the minimally repaired trace $\hat{\sigma}$ which is conformant to $\mathcal{M}$ (Sect. 5.4).

---

[2] To allow multiple labels as customary of big-data scenarios [5], we could simulate such a situation by choosing only the most relevant label as the actual label and using other fields in the payload to hold the remaining ones.

Table 2. Intermediate steps for generating distinct atoms for B labeled events by partitioning the data space via intervals in Declare clauses.

$\mu(B,x)$		|| $\mu(B,y)$	
$B.x > 3$	$B.x > 3$	$B.y = 0$	$0 \le B.y \le 0$
$B.x > 0$	$0 < B.x \le 3,\ B.x > 3$	$B.y \ne 0$	$B.y < 0 \lor B.y > 0$
$B.x \le 0$	$B.x \le 0$		

(a) Interval decomposition in $\mu(\cdot,\cdot)$

B	$B.y < 0$	$B.y = 0$	$B.y > 0$
$B.x \le 0$	p_1	p_2	p_3
$0 < B.x \le 3$	p_4	p_5	p_6
$B.x > 3$	p_7	p_8	p_9

(b) Atom generation for B by data space partitioning via $\times_{k \in}\ \mu(B, k)$

5.1 Σ-encoding for Conformance Checking

As per the previous considerations, we want to show that, to solve the trace alignment problem for data-aware declarative conformance checking, it is sufficient to provide a specific characterization of Σ. Σ will be used to generate an automaton accepting symbols in Σ and the automaton will be used to test log traces represented as finite sequences in Σ^*. The proposed approach for obtaining Σ from a (data-aware) Declare model $\mathcal{M}$ is sketched in Fig. 2, and described in detail in the following.

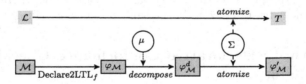

Fig. 2. Intermediate steps required for obtaining Σ from $\mathcal{M}$ and transforming $\mathcal{L}$ into a set of finite sequences T, as well as replacing atoms in $\varphi_{\mathcal{M}}^d$ with equivalent atoms in Σ ($\varphi'_{\mathcal{M}}$).

In the first *Declare2LTL$_f$* step, we exploit the usual conversion of each single Declare clause into an LTL$_f$ formula (see Table 1) in the *negated normal form* [14], where negations are possibly pushed inside atoms "A.$k \Re c$" by replacing $\Re$ with its negation.

Example 1. *The Declare model $\mathcal{M}$ containing clauses* Response(C, B, $B.x > 0$) *and* Existence(B, $B.x > 3 \land B.y = 0$) *is represented as the intermediate LTL$_f$ formula* $\varphi_{\mathcal{M}} = \mathbf{G}(\neg C \lor \mathbf{F}(B \land B.x > 0)) \land \mathbf{F}(B \land B.x > 3 \land B.y = 0)$.

In the second *decomposition* step, for each compound condition $\psi = \mathsf{A} \wedge \phi^d$ over labels $\mathsf{A} \in \mathsf{Act}$, we collect all the atoms in ϕ_d in the form "$\mathsf{A}.k \; \Re \; c$" for each $k \in K$ in a map $\mu(\mathsf{A}, k)$. Contextually, we represent atoms as intervals, and we *decompose* them into a disjunction of maximal non-overlapping data-aware predicates. This task can be efficiently computed via interval trees [4]. Last, we replace the atoms in each LTL_f formula by its decomposed representation.

Example 1 (continued). *Table 2a shows the interval decomposition results for the conditions ψ extracted from $\mathcal{M}$. E.g., predicates $B.x > 3$ and $B.x > 0$ are first represented as intervals $(3, +\infty)$ and $(0, +\infty)$, and then decomposed into disjoint sub-intervals $(-\infty, 0]$, $(0,3]$, and $(3, +\infty)$. As a result, $\varphi_{\mathcal{M}}$ is decomposed into $\varphi_{\mathcal{M}}^d = \mathbf{G}(\neg C \vee \mathbf{F}(B \wedge B.x > 0)) \wedge \mathbf{F}(B \wedge (0 < B.x \leq 3 \vee B.x > 3) \wedge B.y = 0).$*

In the third *atomization* step, we put an atom $\mathsf{A} \in \mathsf{Act}$ in Σ if the map $\mu(\mathsf{A}, k)$ is empty for each key $k \in K$; otherwise, given all the keys $k_{\mathsf{A}_1}, \dots, k_{\mathsf{A}_h} \in K$ for which the map $\mu(\mathsf{A}, k_{\mathsf{A}_i})$ is not empty, we partition the data space by combining the non-overlapping intervals obtained from the previous step as $\mu(\mathsf{A}, k_{\mathsf{A}_1}) \times \cdots \times \mu(\mathsf{A}, k_{\mathsf{A}_h})$. For each of these interval combinations, we generate a fresh atom and put it in Σ.

Example 1 (continued). *Label C is never associated to a data condition, and therefore it will be associated to one single atom C. On the other hand, label B is associated to several atoms obtained by partitioning the data space via the intervals in Table 2a. Table 2b shows the atom decomposition of B via data intervals over keys x and y, which induce a space partitioning of 9 intervals, for which we generate nine distinct atoms $p_1 \dots p_9$. As a result, we obtain $\Sigma = \{ p_i \mid 1 \leq i \leq 9 \} \cup \{ C \}$ in Fig. 2.*

Starting from these atoms, we firstly replace the compound conditions in $\varphi_{\mathcal{M}}^d$ with a disjunction of atoms from Σ as described in Table 2b, thus obtaining an equivalent LTL_f formula $\varphi_{\mathcal{M}}'$. Secondly, we generate a finite sequence $t_\sigma \in T$ for each log trace $\sigma \in \mathcal{L}$ by replacing each event σ_i in σ with the only atom $t_i \in \Sigma$ such that $\sigma_i \models t_i$.

Example 1 (continued). *With reference to our running example, we replace the compound conditions in $\varphi_{\mathcal{M}}^d$ with the previously generated atoms; the compound cond ition $B \wedge B.x > 0$ is replaced by all the possible configurations of y and data intervals $0 < B.x \leq 3$ and $B.x > 3$, which are identified by the disjunction $p_4 \vee p_5 \vee p_6 \vee p_7 \vee p_8 \vee p_9$. On the other hand, $B \wedge B.x > 3 \wedge B.y = 0$ can be directly replaced by atom p_8: this results into an equivalent formula $\varphi_{\mathcal{M}}' = \mathbf{G}(\neg C \vee (\mathbf{F}(p_4 \vee p_5 \vee p_6 \vee p_7 \vee p_8 \vee p_9))) \wedge \mathbf{F}p_8$. Given a log $\mathcal{L} = \{B\{x = 1, y = 0\} C\{x = 6\} C\{x = 4\}, \; C\{x = 8\} B\{x = 10, y = 0\}\}$, all the events labeled as C are replaced with atom C, as there are no (data) conditions related to C in $\mathcal{M}$ that we can exploit to partition the data space. On the other hand, each event labeled as B is replaced by an equivalent atom in Σ: event $B\{x = 1, y = 0\}$ is uniquely represented by p_5, while event $B\{x = 10, y = 0\}$ is uniquely represented by p_8. This transformation results into a set of string sequences $T = \{p_5 CC, Cp_8\}$.*

After generating $\varphi_{\mathcal{M}}'$, we can exploit existing approaches [25] to generate a DFA that only accepts sequences satisfying $\varphi_{\mathcal{M}}'$. With reference to the previous example, the first trace is not conformant to $\mathcal{M}$, since the first sequence is not accepted by the associated automaton. Instead, the second trace is conformant to $\mathcal{M}$, since the second sequence is accepted by the associated DFA. In the forthcoming subsection, we will discuss how to generate repaired sequences that are accepted by the reference model.

5.2   Automaton Manipulation for Trace Alignment

Consider a sequence $t_\sigma = t_1 \cdots t_n$ generated from a trace σ, and the constraint automaton $\mathcal{A}_{\varphi_\mathcal{M}}$ generated from the Declare model $\mathcal{M}$. If the trace is deviant with respect to the model, we are interested in generating a repair sequence $\varrho = \varrho_1 \cdots \varrho_m$ from t_σ describing the operations to perform over σ to make it conformant to $\mathcal{M}$. To realize this transformation, we consider two types of atomic violations, which can be caused by wrong (*deletion*) or missing (*insertion*) atoms in Σ. Differently from the non-data aware case [8], we also need to model *replacement* operations, defined as a data update within one single trace event: these operations can be mimicked by a delete operation followed by an insertion, as they substitute an event within a trace with the same event where a data value has been updated. The above operations, that will be later on encoded as PDDL actions, can be defined as follows:

- *deletion*/`del` $[\#\sigma_k \leftarrow \phi] ::= \sigma_1 \cdots \sigma_{k-1}\sigma_{k+1} \cdots \sigma_n$, for $n = |\sigma|$, $1 \le k \le n$, and $\phi = \sigma_k$
- *insertion*/`ins` $[@\sigma_k \leftarrow \phi] ::= \sigma_1 \cdots \sigma_{k-1}\phi\sigma_k \cdots \sigma_n$, for $n = |\sigma|$ and $1 \le k \le n$
- *replacement*/`repl` $[\sigma_k[\phi \mapsto \phi']] ::= \sigma_1 \cdots \sigma_{k-1}\phi'\sigma_{k+1} \cdots \sigma_n$, for $n = |\sigma|$, $1 \le k \le n$, and $\phi = \sigma_k$

Similarly to customary cost-based trace aligners, each of these operations has an associated cost, either quantifying the severity of the found violation or determining which operations shall be preferred. E.g., by assigning a higher cost to insertions and deletions and a lower one to replacements, we will favor replacements when possible. The *alignment cost* is defined as the number of deletions multiplied by their cost, plus the number of insertions multiplied by their cost, plus the number of replacements multiplied by their cost. We can now define the conformance checking problem as follows:

Definition 1 (Log/Declare Conformance Checking). *Given a trace σ and a Declare model $\mathcal{M}$, checking the conformance of σ against $\mathcal{M}$ is the task of verifying whether σ conforms to $\mathcal{M}$, or σ is deviant and there exists a repair sequence ϱ making σ non-deviant for $\mathcal{M}$ and guaranteeing a minimal transformation cost.*

The process of generating a repair sequence can be addressed by resorting to DFAs (Sect. 4). Let $t_\sigma = t_1 \cdots t_n$ be a string sequence generated from a log trace σ via Σ, $\mathcal{A}_{\varphi_\mathcal{M}} = (\Sigma, Q, q_0, \rho, F)$ the constraint automaton to check t_σ against. From t_σ, we define a further automaton, called the *trace automaton* $\mathcal{T} = (\Sigma_t, Q_t, q_0^t, \rho_t, F_t)$ having a) $\Sigma_t = \{ t_i \mid t_i \in t_\sigma \}$, b) $Q_t = \{ q_0^t, \cdots, q_n^t \}$ as a set of $|t_\sigma| + 1$ states, c) $\rho(q_i^t, e_{i+1}) = q_{i+1}^t$ for $0 \le i \le n - 1$, and d) $F_t = q_n^t$. By definition, such a graph accepts only t_σ.

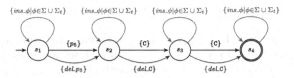

Fig. 3. Augmented trace automaton $\mathcal{T}^+$ for $t_\sigma = p_5\text{CC}$.

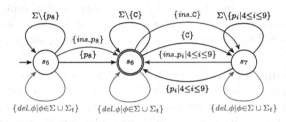

Fig. 4. Augmented constraint automaton $\mathcal{A}^+_{\varphi_\mathcal{M}}$ for $\mathcal{A}_{\varphi_\mathcal{M}}$.

Next, we augment $\mathcal{T}$ and $\mathcal{A}_{\varphi_\mathcal{M}}$ by adding transitions related to the atomic operations of insertions and deletions. Thus, from $\mathcal{T}$ we generate the automaton $\mathcal{T}^+ = (\Sigma_t^+, Q_t, q_0^t, \rho_t^+, F_t)$ having:

- Σ_t^+ extending $\Sigma_t \subseteq \Sigma$ by adding an insertion ins_ϕ for each atom $\phi \in \Sigma_t \cup \Sigma$ and a deletion del_ϕ for each atom $\phi \in \Sigma_t$.
- ρ_t^+ extending ρ_t by adding deletions $\rho_t^+(p, del\_\phi) = q$ for each transition $\rho_t(p, \phi) = q$, and insertions $\rho_t^+(q, ins\_\phi) = q$ for all atoms $\phi \in \Sigma \cup \Sigma_t$ and states $q \in Q_t$.

Figure 3 shows the trace automaton generated from the deviant trace $\sigma = \text{B}\{\text{x=1,y=0}\}\text{C}\{\text{x=6}\}\text{C}\{\text{x=4}\}$ from Example 1. Similarly, from $\mathcal{A}_{\varphi_\mathcal{M}}$, we obtain $\mathcal{A}^+_{\varphi_\mathcal{M}} = (\Sigma^+, Q, q_0, \rho^+, F)$ having:

- Σ^+ extending Σ by adding an insertion ins_ϕ for each atom $\phi \in \Sigma$ and a deletion del_ϕ for each atom $\phi \in \Sigma \cup \Sigma_t$.
- ρ^+ extending ρ_t by adding insertions $\rho^+(p, ins\_\phi) = q$ for each transition $\rho(p, \phi) = q$ and deletions $\rho_t^+(q, del\_\phi) = q$ for all atoms $\phi \in \Sigma \cup \Sigma_t$ and states $q \in Q$.

Figure 4 shows the automaton augmented with the repair operations $\mathcal{A}^+_{\varphi_\mathcal{M}}$ obtained for the model $\mathcal{M}$ from Example 1. This automaton does not accept $t_\sigma = p_5\text{CC}$. In this case, one alignment strategy adds p_8 at the end of the trace; by explicitly marking such a repair with ins_p_8, both augmented automata now accept $\hat{t}_\sigma = p_5\text{CC}ins\_p_8$.

Next, we show how planners can efficiently identify the repair operations ϱ needed to repair the trace σ using the augmented automata just defined.

5.3   Encoding in PDDL

In this section, we show how, given an augmented constraint automaton $\mathcal{A}^+_{\varphi_{\mathcal{M}}}$ obtained from an LTL$_f$ formula $\varphi_{\mathcal{M}}$, and an augmented trace automaton $\mathcal{T}^+$ obtained from a trace t, we build a cost-optimal planning domain $\mathcal{P}_{\mathcal{D}}$ and a problem instance $\mathcal{P}$ in PDDL. $\mathcal{P}_{\mathcal{D}}$ and $\mathcal{P}$ can be used to feed any state-of-the-art planners accepting PDDL 2.1 specifications, as discussed in Sect. 3.3. A solution plan for $\mathcal{P}$ amounts to the set of interventions of minimal cost to repair the trace with respect to $\varphi'_{\mathcal{M}}$, and generates a repair sequence ϱ that is going to be exploited in the forthcoming subsection for finally repairing the trace.

Planning Domain. In $\mathcal{P}_{\mathcal{D}}$, we provide two abstract types: `activity` and `state`. The first captures the activities involved in a transition between two different states of a constraint/trace automaton. The second is used to uniquely identify the states of the constraint automaton (through the sub-type `automaton_state`) and of the trace automaton (through the sub-type `trace_state`). To capture the structure of the automaton and to monitor its evolution, we defined five *domain propositions* as boolean predicates in $\mathcal{P}_{\mathcal{D}}$:

- (trace ?t1 - trace_state ?e - activity ?t2 - trace_state) holds if there exists a transition in the trace automaton between two states t1 and t2, being e the activity involved in the transition.
- (automaton ?s1 - automaton_state ?e - activity ?s2 - automaton_state) holds if there exists a transition between two states s1 to s2 of a constraint automaton, being e the activity involved in the transition.
- (atoms ?e1 - activity ?e2 - activity) holds if e1 and e2 are two atoms in Σ associated to a same activity label.
- (cur_state ?s - state) holds if s is the current state of a constraint/trace automaton.
- (final_state ?s - state) holds if s is a final state of a constraint/trace automaton.

It is worth to notice that, if a generic activity A is associated to some data condition, A will be represented as a set of atoms p_1, p_2, p_3, etc. in $\mathcal{P}_{\mathcal{D}}$, see for example Table 2b. This means that, for any combination of atoms p_i - p_j associated to A, there will exist an instance of the predicate (atoms) that will hold for p_i and p_j. Furthermore, we define a *numeric fluent* `total-cost` to keep track of the cost of the violations. Notice that: *(i)* in PDDL, parameters are written with a question mark character '?' in front, and the dash character '-' is used to assign types to parameters; and *(ii)* we remain consistent with the PDDL syntax, which allows the values of both predicates and fluents to change as a result of the execution of an action.

Planning actions are used to express the *repairs* on the original trace t. In our encoding, we have defined four actions to perform *synchronous moves* both in the trace/constraint automaton, or to add/remove/replace activities to/from/in the constraint and trace automata. In the following, we suppose that actions `ins`, `del` and `repl` have cost equal to 1. However, their cost can be customized to define the severity of a violation or to force priorities among actions.

```
(:action sync
 :parameters (?t1 - trace_state ?e - activity ?t2 - trace_state)
 :precondition (and (cur_state ?t1) (trace ?t1 ?e ?t2))
 :effect(and (not (cur_state ?t1)) (cur_state ?t2)
             (forall (?s1 ?s2 - automaton_state)
             (when (and (cur_state ?s1)
                        (automaton ?s1 ?e ?s2))
                   (and (not (cur_state ?s1))(cur_state ?s2)))))))
```

```
(:action ins                             (:action del
 :parameters (?e - activity)              :parameters (?t1 - trace_state
 :effect (and (increase (total-cost) 1)             ?e - activity
             (forall (?s1 ?s2 - automaton_state)     ?t2 - trace_state)
             (when (and (cur_state ?s1)      :precondition (and (cur_state ?t1)
                        (automaton ?s1 ?e ?s2))              (trace ?t1 ?e ?t2))
                   (and (not (cur_state ?s1))   :effect(and (increase (total-cost) 1)
                        (cur_state ?s2))))))          (not (cur_state ?t1))(cur_state ?t2)))
```

```
(:action repl
 :parameters (?t1 - trace_state ?e1 - activity ?t2 - trace_state ?e2 - activity)
 :precondition (and (cur_state ?t1) (trace ?t1 ?e1 ?t2) (atoms ?e1 ?e2))
 :effect(and (increase (total-cost) 1) (not (cur_state ?t1)) (cur_state ?t2)
             (forall (?s1 ?s2 - automaton_state)
             (when (and (cur_state ?s1)
                        (automaton ?s1 ?e2 ?s2))
                   (and (not (cur_state ?s1))(cur_state ?s2)))))))
```

We modeled sync and del in such a way that they can be applied only if there exists a transition from the current state t1 of the trace automaton to a subsequent state t2, being e the activity involved in the transition. Notice that, while del [#t1 ← e] yields a *single* move in the trace automaton, sync yields, in addition, one move on the constraint automaton, to be performed synchronously. In particular, a synchronous move is performed in the constraint automaton if there exists a transition involving activity e connecting s1 – the current state of the automaton – to a state s2. Then, ins [@t1 ← e] is performed only for transitions involving activity e connecting two states of the constraint automaton, with the current state of the trace automaton that remains the same after the execution of the action. Finally, repl [t1[e1 ↦ e2]] can be seen as a synchronous combination of a del and an ins. It yields one move on the trace automaton and one on the constraint automaton, involving two atoms e1 and e2 associated to a same activity label, i.e., such that the predicate (atoms ?e1 ?e2) holds.

Planning Problem. In $\mathcal{P}$, we first define a finite set of constants required to properly ground all the domain propositions defined in $\mathcal{P}_\mathcal{D}$. In our case, constants correspond to the state and activity instances involved in the trace/constraint automaton. Secondly, we define the *initial state* of $\mathcal{P}$ to capture the exact structure of the trace/constraint automaton. This includes the specification of all the existing transitions that connect two states of the automaton, and the definition of all the pairs of atoms belonging to a same activity label. The current state and the final states of the trace/constraint automaton are identified as well. Thirdly, to encode the goal condition, we first pre-process the constraint automaton by: *(i)* adding a new dummy state with no outgoing transitions; *(ii)* adding a new special action, executable only in the final states of the original automaton, which makes the automaton move to the dummy state; and *(iii)* including in the set of final states only the dummy state. Then, we define the goal condition as the conjunction of the final states of the trace automaton and of the constraint automaton. In this way, we avoid using disjunctions in goal formulas, which are not supported by all planners. Finally, as our purpose is to minimize the total cost of the plan, $\mathcal{P}$ contains the following specification: (:metric minimize (total-cost)). As the goal requires that in both augmented automata an accepting state is reached, the actions will encode the strategies to successfully visit both automata via their transition functions, while assigning different alignment costs to each of the strategies. When the goal is reached, the resulting action sequence (where syncs are stripped) represent the repair sequence ϱ that we are going to exploit in the next section.

5.4 Trace Repair

Last, we need to leverage the repair actions generated by the planner to repair the entire trace so to make it conformant to the model as a whole. In particular, the generated repair actions are always ordered based on their positions within the trace. By removing all the sync actions provided by the planner, we will obtain a sequence of insertions [@t1 ← e], deletions [#t1 ← e], and replacements [t1[e1 ↦ e2]] for a trace σ via its associated t_σ. While deletions [#t1 ← e] can be trivially implemented in the data-aware scenario by simply removing the problematical event, for insertions (or replacements), we need to add events with their associated payloads (or adapt the contained data values). Replacements [t1[e1 ↦ e2]] can be implemented by replacing the values in t1 violating the data condition e2 with the nearest values satisfying e2. On the other hand, insertions require to generate totally new values: the insertion [@t1 ← e] of a new event t1 satisfying e can be modeled by generating a new event having the label induced by e, which is then instantiated with the same data values present in the last occurrence of an event equally labeled if any, and instantiated with default values otherwise; then, such values are repaired by choosing the nearest values satisfying e. E.g., the alignment result $\hat{t_\sigma} = p_5 \text{CC} ins\_p_8$ of trace $\sigma = \text{B}\{x=1,y=0\}\text{C}\{x=6\}\text{C}\{x=4\}$ generates the repair $\varrho = [@\sigma_4 ← p_8]$ after removing the sync operations. Then, we obtain a new trace $\sigma' = \text{B}\{x=1,y=0\}\text{C}\{x=6\}\text{C}\{x=4\}\text{B}\{x=4,y=0\}$, where 4 is the nearest integer to B.x = 1 (taken from the first event) that satisfies $p_8 \equiv \text{B}.x > 3 \wedge \text{B}.y = 0$.

6 Experiments

We have developed a planning-based alignment tool that implements the approach discussed in Sect. 5. The tool allows us to load logs formatted with the XES standard and to import data-aware models previously designed using RuM [3]. To find the minimum cost trace alignment against a pre-specified data-aware Declare model, our tool makes use of the SymBA*-2 [24] planning system, which produces optimal alignments performing a bidirectional A* search. We tested our approach on the grounded version of the problem presented in Sect. 5.3. We performed our experiments with a PC consisting of an Intel Core i7-4770S CPU

3.10 GHz Quad Core and 4 GB RAM. We used a standard cost function with unit costs for any alignment step that adds/removes activities in/from the input trace or changes a data value attached to them, and cost 0 for synchronous moves.

Table 3. Experimental results. The time (in *ms.*) is the average per trace.

Trace length	Alignment Time	Alignment Cost	Alignment Time	Alignment Cost	Alignment Time	Alignment Cost	Alignment Time	Alignment Cost
0 const. modified	3 constraints		5 constraints		7 constraints		10 constraints	
10	599.7	0	772.92	0	-	-	-	-
15	767.23	0	978.38	0	1,887.29	0	-	-
20	854.12	0	1,127.25	0	2,093.71	0	18,421.26	0
25	950.04	0	1,268.54	0	2,297.12	0	20,525.71	0
30	1,026.91	0	1,392.93	0	2,381.38	0	25,394.29	0
1 const. modified	3 constraints		5 constraints		7 constraints		10 constraints	
10	603.84	1	797.16	1	-	-	-	-
15	728.83	1	898.53	1	1,932.31	1	-	-
20	851.62	1	1,094.13	1	2,113.08	1	17,770.91	1
25	929.72	1	1,280.61	1	2,296.76	1	24,023.28	1
30	1,114.75	1	1,379.26	1	2,499.32	1	27,232.07	1
2 const. modified	3 constraints		5 constraints		7 constraints		10 constraints	
10	601.04	1.06	856.71	1.18	-	-	-	-
15	736.93	1.13	934.45	1.23	1,875.37	1.44	-	-
20	864.06	1.06	1,112.61	1.38	2,112.51	1.33	18,370.95	1.55
25	973.28	1.24	1,230.41	1.53	2,299.19	1.38	21,152.86	1.7
30	1,066.69	1.04	1,346.02	1.52	2,453.52	1.58	25,882.66	1.61
3 const. modified	3 constraints		5 constraints		7 constraints		10 constraints	
10	623.85	2.14	937.88	2.22	-	-	-	-
15	748.5	2.25	1,012.5	2.56	1,893.64	2.5	-	-
20	877.4	2.1	1,026.11	2.44	2,095.72	2.63	18,918.48	2.41
25	1,007	2.55	1,115.53	2.34	2,287.93	2.66	22,010.35	2.5
30	1,114.46	2.06	1,230.54	2.33	2,462.62	2.35	26,178.43	2.75

To have a sense of the scalability with respect to the "size" of the model and the "noise" in the traces, we have tested the approach on synthetic logs of different complexity. Specifically, we generated synthetic logs using the log generator presented in [23]. We defined four Declare models having the same alphabet of activities and containing 3, 5, 7 and 10 data-aware constraints respectively. Then, to create logs containing noise, i.e., behaviors non-compliant with the original Declare models, we changed some of the constraints in these models and generated logs from them. In particular, we modified the original Declare models by replacing 1, 2, and 3 constraints in each model using different strategies. In some cases, we replaced a constraint with its negative counterpart (see Table 1); in other cases, we replaced a constraint with a weaker constraint; in other cases, we replaced a data condition with its negation. Each modified model was used to generate 5 logs of 1000 traces containing traces of different lengths (i.e., containing 10, 15, 20, 25, and 30 events, respectively).

The results of the experiments can be seen in Table 3. The alignment time (in ms.) and cost (that corresponds to the amount of `ins`/`del`/`repl` activities in an alignment) refers to the average per trace. The missing values in the table refer to experiments that could not be carried out because traces of certain lengths (e.g., 10) could not be generated by specific models (e.g., including 7 or 10 constraints), i.e., traces of those lengths satisfying those models do not exist. It is evident from the table that the alignment cost does not affect the performance of the alignment tool as, when the noise increases, the execution time does not change. As expected, however, the execution time is slightly sensible to the trace length, and grows exponentially with the number of (data-aware) constraints in the reference model. However, the results suggest that the heuristics adopted by the planner is able to efficiently cope with the above complexity enabling to perform off-line analysis with acceptable performance in case of a reasonably large number of data-aware constraints. The models and the logs used for the experiments are available for reproducibility at: https://tinyurl.com/ezd788bb.

7   Conclusions

In this paper, we presented an approach tackling conformance checking of log traces over data-aware Declare models. The proposed approach exploits Automated Planning for aligning the log traces and the reference model via a preliminary partitioning of the data space. The experiments show that the performance of the approach is acceptable even when the reference model contains a reasonably large number of data-aware constraints. In addition, since the implemented tool is independent of the planner used to solve the alignment problem, forthcoming improvements in the efficiency of the planners will be automatically transferred to the tool.

Future works will investigate the relationship between planners and approximate path matching techniques [18] in order to use these techniques in the context of the alignment problem defined in this paper. We will also investigate the possibility of performing alignments over data-aware knowledge bases [22], which potentially quicken the time required to test the satisfiability of the data conditions by conveniently indexing (i.e., pre-ordering) the payload space. The use of these approaches could allow us to tackle correlation conditions (i.e., data predicates involving attributes belonging to the payload of the activation and of the target, simultaneously) [7] that we did not consider in the current contribution. In fact, the presented approach is not able to cope with the state space explosion, caused by the presence of correlation conditions in the constraints to be checked, when searching for the optimal alignments.

Acknowledgements. The work of G. Bergami has been supported by the project IDEE (FESR1133) funded by the Eur. Reg. Dev. Fund (ERDF) Investment for Growth and Jobs Prog. 2014–2020. The work of A. Marrella has been supported by the H2020 project DataCloud and the Sapienza grant BPbots.

References

1. Acampora, G., Vitiello, A., Di Stefano, B., van der Aalst, W., Gunther, C., Verbeek, E.: IEEE 1849: the XES standard: the second IEEE standard sponsored by IEEE Computational Intelligence Society. IEEE Comp. Int. Mag. **12**(2), 4–8 (2017)
2. Adriansyah, A., van Dongen, B.F., van der Aalst, W.M.P.: Conformance checking using cost-based fitness analysis. In: EDOC 2011 (2011)
3. Alman, A., Di Ciccio, C., Haas, D., Maggi, F.M., Nolte, A.: Rule mining with RuM. In: ICPM 2020 (2020)

4. Bentley, J.: Solutions to Klee's rectangle problems. Carnegie-Mellon University, Technical report (1977)
5. Bergami, G., Magnani, M., Montesi, D.: A join operator for property graphs. In: Workshops of the EDBT/ICDT 2017 Joint Conference (2017)
6. Borrego, D., Barba, I.: Conformance checking and diagnosis for declarative business process models in data-aware scenarios. Exp. Syst. Appl. **41**(11), 5340–5352 (2014)
7. Burattin, A., Maggi, F.M., Sperduti, A.: Conformance checking based on multi-perspective declarative process models. Exp. Syst. Appl. **65**, 194–211 (2016)
8. De Giacomo, G., Maggi, F.M., Marrella, A., Patrizi, F.: On the disruptive effectiveness of automated planning for LTLf-based trace alignment. In: AAAI 2017. AAAI press (2017)
9. De Giacomo, G., Vardi, M.Y.: Linear temporal logic and linear dynamic logic on finite traces. In: IJCAI 2013. AAAI press (2013)
10. Fox, M., Long, D.: PDDL2.1: an extension to PDDL for expressing temporal planning domains. J. Artif. Intell. Res. (JAIR) **20**, 61–124 (2003)
11. Ghallab, M., Nau, D.S., Traverso, P.: Automated Planning - Theory and Practice. Elsevier (2004)
12. Hopcroft, J.E., Motwani, R., Ullman, J.D.: Introduction to Automata Theory, Languages, and Computation, 3rd edn. Addison-Wesley (2007)
13. de Leoni, M., Maggi, F.M., van der Aalst, W.M.P.: Aligning event logs and declarative process models for conformance checking. In: Barros, A., Gal, A., Kindler, E. (eds.) BPM 2012. LNCS, vol. 7481, pp. 82–97. Springer, Heidelberg (2012). https://doi.org/10.1007/978-3-642-32885-5_6
14. Li, J., Pu, G., Zhang, Y., Vardi, M.Y., Rozier, K.Y.: Sat-based explicit LTL$_f$ satisfiability checking. Artif. Intell. **289**, 103369 (2020)
15. Maggi, F.M., Montali, M., Bhat, U.: Compliance monitoring of multi-perspective declarative process models. In: EDOC 2019, pp. 151–160. IEEE (2019)
16. Mannhardt, F., de Leoni, M., Reijers, H.A., van der Aalst, W.M.P.: Balanced multi-perspective checking of process conformance. Computing **98**(4), 407–437 (2015). https://doi.org/10.1007/s00607-015-0441-1
17. Marrella, A.: Automated planning for business process management. J. Data Semant. **8**(2), 79–98 (2018). https://doi.org/10.1007/s13740-018-0096-0
18. Myers, E.W., Miller, W.: Approximate matching of regular expressions. Bull. Math. Biol. **51**(1), 5–37 (1989)
19. Pesic, M., Schonenberg, H., van der Aalst, W.M.P.: DECLARE: full support for loosely-structured processes. In: EDOC 2007, pp. 287–298 (2007)
20. Petermann, A., Junghanns, M., Müller, R., Rahm, E.: FoodBroker - generating synthetic datasets for graph-based business analytics. In: WBDB 2014 (2014)
21. Rozinat, A., van der Aalst, W.M.P.: Conformance checking of processes based on monitoring real behavior. Inf. Syst. **33**(1), 64–95 (2008)
22. Schönig, S., Rogge-Solti, A., Cabanillas, C., Jablonski, S., Mendling, J.: Efficient and customisable declarative process mining with SQL. In: CAiSE 2016 (2016)
23. Skydanienko, V., Di Francescomarino, C., Ghidini, C., Maggi, F.M.: A tool for generating event logs from multi-perspective Declare models. In: BPM 2018 (2018)
24. Torralba, A., Alcazar, V., Borrajo, D., Kissmann, P., Edelkamp, S.: SymBA*: A symbolic bidirectional A* Planner. In: International Planning Competition (2014)
25. Westergaard, M.: Better algorithms for analyzing and enacting declarative workflow languages using LTL. In: Rinderle-Ma, S., Toumani, F., Wolf, K. (eds.) BPM 2011. LNCS, vol. 6896, pp. 83–98. Springer, Heidelberg (2011). https://doi.org/10.1007/978-3-642-23059-2_10

A Discounted Cost Function for Fast Alignments of Business Processes

Mathilde Boltenhagen[1(✉)], Thomas Chatain[1(✉)], and Josep Carmona[2(✉)]

[1] Université Paris-Saclay, CNRS, ENS Paris-Saclay, Inria, LMF,
Gif-sur-Yvette, France
{boltenhagen,chatain}@lsv.fr
[2] Universitat Politècnica de Catalunya, Barcelona, Spain
jcarmona@cs.upc.edu

Abstract. Alignments are a central notion in conformance checking. They establish the best possible connection between an observed trace and a process model, exhibiting the closest model run to the trace. Computing these alignments for huge amounts of traces, coming from big logs, is a computational bottleneck. We show that, for a slightly modified version of the distance function between traces and model runs, we significantly improve the execution time of an A*-based search algorithm. We show experimentally that the alignments found with our modified distance approximate very nicely the optimal alignments for the classical distance.

1 Introduction

Conformance checking techniques establish relations between modeled and observed behavior [6]. The techniques on this field are grounded on solving a very particular problem, known as *alignment* [1]: given a process model that describes a certain process, and a trace which contains a potential observation of this process, to decide if the trace is in the language of the model, and if not, to pinpoint where it deviates. Computing alignments is not necessarily the ultimate goal of an analysis, but instead can be used to further enhance a process model with the evidences found in the data, e.g. depicting explicitly in the model the bottlenecks of the underlying process [23].

The current process mining field is living an interesting paradox: whilst it is widely accepted that the capabilities of discovering huge process models exist, when it comes to analysing these discovered models through conformance checking techniques, only approximate techniques for deriving alignments are used in practice. In the next section we provide a complete overview of current alternatives for alignment computation.

In this paper, however, we somehow go back to the roots, and adopt the seminal work from Arya Adriansyah's PhD thesis [1] as main alignment algorithm. It consists of an A^* graph search algorithm over the state space of a *synchronous product net* made out of the initial process model and a *trace net* corresponding to the input trace. The cost function that governs the A^* search is typically a *standard* cost function which assigns unitary costs to all the possible types of deviations.

© Springer Nature Switzerland AG 2021
A. Polyvyanyy et al. (Eds.): BPM 2021, LNCS 12875, pp. 252–269, 2021.
https://doi.org/10.1007/978-3-030-85469-0_17

We consider a rather simple, yet powerful idea that is motivated from the following use case: for certain processes, the costs associated to deviations at early stages of the process' execution are more important than the ones at the end. For instance, consider a loan application process that has two decisions: one at the beginning, assessing the type of customer (gold, silver, normal), and one at the end, determining whereas the loan was received in a labour day or not. It is normal that the stage in which these decisions are made in any possible execution of the process reveal their importance. For instance, if for the company it is very important to know the type of the customer because further information needs to be gathered depending on the customer's type, then it is likely that the corresponding process has the type of customer decision close to the start of any possible execution. On the contrary, if the day when the loan was received is not so important, then it is likely that the corresponding events will be pushed to the end of the traces.

The aforementioned situation holds for *knock-out processes* [24], representing processes where two outcomes are possible: OK or NOK. In these processes, ordered checks are usually observed, because it allows faster process executions. Indeed, as many tasks of those processes aim at determining the final output, the knock-out decisions should be taken at the beginning of the process, in growing order [14].

Having this in mind, one can instantiate the A^* algorithm to make the cost function exponentially biased to this use case: giving more importance (higher cost) to the deviations that occur in early stages of the alignments, and exponentially reducing the cost as the search algorithm progresses. Importantly, this *discounted* cost function has a huge impact on the size of the search space required for the A^* search, since the cost asymmetry makes the search space rapidly shrink after the first alignment steps are made. For processes which follow the aforementioned use case, this cost function puts the search focus in the right place, deriving alignments that aim at synchronizing modeled and observed behavior in the important decisions that are made at the beginning. Interestingly, this idea can also be used for processes that are not following this trend, since although putting the focus at the beginning may not be the most likely explanation, the computational alleviation can make the problem tractable, where other techniques fail.

In this paper we formalize this simple idea, and show the great impact in performance with respect to several variations of the A^* search proposed in the last years. Interestingly, this improvement causes only a very minor loss in quality: as we will see in the experiments, for well-known and accepted benchmarks, the proposed techniques are often able to produce alignments very close to the optimal ones.

This paper is organized as follows: in the next section we provide a detailed overview of the different techniques to compute alignments. Then in Sect. 3 we provide the necessary definitions to understand the technique of this paper. In Sects. 4 and 5 we provide the formal definition and corresponding algorithmic adaptations for the discounted cost function presented in this paper. Then in Sect. 6 an evaluation of the proposed technique is reported, and Sect. 7 concludes the paper.

2   Related Work

The seminal work in [1] proposed the notion of alignment and developed a technique based on A* to compute optimal alignments for a particular class of process models. The approach represents the state-of-the-art technique for computing alignments, and can be adapted (at the expense of increasing significantly the memory footprint) to provide all optimal alignments. Alternatives to A* have appeared in recent years: in the approach presented in [7], the alignment problem is mapped as an *automated planning* instance. Automata-based techniques have also appeared [10,15]. The techniques in [15] (recently extended in [16]) rely on state-space exploration and determination of the automata corresponding to both the event log and the process model, whilst the technique in [10] is based on computing several subsets of activities and projecting the alignment instances accordingly.

The work in [19] presented the notion of *approximate* alignment to alleviate the computational demands by proposing a recursive paradigm on the basis of the structural theory of Petri nets. In spite of resource efficiency, the solution is not guaranteed to be executable. Alternatively, the technique in [20] presents a framework to reduce a process model and the event log accordingly, with the goal of alleviating the computation of alignments. The obtained alignment, called *macro-alignment* since some of the positions are high-level elements, is expanded based on the information gathered during the initial reduction. Techniques using local search have been also proposed very recently [21].

Decompositional techniques have been presented [12,22,27] that, instead of computing optimal alignments, focus on the *crucial problem* of whether a given trace fits or not a process model. These techniques vertically decompose the process model into pieces satisfying certain conditions (so only *valid* decompositions [22], which satisfy restrictive conditions on the labels and connections forming a decomposition, guarantee the derivation of a real alignment). Later on, the notion of *recomposition* has been proposed on top of decompositional techniques, in order to obtain optimal alignments whenever possible by iterating the decompositional methods when the required conditions do not hold [9]. In contrast to the aforementioned vertical decomposition techniques, our methodology does not require this last consolidation step of partial solutions, and therefore can be a fast alternative to these methods at the expense of loosing the guarantee of optimality.

We believe our work has similarities and synergies with two recent works. In [5], a symbolic algorithm to maximize the number of synchronous moves in the alignment is proposed, by changing the cost function to only penalize log moves, thus allowing an arbitrary number of model moves if this contributes to maximizing synchronous moves. We believe the discounted cost function of this paper may be used in the context of [5], to balance better the solutions found. Recently, in [25], an online alignment technique with a window-based backwards exploration is proposed. Again, by discounting this window-based exploration, a speedup of the online technique can be obtained so that it can be applied on a larger problem instances.

3   Preliminaries

We represent event data as log traces and process models as labeled Petri nets.

Definition 1 (Log Traces). *Let Σ be a set of activities. We define a log L as a finite multiset of sequences $\sigma \in \Sigma^*$, which we refer to as* log traces.

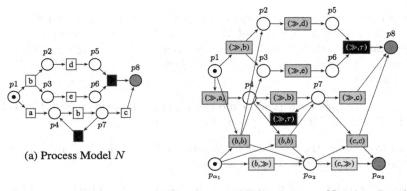

(a) Process Model N

$\langle b, c \rangle$

(b) Log trace σ

(c) Synchronous Product between N and σ. Transitions in purple correspond to the model moves, green transitions are the synchronous moves and yellow transitions the log moves. Black transitions are silent.

Fig. 1. Synchronous product for alignments between N and σ that has the marking reachability problem.

Definition 2 (Process Model (Labeled Petri Net) [13]). *A Process Model defined by a labeled Petri net system (or simply Petri net) is a tuple $N = \langle P, T, F, m_0, m_f, \Sigma, \lambda \rangle$, where P is the set of places, T is the set of transitions (with $P \cap T = \emptyset$), $F \subseteq (P \times T) \cup (T \times P)$ is the flow relation, m_0 is the initial marking, m_f is the final marking, Σ is an alphabet of actions and $\lambda : T \to \Sigma \cup \{\tau\}$ labels every transition by an activity or as silent.*

Semantics. The semantics of Petri nets is given in term of *firing sequences*. Given a node $x \in P \cup T$, we define its pre-set $^\bullet x \stackrel{\text{def}}{=} \{y \in P \cup T \mid (y, x) \in F\}$ and its post-set $x^\bullet \stackrel{\text{def}}{=} \{y \in P \cup T \mid (x, y) \in F\}$. A marking is an assignment of a non-negative integer to each place. A transition t is *enabled* in a marking m when all places in $^\bullet t$ are marked. When a transition t is enabled, it can *fire* by removing a token from each place in $^\bullet t$ and putting a token to each place in $t^\bullet$. A marking m' is *reachable* from m if there is a sequence of firings $\langle t_1 \ldots t_n \rangle$ that transforms m into m', denoted by $m[t_1 \ldots t_n \rangle m'$. The set of reachable markings from m_0 is denoted by $[m_0\rangle$. A Petri net is k-*bounded* if no marking in $[m_0\rangle$ assigns more than k tokens to any place. A Petri net is *safe* if it is 1-bounded. A *full run* of a Petri net N is a firing sequence $m_0[t_1 \ldots t_n \rangle m_f$ from the initial marking m_0 to the final marking m_f. A Petri net is *easy sound* [2] if it has at least one full run, i.e. m_f is reachable from m_0.

In this paper we assume safe and easy sound Petri nets.

Definition 3 (Alignments). *Given a log trace $\sigma = \langle \sigma_1, \ldots, \sigma_m \rangle \in L$ of alphabet Σ, and a process model $N = \langle P, T, F, m_0, m_f, \Sigma, \lambda \rangle$, an alignment of σ with N is a finite sequence $\varphi = \langle (\sigma_1', u_1'), \ldots, (\sigma_p', u_p') \rangle$ of moves such that:*

- *each move is either: a synchronous move $(a, t) \in \Sigma \times T$ with $a = \lambda(t)$, a log move $(a, \gg)$ (where $\gg$ is a special 'skip' symbol), or a model move $(\gg, t)$,*
- *dropping the $\gg$ symbols from the left projection $\langle \sigma_1', \ldots, \sigma_p' \rangle$ of φ, yields σ;*
- *dropping the $\gg$ symbols from the right projection $\langle u_1', \ldots, u_p' \rangle$ of φ, yields a full run u of N.*

Example 1. Figure 1 shows a process model (Fig. 1a) and a log trace (Fig. 1b). An alignment of N and σ is $\varphi = \langle (\gg, a), (b, b), (c, c) \rangle$.

In order to compare the quality of alignment quality, we define a cost function which penalizes log moves and model moves.

Definition 4 (Classical Alignment Cost Function, Optimal Alignments). *For every alignment φ between a model N and a log trace σ, the Classical Alignment Cost Function $\mathcal{C}$ assigns a cost 0 to synchronous moves and a cost 1 to log moves or model moves. The cost of an alignment is the sum of the costs of its moves. An alignment between a model N and a log trace σ is optimal if it minimizes the cost.*

Example 2. The alignment $\varphi = \langle (\gg, a), (b, b), (c, c) \rangle$ between N of Fig. 1a and σ of Fig. 1b costs 1 and is optimal. We recognize the Petri net transformation of σ which are the bottom places and the yellow transitions. The synchronous moves are drawn in green. From the initial state, possible moves are $(\gg, b)$, $(\gg, a)$, (b, b) or $(b, \gg)$.

The optimal alignment cost given with the classical alignment cost function $\mathcal{C}$ gives the Levenshtein edit distance between a run of M and the trace σ.

Definition 5 (Levenshtein Edit distance). *The Levenshtein Edit Distance $dist(u, v)$ between two words u and $v \in \Sigma^*$ is the minimal number of edits needed to transform u to v. In our case, edits can be deletions or insertions of a letter in words,*

$$
\begin{cases}
\mathcal{L}(\langle \rangle, \langle \rangle) = 0 \\
\mathcal{L}(u, \langle \rangle) = |u| \\
\mathcal{L}(\langle \rangle, v) = |v| \\
\mathcal{L}(a.u', b.v') = \mathcal{L}(u', v') & \text{if } (a = b) \\
\mathcal{L}(a.u', b.v') = \min \begin{cases} \mathcal{L}(a.u', v) + 1, \\ \mathcal{L}(u, b.v') + 1 & \text{otherwise.} \end{cases}
\end{cases}
$$

The main methods of the literature to compute optimal alignments are Dijkstra-based algorithms which often implies the construction of the *Synchronous Product* between the given process model and a sequential Petri net representing the log trace [1].

Definition 6 (Synchronous Product for Alignments). *For a process model* $N = \langle P, T, F, m_0, m_f, \Sigma, \lambda \rangle$ *and a log trace* $\sigma = \langle \sigma_1, \ldots, \sigma_m \rangle \in \Sigma^*$, *the Synchronous Product used for computing alignments is the Petri net* $SN = \langle P_{SN}, T_{SN}, F_{SN}, m_{SN_0}, m_{SN_f}, (\Sigma \cup \{\gg\})^2, \lambda_{SN} \rangle$ *defined as:*

- $N_\sigma = \langle P_\sigma, T_\sigma, F_\sigma, m_{\sigma 0}, m_{\sigma f}, \Sigma, \lambda_\sigma \rangle$ *is a translation of* σ *to a sequential Petri net with:* $P_\sigma = \{P_{\sigma_0}, \ldots P_{\sigma_m}\}$, $T_\sigma = \{t_{\sigma_i} = \lambda_\sigma(\sigma_i) \mid i \in \{1, \ldots, m\}\}$, $F_\sigma = \{(P_{\sigma_{i-1}}, t_{\sigma_i}), (t_{\sigma_i}, P_{\sigma_i}) \mid i \in \{1, \ldots, m\}\}$, $m_{\sigma 0} = \{P_{\sigma 0} : 1\}$, $m_{\sigma f} = \{P_{\sigma_m} : 1\}$,
- $P_{SN} = P \cup P_\sigma$
- $T_{SN} = T^{\gg} \cup T_\sigma^{\gg} \cup T_S$, *where* $T^{\gg} = \{(\gg, t) \mid t \in T\}$ *represents the model moves,* $T_\sigma^{\gg} = \{(t, \gg) \mid t \in T_\sigma\}$ *represents the log moves,* $T_S = \{(t_1, t_2) \mid t_1 \in T, t_2 \in T_\sigma$ *and* $\lambda(t_1) = \lambda_\sigma(t_2)\}$ *represents the synchronous moves,*
- $F_{SN} = F \cup F_\sigma \cup \{(P_i, t_i) \mid t_i = (t_1, t_2) \in T_{SN}, t_1 \neq \gg, t_2 \neq \gg, P_i \in {}^\bullet t_1 \cap {}^\bullet t_2\}$ $\cup \{(t_i, P_i) \mid t_i = (t_1, t_2) \in T_{SN}, t_1 \neq \gg, t_2 \neq \gg, P_i \in t_1{}^\bullet \cap t_2{}^\bullet\}$
- $m_{SN_0} = m_0 \cup m_{\sigma 0}$,
- $m_{SN_f} = m_f \cup m_{\sigma f}$,
- λ_{SN} *maps every* $t \in T_{SN}$ *to its move.*

Example 3. Figure 1 shows the synchronous product for alignments of the process model N given in Fig. 1a and the log trace σ of Fig. 1b.

The Dijkstra-based algorithm for finding optimal alignments, explores the reachability graph of the synchronous product of Definition 6. Weights are given by the transitions fired to reach the markings, according to the type of move that they represent. The best firing sequences found for reaching a marking is the less costly one. The algorithm that we present in Sect. 5 is an adaptation of this classical Dijkstra-based algorithm for alignments. As we are using easy-sound Petri nets as process models, the Synchronous Products for Alignments are easy-sound which implies termination of the Dijkstra algorithm with the condition to reach the final marking m_{SN_f} [28].

4 Discounted Cost Function and Properties

The classical alignment cost function corresponds to Levenshtein edit distance between a run of a process model and a log trace, where additions and deletions represent model and log moves. In this section, we introduce the *Discounted Edit Distance* and its impact when using it as alignment cost function.

The idea of this Discounted Edit Distance is to penalize more insertions and deletions when they occur at the beginning of the strings, and less when they occur later.

Definition 7 (Discounted Edit Distance). *We define the* Discounted Edit Distance *between two strings u and v (of length $|u|$ and $|v|$ respectively) with discount parameter $\theta \geq 1$ by $\mathcal{D}_\theta(u, v) \overset{\text{def}}{=} \mathcal{D}_\theta^0(u, v)$ where:*

$$
\begin{cases}
\mathcal{D}_\theta^k(\langle\rangle, \langle\rangle) = 0 \\
\mathcal{D}_\theta^k(\langle\rangle, b.v') = \mathcal{D}_\theta^{k+1}(\langle\rangle, v') + \theta^{-k} \\
\mathcal{D}_\theta^k(a.u', \langle\rangle) = \mathcal{D}_\theta^{k+1}(u', \langle\rangle) + \theta^{-k} \\
\mathcal{D}_\theta^k(a.u', b.v') = \mathcal{D}_\theta^{k+2}(u', v') \qquad\qquad\quad \text{if } (a = b) \\
\mathcal{D}_\theta^k(a.u', b.v') = \min \begin{cases} \mathcal{D}_\theta^{k+1}(u', v) + \theta^{-k} \\ \mathcal{D}_\theta^{k+1}(u, v') + \theta^{-k} \quad \text{otherwise.} \end{cases}
\end{cases}
$$

thus allowing equation $((u_i = v_j))$ for free and insertions and deletions at cost θ^{-k} where k refers to the position where the edit occurs.

Lemma 1. *For $\theta = 1$, the Discounted Edit Distance corresponds to the Levenshtein distance.*

Proof. With $\theta = 1$, we have $\theta^{-k} = 1$ for any k and we obtain Definition 5 from Definition 7. $\qquad\square$

In practice, relevant values for the discount parameter θ are slightly larger than 1. For $\theta \geq 2$, the discount is already very severe since an edit at position k costs more than the sum of all the following edits.

Lemma 2. *With the Discounted Edit Distance, for $\theta \geq 2$, an edit at position k costs more than the sum of all the following edits.*

Proof. For u and v, two words, let k be the position of a non-free cost in $\mathcal{D}_\theta(u, v)$. We note its cost $c(k) = \theta^{-k}$.

The next edits can occur at positions $j \in \{k+1, \ldots, n\}$ where, in the worst case, $n = |u| + |v|$. We write $S(j, n)$ the sum of costs. The maximal value of this sum appears when only non-free edits are used by the discounted edit distance:

$$
S(k, n) = \sum_{j=k+1}^{n} c(j) = \theta^{-(k+1)} + \theta^{-(k+2)} + \cdots + \theta^{-n} = \frac{\theta^{-k} - \theta^{-n}}{\theta - 1}
$$

Hence, $c(k) = \theta^{-k} > S(k, n)$ for $\theta \in [2, \infty[$. Otherwise, in the best case, there is no edit after position k and the cost of the edit at position k is higher than a null sum. $\qquad\square$

Example 4. Let $u = \langle x, a, b\rangle$ and $v = \langle a, y, b\rangle$. The discounted edit distance between u and v is $\mathcal{D}_\theta(u, v) = \theta^{-1} + \theta^{-3}$. If $\theta = 1$, the distance equals to 2 and is the Levenshtein edit distance where deleting x costs 1 and adding y costs 1.

Similarly to the Levenshtein edit distance, the Discounted Edit Distance can be applied to alignments.

Definition 8 (Discounted Cost Function for Alignments). *For an alignment* $\varphi = \langle(\sigma_1', u_1'), \ldots, (\sigma_p', u_p')\rangle$ *between a process model N and a log trace* σ, *the Discounted Cost Function for Alignments assigns a cost 0 to every synchronous move and* θ^{-k} *to every pair* (σ_k', u_k') *that is either a log move or a model move, where* $k \in \{1, \ldots, p\}$, $p \in \mathbb{N}$ *is the length of the alignment, and* $\theta \geq 1$ *is the discount parameter.*

For $\theta = 1$, the Discounted Cost Function for Alignment is equivalent to the Classical Alignment Cost Function. However when $\theta > 1$, the costs of moves are dynamic and depend on the number of previous moves of the alignment.

Example 5. For the alignment $\varphi = \langle(\gg, a), (b, b), (c, c)\rangle$, presented in the first example, the cost of $(\gg, a)$ is θ^{-1} because it is the first move of the alignment. For $\varphi' = \langle(b, b), (\gg, d), (\gg, e), (\gg, \tau)\rangle$ which is certainly not an optimal alignment but still an alignment of $\sigma = \langle b, c\rangle$ and the Petri net N of Fig. 1a, the cost of $(\gg, e)$ is θ^{-3}.

Lemma 3. *For* $\theta > 1$, *a non-free move t of position j, any move of position* $k > j$ *costs less than t.*

Proof. Any function $f : k \to \theta^{-k}$ where $\theta > 1$ is strictly decreasing. Then for $j < k$, we have $\theta^{-j} > \theta^{-k}$. □

As a consequence, algorithms for computing optimal discounted alignments will tend to align in priority the prefixes of the log traces. Suffixes are less costly. From Lemma 2, when the discount parameter is $\theta = 2$, a non-free move of position j is more costly than the sum of all the next costs.

Example 6. In Example 2, we saw that the optimal alignment by using the classical alignment cost function between $\sigma = \langle b, c\rangle$ and the model N of Fig. 1a is $\varphi = \langle(\gg, a), (b, b), (c, c)\rangle$ of cost 1. However, by using the discounted cost function with $\theta = 2$, optimal alignments are $\varphi' = \langle(b, b), (\gg, d), (\gg, e), (\gg, \tau)\rangle$ and $\varphi'' = \langle(b, b), (\gg, e), (\gg, d), (\gg, \tau)\rangle$ of cost $2^{-2} + 2^{-3}$, where $(\gg, \tau)$ is a free model move. This is due to the discounted cost function which penalizes the model move $(\gg, a)$ at first position.

5   Using the Discounted Cost Function in an A*-Based Algorithm for Discounted Alignments

To compute alignments by using the discounted cost function, we present an A*-based algorithm which assigns weights to the explored states according to the discounted cost function for alignment. Let θ be the discount parameter. Then, to a state reached by a move t occurring in position i, will be assigned the weight of its predecessor, increased by the cost

$$h(t, i, \theta) \stackrel{\text{def}}{=} (0 \text{ if } t \text{ is a synchronous move}, \theta^{-i} \text{ otherwise}).$$

As a result of Lemma 3, this heuristic aims at aligning prefix first more than suffixes.

The function h, based on the discounted cost function, is easily incorporated in the state-of-the-art algorithms for computing alignments. We present two versions of the incorporation, one by using the synchronous product of the process model and the log trace, and another one that avoids the computation of the product by exploring the process model along with the trace.

5.1 Algorithm for Computing Optimal Discounted Alignments

Our algorithm Algorithm 1, noted $A^*SP_{\mathcal{D}=\theta}$, is inspired from [6]. It proceeds by exploring the state space of the synchronous product of the process model with a sequential Petri net representing the log trace as defined in Definition 6. An optimal alignment corresponds to the shortest path between the initial marking to the final marking of the synchronous product. For this purpose, our A* algorithm maintains a priority queue Q of prefixes of runs, implemented as a heap of tuples $\langle \gamma, m, d \rangle$, for a prefix γ reaching marking m at cost d, such that the tuple with minimal cost d pops first. Line 1 initializes the heap with the empty prefix reaching the initial marking at cost 0, i.e. $\langle \langle \rangle, m_0, 0 \rangle$.

Algorithm 1: Computation of Optimal Alignments by using the Discounted Edit Distance ($A^*SP_{\mathcal{D}=\theta}$)

Input : $SP = ((P, T, F, m_0, m_f, (\Sigma \cup \{\gg\})^2, \lambda))$: synchronous product, θ: discount parameter

1 $Q \leftarrow \{\langle \langle \rangle, m_0, 0 \rangle\}$ ▷ Heap of open states ordered by distance
2 $A \leftarrow \emptyset$ ▷ Initialize closed set
3 **while** $Q \neq \emptyset$ ▷ While not all reachable states visited
4 **do**
5      $\langle \gamma, m, d \rangle \leftarrow Q.pop()$ ▷ Get next state minimizing d
6   **if** $m = m_f$ **then**
      Return: $\langle d, \gamma \rangle$
7      $A \leftarrow A \cup \{\langle m, |\gamma| \rangle\}$ ▷ Add state to closed set
8   **for** $t \in T$ *with* $m[t\rangle m'$ **do**
9        $\gamma' \leftarrow \gamma \bullet t$ ▷ Get new prefix
10   **if** $\langle m', |\gamma'| \rangle \notin A$ ▷ Reaching a not yet visited state
11   **then**
12         $d' \leftarrow d + h(t, |\gamma'|, \theta)$ ▷ Compute cost of γ'
13         $Q \leftarrow Q.insert(\langle \gamma', m', d' \rangle)$ ▷ Insert new prefix in heap
    Raise : m_f is not reachable

Line 3 starts a *while* loop that ends only when the final marking is reached (line 6) or when the priority queue is empty (line 3). Line 9 gets the next firing transitions of the synchronous product. Some transitions correspond to the log and model moves and are costly. The other transitions are the synchronous moves and are free, like in the original algorithm.

Our discounted cost function h appears on line 12 and determines the cost of the new prefix. Line 13 adds the new discovered state in the priority queue with its prefix γ' and it cost d' for reaching m'.

When the algorithm reaches the final marking, line 6, the while loop is broken and the algorithm returns the sequence of firing transitions to reach the final marking. In fact, this sequence of transitions gives the sequence of moves of the alignment.

Role of Length in States. In the classical version of alignment computation, the closed set contains the markings only. However, the length of the current alignment plays an important role in the discounted cost function (line 8). Indeed, the first visit of a marking might not be the optimal one, as it is the case in the classical version of alignments. A same marking m can be reached with different firing sequences of moves of different lengths. The first path that gives the first visit of the marking m is the shortest one. Let's call this short path γ_{short}, and γ_{long} a longer path from the initial marking to this marking m. We have $|\gamma_{long}| > |\gamma_{short}|$. However, γ_{short} might contain future costly moves to reach the final marking. If those moves are of position lower than $|\gamma_{long}|$, it questions the optimality of γ_{short}. We give an example of this situation below.

Example 7. Let's suppose that silent transition labelled by τ costs for this example. To reach marking $m = \{p4 : 1, p_{\alpha_2} : 1\}$, the algorithm can play $\gamma = \langle (\gg, a), (\gg, b), (\gg, \tau), (b, b) \rangle$ whose cost is $\theta^{-1} + \theta^{-2} + \theta^{-3}$. This firing sequence costs as much as $\gamma' = \langle (\gg, a), (\gg, b), (b, \gg) \rangle$ which reaches the same marking m. However we notice that γ has a synchronisation at position 4 but we don't know yet what appears at position 4 for γ'. Then both paths should be kept.

Note that we tackled the problem of optimality of the alignment with the discounted cost function. For $\theta > 1$, this optimality does not correspond to the optimal classical alignment.

Comparison to Classical Alignments. Due to the discount parameter θ in the discounted cost function, our heuristic prioritizes the alignment of the beginning of the log trace. In the algorithm, this difference with the classical alignment algorithm appears in line 11 of Algorithm 1, where the markings that minimize the cost are much more different with the discounted cost function than by using the classical cost function for alignments. Indeed, when costs are all equivalent, many paths compete in the search for the optimal alignment. However, with very different costs, the number of paths with similar costs is low, thus reducing the search space.

Example 8. For the example of Fig. 1, there is a first choice between a and b. For large θ, the decision is quickly given thus disabling testing the depth of the other paths. For instance, with $\theta = 2$, the log sequences of type $\langle a, b, c \rangle$, $\langle a, b, \tau, b, c \rangle$, $\langle a, b, \tau, b, \tau, b, c \rangle$ won't be explored because they cannot have a better discounted cost.

5.2   A Heuristic for Reducing the Search Space of the Algorithm

The search space of $A^*SP_{\mathcal{D}=\theta}$ is large and even larger than the Dijsktra-based algorithm for alignments due to the incorporation of the lengths of the runs that reach the same marking. To reduce it, we come back to the classical closed set that contain the markings only. Every $\langle m, |\gamma| \rangle$ of the closed set A is reduced to m (like in [6]).

With this reduction, only the first paths that reaches the marking are used. When several concurrent firing sequences of equal cost exist, line 5 picks one as the optimal path and line 8 classifies the marking in A. Then the other firing sequences of equal cost for this marking are not considered anymore (line 10).

Example 9. For the marking $m = \{p4 : 1, p_{\alpha_2} : 1\}$ of the synchronous product given in Fig. 1c, two firing sequences compete for the minimization of the cost (in case that silent transition costs). Indeed both $\gamma = \langle (\gg, a), (\gg, b), (\gg, \tau), (b, b) \rangle$ and $\gamma' = \langle (\gg, a), (\gg, b), (b, \gg) \rangle$ have a cost of $\theta^{-1} + \theta^{-2} + \theta^{-3}$ and reach the marking m. Hence, when using markings only in the states, the algorithm picks one of the sequence as the optimal one and adds m in the closed set. Later, it does not consider the other firing sequence. However, we saw in Example 7 that γ' is better than γ by using the discounted cost function but it can go to the hatch in the reduced version.

With this reduction of the search space, the modified algorithm is not guaranteed any more to return the optimal discounted alignments, but the gain in runtime is extremely significant. Moreover, in practice, the loss of quality is very limited: we observed that the alignments found by the modified algorithm have very similar discounted cost than the optimal discounted alignments.

Process Model Exploration Along with Trace Exploration (Noted $A^*PT_{\mathcal{D}=\theta}$). In order to speed up the exploration, the alignment algorithm can simulate the synchronous product without explicitly constructing it. The synchronous product allows to easily play the moves of alignment. However, those moves can be found by exploring the process model and the trace separately. By comparing the next activity of the process model, given by the semantic of the net, and the next activity of the trace, we obtain the type of move. For instance, at the initialization, one possible next activity of N of Fig. 1a is b and the first activity in σ is also b. Then, we can move forward with a synchronous move, like in the synchronous product but without constructing the corresponding transition of the move. Then the m in the algorithm (for the marking of the synchronous product) is replaced by a pair $\langle m, p \rangle$ where m is the marking of the process model and p the position in the trace. Any marking of $A^*SP_{\mathcal{D}=\theta}$ can be given into a couple $\langle m, p \rangle$ for $A^*PT_{\mathcal{D}=\theta}$. For instance, marking $\{p4 : 1, p_{\alpha_2} : 1\}$ of the synchronous product given in Fig. 1c corresponds to $\langle \{p4 : 1\}, 1 \rangle$ where $\{p4 : 1\}$ is the marking in N and 1 the position in σ. The final marking becomes $\langle m_f, |\sigma| \rangle$ where the trace has been read and the process model reaches its final places.

6   Experiments: Discounted Alignments as a Heuristic for Approximating Classical Alignments

The algorithms presented in the previous section for computing alignment have been implemented in a branch of pm4py[1]. In this section we present general comparisons of quality and runtimes between them and existing methods, where the runtime reflects the search space. We also stress the impact of the discounted parameter by zooming on particular cases.

6.1   Comparison with Respect to Baselines

Inputs. We played the algorithms for both artificial and real-life logs and the corresponding models. Artificial set is taken from [18] and contains large models. For real-life logs, we used data given in the Business Process Intelligence Challenges from 2012 to 2020. We mined the process models of those logs with methods of the literature[2]. First, we applied a preprocessing method introduced by [8] to extract good prototypes of the logs[3]. This preprossessing step allows us to obtain not perfectly fitting models when using miners, interesting for alignments comparison. In fact, the method aims at finding more precise models. Then, we launched two different discovery algorithms on the found prototypes: the inductive miner [11] and the split miner 2.0 [3]. As the latter tool gives BPMN models, we use ProM plugins to transform them into Petri nets.

We computed the alignments on *variants* only, i.e., unique sequences of activities. This choice of using variants only allows to correctly compare the method's runtimes and prevents the situation where one method reduces the log to variants and not another one. Indeed alignment of log sequences of the same variant

Log	#variants	$|\Sigma|$	$\max\limits_{\sigma \in Log} len(\sigma)$	Model	$|T|$	$|P|$	$|F|$
L1	453	36	37	M1	39	40	92
L2	500	32	52	M2	34	34	80
L3	462	109	217	M3	123	108	276
L4	496	44	176	M4	52	36	106
L5	500	32	71	M5	33	35	78

(a) Artificial Logs and Models

Log	#variants	$|\Sigma|$	$\max\limits_{\sigma \in Log} len(\sigma)$	Model Miner	$|T|$	$|P|$	$|F|$
BPI2012	4366	24	175	IM	34	24	68
				SM	30	23	60
BPI2018$_{pa}$	3832	24	100	IM	22	24	60
				SM	20	15	40
BPI2019	11973	42	990	IM	18	13	38
				SM	13	10	26
BPI2020$_{dd}$	99	17	24	IM	15	11	32
				SM	14	9	28
BPI2020$_{rp}$	89	19	20	IM	31	26	74
				SM	23	12	46

(b) Real-life Logs and Models

Fig. 2. Input Description, where Σ is the alphabet of activities in the log, T the set of transitions of the model, P the set of places of the model and F the flow relations between the nodes in the model.

---

[1] Currently available at https://github.com/BoltMaud/pm4py-core.

[2] Available at https://github.com/BoltMaud/A-Discounted-Cost-Function-for-Fast-Alignments-of-Business-Processes-Sources.

[3] Prototype Selection plugin of ProM software with default settings.

is equivalent but this optimization can be used for any algorithm. Figure 2 gives an overview of the inputs.

Comparison. We compare our alignment results to the four current methods of the state-of-the-art implemented in pm4py which are: – the Dijkstra search on the Synchronous Product without heuristic (DSP) [1], – a Disjkstra that consumes less memory by using a similar idea of our second algorithm (DLM), – an A*-based algorithm on the state-space of the synchronous product that incorporates an heuristic on reaching the final marking (A^*SP_{mf}) [26] and – its less-memory version (A^*LM_{mf}). To compare the runtimes, we exclude log-based implementations and used the trace-based version to avoid the use of the parallelism between variants that can be added to any version at the case level. We recall notation of our methods $A^*SP_{\mathcal{D}=\theta}$, for the version that uses the synchronous product, and $A^*PT_{\mathcal{D}=\theta}$, for the second one that explores only the process model and the trace.

Results. The *quality* of an alignment found by a heuristic method, is defined as the ratio (in %) between the classical cost (number of model or log moves) of the optimal alignment (given by the DSP method) and the classical cost of the alignment found by the method. In Fig. 3a we give the quality of each method.

Similarly, in Fig. 3b, each line shows the sum of the runtimes of alignment computations by a method, expressed in percentage of the runtime of the DSP method. The runtime reflects the space of search. The box charts have wide range because they summarize the results of all the alignments which are very different (depending on both the model and the log involved).

We see in Fig. 3b that the runtime of the DLM algorithm is 20% of the runtime of the DSP method. For our heuristic $A^*PTD = 2$, the average runtime is around 10% of the reference method DSP (which corresponds to a gain of 90% of runtime, the result of a large reduction of the search space), for an average quality between 90 and 85% of the optimal alignments.

We did not represent in the charts the runtimes for methods A^*SP_{mf} and A^*LM_{mf} (implemented in pm4py) since they are much higher than the others: A^*SP_{mf} ran up to 30 times longer than the DSP and A^*LM_{mf} up to 7 times longer. We invite the reader to find the results and scripts on github[4].

6.2   Influence of the Discount Parameter θ on the Quality and Runtime

Figure 3a shows that the quality decreases when the parameter θ of the discounted cost function raises. However the gain in term of search space is high when $\theta > 1$ (depicted in practice with a gain in runtime). The output of those experiments is the correlation between the parameter θ and the compromise

---

[4] Available at https://github.com/BoltMaud/A-Discounted-Cost-Function-for-Fast-Alignments-of-Business-Processes-Sources.

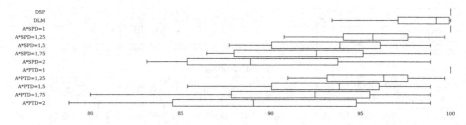

(a) Quality of the alignments obtained by different methods. Quality is defined as the ratio (in %) between the classical cost (number of model or log moves) of the optimal alignment and the classical cost of the alignment found by the method. The first line is the baseline and present the optimal approach which has no lost in quality, i.e., we observe 100% of quality. In general, one can see that the loss of quality with our heuristics is rather limited.

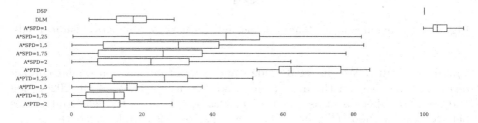

(b) Runtime (in % of the runtime of the DSP Algorithm). A percentage lower than 100 corresponds to a gain of runtime compared to the DSP method.

Fig. 3. Comparison of quality and runtimes of different methods.

between quality and runtime of alignments. For $\theta = 1$, one gets exact alignments but runtimes are slow because the search space is large. For higher θ one can extract very fast alignments but the quality is reduced. In practice, we recommend to try θ slightly higher than 1 and not larger than 2 (which is already a very severe discount factor). Values around 1.1–1.5 should give good results.

On another hand, we want to raise awareness on the method $A^*PTD = 1$ which corresponds to optimal alignment without the construction of the synchronous product. The method gives exact alignments for reduced runtimes because it disables the construction of the synchronous product. Method DLM also does not construct the synchronous product but we see in Fig. 3a that there is a lost of quality.

Additive Comparisons. The omission of ProM and other tool results in the previous section is due to the differences between the output formats which made difficult the comparison of quality and runtimes. However, in this section we zoom in particular cases, i.e., by running a log sequence only, thus making human interpretation possible. We add PNR the results given by the PNetReplayer package of [2] in ProM and REC_{ilp} the results given by [19].

Method	DSP	DLM	A^*SP_m	A^*LM_m	PNR	REC_{ilp}	A^*SPD					A^*PTD				
							1	1.25	1.5	1.75	2	1	1.25	1.5	1.75	2
Number of Asynchronous Moves	14	14	14	14	14	–	14	14	14	15	15	14	14	14	15	15
Runtime (s)	0.14	0.62	0.73	0.02	0.01	–	0.10	0.10	0.04	0.04	0.02	0.13	0.12	0.06	0.04	0.04

(a) BPI2020$_{rp}$

Method	DSP	DLM	A^*SP_m	A^*LM_m	PNR	REC_{ilp}	A^*SPD					A^*PTD				
							1	1.25	1.5	1.75	2	1	1.25	1.5	1.75	2
Number of Asynchronous Moves	11	11	11	11	11	11	11	11	11	11	11	11	11	11	11	11
Runtime (s)	47.78	628.75	3385.59	1.55	0.06	1.38	13.28	0.02	0.01	0.01	0.01	43.41	0.03	0.02	0.02	0.01

(b) M5

Method	DSP	DLM	A^*SP_m	A^*LM_m	PNR	REC_{ilp}	A^*SPD					A^*PTD				
							1	1.25	1.5	1.75	2	1	1.25	1.5	1.75	2
Number of Asynchronous Moves	36	38	36	36	36	–	36	886	2137	1898	4265	36	161	146	330	338
Runtime (s)	6.19	2121.98	16011.60	0.76	1.94	–	4.38	0.07	0.14	0.13	0.45	8.24	0.10	0.12	0.07	0.12

(c) M3

Fig. 4. Particular alignments that draws advantages and disadvantages of our methods.

Specific Inputs. We choose 3 models and traces that have particular characteristics. First, we run the alignment between the first trace of BPI2020$_{rp}$ log and model IM because this couple (BPI2020$_{rp}$, IM) gives the least differences between the methods (Fig. 4a). The model has only 2 parallelism patterns and no loop. Then, we run the alignment of the first trace of $L5$ and model $M5$ where our method specifically works well (Fig. 4b). This model contains a concurrent pattern including 28 transitions and one loop. Finally we present an alignment of the fifth trace of L3 which is very long (215 activities) and its model which has many loops and many parallelism patterns (Fig. 4c). The latter aims at showing the weakness of our method.

Results. From the three tables of Fig. 4, we observe that the methods usually find exact alignments. This is not true for the last experiment given in Fig. 4c which highlights our weakness. This due to the size of the trace (215) that, for the high base of logarithm θ, the algorithms face a situation where all the markings have the same cost (θ^n where n is very large borders zero). At this point, we already advise the user to check the length of the traces to set the discounted parameter θ (or to tackle very small differences between costs with an implementation where more decimal are allowed).

Observe now that for Fig. 4a and b using high value of θ brings very fast result for nearly optimal alignment in Fig. 4a and optimal alignment in Fig. 4b. Moreover, this latter result even beats all the other methods including the ProM implementation (noted PNR). The particularity of model M5 is the large concurrency pattern that creates many paths of different behaviors. Most methods have to explore the different combinations created by the concurrency pattern. Our discounted function favors only the path that align at the beginning of this pattern and does not consider the other combinations of the activities.

The versions using less memory seem to be much less efficient sometimes even for less quality (see DLM for $M3$). The method REC_{ilp} worked only for the second model. $M3$ is too large for the Gurobi open source version and format of model 2020_{rp} is not accepted by the tool.

Comparison with the Token Replay Approach. Last but not least we give a comparison of runtimes between our algorithms for computing alignment and the token replay approach given in [4] because it also computes an approximation of conformance (more precisely fitness) of process models for a given log. For those experiments, we set our method with $\theta = 2$. We observe in Table 1 that our second algorithm gives faster results in most times. The token replay is however much faster for $BPI2018_{p}a$. We plan to compare fitness approximation in future works.

Table 1. Runtime Comparison (in seconds) between the Algorithms for computing Discounted Alignments and the Token Replay Method given in [4] run on a un on a MacBook air 2017 model with a 1.8 GHz Intel ® Core^{TM} i5 CPU and 8 GB RAM.

Method	BPI2012		BPI2018$_{pa}$		BPI2019		BPI2020$_{dd}$		BPI2020$_{rp}$	
	IM	SM	IM	SM	IM	SM	IM	SM	IM	SM
A^*SP	78.18	69.39	493.96	43.92	143.25	103.99	0.43	0.23	1.08	0.24
A^*PT	25.03	19.71	419.37	11.15	42.14	26.61	0.14	0.09	0.70	0.09
Token replay	35.41	36.86	36.11	31.01	45.99	49.40	0.20	0.19	0.22	0.18

7 Conclusion

In this paper, we present a novel cost function for alignments. By using the position of the moves, our discounted cost function penalizes deviations of business processes that appear at early stage of the process execution. While the first aim is to align prefixes first, we nicely see that the proposed discounted cost function gives a heuristic for classical alignments. We implemented two versions of an A*-based algorithm that incorporate this heuristic and we experimented with artificial and real-life logs. The outputs of the experiments clearly show that the lost of quality, in term of log and model moves, is correlated to the gain of runtime, the result of the reduction of the search space. This is due to the parameter θ of our discounted cost function that forces prefix-first alignments. The compromise between quality and runtime can easily be set by using this parameter.

As future work, we suggest to combine the discounted cost function with other heuristics used for alignments. Also, the idea of using a discounted cost for alignments may be more or less relevant depending on the application that one is targeting. Among the multiple applications of alignments in conformance checking, some may be more or less resilient to the little loss of quality that we accept when using heuristics. In some settings, even, the alignments obtained for our discounted cost function may be more relevant than classical alignments, typically when the application justifies to penalize early deviations more than late ones.

Another interesting research line would be to use a machine learning approach (like it was done in [17] for the case of predicting the best process discovery technique), for learning the best parameter setting (mainly, the θ value used for discounting) as a previous step to our alignment technique.

References

1. Adriansyah, A.: Aligning observed and modeled behavior, Ph.D. thesis. Technische Universiteit Eindhoven (2014)
2. Adriansyah, A., van Dongen, B.F., van der Aalst, W.M.P.: Memory-efficient alignment of observed and modeled behavior. BPM Center Report, vol. 3, pp. 1–44 (2013)
3. Augusto, A., Conforti, R., Dumas, M., La Rosa, M., Polyvyanyy, A.: Split miner: automated discovery of accurate and simple business process models from event logs. Knowl. Inf. Syst. **59**(2), 251–284 (2019)
4. Berti, A., van der Aalst, W.M.P.: Reviving token-based replay: increasing speed while improving diagnostics. In: ATAED@ Petri Nets/ACSD, pp. 87–103 (2019)
5. Bloemen, V., van Zelst, S.J., van der Aalst, W.M.P., van Dongen, B.F., van de Pol, J.: Maximizing synchronization for aligning observed and modelled behaviour. In: Proceedings of the 16th International Conference on Business Process Management, BPM 2018, Sydney, NSW, Australia, 9–14 September 2018, pp. 233–249 (2018)
6. Carmona, J., van Dongen, B.F., Solti, A., Weidlich, M.: Conformance Checking - Relating Processes and Models. Springer, Switzerland (2018). https://doi.org/10.1007/978-3-319-99414-7
7. de Leoni, M., Marrella, A.: Aligning real process executions and prescriptive process models through automated planning. Exp. Syst. Appl. **82**, 162–183 (2017)
8. Sani, M.F., Boltenhagen, M., van der Aalst, W.: Prototype selection based on clustering and conformance metrics for model discovery. arXiv (2019)
9. Lee, W.L.J., Verbeek, H.M.W., Munoz-Gama, J., van der Aalst, W.M.P., Sepúlveda, M.: Recomposing conformance: closing the circle on decomposed alignment-based conformance checking in process mining. Inf. Sci. **466**, 55–91 (2018)
10. Leemans, S.J.J., Fahland, D., Wil, M.P.: van der Aalst. Scalable process discovery and conformance checking. Softw. Syst. Model. **17**(2), 599–631 (2018)
11. Leemans, S.J.J., Fahland, D., van der Aalst, W.M.P.: Discovering block-structured process models from event logs containing infrequent behaviour. In: Lohmann, N., Song, M., Wohed, P. (eds.) BPM 2013. LNBIP, vol. 171, pp. 66–78. Springer, Cham (2014). https://doi.org/10.1007/978-3-319-06257-0_6
12. Munoz-Gama, J., Carmona, J., van der Aalst, W.M.P.: Single-entry single-exit decomposed conformance checking. Inf. Syst. **46**, 102–122 (2014)
13. Murata, T.: Petri Nets: properties, analysis and applications. Proc. IEEE **77**(4), 541–574 (1989)

14. Reijers, H.A., Liman Mansar, S.: Best practices in business process redesign: an overview and qualitative evaluation of successful redesign heuristics. Omega **33**(4), 283–306 (2005)
15. Reißner, D., Conforti, R., Dumas, M., Rosa, M.L., Armas-Cervantes, A.: Scalable conformance checking of business processes. In: OTM CoopIS, Rhodes, Greece, pp. 607–627 (2017)
16. Reißner, D., Armas-Cervantes, A., Conforti, R., Dumas, M., Fahland, D., La Rosa, M.: Scalable alignment of process models and event logs: an approach based on automata and s-componentsd. Inf. Syst. **94**, 101561 (2020)
17. Ribeiro, J., Carmona, J., Mısır, M., Sebag, M.: A recommender system for process discovery. In: Sadiq, S., Soffer, P., Völzer, H. (eds.) BPM 2014. LNCS, vol. 8659, pp. 67–83. Springer, Cham (2014). https://doi.org/10.1007/978-3-319-10172-9_5
18. Taymouri, F., Carmona, J.: Model and event log reductions to boost the computation of alignments. In: Ceravolo, P., Guetl, C., Rinderle-Ma, S. (eds.) SIMPDA 2016. LNBIP, vol. 307, pp. 1–21. Springer, Cham (2018). https://doi.org/10.1007/978-3-319-74161-1_1
19. Taymouri, F., Carmona, J.: A recursive paradigm for aligning observed behavior of large structured process models. In 14th International Conference of Business Process Management (BPM), Rio de Janeiro, Brazil, 18–22 September, pp. 197–214 (2016)
20. Taymouri, F., Carmona, J.: Model and event log reductions to boost the computation of alignments. In: Ceravolo, P., Guetl, C., Rinderle-Ma, S. (eds.) SIMPDA 2016. LNBIP, vol. 307, pp. 1–21. Springer, Cham (2018). https://doi.org/10.1007/978-3-319-74161-1_1
21. Taymouri, F., Carmona, J.: Computing alignments of well-formed process models using local search. ACM Trans. Softw. Eng. Methodol. **29**(3), 15:1–15:41 (2020)
22. van der Aalst, W.M.P.: Decomposing Petri Nets for process mining: a generic approach. Distrib. Parallel Databases **31**(4), 471–507 (2013)
23. van der Aalst, W.M.P.: Process Mining - Data Science in Action, 2nd edn. Springer, Heidelberg (2016). https://doi.org/10.1007/978-3-662-49851-4
24. van der Aalst, W.M.P.: Re-engineering knock-out processes. Decis. Support Syst. **30**(4), 451–468 (2001)
25. van Zelst, S.J., Bolt, A., Hassani, M., van Dongen, B.F., Wil, M.P.: van der Aalst. Online conformance checking: relating event streams to process models using prefix-alignments. Int. J. Data Sci. Anal. **8**(3), 269–284 (2019)
26. van Zelst, S.J., Bolt, A., van Dongen, B.F.: Tuning alignment computation: an experimental evaluation. In: ATAED@ Petri Nets/ACSD, pp. 6–20 (2017)
27. Verbeek, H.M.W., van der Aalst, W.M.P.: Merging alignments for decomposed replay. In: Kordon, F., Moldt, D. (eds.) PETRI NETS 2016. LNCS, vol. 9698, pp. 219–239. Springer, Cham (2016). https://doi.org/10.1007/978-3-319-39086-4_14
28. Winskel, G.: Petri Nets, algebras, morphisms, and compositionality. Inf. Comput. **72**(3), 197–238 (1987)

Blockchain and Robotic Process Automation

Task Clustering Method Using User Interaction Logs to Plan RPA Introduction

Yuki Urabe$^{(\boxtimes)}$, Sayaka Yagi$^{(\boxtimes)}$, Kimio Tsuchikawa$^{(\boxtimes)}$, and Haruo Oishi$^{(\boxtimes)}$

NTT Access Network Service Systems Laboratories,
Hikarinooka 1-1, Yokosuka 239-0847, Japan
{yuuki.urabe.ue,sayaka.yagi.aw,kimio.tsuchikawa.eu,
haruo.oishi.nw}@hco.ntt.co.jp

Abstract. Robotic process automation (RPA) software is a powerful tool that can automate business operations to reduce manual labor while improving operational quality by eliminating input errors. In order to efficiently and effectively improve business operations with RPA, it is necessary to clarify the types and volumes of actual business operations being performed by the employees and improve operations that have a large volume and are performed repeatedly. User interaction (UI) logs consist of users' activities performed on the computer and can be collected regardless of the business system or application to understand how employees work. However, it is difficult to understand the types and volumes of the executed tasks from such data because the task types are not recorded explicitly. In this work, we propose a method that clusters UI logs into task types to help analyzers identify high-volume and repetitive tasks for RPA introduction. As the operation types differ by task type, we utilize this characteristic to analyze the co-occurrence of operations and segment UI logs into a sequence of the same task types. Then, we perform clustering based on the operation types contained in the segments. We evaluated our approach using UI logs generated from actual scenarios in a workplace, and report the results and limitations.

Keywords: Business process analysis · User interaction log · Robotic process automation

1 Introduction

In the rapidly changing business environment of the modern era, companies are constantly searching for the best way to improve efficiency in business operations to make the company more productive. Generally, business process improvement is done by clarifying the existing processes, identifying operational problems, redesigning the processes, and evaluating the improvement [1]. For a company to improve efficiency rapidly and maximize the effect of the improvement, it needs to understand the As-Is processes performed by employees and prioritize

© Springer Nature Switzerland AG 2021
A. Polyvyanyy et al. (Eds.): BPM 2021, LNCS 12875, pp. 273–288, 2021.
https://doi.org/10.1007/978-3-030-85469-0_18

the ones that need to be improved, rather than just changing the way of working without thinking of a strategy.

Robotic Process Automation (RPA) software applications such as WinActor[1] and UI Path[2] are powerful tools that can automate business operations, and they have been introduced to many types of work performed on the computer. The automation of business operations using RPA software can improve the productivity of companies by reducing manual labor while improving the operational quality by eliminating input errors. However, introducing an RPA software requires the implementation of RPA robots, and if the robots are not designed for the appropriate scope of work (e.g., a robot created for low-volume operations), the cost of the implementation will increase while no clear business improvement effect will be achieved. Therefore, in order to maximize the effect of the business operation improvement using RPA software, analyzers need to understand the actual state of business operations and identify which operations have a large volume and are performed repeatedly to determine which business operations to improve [2,3]. Process mining using event logs collected from enterprise systems can be one of the options to clarify how employees work and to determine processes for RPA implementation [4–6]. However, in reality, some business operations use enterprise systems or other applications that do not output event logs. Thus, using data only available from some systems may not allow analyzers to understand employees' work thoroughly. On the other hand, user interaction (UI) logs can be collected from workers' computers accurately and exhaustively regardless of the type of business system or application [7,8]. UI logs are sequential data of users' activities performed on the graphical user interface (GUI) (e.g., button click, textbox entry, etc.). As UI logs contain detailed data on operations but do not explicitly contain task names, it is necessary to establish a method that can group the UI logs into task types to discover the workload of each task. A manual method, a supervised method, and an unsupervised method that can segment UI logs into smaller sequences of tasks have been proposed [9–11]. However, the manual and the supervised methods cannot be realized unless the analyzer knows the content of tasks existing in the data. The conventional unsupervised method is also not possible to properly segment UI logs into smaller sequences of tasks if the task is interrupted or restarted and another task is executed in between, or if the order of the operations varies greatly for each task execution, which is common in real-world operations.

In light of the above background, we propose a method that helps analyzers identify high-volume and repetitive operations from a UI log to determine which process has the potential to effectively improve business operations by introducing RPA software. Our method segments the UI log into smaller sequences and clusters them into groups of tasks. In this way, analyzers can understand the variety of tasks executed by employees and their overall workload. We presume that the same task generally consists of the same operations, so our method analyzes the co-occurrence of operations and segments the UI log into a sequence of

---

[1] WinActor: https://winactor.biz/en/.
[2] UI Path: https://www.uipath.com/.

operations under the same task by dividing the non-co-occurring area within the operations. Then, clustering is performed in accordance with the type of operations in the segmented sequences. Our method is unsupervised, which means it does not require the analyzers to have knowledge of the tasks contained in the UI log or to set up any rules. It is also robust for situations where the order of operations is varied among each task execution or when tasks are not executed from start to end due to interruptions.

In Sect. 2 of this paper, we present related research on process selection for RPA introduction, UI logs, and techniques for classifying/clustering sequential data. In Sect. 3, we present our proposed method, and in Sect. 4, we report the details of our evaluation and discuss the results. We conclude in Sect. 5 with a brief summary and mention of future work.

2 Related Work

Process selection for RPA implementation is crucial when it comes to increasing the effectiveness of business improvement [5]. Wanner *et al.* [6] proposed a method to quantitatively measure the number of task executions, execution time, etc. by using the event logs in Process-Aware Information Systems (PAIS) accumulated from various enterprise systems. Measuring the number of task executions is also emphasized in other research [2,3], as it is clearly linked to cost reduction through automation. Our study also focuses on measuring the workload of the task executions, but we use UI logs rather than event logs because they can be obtained from a computer regardless of the type of business system or applications, as mentioned in the previous section.

A UI log is essentially a collection of interactions done on GUI components [7,12] (see Sect. 3.1 for details). Since RPA robots execute operations on GUI components, the UI log is very compatible with RPA and is considered very useful for extracting repetitive operations in the same task [11,13] and understanding the flow of operations [8]. When collecting the UI logs from employees' computers, turning on the logging tool right before a worker executes a single task and turning it off after finishing the task is inconvenient, so the UI log is generally obtained continuously while the terminal is running. Unlike event logs, UI logs do not have any data to identify task types, so it is necessary to classify the data into groups of tasks to measure task types and their workload.

There are several approaches to classifying/clustering sequential data, which can be divided into manual approaches, supervised approaches, and unsupervised approaches. For the manual approach, Urabe *et al.* [9] proposed a method that visualizes the UI log with nodes and edges to enable analyzers to visually check the flow of operations and group various data in accordance with tasks. For the supervised approach, methods such as trace alignment [10] or dynamic time warping [14] can detect sequences that are similar to labeled sequences prepared in advance. However, manual and supervised methods are time-consuming in terms of manually grouping data and/or preparing labeled sequences for each task type, and they cannot be implemented correctly unless the analyzers have

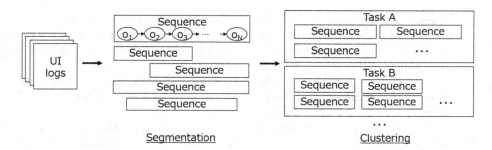

Fig. 1. Overview of our proposed method. "Sequence" comprises of one or more operations. "o_1, o_2, o_3, and o_N" shown in the "Sequence" box represent operations.

knowledge of the data (e.g., knowledge of the operation type for each task). As for the unsupervised approach, Leno *et al.* [11]'s method which detects back-edge operations in tasks in order to segment sequential data into a smaller sequence of operations, could be an option for segmenting data before clustering data into groups of tasks. Their method seems to work well if the order of the operations of a task doesn't vary in every task execution or if there are no interruptions during task execution. However, when the order of operations varies greatly or when an interruption occurs and another task is executed before the current one is finished, this method fails to identify back-edge operations and cannot perform segmentation. Frequent sequential pattern mining algorithms (e.g. Prefix-Span, SPADE) [15] is also insufficient to accomplish our goal because the order of the operations in the task may vary for every task execution.

3   Proposed Method

In this section, we describe our approach to cluster a UI log into a group of tasks (Fig. 1). Input data is a UI log collected from workers ("**UI logs**" in Fig. 1; details provided in Sect. 3.1). The UI log is segmented into smaller sequences using the co-occurrence feature of operations ("**Segmentation**" in Fig. 1: details provided in Sect. 3.2). Finally, the segmented logs are clustered in accordance with the type of operations contained in each segment ("**Clustering**" in Fig. 1; details provided in Sect. 3.3).

3.1   UI Log

The UI log is composed of operation time, user information, operated area (e.g., application name, window title, file name, information of GUI components, etc.), and input content (see Fig. 2 for an example). These are collected at the timing of workers' interactions with GUI components (e.g., button, link, textbox, select box, checkbox, cell, etc.) that cause changes on the computer screen [7,12]. Information of the GUI components can be, for example, id property, name property, GUI coordinate, or values shown on the webpage that can be extracted

	A	B	C	D	E	F
1	time	user ID	application	window title	html_name	content
2	2020/10/1 9:00:33	157925	IEXPLORE.EXE	Search theme number	ref_pro	reference button
3	2020/10/1 9:01:02	157925	IEXPLORE.EXE	Search theme number	bureau_type	AS Labs
4	2020/10/1 9:01:40	157925	IEXPLORE.EXE	Search theme number	department_type	Access Operation Project
5	2020/10/1 9:02:25	157925	IEXPLORE.EXE	Search theme number	division_type	Navigation Group
6	2020/10/1 9:03:03	157925	IEXPLORE.EXE	Search theme number	search	search_button

Fig. 2. Example of a UI log. Each column represents operation time (*time*), user information (*user ID*), application name (*application*), window name (*window title*), name property of an interacted GUI component (*html name*), and input content (*content*).

from a document object model (DOM) for webpages. This information can also be an identifier of GUI objects extracted using UI Automation[3] or Microsoft Active Accessibility (MSAA)[4] for Windows applications.

3.2 Segmentation

Our approach to UI log segmentation is based on the idea of topic segmentation in the field of natural language processing [16]. In topic segmentation, the assumption is that the types of words appearing in a topic change as the topic in the text changes. In Bessho's work [16], a co-occurrence vector is created by counting the co-occurring words in each sentence in a corpus. Then, the words in the text are processed in each defined window width in the order of appearance, and the similarity of window widths before and after is calculated. Finally, the part where the similarity drops is judged to be the part where the topic has changed, and the text is then split into smaller segments. In the same way that the types of words change as the topic changes, we hypothesize that the types of operations change as the task changes in the UI log. Our segmentation method is described below.

1. **Create operation ids from a UI log to identify the same operations.**
   We combine the name of application (*application name*), name of window (*window title*), and information of GUI components (*html name, html id, html type, coordinate*, etc.) to create an id (e.g., "IEXPLORE.EXE_Search theme number_ref_pro" in row 2 in Fig. 2). We do not include operation time (*time*), user information (*user id*), or input content (*content*), as they are not necessary for identifying the location of the operation.
2. **Create a co-occurrence matrix with operation ids.** Unlike natural language texts, which can be segmented by sentences, there is no clue for segmenting operations in the UI log at this stage, so we count the co-occurrence of operations by focusing on the N operations that appear before and after

---

[3] UIAutomation: https://docs.microsoft.com/en-us/windows/win32/winauto/entry-uiauto-win32.

[4] MSAA: https://docs.microsoft.com/en-us/windows/win32/winauto/microsoft-active-accessibility.

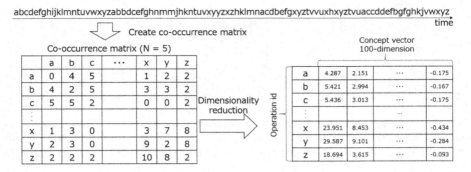

Fig. 3. Example of a co-occurrence matrix. Each letter in the string ("abcdefg...") represents an operation id.

the target operation. N is defined manually (e.g., 10 operations). The target operation is each operation that appears in chronological order in the UI log. Figure 3 shows an example of the co-occurrence matrix. For example, if N is set to 5, five operations existing before and after the target operation are counted. Therefore, in Fig. 3, when the target operation id is "a", it means the operation id "b" has co-occurred four times before and after the operation id "a", and once for the operation id "x".

3. **Create a co-occurrence vector for each operation.** We apply a dimensionality reduction method, namely, singular value decomposition (SVD) [17], to reduce the computation time of the vectors when the operation type is large. SVD is a method for automatically extracting the characteristic dimensions from the co-occurrence matrix. With this method, the vectors of operations that tend to co-occur will be similar to each other. For example, if there are 1,000 types of operations, the dimension of the vector for each operation is 1,000. We reduce the dimensions to 100 using SVD and call it a "concept vector" for each operation (Fig. 3).

4. **Compute similarity between two sequences.** In order to find task boundaries in the UI log, we calculate the similarity of two M-length sequences that are adjacent to each other. M is set manually (e.g., 10 operations). For example, Fig. 4 shows how we calculate the similarity between the M-length sequences which the first sequence ends with operation id "a" and the second sequence starts with operation id "c". If we set M to 3, we compute the similarity of two sequences that each contain three operations (i.e. "[m, n, a]" and "[c, d, b]" in black-bordered boxes in Fig. 4). The similarity is computed by first creating a centroid vector for each sequence by using the concept vector of each operation contained in the sequences (Eq. 1). In Eq. 1, C denotes the centroid vector, M is the length of a sequence, cv_j means the concept vector of the j-th number of the operation id in the sequence, and k is the size of the dimension of the concept vector. Then, the similarity of two sequences is calculated by using cosine similarity in Eq. 2, where C_1 and C_2 denote the first and the second centroid vectors and k means the size of the

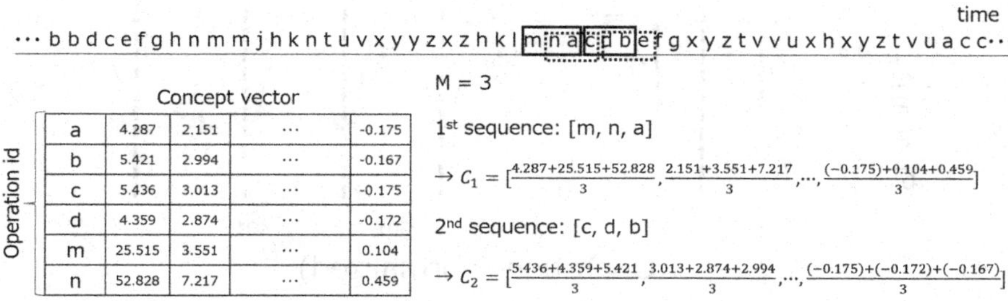

time
··· b b d c e f g h n m m j h k n t u v x y y z x z h k l m n a c d b e f g x y z t v v u x h x y z t v u a c c···

Concept vector

M = 3

		Concept vector		
a	4.287	2.151	···	-0.175
b	5.421	2.994	···	-0.167
c	5.436	3.013	···	-0.175
d	4.359	2.874	···	-0.172
m	25.515	3.551	···	0.104
n	52.828	7.217	···	0.459

Operation id

1st sequence: [m, n, a]

$$\rightarrow C_1 = [\frac{4.287+25.515+52.828}{3}, \frac{2.151+3.551+7.217}{3}, ..., \frac{(-0.175)+0.104+0.459}{3}]$$

2nd sequence: [c, d, b]

$$\rightarrow C_2 = [\frac{5.436+4.359+5.421}{3}, \frac{3.013+2.874+2.994}{3}, ..., \frac{(-0.175)+(-0.172)+(-0.167)}{3}]$$

Fig. 4. Example of centroid vector computation.

dimension. We continue this process from the beginning to the end of the UI log in chronological order by sliding one operation at a time. For example, after computing the sequences "[m, n, a]" and "[c, d, b]", it will then slide to "[n, a, c]" and "[d, b, e]" (black dotted boxes in Fig. 4).

$$C = [\frac{\Sigma_{j=1}^{M} cv_{j,1}}{M}, \frac{\Sigma_{j=1}^{M} cv_{j,2}}{M}, \cdots, [\frac{\Sigma_{j=1}^{M} cv_{j,k}}{M}] \tag{1}$$

$$Similarity(C_1, C_2) = \frac{\Sigma_{i=1}^{k} C_{1k} \times C_{2k}}{\sqrt{\Sigma_{i=1}^{k} C_{1k}^2} \sqrt{\Sigma_{i=1}^{k} C_{2k}^2}} \tag{2}$$

5. **Segment the data where the similarity drops.** At the task boundary, the similarity of the adjacent sequences is expected to be at the minimum. Therefore, we find the minima and the maxima of the similarity in the UI log and identify d_1, a depth from the first maxima to the minima, and d_2, a depth from the minima to the next maxima. The sequence of the data is segmented when both d_1 and d_2 are larger than a threshold t (Fig. 5). The threshold t is set manually between 0 and 1. For example, if the threshold is set to 0.2, we split the sequence where both d_1 and d_2 are larger than 0.2 (vertical dotted lines in Fig. 5). The similarity is normalized to remove weak oscillations by calculating the average value of a certain number of operations before and after the target operation. For example, if the target operation is the 20th operation in the UI log and we set five operations for normalization, we calculate the average similarity from the 15th to 25th operations.

3.3 Clustering

After the data is segmented into sequences of a smaller number of operations, we cluster these segments into groups based on the type of operations they contain. Generally speaking, there are two types of clustering methods: hierarchical clustering and partitioning (e.g., k-means [18]). We opted to use a hierarchical

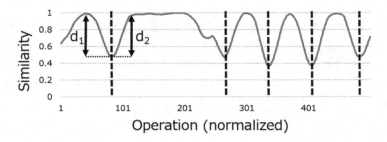

Fig. 5. Similarity score of the operations in a UI log.

clustering method, namely, agglomerative hierarchical clustering (AHC), because the partitioning method requires knowledge of the number of clusters in advance, which we cannot determine in our research setting. The process for clustering is described below.

1. **Create feature vector.** We create a feature vector for each segment that has a dimensionality equal to the type of operation ids contained in the UI log. Then, when we find an operation id in the segment, we increase the count of its element. For example, in Fig. 6, the feature vector of the segment "[a, c, c, d, d, e, f, b, g, f, g]" is "[1, 1, 2, 2, 1, 2, 2, 0, 0, 0, 0, 0, 0, 0, 0, 0, 0, 0, 0, 0]", counting the operation ids existing in the segment and leaving those that do not exist as 0.
2. **Cluster segments.** The segments are clustered into groups using the feature vectors created in the previous step. With the AHC method, we have to define a linkage category (e.g., single-linkage, complete-linkage, and group-average-linkage, etc.) to link the data to create a hierarchy of clusters and implement a method for calculating the distance between two items of data (e.g., cosine similarity, Euclidean distance). We tried these methods and chose the group average linkage method and the cosine similarity method as they worked the best. The input for clustering is a matrix of feature vectors; the size of the number of segments × the type of operation ids. An example of the clustering result is shown as a dendrogram in Fig. 6. The labels shown on the x-axis correspond to the labels of the segments shown on the left side of the figure. Finally, we manually set a threshold (e.g., 0.7) to divide the dendrogram into a group of segments. For example, in Fig. 6, if we set the threshold to 0.7 (horizontal line in the dendrogram), we obtain three groups that contain four segments each.

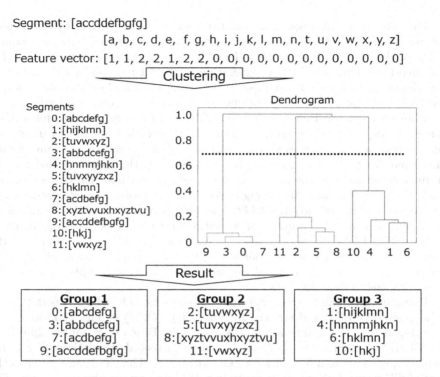

Fig. 6. Example of clustering. The labels shown on the x-axis in the dendrogram figure correspond to the labels (0 to 11) of the segments.

4 Evaluation

We implemented and evaluated our method to investigate how well it can segment and cluster a UI log into tasks, how it is influenced by various parameters, and any limitations it may have. We also visualized the results it provided and examined whether we can comprehend the number of task types and their workload and if they are close to the correct answer. The datasets we used and the evaluation method are described in Sects. 4.1 and 4.2, respectively. We report the results in Sect. 4.3 and discuss the limitations in Sect. 4.4.

4.1 Datasets

We collected two datasets for our evaluation. The first dataset (**Dataset 1**) contains five types of task executions that use web-based enterprise systems running in our company. We implemented a logger tool that extracts user interactions on GUI components from Internet Explorer. The second dataset[5] (**Dataset 2**) was collected from [11]. The details of each dataset are described below.

---

[5] The data was obtained from https://figshare.com/articles/dataset/UI_logs/12543587.

Dataset 1 contains operations of five task types performed by one person for two days. These tasks are: business travel request (BTR), purchase request (PR), publication approval request (PubAR), patent approval request (PatAR), and meeting setting (MT). Each operation in the UI log contains the information described in Sect. 3.1. We created operation ids based on the rule given in Sect. 3.2. Each task is basically completed by entering necessary information on each business system. However, in the (BTR) log, the user searched for a route and its transportation fee on an external transportation website to input this information on the business system, and the timing to search the route varied each time the task was executed. In the (PR) log, the user searched for the product name and code on the Internet to find product information to input on the business system, and the timing to search these information also varied. The total number of operations was 3,422. The number of task executions, minimum, maximum, and average number of operations for each task type, are listed in Table 1. As a UI log file was created for each task execution, we annotated the task names into the UI log in order to use them to compare the result given by our proposed system. We shuffled the order of the files and created one long UI log file for the evaluation.

Dataset 2 contains the execution of three tasks: colored Petri nets (CPN), reimbursement (RT), and student records (SR). (CPN) is data containing one task that is repeated 100 times. It was created by Bosco *et al.* and is equivalent to "CPN1" in their paper [13]. (RT) and (SR) record simulations of real-life scenarios, each created 50 times by Leno *et al.* [11]. The (RT) log simulates the task of filling in reimbursement requests with data provided by a claimant. The (SR) log simulates the task of transferring students' data from a spreadsheet to a web form. All of these logs contained data equivalent to time, user information, application name, and information to identify the interacted GUI components, and we used some of the data to create operation ids. These data contained a case id to identify task execution, which is not included in **Dataset 1**. The total number of operations was 7,180. The number of task executions, along with the minimum, maximum, and average number of operations for each task type, are listed in Table 1. As the original data in the file was separated by tasks, we added the task names into each operation data to use them in the evaluation. We divided the UI logs by case id and shuffled the data to create one long UI log file.

4.2 Evaluation Method

We input each dataset into our system and retrieved the outputs provided. As we wanted to investigate how the parameters influenced the result, we combined the values within a certain range and evaluated how the result changed. The range we set for parameter N and M was from 10 to 100 in increments of 10, and from 0 to 0.5 in increments of 0.1 for t (the details of these parameters are given in Sect. 3.2). The threshold we set for dividing the dendrogram was 70% of the maximum linkage, which is the default of the dendrogram function in the

Table 1. Number of tasks executed and minimum (Min.), maximum (Max.), and average (Avg.) number of operations for each task type. The tasks include a business task request (BTR), purchase request (PR), publication approval request (PubAR), patent approval request (PatAR), meeting setting (MS), colored petri nets (CPN), reimbursement (RT), and student records (SR).

	Dataset 1					Dataset 2		
	(BTR)	(PR)	(PubAR)	(PatAR)	(MS)	(CPN)	(RT)	(SR)
No. of tasks	6	17	9	10	13	100	50	50
Min.	76	19	50	43	8	14	73	37
Max.	127	103	89	105	41	14	81	43
Avg.	96.8	74.8	67.2	68.3	21.6	14.0	74.6	41.0

Scipy library[6] (Python). Since the clustering results were not assigned a specific task name, we examined each cluster in the order of the highest number of operations contained and gave the name of the task that contained the most types of operations in the cluster. In cases where the number of clusters was greater than the number of tasks and a task name was already given to another cluster, we gave a name such as "other 0" or "other 1". We utilized precision, recall, and F-score to quantitatively evaluate whether the clustering was performed accurately and without omissions, as calculated with Eqs. 3, 4, and 5, respectively. In these equations, "Number of Task A operation that was correctly classified" was determined by comparing the task names annotated in the data to the task names given by the aforementioned method in this paragraph. "Number of operation classified as Task A" was decided by counting the number of task names given by the system. We also counted the number of each task name annotated in the data for "Number of Task A operation".

$$Precision = \frac{Number\ of\ Task\ A\ operation\ that\ was\ correctly\ classified}{Number\ of\ operation\ classified\ as\ Task\ A} \tag{3}$$

$$Recall = \frac{Number\ of\ Task\ A\ operation\ that\ was\ correctly\ classified}{Number\ of\ Task\ A\ operation} \tag{4}$$

$$F - score = \frac{2 \times Precision \times Recall}{Precision + Recall} \tag{5}$$

4.3 Result

Figure 7 shows how the F-score changed when the parameters changed in order to clarify the influence of the parameters on the clustering results. The best F-score is shown with a markup balloon in each figure including the precision and

---

[6] scipy.cluster.hierarchy.dendrogram: https://docs.scipy.org/doc/scipy/reference/generated/scipy.cluster.hierarchy.dendrogram.html.

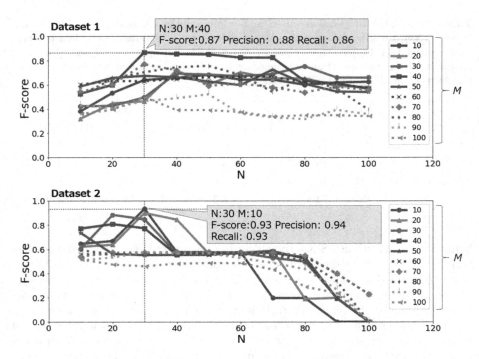

Fig. 7. F-score of **Dataset 1** (upper) and **Dataset 2** (lower). X-axis is the parameter for N. Each line represents the parameter for M. t is set to 0.1.

recall results. The best result for **Dataset 1** was $\{Precision, Recall, F\text{-}score\} = \{0.88, 0.86, 0.84\}$ when the parameters were $\{N, M, t\} = \{30, 40, 0.1\}$. For **Dataset 2**, it was $\{Precision, Recall, F\text{-}score\} = \{0.94, 0.93, 0.93\}$ when the parameters were $\{N, M, t\} = \{30, 10, 0.1\}$.

As we can see in the figure, the F-score tended to get a higher score when N was set larger than 30 and get lower scores at 10 and 20 for **Dataset 1**. For **Dataset 2**, the F-score was higher when N was set between 10 and 50 and was lower as the parameters grew larger. For parameter M, the F-score tended to be lower when M was large (around 90 and 100) for **Dataset 1** (see M lines at "90" and "100" in Fig. 7) and when M was larger than 60 for **Dataset 2** (see M lines from "60" to "100"). For parameter t, we found that a larger value tended to result in a failure to segment the UI logs, as the similarity of the UI log did not create a big drop (this can be clearly seen when parameter M was larger). However, if parameter t is too small (e.g., less than 0.1), it may segment the UI log which is not a point of a task change. When comparing the two datasets, the tendency of the parameters that resulted in higher F-scores was somewhat different: namely, parameters $\{N, M\}$ for **Dataset 1** were larger than those for **Dataset 2**. We conclude that the best parameters to achieve better clustering results will vary depending on the length of the operations contained in the tasks. For example, the number of operations in the tasks for **Dataset 1** ranged from 21.6 to 96.8, which is in contrast to the lower number of operations, 14.0 to 74.6, for **Dataset 2**.

4.4 Limitations of Our Approach

We further investigated the clustering results and discovered two limitations to our approach.

- **Optimization of parameters $\{N, M\}$ is necessary to achieve best clustering result.** From **Dataset 1**, we discovered that the segmentation of the UI logs tended to fail when the operation order varied largely in the task when parameters N and M were set smaller to 10—a failure that was not seen in the best clustering result. For example, in the (BTR) log, there were cases where the user searched for the business travel route before any data had been entered on the business system or right before the person entered data about the route. When the parameters were $\{N, M\} = \{10, 10\}$, our approach segmented the UI log right before the route was entered on the system for cases where the user searched for the route before using the system and then input all the required information. As a smaller parameter N counts the co-occurrence of the smaller range of operations, we assume that if the order of the operation varies greatly for every task execution, the system cannot deduce that the operations of the same task co-occur together. On the other hand, if parameter N is larger, our approach counts a longer range of operations so it can consider that the operations of the same task co-occur together. However, we must note that parameter N should not be too big, as it will count the co-occurrence of other tasks. Parameter M sets the range of operations to create a centroid vector and we assume that if the parameter is too large, the centroid vector will become a vector containing operations of multiple tasks, which may result in making a smaller and vague depth of drop at the task boundary that will then fail to be segmented. From these observations, it is important to optimize the parameters, especially $\{N, M\}$, to achieve better clustering results for every dataset. However, when using this system in the real world, we generally would not know the characteristics of the UI logs. Therefore, a method to optimize these parameters needs to be established. Since operations occur only in a certain task(s), examining how the operations appear in one or more clusters from the clustering result may be one of the clues to optimize the parameters $\{N, M\}$.
- **Segmentation failure occurs when the UI log contains a task where the number of operations is explicitly smaller than others.** To be more precise, when a task that contains a smaller number of operations (e.g., (MS) in **Dataset 1** or (CPN) in **Dataset 2**) exists between the other tasks of a larger number of operations, our system tends to only segment at the first task change, and the task of a smaller number of operations tends to be in the same segment of the second task of longer operations instead of segmenting the data at the point of every task change (Fig. 8). This is potentially because, when computing the similarity of two sequences in this situation, our approach

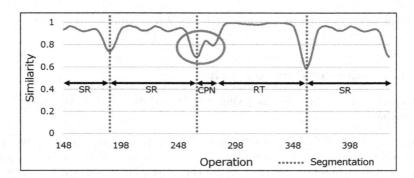

Fig. 8. Example of segmentation failure (circled area). The X-axis represents the 148 th to 432 th operation in the UI log of **Dataset 2**. The blue line represents the similarity of the operations when parameters were $\{N, M, t\} = \{30, 10, 0.1\}$. The black both-direction arrows represent the range of each task (SR: Student records, RT: Reimbursement, CPN: Colored Petri Nets). The red dotted lines represent the segmentation point given by our approach. (Color figure online)

computes the sequences that contain the operations of two or more tasks (i.e., the first sequence containing the operations of the first and second tasks and the second sequence containing those of the second and third tasks), and as such, the similarity will not score lower compared with when computing the similarity of sequences containing operations of different tasks. Our approach does not also compute the similarity of two sequences where they both belong to the same task for the task with a smaller number of operations because the operational length of the task is too small, which results in not scoring a higher value of similarity. These reasons result in not making a significant drop at the point of the task change and cannot be segmented.

4.5   Visualization Result

Figure 9 shows the percentage of operations contained in each task type for each dataset where the left column ("Clustering result") shows the result given by our approach and the right column ("Correct") shows the correct data. Overall, our approach could accurately show the quantitative result of task types and their ratio of operations, and the visualization result was quite similar to the correct data. From this visualization, we can conclude that our method achieves the goal of helping analyzers understand the number of task types and their workloads. However, if using our approach in the real world, it would not give the appropriate names for each task type, so analyzers would have to look through the operation types in each cluster to determine the task name.

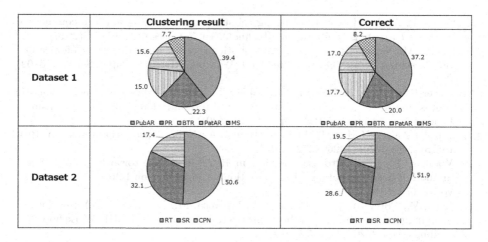

Fig. 9. Percentage of operations contained in each task type for **Dataset 1** and **Dataset 2**. The left column ("Clustering result") represents the clustering result given by our system and the right column ("Correct") shows the correct visualization.

5 Conclusion

In this work, we introduced a method that clusters a UI log into a group of tasks to quantitatively discover the type of the tasks and their workload. Our aim with this method was to help analyzers to clarify high-volume and repetitive tasks to make decisions for RPA introduction. Our approach consists of two main processes: segmentation and clustering. We hypothesized that a task comprises a certain type of operations and therefore segmented the UI log by analyzing the co-occurrence of the operations in the UI log to determine the point where the characteristic of the operations changes in the sequence. Then, we clustered the segments based on the type of operations.

We evaluated our approach with two different datasets and found that it can provide a high-quality clustering result when the parameters are optimized appropriately. Moreover, we were able to understand the number of task types and their workload quantitatively, which demonstrates that our system can achieve the main goal of this paper. However, at present, there is no method to optimize the parameters automatically, and when the number of operations of a certain task type differs greatly from that of the other task types, our approach fails to segment at the time the task changes. We also plan to evaluate our system in an environment where business operations are being conducted to investigate whether it helps the analyzers and clarify what else might be necessary to support them in improving business operations.

References

1. Adesola, A., Baines, T.: Developing and evaluating a methodology for business process improvement. Bus. Process Manage. J. **11**(1), 37–46 (2005)

2. Asatiani, A., Pentinnen, E.: Turning robotic process automation into commercial success - case OpusCapita. J. Inf. Technol. Teach. Cases **6**(2), 67–74 (2016)
3. Lacity, M., Willcocks, L., Craig, A.: Robotic process automation at Telefónica O2. In: Presented at the Outsourcing Unit Working Research Paper Series (15/02) (2015)
4. Geyer-Klingeberg, J., Nakladal, J., Baldau, F., Veit, F.: Process mining and robotic process automation: a perfect match. In: 16th International Conference of Business Process Management (BPM), pp. 124–131 (2018)
5. van der Aalst, W.M.P., Bichler, M., Heinzl, A.: Robotic process automation. Bus. Inf. Sys. Eng. **60**(4), 269–272 (2018)
6. Wanner, J., et al.: Process selection in RPA projects - towards a quantifiable method of decision making. In: International Conference on Information Systems, vol. 1–17 (2019)
7. Leno, V., Polyvyanyy, A., Dumas, M., La Rosa, M., Maggi, F.M.: Action logger: enabling process mining for robotic process automation. In: CEUR Workshop Proceedings, vol. 2420, pp. 1–5 (2019)
8. Yokose, F., et al.: Operation-visualization techonology to support digital transformation. NTT Tech. Rev. **18**(5), 1–6 (2020)
9. Urabe, Y., Yagi, S., Tsuchikawa, K., Masuda, T.: Visualizing user action data to discover business process. In: Asia-Pacific Network Operations and Management Symposium (APNOMS), vol. 2019, pp. 1–4 (2019)
10. Agostinelli, S.: Automated segmentation of user interface logs using trace alignment techniques (extended abstract). In: ICPM Doctoral Consortium and Tool Demonstration Track (ICPM-D 2020), pp. 13–14 (2020)
11. Leno, V., et al.: Identifying candidate routines for robotic process automation. In: 2nd International Conference of Process Mining (ICPM), pp. 153–160 (2020)
12. Nakajima, H., Masuda, T., Takahashi, I.: Hybrid approach on GUI information logging methods for visualization of operations in business applications [in Japanese]. In: ICM 2011-28, vol. 111, no. 279, pp. 49–54 (2011)
13. Bosco, A., Augusto, A., Dumas, M., La Rosa, M., Fortino, G.: Discovering automatable routines from user interaction logs. In: Hildebrandt, T., van Dongen, B., Röglinger, M., Mendling, J. (eds.) Business Process Management Forum. BPM 2019. Lecture Notes in Business Information Processing, vol. 360 (2019)
14. Keoth, E., Chu, S., Hart, D., Pazzani, M.: An online algorithm for segmenting time series. In: Proceedings 2001 IEEE International Conference on Data Mining, pp. 289–296 (2001)
15. Fournier-Viger, P., et al.: A survey of sequential pattern mining. Data Sci. Pattern Recognit. **1**(1), 54–77 (2017)
16. Bessho, K.: Text segmentation using word conceptual vectors [in Japanese]. J. Inf. Process. **42**, 2650–2662 (2001)
17. Wall, M.E., Rechtsteiner, A., Rocha, L.M.: Singular value decomposition and principal component analysis, pp. 91–109 (2003)
18. Xu, D., Tian, Y.: A comprehensive survey of clustering algorithms. Ann. Data Sci. **2**, 165–193 (2015)

From Symbolic RPA to Intelligent RPA: Challenges for Developing and Operating Intelligent Software Robots

Lukas-Valentin Herm[1]([☒]) [iD], Christian Janiesch[1,2] [iD], Hajo A. Reijers[3,4] [iD],
and Franz Seubert[1]

[1] Julius-Maximilians-Universität, Würzburg, Germany
{lukas-valentin.herm,christian.janiesch,
franz.seubert}@uni-wuerzburg.de
[2] HAW Landshut, Landshut, Germany
[3] Utrecht University, Utrecht, The Netherlands
h.a.reijers@uu.nl
[4] Eindhoven University of Technology, Eindhoven, The Netherlands

Abstract. Robotic process automation (RPA) is a novel technology that automates tasks by interacting with other software through their respective user interfaces. The technology has received substantial business attention because of its potential for rapid automation of process-driven tasks that would otherwise require tedious manual labor. This article explores the dichotomy between the practical reality of symbolic RPA, which requires handcrafting robots using process models and rulesets, and the promise of intelligent RPA, which relies on artificial intelligence technology to implement intelligent robots. Our research is based on a scholarly literature review as well as an interview study to derive and discuss challenges for this transition. We found that issues such as the lack of training data, human bias in data, compliance issues with transfer learning, poor explainability of robot decisions, and job-security-induced fear of AI robots all need to be addressed to enable the transition from symbolic to intelligent RPA.

Keywords: Robotic process automation · Artificial intelligence · Symbolic RPA · Intelligent RPA · Challenges

1 Introduction

Due to its heavyweight development load and the lack of application programming interfaces (APIs) of legacy software, it has become apparent that BPM software does not provide suitable automation solution for every business process [1, 2]. This has triggered the emergence of lightweight techniques for automating digital and manual tasks such as robotic process automation (RPA) [3]. In essence, RPA uses software robots that are designed to mimic human employee behavior by relying on existing user interfaces (UI) of legacy software instead of using APIs. In practice, this technology allows for the rapid automation of simple, repetitive tasks and, consequently, a fast

© Springer Nature Switzerland AG 2021
A. Polyvyanyy et al. (Eds.): BPM 2021, LNCS 12875, pp. 289–305, 2021.
https://doi.org/10.1007/978-3-030-85469-0_19

return on investment, since employees are no longer required to operate monotonous, non-value-added processes [1, 2].

The application of RPA, however, faces several challenges. Since not every process is predestinated for RPA-based automation, identifying suitable processes can be quite difficult [3]. Likewise, due to the symbolic character of current RPA practices, which means that it relies on handcrafted flow models and rulesets, the process of identification and development is still time-consuming and limited by the abilities of the involved designer [4]. There is a cut-off point at which RPA development becomes inefficient due to the large and complex variants and rulesets [3, 4].

A reflection on these challenges reveals similarities with early artificial intelligence (AI) research on expert systems. These systems are commonly referred to as *symbolic AI* [5]. AI is nowadays a highly successful technology by advances in machine learning (ML), leading to AI applications that outperform humans [6]. ML encompasses algorithms to build models for data-driven task solving that do not require explicit programming. Instead, data is used for autonomous learning [5]. Considering this successful transition of AI, it is only logical to explore a similar path for RPA: by infusing AI capabilities into RPA, it seems feasible to overcome the limitations of *symbolic RPA* and arrive at what we refer to as *intelligent RPA*.

There are already various proposals that point to AI as the future of RPA, which may eventually lead to the approach of hyperautomation [7, 8]. Likewise, comprehensive surveys, for example Syed et al. [1], identify the need for future research to develop innovative solutions for AI-assisted RPA. Nevertheless, they also note that it is not apparent what challenges need to be addressed to enable its productive use. Agostinelli et al. [9] and Chakraborti et al. [4] have proposed several research challenges and tool-oriented challenges, but their validity and practical relevance has not been assessed.

In this paper, we derive and investigate the relevance of challenges for the amalgamation of RPA and AI, and consequently for intelligent RPA. This results in the following research question:

RQ: Which challenges exist for the development and operation of software robots based on intelligent RPA?

The contribution of our paper is an overview of ten concrete and distinct challenges, which we assessed with respect to their relevance, severity, and longevity. One significant improvement over the state-of-the-art is that our work brings a specific focus and deeper layer to more abstract RPA challenges identified before. Furthermore, the challenges we describe are not just grounded in theory but firmly rooted in the industrial application of RPA. This is important since the practice of RPA is at times well ahead of rigorous theory-grounded research in academia.

This paper is structured as follows: In Sect. 2, we present the theoretical foundation for RPA and our conceptualization of intelligent RPA. Section 3 presents the research design, including details on the conducted literature review and expert interviews. In Sect. 4, we introduce existing RPA and AI challenges as well as intelligent RPA challenges, which we discuss in Sect. 5 in detail. Section 6 provide a discussion of theoretical and practical implications. Lastly, in Sect. 7 we conclude with a summary, limitation, and outlook.

2   Theoretical Background

2.1   Symbolic Robotic Process Automation

Following the idea of the long tail of processes [10], van der Aalst et al. [3] proposed a Pareto distribution for the applicability of RPA. Depending on case frequency and possible types of cases, they motivate the application of traditional backend automation with BPM, automation with RPA, and the continued manual execution of specialized manual human processes.

In this respect, RPA is an umbrella term that comprises many different automation tools, which operate on the UI layer of off-the-shelf, legacy software in an "outside-in" manner. They have in common that they enable software robots to mimic human knowledge workers and perform their digital yet manual tasks with no adjustments to existing software [1–3].

Currently, most state-of-the-art software requires users to implement their software robots in a symbolic fashion [9]. This means that processes or simple sequences of tasks need to be explicitly modeled and decisions need to be documented in handcrafted rulesets [2]. While being simpler and timelier to realize than business processes using traditional BPM software, these factors still limit the development of RPA. It entails that implementing a robot must also be carried out by business users with knowledge about variants and decisions as well as technical users with the ability to codify this knowledge. In analogy with symbolic AI, which describes the handcrafting of explicit if-then rules in early AI applications [11], we denominate this type of RPA as *symbolic RPA*, since RPA is currently constrained by the inability of humans to manually code complex and shared tacit experiences in comprehensive explicit rulesets [5].

2.2   Intelligent Robotic Process Automation

Using AI for RPA can help to mitigate the limitations of the rule-based specification of software robots and leverage the ability to apply flexible AI-based pattern recognition techniques representing human-like cognitive abilities to solve problems [12]. Hereby, we use the umbrella term AI, for the application of ML and deep learning (DL). While, ML relies on statistical algorithms to train analytical models, which can solve problems without being explicitly programmed to do so [6], DL refers to complex models using (deep) artificial neural networks whose inner workings are intransparent to human users. The latter are especially useful for high-dimensional datasets [5]. DL models tend to outperform shallow ML models and even humans for specific applications [6].

Ultimately, this entails, that robots will not only be able to complete tasks by themselves without the necessity of explicit process models or rulesets, but that they will be able to perform tasks that require cognitive abilities, such as perceiving and reasoning. Consequently, they will become more convenient to create and more versatile in their deployment since they can complete tasks so far unsuitable for robots developed through symbolic RPA. Examples include process identification, image recognition, (process) prediction, natural language processing (NLP), chatbot functionality, or automated reasoning [1, 4]. Currently, RPA vendors have begun to include AI capability into their RPA software to unearth some of these potentials [12]. Yet in academic literature, there is only little information on how to combine RPA and AI successfully and which challenges need to be addressed in the course [1].

Closely related to intelligent RPA is the term hyperautomation [8]. Gartner defines it as the joint application of advanced technologies such as ML or DL to automate processes and augment humans. While our focus is on RPA as an automation technology augmented by the use of various AI technologies, hyperautomation also refers to the sophistication of the automation process itself. Hence, we include this concept in our search for relevant work.

3   Research Design

3.1   Overview

In general, we followed an iterative, design-oriented procedure that uses theory-building elements for data collection, specifically (1) a structured literature review and (2) expert interviews [13, 14]. As shown in Fig. 1, our research can be divided into four distinct phases.

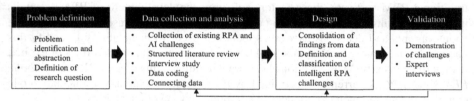

Fig. 1. Research procedure

Problem Definition. Syed et al. [1] and Gotthardt et al. [7] demonstrate the need for more clarity in how the combination of AI and RPA can successfully be applied. While Agostinelli et al. [9] discuss a lack of learning capabilities, they do not explore ML in detail. Chakraborti et al. [4] discuss only abstract and general AI challenges and opportunities. In contrast, our aim is to derive theoretical and practical challenges at the intersection of RPA and AI that must be addressed in concert.

Data Collection and Analysis. First, we aim for saturation in theoretical knowledge. We connect existing RPA, ML, and DL challenges from seminal review literature as well as with a structured literature review according to vom Brocke et al. [13], in which we focus on the combination of RPA and AI towards intelligent RPA. Second, we propose initial challenges derived from this analysis. Note that Sect. 4.3 contains an overview that has already been revised based on the feedback from the last phase. Third, since practice is at least on par if not ahead of academia, we conduct an interview study with practitioners to investigate and assess these challenges further.

Design. Through the connection of our findings, we can formulate and assess different challenges for intelligent RPA, which future research and practice must solve. Thereby, we also include a ranking, severity, and estimation from practitioners, who are facing these challenges in real life. See Sect. 5 for a detailed presentation.

Demonstration. Lastly, we demonstrate and discuss our findings. Here, the experts were able to validate or dispute our findings. Following that, we discuss implications (see Sect. 6).

3.2 Literature Review

Procedure Literature Review. To investigate the state-of-the-art of applications and challenges in the field of intelligent RPA, we conducted a structured literature review according to vom Brocke et al. [13]. In this vein, we examine the state-of-the-art in challenges associated with it. Consequently, we screened for theoretical and practical contributions that use RPA and any kind of AI for process automation.

Within our literature search, we focused on the computer science-related databases IEEE Xplore and ACM Digital Library, information systems-related databases Science Direct, AIS eLibrary, and Web of Science, as well as economics-related databases such as EBSCOhost and Emerald Insight. Due to the novelty of the topic and its practical nature, we did not restrict our search by rankings and considered industry reports as relevant. For our literature review, we used the following search string: *"(IPA | intelligent process automation | cognitive automat* | hyperautomat*) OR ((AI | artificial intelligence | deep learning | machine learning | (natural language processing) AND (RPA | robotic process automation | desktop automation))"*. Hereby, we included the topics of intelligent process automation and related fields such as cognitive automation and hyperautomation. In addition, we considered contributions relevant that deal with the combination of RPA and different kinds of AI such as ML or DL, including NLP. We derived these terms iteratively from literature on intelligent RPA and intelligent automation to ensure comprehensiveness of our results.

Using the proposed search string resulted in the identification of 642 contributions. Then, we performed a reduction based on title, keywords, and abstract, followed by a full-text analysis. Lastly, we applied a forward and backward search on the remaining contributions. This resulted in 47 contributions classified as relevant for our research. A summary of the procedure is shown in Fig. 2.

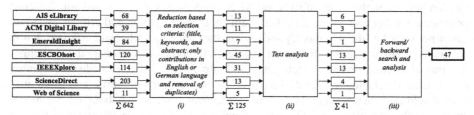

Fig. 2. Results of literature review according to vom Brocke et al. [13]

Meta-synthesis. In the following, we present a meta-synthesis of the 47 contributions. For this purpose, we grouped them based on their year of publication and their type of contribution.

For 2019 ($n = 18$) and 2020 ($n = 19$), the number of contributions on intelligent RPA rose rapidly. Before 2019, we identified only $n = 10$ contributions dealing with intelligent RPA or related topics. Considering the different types of contributions, it becomes apparent that since 2019 the number of contributions presenting a proof of concept, or an implementation project has increased markedly. Nevertheless, many contributions still provide more theoretical contributions such as design principles, interview studies, or literature reviews (2019: ≈46%; 2020: ≈65%). Related to this predominance of theoretical contributions, we identified only a few relevant practical reports (Fig. 3).

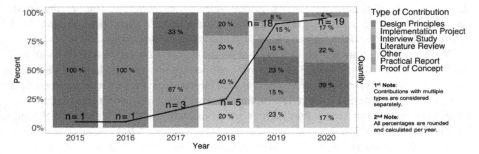

Fig. 3. Meta-synthesis of literature review

3.3   Expert Study on Intelligent RPA in Current and Future Business Practice

To gain further insights into intelligent RPA challenges, we conducted four expert interviews. These lasted between 60 and 90 min. All interviewees currently work in the field of RPA and engage with issues of intelligent RPA implementations. We spoke with experts from Germany, the Netherlands, and Belgium. Therefore, the interviews were multilingual, and the discussion of the concepts were later translated into English.

Due to the novelty of the topic, we followed a semi-structured interview guide divided into four parts. First, we asked for information about their (company) background and their confidence in the topics of RPA and AI. Second, we openly discussed our challenge proposals (see Sect. 4). Here, we asked them about their opinion and critical appraisal. Likewise, we asked them to modify and rename the challenges where appropriate. Third, we invited them to rank the challenges in order of importance, to classify the challenges in terms of severity, timing of occurrence, and implementation, to provide their opinion on whether the challenges should be solved in the short or long term, and to identify who should approach solving these challenges. Finally, we asked about any additional challenges they could think of. Thereby, through a result discussion, the experts validated or disputed our initial findings.

Following [14], the interviews were recorded and analyzed. This approach allowed us to overview and compare expert perceptions across all interviews. In total, the audio recordings of our interviews have a length of 295 min. While the small number of interviews could be considered a limitation, we noticed a saturation for most topics. See the Table 1 for an overview of the interviewees.

Table 1. Overview of interviewees

I#	Focus of company	Role	Years of experience	Confidence in RPA[*]	Confidence in AI[*]
1	Software development and IT consulting	Head of department and product manager for automation	5–10	Agree	Neutral
2	IT consulting	Lead developer	2–5	Agree	Neutral
3	Intelligent automation	Founder, director, and product manager	2–5	Strongly agree	Agree
4	Intelligent automation	Managing partner	>2	Strongly agree	Agree

[*]On a 5-point Likert scale: *"I'm confident in the field of [...]"*, metric: *strongly disagree,..., strongly agree.*

4 Proposed Challenges for RPA, AI, and Intelligent RPA

4.1 RPA Challenges Impacting Intelligent RPA

The rapid deployment of robots in practice has left research catching up with practice to rationalize what is happening. There are several authors that have formulated challenges or opportunities for RPA development and use. We have consolidated the works of several authors [1, 7, 15–18] and systematize them along the meta themes introduced by Syed et al. [1].

RPA1: Realization of Needs and Benefits. Companies must be committed to identify and justify the need to implement RPA. The development of guidelines and best practices can ensure the consideration of RPA to realize cooperative strategies [15]. Likewise, metrics must be defined to measure benefits and ensure long-term support [2].

RPA2: Readiness. Companies must not only identify the need for applying RPA, but companies must also be prepared for new automation technologies. For example, they need frameworks for maturity and technology infrastructure assessments [1]. These frameworks can be used to support implementation projects [2].

RPA3: Capabilities. Similarly, companies need to be aware of what intelligent RPA can and cannot do [17]. Only by doing so, they can use appropriate technologies for given projects and organizational contexts. This includes building organizational and analytical capabilities to gather specialized knowledge to develop innovative and intelligent solutions [1, 2].

RPA4: Methodologies. Methodological support is necessary for a successful integration of RPA. Therefore, companies must develop such support for adoption and implementation to ensure success. This entails the definition of critical success factors [1].

Lastly, companies have to brief employees, so that they will consider RPA as an assistance rather than as a substitution as using software robots can have socio-technical implications that need to be approached [15, 17].

RPA5: Technologies. There are several technology issues to consider. First, task selection for automation is still highly subjective. Also, companies need to develop templates and guidelines for implementing and reusing technologies as well as maintaining robots [2]. This includes procedures for exception handling. Likewise, they need to define metrics to evaluate their implementations [18]. Lastly, while the initial use of robots works well on a small scale with limited resources, scaling them is highly dependent on the elasticity of resources [7].

4.2 AI Challenges Impacting Intelligent RPA

Several socio-technical challenges for ML and DL applications have been formulated [19–22]. Janiesch et al. [6] condense and highlighted several technology-related meta themes related to analytical model building and use in intelligent systems. We employ them to systematize the impact of AI on intelligent RPA engineering and use.

AI1: Model and Training Data Selection. Comparing or assessing ML and DL models for automated decision making is difficult, due to limitless options for algorithms, hyperparameter tuning, and the handling of training data [23]. Further, companies must consider economic limitations resulting in a trade-off between a models' ability to uncover all patterns within data and compute costs for training and execution [23]. Lastly, results of test system and live system can differ making it difficult to assess the suitability of implementation in real-life.

AI2: Bias in Data. ML and DL models learn from data. Biases within this data will be adopted and reinforced by the model's decision logic. This means that an AI trained on human data is not as impartial as an explicit ruleset but will mirror the subjective nature of cognitive decisions taken in the past. Thus, training data for analytical model building must be carefully reviewed and preprocessed [24].

AI3: Drift in Data. Similar to bias, drift in data can lead to insufficient or wrong decisions over time. Drift means that the historical data used for training does not correspond well to current data and trends [25]. Drift in real life is constant may be more subtle than explicit changes to business rules.

AI4: Transfer Learning. To overcome the "cold start" problem of DL models, companies either need to have gathered large datasets for their initial training or they have to resort to pre-trained models [19]. For the latter, a pre-trained general model is tuned for its new task with comparably few specific observations in a process called transfer learning [26]. However, acquiring and using third-party pre-trained models, such as NLP models for chatbots, often means using a black box, which can exhibit any kind of prejudicial behavior such as local social or geographical biases or even susceptibility to adversarial attacks or [27].

AI5: Model Explainability. The so-called black-box nature of DL models is rooted in their inherent complexity. As a result, these analytical models are intransparent to humans. However, in many cases, decision making must be traceable [22]. Thus, companies must either use inherently transparent white-box models or integrate explainable AI (XAI) augmentations to explain the decision-making process of the models [20, 22].

AI6: Effect on Employees. Fear about job security due to RPA implementations (see RPA4) goes hand in hand with the effect of AI implementation in workplaces. Arguably, this extends even further with AI as AI can solve more complex tasks and is often perceived as anthropomorphic [28].

4.3 Derivation of Challenges at the Intersection of RPA and AI

Using the 11 meta themes (*RPA1–5* and *AI1–6*) as a guideline, we reviewed the 47 articles of our literature search. This led to the formulation of 10 distinct challenges that need to be addressed for intelligent RPA to materialize successfully. In Sect. 5, we describe and discuss each challenge in more detail. See Table 2 for an overview of the

Table 2. Proposed challenges for intelligent RPA

C#	Proposed challenges	Challenge rationale		
		RPA[1]	AI[2]	Intelligent RPA[3]
1	Transfer learning causes trust and compliance concerns	–	*AI4* [26, 27]	[12]
2	Employees with knowledge at the intersection of RPA and AI are scarce	*RPA2–3* [1, 2]	*AI6* [29]	[1]
3	Intelligent RPA is not (yet) a commodity	*RPA4* [2]	–	[30, 31]
4	Insufficient training data obstructs intelligent robot development	–	*AI1* [19]	[7, 32]
5	Automated learning of task sequences is an un(der)explored issue	–	*AI1* [23]	[9, 33]
6	Intelligent robot performance is hard to assess and compare	*RPA5* [34]	*AI1* [6]	[35]
7	Intelligent robots reinforce human biases	–	*AI2* [24]	[36]
8	Businesses evolve but robot training is static	*RPA5* [16, 37]	*AI3* [25]	[4, 38]
9	Fear of AI and robots can cause job-security-induced distrust	*RPA1 & 4* [17]	*AI6* [28]	[7, 39]
10	Robot decisions need to be interpretable or explainable	–	*AI5* [20]	[4, 7, 40]

Legend: [1]Based on Sect. 4.1, [2]Based on Sect. 4.2, [3]Based on literature review (Sect. 3.2).

challenges and their rationale. In the table, we also provide the meta themes and key references that we used to derive the various challenges. The ordering of the challenges only serves the purpose of conveniently referring to each of these.

Using the 11 meta themes allowed us to identify and structure if and how pre-existing RPA and AI challenges might be relevant for intelligent RPA. Also, we aimed at exploring yet unknown challenges that may arise from the combined context of intelligent RPA yet are not apparent from the domains is isolation. While we could not identify further intelligent RPA challenges that were unrelated to pre-existing RPA and AI challenges, we found that the priority or emphasis of challenges in their combination as intelligent RPA differs from their isolated consideration in either domain. Since many challenges intersected with each other, we merged closely related challenges through a consensus of experts to obtain a manageable number of distinct challenges. We validated the results through our literature review (see Sect. 3.2) and performed a subsequent interview study (see Sect. 3.3) to assess the practical validity.

With this result, it becomes apparent that we have not merely repeated the challenges of symbolic RPA or AI. While we contextualized some AI challenges specifically for RPA, in many cases prospective solutions for existing symbolic RPA challenges can be used as a baseline to solve similar challenges for intelligent RPA. In response, we have focused only on those pre-existing RPA challenges that we deem to be at the core of intelligent RPA since they extend beyond the challenges of symbolic RPA.

5   Consolidated Challenges Impacting Intelligent RPA

5.1   Overview of Challenges

In the following, we describe and discuss the findings from our literature review and expert interviews. In doing so, we go into more detail about the challenges that we derived and provide further classifications.

To provide a structured overview of our findings, we classify the challenges into one or more of four lifecycle phases of intelligent RPA in a 2×2 matrix. These phases based on extant intelligent RPA literature [4, 7, 32]. The first phase, *organizational and socio-technical challenges during build-time*, describes all organizational and socio-technical challenges that occur when considering intelligent RPA as a potential automation technique from an organizational perspective. The *technical challenges during build-time* phase relates to all technical challenges during the implementation of intelligent robots. Similarly, all technology-related challenges during the operation of robots are summarized in *technical challenges during run-time* phase. The last phase, *organizational and socio-technical challenges during run-time*, relates to all human-robot-related challenges during the operation of intelligent RPA.

As challenges may not be attributed to only one of those phases, they can occur in multiple phases. We asked the experts about the severity of challenges and who should approach solving them. The results are shown in Fig. 4 using a median calculation. Since many challenges occur and impact over several phases, we describe them according to the time of their occurrence, which is not necessarily their root-cause.

Based on these findings, we describe our ten derived challenges in the following subsections. For each challenge, we describe supporting arguments from literature and from the experts. Likewise, we show how these challenges should be solved and whether they will occur in the short or long term in an intelligent RPA implementation project.

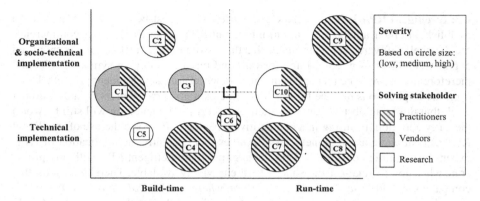

Fig. 4. Classification of challenges for intelligent RPA

5.2 Organizational and Socio-Technical Challenges During Build-Time

C1: Transfer Learning Causes Trust and Compliance Concerns. While the use of AI models acquired from transfer learning for intelligent RPA reduces development time and can also overcome a lack of training data (see C4), this process also causes trust and compliance concerns [26, 27]. In this context, companies need to build trust with vendors and developers that their AI models are unbiased and robust against adversarial attacks [12]. In our expert interviews, we found that I1 and I4 are concerned about sending customer data to AI cloud solutions for analysis mainly due to governance regulations. As a result, at this point transfer learning is not realistic (I1). As I3 noted, *"all of the time there is something about being compliant and being sure that you know where and how the model trained."* In contrast, I2 considers this only as an issue for high-stake use cases. Further, I3 is especially concerned about dealing with personal data. Using locally trained models for transfer learning would be possible in all cases. Summarizing, I1–3 all note that this challenge must be solved by practice, may involve contracts or certifications, and constitutes a long-term challenge.

C2: Employees with Knowledge at the Intersection of RPA and AI Are Scarce. While Syed et al. [1] and Herm et al. [2] state that finding experts in the field of RPA is quite difficult, the same is true for the field of AI [29]. Our literature review revealed that finding experts experienced in both fields exacerbates this issue [1]. As an example, I1 has *"exactly one [employee] in my team [...] who could do that."* Therefore, I1 sees this challenge as the most important challenge to be solved by universities through intensified teaching in the respective areas and by practitioners through training their employees. I4 interjects that specialized knowledge in AI and RPA engineering can reside in different people and only needs to be bridged by at least one expert when applied. In contrast, I3 notes that in today's business practice, deep knowledge in AI implementations may not be necessary. Instead, a rough understanding of application and evaluation is sufficient. Consequently, I1–3 expect this challenge to impact intelligent RPA in the long term.

C3: Intelligent RPA Is Not (Yet) a Commodity. Clear cost-benefit metrics are hard to establish and their amalgamation into intelligent RPA is not available as commercial-off-the-shelf software [31]. This entails that the use of intelligent RPA, with its enhanced cognitive abilities, is not as straightforward and rapid as applying symbolic RPA and therefore may have to be managed similar to other custom development projects. However, the implications may be far-reaching. Interestingly, practitioners I1 and I4 do not think that this is an obstacle as own intelligent RPA implementation will still be worth the early adoption, resulting in a competitive advantage. Both see the use of intelligent RPA as a strategic asset. Nonetheless, I2 notes that currently the application of AI is expensive and time-consuming. Thus, he assumes that intelligent RPA will only proliferate when commercial-off-the-shelf software is widely available. Thereby, I3 adds, that companies should *"use a [low-code] platform where you basically have a way to scale it up, because you need less technical experience"* and therewith also alleviate C2. I3 predicts that this will take at least five years.

5.3 Technical Implementation Challenges During Build-Time

C4: Insufficient Training Data Obstructs Intelligent Robot Development. The development of intelligent robots faces several challenges due to a lack of data availability. Many highlight customer privacy concerns or data regulation limitations when sharing their data [7, 18]. However, as AI models are data-driven, they need to learn from data [5]. This may result in a situation where intelligent RPA is not applicable as an automation technique as not enough data is available for training robots with sufficient accuracy [7]. This is in line with our interviewees. I1–2, I4 state that generally no AI implementation is possible without sufficient data (see C1 for a possible remedy). This is most serious for new processes (I3). To generate enough data for intelligent RPA, humans must label and validate data manually, by staying in-the-loop (I3), which incurs cost. Nonetheless, I3 and I4 believe that this challenge will only affect most companies in the short-term.

C5: Automated Learning of Task Sequences Is an Un(der)Explored Issue. Although the application of AI models for single tasks within otherwise handcrafted robots is showcased in many papers [9], automated pattern learning for task sequences within processes is a difficult and not always feasible problem of cross-modal learning [23]. I1–3 all state that this challenge is far head of current business practice and not yet of their concern. Instead, the current focus is on enriching individual tasks with AI and then extending the integration to closely related tasks (I1–2) or using technologies such as process mining to detect potential processes for automation in the first place (I4). I1–4 all agree that this challenge will establish as a long-term challenge and currently is predominantly a research issue.

C6: Intelligent Robot Performance Is Hard to Assess and Compare. While most AI and RPA implementations are performed in a test environment, transferring them to a production environment can cause problems due to differences in data volume and permission management [34]. This can further lead to inappropriate models being used and insufficient results in terms of robot accuracy or latency [6]. Further, the suitability of replacing of legacy robot with new robots can only be assessed in production (I3). While I1–2 both notice a similar behavior in symbolic RPA projects, they assume that the issue will aggravate significantly in intelligent RPA projects. They suggest that AI models should be trained on data from live environments (I3) and different models must be considered (I4). I1 states that comparability is currently not a challenge at all, since RPA is not a market characterized by eliminatory competition. He adds that this may change in the future though. Therefore, we assume to be a mid- to long-term challenge.

5.4   Technical Implementation Challenges During Run-Time

C7: Intelligent Robots Reinforce Human Biases. AI models learn patterns from training data [24], which leads to intelligent robots mimicking human-biased observations in process execution. This impacts cognitive decision-making but furthermore, this can lead to non-optimized processes, workarounds, or to activities that are not relevant to the core of the process, as employees sometimes perform unnecessary tasks [36]. I1 notes that noise reduction can be achieved by monitoring data collection for ML or doing post-hoc processing (I4). Nonetheless, this data has to be investigated in detail before model training and during operation (I3). This results in a long-term challenge.

C8: Businesses Evolve But Robot Training Is Static. Robots have to be adjusted, when processes and their data are changing [37]. This drift in process execution, when businesses are evolving, also becomes apparent in intelligent robots, when current data does not correspond well to the data used for training [25]. In our literature review, we noticed that this issue is prominent for intelligent RPA [4, 38]. Further, I2 state, that they *"monitor the performance of a bot over the time"*, as this is necessary for the continuous maintenance of intelligent robots in operation for longer-term use (I1–2, 4). As a result, this challenge must be handled by companies individually on a long-term basis. I2–3 both assume that companies must define an error margin for when robots should be reevaluated and retrained.

5.5   Organizational and Socio-Technical Challenges During Run-Time

C9: Fear of AI and Robots Can Cause Job-Security-Induced Distrust. The integration of intelligent robots in companies can be accompanied by many benefits. Yet the automation of processes can also cause distrust regarding the job security of employees [17]. Likewise, the use of AI can exacerbate these concerns, due to the seemingly infinite potential of AI [28]. These findings go hand in hand with the combination of both, with AI's anthropomorphic properties enabling it to perform not only monotonous, repetitive tasks, but also complex, cognitive tasks [7, 17, 39]. While this is already a critical challenge in practice, I1 notes that a work council's approval must be obtained for any current RPA implementation. Nevertheless, if the work council stalls the rollout of intelligent robots, companies may start to consider outsourcing their processes altogether. Nevertheless, I3 state that *"If a work council would block these kinds of implementations, [...] we will see that this kind of work will move to other countries in the long term."* As a result, balance is crucial (I3). Furthermore, I2 states that this distrust results from using top-down approaches in integrating intelligent robots, instead of seeing the need of automation within the departments. In today's practice AI is not (yet) capable to automate every task (I3–4) and, thus, this poses a long-term challenge.

C10: Robot Decisions Need to be Interpretable or Explainable. Although the development of intelligent robots offers many advantages [12], the use of black-box models entails drawbacks as their decision logic is not interpretable by users [20]. This results in a lack of trust and confidence that must be minimized to enable broad adoption [21], since *"trust issues will be one of the biggest challenges of intelligent RPA"* (I2). For example, Lamberton et al. [40] describes an implementation where AI classifications have to be verified by a human at the end of each day. In our literature review, we noticed two different approaches to overcome this issue. On the one hand, more interpretable, white-box ML models such as decision trees can be used (even though a DL model may perform better) (I4). On the other hand, XAI can be used to explain the decision logic and prediction to users [4, 7]. Currently, per-se interpretable ML models are common as practitioners such as I3 *"would always start with a white-box model"*. However, the use of DL with XAI is also a highly targetable option. In the end, decisions have to be explainable at all times (I2–4), due to continuous model performance assessment or legal regulations such as general data protection regulation (GDPR) especially in areas such as finance (I3–4). However, implementations in practice are hampered by the novelty of the issue (I1). Lastly, I1 and I3 note that the main goal is to gain the customers' trust and provide a well-performing solution.

6   Discussion

Through our interview study, we found that the primary challenges of intelligent RPA today are the lack of training data, human bias in data, compliance issues with transfer learning, poor explainability of robot decisions, and job-security-induced fear of AI robots – all of which stem primarily from the AI domain. They all need to be addressed to enable the successful transition from symbolic RPA to intelligent RPA.

Theoretical Implications. With our research, we create awareness for the specificities of RPA as well as of AI research so that researchers from each domain can better attune to the issues of the other. Specifically, RPA and BPM researchers must understand that ML and DL do not provide a silver bullet for cognitive problem-solving and remove the need for handcrafting models in any context. While the application of AI technology comes with many benefits to solve issues that seemed unsolvable before, it comes with new challenges. Particularly, joint efforts are necessary to address the automated learning of task sequences across applications, as well as making process-based cognitive decisions explainable to business users. The latter needs to be supported with suitable and, possibly, novel metrics and visualizations, which are not only relevant for intelligent RPA but also for predictive process monitoring.

Practical Implications. Our challenges paint a clear picture that process automation and AI skills are relevant but also scarce. University teaching and professional training must pick up on these opportunities to equip the (future) workforce with appropriate abilities to automate tasks using intelligent RPA by introducing novel modules and degree courses. Furthermore, companies must introduce means to capture manual yet digital activities in a non-invasive, privacy-preserving manner to generate enough data for intelligent RPA. While the availability of such data is a practical problem, the means to collect it may require further research as well. In addition, vendors must approach the issue of trust and compliance for transfer learning to ensure that intelligent RPA products will eventually become a useful commodity. Lastly, the socio-technical issue of employee distrust in intelligent robots must be addressed openly and proactively.

Limitations. Our research is not without limitations. While we consolidated our challenges through an interview study and thereby assessed the comprehensiveness of our results, we did not test their usefulness. Implementing multiple use cases could close this gap and serve to reassess their completeness. As consequence, for future research, we plan to evaluate validity and reliability in more detail. Subsequently, we aim to provide guidelines for the successful implementation of intelligent RPA to create a foundation for future research on the constituent properties of hyperautomation.

7 Conclusion

While the amalgamation of RPA and AI will enable companies to automate more complex, cognitive tasks overcoming the limited, handcrafted behavior of symbolic RPA, intelligent RPA faces several challenges. We reviewed related challenges from the fields of symbolic RPA and AI (represented by ML and DL) and performed a literature review as well as an expert interview study to devise challenges that have the potential to shape the future discussion of intelligent RPA. In doing so, we determined the severity and the longevity of the challenges and pointed to possible solutions.

In total, we compiled ten challenges that illustrate how practice was ahead realizing symbolic RPA but has so far not completely grasped the implications that intelligent robots will entail. Currently, this results in applications that do not yet take full advantage of the affordances of AI technology. However, we observed that practice has already developed solutions and workarounds for some challenges, for example to deal with biases and drift in process execution, and mistrust and fear of job security.

Much of our research has been evaluated in the interview study with a focus on contemporary challenges of intelligent RPA. Future challenges of any type of RPA will eventually materialize when long-term effects and side-effects of replacing or augmenting manual processes with software robots become apparent.

References

1. Syed, R., et al.: Robotic process automation: contemporary themes and challenges. Comput. Ind. **115**, 103162 (2020)
2. Herm, L.-V., et al.: A consolidated framework for implementing robotic process automation projects. In: Fahland, D., Ghidini, C., Becker, J., Dumas, M. (eds.) BPM 2020. LNCS, vol. 12168, pp. 471–488. Springer, Cham (2020). https://doi.org/10.1007/978-3-030-58666-9_27
3. van der Aalst, W.M., Bichler, M., Heinzl, A.: Robotic process automation. Bus. Inf. Syst. Eng. **60**, 269–272 (2018)
4. Chakraborti, T., et al.: From robotic process automation to intelligent process automation. In: Asatiani, A., et al. (eds.) BPM 2020. LNBIP, vol. 393, pp. 215–228. Springer, Cham (2020). https://doi.org/10.1007/978-3-030-58779-6_15
5. Goodfellow, I., Bengio, Y., Courville, A., Bengio, Y.: Deep Learning. MIT Press, Massachusetts (2016)
6. Janiesch, C., Zschech, P., Heinrich, K.: Machine Learning and Deep Learning. Electronic Markets Forthcoming (2021). https://doi.org/10.1007/s12525-021-00475-2
7. Gotthardt, M., Koivulaakso, D., Paksoy, O., Saramo, C., Martikainen, M., Lehner, O.: Current state and challenges in the implementation of smart robotic process automation in accounting and auditing. ACRN J. Finance Risk Perspect. **9**, 90–102 (2020)
8. Panetta, K.: Top strategic technology trends for 2021 (2020), https://www.gartner.com/en/publications/top-tech-trends-2021. Accessed 19 Jan 2021
9. Agostinelli, S., Marrella, A., Mecella, M.: Research challenges for intelligent robotic process automation. In: Di Francescomarino, C., Dijkman, R., Zdun, U. (eds.) BPM 2019. LNBIP, vol. 362, pp. 12–18. Springer, Cham (2019). https://doi.org/10.1007/978-3-030-37453-2_2
10. Imgrund, F., Fischer, M., Janiesch, C., Winkelmann, A.: Managing the long tail of business processes. In: European Conference on Information Systems, Guimarães, AIS (2017)
11. Haugeland, J.: Artificial Intelligence: The Very Idea. MIT Press, MA, Boston (1989)
12. Le Clair, C.: The forrester wave™: robotic process automation, Q2 2018 (2018), http://rpa.innavatar.ca/The_Forrester_Wave_RPA_2018.pdf. Accessed 19 Jan 2021
13. vom Brocke, J., Simons, A., Riemer, K., Niehaves, B., Plattfaut, R., Cleven, A.: Standing on the shoulders of giants: challenges and recommendations of literature search in information systems research. Commun. Assoc. Inf. Syst. **37**, 205–224 (2015)
14. Schultze, U., Avital, M.: Designing interviews to generate rich data for information systems research. Inf. Organ. **21**, 1–16 (2011)
15. Asatiani, A., Penttinen, E.: Get ready for robots: why planning makes the difference between success and disappointment. J. Inf. Technol. Teach. Cases **6**, 67–74 (2016)
16. Noppen, P., Beerepoot, I., van de Weerd, I., Jonker, M., Reijers, H.A.: How to keep RPA maintainable? In: Fahland, D., Ghidini, C., Becker, J., Dumas, M. (eds.) BPM 2020. LNCS, vol. 12168, pp. 453–470. Springer, Cham (2020). https://doi.org/10.1007/978-3-030-58666-9_26
17. Syed, R., Wynn, M.T.: How to trust a bot: an RPA user perspective. In: Asatiani, A., et al. (eds.) BPM 2020. LNBIP, vol. 393, pp. 147–160. Springer, Cham (2020). https://doi.org/10.1007/978-3-030-58779-6_10
18. Abdulla, Y., Ebrahim, R., Kumaraswamy, S.: Artificial intelligence in banking sector: evidence from Bahrain. In: Proceedings of the International Conference on Data Analytics for Business and Industry (ICDABI), pp. 1–6. IEEE, Virtual (2020)
19. Mazurek, G., Małagocka, K.: Perception of privacy and data protection in the context of the development of artificial intelligence. J. Manag. Analytics **6**, 344–364 (2019)
20. Herm, L.-V., Wanner, J., Seubert, F., Janiesch, C.: I don't get it, but it seems valid! The connection between explainability and comprehensibility in (X)AI research. In: European Conference on Information Systems (ECIS), Virtual Conference, AIS (2021)

21. Miller, T.: Explanation in artificial intelligence: insights from the social sciences. Artif. Intell. **267**, 1–38 (2019)
22. Adadi, A., Berrada, M.: Peeking inside the black-box: a survey on explainable artificial intelligence (XAI). IEEE Access **6**, 52138–52160 (2018)
23. Heinrich, K., Zschech, P., Janiesch, C., Bonin, M.: Process data properties matter: introducing GCNN and KVP for next event prediction with deep learning. Decis. Support Syst. **143**, 113494 (2021)
24. Mehrabi, N., Morstatter, F., Saxena, N., Lerman, K., Galstyan, A.: A survey on bias and fairness in machine learning. arXiv preprint arXiv:1908.09635 (2019)
25. Gama, J., Žliobaitė, I., Bifet, A., Pechenizkiy, M., Bouchachia, A.: A survey on concept drift adaptation. ACM Comput. Surv. (CSUR) **46**, 1–37 (2014)
26. Wang, S., Nepal, S., Rudolph, C., Grobler, M., Chen, S.: Backdoor attacks against transfer learning with pre-trained deep learning models. IEEE Trans. Serv. Comput. **1** (2020)
27. Amors, L., Hafiz, S.M., Lee, K., Tol, M.C.: Gimme that model!: a trusted ML model trading protocol. arXiv preprint arXiv:2003.00610 (2020)
28. Davenport, T.H., Ronanki, R.: Artificial intelligence for the real world. Harv. Bus. Rev. **96**, 108–116 (2018)
29. Zschech, P., Fleißner, V., Baumgärtel, N., Hilbert, A.: Data science skills and enabling enterprise systems. HMD Praxis der Wirtschaftsinformatik **55**, 163–181 (2018)
30. Daugherty, P.R., Wilson, H.J.: Human+ Machine: Reimagining Work in the Age of AI. Harvard Business Press, Boston (2018)
31. Pantano, E., Pizzi, G.: Forecasting artificial intelligence on online customer assistance: evidence from chatbot patents analysis. J. Retail. Consum. Serv. **55**, 102096 (2020)
32. Martins, P., Sá, F., Morgado, F., Cunha, C.: Using machine learning for cognitive Robotic Process Automation (RPA). In: Proceedings of the 15th Iberian Conference on Information Systems and Technologies (CISTI), Seville, pp. 1–6. IEEE (2020)
33. Marrella, A.: Automated planning for business process management. J. Data Semant. **8**, 79–98 (2019)
34. Schuler, J., Gehring, F.: Implementing robust and low-maintenance Robotic Process Automation (RPA) solutions in large organisations. Available at SSRN 3298036 (2018)
35. Koch, J., Trampler, M., Kregel, I., Coners, A.: Mirror, mirror, on the wall': robotic process automation in the public sector using a digital twin. In: European Conference on Information Systems (ECIS), Virutal, AIS (2020)
36. Richardson, S.: Cognitive automation: a new era of knowledge work? Bus. Inf. Rev. **37**, 182–189 (2020)
37. Seasongood, S.: A case for robotics in accounting and finance. Financ. Executive **31**, 31–39 (2016)
38. Yatskiv, N., Yatskiv, S., Vasylyk, A.: Method of robotic process automation in software testing using artificial intelligence. In: International Conference on Advanced Computer Information Technologies (ACIT), pp. 501–504, IEEE (2020)
39. Lasso-Rodriguez, G.W.K.: Hyperautomation to fulfil jobs rather than executing tasks: the BPM manager robot vs human case. Rom. J. Inf. Technol. Autom. Control **30**, 7–22 (2020)
40. Lamberton, C., Brigo, D., Hoy, D.: Impact of robotics, RPA and AI on the insurance industry: challenges and opportunities. J. Financ. Perspect. **4**, 8–20 (2017)

Process Mining on Blockchain Data:
A Case Study of Augur

Richard Hobeck[1]([✉]), Christopher Klinkmüller[2], H. M. N. Dilum Bandara[2],
Ingo Weber[1], and Wil M. P. van der Aalst[3]

[1] Chair of Software and Business Engineering, Technische Universitaet Berlin,
Berlin, Germany
{richard.hobeck,ingo.weber}@tu-berlin.de
[2] Data61, CSIRO, Sydney, Australia
{christopher.klinkmueller,dilum.bandara}@data61.csiro.au
[3] RWTH Aachen University, Aachen, Germany
wvdaalst@pads.rwth-aachen.de

Abstract. Through its smart contract capabilities, blockchain has
become a technology for automating cross-organizational processes on
a neutral platform. Process mining has emerged as a popular toolbox for
understanding processes and how they are executed in practice. While
researchers have recently created techniques for the challenging task of
extracting authoritative data from blockchains to facilitate the analysis
of blockchain applications using process mining, as yet there has been no
clear evaluation of the usefulness of process mining on blockchain data.
With this paper, we close that gap with an in-depth case study of process
mining on the popular Ethereum application *Augur*, a prediction
and betting marketplace. We were able to generate value-adding insights
for application-redesign and security analysis, as validated by the application's chief architect and revealed blind spots in Augur's white paper.

Keywords: Blockchain · Process mining · Case study · Process
discovery · Conformance checking · Ethereum

1 Introduction

A blockchain can be characterized as a distributed, append-only data store for
transactions [31]. Second-generation blockchains have comprehensive smart contract capabilities, i.e., allow for the deployment and execution of user-defined
programs. On this basis, blockchain has emerged as a technology allowing the
automation of cross-organizational processes on a neutral platform [20,29].

Process mining [1] has become popular as a toolbox for understanding processes and how they are executed in practice. For example, many case studies ranging from healthcare [5,19,25,27], finance [8,12], manufacturing [26],
and public services [3,17] to software development [18] applied process mining to analyze processes from different perspectives including aspects, such as

© Springer Nature Switzerland AG 2021
A. Polyvyanyy et al. (Eds.): BPM 2021, LNCS 12875, pp. 306–323, 2021.
https://doi.org/10.1007/978-3-030-85469-0_20

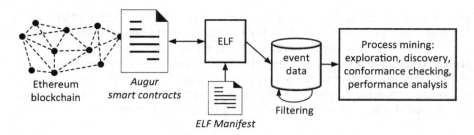

Fig. 1. Overview of the approach.

control flow, conformance, drifts, and performance [24]. Nevertheless, process mining on blockchain data turned out to be a challenging task [10]. Hence, recently researchers have created techniques to extract authoritative data from blockchains [13,14]. On that basis, concepts were introduced that can put extracted blockchain data into use, e.g., for monitoring business processes executed on a blockchain [9]; validating smart contracts on Hyperledger Fabric [11]; auditing blockchain applications on Ethereum [7]; analyzing transactions stored on the Ethereum network without focusing on specific *decentralized applications* (DApps) [21]; and using process mining on blockchain-wide data [22] but no single process in particular. As yet, there has been no clear evaluation of the usefulness of process mining on blockchain data. All of the above process-specific approaches have been evaluated with small examples, demonstrating technical feasibility more than the usefulness and business value.

With this paper, we close that gap and analyze the usefulness of process mining on blockchain data with an in-depth case study of process mining on the popular Ethereum application *Augur*[1]. Augur is a prediction and betting marketplace, where users can create bets (e.g., "Will Donald Trump win the 2020 U.S. presidential election?"), and other users can bet on the outcomes. Because Augur smart contracts run on the public Ethereum blockchain, all data are time-stamped, transparent, and available. We used our *Ethereum Logging Framework* (ELF) [13,14] to extract Augur data. This extraction resulted in nearly 3000 traces and more than 23000 events. As shown in Fig. 1, we then filtered the data and applied various process mining techniques to analyze Augur from control flow, conformance, and performance perspectives.

In our study, we were able to generate insights of value to the business. In more detail, we provide a clear view of how Augur is used, verify its design mechanisms, and check for unintended behavior and bugs in the (immutable) code; immutability poses a challenge from a *business process management* (BPM) perspective [20], and software engineering in general [28]. The usefulness of the insights was confirmed by anecdotal evidence of Augur's chief architect, particularly in terms of understanding user behavior and code validation, which is

---

[1] https://augur.net/, accessed 2021-03-05.

especially relevant for security aspects in an open-source application that can be invoked (and thus potentially attacked) by anyone with Internet access.

The paper is structured as follows. Next, we introduce the object of our case study, Augur. Then, Sect. 3 outlines the data extraction and pre-processing procedures. The focal point of the paper is the data analysis in Sect. 4, covering data exploration, process discovery, conformance checking, and performance analysis. Finally, we discuss the results in Sect. 5 and conclude in Sect. 6.

2 The Case of Augur

Augur is a betting platform and prediction marketplace that is implemented as a set of smart contracts on the public Ethereum blockchain. Augur's white paper characterizes the mechanics of a prediction and betting market: "individuals can speculate on the outcomes of future events; those who forecast the outcome correctly win money, and those who forecast incorrectly lose money." As a betting market organized on Ethereum, the developers claim that Augur bypasses disadvantages of traditional betting markets, such as trusted market operator and limited participation [23].

Currently, there are two versions of Augur available in parallel: Augur v1.0 (launched 2018-07-09) and Augur v2.0 (details announced April 2020[2], launched 2020-07-28[3]). Interestingly, to gain user trust, the Augur developers open-sourced the smart contracts and deployed both versions without any option to update or stop them – giving themselves the privilege to do either might result in the loss of users' cryptocurrency and omitting such a possibility; therefore, increases trustworthiness. Hence, the new version is deployed in parallel to the old one, as such *not comprising an update* in any traditional sense. However, once the new version was deployed and users migrated to it, the old version became "economically insecure" according to the developer team, and therefore should not be used anymore. Because prediction markets are long-running, and hence extended observation time frames are crucial for their analysis, we nevertheless focused on Augur v1.0 and considered the data from its launch until its use was no longer recommended in July 2020 (see Sect. 3 for details).

Augur was chosen for this case study for several reasons. *Data availability.* Augur v1 was among the most popular Ethereum DApps at times, resulting in the availability of substantial amounts of data to analyze. *Application design.* Augur is designed so that events are tracked and stored by a central logging contract with a high level of detail, which allowed insights in user behavior and simplified the extraction of data with ELF (in contrast to other DApps, in which logging is fragmented over multiple contracts). *Subsidiary information.* Information on Augur is widely available, such as in the Whitepaper [23], which served as basis, e.g., for conformance checking. Thus, Augur promised to be an interesting candidate for deeper analysis.

---

[2] https://twitter.com/AugurProject/status/1245715269042888706, accessed 2021-03-14.

[3] https://www.augur.net/blog/augur-v2-launch/, accessed 2021-03-14.

Markets are distinguished based on their outcome: *yes/no-markets* deal with binary questions, while *categorical* and *scalar markets* expect discrete and numeric answers, respectively. For each type, the Augur market process follows a procedure organized in four stages: market creation, trading, reporting, and settlement. *Market creation*: a market is set up for a future event, i.e., "market event." *Trading*: traders place bets on the outcome of the market by buying shares for that outcome. *Reporting*: a user reports the outcome of the event the market revolves around. The report can be challenged in *disputes* that are part of the reporting. *Settlement*: traders resolve their positions. Within these four stages, the Augur smart contracts specify 35 different types of events.

Participants can be active in an Augur market in five roles: market creator, traders, designated reporter, public reporters, and disputants. A *market creator* instantiates markets, including choosing a market question that revolves around a market event and appointing a designated reporter. *Traders* place bets by buying and selling shares of market outcomes. A *designated reporter* reports on the market event, thus creating the first tentative outcome of the market. If the designated reporter fails to submit a report within three days of the market event, reporting opens to *public reporters* who can report on the market outcome. Once an initial report is submitted, *disputants* can challenge the reported outcome of an event by crowd-sourcing a dispute bond with Augur's native token called "Reputation" (REP). If the dispute bond crosses a threshold, the crowd-funded outcome becomes the new tentative outcome. If disputes against an outcome remain unsuccessful, the tentative outcome becomes the final outcome. Depending on the dispute's success, disputants are redeemed after the dispute round (unsuccessful) or after the market is finalized (successful). A market finalizes if a tentative market outcome has not been successfully disputed within seven days. After it finalizes, market creators receive the market creation fee, designated reporters receive a fee if their report represents the final outcome, and traders settle their positions. As a final resolution mechanism for disputes, Augur also offers a fork event, which creates parallel instantiations of Augur based on each possible outcome of the forking market to which users can migrate. Forking is considered "very disruptive" and has not been triggered yet [23].

The Normative Process Model. Conformance checking requires a normative process model, which we created from information in the white paper [23]. We enriched it with information gained from discovery and conformance checking where the information in the white paper was not detailed or precise enough for our purposes. The resulting process model is shown in Fig. 2. Additional information on initial discrepancies is discussed in Sect. 5. We restricted the model to activities where the corresponding events were triggered.

3   Data Extraction and Pre-processing

On a second-generation blockchain like Ethereum, that allows for deploying and executing arbitrary smart contracts, log entries are the primary means for passing information to off-chain components. Commonly, log entries communicate

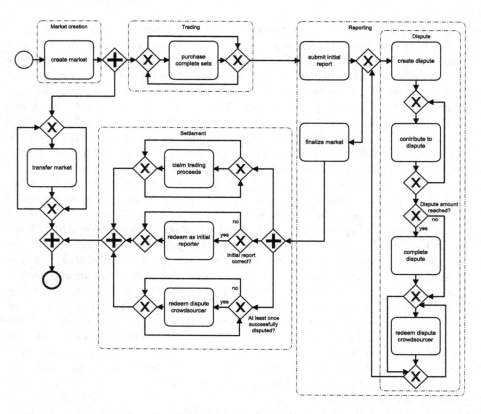

Fig. 2. Normative BPMN model.

information related to results of and events occurring during the execution of smart contract invocations. The developers of Augur v1.0 made extensive use of this feature and implemented a central logging contract that handles the emission of log entries. This contract defines a range of log event types intended to share detailed information about all possible events. Due to the level of detail provided by these log entries, we decided to solely focus on information from Augur's log entries for this case study. Hence, we typically did not consider additional information from the transactions or the states of Augur's smart contracts, as the information we could obtain this way is largely included in the log entries; deviations from this rule are marked.

We extracted the data using the publicly available Ethereum Logging Framework[4] [13,14]. ELF enables analysts to extract, transform, and format information from blocks, transactions, log entries, and smart contracts stored on Ethereum-based networks. ELF takes as input a manifest file, which contains instructions that define which data to extract and how to process it – see also Fig. 1. We defined such a manifest file for Augur v1.0 based on its source code,

---

[4] https://github.com/ChrisKlinkmueller/Ethereum-Logging-Framework

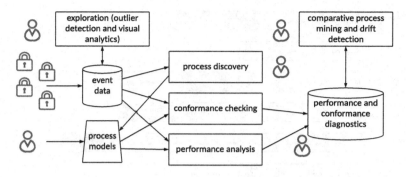

Fig. 3. Process mining techniques applied to the Augur v1.0 data extracted with ELF.

which provided us with the definitions for all the log entries. The execution of the manifest resulted in an event log in the XES format [4], where for each log entry, there is an XES event containing the information from Augur's log entry. We grouped the events into traces based on the notion of a market.

We extracted information related to 2897 markets stemming from the period of 2018-07-09 to 2020-11-10. The former date marks the date of the first execution of Augur v1.0. Regarding the latter, we ran the data extraction from 2020-11-12 to 2020-11-16, and the last event that we extracted was from 2020-11-10. However, as outlined in Sect. 2, the launch of Augur v2.0 in July 2020 rendered Augur v1.0 "economically insecure" and unsurprisingly caused a decline in user interest which already started after the announcement of Augur v2.0 in April 2020. To account for this decrease, we removed 162 cases that were either created after v2.0 was announced on 2020-04-02 or that were not finalized before its actual launch, leaving us with a total of 2735 cases and 22772 events.

For purposes of replication, all data and code used in this study are available publicly, including the source code of ELF (See Footnote 4), the manifest, the normative process model and the resulting XES log[5], the source code of Augur v1.0[6], the Augur white paper [23], and the data on the public Ethereum blockchain.

4   Process Mining Analysis and Results

As discussed in Sect. 3, we used ELF to extract an XES event log [4] for Augur v1.0. As a result, we can apply a range of process mining techniques, as illustrated by Fig. 3. It is possible to discover the actual betting/prediction process, check conformance of the process with respect to a normative model, analyze performance, and compare process variants [1]. In the remainder, we will mainly use the ProM process mining platform. We could apply any other process mining tool, e.g., open-source tools like PM4Py, Apromore, bupaR, and RapidProM, or

---

[5] https://github.com/ingo-weber/dapp-data.
[6] https://github.com/AugurProject/augur-core, accessed 2021-03-19.

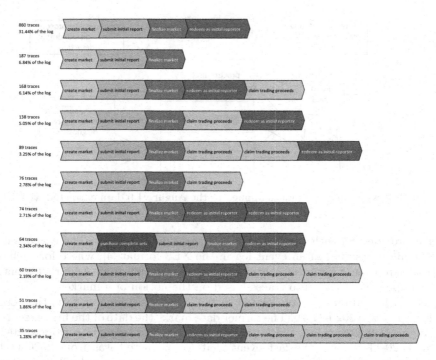

Fig. 4. Some of the most frequent variants, e.g., 860 markets follow the most frequent variant having only four events. The event data have a Pareto distribution with 35 variants (i.e., 8.5% of variants) explaining 80% of all cases.

commercial closed-source tools like Celonis, Disco, ProcessGold (UiPath), Minit, QPR, myInvenio, PAFnow, Lana, Software AG, Signavio (SAP), ABBYY Timeline, and Mehrwerk. However, our goal is not to present specific process mining algorithms or tools. Instead, we demonstrate that event data extracted from Ethereum using ELF can be used to analyze marketplaces like Augur.

4.1   Exploring the Event Data

All process mining tools start from event data [1]. An *event log* is a collection of events stored in a format like XES. An event may have many different attributes, but at least a *case identifier*, an *activity name*, and a *timestamp*. Additional attributes may refer to locations, resources, costs, transactional information, and on Ethereum blockchain, the consumed gas. Events are grouped using the case identifier and sorted using the timestamps. Hence, each case corresponds to a *trace*, i.e., a sequence of events. By focusing only on the activity names, these traces can be grouped into *variants*, i.e., sequences of activities. Most event logs have a Pareto distribution, i.e., a few variants explain a large proportion of the event log.

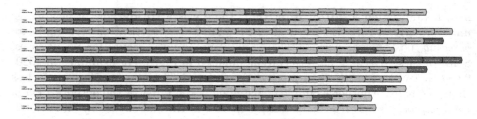

Fig. 5. Some of the unique variants that only have one corresponding market. The figure is not intended to be readable but gives an idea of the variability. 319 of the 414 variants are unique, covering 11.7% of all markets.

The event log we extracted and filtered as per Sect. 3 has 2735 cases (each case refers to a market), 22772 events, and 11 unique activities. There are 414 variants where 35 variants have at least ten corresponding cases and describe 2203 cases. This implies that 80% of the cases are described by less than 8.5% of variants. Some of the most frequent variants are shown in Fig. 4. 319 cases have a unique sequence of activities. A few of the shorter unique variants are shown in Fig. 5. The length varies from three to 226 events per case.

The event log contains 11 activities having the following frequencies: *claim trading proceeds* (6046), *redeem as initial reporter* (3259), *submit initial report* (2735), *create market* (2735), *finalize market* (2735), *contribute to dispute* (1598), *redeem dispute crowdsourcer* (1412), *create dispute* (901), *complete dispute* (780), *purchase complete sets* (570), and *transfer market* (1).

Figure 6 shows a so-called *dotted chart* where each dot refers to an event (i.e., 22772 dots). In a dotted chart, we can configure the two axes and the coloring of the dots [1]. In Fig. 6, the x-axis refers to the time of the event, the y-axis corresponds to the cases (i.e., markets) sorted by the time of the first event, and the color of the dot refers to the activity name (e.g., blue is the creation of the market). The dotted chart shows that many markets were created in the first

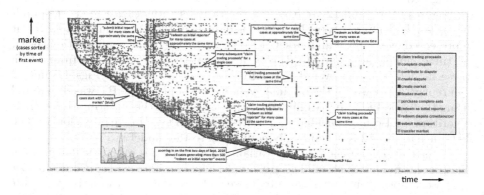

Fig. 6. Dotted chart showing all 22772 events. The vertical patterns indicate batching. (Color figure online)

month (July/August 2018). After that, there was a steady flow of new cases, until the arrival rate decreased after May 2019. The vertical patterns indicate *batching*, i.e., shorter periods where the same activity occurs for many cases. Some of these batching patterns are highlighted in Fig. 6. For example, on 2020-02-11, activity *claim trading proceeds* is executed 63 times for 53 cases in less than one hour. Another example of batching is the burst of the activities *claim trading proceeds* and *redeem as initial reporter* at the end of the day on 2019-07-07. These occur respectively 148 and 98 times in a three hours. There are also horizontal patterns indicating a sequence of events for the same case in a short period. For example, for the market "Ethereum Price at end of March 2019" we witnessed *redeem dispute crowdsourcer* and *claim trading proceeds* four and 132 times, respectively, within a period of a few weeks. Although one can already visually spot exceptional cases, we discuss these further when presenting the conformance checking results.

4.2   Process Discovery

Figures 7, 8, and 9 are based on the whole event log (i.e., 2735 markets generating 22772 events). Figure 7 shows a so-called Directly-Follows Graph (DFG) without filtering [1, 2]. The nodes are activities and show the frequencies of each activity. The connections show how often one activity is followed by another. DFGs are the most-widely used discovery technique in commercial process mining tools due to their simplicity. However, there are several know problems, as demonstrated in [2]. These can be witnessed in Fig. 7, where there are many loops in the diagram because activities are not performed in a fixed order.

Figure 8 shows the Process Tree (PT) obtained by the Inductive Miner in ProM for the whole event log using the default settings [16]. The model is not intended to be readable, but one can see that the process model has more structure. 1771 of all cases (65%) can be explained by this model (the average trace fitness is 94%). Figure 9 shows the same model but now with timing information rather than frequencies. Two activities that have a longer sojourn time are highlighted.

Figures 10, 11, and 12 are based on the variants with at least ten corresponding cases. This filtered event log contains only 35 of the 414 variants; however, it represented over 80% of all markets (2203 cases). Due to the configurations used, all three models are guaranteed to be able to replay all 2203 cases from which these models were discovered. Actually, the process models in Figs. 11 and 12 can replay 2501 cases in the original event logs. Note that the PT was discovered using the basic Inductive Mining algorithm without further filtering [1, 15]. This algorithm is also implemented in a few commercial systems (e.g., Celonis). The Petri net in Fig. 12 is semantically equivalent to the model in Fig. 11.

After focusing on the frequent variants, one can focus on particular parts of the process model. Such models are simpler and can be used to drill down. Let us, for example, focus on the dispute phase and consider only the activities *create dispute*, *contribute to dispute*, and *complete dispute*. Figures 13 and 14 show two process models explaining the dispute subprocess. This example illustrates that

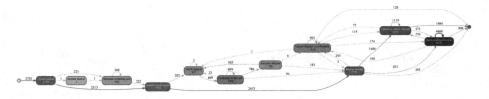

Fig. 7. Directly-Follows Graph (DFG) for the whole event log without filtering.

Fig. 8. Process Tree (PT) for the whole event log using default settings.

Fig. 9. Process Tree (PT) for the whole event log showing sojourn times.

process mining tools like ProM provide various ways to reduce the complexity and either focus on a particular part of the process or zoom-out (e.g., using aggregation) to see the overall process.

4.3 Conformance Checking and Unusual Cases

Figure 2 shows a normative process model that can be used for *conformance checking* [1,6]. The goal of conformance checking is to identify commonalities and differences between the modeled process and the actual process. Figures 15 and 16 show the reference model in the form of a process tree and a Petri net to allow for easy comparison with the discovered process models. A visual comparison shows that the reference model is close to the discovered models, but there are some notable differences. Compare, for example, Fig. 16 (Petri-net version of the reference model) with Fig. 12 (Petri-net able to replay all traces that happened at least ten times). Some of the striking differences: *transfer market* is missing in the discovered model (it was only executed in one trace); in the discovered process model, the activities *contribute to dispute* and *complete dispute* both occur precisely once after creating the dispute; and *redeem dispute crowdsourcer* can occur before *claim trading proceed* and *redeem as initial reporter*, but not after.

The representations shown in Figs. 15 and 16 can be used in ProM to perform a range of conformance checking techniques. Here, we limit ourselves to alignment-based conformance checking [1,6], i.e., for each trace in the event log, we searched for a path through the model that is closest.

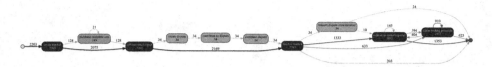

Fig. 10. Directly-Follows Graph (DFG) for 8.5% of variants covering 91.4% of the cases.

Fig. 11. Process Tree (PT) discovered for the filtered event log showing all paths.

Fig. 12. The Petri net discovered for the filtered event log.

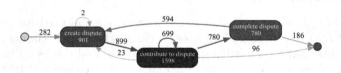

Fig. 13. Directly-Follows Graph (DFG) discovered for the dispute phase.

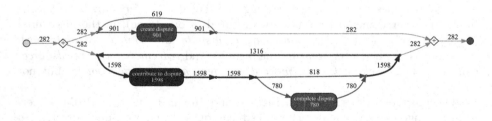

Fig. 14. Process Tree (PT) discovered for the dispute phase.

Fig. 15. Normative Process Tree based on the BPMN reference model.

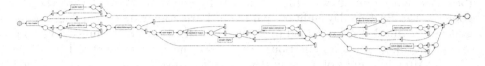

Fig. 16. Normative Petri net model.

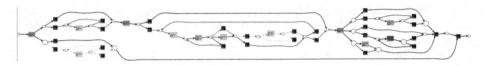

Fig. 17. Replay results after aligning event logs and process model: 2511 of the 2735 cases are perfectly fitting the reference model.

ProM's diagnostics show that the reference model in Fig. 2 explains 2511 of the 2735 cases, i.e., 224 cases have at least one deviation. Figure 17 shows the same diagnostics after aligning event log and process model. There are 21647 synchronous moves (i.e., events in the log that fit the model) and 1125 moves on the log (i.e., events in the log that do not fit the model). However, there are no moves on the model (i.e., missing events). 223 of the 224 deviating cases have multiple *redeem as initial reporter* events, and 1119 of the 1125 log-only moves fall into this category. Almost all of these are instantaneous: using Disco's performance view, we see a median duration of 0 ms, a total duration over all 1119 moves of 42 days, and a maximum of 35 days – i.e., much of the whole duration can be accounted for with a single of the 1119 occurrences.

For a random sample of 20 of these 1119 occurrences, we inspected the underlying blockchain transactions, and observed the following pattern in all 20 instances: the first *redeem as initial reporter* event resulted in a payout, the second did not; the first and second transaction came from the same account in all 20 pairs; and the pairs were close together (between 0 and 47 blocks, the large majority with less than ten blocks). We also observed two cases with 108 *redeem as initial reporter* events ("Who will win the second democratic primary debate?" and "Will Tulsi Gabbard poll higher than Andrew Yang on August 12th?").

Like in discovery, there is the possibility to focus on selected parts of the process. Figure 18 shows conformance checking results for the dispute subprocess. There is only a single deviating case (see the upper part of Fig. 18) where there are two instances of two subsequent occurrences of create dispute without any contributions in between. This is not possible according to the reference model. We discuss possible reasons for non-conformance in Sect. 5.

Next to the non-conforming cases, we identified the following *unusual cases.* In our data, we observed 13 cases with nine or more *complete dispute* events created in 2018. Ten of those were created in July 2018, the month the application was launched. The market with the highest number of contributions to disputes (98) was created on 2018-07-13 and posed the question, "Will the weather be good for the Bastille day military parade in Paris tomorrow?" The high ambiguity of the market question led to a debate in the Augur community revolving around wording of market questions and forking the application shortly after its launch. After 15 rounds of dispute[7], the market resolved as invalid and remained a familiar quotation. Soon after the debate around the Bastille Day market gained momentum, a meta-market was created ("Will the weather good when the *"Will the weather be good for the Bastille day military parade in Paris tomorrow?"* market resolve?"), betting on the events based on existing markets. That phenomenon, however, did not become a trend.

On 2018-07-10, four identical markets were created within 17 s, asking the question "Will Bitcoin go below \$6000". One of the markets resolved as invalid after five weeks, while the other three went through dispute rounds until mid-September 2018, before also resolving invalid, all on the same day. In sum, this market question went through the highest number of dispute rounds (20).

4.4   Performance Analysis

Events have timestamps; therefore, it is trivial to enrich process models with timing information (e.g., waiting times and service times). This is a key capability of process mining and often used to improve operational processes, e.g., to reduce the time needed to produce a car or process a claim. For marketplaces like Augur, standard measurements like waiting times are less relevant, because the duration is related to the nature of the particular bet. For example, users can create markets for future events, no matter how far into the future the event is expected to take place. In this regard, we inspected the top 100 completed

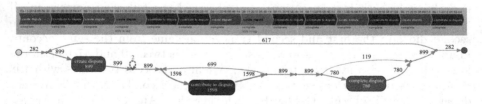

Fig. 18. Conformance checking results for the dispute phase including the activities *create dispute, contribute to dispute,* and *complete dispute.* Only one case is non-fitting.

---

[7] https://themajority.report/market/0x67ef420c045f3561d11ef94b24da7e2010650cc3, accessed 2021-03-05.

traces concerning the waiting time before submitting the initial report. All these markets were created in 2018 but referred to events that took place in 2019 and 2020. We also noted that there is a market with a prospected market event in 2070. In addition to these analyses, we zoomed into the dispute phase and only considered the activities *create dispute*, *contribute to dispute*, and *complete dispute* shown in Figs. 13 and 14. The mean duration of this phase is 15.4 days, the median duration is 7.1 days, and the longest duration is 111 days. This illustrates that time also plays a role in the analysis of markets.

5   Discussion

The Augur logging smart contract specifies 35 activities, of which only 11 activities could be observed after the data extraction. Partially, this discrepancy can be explained by events not being triggered throughout the application's life-cycle, such as the fork event. The option to fork serves as a final resolution mechanism in case a dispute could not be resolved over many rounds, and forms the last resort. Thus, not observing it was expected, and can indeed be seen as a sign that the incentive mechanism (geared towards avoiding forks) work. However, other events such as `DisputeWindowCreated` could be expected to be triggered frequently but were not part of the logged data, although specified in our ELF manifest.

Additionally, the white paper did not cover all events included in the smart contract (e.g., `DisputeCrowdsourcerCompleted` or `TradingProceedsClaimed`). That led to multiple iterations for creating the normative process model, where we started with the information in the white paper, ran discovery and conformance checking, found discrepancies, and resolved those by reconsidering the white paper and inspecting the source code. One observation was that the white paper in part turned out to be too abstract to model the normative process, as some information on the workings of Augur was not contained in it. For instance, `completeDispute` only happens if a sufficient amount of stakes is contributed to a dispute; this information is not contained in the white paper.

As pointed out in Sect. 4, cases with many dispute events were observed mainly in 2018, and mainly had creation dates in July 2018, the month of the Augur v1.0 launch. Disputes delay resolving a market and hint towards disagreement in the community. Their occurrence in the early days of the application indicates that the user group needed to build up experience in using the application. At times, users seemingly tested the resilience of the application (e.g., a market for "Did this market need a fork to be resolved?", created 2018-07-27, led to 12 complete dispute rounds but no fork). Eventually, the users learned to pose less ambiguous market questions, leaving less wiggle room for interpretation and reducing the potential for disputes.

Comparing the normative and discovered models in Fig. 16 and Fig. 12, we observed paths that were executed infrequently. Recall that the model in Fig. 12 was discovered from the 35 most frequent variants, and hence represents typical (but not all) observed behavior. Some paths, however, occurred very rarely if at all: According to the white paper, after unsuccessful disputes crowdsourcers are redeemed at the end of the dispute round, while for successful disputes redeeming happens after the market finalized [23]. The sequence for redeeming unsuccessful disputes occurred only four times, and the log does not show a single case of *contribute to dispute* being directly followed by *redeem dispute crowdsourcer*. That poses the question why users did not make use of that option.

The most striking result from conformance checking was the frequent occurrences of *redeem as initial reporter* more than once, where we observed for a sample that the first event resulted in a payout and the second did not, and both originated from the same account within a short time frame. The logging on Augur could be made more precise here, and differentiate successful, legitimate transactions from others. Note that transaction inclusion may be subject to delay [30], and the timestamp for a transaction to be finally included in the ledger may be significantly after the transaction had been announced to the network. There are multiple possible explanations for the phenomenon of the repeated *redeem as initial reporter* events, including: (i) the reporter was impatient; (ii) the reporter used an automated tool with a time-out before retry, but the tool did not implement *retry* correctly (as per [30]); or (iii) the reporter tried to cheat or hack the system. Given that these attempts were unsuccessful and the reporter had to pay fees, and the same reporter accounts showed the same behavior repeatedly, we find (ii) the most plausible of the three scenarios.

The non-conforming repeated *create dispute* events happened in the same categorical market "2018 MLB World Series Champion". All four transactions (two pairs of two) were sent from the same blockchain account, and each pair was included in the ledger in direct succession in the same block. The two pairs were 95 blocks apart. The four transactions initialized four different dispute rounds, although at any time only one of those was active. By initializing future dispute rounds, the user "pre-staked" tokens for these future rounds. This was a *bug* in Augur v1.0, but turned out to be useful and was made a feature in v2.0, as we established in discussion with Augur's chief architect (see below).

Note that we did not aim to apply process mining as a design time or predeployment test for software vulnerabilities. However, we were able to show that process mining can serve as a tool to discover bugs and performance issues for blockchain applications post-deployment (based on actual user behavior), which enables developers to patch weaknesses or formalize unexpected behavior in updates. Methods for design time checks of vulnerabilities are nevertheless very important, particularly for DApps, but can be complemented with analyses such as ours.

To validate the veracity and assess the usefulness of the insights generated by our analyses, we interviewed Paul Gebheim, the chief architect of Augur. Given that we only interviewed one person, we classify results from this interview as *anecdotal evidence*; but given his position, we believe this evidence to be of value. We asked him to check assumptions we had – all of which he confirmed – and presented intermediate results from our analyses to him. From his perspective, using process mining for the analysis of blockchain applications generally, and Augur, in particular, provides value in three ways. First, it helps to verify the design mechanisms and check for unintended behavior and bugs in the (immutable) code; immutability poses a challenge from a BPM perspective [20] and software engineering in general [28]. Second, process mining provides a clear view of how an application is used, which is also helpful for designing updated versions of an application. Third, it has great potential for technical and economic security analysis, e.g., in that, an auditor could create a model and conformance-check it against actual user behavior. Also, even though a smart contract typically implements a fixed set of rules, analyses of process variability may reveal valuable insights that could help evolve future versions of the smart contract, e.g., to align them better with changed user expectations.

The validity of this case study faced several threads to validity. As an internal thread, we might have introduced a bias in our conformance checking approach. As a basis for conformance checking, we used the entire normative process model (Fig. 2) and thus the overall control flow without checking the gate conditions for individual cases. That might have led to overly generalized results, ignoring non-conforming cases. Additionally, we largely observed the user behavior as a whole and not over time, which might have compromised awareness of maturation effects. An external thread to the study may be that the data we performed our analysis on was incomplete or its quality corrupted. We did, however, take precautions in reducing these threads by validating intermediate results and findings with Augur's user interface and their chief architect, as described above.

6   Conclusion and Future Work

In this paper, we conducted a case study on process mining for data extracted from the blockchain application Augur. To this end, we used ELF to extract data over essentially the entire lifecycle of Augur v1.0. We used process mining methods and tools to explore the data, discover models for a set of variants, and conducted conformance checking and performance analyses. Finally, we interviewed the chief architect of Augur to validate our insights and understand their usefulness. As stated in Sect. 3, we followed open science principles and made all data and code from our study available publicly.

In summary, we conclude that there is clear evidence for the usefulness of process mining on blockchain data. Main areas of interest for software developers may include user behavior analysis and security audits, for which we demonstrated the applicability of process mining tools. Indeed, we discovered a bug in Augur's smart contracts – albeit a non-critical one. Future research can be done evaluating other applications which might run on other blockchains, such as Hyperledger Fabric. The analysis method could be extended for blockchain-specific security and user studies, e.g., through drift detection and cohort analysis.

Acknowledgments. We are very thankful for the input of Paul Gebheim, chief architect at the Augur Project. We would also like to thank Martin Rebesky for writing the first version of the ELF manifest to extract an Augur event log.

References

1. van der Aalst, W.M.P.: Process Mining: Data Science in Action. Springer, Heidelberg (2016). https://doi.org/10.1007/978-3-662-49851-4
2. van der Aalst, W.M.P.: A practitioner's guide to process mining: Limitations of the directly-follows graph. In: International Conference on Enterprise Information Systems (Centeris 2019), Procedia Computer Science, vol. 164, pp. 321–328 (2019)
3. van der Aalst, W.M.P., et al.: Business process mining: an industrial application. Inf. Syst. **32**(5), 713–732 (2007)
4. Acampora, G., Vitiello, A., Stefano, B., van der Aalst, W.M.P., Günther, C., Verbeek, E.: IEEE 1849: the XES standard. IEEE Comput. Intell. Mag. **12**(2), 4–8 (2017)
5. Andrews, R., Suriadi, S., Wynn, M., ter Hofstede, A.H.M., Rothwell, S.: Improving patient flows at St. Andrew's War Memorial Hospital's emergency department through process mining. In: Business Process Management Cases, pp. 311–333. Digital Innovation and Business Transformation in Practice (2018)
6. Carmona, J., Dongen, B., Solti, A., Weidlich, M.: Conformance Checking: Relating Processes and Models. Springer, Berlin (2018). https://doi.org/10.1007/978-3-319-99414-7
7. Corradini, F., Marcantoni, F., Morichetta, A., Polini, A., Re, B., Sampaolo, M.: Enabling auditing of smart contracts through process mining. In: ter Beek, M.H., Fantechi, A., Semini, L. (eds.) From Software Engineering to Formal Methods and Tools, and Back. LNCS, vol. 11865, pp. 467–480. Springer, Cham (2019). https://doi.org/10.1007/978-3-030-30985-5_27
8. De Weerdt, J., Schupp, A., Vanderloock, A., Baesens, B.: Process mining for the multi-faceted analysis of business processes - a case study in a financial services organization. Comput. Ind. **64**(1), 57–67 (2013)
9. Di Ciccio, C., Meroni, G., Plebani, P.: Business process monitoring on blockchains: potentials and challenges. In: Enterprise, Business-Process and Information Systems Modeling, pp. 36–51 (2020)
10. Di Ciccio, C., et al.: Blockchain-based traceability of inter-organisational business processes. In: Business Modeling and Software Design, pp. 56–68 (2018)
11. Duchmann, F., Koschmider, A.: Validation of smart contracts using process mining. In: Central European Workshop on Services and their Composition, pp. 13–16 (2019)
12. Jans, M., van der Werf, J.M., Lybaert, N., Vanhoof, K.: A business process mining application for internal transaction fraud mitigation. Expert Syst. Appl. **38**(10), 13351–13359 (2011)
13. Klinkmüller, C., Ponomarev, A., Tran, A.B., Weber, I., van der Aalst, W.M.P.: Mining blockchain processes: extracting process mining data from blockchain applications. In: BPM Blockchain Forum, pp. 71–86 (2019)
14. Klinkmüller, C., Weber, I., Ponomarev, A., Tran, A.B., van der Aalst, W.M.P.: Efficient logging for blockchain applications. CoRR abs/2001.10281 (2020). https://arxiv.org/abs/2001.10281, Accessed 21 Mar 2021
15. Leemans, S.J.J., Fahland, D., van der Aalst, W.M.P.: Discovering block-structured process models from event logs - a constructive approach. In: Colom, J.-M., Desel, J. (eds.) PETRI NETS 2013. LNCS, vol. 7927, pp. 311–329. Springer, Heidelberg (2013). https://doi.org/10.1007/978-3-642-38697-8_17
16. Leemans, S.J.J., Fahland, D., van der Aalst, W.M.P.: Scalable process discovery and conformance checking. Softw. Syst. Model. **17**(2), 599–631 (2018)

17. Leemans, S.J.J., Poppe, E., Wynn, M.T.: Directly follows-based process mining: exploration a case study. In: 2019 International Conference on Process Mining, pp. 25–32 (2019)
18. Lemos, A.M., Sabino, C.C., Lima, R.M.F., Oliveira, C.A.L.: Using process mining in software development process management: a case study. In: 2011 IEEE International Conference on Systems, Man, and Cybernetics, pp. 1181–1186 (2011)
19. Mans, R., Schonenberg, M.H., Song, M., van der Aalst, W.M.P., Bakker, P.: Application of process mining in healthcare: a case study in a Dutch hospital. Biomed. Eng. Syst. Technol. **25**, 425–438 (2009)
20. Mendling, J., et al.: Blockchains for business process management - challenges and opportunities. ACM Trans. Manag. Inf. Syst. (TMIS) **9**(1), 41–416 (2018)
21. Mühlberger, R., Bachhofner, S., Di Ciccio, C., García-Bañuelos, L., López-Pintado, O.: Extracting event logs for process mining from data stored on the blockchain. In: Business Process Management Workshops, pp. 690–703 (2019)
22. Müller, M., Ruppel, P.: Process mining for decentralized applications (2019)
23. Peterson, J., Krug, J., Zoltu, M., Williams, A.K., Alexander, S.: Augur: A decentralized oracle and prediction market platform. Technical report, Forecast Foundation (2018). https://github.com/AugurProject/whitepaper/blob/master/v1/english/whitepaper.pdf, Accessed 05 Jan 2021
24. Reinkemeyer, L.: Process Mining in Action: Principles, Use Cases and Outlook. Springer, Berlin (2020). https://doi.org/10.1007/978-3-030-40172-6
25. Rovani, M., Maggi, F.M., Leoni, M., van der Aalst, W.M.P.: Declarative process mining in healthcare. Expert Syst. Appl. **42**(23), 9236–9251 (2015)
26. Rozinat, A., de Jong, I.S.M., Günther, C.W., van der Aalst, W.M.P.: Process mining applied to the test process of wafer scanners in ASML. IEEE Trans. Syst. Man Cybern. Part C **39**(4), 474–479 (2009)
27. Suriadi, S., Mans, R.S., Wynn, M.T., Partington, A., Karnon, J.: Measuring patient flow variations: a cross-organisational process mining approach. In: Asia Pacific Business Process Management, pp. 43–58 (2014)
28. Weber, I., Staples, M.: Programmable money: next-generation conditional payments using blockchain - keynote paper (2021)
29. Weber, I., Xu, X., Riveret, R., Governatori, G., Ponomarev, A., Mendling, J.: Untrusted business process monitoring and execution using blockchain. In: International Conference on Business Process Management, Rio de Janeiro, Brazil (2016)
30. Weber, I., et al.: On availability for blockchain-based systems (2017)
31. Xu, X., Weber, I., Staples, M.: Architecture for Blockchain Applications. Springer, Heidelberg (2019). https://doi.org/10.1007/978-3-030-03035-3

Process and Resource Analytics

Multivariate Business Process Representation Learning Utilizing Gramian Angular Fields and Convolutional Neural Networks

Peter Pfeiffer[✉], Johannes Lahann, and Peter Fettke

German Research Center for Artificial Intelligence (DFKI) and Saarland University,
Saarbrücken, Germany
{peter.pfeiffer,johannes.lahann,peter.fettke}@dfki.de

Abstract. Learning meaningful representations of data is an important aspect of machine learning and has recently been successfully applied to many domains like language understanding or computer vision. Instead of training a model for one specific task, representation learning is about training a model to capture all useful information in the underlying data and make it accessible for a predictor. For predictive process analytics, it is essential to have all explanatory characteristics of a process instance available when making predictions about the future, as well as for clustering and anomaly detection. Due to the large variety of perspectives and types within business process data, generating a good representation is a challenging task. In this paper, we propose a novel approach for representation learning of business process instances which can process and combine most perspectives in an event log. In conjunction with a self-supervised pre-training method, we show the capabilities of the approach through a visualization of the representation space and case retrieval. Furthermore, the pre-trained model is fine-tuned to multiple process prediction tasks and demonstrates its effectiveness in comparison with existing approaches.

Keywords: Predictive process analytics · Representation learning · Multi-view learning

1 Introduction

Current machine-learning-based methods for predictive problems on business process data, e.g., neural-network-based methods like LSTMs or CNNs, achieve high accuracies in many tasks such as next activity prediction or remaining time prediction on many publicly available datasets [15]. In recent time, a large variety of new architectures for next step and outcome prediction have been proposed and evaluated [17, 19, 24]. These machine-learning-based methods are mostly task-specific and not generic, i.e., they are designed and tested on predictive process analytics tasks like next step prediction, outcome prediction,

© Springer Nature Switzerland AG 2021
A. Polyvyanyy et al. (Eds.): BPM 2021, LNCS 12875, pp. 327–344, 2021.
https://doi.org/10.1007/978-3-030-85469-0_21

anomaly detection, or clustering. Moreover, most of the proposed approaches process only one or a limited set of attributes including activity, resource [6] or timestamp [23]. On one hand, predicting the next activity in an ongoing case using the control-flow information is very similar to predicting the next word in a sentence. On the other hand, data in an event log recorded from business process executions is very rich in information. Usually, there are various attributes with different types, scales, and granularity, which makes generating good representations containing all characteristics a difficult tasks. Characteristics of a process instance that are embedded in the data attributes, can improve the performance of predictive models [13]. For example, the next activity in a business process can depend on multiple attributes in previous events and complex dependencies between these attributes [2].

Inspired by recent research in the language modeling domain [5], we propose and evaluate a novel and generic network architecture and training method – the Multi-Perspective Process Network (MPPN) – which learns a meaningful, multi-variate representation of a case in a general-purpose feature vector that can be used for a variety of tasks. The research contributions of this paper is threefold:

1. We introduce a novel neural-network-based architecture to process a flexible number of process perspectives of a process instance that examines all of its characteristics using gramian angular fields.
2. For this architecture, we propose an self-supervised pre-training method to generate a feature-vector representation of a process instance that can be fine-tuned to various tasks, thus making a contribution to representation learning for predictive process analytics.
3. We show the effectiveness of this approach by analyzing the representation space and performing an unsupervised case-retrieval task. Furthermore, we fine-tune and compare the model on a variety of predictive process analytic tasks such as next step and outcome prediction against existing approaches.

The structure of the remaining chapters unfolds as follows: Sect. 2 introduces the reader to preliminary concepts. Section 3 discusses related work on the use of machine learning in predictive process analytics and representation learning for business process data. Section 4 and 5 present the proposed approach and the evaluation on a variety of predictive process analytic tasks. Section 6 closes the paper with a summary of the main contributions and findings as well as an outline of future work.

2   Foundations

2.1   Business Process Event Log and Perspectives

Event logs contain records from process-aware information systems in a structured format. These recordings contain information about what activities have been conducted by whom at what time as well as additional contextual data. The following definitions will be used in later sections of the paper.

Definition 1. *Event Log*
An event log is a tupel $L = (E, <, V_1, \ldots, V_n, a_1, \ldots, a_n)$, where

- *E is the set of events*
- *$<$ is a total order on E*
- *$V_1, \ldots, V_n$ are the sets of the attribute values*
- *attributes $a_i : E \to V_i$, maps an event to an attribute value.*

In the following, we expect an event log to have at least the attributes *case-id*, *activity*, *resource*, and *timestamp*.

Definition 2. *Case*
Let a_j be the attribute case-id and $v \in V_j$. C is the set of events of one case, iff

1. *$C \subseteq E$*
2. *For each $e \in C : a_j(e) = v$*
3. *For each $e \in E \setminus C : a_j(e) \neq v$*

Let $C = \{e_1, \ldots, e_n\}$ be the events of a case c. These events follow the order $<$. We use the notation: $c = <e_1, \ldots, e_n>$, where $e_i < e_j$ if $i < j$.

Definition 3. *Business Process Perspective*
Given $L = (E, <, V_1, \ldots, V_n, a_1, \ldots, a_n)$ and a sequence of events $\langle e_1, \ldots, e_n \rangle$, we define a perspective on each attribute a_i as $\Pi_{a_i} := \langle a_i(e_1), \ldots, a_i(e_n) \rangle$

In the next sections, we frequently use the control-flow perspective $\Pi_{control-flow}$, the resource perspective $\Pi_{resource}$ and the temporal perspective Π_{time}.

Last, we distinguish between event attributes and case attributes. A case attribute returns the same value for all events in a case, i.e. it fulfils Eq. 2 in Definition 2. Otherwise, it is an event attribute.

2.2   Business Process Data and Representation Learning

Representation learning is the task of learning "representations of data that make it easier to extract useful information when building classifiers or other predictors" [1]. For example, embeddings are utilized in natural language processing to learn a vectorized representation of words. In recent times, attention-based networks [25] have shown superior performance in many language tasks such as machine translation, mainly due to their ability to generate meaningful representations. Usually, these types of networks are pre-trained in an unsupervised fashion on extensive datasets. For business process data, embeddings are commonly used in predictive process analytics to represent the control-flow [3], or certain perspectives [6] in a vector space. Thus, it should allow the model to exploit the vector representation more effectively than a one-hot or integer encoding. When learning good representations of cases, one tries to represent all relevant characteristics within the representation. For predictive tasks, this includes the underlying distribution of the exploratory factors, i.e., attributes that influence the prediction [2]. Usually, there are several attributes with different types of data – categorical, numerical, and temporal ones. Within each type, the dimensions, scales, and variabilities can be different. For instance, there can be a numerical attribute *cost* ranging from [0, 1.000.000] and another one, e.g., *discount* that is in range [0, 30]. Temporal attributes also have different scales (daily, weekly, monthly, etc.) and high variability. Categorical attributes often vary in their dimensionality. While the *activity* has few different values, the *resource*, e.g., persons involved in a process, often has much more distinct values. Some perspectives are very spare while others are rich. Furthermore, different from event-related attributes, there are also case-related attributes. Some attributes change their values only in certain events of a case, while others have a different value for each event. This, in turn, means that perspectives have different levels of granularity. When learning representations of cases, the multivariate, multi-scalar, and multi-granular nature of the data must be considered and depicted.

3   Related Work

In [4], the authors introduced methods to learn representations of activities, cases, and process models. They trained a model on the next step prediction task to learn representations similar to obtaining embeddings for words, sentences, and documents. Although they explained that other attributes besides activity are important, they only consider the control-flow perspective. Furthermore, they did not include an extensive evaluation to elaborate on the effectiveness of the proposed representations. Apart from that, representation learning is not explicitly tackled in existing predictive analytic approaches. However, these approaches learn a representation alongside a specific prediction task. [6] was the first to introduce neural networks to the field of process prediction. They applied recurrent neural networks to next activity and remaining time prediction. They trained separate neural networks considering the control-flow, resource, and time perspectives. [23] examined the next step and remaining time prediction task. They used an LSTM-based approach that optimized both tasks simultaneously and elaborated on the effect of separated or shared LSTM network layers. [3] elaborated three different LSTM architectures for predicting the next activity, resource, and timestamp. In their first architecture, they used specialized layers for each attribute to predict. The second version combines the categorical attributes in a shares layer, while the third version shares categorical attributes and the timestamp. In [17], the authors proposed an LSTM-based method that can combine multiple attributes. In their model, the authors use embeddings for each categorical attribute while non-categorical attributes are concatenated with the categorical ones' embedded representation. Other approaches for next step prediction used different techniques such as decision trees (DT) [9], autoencoder (AE) with n-grams [10], attention networks [12], CNNs [18] or generative adversarial networks (GAN) [24]. Similarly, CNNs [19], LSTMs [14] or autoencoder [11] are used for outcome prediction. In order to detect anomalies in business

Table 1. Overview of encoding techniques used in literature. *duration*: timestamps to duration after a certain timestamp, *IMG*: one or multiple perspectives Π to a single or multiple matrices $M^{h \times w \times c}$ of size *height* $\times$ *width* $\times$ *#channels*.

Task	Approach	ML method	Encoding techniques for event attributes					
			Most common perspectives			Other event log attributes		
			$\Pi_{control-flow}$	$\Pi_{resource}$	$\Pi_{timestamp}$	Categorical	Numerical	Temporal
Next step prediction	[6]	LSTM	Embedding		–	–	–	–
	[23]	LSTM	One-hot	–	Custom	–	–	–
	[10]	AE + FF	N-gram	One-hot	–	One-hot	As-is	–
	[9]	DT	Integer			Integer		
	[18]	CNN	IMG			–	–	–
	[12]	Attention	One-hot	One-hot	–	One-hot	As-is	–
	[17]	LSTM	Embedding	Embedding	Duration	Integer	As-is	Duration
	[3]	LSTM	Embedding	Embedding	Duration	–	–	–
	[24]	GAN	One-hot	–	Duration	–	–	–
Outcome prediction	[19]	CNN	IMG			–	–	–
	[11]	FF	Custom	Custom	Custom	Custom	Custom	Custom
	[14]	LSTM	One-hot	One-hot	Custom	One-hot	–	–
Anomaly detection	[16]	LSTM	Integer	Integer	–	Integer	–	–
	[20]	Bayesian NN	Probability	Probability	Probability	Probability	Probability	Probability
All	MPPN	CNN	IMG	IMG	IMG	IMG	IMG	IMG

process data, LSTMs [16] or Bayesian neural networks [20] were applied. Table 1 gives an overview of existing predictive approaches and categorizes them by prediction task, examined perspective, encoding technique per perspective, as well as used machine learning method. Also, it clarifies what information is available to which model in what form. While all predictive approaches use at least information from two perspectives, only a few approaches are able to encode and process all types of attributes. We differentiated between the most commonly used perspectives and other attribute types to delimit generic and non-generic approaches. Only [17] used a generic encoding approach that can process and represent all types of attributes. However, the approach is tailored towards next step prediction and does not focus on the learned representation within the model. Thus, we propose a generic multi-attribute representation learning approach that is not tailored to a specific prediction task.

4 Multi-Perspective Process Network (MPPN)

The MPPN approach for representation learning is mainly built on two concepts – graphical event log encoding and neural-network-based processing. The first part is to encode the perspectives of interest $\hat{\Pi}$ in the event log L uniformly as 2D images by transforming them to distinct gramian angular fields (GAF) – no matter if the perspective contains categorical, numerical or temporal information. The second part is a convolutional neural network architecture and training method that learns representations of cases using the GAF-encoded perspectives. Figure 1 shows the architecture and processing pipeline of the MPPN approach. In this example, the six perspectives of interest $\hat{\Pi} = \{\Pi_{control-flow}, \Pi_{timestamp}, \Pi_{type}, \Pi_{resource}, \Pi_{travel\_start}, \Pi_{cost}\}$ of

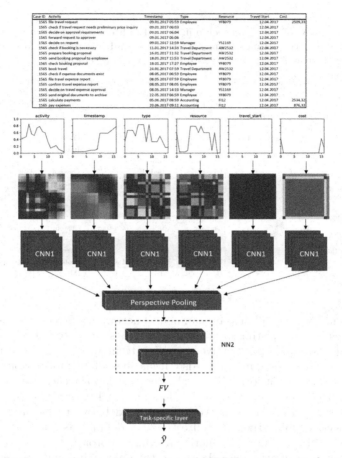

Fig. 1. Architecture and processing pipeline of MPPN using a case from the MobIS event log [7].

the case with *case-id* 1565 are first encoded as six individual GAFs, which can then be processed by the MPPN. CNN1 extracts the features of each perspective $\hat{\Pi}$ which are combined in the perspective pooling layer. The combined features capture all characteristics of interest of a particular case. The forwards pass in MPPN of a single case c is as follows: For each GAF-encoded perspective, *CNN1* extracts a feature vector that is pooled before being passed to *NN2*. *NN2* then takes the pooled features from all perspectives, processes them, and produces a single feature vector *FV*. This two-stage architecture allows *CNN1* to focus on the features within each perspective while *NN2* captures and models the dependencies between perspectives. By transforming all perspectives uniformly to GAFs, all attributes lie within the same range, no matter what scale or variability they had before. At the same time, *NN2* can learn what features from what perspectives are important. Unlike RNN-based models, MPPN consumes the whole case at once instead of being fed with cases event by event.

Inspired by multi-view learning, e.g., Multi-View Convolutional Neural Networks (MVCNN) for 3D object detection using 2D renderings [22], the Multi-Perspective Process Network creates a feature vector FV for a case using the GAF-encoded perspectives. Analogous to using multiple renders from different views to represent 3D structures, we use different perspectives of a process to represent a case. Another important aspect of MPPN is its ability to be used for several tasks instead of being task-specific. This is achieved by an self-supervised pre-training phase, as also done in[10], that learns a representation in the form of a feature vector FV. Afterwards, a task-specific layer can be added to the pre-trained model allowing to fine-tune the model on different tasks. The learned representation FV thus serves as the basis for any downstream task.

4.1   Graphical Representation of Event Log Data

In order to encode all types of attributes into a single representation in a generic way, we decided to choose a graphical encoding instead of the methods used in related work shown in Table 1. We see a strong similarity in the characteristics of time-series and a single perspective of a process case. Furthermore, all types of attributes in a case can easily be transformed to time-series. For this reason, we treat the perspectives $\hat{\Pi}$ as multivariate time series. A naive way to get a both machine-readable and visualizable representations of perspectives Π is to represent and plot them as time series. Thus, each value of a perspective is encoded as a real number and visualized in a 2D representation. The y-coordinate corresponds to the value v, and the x-coordinate to t. In Fig. 1, one can see the 6 perspectives $\hat{\Pi}$ of case 1565 encoded and plotted as 6 distinct time series. Although this representation is a nice visualization for humans, presenting the perspectives Π as a time series plot is a very naive way. Such a plot is very sparse, i.e., most of the plot is empty with just a fine line drawn, containing only little information for convolutional neural networks.

Gramian angular fields (GAF), originally proposed for time-series classification, transform sequential data to 2D images, which contain more information for machine learning methods as time-series plots [26]. For a sequence $\langle v_1, ..., v_n \rangle$, a gramian angular field is a matrix of size $n \times n$ where each entry is the cosine of the sum of two polar coordinates in time – the polar coordinate of v_i plus v_j. This projection is bijective and preserves temporal relations. To transform event log data, i.e., all perspectives $\hat{\Pi}$ of categorical, numerical, and temporal event log attributes and case attributes into gramian angular fields, they must be treated and transformed to distinct sequences of numerical values. In order to get numerical sequences from each type, the following transformations and encodings are performed. Other types of attributes can also be used (e.g., textual data) if they are encoded as numerical sequences.

1. For categorical attributes a_i, we applied an integer encoding $integer : \mathcal{V}_i \rightarrow int$ where $int \in [0, 1, 2, .., |\mathcal{V}_i| - 1]$.

2. Timestamps are transformed into the duration in seconds from the earliest timestamp.
3. Numerical attributes are used unchanged.

Case attributes are first duplicated to the case length before being encoded in the same way as event attributes. Once encoded as numerical sequences, each perspective can easily be encoded as a gramian angular field after scaling them to a $[-1, 1]$ range. To ensure equal size images where characteristics are equally represented, the sequences are adjusted to equal length, either by padding or truncating. This results in distinct GAF-representations for each perspective $\hat{\Pi}$ of a case as shown in Fig. 1.

By using graphical encodings we can transform attributes of different types to images and use state-of-the-art image processing neural networks. This way we avoid building networks that process cases with customized architectures for specific attribute types as well as the complexity of training embeddings.

4.2 Architecture

The MPPN architecture consists of three parts as shown in Fig. 1: *CNN1* for feature extraction, *NN2* for modeling dependencies and relations between perspectives, and one or multiple task-specific layers called *HEAD*. Between *CNN1* and *NN2*, a pooling layer combines the features produced by *CNN1* for each GAF-encoded perspective to a single vector. The weights in *CNN1* are shared between all perspectives, i.e. the same *CNN1* is applied on all perspectives. For *CNN1*, we use Alexnet [8]. However, as gramian angular fields are different from natural images, pre-training *CNN1* on GAFs significantly reduces the later training time. *NN2* is a fully-connected neural network. Together, *CNN1* and *NN2* form the model used for representation learning that produces *FV*. *FV* can either be used directly or by any other task-specific layer; e.g., a fully-connected *HEAD* with *softmax* for next step prediction or a *HEAD* for remaining time prediction.

4.3 Training Method

One integral part of MPPN is its ability to learn representations of all perspectives $\hat{\Pi}$ of cases in an event log. In order to obtain good feature vectors *FV*, one must ensure that all relevant characteristics are fully captured in the model. We distinguish three stages of training that should be performed successively.

Pre-Training CNN1 on GAFs. As GAFs are very different from natural images, pre-trained CNNs like Alexnet need to be fine-tuned. While lower-level features like edges and corners are present in GAFs too, higher-level features differ. In order to make the MPPN sensitive to GAF-specific feature, we fine-tuned the *CNN1* once by classifying cases according to their variant. This task has been chosen as the process variant is always directly derivable from the sequence of events and the model can focus on learning features from the single GAF-encoded perspective. All relevant information for this task is entailed in the GAF image which is what we want the model to focus on. However, many other tasks are also possible. In detail, we build a MPPN with a pre-trained Alexnet consuming only $\Pi_{control-flow}$ and predicting the variant on the MobIS dataset. For each case c the whole sequence of *activity* was used as input and the variant used as the target. Afterwards, the weights of *CNN1* are saved on disk and can be used on any dataset, any perspective, and any task for MPPN in the future.

Representation Learning. To obtain meaningful feature vectors *FV* of business process cases, MPPN must be trained to hold all characteristics of a case in it. One can train MPPN on next step prediction tasks, e.g., to predict the next activity in an ongoing case given $\hat{\Pi}$. This works fine, but the model will learn the relation in the data, which are important for the next activity. This leads to a feature vector *FV* that by design holds features that are important to predict the next activity. Attributes that do not have relevance for the next activity will be less present in *FV*.

To obtain more generic feature vectors of cases, a self-supervised multi-task next event prediction training method is applied that trains the network to predict $a_i(e_{t+1})$ for each attribute in $\hat{\Pi}$. For this task, the MPPN architecture is extended by small networks $HEAD_{a_i}$ – one for each attribute a_i to predict. Each *HEAD* is a task-specific layer that consumes *FV* and predicts $a_i(e_{t+1})$. During representation learning, the task's criterion is to minimize the sum of all losses of all predictions, measured as mean absolute error (for numerical and temporal attributes) and cross-entropy (for categorical attributes). During training, all *HEADs* are trained in parallel and in conjunction with the rest of MPPN. Thereby, the MPPN and especially *NN2* learns to focus on important features in all perspectives $\hat{\Pi}$ and produces a *FV* that holds information relevant for the attributes in the next event. Using this method, a representation can be learned without the need for manual labeled data. However, depending on the final task to be solved, other training methods are also possible. As long as all relevant characteristics of the case are enclosed in *FV*, any training method is appropriate. We chose the multi-task next event prediction task as it allows the model to incorporate all attributes for each prediction. While making predictions for each attribute the model is forced to not drop relevant characteristics of a case. Afterwards, the weights of MPPN (without the heads) are saved on disk. The *FV* produced in this state can directly be used for tasks where additional labels are hard to obtain or unavailable, such as clustering, retrieval or anomaly detection using the same dataset.

Fine-Tuning on Specific Tasks. After being trained to learn good representations, MPPN can also be fine-tuned on other tasks using the same event log and given appropriate labels. Therefore, one or multiple *HEADs* are added that consume *FV*. With each *HEAD*, the model and especially the *HEAD* can be trained on a large variety of tasks, e.g., outcome prediction, next step prediction or (supervised) anomaly detection. Thereby, the model makes use of the representation in FV to solve a certain problem.

4.4 Implementation Details

We implemented MPPN with the following hyperparameter choices: We padded or truncated all cases c to length 64 which results in GAF images of size 64×64 pixel. *CNN1* consists of four CNN layers with max-pooling and dropout. *NN2* is a two-layer fully-connected network with dropout. We pooled the perspectives behind *CNN1* by concatenation. The *HEADs* consist of shallow fully-connected networks with a softmax or regression layer. More details can be found in the implementation.

5   Evaluation

This section elaborates on two experiments. The first experiment visualizes the learned representations during the self-supervised pre-training phase and demonstrates a contextual retrieval task. In the second experiment, we compare the MPPN model to existing approaches on next event and outcome prediction tasks by fine-tuning the pre-trained model.

5.1   Representation Visualization and Retrieval

In the following, we demonstrate how MPPN's internal representations FV can be used for case-based case retrieval. Figure 2 visualizes FVs of each cases after they were reduced to a two-dimensional representation space using PCA. The training of the MPPN was performed analog to Sect. 4.3 using the same input attributes as described in Table 3[1] but complete cases c instead of prefixes. Note that the feature vectors hold information of all perspectives. Therefore, the clusters do not solely depend on the control-flow.

Figure 2 shows that some clusters consist of cases with the same process variant. Other clusters are formed based on specific attribute combinations. For example, the biggest bulk shows all finished cases, i.e., complete cases from start to end containing the most common variant, represented by case 3006. One can make use of this representation for case-based case retrieval. Given L and a query case c_{query}, the task is to generate an ordered set of cases $\hat{C}$ such that all cases in $\hat{C}$ have similar characteristics as c_{query}. Instead of applying different filters on an event log to retrieve cases with particular characteristics, one can also retrieve cases starting with a specific case of interest. For this, the same feature vectors FVs can now be used for retrieving such cases that share similar characteristics as a query case. First, the feature vector of the query case FV_{query} is computed and compared to all other FV of cases in L using the cosine similarity. Next,

---

[1] We added *travel_start* as another attribute.

Table 2. Similarities in the perspectives of the retrieved cases

c_{query}	$\hat{C}$ ID	FV distance	DLD	MAE		
				Timestamp	Cost	TraveLstart
5523	5511	0.00411	0	101.66	240	0.53
	5613	0.00479	0	154.82	154	6.47
	5036	0.01665	5	1307.83	244	28.53
	5911	0.01755	8	1004.02	203	24.47
	6034	0.01937	8	917.40	253	31.93
	5980	0.02088	8	933.96	237	28.55
	5868	0.02115	8	1045.91	69	21.55
2056	4819	0.01388	0	2066.35	49	174.00
	4960	0.02068	5	3587.52	218	181.33
	4765	0.02295	5	729.69	253	169.15
	4497	0.02340	5	632.51	217	153.00
	4715	0.02428	5	717.51	263	167.00
	5044	0.02453	5	847.96	375	188.00
	4657	0.02465	5	689.45	233	162.39
7222	7109	0.00006	0	14.71	97	7.35
	7092	0.00006	0	16.86	94	8.42
	7073	0.00012	0	18.01	77	9.00
	7090	0.00015	0	17.10	24	8.54
	7133	0.00016	0	11.72	32	5.86
	7231	0.00017	0	0.54	100	0.27
	7052	0.00021	0	18.01	41	9.00
3006	3227	0.00048	0	55.97	392	153.00
	2403	0.00105	0	164.74	1123	0.00
	2624	0.00118	0	54.72	501	30.00
	3748	0.0012	0	206.65	662	153.00
	2859	0.00123	0	103.17	629	38.00
	2861	0.0014	0	89.77	474	52.00
	2116	0.00153	0	287.39	250	40.00

Fig. 2. Visualization of the representation space learned by the MPPN on all MobIS cases. Different colors indicate different control-flow variants.

the cases are sorted by their similarity, and those with the highest similarity are returned. We picked four cases as shown in Table 2 for retrieval and marked the retrieved cases with bold symbols in Fig. 2. We see that the control-flow still is the deciding feature for the model as most of the retrieved cases have the same sequence of activities. Additionally, the retrieved cases have similar other characteristics as the query case:

- 5523: Different process variants starting and ending with the same activities performed around the same date with cost below 1000.
- 2056: Cases that looped through the same activities with various number of this loop.
- 7222: Cases consisting of the first two events in the process performed around the same date with costs around 200.
- 3006: Complete cases from start to end of the most common variant.

From Table 2 one can see that the retrieved cases $\hat{C}$ are similar in all perspectives to the query cases. We calculate the cosine distance of the FV, the Damerau-Levenshtein distance (DLD) and the mean absolute error for the three perspectives Π_{cost}, Π_{travel_start} and $\Pi_{timestamp}$ (the MAE is computed after transforming the timestamps to durations).

5.2   Next Step and Outcome Prediction

This experiment evaluates the performance of the fine-tuned MPPN model in comparison to four baselines on the tasks next activity, last activity, next resource, last resource, event duration, and remaining time prediction.

Datasets. In this experiment, we consider seven event logs from different application domains. The Helpdesk[2] event log contains events from a ticketing management process of the help desk of an Italian software company. Five event logs from the BPI Challenge 2012[3]. The original event log is taken from a Dutch Financial Institute and represents the application process for a personal loan or overdraft within a global financing organization. We included the original log as well as each sub-process individually. The event log within BPI Challenge 2013[4] is an export from Volvo IT Belgium and contains events from an incident and problem management system called VINST. The event log within BPI Challenge 2017[5] is an updated, richer version of BPI Challenge 2012. The event log from BPI Challenge 2020[6] was collected data from the reimbursement process at TU/e. We only included the request-for-payment log. The MobIS event log[7] was elaborated in the MobIS Challenge [7]. It describes the execution of a business travel management process in a medium-sized consulting company. We chose Helpdesk, BPIC 2012, and BPIC 2013 to achieve high comparability with existing approaches. BPIC 2017 and BPIC 2020 are selected as significantly more complex event logs that pose new challenges to prediction approaches while also revealing weaknesses of current approaches. MobIS contains several attributes and relationships, making it well-suited to demonstrate MPPN's multi-perspective approach's benefits. Table 3 lists characteristics of each log and presents the attributes used as inputs for the process prediction tasks.

Experimental Setup. We compare MPPN with four different approaches [3, 6,17,23]. For each task, the models receive as input case prefixes of increasing length, starting with the prefix that contains only the first event of a case up to the prefix that omits just the last event; i.e., for each case $\langle e_1, ..., e_n \rangle$ we create n prefixes $\langle e_1, \ldots, e_t \rangle$ with $0 <= t < n$. In addition, we front-padded all prefixes to equal length. To make the results reproducible, we apply a random split between training, validation, and test cases for each data set, utilizing 20% of the cases as test and 10% of the cases as validation data. While the test set is fixed through all experiments and runs, the split between train and validation is performed randomly from run to run. All models were trained and validated

[2] https://doi.org/10.17632/39bp3vv62t.1.

[3] https://doi.org/10.4121/uuid:3926db30-f712-4394-aebc-75976070e91f.

[4] https://doi.org/10.4121/uuid:a7ce5c55-03a7-4583-b855-98b86e1a2b07.

[5] https://doi.org/10.4121/uuid:5f3067df-f10b-45da-b98b-86ae4c7a310b.

[6] https://doi.org/10.4121/uuid:52fb97d4-4588-43c9-9d04-3604d4613b51.

[7] https://doi.org/10.13140/RG.2.2.11870.28487.

Table 3. Event logs, statistics and attributes used

	#Traces	#Events	Avg. trace length	Avg. trace duration	Input attributes		
					Categorical	Numerical	Temporal
Helpdesk	4580	21348	4.66	62.9 days	activity, resource		timestamp
BPIC12	13087	262200	20.04	150.2 days	activity, resource	AMOUNT_REQ	timestamp
BPIC12_Wc	9658	72413	7.50	95.6 days	activity, resource	AMOUNT_REQ	timestamp
BPIC13_CP	1487	6660	4.48	426.5 days	activity, resource, resource country, organization country, organization involved, impact, product, org:role		timestamp
BPIC17_O	42995	193849	4.51	23.9 days	activity, Action, NumberOfTerms, resource	FirstWithdrawalAmount, MonthlyCost, OfferedAmount, CreditScore	timestamp
BPIC20_RFP	6886	36796	5.34	31.6 days	org:role, activity, resource, Project, Task, Organiza-tionalEntity	RequestedAmount	timestamp
MobIS	6555	166512	25.40	1194.4 days	activity, resource, type	cost	timestamp

with the same sets in each run. Each model was trained in the same fashion with a batch size of 512 while utilizing cyclical learning rates and early stopping [21]. The learning rate was picked with the learning rate finder algorithm as defined in [21]. Other than that, we picked the hyper-parameters of the baselines as mentioned in the corresponding papers. While [3,6,23] only considered control flow, resource and timestamp perspectives, the MiDA and the MPPN model is fed with all attributes listed in Table 3. We only removed attributes that contained duplicated information. Last, we decided to remove all cases that are longer than 64 events since these are mostly outliers that falsify the prediction results and significantly increase training time. Each model was trained and tested ten times on all datasets and tasks.

Prediction Tasks and Evaluation Metrics. For this experiment, we formalize the prediction tasks and evaluation metrics as follows:

Given a prefix $p_t = \langle e_1, ..., e_t \rangle$ of a case $c = \langle e_1, ..., e_n \rangle$ with $0 <= t < n; t, n \in \mathbb{N}$, we define *next step prediction* of an attribute a as the task $NSP_a(p_t)$ that predicts $a(e_{t+1})$ based of the prefix p_t. We define *outcome prediction* analogously to next step prediction as the task $OUT_a(p_t)$ that predicts $a(e_n)$ based on a prefix p_t. We measure the prediction performance of a model through a metric function, which is pairwise applied to all predictions and ground truth values for all prefixes over all cases and afterward combined to a final score. According to the type of the predicted attribute, it is necessary, to use different metric functions. In this experiment, we predict activity, resource, and timestamp. For activity and resource, we select the metric function accuracy. For timestamp, we convert it in the duration in days and then compute the mean absolute error.

Baselines. We re-implemented eight models as baselines from [3,6,17,23] based on the original papers and the corresponding source code. Our main objective is to reproduce the different network architectures, to be able to compare them in a fair and unified test setting with our MPPN.

Thus, we deviate from the original work in some aspects regarding train-test splitting, sequence generation, and pre-processing, which also leads to different prediction results. Unfortunately, we cannot guarantee that we have correctly reproduced all the details of the specifications of the models, due to missing source code, documentation or test data.

Interpretation of Results. For the final comparison, we averaged the prediction scores over ten runs. Table 4 presents the final results. There is no superior model that performs best in all tasks on all datasets. However, the results suggest the effectiveness of the MPPN. This yields in particular for the $NSP_{activity}$ and the $NSP_{resource}$ tasks, where it achieves the highest scores on nearly all datasets. The MPPN also performs well on the $OUT_{activity}$ and the $OUT_{resource}$ tasks. However, there is not such a wide performance variety between the models. Most of the examined processes only have a few outcome classes. Therefore, the tasks are supposed to be simpler and lead to similar results. At the same time, the available information in the prefixes may not always allow for a adequate prediction. For the two regression tasks, the MPPN achieves solid but no outstanding results. Overall, the results suggest that the MPPN model is more robust than the other models and does not require extensive hyper-parameter tuning. One explanation might be that the MPPN utilizes gramian angular fields in combination with CNNs instead of embeddings and recurrent layers. Also, the CNN in MPPN is based on the Alexnet architecture, which has been carefully optimized for image recognition tasks. [3,17,23] utilize multi-task learning without fine-tuning, which seem to fail occasionally to optimize one particular task fully. In contrast, through the fine-tuning step of the MPPN, it can focus on one task at a time. Additionally, the MPPN performs reasonable overall tasks and datasets which is a strong indicator that it can learn effective, general representations of the underlying process. Another interesting aspect is the influence of the different perspectives on the process predictions. The MPPN and the MiDA model utilized almost all available perspectives, while the other models only examined activity, resource, and timestamp. In the datasets containing contextual attributes, the MPPN can often outperform other methods indicating that the model can make use of the additional information and embed them into the representation. In the future, we plan to further investigate the influence of different datasets and subsets of perspectives. For example, in the case of BPI17, we expect that contextual information such as application type and event origin can positively affect the prediction quality.

Table 4. Process prediction results

Dataset	Model	$NSP_{activity}$	$NSP_{resource}$	$OUT_{activity}$	$OUT_{resource}$	$NSP_{timestamp}$	$OUT_{timestamp}$
Helpdesk	Evermann [6]	0.651+-0.128	0.222+-0.005	**0.994+-0.000**	0.811+-0.000	—	—
	Ca_Spez. [3]	0.693+-0.168	0.289+-0.071	**0.994+-0.000**	0.811+-0.000	7.95+-0.576	6.654+-0.101
	Ca_concat [3]	0.696+-0.116	0.421+-0.035	**0.994+-0.000**	0.811+-0.000	7.63+-0.052	6.739+-0.253
	Ca_full [3]	0.774+-0.077	0.432+-0.000	**0.994+-0.000**	0.811+-0.000	5.308+-0.288	7.018+-0.225
	Tax_Spez. [23]	0.763+-0.082	—	**0.994+-0.000**	—	7.777+-0.526	6.895+-0.253
	Tax_Mixed [23]	0.3+-0.003	—	**0.994+-0.000**	—	14.849+-0.034	7.197+-0.101
	Tax_Shared [23]	0.793+-0.004	—	**0.994+-0.000**	—	5.088+-0.129	6.67+-0.100
	MiDA [17]	0.693+-0.120	0.263+-0.089	**0.994+-0.000**	0.811+-0.000	**4.898+-0.043**	**6.629+-0.166**
	MPPN	**0.805+-0.003**	**0.691+-0.006**	**0.994+-0.000**	**0.847+-0.008**	5.197+-0.126	6.691+-0.089
BPIC12	Evermann [6]	0.595+-0.107	0.149+-0.000	0.417+-0.000	0.172+-0.000	—	—
	Ca_Spez. [3]	0.795+-0.030	0.333+-0.282	0.417+-0.000	0.177+-0.015	0.693+-0.208	7.82+-0.033
	Ca_concat [3]	0.74+-0.071	0.426+-0.164	0.417+-0.000	0.172+-0.000	0.722+-0.206	7.849+-0.076
	Ca_full [3]	0.756+-0.064	0.283+-0.197	0.417+-0.000	0.184+-0.025	0.687+-0.226	6.649+-0.084
	Tax_Spez. [23]	0.585+-0.194	—	0.417+-0.000	—	0.734+-0.155	7.477+-0.127
	Tax_Mixed [23]	0.615+-0.182	—	0.417+-0.000	—	0.544+-0.205	6.678+-0.101
	Tax_Shared [23]	0.824+-0.008	—	0.487+-0.019	—	**0.542+-0.167**	6.693+-0.080
	MiDA [17]	0.565+-0.123	0.149+-0.000	0.417+-0.000	0.172+-0.000	0.625+-0.041	**6.587+-0.047**
	MPPN	**0.846+-0.006**	**0.775+-0.002**	**0.53+-0.005**	**0.316+-0.004**	0.82+-0.079	6.694+-0.066
BPIC12_Wc	Evermann [6]	0.774+-0.000	0.104+-0.000	0.435+-0.000	0.11+-0.000	—	—
	Ca_Spez. [3]	0.775+-0.002	0.104+-0.000	0.435+-0.000	0.113+-0.005	1.799+-0.088	8.31+-0.058
	Ca_concat [3]	0.794+-0.027	0.104+-0.000	0.435+-0.000	0.115+-0.013	1.843+-0.169	8.333+-0.041
	Ca_full [3]	0.792+-0.026	0.104+-0.000	0.443+-0.026	0.112+-0.005	1.81+-0.125	7.455+-0.063
	Tax_Spez. [23]	0.713+-0.081	—	0.435+-0.000	—	1.765+-0.098	7.932+-0.086
	Tax_Mixed [23]	0.774+-0.000	—	0.435+-0.000	—	**1.595+-0.064**	7.51+-0.106
	Tax_Shared [23]	0.773+-0.001	—	0.537+-0.057	—	1.645+-0.070	**7.409+-0.110**
	MiDA [17]	0.805+-0.022	0.104+-0.000	0.435+-0.000	**0.155+-0.028**	1.767+-0.115	7.424+-0.103
	MPPN	**0.815+-0.006**	**0.237+-0.011**	**0.558+-0.01**	0.147+-0.009	1.761+-0.061	7.528+-0.072
BPIC13_CP	Evermann [6]	0.417+-0.113	0.082+-0.005	**1.0+-0.000**	0.211+-0.000	—	—
	Ca_Spez. [3]	0.481+-0.090	0.086+-0.000	**1.0+-0.000**	0.211+-0.000	50.927+-2.339	137.718+-3.125
	Ca_concat [3]	0.524+-0.004	0.086+-0.000	**1.0+-0.000**	0.211+-0.000	51.672+-3.62	139.412+-5.032
	Ca_full [3]	0.493+-0.065	0.106+-0.035	**1.0+-0.000**	0.211+-0.000	67.168+-7.233	137.193+-6.280
	Tax_Spez. [23]	0.502+-0.067	—	**1.0+-0.000**	—	50.785+-4.395	140.481+-4.913
	Tax_Mixed [23]	0.309+-0.003	—	**1.0+-0.000**	—	112.867+-0.279	176.167+-0.930
	Tax_Shared [23]	0.51+-0.011	—	**1.0+-0.000**	—	**47.741+-1.217**	144.528+-21.964
	MiDA [17]	0.434+-0.110	0.083+-0.005	**1.0+-0.000**	0.211+-0.000	54.949+-4.044	128.185+-10.555
	MPPN	**0.562+-0.009**	**0.178+-0.024**	**1.0+-0.000**	**0.216+-0.008**	54.922+-3.948	**127.824+-3.806**
BPIC17_O	Evermann [6]	0.818+-0.000	0.067+-0.005	0.509+-0.032	0.186+-0.041	—	—
	Ca_Spez. [3]	0.818+-0.000	0.064+-0.000	0.513+-0.018	0.192+-0.000	3.628+-0.057	9.604+-0.017
	Ca_concat [3]	0.818+-0.000	0.226+-0.261	0.501+-0.027	0.192+-0.000	3.611+-0.082	9.606+-0.014
	Ca_full [3]	0.818+-0.000	0.081+-0.048	0.52+-0.001	0.192+-0.000	3.627+-0.105	9.519+-0.025
	Tax_Spez. [23]	0.67+-0.065	—	0.454+-0.019	—	3.529+-0.019	9.688+-0.145
	Tax_Mixed [23]	0.726+-0.178	—	0.458+-0.014	—	3.999+-0.503	9.768+-0.184
	Tax_Shared [23]	0.818+-0.000	—	0.519+-0.000	—	3.531+-0.037	9.47+-0.021
	MiDA [17]	**0.836+-0.030**	0.064+-0.000	**0.828+-0.002**	0.192+-0.000	**3.297+-0.037**	**8.946+-0.059**
	MPPN	0.818+-0.000	**0.553+-0.061**	0.518+-0.001	**0.208+-0.001**	3.567+-0.068	9.534+-0.016
BPIC20_RFP	Evermann [6]	0.699+-0.099	0.817+-0.084	**0.957+-0.000**	**0.958+-0.000**	—	—
	Ca_Spez. [3]	0.756+-0.087	0.841+-0.020	**0.957+-0.000**	**0.958+-0.000**	2.556+-0.142	6.068+-0.185
	Ca_concat [3]	0.704+-0.09	**0.997+-0.000**	**0.957+-0.000**	**0.958+-0.000**	2.631+-0.199	6.062+-0.079
	Ca_full [3]	0.804+-0.025	**0.997+-0.001**	**0.957+-0.000**	**0.958+-0.000**	2.634+-0.252	5.931+-0.117
	Tax_Spez. [23]	0.791+-0.085	—	**0.957+-0.000**	—	2.269+-0.085	5.933+-0.087
	Tax_Mixed [23]	0.431+-0.252	—	**0.957+-0.000**	—	3.827+-2.194	8.55+-0.058
	Tax_Shared [23]	**0.849+-0.001**	—	**0.957+-0.000**	—	**2.12+-0.095**	**5.468+-0.181**
	MiDA [17]	0.55+-0.109	**0.997+-0.001**	**0.957+-0.000**	**0.958+-0.000**	2.673+-0.173	5.842+-0.086
	MPPN	**0.849+-0.001**	**0.997+-0.000**	**0.957+-0.000**	**0.958+-0.000**	3.018+-0.849	6.495+-0.909
MobIS	Evermann [6]	0.767+-0.140	0.163+-0.000	0.798+-0.000	0.075+-0.000	—	—
	Ca_Spez. [3]	0.87+-0.040	0.163+-0.000	0.798+-0.000	0.075+-0.000	4.648+-0.560	30.106+-0.814
	Ca_concat [3]	0.836+-0.034	0.163+-0.000	0.798+-0.000	0.075+-0.000	4.801+-0.525	30.133+-0.526
	Ca_full [3]	0.838+-0.038	0.163+-0.000	0.798+-0.000	0.075+-0.000	3.966+-0.922	24.449+-0.354
	Tax_Spez. [23]	0.85+-0.079	—	0.798+-0.000	—	3.919+-0.968	28.236+-1.569
	Tax_Mixed [23]	0.545+-0.188	—	0.798+-0.000	—	2.333+-0.602	21.384+-0.977
	Tax_Shared [23]	0.926+-0.008	—	0.805+-0.009	—	**2.323+-0.638**	**20.963+-0.420**
	MiDA [17]	0.7+-0.154	0.163+-0.000	0.798+-0.000	0.075+-0.003	2.992+-0.372	24.498+-0.405
	MPPN	**0.934+-0.003**	**0.536+-0.026**	**0.812+-0.002**	**0.121+-0.023**	4.827+-0.420	22.454+-1.011

Reproducibility. All code used for this paper, including the implementation of MPPN as well as the case retrieval and the prediction experiments, can be found in our git repository[8].

6   Conclusion

In this work, we have proposed a novel approach for multivariate business process representation learning utilizing gramian angular fields and convolutional neural networks. MPPN is a generic method that generates multi-purpose vector representations by exposing important characteristics of process instances without the need for manually labeled data. We showed how these representations can be exploited for analytics tasks such as clustering and case retrieval. Furthermore, our work demonstrated the advantages of meaningful, general representations for later downstream tasks such as next step and outcome prediction. In the performed experiments, we were able to outperform existing approaches and generate robust results over several datasets and tasks. This demonstrates that representation learning can successfully be applied on business process data. Furthermore, the self-supervised pre-training makes the model robust and helps in cases where contextual information is given. Additionally, in spite of recent advances in NLP, our result indicate that a non-recurrent neural network outperforms other architectures that use recurrent layers.

One limitation of this paper is a missing systematic hyper-parameter tuning. In this paper, we investigated the robustness of the models on multiple datasets and tasks making it a generic approach. In the future, we want to elaborate on how hyper-parameter tuning can improve the performance of a specific model on a given dataset. Furthermore, we plan to investigate how the approach can explain the impact of certain attributes on other events in a process. The "black box" nature of deep learning models is still a major issue in the context of predictive process analysis. Last, we want to elaborate more approaches and ideas from other domains such as natural language processing and computer vision to learn richer representations capturing more and finer characteristics.

References

1. Bengio, Y., Courville, A., Vincent, P.: Representation learning: a review and new perspectives. IEEE Trans. Pattern Anal. Mach. Intell. **35**, 1798–1828 (2013)
2. Brunk, J., Stottmeister, J., Weinzierl, S., Matzner, M., Becker, J.: Exploring the effect of context information on deep learning business process predictions. J. Decis. Syst. (2020)
3. Camargo, M., Dumas, M., González-Rojas, O.: Learning accurate LSTM models of business processes. In: Hildebrandt, T., van Dongen, B.F., Röglinger, M., Mendling, J. (eds.) BPM 2019. LNCS, vol. 11675, pp. 286–302. Springer, Cham (2019). https://doi.org/10.1007/978-3-030-26619-6_19

---

[8] http://bit.do/fQRbF.

4. De Koninck, P., vanden Broucke, S., De Weerdt, J.: act2vec, trace2vec, log2vec, and model2vec: representation learning for business processes. In: Weske, M., Montali, M., Weber, I., vom Brocke, J. (eds.) BPM 2018. LNCS, vol. 11080, pp. 305–321. Springer, Cham (2018). https://doi.org/10.1007/978-3-319-98648-7_18

5. Devlin, J., Chang, M.W., Lee, K., Toutanova, K.: Bert: Pre-training of deep bidirectional transformers for language understanding. arXiv preprint arXiv:1810.04805 (2018)

6. Evermann, J., Rehse, J.R., Fettke, P.: Predicting process behaviour using deep learning. Decis. Supp. Syst. **100**, 129–140 (2017)

7. Houy, C., Rehse, J.R., Scheid, M., Fettke, P.: Model-based compliance in information systems - foundations, case description and data set of the mobis-challenge for students and doctoral candidates. In: Tagungsband der Internationalen Tagung Wirtschaftsinformatik 2019, Siegen, Germany, 24–27 February 2019, pp. 2026–2039. Universität Siegen

8. Krizhevsky, A., Sutskever, I., Hinton, G.E.: Imagenet classification with deep convolutional neural networks. NIPS **25**, 1097–1105 (2012)

9. Maggi, F.M., Di Francescomarino, C., Dumas, M., Ghidini, C.: Predictive monitoring of business processes. In: Jarke, M., Mylopoulos, J., Quix, C., Rolland, C., Manolopoulos, Y., Mouratidis, H., Horkoff, J. (eds.) CAiSE 2014. LNCS, vol. 8484, pp. 457–472. Springer, Cham (2014). https://doi.org/10.1007/978-3-319-07881-6_31

10. Mehdiyev, N., Evermann, J., Fettke, P.: A novel business process prediction model using a deep learning method. Bus. Inf. Syst. Eng. **62**(2), 143–157 (2020)

11. Mehdiyev, N., Fettke, P.: Local post-hoc explanations for predictive process monitoring in manufacturing. arXiv preprint arXiv:2009.10513 (2020)

12. Moon, J., Park, G., Jeong, J.: Pop-on: Prediction of process using one-way language model based on nlp approach. Appl. Sci. **11**(2), 864 (2021)

13. Márquez-Chamorro, A.E., Resinas, M., Ruiz-Cortés, A.: Predictive monitoring of business processes: a survey. IEEE Trans. Serv. Comput. **11**, 962–977 (2018)

14. Navarin, N., Vincenzi, B., Polato, M., Sperduti, A.: In: Lstm networks for data-aware remaining time prediction of business process instances, pp. 1–7. IEEE (2017)

15. Neu, D.A., Lahann, J., Fettke, P.: A systematic literature review on state-of-the-art deep learning methods for process prediction. Artif. Intell. Rev. (2021)

16. Nolle, T., Seeliger, A., Mühlhäuser, M.: Binet: multivariate business process anomaly detection using deep learning. In: Business Process Management, pp. 271–287 (2018)

17. Pasquadibisceglie, V., Appice, A., Castellano, G., Malerba, D.: A multi-view deep learning approach for predictive business process monitoring. IEEE Trans. Serv. Comput. (2021)

18. Pasquadibisceglie, V., Appice, A., Castellano, G., Malerba, D.: Predictive process mining meets computer vision. In: Fahland, D., Ghidini, C., Becker, J., Dumas, M. (eds.) BPM 2020. LNBIP, vol. 392, pp. 176–192. Springer, Cham (2020). https://doi.org/10.1007/978-3-030-58638-6_11

19. Pasquadibisceglie, V., Appice, A., Castellano, G., Malerba, D., Modugno, G.: Orange: outcome-oriented predictive process monitoring based on image encoding and CNNs. IEEE Access **8**, 184073–184086 (2020)

20. Pauwels, S., Calders, T.: Detecting anomalies in hybrid business process logs. ACM SIGAPP Appl. Comput. Rev. **19**, 18–30 (2019)

21. Smith, L.N.: A disciplined approach to neural network hyper-parameters: Part 1-learning rate, batch size, momentum, and weight decay. arXiv preprint arXiv:1803.09820 (2018)
22. Su, H., Maji, S., Kalogerakis, E., Learned-Miller, E.: Multi-view convolutional neural networks for 3D shape recognition. In: Proceedings of the IEEE international conference on computer vision, pp. 945–953 (2015)
23. Tax, N., Verenich, I., La Rosa, M., Dumas, M.: Predictive business process monitoring with LSTM neural networks. In: Dubois, E., Pohl, K. (eds.) CAiSE 2017. LNCS, vol. 10253, pp. 477–492. Springer, Cham (2017). https://doi.org/10.1007/978-3-319-59536-8_30
24. Taymouri, F., Rosa, M.L., Erfani, S., Bozorgi, Z.D., Verenich, I.: Predictive business process monitoring via generative adversarial nets: the case of next event prediction. In: Fahland, D., Ghidini, C., Becker, J., Dumas, M. (eds.) BPM 2020. LNCS, vol. 12168, pp. 237–256. Springer, Cham (2020). https://doi.org/10.1007/978-3-030-58666-9_14
25. Vaswani, A., et al.: Attention is all you need. arXiv preprint arXiv:1706.03762 (2017)
26. Wang, Z., Oates, T.: Encoding time series as images for visual inspection and classification using tiled convolutional neural networks. In: Workshops at the twenty-ninth AAAI conference on artificial intelligence (2015)

Seeing the Forest for the Trees:
Group-Oriented Workforce Analytics

Jing Yang[1]([✉]), Chun Ouyang[1], Arthur H. M. ter Hofstede[1],
Wil M. P. van der Aalst[2,1], and Michael Leyer[3,1]

[1] Queensland University of Technology, Brisbane, Australia
roy.j.yang@qut.edu.au
[2] RWTH Aachen University, Aachen, Germany
[3] University of Rostock, Rostock, Germany

Abstract. Workforce analytics brings data-driven methods to organizations for deriving insights from employee-related data and supports decision making. However, it faces an open challenge of lacking the capability to analyze the behavior of employee groups in order to understand organizational performance. This paper proposes a novel notion of work profiles of resource groups, informed by the management literature, for characterizing resource group behavior from multiple aspects relevant to workforce performance. This notion is central to the design of a new, systematic approach that supports resource group analysis by exploiting business process execution data. The approach also provides managers and business analysts with an intuitive means of group-oriented resource analysis by applying visual analytics. We demonstrate the applicability of the approach and usefulness of the proposed notion of resource group work profiles using real datasets from five Dutch municipalities.

Keywords: Workforce analytics · Resource groups · Process mining · Event logs · Visual analytics

1 Introduction

Achieving excellent business process performance within the management of operations is a demanding and crucial challenge for any organization to maintain competitive advantage. The prevalence of information systems has led to many data science applications supporting analyses of organizational performance to address this challenge. Business processes are often at the core of such analyses as they describe how resources of an organization (employees, machines, systems) are connected with each other [3]. The focus of business process analytics is often on the control-flow perspective and process design. However, the aspect of how employees work together in processes to achieve efficiency is also important [21].

Employees are the key resources of an organization. Not only their individual but also collective performance as different units or teams has a direct impact on the outcomes delivered by the organization [33]. Data science applications in this regard are termed *workforce analytics*, which aim at extracting

© Springer Nature Switzerland AG 2021
A. Polyvyanyy et al. (Eds.): BPM 2021, LNCS 12875, pp. 345–362, 2021.
https://doi.org/10.1007/978-3-030-85469-0_22

insights from analyzing employee-related data and thus support evidence-based decisions on human resources [23]. The success of Google's Project Oxygen and other leading-edge enterprises illustrates the value of workforce analytics as an important organizational capability to improve resource planning and performance evaluation. However, as workforce analytics receives growing attention, several challenges have been identified regarding its current practice [20]. One of these challenges concerns the absence of group-level analysis pivotal to strategy execution and organizational effectiveness. For example, current workforce analytics has not yet enabled consistent comparisons across internal groups within organizations [12].

Our research aims to explore a possible solution to improving organizations' capability to conduct group-oriented workforce analytics by systematically exploiting business process execution data. The *motivation* is two-fold. First, business processes often cut across functional boundaries in an organization and collectively involve employees from different functional units to deliver outcomes to customers [18]. The end-to-end nature of processes makes it viable to analyze and compare different resource groups by linking their performance with process outcomes. Second, data recording actual process execution is readily available in many organizations in the form of event logs. With time-stamped information on process instances (e.g., an insurance claim), process activities, and relevant organizational groups (e.g., a group of claim processors), event logs can serve as a valuable and objective data source complementary to survey data commonly used by current workforce analytics in practice [23].

Process mining is the field that studies data-driven process analytics using event logs. With regard to human resources in organizations, the state-of-the-art literature focuses on analyzing individual resources or discovering the formation of resource groups. Studying human resources at the group-level to extract insights on how resources work in groups and how resource groups perform in business processes is underexplored. This leads to the following research question for workforce analytics in process-related digitalization: *how to utilize process execution data for analyzing the behavior of resource groups working in business processes?*

In this paper, we propose a novel notion of *work profile of resource groups*, drawing on relevant studies in the management literature. It comprises an extensible set of quantitative measures for characterizing resource group behavior from multiple aspects, including workload, performance, goal achievement, participation, distribution, and collaboration. Based on this notion, we develop an approach to identify and analyze resource groups' work profiles using event log data. The approach provides managers and business analysts with an intuitive means of group-oriented resource analysis by applying visual analytics. We demonstrate the applicability of the implemented approach and usefulness of the proposed notion of resource group work profiles by analyzing real event logs from five Dutch municipalities.

Our research contributes to addressing the gap of resource-group level analysis in business process management research on a conceptual and also methodological level. From a practical perspective, our research provides the possibility of strengthening an organization's process-oriented capability in terms of coordinating groups to increase efficiency.

The paper is organized as follows. Section 2 reviews existing literature related to resource group analysis. Section 3 proposes the notion of work profiles of resource groups. Section 4 presents the design of an approach for identifying and analyzing work profiles. Section 5 discusses results and findings from evaluating the approach over real-life datasets. Section 6 concludes the paper and outlines future work.

2 Resource Group Analysis: Theory and Related Work

The organization of employees in terms of teams or groups and the comparison of their collective performance constitute important topics in management [16]. A team is formed by engaging individuals in collective work with joint effort, whereas a group only represents individuals tied together by certain criteria, not necessarily working jointly [26]. For example, there can be employees from a function-oriented group who work together with those from other function-oriented groups in a team performing a particular process, but having limited interaction with their own group members. In this work, we focus on groups rather than teams.

Groups of employees can be characterized by the interaction between group members. This is addressed by the interactionist theory of behavior, which states that the interaction between individuals in a group determines the performance of the group [24]. Malinowski et al. [22] provide a comprehensive overview of the challenges regarding decision support to identify influencing factors and the related concepts. Next to a person-job fit and a person-vocation fit, individuals interact with their group members, and thus a person-group fit has to be ensured. Whether all group members have an adequate person-group fit can be determined from their interaction and performance [22]. Hence, there are two levels of workforce analysis—group performance and interaction within a group, i.e., the way a group is organized internally.

Within management research, much work has focused on defining general practices while neglecting individual interactionist fits in a group context [14]. An example of such a general practice would be the grouping of employees around the processes they are involved in rather than around the types of tasks they perform. Other general practices state that high performance groups should have, e.g., clearly defined goals, aligned values, and adequate collaboration [8]. In particular, the collaboration aspect remains opaque in such work. The problem with such practices is that they are based on generic assumptions and may not be the best for a specific organization or parts of it. Research in the field of psychology includes individual differences, perceived psychological states regarding various dimensions and aspects, e.g., group cohesion [9]. However, such psychological aspects are often subjectively measured through questioning, conducted sporadically. Hence, these aspects are not considered in this article as focus is on objective measures using process data. Moreover, organizations nowadays are required to be flexible as they are faced with dynamic and ongoing changes of the environment [32]. Organizational structures need to reflect this by being able to evaluate groups on an ongoing basis—providing data on group comparisons.

Group performance is typically described from a measurement perspective without specifying how to gather and analyze data. Brignall and Ballantine [5] review different performance management models and point out that the utilization of human resources is an essential aspect. The literature reviews conducted by Haynes [13] and Bortoluzzi [4] discuss the measurement of productivity in organizations and identify certain productivity indicators, e.g., working hours, time to completion, and amount of satisfactory outcomes vs. errors. Gibson et al. [10] review the existing measures of group effectiveness in the literature and conduct interviews in several multinational organizations, summarizing five dimensions for measuring the "outcome effectiveness" of groups. Charlwood [6] reports the results from a literature review that identifies theory and evidence on the use of Human-Capital metrics by organizations. The review extracts more than 600 Human-Capital metrics from the literature describing workforce characteristics and the evaluation of workforce efficiency.

With regard to the internal organization of the group, first there are approaches which consider the interaction between groups referring to handovers in processes [21], role descriptions and expertise [1], or communication and control structures [11]. Second, approaches using business process execution data to study human resource groups can be categorized into two topics. One concerns using event logs for analyzing the formation of resource groups, e.g., Schönig et al. [28] propose an approach that uncovers the composition rules of human resource groups in process executions, and Appice [2] proposes a method that reveals the construction and destruction of organizational groups over time using event logs. The other topic concerns the discovery of organizational groups (e.g., [30]), which aims at extracting the grouping structures around resources. Third, there exists research (e.g., [17,25]) focusing on analysis of individual resource behavior by building resource "profiles" from event logs, which represent objective descriptions of how individual resources were involved in process execution. However, it still remains an open question as to what and how to characterize the behavior of resource groups working in processes.

3   Work Profile of Resource Groups

Drawing on the theoretical and conceptual background in the prior section, this section presents the notion of *work profile of resource groups*. A work profile of a resource group can be defined as a collection of *indicators* used to measure different *aspects* of that group of resources in terms of their interaction with relevant work. As with any indicators related to performance, the measurement of indicators includes a connection to time, i.e. a time interval (between t_1 and t_2) in which the respective performance of a group is measured [6]. By specifying the relevant interval, work profiles can reflect the fact that the performance of resource groups is often dynamic due to having shifts and turnover. Hence, the definition of a work profile is as follows:

Definition 1 (Work Profile of a Resource Group). *Let RG be a set of resource group identifiers, $\mathcal{T}$ the universe of timestamps, and $[t_1, t_2)$ a half-open time interval with $t_1, t_2 \in \mathcal{T}$ and $t_1 < t_2$. Let $\mathcal{I}$ be a set of names for possible indicators. Given a resource group $rg \in RG$, $WP = (rg, t_1, t_2, \mathcal{I}, \sigma)$ is a work profile for the resource group during time period $[t_1, t_2)$ where $\sigma : \mathcal{I} \to \mathbb{R}$ specifies the quantified measures of the indicators.*

The definition provides a general representation of indicators measuring different aspects of a resource group over a specific time-frame. By reviewing the management literature, we identified a number of relevant studies [4–6,10,13] which can inform the proposal of a resource group's work profile useful for workforce analytics. The indicators refer to the input-throughput-output view on processes [7]. Performance regarding input-output can be measured with indicators related to productivity and efficiency. Whether a specific output is achieved is referred to as goal achievement. Finally, the throughput is reflected by the summation of employee workload in a group. As a result, we present a collection of three general aspects and associated indicators, focusing on a resource group in its entirety.

- **Workload** [5]: *What and how much work is a resource group involved in?*
  - allocation – overall amount of work allocated to the group
  - assignment – amount of the group's workload assigned to specific work
  - relative focus – % of the group's workload assigned to specific work
  - relative stake – amount of contribution by the group to specific work
- **Performance** [4,6,10,13]: *How does a group perform?*
  - amount-related productivity – amount of work completed by the group
  - time-related productivity – time needed by the group to complete work
  - efficiency – amount of satisfactory work produced by the group
- **Goal achievement** [4,10]: *To what extent does a group adhere to goals?*
  - effectiveness – % of established goals accomplished by the group

In this research, we also consider how resource groups interact with work in terms of their involvement in business process execution captured by process event logs. This theoretical focus is reflected in the following aspects and indicators, which measure how group members interact with relevant work in a process, and with each other.

- **Participation** [4,6]: *How do group members commit to work?*
  - attendance – number or % of members in the group committing to work
- **Distribution** [4]: *How is work distributed over group members?*
  - member load – amount of work allocated to individual group members
  - member assignments – amount of members' workload allocated to specific work
- **Collaboration** [6]: *How is the collaboration among group members?*
  - cooperation – extent of collaboration between group members

The above collection of six aspects and associated indicators can be used to form the structure (or template) of a group's work profile for group-oriented analysis. Note that the term "work" here refers to either activities (tasks) or cases of a business process. Analysts can build their own sets of indicators according to different problems and contexts. However, to enumerate a comprehensive, universal set of aspects and indicators would be unrealistic [6] and is beyond this paper's scope.

4   Identifying and Analyzing Work Profiles

We introduce the design of an approach for identifying and analyzing work profiles of resource groups using process event log data. Figure 1 depicts an overview of the proposed approach consisting of two main phases.

4.1   Identifying Work Profiles

Identify Resource Groups. The starting point is an event log. As a minimum requirement, the input event log should provide information on cases (instances of process execution), activities, resources, and time. These are satisfied by many event logs as they often record case identifiers, activity labels, resource identifiers, and timestamps as the basic event attributes. Additionally, the input event log may also carry an attribute indicating the group identities of resources.

Given such an event log, the first task is to identify different resource groups. This is straightforward when a group identity attribute is present in the log. Otherwise, organizational group discovery (e.g., [30]) can be applied to extract group identities of resources. In either situation, one can determine the number of resource groups, their members, and thus the associated event data in the log.

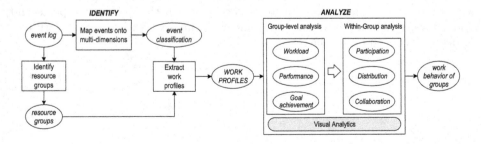

Fig. 1. Overview of the approach to identifying and analyzing work profiles

Map Events onto Multiple Dimensions. Event logs contain complex and multi-dimensional data capturing the information on various perspectives of process execution. Consider an example of an insurance claim process: a manager (organizational dimension) is in charge of the final review of a claim (activity dimension), and several groups are formed to work on different weekdays (time dimension) to serve customers lodging different types of claims (case dimension). Moreover, from the perspective of resource groups, members in the same group are likely to share common characteristics, e.g., all managers conduct reviews, despite that they may be specialized in handling certain types of claims.

To study the work behavior of resource groups in process execution, we organize events into classes of events based on different dimensions (such as case, activity, time dimensions). Depending on the purpose of an analysis and available information in the input log, analysts can specify different case types, activity types, and time types. For example, to compare the performance of employee groups on different weekdays, seven time types may be defined (e.g., "Monday", "Tuesday"). Consequently, ("car insurance claims", "contact", "Friday") refers to all events on Fridays concerning the work behavior of employees when they contacted customers that had lodged car insurance claims.

Based on the classification of events according to various process dimensions, indicators of work profiles can be calculated respectively. It therefore enables more targeted analyses on the work behavior of groups. For instance, given case type "gold customer" and activity type "contact", ("CityS.", 2020-09-27, 2020-10-25, attendance, 60%) indicates to HR analysts that 60% of members in employee group "CityS." worked on contacting gold customers between September and October 2020.

Extracting Work Profiles. We describe the pre-defined work profile indicators (Sect. 3) that can be directly extracted given a typical event log with essential information recorded. Note that all indicators are measured given a resource group and a time interval (see Definition 1).

Workload: The indicators of group workload capture the amount of different types of work carried out by a resource group. With respect to an event log, the amount of work can be quantified by considering either the number of activities (which can be inferred from the event number) or the number of cases (which can be inferred from the case identifiers).

- allocation is measured by the total number of activities conducted by a group, or the total number of cases involving the group;
- assignment is measured by the number of activities conducted by a group that are specific to some case type, activity type, and time type, or the number of cases involving a group that are specific to some case type;
- rel_focus measures the assignment of specific activities or cases to a group, compared with the total allocation to the group;
- rel_stake measures the assignment of specific activities or cases to a group, compared with the total number of activities or cases of the specific types.

Performance: The indicators of group performance can be quantified by considering activities and cases *completed* in a given time interval. Note that they are different from the workload indicators which do not consider completion.

- amount-related productivity is measured by the total number of completed activities or completed cases by a group;
- time-related productivity is measured by the average time taken by a group to complete an activity or a case;
- efficiency extends amount-related productivity by including some normative pre-defined criteria. For example, an analyst can specify that only cases completed within 10 days are considered "satisfactory", and therefore efficiency will be calculated based on the number of satisfactory cases by the group only.

Goal Achievement: The effectiveness indicator measuring the *goal achievement* of a resource group can be quantified based on other aspects and their indicators. For example, when two goals are established in terms of the maximum amount of allocation (measuring workload) and the minimum level of efficiency (measuring performance), the effectiveness of a group can be measured by considering whether the group accomplishes these goals, respectively.

Participation: The indicator attendance can be quantified by considering the occurrences of group members carrying out activities or cases. Note that the measure may only be a rough estimate since an event log may not accurately capture the time when employees start working on a process.

- attendance is measured by the number of member resources in a group who originated at least one event (for a relevant activity or case).

Distribution: The indicators for distribution are defined over group members by calculating the portion of workload of the group. Thus, the following indicators consider a given resource in a group.

- member_load is measured by the number of activities conducted by a resource. Therefore, the sum of member_load across all members of a group should be equal to the allocation of the group (measured by activities);
- member_assignment is measured similarly to member_load, but using case types, activity types, and time types to characterize the work by different dimensions.

Collaboration: Quantifying the extent of collaboration among employees using event logs can be challenging since (1) event logs usually do not capture the communication between employees and (2) the way how collaboration happens in different processes and organizations may differ. In the following, we discuss a possible estimate of cooperation based on how frequently group members transfer work between each other in process execution (known as handovers).

- cooperation within group members can be estimated by the density of handovers of work between group members [31].

4.2 Analyzing Work Profiles

Building on work profiles extracted from event logs, different data analytics techniques can be applied to discover patterns from the measurement of indicators. In our approach, we discuss the use of visual analytics as an intuitive and proven means [15] for analyzing work profiles.

Following the definition of work profiles and the relevant aspects and indicators, we consider the following requirements for visually analyzing work profiles:

- Users should be able to interactively extract work profiles related to different time intervals in an event log and at different granularity (e.g., daily, monthly), thus be able to track changes of work profiles over time;
- Users should be able to have an integrated view of interrelated indicators (e.g., allocation and assignments) to derive findings on interactions between different aspects (or dimensions);
- Users should be able to compare indicators measured among different groups at different times; and
- Users should be able to correlate indicators of group-level analysis with those of within-group analysis to obtain a holistic view on groups' work behavior.

Based on these requirements and guided by the general principles in visual analytics [19], we developed a design composed of several types of charts combined with interactive filters. The design aims at providing an integrated and purposeful visualization on multiple aspects of a resource group's work profiles.

The design includes the following. (1) A *stacked area chart* and a *line chart* are chosen for analyzing workload and performance, considering their advantages in capturing indicator values as time-series and showing the evolution patterns. For these two charts, interactive filters are embedded to allow users to explore the workload and performance indicators at different times and at different levels of granularity. (2) A *heatmap* is used for supporting the analysis on workload and distribution with regard to different case, activity, and time types, for its usefulness in simultaneously presenting values related to two-dimensional data attributes. (3) A *stacked bar chart* is used for intuitively presenting the attendance of group members with respect to group size. By connecting different charts using the same set of interactive filters, users are provided with an overall picture of work profiles of resource groups in a selected time interval of interest.

The design shows a possible way of applying visual analytics to analyze work profiles. While the aspects and indicators of a work profile may be further extended, other visualization techniques can also be adopted accordingly.

5 Evaluation

The purpose of our evaluation is to demonstrate how the proposed approach can be used for resource group-oriented analysis. To this end, we have developed a prototype with interactive visualization, built upon Vega-Lite [27], as a realization of the design of the approach in Sect. 4. The tool is publicly available (https://royjy.me/to/gwp-demo). Figure 2 and Fig. 3 illustrate the prototype's interactive visualization interface.

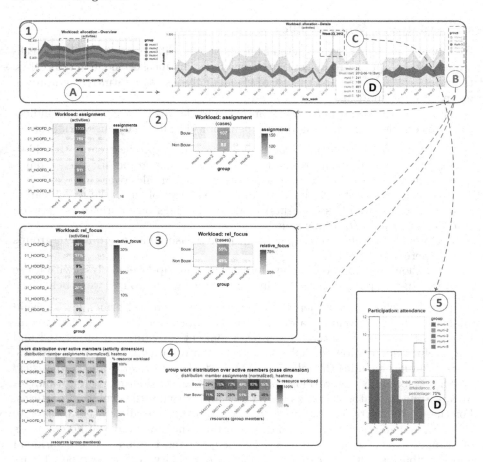

Fig. 2. Annotated screenshots of the prototype's interactive interface for analyzing work profiles regarding workload, participation and distribution. The numbers mark different views: (1) workload by allocation; (2) workload by assignment measuring either activities or cases; (3) workload by rel_focus measuring either activities or cases; (4) distribution by member_assignment; (5) participation by attendance. The views respond to user interactions simultaneously: (A) selecting a time interval and zoom-in; (B) highlighting specific groups; (C) focusing on a specific time period (week); and (D) showing specific numbers via a tooltip

5.1   Design of Experiments

We conducted an evaluation by experimenting on a real-life dataset[1] with five event logs. The event logs record a process of handling building permit applications in an approximate four-year period, and contain typical event attributes satisfying the minimum requirements on an input event log (Sect. 4.1). Note that the event logs only record the end timestamp for each activity conducted in the

---

[1] BPIC 2015: https://data.4tu.nl/collections/BPI_Challenge_2015/5065424/1.

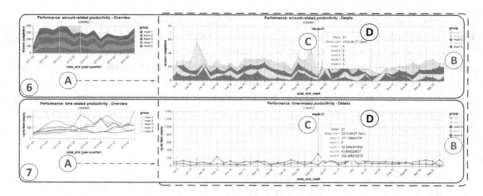

Fig. 3. Annotated screenshots of the prototype's interface for analyzing work profiles regarding performance. Views of (6) amount-related productivity and (7) time-related productivity respond simultaneously to user interactions (A–D)

process. Therefore, only activity occurrences can be considered in the subsequent analysis, not the activity duration time.

Still, this dataset can serve as a representative example of how our approach can contribute to workforce analytics centered around resource groups. This is because the dataset captures how an identical process was performed in five different municipalities, and thus representing scenarios where *different resource groups participate in executing the same process*. Moreover, the process owners raised a few questions originally, with a particular focus on the differences between the municipalities' performance and the roles of their employees. Given this context, we consider each municipality as a separate resource group in our experiments[2], and apply the approach to extract and analyze their work profiles.

5.2 Group-Level Analysis

We first conduct the group-level analysis and focus on the workload and performance aspects, motivated by one of the process owner's original questions: *Where are differences in throughput times between the municipalities and how can these be explained?* For simplicity, we refer to the five municipalities (i.e., the resource groups) by short names, e.g., "muni-1" denotes the first municipality.

Workload Analysis. We organize cases and events by three process dimensions (activity, time, case) to compare the workload of resource groups. Figure 4 shows the visualization of group workload in regard to different activity, time, and case types. The five groups exhibit very similar patterns in terms of assigning their group workload according to different types of activities (Fig. 4a). Slight differences can be observed as neither of muni-4 nor muni-5 has worked on activities of type 6. Also, employees from muni-2 and muni-5 seem to have committed to

---

[2] Experiment details: https://git.io/Jq9uC.

more workload in executing activities of type 8. These groups also show similarities regarding the types of cases they processed (Fig. 4c), as the majority
leaned towards handling the construction-related applications ('Bouw'), especially muni-1 and muni-5. An interesting observation can be made regarding the
weekday pattern shown in Fig. 4b. Muni-1 differs from others as it had only 12%
of its total workload assigned on Wednesdays. In the meantime, muni-2, muni-3
and muni-5 seem to form another cohort as Fridays were their least busy day.
This observation may link to different arrangements of office hours in the groups.

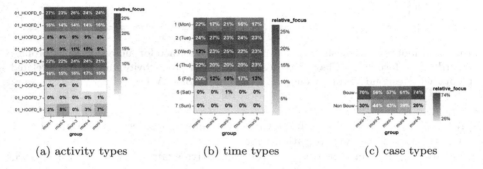

(a) activity types   (b) time types   (c) case types

Fig. 4. Workload of the groups measured by rel_focus in 2011–2014

Performance Analysis. Figure 5 presents an overview of group performance by
calculating indicator **amount-related productivity** and **time-related productivity** for
different year-quarters. For analyses in this part, we base our observations on
work profiles starting from 2012 Q1, since we only included cases started after
2010-12-31 in our evaluation, and hence the numbers related to case completion
in 2011 may not reflect the actual performance[3].

From Fig. 5a we can see that five groups follow a highly similar pattern in
terms of **amount-related productivity** (as the number of completed cases)—most
of the cases were completed in Q1, followed by that in Q4 and Q3, while the
least throughput happened in Q2. Compared across years, 2012 saw the most
completed cases. The groups' performance decreased in 2013 and went slightly
higher in 2014. An observation worth mentioning is that muni-4 had a sudden
increase of performance after 2013 Q1 until 2014 Q2, and later dropped to the
same level as the other groups.

Figure 5b provides another perspective on group performance visualizing
time-related productivity. Note that it is calculated by the average cycle time
of completed cases, hence the performance is high when the value is low, and
vice versa. We can see that muni-3 delivered steadily high performance in terms
of shorter cycle time. Muni-5 also had a relatively consistent level of performance, which slightly improved during the year 2013. The performance of muni-
2 changed across the four quarters, while within each year it follows a pattern:

---

[3] The mean case cycle time in the dataset is 91.1 days (std. 105.8 days).

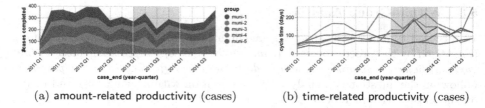

(a) amount-related productivity (cases)   (b) time-related productivity (cases)

Fig. 5. Performance of the groups in 2011–2014

starting low in Q1, improving in Q2, and gradually decreasing towards the end of a year (Q3 and Q4). This highlighted pattern of muni-2 would be interesting to investigate, as this group is not unique in terms of amount-related productivity.

Meanwhile, the spike of case cycle time in muni-1 and muni-4 in 2013 also deserves further attention. With our previous observation on the increase of throughput of muni-4 in the same period, we selected the interval of 2013 and used the detailed view to drill down the performance values of muni-4.

Figure 6 depicts the visualization. The upper view clearly shows four sharp increases of amount-related productivity. In each of the four weeks, muni-4 completed significantly more cases (more than 30) compared to all other groups (less than 10). This explains the spike in the overview (Fig. 5a) and may link to the existence of batching behavior of muni-4. Interestingly, the increase of amount-related productivity seems unrelated to the group's time-related productivity as shown in the lower view. Cross-checking the same weeks in the two charts, we can see that the potential batching completion did not directly link to a significantly longer case cycle time of muni-4.

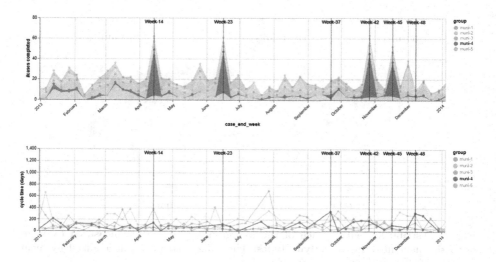

Fig. 6. Muni-4's performance by amount-related and time-related productivity

5.3   Within-Group Analysis

We proceed to analysis at the group-member level, motivated by another question raised by the process owner: *What are the roles of the people involved in the various stages of the process and how do these roles differ across municipalities?* Following the question, we analyze the distribution within each group and focus on the most active members.

Distribution Analysis. Figure 7 presents how individual resources within each group handled different types of activities distributed to them, which reflects the involvement of resources at different phases in the process. Comparing across the columns in the heatmaps, we noticed two major patterns in all five groups, which are more significant in muni-4 and muni-5. There exists a cohort of resources focusing primarily on the executions of activities of type 0, 4, and 5, while they seldom carry out activities in the middle of the process (type 1, 2, and 3). Also, there is another cohort of resources that exhibits a different pattern as their workload was mostly on executing activities from phases in the middle (type 1, 2, 3, and 4) in a balanced manner. This second cohort of resources was less

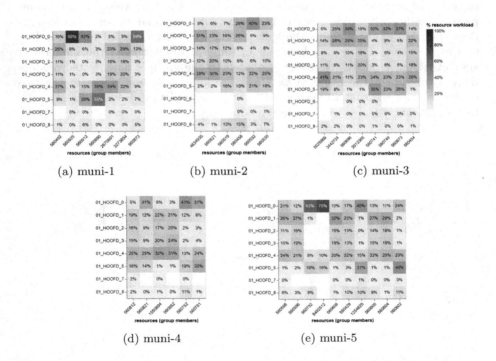

Fig. 7. Distribution within each of the five groups (2011–2014) measured by member_assignment in terms of activity types. The values have been normalized by member_load of each individual for role analysis

involved in executing activities of type 0 and 5. The two different yet possibly complementary patterns may relate to two business roles in the process.

The heatmaps also highlight patterns unique to some municipalities. For example, resource '560925' in muni-1 carried over 89% of its total workload in executing activities of type 0, and 8% in conducting activities of type 1. The resource was rarely involved in activities during the later phases in the process. While such a pattern is not observed in the other groups, it implies that in muni-1 there was a specific role for dealing with the initial processing of the received applications. As another example, resource '8492512' in muni-5 only executed activities of type 0, 4, and 5 in the four-year period, and may have acted as a specialist supporting the first major role identified before (i.e., focused mainly on activities of type 0, 4, and 5).

Summary. The above analyses on group work profiles using visual analytics reveal interesting patterns regarding how five different resource groups worked on the same process, and identify areas that require further investigation. While we do not aim at a thorough case study on these municipalities, we demonstrate how the proposed notion of work profiles and the approach to identifying and analyzing them can contribute to answering questions related to group-oriented workforce analytics, through utilizing event logs.

6   Discussion, Implications, and Conclusion

Our study is inspired by research on analyzing resource group characteristics and on mining individual resource behavior. The results of demonstrating the proposed approach show that it can be applied successfully and provides interesting insights with regard to workforce analytics. Compared to prior work, we provide an approach that is based on theory and a subsequent conceptualization on the group level. It allows the use of a minimum of information from event logs to enable relevant workforce analysis on the group level and describes how visual analytics can be used to support the analysis.

Our research has several theoretical implications. First, we contribute to the discussion of connecting human resource management to the domain of BPM [29]. We introduce the interactionist theory to the domain of analyzing groups in a BPM context and demonstrate how it is relevant for workforce analytics for group performance and organization. We show how performance indicators can be connected with interactionist-related parameters, using process data to extract knowledge about how interaction leads to performance. Second, our research provides insights on workforce analytics in the context of business processes by conceptualizing the notion of work profiles of resource groups. As such, we provide a better understanding of how such an organizational capability can be fostered to enable high performance. The conceptualization of work profiles allows the characterization and comparison among different groupings of employees over time. Such information is important to continually evaluate existing organizational structures which might not reflect optimal interaction between employees and have to be adapted. Hence, measuring and managing resource groups is an important organizational capability as organizations continuously have to decide how to group employees to adapt to changing requirements. Third, we provide an analytical approach using actual process execution data that can be used to determine the performance of groups over time and identify possible root causes related to the internal group interaction for the performance observed. Fourth, we show how the analytical results on the group level can be visualized.

From a practical perspective, process managers and analysts can benefit from the research outcomes which enable them to use event log data to objectively evaluate work behavior of their resource groups. The analysis can pinpoint the areas of interest across different periods, different levels of resources, and different process dimensions. The use of visualizations facilitates the interpretation of analysis results in daily operations.

As with any research, our work is subject to limitations. First, the dataset used in the evaluation only records end timestamps. Richer insights can be derived if both start and end timestamps are recorded. Second, the proposed indicators are based on standard event log information. While this allows for broad applicability, other attributes, e.g., capturing the collaboration aspect of human resource groups, can be defined and exploited to derive additional insights. Third, factors related to other aspects of the interactionist theory, e.g., psychological factors, can be taken into consideration. For this, however, data sources beyond event logs need to be included.

References

1. Alvarez, C., et al.: Discovering role interaction models in the Emergency Room using Process Mining. J. Biomed. Inf. (2018)
2. Appice, A.: Towards mining the organizational structure of a dynamic event scenario. J. Intell. Inf. Syst. **50**(1), 165–193 (2018)
3. Bititci, U.S., Ackermann, F., Ates, A., Davies, J., et al.: Managerial processes: business process that sustain performance. Int. J. Oper. Prod. Manag. **31**(8), 851–887 (2011)
4. Bortoluzzi, B., Carey, D., McArthur, J.J., Menassa, C.: Measurements of workplace productivity in the office context: a systematic review and current industry insights. J. Corporate Real Estate **20**(4), 281–301 (2018)
5. Brignall, S., Ballantine, J.: Performance measurement in service businesses revisited. Int. J. Serv. Ind. Manag. **7**(1), 6–31 (1996)
6. Charlwood, A., Stuart, M., Trusson, C.: Human capital metrics and analytics: assessing the evidence of the value and impact of people data. Loughborough University, Technical report (2017)
7. Coelli, T., Rao, D., O'Donnell, C.: An Introduction to Efficiency and Productivity Analysis, 2nd edn. Springer, Boston (2005). https://doi.org/10.1007/b136381
8. Flood, F., Klausner, M.: High-performance work teams and organizations. Global Encyclopedia of Public Administration, Public Policy, and Governance; Springer Science and Business Media LLC: Berlin, Germany, pp. 1–6 (2018)

9. Furnham, A.: Personality and Intelligence at Work: Exploring and Explaining Individual Differences at Work. Routledge, London (2008)
10. Gibson, C.B., Zellmer-Bruhn, M.E., Schwab, D.P.: Team effectiveness in multinational organizations. Group Org. Manag. **28**(4), 444–474 (2003)
11. Hanachi, C., Gaaloul, W., Mondi, R.: Performative-based mining of workflow organizational structures. In: Huemer, C., Lops, P. (eds.) EC-Web 2012. LNBIP, vol. 123, pp. 63–75. Springer, Heidelberg (2012). https://doi.org/10.1007/978-3-642-32273-0_6
12. Harris, J.G., Craig, E., Light, D.A.: Talent and analytics: new approaches, higher ROI. J. Bus. Strateg. **32**(6), 4–13 (2011)
13. Haynes, B.P.: An evaluation of office productivity measurement. J. Corporate Real Estate **9**(3), 144–155 (2007)
14. Hellström, A., Eriksson, H.: Among fumblers, talkers, mappers and organisers: four applications of process orientation. Total Qual. Manage. Bus. Excellence **24**(5–6), 733–751 (2013)
15. van den Heuvel, S., Bondarouk, T.: The rise (and fall?) of HR analytics: a study into the future application, value, structure, and system support. J. Organizational Effectiveness **4**(2), 157–178 (2017)
16. Higgs, M., Plewnia, U., Ploch, J.: Influence of team composition and task complexity on team performance. Team Performance Manage. **11**(7–8), 227–250 (2005)
17. Huang, Z., Lu, X., Duan, H.: Resource behavior measure and application in business process management. Expert Syst. Appl. **39**(7), 6458–6468 (2012)
18. Jones, G.R.: Organizational Theory, Design, and Change. Pearson, 7th edn. (2013)
19. Keim, D.A., Mansmann, F., Schneidewind, J., Thomas, J., Ziegler, H.: Visual analytics: scope and challenges. In: Simoff, S.J., Böhlen, M.H., Mazeika, A. (eds.) Visual Data Mining. LNCS, vol. 4404, pp. 76–90. Springer, Heidelberg (2008). https://doi.org/10.1007/978-3-540-71080-6_6
20. Levenson, A.: Using workforce analytics to improve strategy execution. Hum. Resour. Manage. **57**(3), 685–700 (2018)
21. Leyer, M., Iren, D., Aysolmaz, B.: Identification and analysis of handovers in organisations using process model repositories. Bus. Process. Manag. J. **26**(6), 1599–1617 (2020)
22. Malinowski, J., Weitzel, T., Keim, T.: Decision support for team staffing: an automated relational recommendation approach. Decis. Support Syst. **45**(3), 429–447 (2008)
23. Marler, J.H., Boudreau, J.W.: An evidence-based review of HR analytics. Int. J. Hum. Resource Manage. **28**(1), 3–26 (2017)
24. Muchinsky, P.M., Monahan, C.J.: What is person-environment congruence? supplementary versus complementary models of fit. J. Vocat. Behav. **31**(3), 268–277 (1987)
25. Pika, A., Leyer, M., Wynn, M.T., Fidge, C.J., ter Hofstede, A.H.M., van der Aalst, W.M.P.: Mining resource profiles from event logs. ACM Trans. Manage. Inf. Syst. **8**(1), 1:1-1:30 (2017)
26. Robbins, S.P., Judge, T.A.: Essentials of Organizational Behavior, 14th edn. Pearson Education Limited, Harlow, England (2018)
27. Satyanarayan, A., Moritz, D., Wongsuphasawat, K., Heer, J.: Vega-lite: a grammar of interactive graphics. IEEE Trans. Visual Comput. Graph. **23**(1), 341–350 (2017)
28. Schönig, S., Cabanillas, C., Ciccio, C.D., Jablonski, S., Mendling, J.: Mining team compositions for collaborative work in business processes. Softw. Syst. Model. **17**(2), 675–693 (2018)

29. Shafagatova, A., Van Looy, A.: Alignment patterns for process-oriented appraisals and rewards: using HRM for BPM capability building. Bus. Process. Manag. J. **27**(3), 941–964 (2020)
30. Song, M., van der Aalst, W.M.P.: Towards comprehensive support for organizational mining. Decis. Support Syst. **46**(1), 300–317 (2008)
31. van der Aalst, W.M.P., Reijers, H.A., Song, M.: Discovering social networks from event logs. Comput. Support. Cooperative Work. **14**(6), 549–593 (2005)
32. van Vianen, A.E.: Person-environment fit: a review of its basic tenets. Annu. Rev. Organ. Psych. Organ. Behav. **5**, 75–101 (2018)
33. Wheelan, S.: Creating Effective Teams: A Guide for Members and Leaders, 4th edn. SAGE, Thousand Oaks (2013)

A Case Study of Inconsistency in Process Mining Use: Implications for the Theory of Effective Use

Rebekah Eden[1(✉)], Rehan Syed[1], Sander J. J. Leemans[1], and Joos A. C. M. Buijs[2]

[1] Queensland University of Technology, Brisbane, Australia
rg.eden@qut.edu.au
[2] Algemene Pensioen Groep, Heerlen, Netherlands

Abstract. Responding to recent and repeated calls in literature, we sought to understand the effective use of business intelligence systems, specifically process mining. The intersection between effective use and business intelligence is pertinent to practice, as these systems do not automatically result in improved organizational outcomes, rather they must first be effectively used. Through a qualitative case study, we examined the effective use of process mining (analytical technique underpinning business intelligence), whereby inconsistency-in-use emerged as salient. We, therefore, shifted our focus to understanding the role of inconsistency-in-use in the effective use of process mining. We identified inconsistencies in: place, meaning, and content (i.e., entanglement of data and information). These types of inconsistency were interrelated and influenced informed action. Inconsistency in content also had implications for representational fidelity. Given, both informed action and representational fidelity are effective use dimensions, these inconsistencies need to be considered for process mining systems to be effectively used.

1 Introduction

Organizations continue to make substantial investments in business intelligence systems and technologies with the objective of improving decision making to yield a competitive advantage [1]. In line with Trieu [2], we view business intelligence as an umbrella term (encapsulating, for example, business analytics, big data, data mining, and process mining) that refers to "a set of concepts and methods based on fact-based support systems for improving decision making". Process mining is a domain of business intelligence [3], consisting of techniques, algorithms, visualizations and methodologies for analyzing business process data, such that these processes can be improved using Business Process Management principles. For instance, process mining enables organizations to monitor performance indicators, discover process models, identify resource constraints and bottlenecks, and determine the extent of regulatory performance [4]. Recently, process mining is gaining traction with its uptake in multiple fields including: healthcare [5], financial services [6], and insurance [7]. Despite the increasing uptake of process mining as a form of business intelligence system, implementations of such systems do not automatically result in improved decisions or organizational enhancements [8].

© Springer Nature Switzerland AG 2021
A. Polyvyanyy et al. (Eds.): BPM 2021, LNCS 12875, pp. 363–379, 2021.
https://doi.org/10.1007/978-3-030-85469-0_23

Based on the theory of effective use, to attain the goals of a system, whether a business intelligence system or otherwise, it must be effectively used [9]. According to this theory, to make informed actions, which is the prime goal of business intelligence systems, users must be able to leverage data that provides an accurate account of the phenomenon of interest. There are repeated and recent calls in literature [2, 10] to understand the effective use of business intelligence systems. The importance of the intersection between these two areas is further compounded with Gartner predicting that self-service analytics (a capability of process mining) is a key future trend [11], which places more onus on business users effectively using these systems.

Due to the nascent state of research, we adopted a grounded theory approach [12] with the broad aim of understanding the effective use of business intelligence systems. We examined process mining as the analytic technique underpinning business intelligence. Process mining provides an evidenced-based foundation to improve an organization's processes by analyzing historical behavior of processes stored in event logs [4]. We investigated the effective use of process mining at a Dutch pension fund services provider. Following grounded theory, the salient theme of inconsistency-in-use (i.e., variations in meaning, content, and place) emerged as critical to the effective use of process mining. We then narrowed our aim to focus on inconsistency and aimed to provide insights into the following: What is the role of inconsistency-in-use in the effective use of process mining?

Although, we follow a grounded theory approach, we present our research sequentially. Next, we present related work followed by the case design. Then, we present our findings into types of inconsistency. We then integrate our findings with literature to show the role of inconsistency of use in the effective use of business intelligence.

2   Related Work

As we will unpack in this section, the notion of "use" in process mining literature is largely absent in the current discourse. Consequently, this section is structured as follows. First, we refer to seminal work grounded in the Information Systems domain investigating "use" and "effective use" of systems. We then examine how such terms have been investigated in conjunction with the umbrella concept of business intelligence narrowing to the specific domain of process mining.

2.1   Information Systems Use

For more than three decades, Information Systems literature has largely rebuked technology determinist assumptions through recognizing that systems must be used for benefits to be attained [13]. This has resulted in system use being a cornerstone of the field [14]. System use is defined as "an individual user's employment of one or more features of a system to perform a task" [15] and has been conceptualized to consist of three components: the technological artifact, the user, and the task. Translating to the process mining domain, the process mining system is the technology artifact; the user is the individual who interacts with the process mining system; and the task centers on the informed decision the user is seeking to attain from their interactions with the process mining system. Yet, while use is a precursor to benefits, it is an insufficient condition as not all use results in benefits [9].

Information Systems literature has started shifting to understanding effective use, defined as "using a system in such a way that helps attains the goals for using a system" [9]. The theory of effective use [9], based on representation theory [16], conceptualizes effective use to consist of three dimensions: 1) Transparent interaction: "The extent to which a user is accessing the system's representations unimpeded by its surface and physical structures"; 2) Representational fidelity: "The extent to which a user is obtaining representations from the system that faithfully reflect the domain being represented"; and 3) Informed action: "The extent to which a user acts upon the faithful representations he or she obtains from the system to improve his or her state".

Thus, for users to effectively use the system, they need to transparently interact with the hardware and software to access representations, determine the faithfulness of the representations they leverage to make informed actions based on these representations to attain their goal for using the system. When conceptualizing effective use, Burton-Jones and Grange [9] provided a generalizable account. As a result, there have been calls to examine effective use in different contexts [17, 18], where emerging insights are providing a more nuanced understanding. For instance, according to Burton-Jones and Volkoff [17] effectively using health information systems requires users using the system in consistent ways. Similar findings emerged in Eden and Burton-Jones [19] who highlighted that effective use involves balancing consistency and inconsistency-in -use. This notion of inconsistency-in-use proved critical to the effective use of the process mining tool within our case organization. While effective use research has begun to explore new contexts, revealing new concepts and insights for how organizations can improve how effectively their systems are used, these studies seldom reflect back on how their context can shed new light on the theory's generalizable dimensions.

2.2 Business Intelligence Use

Business intelligence provides a contemporaneous context for studying system use and in particular, effective use [47]. This is because unlike traditional systems, which were primarily focused on repetitive data entry tasks, business intelligence system enable users to make informed decisions based on the outputted data. According to Ain, Vaia, DeLone and Waheed [20] business intelligence systems "supports decision processes by i) facilitating: more aggregation, systematic integration and management of unstructured data and structured data, ii) dealing with a huge amount of data (e.g., big data), iii) providing end users with increased processing capabilities to discover new knowledge, and iv) offering analysis solutions, ad hoc queries, reporting and forecasting". In a systematic literature review, Ain, Vaia, DeLone and Waheed [20] identified studies have recognized organizational factors, system factors, and user factors influence the adoption, use, and success of business intelligence systems. However, studies investigating business intelligence use did so from the perspective of extent of use [21, 22] or beliefs and attitude towards use [23, 24] seldom were rich conceptualizations of use provided. Notable exceptions include Grublješič and Jaklič [25] who conceptualized that beliefs and attitudes regarding business intelligence, impact individuals intensity of use, extent of use, and embeddedness of use; Trieu [2] who proposed effective use for business intelligence assets translate into impacts; and Surbakti, Wang, Indulska and Sadiq [10] who proposed realizing business value from big data is a function of effective use. However, these studies while highlighting the need for richer conceptualizations of use, particularly effective use, in the context of business intelligence systems are all conceptual in nature.

As previously highlighted, inconsistency-in-use plays a pivotal role in how effectively information systems are used, which per Sect. 4 is salient in our case study data. We therefore, further reflect on how the notion of inconsistency-in-use has been investigated in business intelligence literature. According to [26] "relational database assumes consistency in the way entities and their properties are defined". This is further supported by [27], who highlights the difficulty in creating coherent and consistent data structures. Inconsistency in data [28] can ultimately hamper users ability to analyze data and result in erroneous reports. Despite, consensus over the importance of consistency in the data source, the interrelationships between inconsistent data with other forms of inconsistency (e.g., presentation format) has yet to be addressed nor has the implications of inconsistency for effective use been examined.

The lack of robust investigation of how business intelligence systems are used is compounded in the process mining domain where the behavior and perceptions of individual users is often neglected. Process mining aims to gain insights into processes as run by organizations, by providing analysts with methods and systems to visualize behavior in these processes. Typically process mining literature has focused on the techniques and algorithms to perform analyses although some have examined the adoption of process mining at an organizational level across a variety of settings [5, 29]. Such studies provide details on the analysis performed [5], extent of process mining implementation [30], or techniques used across domains [31]. While process mining literature references notions of 'use' it generally does so from the perspective of 'use cases', which "represent the use of a concrete process mining functionality with the goal to obtain an independent and final result" [32]. This is in line with technology deterministic assumptions as use cases focus on the functionality provided to the user (e.g., discovery, conformance checking, and enhancement) [32]; rather than the actions of users to extract and interpret information to make informed decisions. It is counter-intuitive that process mining literature with its emphasis on unpacking representations of the behavior of individuals through event logs, has not yet explored how individuals adopt the process mining systems. Therefore, in this paper, we extend process mining literature by examining how users adopt these systems to make informed decisions.

3   Grounded Theory Case Study

To investigate effective use of process mining, we adopt a grounded theory approach [12] following the guidelines of Fernandez [33]. Grounded theory is recommended to explore revelatory phenomenon such as process mining and can be used to build novel theories [34, 35]. Algemene Pensioen Groep N.V. (APG) served as our case organization and is a large provider of services to pension funds in the Netherlands.

3.1 Case Organization

APG recognized process mining could provide them with the potential to improve its processes to benefit efficiency, effectiveness and quality of process outcomes. As such, APG formulated a strategy to trial, implement and embed process mining as a business intelligence system.

In 2016, APG commenced adopting Celonis, which is a commercial process mining system organizations adopt to enable business users to analyze business processes to identify inefficiencies and bottlenecks. Through performing process mining techniques on data derived from multiple sources, Celonis visualizes the output of the analysis to the users in the form of graphs and models via dashboards. Initially, Celonis was rolled out using what APG describes as a 'launch and learn' approach, with minimum governance. However, overtime they changed their approach establishing governance frameworks, providing data extraction expertise, and user guidance.

At APG, dashboard development typically involves several stakeholder groups. Dashboard development is done by an 'Actionable Insights' Data Intelligence (AI-DI) team of technical specialists, after which a 'Self Service' data intelligence team takes over user training, guidance, and provides assistance. The work of both teams is managed by the product owner of the 'Actionable Insights' team in APG. Each dashboard has an owner who asks for the dashboard in the first place and prioritizes features. The result is an interactive, custom-built dashboard where data is presented through charts and process graphs to business users. The users can be categorized as viewers or analysts. The viewers directly use the output provided by the system. Whereas, the expert analyst users, can also extend the dashboards to better meet the requirements of all users. Both types of business users are supported when necessary by the self-service data intelligence team where they receive additional training and advice.

Currently, several dashboards are used in APG. The following are referred to by our interview participants:

1. A customer journey analysis dashboard, which is a centralized dashboard that pension administrative teams use to analyze their administrative processes such as clients starting retirement, starting a new job, and other life events. The dashboard is also used to determine the fraction of cases that follow straight-through processing (STP, i.e., a fully automated process), and determine where STP fails. This dashboard has been developed by the AI-DI team and is now supported via the self-service team. This dashboard uses data prepared in a central data warehouse by AI-DI. The central data warehouses enables cross-process analysis, such as tracking process-chains for a customer. The dashboard also includes client satisfaction scores and number of contacts in order to analyze the customer journey in full.
2. A series of dashboards for specific pension-related processes, which were built by business users before the existence of the self-service team and without the help of the AI-DI team. The data used is taken directly from the pension administration system and therefore the dashboards have a process-specific scope.
3. An auditing dashboard to analyze the 4-eyes principle of a specific financial process. This dashboard was built by the AI-DI team as a one-time analysis on static as-is

data directly from the source system. Further development of the dashboard by the business analysts is supported via the self-service team.

In all cases Celonis is used as a self-service process analytics dashboard tool, allowing almost all employees of APG to make use of the dashboards. Furthermore, in all three cases, the dashboards are also maintained by a group of users, allowing them to adjust the dashboards to their changing needs. Therefore, Celonis is available company-wide, and not just of one department or legal entity. The same holds for the AI-DI availability, which performs projects for the whole of APG.

3.2 Data Analysis

Our objective was to understand the effective use of Celonis as a process mining system at APG. To collect data, we conducted semi-structured interviews and analyzed relevant archival data (e.g., presentations, training materials, and governance structures). We used purposeful sampling [36] and selected participants from each role, who had worked with one or more of the dashboards (excluding the product team owner). In total, 15 individuals participated across 14 interviews (see Table 1), which each lasted between 30 and 45 min on average.

The interviews were conducted in English. However, participants could switch to Dutch (native language) to explain key concepts. This was possible as two of the interviewers were fluent in Dutch. All interviews were recorded. The recordings were transcribed and uploaded into NVivo (v12), which was used as a data repository system, with coding and analysis manually performed [37].

Table 1. Overview of interview participants*

Role	Participant count	Identifier
Actionable Insights Data Intelligence (AI-DI) member	5	P1–P5
Self-service Data Intelligence team member (SS-DI)	3	P6–P8
Dashboard owner	1	P9
Dashboard analyst (expert users)	4	P10–P13
Dashboard viewers (basic users)	2	P14–P15

*The participant count is greater than the interview count as in an interview two individuals participated.

To analyze our data, we performed open coding [33] to enable key themes to emerge. As such, we did not have a preconceived framework for analyzing interviews. We used coder-corroboration to maintain reliability of the coding in which three researchers independently coded interviews followed by corroboration sessions to identify any differences and to attain consensuses [38]. As a result of open coding, rather than effective use, the most salient themes pertained to 'inconsistency of use' emerged centering on the data within the system and the information extracted from the system. We then on-coded the data comparing the quotes related to inconsistency to one another [37]. In doing so, we identified three types of inconsistency: 1) inconsistency in meaning, 2) inconsistency in content, and 3) inconsistency in place.

Next, we performed on-coding with constant comparison to literature. We discovered inconsistency in content was more complex than considered in past literature. Specifically, we identified it was important to consider inconsistency at the data layer and at the output layer (termed inconsistency in data and inconsistency in information respectively). We then progressed to theoretical coding, identifying the relationships between the types of inconsistency, as well as potential antecedents and consequences. We continued this process until theoretical saturation was reached [12], which was when no new themes nor relationships relating to inconsistency emerged.

4   Findings

In our case study, inconsistency related to meaning, content, and place were apparent in the use of Celonis. We identified that inconsistency in content is comprised of the entanglement of inconsistency in data and inconsistency in information. The types of inconsistency observed are defined with examples provided in Table 2.

Table 2. Examples of types of inconsistency

Inconsistency	Definition*	Example
Data	Variations in the completeness and accuracy of the data that is loaded into the process mining system	*"We find it very difficult to get the data we want. ...There are number of reasons for that sometimes its hard to get extractions from the systems, sometimes data is not available because it is not logged, sometimes the application managers dont know how to generate reports for data we are looking for. ...Another problem is that we want to have data from different systems because we want to have a look at the whole process in which more than one system is used ...making sure that the definitions from one application are [the] same in the other."* (P12)
Information	Variations in the completeness and accuracy of output provided to the user by the system	*"If we know that if we selected one item or two cases ...then you have a more narrow item in your process flow and ...that gives a more [specific] overview...it's not a whole spaghetti of things it was only one or two items. Which makes it easier to understand what we were looking for"* (P13)

(*continued*)

Table 2. (*continued*)

Inconsistency	Definition*	Example
Meaning	Variations in how individuals interpret the content present in either the data structure or output provided	*"The definition of straight-through processing (STP) only applies to processes in which no manual interference comes in. ...At assets management, they use straight processing for processes with a high automation degree. That's already a difference in definition, because ...an STP process is 100% automatic. If a process has 10 steps, and 9 are automatic, that isn't STP..., it is a process with a 90% degree of automation."* (P10)
Place	Variations in where individuals perform their process mining analysis (i.e., Celonis or other software)	*"Celonis can provide a lot, it's just due to a lack of understanding of what Celonis can be and the fact that we constantly have to ask...can you build this. ...That's the reason why we chose to extract to Excel and we can do it ourselves in the timeframe that is working for us."* (P13)

Definitions formed through constant comparison with literature. Adapted from [26].

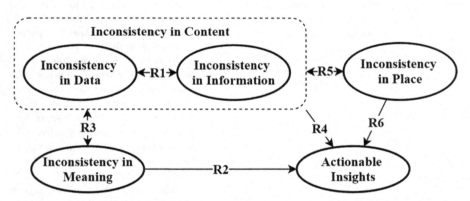

Fig. 1. Conceptual model of the interrelationships between the types of inconsistency-in-use and influence on actionable insights

These types of inconsistencies had implications for the goal of using the process mining system, Celonis, which was to form actionable insights. The participants described actionable insights as *"insights actionable for the business...where the business can translate those insights into actions"* (P7). We also identified interrelationships between the types of inconsistency. Below we describe the relationships between the types of inconsistency and actionable insights and the interrelationships between the types of inconsistency (Fig. 1).

4.1 Interrelationship Between Inconsistency in Data and Inconsistency in Information (R1)

We define inconsistency in content as variations in the completeness and accuracy of the data/information in a process mining system. Through constant comparison, we identified the entanglement between inconsistency in data and inconsistency in information. Inconsistency in data refers to variation of the completeness and accuracy of the data that is loaded into a process mining system, whereas inconsistency in information refers to the variations in the completeness and accuracy of output provided to the user by the system. As the participants describe:

> "The corporate actions audit is [based on] predefined audit criteria ...The difficulty for us is ...we are telling somebody please build it for us [but] he doesn't understand or ...know what we would really like to see. So he just builds something that he thinks is the best of course. Every outcome is also checked by us. ...We first check ...is it the right analysis that we intended ... or is it something completely different built that we didn't really want." (P13)

> "Because we want to make the data as good as possible...we have to change something so the data becomes better then we have a straight through processing figure that's accurate and we can all rely on it." (P1)

4.2 Relationships Between Inconsistency in Meaning and Actionable Insights (R2)

Based on our data and constant comparison with literature, we defined inconsistency in meaning as variations in how individuals interpret the content present in either the data structure or output provided by process mining system. For instance, there are multiple ways a process can start, yet all of these starting points were collapsed under the one field in the data structure. Yet these starting points mean different things to different users. Therefore, users can ultimately attribute different meanings to the output and misinterpretations can result. As one participant describes:

> "And of course, you can interpret yourself what you think is the real name for a data element. ...I have already seen 4 or 5 process with the same name. ...For instance the first letter people get, startbrief (initial letter), three processes startbrief exactly the same name, [..] startbrief 1, and there are a lot of other data elements that sound ...like startbrief, so a lot of risk for misinterpretation when people combine those things. I even don't think DI [data intelligence] has all the knowledge what people made in 25 years which startbrief is the real one." (P9)

Concerns regarding the terminology used to denote the phenomenon being represented in the dashboard was highlighted as a core impediment to actionable insights.

This was evident as different departments had different definitions for the term 'straight through processing' and it was feared users would act on their interpretation of STP rather than the dashboards fundamental meaning, as a participant highlights:

> *User's definitions of straight through processes will differ from AI-DI's definition of straight through processes and then we implement AI-DI's definition of straight through process and you will look at our dashboards you will think this is straight through processes but it doesn't necessary mean its your definition of straight through processes. More like the definitions and the terminologies and the way we implement them in the dashboards that could make the users misinterpret.* (P8)

4.3   Interrelationships Between Inconsistency in Meaning and Inconsistency in Content (R3)

Inconsistency in meaning also has important implications on inconsistency in content. Participants regularly highlighted the difficulties of inconsistent terminology between stakeholder groups (i.e., inconsistency in meaning). For instance, auditors were initially challenged in communicating to the data intelligence team. It was difficult for auditors to communicate what data they required and what analyses needed to be performed. This resulted in inconsistent data being loaded into the system, which could result in data inaccuracy in some cases.

Inconsistency in meaning is further compounded when a dashboard is created for a centralized goal rather than a team-specific goal. For instance, APG developed a dashboard to measure 'straight through processing' (STP) to be used across many departments to improve their processes. However, different teams have different perspectives of how STP should be measured. If a team views the term differently, they could ultimately reach different, and potentially, inappropriate conclusions. Resolving inconsistent terminology is imperative when you have data coming from multiple systems and multiple stakeholder groups, as an auditor states:

> *"...We need data also from an external provider, their definition of its corporate action ...they use as an external provider of data are different from definitions we use internally. So, if you want to connect data that's one thing, we have to get rid of because we have to use same definitions." (P12).*

Recognizing the implications that inconsistency in meaning can have on data, the data intelligence (AI-DI) team have been actively establishing consistent data definitions. As one participant notes:

> *"But, in the DI department we are already working since I think two or three years trying to get the same names for the same data elements." (P9)*

4.4   Relationships Between Inconsistency in Content and Actionable Insights (R4)

It was often described that it is not possible to have data in the system that is entirely complete and correct, with challenges associated with extracting data and required data not always being logged. Responding to this challenge, the data intelligence team tries to provide insights in the accuracy and completeness of the data, terming this golden data. This inconsistency makes it difficult for people to trust the data and the output. This can make business users reluctant to use the system, potentially impeding decision making. To resolve the inconsistency in the data, the DI team has been working on establishing a data core as a single source of truth. As one participant notes:

> *"But [the AI-DI] team says, "hey its golden data", but golden data doesn't necessarily mean its correct. It means, there is data and you know what's wrong with the data. Where do you draw the line, when is the data correct enough, who says it correct enough, who tests the data. That's why I say the dashboard is great, but people are still like hmmm can I honestly trust what I am seeing. That's what people are still wondering about." (P8)*

Asides from inconsistency in meaning and inconsistency in data, inconsistency in information can also result from different visualization approaches being adopted. While these differing visualization approaches may result in interesting actionable insights. If the users filter down to such a small level, the misinterpretations can result or the insight may not be feasible to address. As one participant notes,

> *"It's one of the most difficult things to compare processes because what I saw once was people filter so much on that particular group, the group becomes so small that you can ask if they are still representative enough for the whole group. ...Sometimes you see activities which appear less frequently and are focusing on exceptions or are you focusing on the major things that go wrong. And if you try to compare and you can filter everything you want of course you get a difference is it still making sense to invest in this difference." (P5).*

4.5 Interrelationships Between Inconsistency in Content and Inconsistency in Place (R5)

When challenges arise with respect to inconsistency in data, workarounds occur, which ultimately results in people using different systems to perform their analysis (i.e., inconsistency in place). These workarounds can result in actionable insights being formulated but can result in inefficiencies in deriving the insights, as one participant notes:

> *"We had 46,000 payments and we should change in some cases, ...you need to use the bank account number and in some cases you need to use the bank account name. And those should be switched. ...We thought it was already done in Celonis but we find out that it wasn't already done. So we thought ok let's extract in to excel and we will do it by ourselves, but filtering in excel with 46000 payments it just didn't work out. And in the end we thought we might just check if [AI-DI] can do this in Celonis. And he could do it in just five minutes. But we just maybe three days we spent over Excel changing all these things" (P13)*

4.6   Relationship Between Inconsistency in Place and Actionable Insights (R6)

Inconsistency in place does not solely originate from inconsistency in data, but it was also a direct effect of participants having previous expertise in other systems, in some cases Excel. In other cases, they have extracted their own data sources to be used in the analysis and created bespoke analysis for themselves and their teams. This creates the need for data governance practices to be put into place as it can lead to inappropriate actionable insights.

> *"Someone [is] making new stuff on the views ...on the base tables. ...It is a person who can do very good SQL. ...But then you have two, you have this one, and the Celonis one. ...In this new world, we want to have data governance. ...We are eager to have a metadata agreement.... If someone is going to make his own connections, joins, calculations, then you don't know whether it is the same calculation as we do in Celonis, which represents the definition of how we want to use it in this company. ...We are fading away from the goal." (P6)*

In other cases, they extracted their own data sources to be used in the analysis and created bespoke analysis for themselves and their teams. This creates the need for data governance practices as it can lead to inappropriate actionable insights.

> *The second risk I see is that they are used to their own dashboards, they worked on it for months to make their own dashboards. ...but when they are combining them in their own dashboards, we are not sure they will get all the data. I'm not sure that managers' [personal dashboards] has all the data in it. In this new world, we want to have data governance about our stuff. (P6)*

4.7   Summary of Findings

In summary, inconsistency was present in terms of meaning, data, information, and place. However, this inconsistency was not always detrimental. For instance, inconsistent presentation of information allowed for more specific conclusions to be drawn, inconsistency in place allowed for limitations associated with the data structure to be overcome. Moreover, inconsistency in data is an inevitability. Some actions have been put into place by the organization to minimize the detrimental effects that result from inconsistency. Including iterative development of dashboards to optimize data correctness; visualization training to minimize poor data visualization practices; establishment of a self-service team to quickly respond to issues minimizing the need for workarounds; and active collaboration to form an agreed upon data dictionary.

5   Discussion

In examining the effective use of process mining, we identified the importance of the interdependent nature of inconsistency in meaning, content, and place in attaining actionable insights. This notion of actionable insights mirrors the definition of informed action a key dimension of effective use. As such, our findings highlight that inconsistency in meaning, content, and place all influence the "extent to which a user acts upon the faithful representations he or she obtains from the system to improve his or her state" [9]. However, while our findings largely pointed towards the challenge of inconsistency, inconsistency was not always detrimental and positive outcomes can still be obtained. Our findings extend current literature pertaining to inconsistency-in-use and business intelligence. We discuss these contributions in turn. We then reflect on how our findings contribute to the theory of effective use.

5.1 Importance of Inconsistency-In-Use for Process Mining

The importance of inconsistency-in-use has been identified in previous literature. For example, Burton-Jones and Volkoff [17] found to effectively use health systems, users need to attribute consistent meanings to form fields and input data in a consistent manner. Eden, Akhlaghpour, Spee, Staib, Sullivan and Burton-Jones [26] also identified the importance of inconsistency of use, however unlike Burton-Jones and Volkoff [17], they found effective use requires balancing consistency and inconsistency of use, where perfect consistency was deemed improbable and undesirable. Specifically, Eden, Akhlaghpour, Spee, Staib, Sullivan and Burton-Jones [26] identified five types of inconsistency (process, form, place, meaning, and content) of which the latter three were identified in this research. Our research also identified that in the context of process mining a more nuanced understanding of inconsistency in content is required by decomposing it into inconsistency of data and inconsistency of information.

Separation of data and information is well recognized in information systems and business intelligence literature. Data is often considered as the raw, structured collection of facts, whereas information is the "outcome of extraction and processes activities carried out on data, and it appears meaningful for those who receive it in a specific domain" [39]. Information can also be considered data in context [40]. While recognizing the distinction between data and information, the business intelligence domain does not specifically examine inconsistency in the two, rather it is often implied. For instance, variation in context can result in meaningless output and result in misinterpretation, even in the presence of highly accurate data [41]. The risk of misinterpretation is a key barrier to the adoption and continued use of business intelligence systems [42, 43]. Our findings reinforce the notion of inconsistency present in business intelligence literature, but provides a more nuance view including: 1) defining the specific elements of inconsistency-in-use: data, information, content, and place; 2) demonstrating the interrelated nature of these types of inconsistency and 3) identifying relationships between inconsistency-in-use and effective use.

In the process mining domain, Baier, Mendling and Weske [44] highlight the meaning of different events in a process may have different interpretations at different points in time. While the use of process mining has been advocated [45], how users use process mining systems is seldom explored, with most studies performed from a technical process mining expert's perspective [46]. Our findings highlight the importance of not taking a technology deterministic perspective when examining process mining systems. This is reflected by a participant who stated: "*if you cannot translate what you see into actionable insights then it became something that is gimmick*". As such, rich and robust theorizing from the broader information systems literature could shine light on the relationship between process mining systems and its resultant impacts. We call for researchers to further explore the intersection of information systems and process mining.

5.2 Extending the Theory of Effective Use

As previously discussed, we set out with the objective of understanding the effective use of business intelligence through the examination of process mining. In doing so, the notion of inconsistency arose. Yet, how does this notion of inconsistency contribute to the 'theory of effective use'? In Sect. 2 we mentioned effective use with its foundations in representation theory consist of three dimensions: 1) transparent interaction, 2) representational fidelity: and 3) informed action: As described below, we believe inconsistency in content and meaning has implications for representational fidelity.

Information systems are designed to represent real-world phenomenon. In this case, the process mining system should provide an accurate reflection of the pension fund processes. We observed that in some instances data was required to be extracted from multiple systems and thus each system only provided a partial account of the overarching phenomenon of interest. Integrating the data sources into a centralized data warehouse (APG referred to this as the data core) to be analyzed in an analytical process mining system, such as Celonis, provides a more complete representation. However, while necessary, this can result in inconsistencies in content and meaning. As our interview participants highlighted, data from different sources can have different underlying meanings. Moreover, the data used in the analysis is 'golden data', which means that the data is usable, its limitations are known, but it is not a completely accurate representation of the phenomenon of interest.

Adding complexity to attaining representational fidelity is the data sources used in the analysis are dependent on what the data intelligence team perceives the dashboard owner/users require. This influences the extent the representations contained in the analysis are meaningful. This is due to each team possessing knowledge and skills that are at opposing ends of a spectrum. In the case of APG, the data intelligence team has technical expertise, and the dashboard owner/user has requisite domain knowledge. These differences in knowledge can be expressed as tensions. As Pike, Bateman and Butler [47] notes "tensions represent poles of perspective that frequently work against one another, creating oppositional pulls, or tensions, that vary in degree". Tensions do not have to result in direct conflicts, rather they can be considered as the "push-pull between different poles" [48]. In this case, the data intelligence team and dashboard owners/users need to collaborate regularly in these pull-push activities to derive a shared understanding [49].

Overall, our findings demonstrate the implications that inconsistency in content and meaning have on representational fidelity, in terms of the completeness, accuracy, and meaningfulness of the representations in the system. Our findings also demonstrated that inconsistency in content and meaning (i.e., representational fidelity) can result in misinterpretations hindering actionable insights (i.e., informed action), and therefore provides initial support for the relationship between representational fidelity and informed action proposed by the theory of effective use.

6   Conclusion

In conclusion, this study sought to investigate the effective use of process mining systems. Through conducting a qualitative case study, we identified that inconsistency-in-use (i.e., inconsistency in content, data, information, meaning, and place) plays an important role in the effective use of process mining systems. In analyzing these types of inconsistencies we reveal important implications for the theory of effective use. This research contributes both to the information systems and process mining domains and is one of the first attempts to bridge these two areas together.

Our study is limited as we only investigate a single case in the early stages of process mining adoption. Further, the case design was scoped to the process mining tool, Celonis. As such, broad canvasing statements related to generalizability cannot be made. Nevertheless, the case study provides indicators of how organizations may adopt process mining in effective ways. We encourage others to perform case studies of the adoption of other process mining tools within different settings. In addition, future research should also seek to compare how the effective use of process mining differs to other types of business intelligence systems. We also encourage future research efforts to employ different methodological approaches, for instance experimental and longitudinal survey designs could provide insights into causality of the relationships.

With process mining and other business intelligence systems shifting to self-service modes, the potential for ineffective use and misinterpretations is heightened. Failure to understand this intersection could therefore have detrimental effects on practice hampering the proliferation of process mining at the coalface. Future examination of the effective use of process mining system will, therefore, prove highly desirable to practice.

References

1. Chen, H., Chiang, R.H., Storey, V.C.: Business intelligence and analytics: from big data to big impact. MIS Q. **36**(1), 1165–1188 (2012)
2. Trieu, V.-H.: Getting value from business intelligence systems: a review and research agenda. Decis. Support Syst. **93**, 111–124 (2017)
3. van der Aalst, W., et al.: Process mining manifesto. In: Daniel, F., Barkaoui, K., Dustdar, S. (eds.) BPM 2011. LNBIP, vol. 99, pp. 169–194. Springer, Heidelberg (2012). https://doi.org/10.1007/978-3-642-28108-2_19
4. Van der Aalst, W.: Data Science in Action. Process Mining, Springer Heidelberg, pp. 3–23 (2016). https://doi.org/10.1007/978-3-662-49851-4_1
5. Rojas, E., Munoz-Gama, J., Sepulveda, M., Capurro, D.: Process mining in healthcare: a literature review. J. Biomed. Inform. **61**, 224–236 (2016)
6. Buijs, J.C., Bergmans, R.F., El Hasnaoui, R.: Customer journey analysis at a financial services provider using self service and data hub concepts. In: International Conference on Business Process Management (Industry Forum), pp. 25–36 (2019)
7. Wynn, M.T., et al.: Grounding process data analytics in domain knowledge: a mixed-method approach to identifying best practice. In: Hildebrandt, T., van Dongen, B.F., Röglinger, M., Mendling, J. (eds.) BPM 2019. LNBIP, vol. 360, pp. 163–179. Springer, Cham (2019). https://doi.org/10.1007/978-3-030-26643-1_10
8. Van der Aalst, W., Damiani, E.: Processes meet big data: connecting data science with process science. IEEE Trans. Serv. Comput. **8**, 810–819 (2015)

9. Burton-Jones, A., Grange, C.: From use to effective use: a representation theory perspective. Inf. Syst. Res. **24**, 632–658 (2013)
10. Surbakti, F.P.S., Wang, W., Indulska, M., Sadiq, S.: Factors influencing effective use of big data: a research framework. Inf. Manag. **57**, 103146 (2020)
11. Idoine, C.: How to Enable Self-Service Analytics. Gartner (2019, online)
12. Glaser, B.: Theoretical Sensitivity: Advances in the Methodology of Grounded Theory. Sociology Press, San Francisco (1978)
13. Orlikowski, W.J.: Using technology and constituting structures: a practice lens for studying technology in organizations. Organ. Sci. **11**, 404–428 (2000)
14. Burton-Jones, A., Stein, M.-K., Mishra, A.: MISQ research curation on IS use. MIS Q., 24 (2017)
15. Burton-Jones, A., Straub, D.W., Jr.: Reconceptualizing system usage: an approach and empirical test. Inf. Syst. Res. **17**, 228–246 (2006)
16. Wand, Y., Weber, R.: On the deep structure of information systems. Inf. Syst. J. **5**, 203–223 (1995)
17. Burton-Jones, A., Volkoff, O.: How can we develop contextualized theories of effective use? A demonstration in the context of community-care electronic health records. Inf. Syst. Res. **28**, 468–489 (2017)
18. Eden, R., Fielt, E., Murphy, G.: Advancing the theory of effective use through operationalization. In: European Conference of Information Systems, Marrakesh, Morocco (2020)
19. Eden, R., Burton-Jones, A.: Beyond effective use: a journey to understand inconsistencies in use. In: International Conference on Information Systems, San Francisco, USA (2018)
20. Ain, N., Vaia, G., DeLone, W.H., Waheed, M.: Two decades of research on business intelligence system adoption, utilization and success–a systematic literature review. Decis. Support Syst. **125**, 113113 (2019)
21. Visinescu, L.L., Jones, M.C., Sidorova, A.: Improving decision quality: the role of business intelligence. J. Comput. Inf. Syst. **57**, 58–66 (2017)
22. Han, Y.-M., Shen, C.-S., Farn, C.-K.: Determinants of continued usage of pervasive business intelligence systems. Inf. Dev. **32**, 424–439 (2016)
23. Popovič, A.: If we implement it, will they come? User resistance in postacceptance usage behaviour within a business intelligence systems context. Econ. Res.-Ekonomska istraživanja **30**, 911–921 (2017)
24. Brockmann, T., Stieglitz, S., Kmieciak, J., Diederich, S.: User acceptance of mobile business intelligence services. In: 15th International Conference on Network-Based Information Systems, Melbourne, pp. 861–866. IEEE (2012)
25. Grublješič, T., Jaklič, J.: Conceptualization of the business intelligence extended use model. J. Comput. Inf. Syst. **55**, 72–82 (2015)
26. Eden, R., Akhlaghpour, S., Spee, P., Staib, A., Sullivan, C., Burton-Jones, A.: Unpacking the complexity of consistency: Insights from a grounded theory study of the effective use of electronic medical records. In: 51st Hawaii International Conference on System Sciences (2018)
27. Negash, S., Gray, P.: Business Intelligence. Handbook on Decision Support Systems 2. Springer, Heidelberg, pp. 175–193 (2008). https://doi.org/10.1007/978-3-540-48716-6_9
28. Lennerholt, C., Van Laere, J., Söderström, E.: User-related challenges of self-service business intelligence. Inf. Syst. Manag., 1–15 (2020)
29. Reinkemeyer, L.: Process Mining in Action. Springer Cham (2020). https://doi.org/10.1007/978-3-030-40172-6_1
30. Thiede, M., Fuerstenau, D., Barquet, A.P.B.: How is process mining technology used by organizations? A stystematic literature review of empirical sudies. Bus. Process. Manag. J. **24**, 900–922 (2018)

31. Dakic, D., Stefanovic, D., Cosic, I., Lolic, T., Medojevic, M.: Business process mining application: a literature review. In: Annals of DAAAM & Proceedings, vol. 29, (2018)
32. Ailenei, I., Rozinat, A., Eckert, A., van der Aalst, W.M.P.: Definition and validation of process mining use cases. In: Daniel, F., Barkaoui, K., Dustdar, S. (eds.) BPM 2011. LNBIP, vol. 99, pp. 75–86. Springer, Heidelberg (2012). https://doi.org/10.1007/978-3-642-28108-2_7
33. Fernandez, W.: The grounded theory method and case study data in IS research: issue and design. In: Information Systems Foundations Workshop: Constructing and Criticising, vol. 1, pp. 43–59 (2004)
34. Eisenhardt, K.M.: Building theories from case study research. Acad. Manag. Rev. **14**, 532–550 (1989)
35. Urquhart, C., Lehmann, H., Myers, M.D.: Putting the 'theory' back into grounded theory: guidelines for grounded theory studies in information systems. Inf. Syst. J. **20**, 357–381 (2010)
36. Flick, U.: An Introduction to Qualitative Research. Sage, Thousand Oaks (2014)
37. Glaser, B.G.: Doing Grounded Theory: Issues and Discussions. Sociology Press, Mill Valley (1998)
38. Saldaña, J.: The Coding Manual for Qualitative Researchers. Sage, Thousand Oaks (2015)
39. Vercellis, C.: Business Intelligence: Data Mining and Optimization for Decision Making. Wiley Online Library (2009)
40. Erickson, S., Rothberg, H.: Big data and knowledge management: establishing a conceptual foundation. Lead. Issues Knowl. Manag. **2**, 204 (2015)
41. Kimble, C., Milolidakis, G.: Big data and business intelligence: debunking the myths. Glob. Bus. Organ. Excell. **35**, 23–34 (2015)
42. Khan, A.M.A., Amin, N., Lambrou, N.: Drivers and barriers to business intelligence adoption: a case of Pakistan. In: European and Mediterranean Conference on Information Systems, Abu Dhabi, UAE, pp. 1–23 (2010)
43. Economist Intelligence Unit: Business intelligence: putting enterprise data to work. The Economist (2007)
44. Baier, T., Mendling, J., Weske, M.: Bridging abstraction layers in process mining. Inf. Syst. **46**, 123–139 (2014)
45. Martin, N., Depaire, B., Caris, A.: The use of process mining in a business process simulation context: overview and challenges. In: 2014 IEEE Symposium on Computational Intelligence and Data Mining (CIDM), pp. 381–388 (2014)
46. Emamjome, F., Andrews, R., ter Hofstede, A.H.M.: A case study lens on process mining in practice. In: Panetto, H., Debruyne, C., Hepp, M., Lewis, D., Ardagna, C.A., Meersman, R. (eds.) OTM 2019. LNCS, vol. 11877, pp. 127–145. Springer, Cham (2019). https://doi.org/10.1007/978-3-030-33246-4_8
47. Pike, J.C., Bateman, P.J., Butler, B.: Dialectic tensions of information quality: social networking sites and hiring. J. Comput.-Mediated Commun. **19**, 56–77 (2013)
48. Stein, M., Lim, E.: Tensions to frictions? Exploring sources of ineffectiveness in multi-level IT use. In: International Conference on Information Systems, Auckland, NZ (2014)
49. Arias, E., Eden, H., Fischer, G., Gorman, A., Scharff, E.: Transcending the individual human mind—creating shared understanding through collaborative design. ACM Trans. Comput.-Human Interact. (TOCHI) **7**, 84–113 (2000)

Concept Drift and Anomaly Detection from Event Logs

A Robust and Accurate Approach to Detect Process Drifts from Event Streams

Yang Lu$^{(\boxtimes)}$ (iD), Qifan Chen (iD), and Simon Poon (iD)

School of Computer Science, The University of Sydney, Sydney, NSW 2006, Australia
{yalu8986,qche8411}@uni.sydney.edu.au, simon.poon@sydney.edu.au

Abstract. Business processes are bound to evolve as a form of adaption to changes, and such changes are referred as process drifts. Current process drift detection methods perform well on clean event log data, but the performance can be tremendously affected by noise. A good process drift detection method should be accurate, fast, and robust to noise. In this paper, we propose an offline process drift detection method which identifies each newly observed behaviour as a candidate drift point and checks if the new behaviour can signify significant changes to the original process behaviours. In addition, a bidirectional search method is proposed to accurately locate both the adding and removing of behaviours. The proposed method can accurately detect drift points from event logs and is robust to noise. Both artificial and real-life event logs are used to evaluate our method. Results show that our method can consistently report accurate process drift time while maintaining a reasonably fast detection speed.

Keywords: Process science · Data science · Process mining · Concept drift detection

1 Introduction

Business processes are continuously evolving in order to adapt to changes. Changes are often responses to different factors which can be planned or unexpected. For example, a planned change can be caused by the introduction of a new regulation, and an unexpected change can be caused by an emergency (e.g. the COVID-19 outbreak). In the field of process science, such changes are called process drifts.

It has been argued that assuming a process model to be stable is unrealistic [1]. It is important for us to detect process drifts as accurately as possible. On the one hand, unexpected changes can cause losses to organizations. Detecting such drifts can help us make appropriate responses to changes. On the other hand, most current algorithms to discover process models assume the process to be in a steady-state and ignore process drifts [3]. Detecting and understanding process drifts can help us to understand the evolving nature of processes.

© Springer Nature Switzerland AG 2021
A. Polyvyanyy et al. (Eds.): BPM 2021, LNCS 12875, pp. 383–399, 2021.
https://doi.org/10.1007/978-3-030-85469-0_24

Statistically, a process drift point is a time point when there is a significant difference among the process behaviours before and after the drift point [5,11,22]. Various process drift detection methods have been proposed in the last decade [1,4–14,16–19,22]. However, many of these methods assume the input event log data to be clean, and their abilities to handle noise can vary. In [3], noise is defined as "the event log contains rare and infrequent behaviours not representative the typical behaviour of the process". Such behaviours are infrequent and cannot cause a significant change to the process behaviours. For example, if an activity is skipped only once in one process execution record, it is more likely to be an infrequent behaviour instead of a process change. However, noise is known to have big impacts on process drift detection accuracy.

In this paper, we consider a process drift as either the adding or removing of behaviours which can signify significant changes to the behaviours of the original process. We focus on offline process drift detection from the control-flow perspective. We propose an event-stream based process drift detection method which is accurate, robust to noise and reasonably fast. When a new behaviour is observed in the event log, we treat it as a candidate drift point and verify if it can signify significant changes to the current process through statistical tests. Both artificial and real-life event logs are used to evaluate the method.

The rest of this paper is structured as follows: Sect. 2 is a literature review of related work. Section 3 introduces formal definitions of some terms. Section 4 introduces the proposed method. The evaluation results are presented in Sect. 5 and Sect. 6. We finally conclude the paper in Sect. 7.

2   Background

2.1   Detecting Process Drifts by Statistical Tests

A general approach to detect process drifts is to use a sliding window to obtain two consecutive samples in the event log, naming as reference and detection windows. The two windows are then moving through the event log trace by trace or event by event. Then samples within each window are transformed into a set of features, and if statistical hypothesis tests show that there is a significant difference before/after a certain time point among these features, a drift is reported.

Early approaches such as [1,19] extract features to represent each sample of the event log. Then statistical hypothesis tests are applied to detect process drifts among feature vectors. Based on [1,7] applies adaptive window approaches to automatically adjust window sizes. Those methods require users to select features to be used, which require background knowledge about the drifts in input event logs.

The ProDrift run-based method [5,22] transforms each trace into a partial-order run which is a graph representation of a trace eliminating the order between parallel events. Then chi-square tests are applied to detect if there are any significant changes among the distribution of partial-order runs between two consecutive windows. The method is fully automated with the capability to categorize certain drift types. In addition, [5,22] also aim at eliminating the impact of noise by performing a number of consecutive tests. However, since each trace is only counted once in each window, the samples used for statistical tests are relatively small, returning unreliable results especially when input logs have high variability (e.g. when the event log contains noise). The ProDrift event-based method [11] improves [22] by treating event logs as event streams and using the count of alpha+ relations[1] as features for statistical tests. On the one hand, process drifts during the execution of traces can be detected. On the other hand, since the number of alpha+ relations is much larger than traces in each window, the statistical tests in [11] are more reliable. In addition, the ProDrift event-based method [11] can also filter out infrequent behaviours and can work both in online and offline settings. It is also the basis of the new approach to characterize process drifts in [15]. The ProDrift event-based method [11] requires parameters such as noise filtering thresholds from users.

When using statistical tests to detect process drifts in event logs, the distances between the actual process drift points and the reported drift points are relatively longer, resulting in lower detection accuracy.

2.2   Other Process Drift Detection Methods

To improve detection accuracy, the TPCDD method [4] and the LCDD method [14] are proposed. Both methods can achieve high accuracy. The TPCDD method [4] firstly transforms the whole event log into a relation matrix, and whenever a new behaviour is detected or an existing behaviour is removed, if it lasts for a certain period, a new drift point is reported. The LCDD method [14] firstly finds a time window where the sub-log within the window is locally complete. Then whenever a new behaviour is observed or an existing behaviour is removed, a drift point is reported. Although these two methods can return highly accurate results on artificial logs, they are very sensitive to noise.

Other methods are also proposed to detect process drift points. [18] detects process drifts based on the change of distances between each pair of activities. Loops and parallel behaviours are ignored, resulting in possible failures. [17] abstracts initial traces into a polyhedron and checks if subsequent traces are within the polyhedron, a drift is detected if a trace is outside the polyhedron. [17] is the first concept drift detection method which can be used in online settings, but it suffers from long execution time.

Instead of focusing on detection accuracy, some methods focus more on understanding how the process model evolved over time. [6] mines process models for different time periods and compares graph matrices of different models. [8,13] mine models for the first period of time and perform conformance check on each new trace. A drift point is reported if there is a significant change on the conformance checking results. [16] applies Declare miners to represent the process, and

---

[1] Alpha+ relations define a set of relations between activities which are conflict, concurrency, causality, length-one loop and length-two loop. For their formal definitions, please refer to [20].

a comprehensive visualisation is provided to understand process drifts. These methods provide comprehensive analyses of process drifts, but usually suffer from relatively longer execution time and lower accuracy.

Some methods also focus on process drifts from other perspectives other than the control-flow perspective. For example, [9] detects process drifts from the data value perspective (e.g. the change of activity attribute values), [10] applies the earth mover's distance to detect time and control-flow drifts together (e.g. the change of activity execution time).

In summary, existing methods which are highly accurate are sensitive to noise in event logs. Methods which are capable of handling noise could improve their accuracy. A new method which requires fewer user-inputs and can produce highly accurate results while properly handling noise is needed in this field.

3   Preliminaries

Definition 1. (Process drift point [5,11,22]). *A process drift point is a time point when there is a statistically significant difference among the observed process behaviours before and after the time point.*

Definition 2. (Event log, Trace, Activity, Event). *An event log L is a multiset of traces where each trace t_i is a sequence of events in a set E, i.e. $E = \{e_1, e_2, ..., e_n\}$, and each event corresponds to a single activity A.*

Definition 3. (Directly-follows relation). *Let L be an event log of a process model N, let A, B be two activities in L. Then there is a directly-follows relation from A to B, denoted as $A >_L B$, if there exists a trace $t \in L$ where $t =< ......, A, B, ... >$.*

4   Concept Drift Detection

Figure 1 shows an overview of our proposed method. Our method firstly converts the input event log into a stream of events where events are indexed and ordered by their timestamps. Then a reference window is built and continuously moves through the event stream. A sub-log is built including all events within the reference window. Each time the reference window moves, the sub-log is updated and the event immediately follows the reference window is peeked. If the peeked event brings a new behaviour which cannot be observed in the sub-log corresponding to the reference window, we treat it as a candidate drift point and check if the new behaviour can signify a significant difference to the original behaviours of the process through statistical tests. If so, a drift point is reported.

4.1   Selection of Features

The first step of designing a process drift detection method is to find a feature which can represent the behaviours of the process, and changes of such features should reflect changes in process control-flow structures. As the proposed

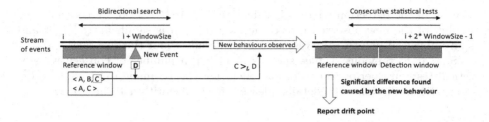

Fig. 1. Overview of the proposed method

method relies on a single event to determine possible process drifts, we decide to use directly-follows relations as features to represent process behaviours for two reasons: 1) Most current process discovery algorithms are based on directly-follows relations [3], changes in process control-flow structures are highly likely to result in changes of directly-follows relations. 2) By peeking one event after the reference window, a directly-follows relation could be obtained. It is worth mentioning that alpha+ relations used by [11] are not suitable for our method as an alpha+ relation cannot be determined by a single peeked event.

4.2 Validation of Candidate Drift Points

Observing a new directly-follows relation means a possible process drift is detected. However, it could also be noise inside the event log. Whenever a new directly-follows relation is observed, we treat it as a candidate drift point. Statistically, a process drift point should be treated as a time point t, and there is a significant difference between process behaviours before and after t [5,11,22]. Although noise can bring new observed directly-follows relations in event logs, significant changes to the process behaviours will not be signified.

To confirm if a candidate drift point is an actual drift point, statistical tests are applied to check if a significant difference is caused. Firstly, a detection window is built after the reference window, and a contingency matrix is built to report the frequencies of each type of directly-follows relations in both the reference and detection windows. Then the G-test of independence[2] [23] is applied and a P-value is returned. If the P-value is less than a certain threshold, which is typically 0.05, we conclude there is a significant difference between process behaviours before and after the candidate drift point.

If the G-test of independence shows there is a significant difference between process behaviours before and after a candidate drift point, it is likely to be an actual drift point. However, if the candidate drift point is close to an actual drift point, the low P-value could be caused by other directly-follows relations instead of the new observed one.

To check if the new observed directly-follows relation contributes to the low P-value, the adjusted standardized residual (ASR) of the new directly-follows

---

[2] The G-test of independence is a non-parametric statistical hypothesis test.

relation in the detection window is calculated. If $ASR > 1.96$, we conclude the number of the new observed directly-follows relation is significantly larger and is an influential point to the test score. For details about this, we refer to [21].

Similar to previous studies such as [5,11,22], a number of consecutive statistical tests are performed before a conclusion can be made to avoid sporadic stochastic oscillations. For details, please refer to Algorithm 1, lines 9–20.

4.3   Bidirectional Searches

A change in process models can cause both the adding and removing of directly-follows relations. Detecting an added directly-follows relation can be simply done by checking if the newly observed directly-follows relation exists in the reference window. However, the removing of directly-follows relations cannot be detected by peeking one event immediately after the reference window. A possible solution is to build a detection window immediately after the reference window and checks if any directly-follows relations are removed. Such a method can affect detection accuracy. Figure 2 shows an example process drift. Suppose model 1 is shifted into model 2 at time t. $E >_L F$ and $C >_L D$ will no longer be observed after t. However, suppose the last appearance of $E >_L F$ is at t_1 which is earlier than t, t_1 could be treated as the drift point by mistake, reducing the detection accuracy.

To solve the problem, we perform both forward and backward searches on the event stream to detect process drifts. When performing backward searches, the removing of directly-follows relations is shown as the adding of directly-follows relations. There are two advantages of performing bidirectional searches: 1) When a process drift causes both adding and removing of directly-follows relations, if the drift is missed by one search, there is one more chance for it to be detected in another search. 2) the accuracy of detection can be improved.

It is worth mentioning that performing bidirectional searches will not double the amount of time required to detect process drifts. Each time a G-test is performed, its resulting P-value will be stored and if another G-test is required at the same position, the P-value can be retrieved within constant time. Furthermore, each time when a G-test is performed, the ASR of each directly-follows relation can also be computed and stored. As a result, no duplicate statistical tests will be performed. We show that our algorithm is efficient to detect process drifts in Sect. 5 and Sect. 6.

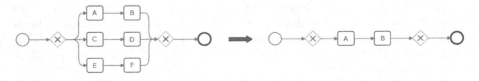

Fig. 2. An example process drift from model 1 (left) to model 2 (right)

4.4   The Framework of the Proposed Method

Finally, we present the forward detection method in Algorithm 1. Since the same approach applies to the backward detection but in a reverse direction, we do not present it separately. Lines 1–8 build a reference window, peek the next event and see if a new directly-follows relation is found (Sect. 4.1). Whenever a new directly-follows relation is observed, the new event is treated as a candidate process drift point. Lines 9–25 perform statistical tests to confirm if a candidate process drift point is an actual drift point (Sect. 4.2).

When a Noise Is Close to the Real Process Drift Point. A challenge to the proposed method is when a new directly-follows relation is observed which is noise but is close to the actual process drift point. Although the problem can be solved by calculating ASRs, it fails to solve the case when the noisy directly-follows relation is the same as one of the added directly-follows relations after the actual drift point. For example, suppose directly-follows relations $A >_L B$ and $C >_L D$ are added to the process after a process drift at time t, if a noisy directly-follows relation $A >_L B$ is observed at time t_0 which is earlier than t, t_0 could be treated as a drift point by mistake. To overcome this issue, two measures are taken: 1) When performing a number of consecutive tests, we not only move the windows forward but also move the windows backward (Algorithm 1, lines 9–20). 2) By moving the window backward, the noisy $A >_L B$ could be differentiated. However, since it is close to the real process drift point, having $A >_L B$ in the reference window can avoid $A >_L B$ from being observed as a new behaviour when arriving at the real drift point. As a result, if a new observed directly-follows relation fails statistical tests, we delete it from the reference window (Algorithm 1, line 28).

5   Evaluation on Synthetic Data

The proposed method is implemented as a stand-alone Java application. All the code, data and results are publicly-available[3].

5.1   Evaluation Design

We firstly collect the 72 artificial event logs from [22] which are generated from an artificial process model containing 1 start event, 3 end events, 8 gateways and 15 activities. [22] systemically alters the base model by 12 simple patterns shown in Table 1. Each simple change pattern can be categorized as Insertion (I), Resequentialization (R) and Optionalization (O). Then the base model is also altered according to 6 composite change patterns (RIO, ROI, IOR, IRO, OIR, ORI). For each change pattern, 4 logs with 2500, 5000, 7500, 10000 traces are

---

[3] https://github.com/bearlu1996/ProcessDrifts.

Algorithm 1: Forward Detection

Input: eventStream, windowSize, numOfConsecutiveTests
1 refStartPosition $\leftarrow$ 0
   // The index of the first event in the reference window
2 refSubLog $\leftarrow$ getSubLog(eventStream, windowSize, refStartPosition)
3 refDfRelations $\leftarrow$ getDfRelations(refSubLog)
   // The directly-follows relations of the sub-log
4 **while** $refStartPosition + 2 \cdot windowSize + numOfConsecutiveTests <$ $eventStreamSize$ **do**
5 | e $\leftarrow$ getNewEvent()
   | // Peek the first event immediately after the reference window
6 | $>_e \leftarrow getNewDfRelation(e, refSubLog)$
   | // Get the new directly-follows relation brought by e
7 | numOfSatisfiedTests $\leftarrow$ 0
8 | **if** $>_e \neq null\ AND\ >_e \notin refDfRelations$ **then**
   | | // A candidate drift point is found
9 | | **for** $i \leftarrow 0$ **to** $2 \cdot numOfConsecutiveTests$ **do**
10 | | | refTestSubLog $\leftarrow$ Sub-log for window starting with event refStartPosition - numOfConsecutiveTests + i
11 | | | decTestSubLog $\leftarrow$ Sub-log for window starting with event refStartPosition - numOfConsecutiveTests + windowSize + i
12 | | | Compute Contigency matrix based on the frequency of directly-follows relations in refTestSubLog and decTestSubLog
13 | | | Perform G-test on the matrix and get pValue
14 | | | **if** $pValue$ *is smaller than the threshold* **then**
15 | | | | Compute ASR for $>_e$
16 | | | | **if** ASR *is significant* **then**
17 | | | | | numOfSatisfiedTests ++
18 | | | | **end**
19 | | | **end**
20 | | **end**
21 | **end**
22 | **if** $numOfSatisfiedTests = 2 \cdot numOfConsecutiveTests$ **then**
23 | | Report drift point e
24 | | RefStartPosition $\leftarrow$ index of e
25 | | Update refSubLog and refDfRelations
   | | // Move the beginning of the reference window to the new detected change point
26 | **else**
27 | | **if** $>_e \neq null\ AND\ >_e \notin refSubLog$ **then**
28 | | | Remove $>_e$ from refDfRelations
29 | | **end**
30 | | RefStartPosition ++
31 | | Update refSubLog and refDfRelations
   | | // Move the reference window by one event
32 | **end**
33 **end**

---

generated with a sudden process drift after every 10% of traces[4]. The synthetic data set has also been used to evaluate drift detection algorithms in [5,14].

Since branching frequency changes cannot be reflected on changes of directly-follows relations, it cannot be detected by our proposed method. We exclude its corresponding four event logs from our evaluation. Then for each event log, we insert noise by randomly adding and removing 10%, 20% and 30% of events. To avoid biases caused by randomly generated noise, we generate 10 logs for each log at each noise level and take the average results in the following parts. In total, we evaluate our algorithm on 4148 synthetic event logs[5] including logs without noise. It has to be noted that inserting noise will not change the trace indexes of process drifts[6].

In this section, when two drift points are reported by searches from different directions, and the distance between them is smaller than the window size, we only take the point with a smaller index.

Finally, since the drifts in the artificial event logs are inter-trace drifts (i.e. drifts occur between complete trace executions), we stream the events in the order from the first event in the first trace to the last event in the last trace[7] in both our method and the baseline so that these drifts can also be detected by event-stream based algorithms. In this section, trace ids are used to represent the location of all process drifts[8].

Table 1. Simple control-flow change patterns.

Code	Simple Change Pattern	Category
re	Add/remove fragment	I
cf	Make two fragments conditional/sequential	R
lp	Make fragment loopable/non-loopable	O
pl	Make two fragments parallel/sequential	R
cb	Make fragment skippable/non-skippable	O
cm	Move fragment into/out of conditional branch	I
cd	Synchronize two fragments	R
cp	Duplicate fragment	I
pm	Move fragment into/out of parallel branch	I
rp	Substitute fragment	I
sw	Swap two fragments	I
fr	Change branching frequency	O

Evaluation Metrics. Standard f-score metric for evaluating process drifts detection approaches is used in our evaluation [4,14] where $precision = TP/(TP + FP), recall = TP/(TP + FN), f - score = 2 * precision *$

---

[4] 9 drift points are included in each log.

[5] $4148 = 68 \times 6 \times 10 + 68$.

[6] We do not add/remove traces into/from the event logs.

[7] For example, event 0 refers to the 1st event in the 1st trace, event 1 refers to the 2nd event in the 1st trace ... the last event refers to the last event in the last trace.

[8] When an event id is reported, we refer to the id of its corresponding trace.

$recall/(precision + recall)$. TP refers to true positive, FN refers to false negative, and FP refers to false positive. To describe the three variables, an error tolerance (ET) is defined. A TP is detected if a change point t is detected where the actual drift point is within the integer interval [t - ET, t + ET]. A FP is detected if a change point t is detected and there is not an actual drift point within the integer interval [t - ET, t + ET]. A FN is detected if an actual process drift exists in the integer interval [t - ET, t + ET] where no change points are detected.

Baseline. Among several existing methods, the ProDrift event-based method [11] seem to be more capable in handling noise than other popular methods such as [4,5,14,22]. As suggested by its documentation, we change the noise filtering threshold to 0 and drift sensitivity to "very high" for noise-free logs, and we use its default settings for all other logs (adaptive window is enabled for all tests).

5.2   Evaluation on Different Parameter Settings

In the first experiment, we evaluate the impact of window sizes and the number of consecutive tests on the detection results. We test a total of 6 different window sizes ranging from 500 to 3000, and we combine them with 4 different number of consecutive tests, ranging from windowSize/5 to windowSize/2. For each of the 24 settings, we run all the synthetic event logs and calculate the average f-scores. Figure 3 shows the average f-scores when the error tolerance is set to 10.

Overall, the impacts of the number of consecutive tests to f-scores are small. When the number of consecutive tests is set to be WindowSize/2, the accuracy is slightly higher and more consistent in most cases unless a small window size is set. We decide to set the number of consecutive tests to WindowSize/2 as the default setting for our method.

With the number of consecutive tests being empirically set, the only user input required is the windowSize, When logs of size 2.5k are included (Fig. 3 left), the average f-Scores drops after the window size of 1000 since the window size becomes larger than the distance between two consecutive process drift points. We then remove logs of size 2.5k from the calculation (Fig. 3 right), results show that f-Scores are less sensitive to the choice of window sizes. Although a larger sample can result in more reliable statistical test results, having a larger window size could increase the chance of treating a new observed noisy directly-follows relation as a real drift point when it is close to the actual drift point, and the noisy directly-follows relation is the same as one of the added directly-follows relations after the drift point (Sect. 4.4). It is worth mentioning that the average f-score of the baseline is only 0.03 when ET = 10, which is much lower than our method. We also calculate average f-scores when ET = 50 and obtain similar observations.

It is also noticed that the choice of window sizes is related to the distance between two consecutive process drifts. For most current window-based process drift detection approaches, the accuracy drops when the window size is larger than the minimal distance between two consecutive drifts, or the window size is too small that event logs within windows are incomplete even if adaptive window approaches are implemented. In the remaining text, we report the results with the number of consecutive tests = WindowSize/2. In Sect. 5.3 and 5.4, we set the window size of our method to 1500.

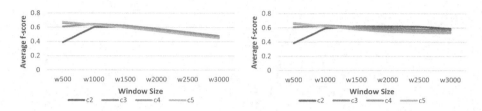

Fig. 3. Average f-scores (ET = 10) under different settings including logs of size 2.5k (left) and excluding logs of size 2.5k (right). Each color represents a setting of number of consecutive tests. For example, c2 means WindowSize/2 consecutive tests required in one direction (Sect. 4.4).

5.3   Comparing with the Baseline on Different Change Patterns

In the second experiment, the accuracy of our proposed method and the baseline is compared for each change pattern and under different noise levels.

We firstly run both methods on the 68 noise-free event logs, and the results are presented in Fig. 4 where each f-score is averaged over 4 logs with different sizes. When ET = 50, our method achieves an average f-score of 0.88 while the baseline achieves 0.58. When ET = 10, our average f-score achieves 0.85, which is close to the results when ET = 50. However, the baseline drops to 0.21, which means our method is more accurate.

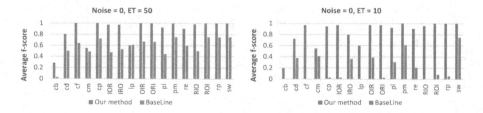

Fig. 4. Average f-scores per change pattern for noise-free logs comparing to the baseline with ET = 50 and 10.

Figure 5 shows the average f-scores for each change pattern under different noise levels when ET = 50 and ET = 10 where each f-score is averaged over

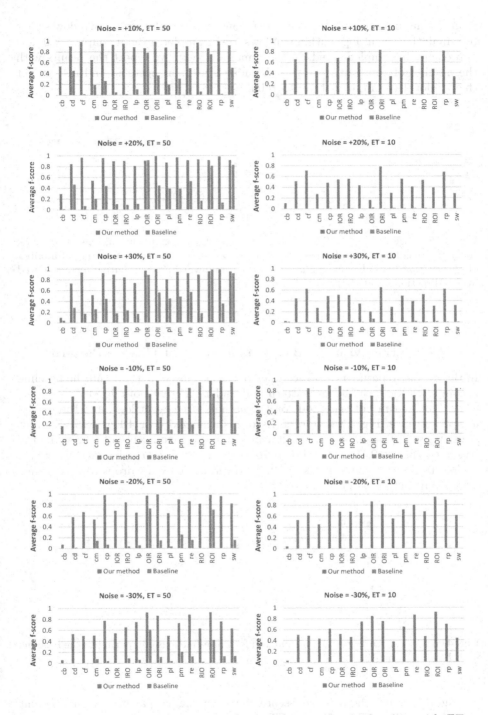

Fig. 5. Average f-scores per change pattern comparing to the baseline with ET = 50 and 10. For noise levels, + refers to inserting activities, and − refers to removing activities.

40 logs. When ET = 50, our method achieves an average f-score[9] of 0.8 and an average of 0.57 when ET = 10. Comparing to the baseline, our method wins in almost all cases. When noise is inserted into the log, the baseline can achieve satisfied f-scores for a few change patterns when ET = 50. However, when ET = 10, the f-scores of the baseline drops dramatically, of which the f-scores are 0 in most cases.

It is also interesting to find that our method performs better when removing events from the event log. The main reason is that when inserting events into logs, the probability that a noisy directly-follows relation is inserted before a drift point which is the same as one of the added directly-follows relation after the drift point is higher (Sect. 4.4). Thus, our method could report process drifts earlier than the actual drift points, causing lower f-scores when ET is small. We find that this is the biggest factor affecting the results.

Finally, we also calculate the average precision among both methods when ET = 50. Our method achieves an average precision of 0.97 among all event logs while the precision of the baseline is only 0.3. A high precision indicates that our method will not return too many results which are not actual process drifts or mistakenly treat infrequent behaviours as process drift points, saving the time it takes to validate each drift point. In conclusion, our method is more accurate and reliable than the baseline for both event logs with or without noise.

5.4   Execution Time

In the last experiment, we run both our method and the baseline on all artificial logs and record their execution time. The platform is equipped with Intel i7-9700 (8 cores, 8 threads) and 32 GB RAM, running Windows 10 (64 bit) with a heap space of 16 GB. Among the 4148 event logs, our method takes 0.03 ms (min 0.01 ms, max 0.13 ms) for each event on average while the baseline takes 0.1 ms (min 0.05 ms, max 0.26 ms) where average execution time for each event = total execution time/number of events. The results indicate that our method can detect process drifts efficiently and can be potentially applied in online settings.

6   Evaluation on Real-Life Data

We evaluate our algorithm on the BPI Challenge 2020 (BPIC2020) data-sets[10]. The BPIC 2020 data-sets collect a total of five event logs of travel reimbursement processes at Eindhoven University of Technology (TU/e) from 2017 to 2018, and each log corresponds to one type of request types. Depending on the specific request type, employees can usually submit three types of documents which are travel declarations, travel permits and payment requests (Some event logs may not contain all document types). As described in the documentation, all documents follow a similar workflow, and the processes in 2017 and 2018 are

---

[9] Among all the logs with noise.
[10] https://icpmconference.org/2020/bpi-challenge/.

different since 2017 is a pilot year. The information suggests that there is a potential process drift for the five logs sometime between the end of 2017 and the beginning of 2018.

We run our method on all five event logs without applying any noise filtering approaches. The description of each event log, window size used for drift detection, total execution time[11] and detection results are presented in Table 2.

Table 2. Process drifts detection results on BPIC2020 data-sets.

Log	Traces	Events	Window Size	Time	Drift Points Detected Event ID (Event Time)
Requests for Payment	6,886	36,796	2,000	1.43s	Forward: 4948(2018-01-06 20:00:55) Backward: 4878(2017-12-22 02:56:06)
Domestic Declarations	10,500	56,437	2,000	1.68s	Forward: 9948(2018-01-06 19:42:04) Backward: 9876(2017-12-22 22:07:12)
Prepaid Travel Cost	2,099	18,246	1,500	1.3s	Forward: 2369(2018-01-07 02:22:19) Backward: 2362(2017-12-19 19:22:00)
International Declarations	6,449	72,151	2,000	6.63s	Forward: 12603(2018-01-06 21:13:26) Backward: 12426(2017-12-22 03:11:38)
Travel Permits	7,065	86,581	2,000	7.79s	Forward: 13749(2018-01-06 21:13:26) Backward: 13630(2017-12-22 03:11:38)

As shown in Table 2, the time for drift points is similar among the five logs. For each event log, the forward detection finds a drift point at the beginning of 2018 (new behaviours added), and the backward detection finds a drift at the end of 2017 (old behaviours removed). Besides, the number of events between the two drift points for each log is small (Although there is a relatively long time interval between the two drift points, we believe this is caused by the Christmas vacation). The results indicate that there is a process drift in each log sometime between the two detected drift points (at the end of 2017 or beginning of 2018) which involves both adding and removing of behaviours. The results conform to the documentation of the data-sets.

To further validate the results, we cut each event log into two sub-logs using the results of backward defections. We observe similar significant changes to all the five logs. Before the process drift, when a document is submitted, it can be sent to "pre-approvers" or supervisors for approval. After the process drift, the submission will be sent to the administration for approval, and if approved by the administration, it will be forwarded to the supervisor or budget owner for further steps. Figure 6 shows the process drift for the Domestic Declarations log.

Finally, it is worth mentioning that our method is efficient to detect process drifts. The time it takes to detect process drifts among all the five logs is within 10 s while three of the logs are completed within 2 s.

---

[11] The time includes converting the event log into event stream, forward detection and backward detection. The platform is the same as Sect. 5.4.

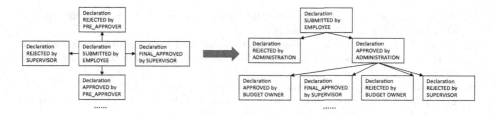

Fig. 6. Simple directly-follows graphs showing the process before (2017) and after (2018) the drift in the Domestic Declarations log.

7   Conclusion

In this paper, we propose a new process drift detection method which can accurately locate the process drift points. If a valid drift can be identified, subsequent comparative analysis can be performed for process improvement. In addition, accurate process drift detection results can also be used as input for process drift characterization methods such as [2,15] to generate more accurate results.

Different from previous work, our method does not rely on statistical tests to detect process drifts but applying statistical tests to differentiate between real process drift points and noise. The advantages of our method are as follows: First, The detection accuracy is high among event logs with different noise levels, and the high precision indicates the method returns very few false positives. Second, There is no need to define a noise filtering threshold, which reduces the need for background knowledge about the data. Lastly, The detection speed is reasonably fast.

It has to be noted that like other current window-based process drift detection algorithms, under different parameter settings, the detection results can still be different among different logs with different noise levels and with different process change types. In addition, process drifts which only contain branching frequency changes cannot be detected by the proposed method.

Future work includes the following aspects: First, we aim to propose a way to determine the window size automatically for different logs. Second, we plan to extend the work to characterize different drift types and provide comprehensive results. Finally, we aim to improve our work to suit online settings.

References

1. Bose, R.P.J.C., van der Aalst, W.M.P., Zliobaite, I., Pechenizkiy, M.: Dealing with concept drifts in process mining. IEEE Trans. NNLS **25**(1), 154–171 (2014)
2. Ostovar, A., Maaradji, A., La Rosa, M., ter Hofstede, A.H.M.: Characterizing drift from event streams of business processes. In: Dubois, E., Pohl, K. (eds.) CAiSE 2017. LNCS, vol. 10253, pp. 210–228. Springer, Cham (2017). https://doi.org/10.1007/978-3-319-59536-8_14
3. van der Aalst, W.M.P.: Process Mining - Data Science in Action. Springer, Heidelberg (2016). https://doi.org/10.1007/978-3-662-49851-4_1

4. Zheng, C., Wen, L., Wang, J.: Detecting process concept drifts from event logs. In: OTM CoopIS, pp. 524–542 (2017)
5. Maaradji, A., Dumas, M., La Rosa, M., Ostovar, A.: Detecting sudden and gradual drifts in business processes from execution traces. IEEE TKDE **29**(10), 2140–2154 (2017)
6. Seeliger, A., Nolle, T., Mühlhäuser, M.: Detecting concept drift in processes using graph metrics on process graphs. In: Proceedings of the 9th Conference on Subject-Oriented Business Process Management, pp. 6:1 (2017)
7. Martjushev, J., Bose, R.P.J.C., van der Aalst, W.M.P.: Change point detection and dealing with gradual and multi-order dynamics in process mining. In: Matulevičius, R., Dumas, M. (eds.) BIR 2015. LNBIP, vol. 229, pp. 161–178. Springer, Cham (2015). https://doi.org/10.1007/978-3-319-21915-8_11
8. Stertz, F., Rinderle-Ma, S.: Process histories - detecting and representing concept drifts based on event streams. In: Panetto, H., Debruyne, C., Proper, H.A., Ardagna, C.A., Roman, D., Meersman, R. (eds.) OTM 2018. LNCS, vol. 11229, pp. 318–335. Springer, Cham (2018). https://doi.org/10.1007/978-3-030-02610-3_18
9. Stertz, F., Rinderle-Ma, S.: Detecting and identifying data drifts in process event streams based on process histories. In: Cappiello, C., Ruiz, M. (eds.) CAiSE 2019. LNBIP, vol. 350, pp. 240–252. Springer, Cham (2019). https://doi.org/10.1007/978-3-030-21297-1_21
10. Brockhoff, T., Uysal, M.S., van der Aalst, W.M.: In: Time-aware Concept Drift Detection Using the Earth Mover's Distance, pp. 33–40. IEEE (2020)
11. Ostovar, A., Maaradji, A., La Rosa, M., ter Hofstede, A.H.M., van Dongen, B.F.V.: Detecting drift from event streams of unpredictable business processes. In: Comyn-Wattiau, I., Tanaka, K., Song, I.-Y., Yamamoto, S., Saeki, M. (eds.) ER 2016. LNCS, vol. 9974, pp. 330–346. Springer, Cham (2016)
12. Hompes, B.F.A., Buijs, J.C.A.M., van der Aalst, W.M.P., Dixit, P.M., Buurman, J.: Detecting changes in process behavior using comparative case clustering. In: Ceravolo, P., Rinderle-Ma, S. (eds.) SIMPDA 2015. LNBIP, vol. 244, pp. 54–75. Springer, Cham (2017). https://doi.org/10.1007/978-3-319-53435-0_3
13. Liu, N., Huang, J., Cui, L.: In: A framework for online process concept drift detection from event streams, pp. 105–112. IEEE, San Francisco, CA, USA (2018)
14. Lin, L., Wen, L., Lin, L., Pei, J., Yang, H.: LCDD: detecting business process drifts based on local completeness. IEEE Trans. Services Comput. (2020)
15. Ostovar, A., Leemans, S.J., Rosa, M.L.: Robust drift characterization from event streams of business processes. ACM Trans. Knowl. Discov. Data (TKDD) **14**(3), 1–57 (2020)
16. Yeshchenko, A., Di Ciccio, C., Mendling, J., Polyvyanyy, A.: Comprehensive process drift detection with visual analytics. In: Laender, A.H.F., Pernici, B., Lim, E.-P., de Oliveira, J.P.M. (eds.) ER 2019. LNCS, vol. 11788, pp. 119–135. Springer, Cham (2019). https://doi.org/10.1007/978-3-030-33223-5_11
17. Carmona, J., Gavaldà, R.: Online techniques for dealing with concept drift in process mining. In: Hollmén, J., Klawonn, F., Tucker, A. (eds.) IDA 2012. LNCS, vol. 7619, pp. 90–102. Springer, Heidelberg (2012). https://doi.org/10.1007/978-3-642-34156-4_10
18. Accorsi, R., Stocker, T.: Discovering workflow changes with time-based trace clustering. In: Aberer, K., Damiani, E., Dillon, T. (eds.) SIMPDA 2011. LNBIP, vol. 116, pp. 154–168. Springer, Heidelberg (2012). https://doi.org/10.1007/978-3-642-34044-4_9

19. Bose, R.P.J.C., van der Aalst, W.M.P., Žliobaitė, I., Pechenizkiy, M.: Handling concept drift in process mining. In: Mouratidis, H., Rolland, C. (eds.) CAiSE 2011. LNCS, vol. 6741, pp. 391–405. Springer, Heidelberg (2011). https://doi.org/10.1007/978-3-642-21640-4_30

20. Alves de Medeiros, A.K., van Dongen, B.F., van der Aalst, W.M.P., Weijters, A.J.M.M.: Process mining: Extending the α-algorithm to mine short loops. BETA Working Paper Series WP 113, Eindhoven University of Technology (2004)

21. Agresti, A.: Categorical Data Analysis, vol. 482. John Wiley, Hoboken (2003)

22. Maaradji, A., Dumas, M., La Rosa, M., Ostovar, A.: Fast and accurate business process drift detection. In: Motahari-Nezhad, H.R., Recker, J., Weidlich, M. (eds.) BPM 2015. LNCS, vol. 9253, pp. 406–422. Springer, Cham (2015). https://doi.org/10.1007/978-3-319-23063-4_27

23. Woolf, B.: The log likelihood ratio test (the G-test). Annal. Hum. Genet **21**(4), 397–409 (1957)

A Framework for Explainable Concept Drift Detection in Process Mining

Jan Niklas Adams[1]([✉])(iD), Sebastiaan J. van Zelst[1,2](iD), Lara Quack[2],
Kathrin Hausmann[2], Wil M.P. van der Aalst[1,2](iD), and Thomas Rose[1,2]

[1] RWTH Aachen University, Aachen, Germany
{niklas.adams,s.j.v.zelst,wvdaalst}@pads.rwth-aachen.de
[2] Fraunhofer Institute for Applied Information Technology (FIT),
Sankt Augustin, Germany
{lara.quack,kathrin.hausmann,thomas.rose}@fit.fraunhofer.de

Abstract. Rapidly changing business environments expose companies to high levels of uncertainty. This uncertainty manifests itself in significant changes that tend to occur over the lifetime of a process and possibly affect its performance. It is important to understand the root causes of such changes since this allows us to react to change or anticipate future changes. Research in process mining has so far only focused on detecting, locating and characterizing significant changes in aprocess and not on finding root causes of such changes. In this paper, we aim to close this gap. We propose a framework that adds an explainability level onto concept drift detection in process mining and provides insights into the cause-effect relationships behind significant changes. We define different perspectives of a process, detect concept drifts in these perspectives and plug the perspectives into a causality check that determines whether these concept drifts can be causal to each other. We showcase the effectiveness of our framework by evaluating it on both synthetic and real event data. Our experiments show that our approach unravels cause-effect relationships and provides novel insights into executed processes.

Keywords: Process mining · Concept drift · Cause-effect analysis

1 Introduction

Digitization poses great threats but also exceptional opportunities to companies. On the one hand, new technologies, business models, and legislation expose companies to high levels of uncertainty. On the other hand, the introduction of information systems over the last decades enables companies to collect and analyze data on their *business processes*. These data can be converted into an *event log* and are used to discover, monitor and improve the underlying business processes. It, thus, helps the companies to deal with the uncertainty they are exposed to. *Process mining* [1] is the discipline of computer science that successfully analyzes and improves business processes by applying concepts of process and data science

© Springer Nature Switzerland AG 2021
A. Polyvyanyy et al. (Eds.): BPM 2021, LNCS 12875, pp. 400–416, 2021.
https://doi.org/10.1007/978-3-030-85469-0_25

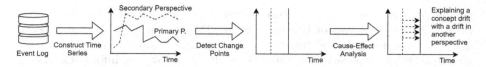

Fig. 1. Our proposed framework transforms event data into two time series representations that can describe various different process perspectives, e.g., the weekly workload. A cause-effect analysis is then conducted using the information of detected concept drifts in the selected perspectives to unravel root causes for these drifts.

to transform event logs into process models and actionable insight for the process owner. When looking at business processes uncertainty is often caused by significant change, called *concept drift*, in some perspective of a business process. For example, due to Covid-19 a lot of companies had to redesign or extend processes by including digital alternatives to previously in-person activities. This resulted in so-called concept drifts. As the quality and profitability of organizations highly depend on their business processes concept drift can have a huge impact on either of these dimensions. The restructuring of a process to meet the health safety regulatory standards could, e.g., lead to increased processing time and thus increased cost. Detecting and handling concept drift has, thus, been named one of the main challenges in process mining [2]. For the process owner the mere knowledge of past occurrences of concept drifts is not sufficient. To derive useful insights it is helpful to know the underlying cause-effect relationships associated with these concept drifts, i.e., the user can either anticipate future concept drifts or use the uncovered relations to further improve the process.

In this paper, we introduce a generic framework that augments concept drift detection in process mining by adding a cause-effect analysis on top of the detected concept drifts. This cause-effect analysis extracts possible explanations for the occurrence of a concept drift. The core idea of the framework is depicted in Fig. 1. Before starting, we choose a perspective of the process to be analyzed for concept drift, i.e., the *control-flow, data, resource* or *performance* perspective. This perspective is called the *primary* perspective. As we are interested in the root causes for these concept drifts, we choose a *secondary* perspective that could contain root causes. This secondary perspective is also analyzed for concept drifts and these are tested for causality with the concept drifts of the primary perspective. In the first step, we transform an event log into two time series for both the chosen primary and secondary perspective. After detecting concept drifts in both perspectives, we conduct a cause-effect analysis and check which concept drifts of the secondary perspective could be causal to a concept drift in the primary perspective. The set of explainable concept drifts forms the output of our framework.

Our framework touches the areas of concept drift detection and cause-effect analysis in process mining which have, thus far, primarily been studied separately. Most of the work on concept drift deals with locating concept drifts and only considers the control-flow perspective of a process. The control-flow perspective describes the structuring and dependencies of activities. Recent work, e.g., the approach of Brockhoff et al. [11] introduces additional perspectives, i.e., the time perspective to concept drift detection. Ostovar et al. [27] add an additional characterization of the drift, i.e., providing information about underlying nature of the drift, on top of the mere detection of the drift. With our work, we include more perspectives and add an explainability level to concept drift detection. Most work on cause-effect analysis uncovers cause-effect relationships on a process-instance-level, e.g., giving recommendations for individual customers to maximize the outcome, as Bozorgi et al. [10] recently introduced. Pourbafrani et al. [31] focus on finding cause-effect relationships on a global-process level and use these to simulate what-if scenarios.

The remainder of this paper is structured as follows. We introduce the related work on concept drift detection and cause-effect analysis in Sect. 2. In Sect. 3, we provide the definitions and background used in the remainder of this paper. We illustrate our framework for explainable concept drift detection in Sect. 4. In Sect. 5, we provide details on our specific implementation and evaluate our framework with synthetic data and conduct a case study on real-life event data. Section 6 concludes the paper.

2   Related Work

A general introduction to the field of process mining is given in [1]. In this section, we introduce related work on concept drift detection and cause-effect analysis in process mining.

Concept drift detection (also: change point detection), has received much attention outside of process mining. A general introduction can be found in [5]. As our use case does not provide labeled data sets for supervised algorithms, we are only interested in unsupervised concept drift detection algorithms as the training data for supervised algorithms is expensive to obtain and the ground truth is hard to define in the setting of real-life event logs. Existing work on concept drift detection in process mining focuses on the detection, localization and characterization of changes, not the explanation of them. Detection refers to the presence of a concept drift, localization to the time of occurrence of the drift and characterization to the nature of the drift, e.g., whether an activity was removed or a performance indicator significantly increased. Explanation refers to the root causes of a drift, e.g., why an activity was removed or why a performance indicator significantly increased. Most of the work aims to detect drifts in the control-flow perspective. Bose et al. [8,9] and Martjushev et al. [24] built representations of the control-flow perspective by using the (directly) follows relations. They employ hypothesis testing to compare a window of values before and after a potential change point for significant differences. Maaradji et al. [22] and Ostovar et al. [27] use the α and α^+-relations [25] to model the control-flow perspective while also using hypothesis testing to determine change points. One notable recent approach is the one of Yeshchenko et al. [38]. The authors use DECLARE constraints to model the control-flow of a process. They define

Table 1. Overview of the related approaches for cause-effect analysis and concept drift detection in process mining. Cause-effect analysis can be performed either on the case- or the process level. Approaches for concept drift detection have different scopes, i.e., they can detect, locate, characterize or explain a concept drift. Our approach detects, locates and explains concept drift and therefore yields insights into process level cause-effects.

	Concept drift				Cause-effect analysis	
	Detect.	Locat.	Char.	Expl.	Case level	Process level
[4, 8, 9, 11, 12, 21, 22, 24, 36, 39]	✓	✓				
[17, 27, 33, 38]	✓	✓	✓			
[10, 16, 18, 19, 28, 34]					✓	
[26, 29–31]						✓
Our approach	✓	✓		✓		✓

a range of time windows and subsequently calculate values for the declarative constraints for each time window, forming a multivariate time series. This time series is analyzed for concept drifts by applying the Pruned Exact Linear Time algorithm. By visualizing the results of this clustering, the user can characterize the occurring concept drifts. Other authors also include other perspectives than control-flow. Leontjeva et al. [20] and Meisenbacher et al. [23] use the data payload of past events to include the data perspective into their representation. Analyzing the related work on concept drift in process mining reveals two shortcomings: The little consideration of additional perspectives other than control-flow and the absence of root cause analysis for concept drifts. With this paper we aim to close this gap.

The area of cause-effect analysis in process mining investigates relationships that are present in a process. One way to define different levels of analysis is to either consider the local intra-trace, i.e., case level, or the global level of the process. The case level deals with individual process instantiations, e.g., a customer running through the process of applying for a loan. The global level is the entirety of components and cases that are associated with the process. Many approaches in cause-effect analysis focus on the case level rather than the global level, providing recommendations and predictions for handling individual cases. De Leoni et al. [19] and Hompes et al. [16] provide methods to extract root causes for performance variations on a case level. In another work, Hompes et al. [18] group events based on certain process performance characteristics and further decompose these groups based on different characteristics. They subsequently test for cause-effects between these characteristics by looking at their development over time and testing for Granger-causality [15] to extract the root causes of performance variations on a case level. This technique works well for identifying causal factors for performance variations, however, other perspectives of the process such as control-flow or resources are, so far, not considered, potentially missing important cause-effects. Bozorgi et al. [10] use techniques from causal machine learning to provide recommendations for handling an individual case that maximize the probability of a certain outcome. These approaches

Table 2. Exemplary event log with two cases and resources handling the activities

Case-id	Activity	Timestamp	Resource
1	Register	2021-06-15 12:30	Peter
1	Submit	2021-06-15 12:35	Sophia
2	Register	2021-06-15 13:12	Peter
1	Reply	2021-06-15 14:21	Christina

provide useful information for individual cases, however, they are not able to detect important cause-effect relationships that happen on a global level, e.g., an increase in customers that leads to longer waiting times. Other authors investigate cause-effect relationships on a global level. Pourbafrani et al. [30,31] use system dynamics as a modeling tool of the process over time and construct a model that contains cause-effect relationships between different metrics. This model is subsequently used to simulate the outcomes for different scenarios. Nakatumba et al. [26] investigate the effect of resource workload on their performance using regression analysis.

A selection of papers on concept drift and cause-effect analysis in process mining is depicted in Table 1. Our framework is the only technique that covers both spectra.

3   Preliminaries

In this section, we introduce the core definitions of this paper and the main notations used for improving the readability. $\mathcal{P}(X) = \{X' | X' \subseteq X\}$ denotes the power set of a set X. A sequence allows enumerating the elements of a set. A sequence of length n over X is a function $\sigma:\{1, \ldots, n\} \to X$ which we write as $\sigma = \langle \sigma(1), \sigma(2), \ldots, \sigma(n) \rangle$.

An event can be considered the "atomic datum" of process mining. An event consists of values that are assigned to attributes, e.g., the executed activity, the timestamp, a case-id and other attributes. Each line in Table 2 corresponds to an event. Each event needs to be assigned a case-id describing the process instance which is the *case* this event belongs to. All lines with the same case-id in Table 2 form a case. The collection of recorded cases forms an event log.

Definition 1 (Events, Cases and Projections). *An event describes the information associated to the execution of an activity. Let $\mathcal{E}$ denote the universe of events. Let $\mathcal{D}$ denote the universe of attributes and let $\mathcal{V}$ denote the universe of possible attribute values. Let $\mathcal{T}$ denote the universe of possible timestamps.*

- *For an attribute $d \in \mathcal{D}$ we assume the existence of a mapping to retrieve the corresponding attribute value $\pi_d^{\mathcal{E}}:\mathcal{E} \nrightarrow \mathcal{V}$.*
- *The activity projection is a total function retrieving the activity of an event $\pi_{act}^{\mathcal{E}} : \mathcal{E} \to \mathcal{A}$, where $\mathcal{A}$ denotes the universe of activities.*

- *The time projection is a total function retrieving the timestamp of an event $\pi_{time}^{\mathcal{E}}:\mathcal{E}\rightarrow\mathcal{T}$.*
- *Each event has an identifier $\pi_{id}^{\mathcal{E}}$ to differentiate between events, that might have the same values for each attribute. Therefore, $e, e'\in\mathcal{E}(\pi_{id}^{\mathcal{E}}(e) = \pi_{id}^{\mathcal{E}}(e') \Rightarrow e = e')$*

Events belong to a case denoting the process instance of this event. Let $\mathcal{C}$ be the universe of all cases.

- *For an attribute $d\in\mathcal{D}$ we assume the existence of a projection function to retrieve the corresponding attribute value $\pi_d^{\mathcal{C}} : \mathcal{C}\nrightarrow\mathcal{V}$.*
- *Each event $e\in\mathcal{E}$ has a case-id describing the case it belongs to. The projection function $\pi_{case}^{\mathcal{E}}(e)$ retrieves the corresponding case-id.*
- *We furthermore assume the existence of an event projection that maps a case on the set of its events $\pi_{events}^{\mathcal{C}}:\mathcal{C}\rightarrow\mathcal{P}(\mathcal{E})$. Cases are non-overlapping, i.e., $\forall c_1, c_2\in\mathcal{C}(\pi_{events}^{\mathcal{C}}(c_1)\cap\pi_{events}^{\mathcal{C}}(c_2)\neq\emptyset \Rightarrow c_1=c_2)$.*

An event log L is a set of cases, thus $L\in\mathcal{P}(\mathcal{C})$.

- *For an attribute $d\in\mathcal{D}$ we assume the existence of the projection functions $\pi_d^{\mathcal{E}}(L)=\{\pi_d^{\mathcal{E}}(e)|\exists_{c\in L}e\in\pi_{events}(c)\}$ and $\pi_d^{\mathcal{C}}(L)=\{\pi_d^{\mathcal{C}}(c)|c\in L\}$ to retrieve the set of values for this attribute.*

4   Generic Framework for Explainable Concept Drift

In this section, we introduce the three steps of our framework. The framework is depicted in Fig. 2. In the first step, we construct time series representations for both chosen perspectives. In the second step, a change point detection algorithm is performed on both perspectives. In the third step, we test pairs of change points for causality by taking the time lag between them and check whether the two time series can be causal given the lag. If this test is positive the detected concept drift together with the cause-effect-relationship are as explanation given to the user. For each of the steps, we provide the input and output specifications.

4.1   Time Series Construction

To express the development of a process perspective over time, we construct a time series. A time series assigns values to subsequent time intervals. We, therefore, need to map an event log onto time intervals and then assign values to these intervals. For assigning values to a set of events that are contained in a specific time interval we first need a way to look at these events in isolation and thus define a selection function for events based on a time interval.

Definition 2 (Time Intervals). *Based on a reference timestamp $t_r\in\mathcal{T}$, e.g., describing the beginning of an event log, we can express every timestamp as a*

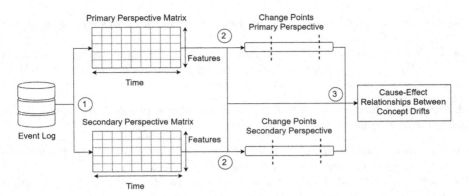

Fig. 2. Our proposed framework for uncovering cause-effect relationships. In Step 1, the event log is transformed into two time series representations of different perspectives. In Step 2, the change points are detected and checked for causality in Step 3.

real number that describes the time, e.g., number of milliseconds or nanoseconds, passed since this reference timestamp. The real-valued representation of a timestamp can be retrieved with the function $r_{t_r}(t) \in \mathbb{R}$. Given two timestamps $t_1, t_2 \in \mathcal{T}$ and $t_1^{\mathbb{R}} = r_{t_r}(t_1), t_2^{\mathbb{R}} = r_{t_r}(t_2)$ we define a time interval $ti = [t_1^{\mathbb{R}}, t_2^{\mathbb{R}})$ where $t_1^{\mathbb{R}} < t_2^{\mathbb{R}}$. Let $\mathcal{TI}$ denote the universe of possible time intervals. $|ti| = t_2^{\mathbb{R}} - t_1^{\mathbb{R}}$ defines the length of a time interval and $start(ti) = t_1^{\mathbb{R}}$. To extract the events of an event log L occurring within a time interval $ti \in \mathcal{TI}$ we define the selection function $sel(L, ti) = \{e \in \mathcal{E} | \exists_{c \in L} e \in \pi_{events}^{\mathcal{C}}(c) \wedge r_{t_r}(\pi_{time}^{\mathcal{E}}(e)) \in ti\}$.

This definition is used to map an event log onto time intervals. To finish constructing the time series we now calculate a value for each time interval. We first need to define a function to map a collection of events onto a real-valued number and can then extend this to multiple functions, mapping a collection of events onto a real-valued vector and finally a time series, doing this for multiple subsequent time intervals.

Definition 3 (Event Log to Time Series). *Given a time interval $ti \in \mathcal{TI}$ and an event log L, we define the function $f(sel(L, ti)) \in \mathbb{R}$ that maps an event log for a specific time interval onto a real-valued number. We use the notation $f(L, ti) = f(sel(L, ti))$ for readability. Let $f_1, f_2, \ldots, f_m$ be functions of the signature of f. We define the function $g(L, ti) = (f_1(L, ti), f_2(L, ti), \ldots, f_m(L, ti))$ with $g(L, ti) \in \mathbb{R}^m$ to construct a real-valued vector for a specific time interval of an event log. Let $TI \in \mathcal{TI}^*$ define a mutually exclusive sequence of time intervals of equal lengths, i.e., $\forall ti_i, ti_j \in TI (|ti_i| = |ti_j| \wedge i \neq j \Rightarrow ti_i \cap ti_j = \emptyset \wedge i < j \Rightarrow start(ti_i) < start(ti_j))$. With $TI = \langle ti_1, \ldots, ti_n \rangle$ we define the time series construction function $h_{g, TI, L} = (g(L, ti_1)^{\intercal}, \ldots, g(L, ti_n)^{\intercal})$ with $h_{g, TI, L} \in \mathbb{R}^{m \times n}$ to retrieve a real-valued matrix, that represents a multivariate time series of an event log.*

For each perspective there are many ways to represent it as a real-valued number. Take the control-flow as an example. We can count the number of distinct activities for subsequent time intervals. If the number of activities suddenly

Table 3. Possible mapping functions to construct a real-valued representation of different perspectives of a business process.

Control-flow	Performance	Data	Resources
Directly-follows frequencies [3]	Service times [26]	Aggregation of case attributes	Workload [26]
α-relations [3]	Overtime cases [34]	Aggregation of activity attributes	Involved resources
α^+-relations [25]	Case durations [18]	Number of events or cases	Number of active resources
Heuristic Miner's $a \Rightarrow_W b$ score [37]	Activity sojourn time [18]	Threshold exceedings	Aggregation of attribute values
Number of activities	Activity waiting time [18]		
DECLARE constraints [38]			
...	...	...	...

increases we know that there is a concept drift in the control-flow since a new activity was added. Different measurements can be combined as a single one can not represent the whole perspective. E.g., if one activity was removed and one was added taking the number of distinct activities as representation could not express this. Table 3 depicts a non-exhaustive list of measurements for each of the introduced perspectives. For a detailed introduction we refer to the corresponding papers.

For the control-flow perspective we can use simple measures as, e.g., the number of distinct activities or intermediate results of mining algorithms like the α-relations obtained from the α-Miner [3].

For the performance perspective we can leverage heavily on the recorded times which can be seen as a proxy for cost or service quality. We can, e.g., calculate the average service times for each activity, i.e., the time from start to completion of an activity. Furthermore, we can define a threshold of processing time and count all the cases that exceed this threshold and are thus classified as overtime.

The measures for the data perspective use the additional attributes associated to events, e.g., the age or credit score of customers. We can use aggregation functions such as average or maximum to map all the values of an attribute in a time interval onto a single number, e.g., the average age of customers for each time interval. We can, furthermore, count the number of events to describe the event volume over time.

Representations for the resource perspective rely on information about the resources, often staff members, handling an activity. We can count the number of events a resource is involved in to calculate the workload and its development over time. By simply counting the number of active resources each time frame we can, furthermore, monitor the number of deployed resources over time.

The question remains which perspectives a user should choose. There is not a general answer for this, domain knowledge and potential assumptions can be used. However, the investigation of certain perspectives might be more promising than others. There are some examples of reoccurring cause-effect themes in process mining. Resources often have an impact onto the performance of a process, e.g., the workload onto the service times [26], the workload onto overtime cases [34] or the associated data onto the case duration [28]. Furthermore, e.g., control-flow changes such as changing prevalence of a choice might influence the performance perspective.

4.2 Change Point Detection

After constructing multivariate time series for each the primary and the secondary perspective, we detect change points in these time series. The change point detection technique maps a time series onto subsets of the time intervals in which the distribution of the features significantly changed.

Definition 4 (Change Point Detection in Multivariate Time Series).
Let $H \in \mathbb{R}^{m \times n}$ be a multivariate time series and $TI = \langle ti_1, \ldots, ti_n \rangle$ be the previously introduced sequence of time intervals used to construct this time series. A change point detection technique CPD maps a time series onto a subset of time intervals, where a significant change of the underlying time series occurred $CPD(H) \subseteq TI$.

The change point detection method has to be able to process a multivariate time series as an input. As mentioned in Sect. 2, this method should be unsupervised, i.e., be able to detect change points without seeing similar kinds of time series with annotated change points before. Examples of change point detection techniques include cost-based techniques [35], hypothesis testing [9] or clustering techniques [17].

4.3 Cause-Effect Analysis

In the first step, two time series for the primary and the secondary perspective are constructed. A set of m_p mapping functions for the primary perspective and m_s for the secondary perspective are applied to construct the time series $H_p \in \mathbb{R}^{m_p \times n}$ and $H_s \in \mathbb{R}^{m_s \times n}$. The change point detection step of the framework calculates two sets of change points $CPD(H_p)$ and $CPD(H_s)$. In the cause-effect analysis step, we look at the change points in the primary perspective and analyse which concept drifts in the secondary perspective potentially have a cause-effect relationship to a concept drift in the primary perspective. We, therefore, look at each primary drift and consider all preceding secondary drifts. We calculate the time lag, i.e., the number of time intervals that lie between the drifts, and test whether the secondary perspective can potentially be causal to the primary perspective given this lag. We, therefore, test all pairs of features between primary and secondary perspective for causality given this lag. A feature is a row of the time series describing a single measurement over time. If a feature pair is tested to be causal we add the change point pair and all causal feature pairs to the output of our framework.

Definition 5 (Cause-Effect Analysis). *Let $H_p \in \mathbb{R}^{m_p \times n}$ and $H_s \in \mathbb{R}^{m_s \times n}$ be time series for the primary and secondary perspective. We define the lag function $l_{TI}(ti_1, ti_2) \in \mathbb{N}$ to retrieve the number of time intervals in TI that lie in between ti_1 and ti_2, i.e., the lag. For a change point of the primary perspective $cp_p \in CPD(H_p)$ and a change point in the secondary perspective $cp_s \in CPD(H_s)$ we retrieve the lag k using the lag function $k = l_{TI}(cp_p, cp_s)$. Given a row, i.e., a feature, of the primary and secondary perspective $h_p \in H_{p,i}, i \in \{1, \ldots, m_p\}$ and $h_s \in H_{s,i}, i \in \{1, \ldots, m_s\}$, where $h_s, h_p \in \mathbb{R}^n$, a cause-effect analysis technique CA maps these two features and a time lag k onto a value between 0 and 1 $CA(h_p, h_s, k) \in [0, 1]$. This value indicates whether a cause-effect relationship with lag k is present or not.*

The set of all change point pairs with all detected cause-effect relationships between feature pairs forms the output of the framework.

5   Evaluation

5.1   Implementation

We implemented our framework on the basis of PM4Py [7]. The implemented version is available at GitHub[1]. In this section, we introduce the techniques in change point detection and cause-effect analysis specific to our implementation.

Similar to Yeshchenko et al. [38], we use the Pruned Exact Linear Time PELT-algorithm [14] as a change point detection technique for multivariate time series. This technique uncovers change points by minimizing a cost function that depends on assigning change points. It is able to process a multivariate time series and computes an optimal solution in linear time and is, therefore, well suited for our experiments. An exact description can be found in [14]. For applying the PELT-algorithm a penalty β has to be chosen that prevents overfitting. The calculated change points are subsequently used to calculate the lags needed for cause-effect analysis. We use the concept of Granger-causality [15]. Granger-causality determines with which probability two time series are correlated given a time lag between them and can, thus, be seen as a type of predictive causality. The user has to provide a p-value that describes the threshold probability at which feature pairs should be classified as Granger-causal.

5.2   Experiments

We evaluate our framework using a synthetic event log and a real-life event log. The synthetic log is used as a means to verify the implementation and a proof of concept. We, then, expand this to conduct a case study on real-life event data and discuss our findings. For both experiments we provide the chosen parameters for the three steps of our framework, i.e., perspectives and measurements in time series construction, change point detection in multivariate time series and cause-effect analysis. To verify our results, we compare our findings to state-of-the-art methods in concept drift detection and cause-effect analysis.

---

[1] https://github.com/niklasadams/explainable_concept_drift_pm.git.

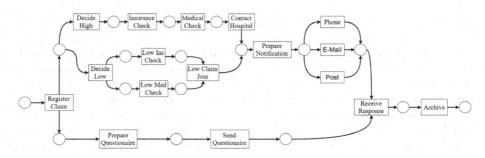

Fig. 3. Synthetic process for claiming insurance. The availability of different ways of notification, phone, e-mail and post, depends on the age of the customer [8].

Table 4. Parameter choices for running the framework on the synthetic event log.

Experimental setup			
Time series construction	Primary perspective	Control-flow	Directly-follows frequencies
	Secondary perspective	Data	Minimum, maximum, sum, average, count, set average
	Time interval duration	1 day	
Change point detection	PELT-algorithm	$\beta_{primary} = 3$	$\beta_{secondary} = 1.5$
Cause-effect analysis	Granger-causality	p-value=1×10^{-12}	

5.3   Synthetic Insurance Event Log

We use CPN Tools [32] to generate an event log based on a simulation model of claiming insurance shown in Fig. 3. The different ways of notification, i.e., postal, phone and email, are available for different ages of customers. When simulating we introduce a drift in the ages of customers that should then cause a succeeding drift in the prevalence of notification activities, especially an increase in email-notification. The chosen parameters for the instantiation of our framework are depicted in Table 4.

For change point detection we retrieve a change point in the primary control-flow perspective at day 133 and in the secondary data perspective at day 132. The lag between this drift is $k = 1$. We, therefore, use a lag of 1 when testing for a cause-effect relationship between the two perspectives.

With a p-value of 10^{-12}, which is especially low due to the artificial setting, we retrieve 25 feature pairs that are Granger-causal with lag $k = 1$. All involved features of the primary control-flow perspective concern the frequency of directly follows relationships between one of the notification activities and either a preceding or succeeding activity. The features of the secondary perspective all describe the distribution of age, i.e., the sum, average, minimum, maximum and average of the set of values. We, therefore, limit our output to only 5 of the feature pairs, which are depicted in Fig. 4. The depicted features propose that a decrease in the age of customers led to an increase in the prevalence of the email

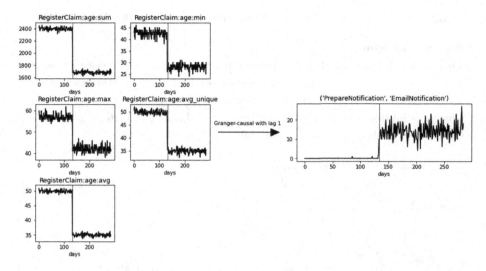

Fig. 4. 5 Granger-causal feature pairs for the cause-effect relationship between data and control-flow perspective. A drift in the age of the customers is responsible for an increase in email notifications and a decrease in other notifications.

notification activity one day later which is exactly the cause-effect relationship we artificially introduced. Our framework has correctly detected and explained the concept drift with the underlying cause-effect relationship.

5.4 Case Study

We also evaluated our framework using data from the Business Process Intelligence (BPI) Challenge 2017 [13]. The event log considered belongs to a loan application process through an online system. A customer can submit loan applications to the financial institute and may receive an offer from the financial institute afterwards. The parameters for applying our framework are depicted in Table 5. We analyze the performance perspective, i.e., the service times, for concept drifts. We search for root causes in the resource perspective, i.e., the workload, as it has shown to often have a significant impact on the service times [26].

For the primary, performance perspective we retrieve a change point in Week 28. For the secondary, workload perspective we retrieve a change point at Week 22. The lag for cause-effect analysis is therefore $k = 6$. The cause-effect analysis with a p-value of 0.015 yields 23 Granger-causal feature pairs with a lag of 6 weeks. Four different primary features are contained in these feature pairs. Since three of them do not exhibit a concept drift around week 28, we drop the corresponding pairs for further analysis. The remaining pairs are depicted in Fig. 5. The average duration of *W_Validate application* shows a significant decrease for week 28. We further analyze the resource workloads that are Granger-causal to

Table 5. Parameter choices for running the framework on the BPI 2017 log.

Experimental setup			
Time series construction	Primary perspective	Performance	Service times [26]
	Secondary perspective	Resource	Workload [26]
	Time interval duration	1 week	
Change point detection	PELT-algorithm	$\beta_{primary} = 3$	$\beta_{secondary} = 1.5$
Cause-effect analysis	Granger-causality	p-value $= 0.015$	

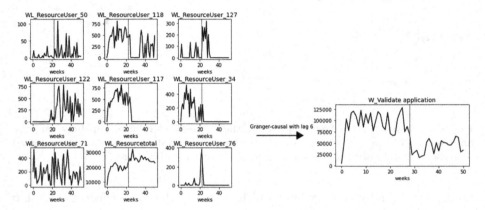

Fig. 5. Granger-causal feature pairs of the cause-effect relationship between resource and performance perspective. The only concept drift for the duration perspective of these features can be observed in *W_Validate application*. An increase of the workload is Granger-causal to the reduction of the service times.

this feature. Most of the resources do not work continuously over the span of the event log. We can see increases and peaks in the workload for some resource. When looking at the total workload of all resources, which is among the Granger-causal features, we can see a significant increase. The detected cause-effect relationship, therefore, states that **an increase in the workload of resources led to a decrease in the service times for *W_Validate application*.**

One submission paper for the BPI Challenge [6], amongst other things, investigates different KPIs of the process over time. This paper also found a significant decrease in the manual validation time, i.e., the service times for validating an application, and an increase in case numbers. Due to the absence or the lack of visibility of other factors such as additional training, change of staff, etc., the paper suggests that the decrease in service times is a reaction to cope with the increased workload.

Table 6. Comparison of results for the concept drift detection

	Our approach	Visual analytics [38]	ProDrift [22]
Synthetic log	Control-flow drift, day 133	✓	✓
BPI 2017	Performance drift, week 28	✗	✗

Table 7. Comparison of results for cause-effect analysis

	Our approach	PMSD [29]
Synthetic log	Data (age) → control-flow	✗
BPI 2017	Resource (workload) → performance	✓

5.5 Comparison

Our proposed framework for explainable concept drift detection touches two areas of research: Concept drift detection and cause-effect analysis. We, therefore, compare the results for the synthetic event log and the BPI 2017 log with the results from state-of-the-art methods from both of these areas. For concept drift detection we compare the results with the visual analytics approach of Yeshchenko et al. [38] and ProDrift by Maaradji et al. [21] as both approaches have shown outstanding results in concept drift detection. For cause-effect analysis we compare our results with the findings of Pourbafrani et al. [29] as they are searching for relations between different process parameters on a system-wide level.

Table 6 depicts the comparison between the detected concept drifts for the synthetic and the real-life event log. The control-flow drift in the synthetic log is detected by both approaches. As ProDrift relies on completed traces, the drift is detected approximately 15 days later compared to our approach. Both approaches very clearly show the existence of a sudden drift through means of their visualization. As both approaches do only focus on control-flow drifts they can not be used to compare results on the detected performance drift for the BPI 2017 log. Table 7 depicts the results retrieved from PMSD compared to our approach. As PMSD does not model the data perspective, we can not use it to detect the cause-effect in the synthetic log. For the BPI 2017 log we apply the PMSD framework and compute a system dynamics log. This log contains, among others, the arrival rate and the service times of the process. We apply the relation detection of PMSD with a lag of 6 weeks. The results show a negative correlation between the lagged arrival rate and the service times. This corresponds to our detected cause-effect as the higher influx of cases determined a decrease in service times.

We verified our findings by applying state-of-the-art methods from both concept drift detection and cause-effect analysis. If the corresponding perspective can be modeled, we are able to verify our findings with these approaches. These are promising results as they show the power of incorporating more perspectives into concept drift detection and using these to find possible cause-effects of concept drifts.

6   Conclusion

In this paper, we combine concept drift detection and cause-effect analysis to create a framework for explainable concept drift detection. We define a primary perspective where concept drifts should be detected and a secondary perspective with which these concept drifts are explained. By applying a cause-effect analysis to the features of both perspectives, we identify feature pairs that can be used to explain the concept drift. We verified our approach using a synthetically generated event log. We furthermore analyzed the event log of the BPI Challenge 2017 and were able to explain a concept drift in the performance with an increase in the resources' workload. These first experiments have shown a great potential for explaining concept drifts.

Future Work. To further improve our conceptual framework the following steps can be taken. First of all, we want to plug different change point detection algorithms and cause-effect analysis tools to detect other types of drifts and, e.g., non-linear relationships. Furthermore, spurious elements and rare signals produce spikes in a signal that can be misleading to cause-effect analysis techniques. We want to investigate whether the general application of noise filtering on the time series is beneficial. Another interesting point for an extension of the framework are non pairwise dependencies. A concept drift could, e.g., be caused by two different concept drift in two other perspective and not by only one of them.

References

1. van der Aalst, W.M.P.: Process mining: Data science in action. Springer (2016). https://doi.org/10.1007/978-3-662-49851-4
2. van der Aalst, W.M.P., et al.: Process mining manifesto. In: Daniel, F., Barkaoui, K., Dustdar, S. (eds.) BPM 2011. LNBIP, vol. 99, pp. 169–194. Springer, Heidelberg (2012). https://doi.org/10.1007/978-3-642-28108-2_19
3. van der Aalst, W.M.P., Weijters, T., Maruster, L.: Workflow mining: discovering process models from event logs. IEEE Trans. Knowl. Data Eng. **16**(9), 1128–1142 (2004)
4. Accorsi, R., Stocker, T.: Discovering workflow changes with time-based trace clustering. In: Aberer, K., Damiani, E., Dillon, T. (eds.) SIMPDA 2011. LNBIP, vol. 116, pp. 154–168. Springer, Heidelberg (2012). https://doi.org/10.1007/978-3-642-34044-4_9
5. Aminikhanghahi, S., Cook, D.: A survey of methods for time series change point detection. Knowl. Inf. Syst. **51**, 339–367 (2017)
6. Berger, F.: Mining event log data to improve a loan application process. BPI Challenge (2017). https://www.win.tue.nl/bpi/lib/exe/fetch.php?media=2017:bpi2017_paper_3.pdf
7. Berti, A., van Zelst, S.J., van der Aalst, W.M.P.: Process mining for python (PM4PY): bridging the gap between process-and data science. arXiv preprint arXiv:1905.06169 (2019)

8. Bose, R.P.J.C., van der Aalst, W.M.P., Žliobaitė, I., Pechenizkiy, M.: Handling concept drift in process mining. CAiSE , 391–405 (2011)
9. Bose, R.P.J.C., van der Aalst, W.M.P., Žliobaitė, I., Pechenizkiy, M.: Dealing with concept drifts in process mining. IEEE Trans. Neural Networks Learn. Syst. **25**(1), 154–171 (2014)
10. Bozorgi, Z.D., Teinemaa, I., Dumas, M., Rosa, M.L., Polyvyanyy, A.: Process mining meets causal machine learning: discovering causal rules from event logs. In: ICPM, pp. 129–136 (2020)
11. Brockhoff, T., Uysal, M.S., van der Aalst, W.M.P.: Time-aware concept drift detection using the earth mover's distance. In: ICPM, pp. 33–40 (2020)
12. Carmona, J., Gavaldà, R.: Online techniques for dealing with concept drift in process mining. IDA **7619**, 90–102 (2012)
13. van Dongen, B.: BPI: Challenge (2017)
14. Gachomo, D.: The power of the pruned exact linear time (PELT) test in multiple changepoint detection. Am. J. Theor. Appl. Stat. **4**, 581 (2015)
15. Granger, C.: Some recent development in a concept of causality. J. Econometrics **39**(1), 199–211 (1988)
16. Hompes, B., Buijs, J.C.A.M., van der Aalst, W.M.P.: A generic framework for context-aware process performance analysis. OTM **10033**, 300–317 (2016)
17. Hompes, B., Buijs, J.C.A.M., van der Aalst, W.M.P., Dixit, P.M., Buurman, H.: Detecting change in processes using comparative trace clustering. SIMPDA **1527**, 95–108 (2015)
18. Hompes, B.F.A., Maaradji, A., Rosa, M.L., Dumas, M., Buijs, J.C.A.M., van der Aalst, W.M.P.: Discovering causal factors explaining business process performance variation. CAiSE **10253**, 177–192 (2017)
19. de Leoni, M., van der Aalst, W.M.P., Dees, M.: A general process mining framework for correlating, predicting and clustering dynamic behavior based on event logs. Inf. Syst. **56**, 235–257 (2016)
20. Leontjeva, A., Conforti, R., Francescomarino, C.D., Dumas, M., Maggi, F.M.: Complex symbolic sequence encodings for predictive monitoring of business processes. BPM **9253**, 297–313 (2015)
21. Maaradji, A., Dumas, M., Rosa, M.L., Ostovar, A.: Fast and accurate business process drift detection. BPM **9253**, 406–422 (2015)
22. Maaradji, A., Dumas, M., Rosa, M.L., Ostovar, A.: Detecting sudden and gradual drifts in business processes from execution traces. IEEE Trans. Knowl. Data Eng. **29**(10), 2140–2154 (2017)
23. Maisenbacher, M., Weidlich, M.: Handling concept drift in predictive process monitoring. SCC , 1–8 (2017)
24. Martjushev, J., Bose, R.P.J.C., van der Aalst, W.M.P.: Change point detection and dealing with gradual and multi-order dynamics in process mining. BIR **229**, 161–178 (2015)
25. de Medeiros, A.K.A., van Dongen, B.F., van der Aalst, W.M.P., Weijters, A.J.M.M.: Process mining: extending the α-algorithm to mine short loops. In: BETA Working Paper Series. vol. WP 113 (2004)
26. Nakatumba, J., van der Aalst, W.M.P.: Analyzing resource behavior using process mining. BPM **43**, 69–80 (2009)
27. Ostovar, A., Maaradji, A., Rosa, M.L., ter Hofstede, A.H.M.: Characterizing drift from event streams of business processes. CAiSE **10253**, 210–228 (2017)
28. Polato, M., Sperduti, A., Burattin, A., de Leoni, M.: Data-aware remaining time prediction of business process instances. In: IJCNN, pp. 816–823 (2014)

29. Pourbafrani, M., van der Aalst, W.M.P.: PMSD: data-driven simulation using system dynamics and process mining. BPM (PhD/Demos) **2673**, 77–81 (2020)

30. Pourbafrani, M., van Zelst, S.J., van der Aalst, W.M.P.: Scenario-based prediction of business processes using system dynamics. OTM **11877**, 422–439 (2019)

31. Pourbafrani, M., van Zelst, S.J., van der Aalst, W.M.P.: Supporting automatic system dynamics model generation for simulation in the context of process mining. BIS **389**, 249–263 (2020)

32. Ratzer, A.V., et al.: CPN tools for editing, simulating, and analysing coloured petri nets. ICATPN **2679**, 450–462 (2003)

33. Seeliger, A., Nolle, T., Mühlhäuser, M.: Detecting concept drift in processes using graph metrics on process graphs. In: S-BPM ONE, p. 6 (2017)

34. Suriadi, S., Ouyang, C., van der Aalst, W.M.P., ter Hofstede, A.H.M.: Root cause analysis with enriched process logs. BPMs **132**, 174–186 (2012)

35. Truong, C., Oudre, L., Vayatis, N.: Selective review of offline change point detection methods. Sign. Process. **167**, 107299 (2020)

36. Weber, P., Bordbar, B., Tiño, P.: Real-time detection of process change using process mining. ICCSW **DTR11−9**, 108–114 (2011)

37. Weijters, A., van der Aalst, W.M.P., Medeiros, A.: Process mining with the heuristics miner-algorithm. CIRP Annal.-Manufact. Technol. **166**, 1–34 (2006)

38. Yeshchenko, A., Ciccio, C.D., Mendling, J., Polyvyanyy, A.: Comprehensive process drift detection with visual analytics. ER **11788**, 119–135 (2019)

39. Zheng, C., Wen, L., Wang, J.: Detecting process concept drifts from event logs. OTM **10573**, 524–542 (2017)

Graph Autoencoders for Business Process Anomaly Detection

Siyu Huo[1]([✉]), Hagen Völzer[2], Prabhat Reddy[1], Prerna Agarwal[3],
Vatche Isahagian[4], and Vinod Muthusamy[5]

[1] IBM Research, Yorktown Heights, NY, USA
{siyu.huo,Prabhat.Reddy}@ibm.com
[2] IBM Research, Rueschlikon, ZH, Switzerland
hvo@zurich.ibm.com
[3] IBM Research, Gurgaon, HR, India
preragar@in.ibm.com
[4] IBM Research, Cambridge, MA, USA
vatchei@ibm.com
[5] IBM Research, Austin, TX, USA
vmuthus@us.ibm.com

Abstract. We propose an approach to identify anomalies in business processes by building an anomaly detector using graph encodings of process event log data coupled with graph autoencoders. We evaluate the proposed approach with randomly mutated real event logs as well as synthetic data. The evaluation shows significant performance improvements (in terms of F1 score) over previous approaches, in particular with respect to other types of autoencoders that use flat encodings of the same data. The performance improvements are also stable under training and evaluation noise. Our approach is generic in that it requires no prior knowledge of the business process.

1 Introduction

Anomaly detection is an unsupervised machine learning technique that has become very popular with the recent advances in AI. An anomaly detector automatically learns correlations, i.e., regularities in its structured input data and flags irregular data as anomalies, where the notion of an anomaly depends on the dataset and use case.

Business process data have many different aspects, such as the activities, their ordering, their duration and waiting times, the acting resources and roles, the business objects and associated values, states, milestones, decisions and process outcomes. Parts or combinations of these data as well as abstractions, transformations and aggregations thereof, such as KPIs, sliding windows, rolling averages etc. can be presented to an anomaly detector which would all result in different notions of anomaly.

In line with recent studies [24, 26, 27], in this paper we consider process activities, their ordering, and their business object attributes in relation to the following anomaly detection use cases:

© Springer Nature Switzerland AG 2021
A. Polyvyanyy et al. (Eds.): BPM 2021, LNCS 12875, pp. 417–433, 2021.
https://doi.org/10.1007/978-3-030-85469-0_26

- Log errors: When the process event log is distorted because parts of it has been collected manually, i.e., subject to human error, or it has been recorded or transmitted by an unreliable mechanism, then an anomaly detector can be used to detect and correct such perturbations, provided they occur with limited frequency.
- Exception analysis: Finding and inspecting rare exceptional cases can help to understand deviations from expected behavior. This is similar to variant analysis and conformance checking [3,35] in traditional process mining [2]. However, the traditional concept of variant is very fine-grained such that normal behaviour can distribute over a large number of variants and exceptional behavior may not always be easily distinguished from rare but normal variants. Conformance checking on the other hand requires a carefully hand-crafted specification of normative (or normal) behavior, either as an imperative (BPMN) model [4,7,8] or, in a more declarative form, as a set of rules. For more complex processes, creating and maintaining such a specification over time may require substantial effort, whereas anomaly detection requires no such specification.
- Process drift: Exceptions can also be detected at run time, and when multiple anomalies occur in succession, they could indicate changes in external conditions, process drift, or unwanted behavior.

Anomaly detectors for the above use cases can be partially evaluated with real event logs that are perturbed with limited random mutations to see how well the anomaly detector identifies these mutations [23,24,27].

A popular type of anomaly detector is an *autoencoder*, which is an artificial neural network that learns an efficient representation of the input data, i.e., an encoding or embedding, together with a decoding that reproduces the input data from that internal representation in a way that minimizes the reproduction error. A threshold on the reproduction error identifies anomalous input data [42]. The learned encoding can be seen as a form of dimensionality reduction of the input data.

Earlier work [24,26,28] has applied *multilayer perceptron-based autoencoders*, *variational autoencoders* and *LSTM-based autoencoders* to business process anomaly detection and showed that they outperform other methods, such as t-STIDE [41], OC-SVM [39], HMM [18], and Likelihood [27] in terms of accuracy, noise endurance, and generalizability. However, their absolute performance is still limited leaving substantial room for improvement.

In this paper, we show that the performance indeed can be substantially improved by enriching the autoencoder input data representation with activity relationships, i.e., edges between different events of a trace. Thus, the autoencoder input becomes a graph, and we then present the graph to a *graph autoencoder* [20] with edge-conditioned convolutions (ECC) [40]. We evaluate the performance of our graph autoencoder on both synthesized and real-life event logs from the Business Process Intelligence Challenge (BPIC) against several earlier methods.

2   Background

To better explain the idea of this paper, we introduce some basic notations and concepts, partially borrowed from [1].

Definition 1 (Universes). *Let U_E be the set of all* event identifiers, *let U_C be the set of all* case identifiers, *let U_A be the set of all* activity identifiers, *let U_T be the totally ordered set of all* timestamp identifiers, *and let $U_F = \{U_{f_1}, ..., U_{f_k}\}$ be the identifier collections of event associated* features *with k categories: $\{f_1, ..., f_k\}$.*

We assume that events are characterized by various properties. For example, an event has a timestamp, corresponds to an activity, is performed by a particular resource with several attributes, etc. Given the focus of this paper, we assume that events should at least contain activity and timestamp properties, and there is a function $\pi_A : U_E \to U_A$ that assigns to each event an activity from the finite set of process activities, and also a function $\pi_T : U_E \to U_T$ that assigns a timestamp to each event.

Definition 2 (Sequence, Trace, Event Log). *Given a set A, a finite sequence over A of length n is a function $\sigma \in A^* : \{1, ..., n\} \to A$, typically written as $\sigma = \langle a_1, a_2, ..., a_n \rangle$, where $\sigma(i) = a_i$. For any sequence σ, we define $|\sigma| = n$. A* trace *is a finite non-empty sequence of events $\sigma \in U_E^*$ such that each event appears at most once and time is non-decreasing, i.e., for $1 \le i \le j \le |\sigma|$, $\sigma(i) \ne \sigma(j)$ and $\pi_T(\sigma(i)) \le \pi_T(\sigma(j))$. Let C be the set of all possible traces. An* event log *is a set of traces $L \subseteq C$ such that each event appears at most once in the entire log, and each trace in the log represents the execution of one case assigned with a case identifier (case ID) by a function $\pi_C : U_E \to U_C$.*

Definition 3 (Directed Graph). *A directed graph $G = (V, E)$ consists of a nonempty set of* nodes *V and a set of directed* edges *$E \subseteq V \times V$, and for a directed edge $e_{u,v} = (u, v), e_{u,v} \in E$, we call u the* tail *node of e and v the* head *node of e. $N_d(v)$ defines* neighbor *(namely predecessor) nodes of v, which returns the nodes that directly connect to v with incoming edge towards v. For example, for a simple graph with three nodes $u \to v \leftarrow w$, $N_d(v)$ returns the node set $\{u, w\}$.*

2.1   Autoencoders and Anomaly Detection

An autoencoder is a type of artificial neural network for unsupervised learning, which contains two main components: an *encoder* and a *decoder* [6]. The encoder takes an input vector $x \in [0, 1]^d$ and maps it to a hidden representation $h \in [0, 1]^{d'}$ by a deterministic mapping function $f_\phi : [0, 1]^d \to [0, 1]^{d'}$ parameterized by ϕ. Symmetrically, the decoder takes the encoder output h and maps it to $z \in [0, 1]^d$ by a mapping function $g_\psi : [0, 1]^{d'} \to [0, 1]^d$ parameterized by ψ. f_ϕ and g_ψ here can be corresponding typical neural networks such as multi-layer perceptrons, recurrent neural networks, etc. Each input x is thus first encoded into h and then decoded into z. During training, the parameters are optimized to minimize the observed *reconstruction loss* $L(x, z)$ of input x and its reconstruction z through backpropagation:

$$
\begin{aligned}
\phi^{\star}, \psi^{\star} &= \arg\min_{\phi,\psi} L(x, z) \\
&= \arg\min_{\phi,\psi} L(x, g_{\psi}(f_{\phi}(x)))
\end{aligned}
\tag{1}
$$

where the reconstruction loss function is traditionally defined as the mean square error:

$$
L(x, z) = \frac{1}{d} \sum_{i=1}^{d} (x^{(i)} - z^{(i)})^2
\tag{2}
$$

An autoencoder based anomaly detector uses reconstruction loss as the anomaly score, i.e., a data point with relatively high reconstruction loss is considered to be an anomaly. During the training phase, the autoencoder learns f_{ϕ} and g_{ψ} through data training split based on Eq. (1), and then a reconstruction loss threshold θ is chosen to classify anomalies during the validation phase based on another independent validation data split. (Our setting details are described in Sect. 4.2.) Finally, the model inference relies on f_{ϕ}, g_{ψ} and θ obtained from the training and validation phases described as above.

2.2   Feature Encoding for Business Process Event Logs

Machine learning always requires an adequate feature extraction and engineering for the target data. In the business process literature, [21] converts the event log into vectors using a method that is similar to continuous bag of words (CBOW), which is a natural language processing (NLP) method for document encoding. These vectors include different encoding levels: activity level, trace level, and the entire log level. These vectors, or their embeddings, are then fed into different neural networks designed for purposes such as anomaly detection, trace clustering, and process comparison. As all event logs record the executed process activities and their ordering, [17] extracts the event ordering from the log. However, these methods do not leverage other business process object attributes.

The greater the variety of process data attributes included in the input vector, the more types of anomalies can be detected by the autoencoder. For example, besides the activity name, a delayed process activity could result in an unusual ending timestamp, which is a numerical attribute in the log. Also several business data attributes are often related to each other, such as the credit score and loan amount in a loan application. Usually it is quite challenging to extract only useful attribute features without any prior domain knowledge about the business process. Some earlier work [24, 26] treats the time series event log as flat structural data, and directly applies one-hot or dummy encoding on categorical features and re-scales numerical features to generate process encoding vectors. These encoding vectors are then concatenated in time series order and fed into the neural network. In the business process anomaly detection literature, the primary difference between existing autoencoder approaches and our work is that we encode both, structural information as well as various kinds of business process attributes by using a graph encoding on them.

2.3   Graph Neural Networks

Over the past few years, there has been a surge of approaches that seek to learn the representations of graph nodes, or entire (sub-)graphs based on Graph Neural Networks (GNN), which extend well-known network architectures, including recurrent neural networks (RNNs) and convolutional neural networks (CNNs), to graph data [10,12,13,15,16,22,25,38]. Most of the existing graph neural networks are instances of the Message Passing Neural Network (MPNN) framework [14] for node aggregation. In a directed graph G, the forward pass consists of two phases, a message passing phase and a readout phase. At the time step t, the message passing function S_t and vertex update function U_t describe how the hidden state h_v^t for each node in the graph is updated:

$$s_v^t = \sum_{u \in N_d(v)} S_t(h_v^{t-1}, h_u^{t-1}, e_{u,v}) \tag{3}$$

$$h_v^t = U_t(h_v^{t-1}, s_v^t) \tag{4}$$

Then the readout phase computes a feature vector for the whole graph using a readout function R according to:

$$\hat{y} = R(\{h_v | v \in G\}) \tag{5}$$

The message functions S_t, vertex update functions U_t, and readout function R are all learned differentiable functions, and associated parameters can be learned by back-propagation based on an error function, such as an error function on a graph classification prediction score $\hat{y}$ where y is the classification label.

3   Method

3.1   Graph Construction on the Process Event Log

The Graph-based representation of business process data has been previously used to improve process discovery [32], build Bayesian networks [33,37], and generate likelihood graphs of causally dependent event attributes [27]. To represent the structural process information of an event trace in the log, we build a directed graph $G = (V, E)$ on it as follows (similar to a Directly-Follows-Graph in process mining). We treat activity names, which are a required property of the events in the log, as nodes V in the graph, and edges E correspond to every pair of adjacent events in the time ordered trace. Thus a trace with n activities results in $n - 1$ directed edges. Since the node is identified by its activity name, an edge that is formed by two adjacent activity names may contain several duplicates in a trace. To leverage this situation, we propose a positional embedding method by using the specific location of the adjacent events in a vector p to represent edge positional information and associated activity attributes, and the vector p is treated as an edge feature vector. This way, duplicate edges are represented by digits in different locations within the same positional vector. Following the graph construction steps below, a trace with n activities potentially results in $k \leq n-1$ positional vectors p corresponding to the unique k edges. The overall graph construction diagram can be represented by k label vectors $m \in \{0,1\}^{t_m-1}$, which record activity occurrence information and are targets of the autoencoder's decoding output.

CaseID	Activity	Timestamp	Variable1	Variable 2
0	A	3/1/2021	1	1
0	B	3/2/2021	2	1.8
0	C	3/3/2021	4	2.5
0	B	3/4/2021	7	3.1
0	C	3/5/2021	11	3.6
0	D	3/6/2021	16	4
0	C	3/7/2021	22	4.3
0	B	3/8/2021	29	4.5
0	E	3/9/2021	37	4.6

(a) An example event log.

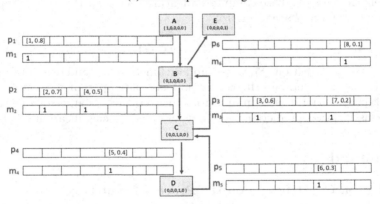

(b) The constructed graph corresponding to the example event log.

Fig. 1. A graph construction example based on the example event log.

The following are the steps of the graph construction algorithm and the feature extraction for one trace with n activities:

1. Compute the maximum trace length $t_m = max\{|\sigma| : \sigma \in U_E\}$ over the whole events U_E in the log, and obtain an event attribute feature embedding with dimension $d_e = d_n + d_c$ by concatenating activity numerical features (rescaling

with dimension d_n) and categorical features (one-hot encoding with dimension d_c) of event attributes (excluding the activity name columns). Meanwhile, track all existing activities as nodes and assign them an initial node embedding h_v^0 (one-hot encoding).

2. Generate $n-1$ activity-activity pairs based on occurrence order, and maintain this order. For example, trace (A, B, C, B, C) ends up in 4 ordered activity-activity pairs (A, B), (B, C), (C, B), and (B, C), which define edges in the graph.

3. Within one activity-activity pair at position $i \in [1, n-1]$ based on the second step, treat the activity that happened first as u, and the other as v. Also compute the edge feature vector based on the event attribute feature embedding distance (subtraction) of u and v, and put this computed vector in index i of the positional vector p which has dimension $d_p = (t_m - 1) \times d_e$ (each computed vector takes d_e space in p initialized with all 0, and $t_m - 1$ is the number of activity-activity pairs for the longest trace). Finally, build a corresponding binary edge label vector $m \in \{0, 1\}^{t_m - 1}$, setting position i to 1 and all other positions to 0.

4. Loop over the third step until the end of the trace. It will end up with $n-1$ positional vectors p and edge label vectors m associated with each edge. As we mentioned, there could be duplicate edges (as the example in step 2), and we deal with this by aggregating (sum) p and m with names of u and v as keys (e.g. 'AB', 'BC', 'CB'). Finally we end up with $k \leq n-1$ positional vectors p as final edge features and edge label vectors m associated with each unique edge that appeared in the trace. The initial node features h_v^0 are specified by one-hot encoding of the activity names.

Figure 1 shows an example of building a graph based on an example event log with 5 nodes and 6 edges. Each node comes with its initial embedding based on its name, and each edge is associated with a positional vector p_i and a label vector m_i. The first element in each cell of p_i stands for the feature computed from the "Variable 1" column, the second is for the "Variable 2" column. The blank space in each cell is filled with $\{0\}^d$ where d is the same dimension for all cells in the vector. In the example, d is 2 (equal to d_e) for p and 1 for m.

Looking more closely at this example, in the constructed graph view, the activity E is more closely related to and affected by A (connected through B). However from the perspective of a flat sequence (such as with LSTM or RNN), E is the farthest event from A. In a hypothetical process, it is possible that event A is a starting event, E is the proceeding event, B corresponds to a "check status" activity, and events C and D happen when B "fails"; otherwise E would directly follow B if A happened. Intuitively, in such a process E should be closely related to A, but the flat sequence where B is near the end of the sequence can not preserve such process logic. Meanwhile in the case where the sequence is very long, the sequence encoder (such as an LSTM or RNN) could suffer from the vanishing gradient problem [30]. These are some of the factors we have considered and lead us to believe that the graph encoding, which takes more structural process information into account, is a better choice than sequence encoding.

3.2   Encoding by the Graph Autoencoder with ECC

To make full use of our graph construction and the converted business process features, we apply edge-conditioned convolution (ECC) filters to obtain a better graph encoding. The ECC filters in the graph autoencoder transform each node representation computed from the previous layer of the neural network and combines them with their transformed neighbor nodes representation conditioning on edge features. Let $l \in \{1, ..., l_m\}$ be the layer index in a feed-forward neural network, h_v^l, $h_{e_{u,v}}^l$ be the vector representation for the node v and edge $e_{u,v}$ at layer l (layer 0 is the input layer). The node representation updating through ECC in the graph can be formulated as:

$$ h_v^l = \phi\Big(F^l(h_v^{l-1}; w) + \sum_{u \in N_d(v)} F_e^l(h_{e_{u,v}}; w_e) h_u^{l-1} + b^l \Big) \tag{6} $$

where ϕ is the activation function, $F^l : \mathbb{R}^{d_{l-1}} \to \mathbb{R}^{d_l}$, and $F_e^l : \mathbb{R}^{d_p} \to \mathbb{R}^{d_l \times d_{l-1}}$ denote a parameterized feature transformation neural network for the node feature and the edge feature, and their corresponding parameters w, w_e. The learnable random initialized bias term $b^l \in \mathbb{R}^{d_l}$ can be learned through backpropagation during training.

The graph reconstruction, i.e., readout, can be treated as an edge label prediction or link prediction similar to the approach introduced in [20]. Based on Eq. (5), the graph reconstruction edge-associated probability of recreating binary edge labels m is formulated as:

$$ m' = \text{sigmoid}\left(F_r(h_u^{l_m} \oplus h_v^{l_m}; w_r) \right) \tag{7} $$

where $u, v \in V, e_{u,v} \in E$, and $F_r : \mathbb{R}^{2d_{l_m}} \to \mathbb{R}^{t_m - 1}$ denotes neural network processing concatenated vector of h_u and h_v with trainable parameter w_r. $\oplus$ denotes vector concatenation.

Finally, instead of Eq. (2), in this paper the reconstruction loss (error) of the target graph is defined by the average of the binary cross entropy loss:

$$ L(m', m) = \frac{1}{k(t_m - 1)} \left(-\sum_{i=1}^{k} \sum_{j=1}^{t_m - 1} m_i^{(j)} \log(m_i'^{(j)}) + (1 - m_i^{(j)})(1 - \log(m_i'^{(j)})) \right) \tag{8} $$

The autoencoder training objective is to minimize the output from (8) through backpropagation. Furthermore, Eq. (8) is used as the anomaly scoring function which is consistent with the approaches in the literature on anomaly detection.

4 Experiments

4.1 Simulated Anomalous Data Sets

As we are not aware of a standard process mining anomaly detection benchmark, we rely on fully or partially simulated data used in the literature. Note that we do not devise our own datasets but borrow the datasets and preprocessing steps from existing work. We consider three types of simulated datasets containing labeled anomalous cases. These anomalous cases are introduced in three ways described below. The dataset details are shown in Table 1. Training, validation, and testing are randomly sampled based on the provided ratios in the table and corresponding data set. Note that the sum may not total to 100% since we used the remainder to create noise cases (mentioned below) based on the original normal and anomalous data.

Table 1. Statistics of event logs we used in our experiments. The 'N' and 'A' in the Test set refer to normal and anomalous cases, respectively. The ratios are counted as a portion of the number of traces. The number of attributes count does not include the activity name.

Event log	No. traces	Max. trace length	No. activities	No. attributes	Training	Validation	Test
BPIC2012	13,087	95	24	2	50%	20%	15%N, 15%A
BPIC2013	7,554	34	11	2	50%	20%	15%N, 15%A
Loan	10,000	63	19	2	25%	10%	15%N, 15%A
BPIC2017	14,289	100	26	1	32%	12%	6%N, 6%A
Large	5,000	14	43	4	32%	12%	6%N, 6%A
Huge	5,000	13	55	4	32%	12%	6%N, 6%A

4.1.1 Log Attributes Anomalies

To evaluate the detection of anomalies in a distorted or wrongly recorded log, we follow [24] by using simulated anomalies injected into two public real event logs, from the BPI challenges of 2012 and 2013 (BPIC2012 and BPIC2013). We use the same original data with the corresponding process to introduce anomalies[1] as described in [24]. Every anomalous trace is simulated by randomly choosing a proportion of $L/2$ activity columns and replacing them with random activities sampled from U_A, and choosing a proportion of $L/2$ activity duration columns and replacing them with uniformly random sampled values ranging from the minimum and maximum activity duration values observed in this column. Thus it will create a proportion of L anomalous values for one anomalous trace. In our experiments we set $L = 0.5$ for these two datasets.

---

[1] Available at BPIC2012 and BPIC2013 data sets with injected anomalies.

4.1.2 Activity Ordering Anomalies

In this case, an anomaly is caused by a variation of the activity ordering [36] or concept drift [9]. During process execution, a change in the activity ordering may happen due to a change in the environment, and it can be seasonal or hourly but only takes up a small portion of all executed cases. This type of anomaly is sampled by a certain pattern or distribution instead of random error. We use the same simulated loan access data set from [23]. The event logs in this work are simulated by the Apromore [34] platform for a loan access process. Anomalies here are introduced as changes of the activity ordering in mainly 3 categories: *Insertion ("I")*, e.g., add/remove fragment or duplicate fragment in the control flow; *Resequentialization ("R")*, e.g., synchronize two fragments or make two fragments sequential in the control flow; and *Optionalization ("O")*, e.g., change the branching frequency or make a fragment skippable in the control flow. The details of these categories are described in [23]. In our experiment, we use six composite operations ("IOR", "IRO", "OIR", "ORI", "RIO", "ROI") to form anomalous traces. For example, the operation "IRO" is obtained by first adding a new activity ("I"), then making this activity in parallel with an existing activity ("R") and finally skipping the latter activity ("O"). Each composite operation of the six forms have the same amount of anomalous traces.

4.1.3 Composite Anomalies

We also evaluated our anomaly detector against the combination of random attribute changes and changes in the activity ordering using the existing three data sets: BPIC2017, 'Large', and 'Huge'[2] simulated by [27], where anomalies are injected by the following 6 types of operations:

1. Skip: A sequence of up to 3 events is skipped.
2. Insert: Up to 3 random activities are inserted in random places in the trace.
3. Rework: A sequence of up to 3 events is repeated.
4. Early: A sequence of up to 2 events is moved backward in the trace.
5. Late: A sequence of up to 2 events is moved forward in the trace.
6. Attribute: An attribute value is mutated in up to 3 events in the trace.

It should be mentioned that in this case the above operations are directly applied to the event log without considering any underlying process model, thus they are not simply mixtures of the previous two anomalous types. For example, the Rework operation applied on a log may not result in an anomalous case if the control flow permits a loop over these events, such as a process model with a 'check' and 'resubmit' control loop until the submission is satisfied.

Meanwhile during training and validation, in order to test the impact of noise as mentioned in the literature [26], we introduce a noise ratio $r \in [0, 0.5]$ to all data sets mentioned above, where r is the proportion of anomalous cases manually added into training and validation sets.

---

[2] Available at: BPIC2017, 'Large', and 'Huge' data sets with injected anomalies.

4.2   Experiment Settings and Results

We compare our *Graph Autoencoder (GAE)* with three baseline autoencoders: the original *multilayer perceptron-based autoencoder (AE)* [24,26–28], a *variational autoencoder (VAE)* [24] and a *LSTM-based autoencoder (LSTMAE)* [24]. Note that a modified version of the latter was also used in [27] as an encoding network. We choose the F1 score, where correctly detected anomaly cases are treated as true positive cases, to measure their detection performance.

For the configurations of the three baseline models, we consider the neural network layer settings used in [24]. For AE and VAE we use two encoding dense layers [31] and two decoding dense layers, and for LSTMAE we use one encoding LSTM layer and one decoding LSTM layer. These layer sizes are adapted to input dimensions. Regarding the graph neural network configurations, initially we use one ECC layer ($l = 1$) for Eq. (6) and 1-layer dense layer for F, F_e and F_r for Eqs. (6) and (7). The hidden embedding $h_v^{l_m}$ is set to be $2\times$ h_v^0 for each dataset.

For the training of the neural networks, we use the Adam optimizer [19] with a learning rate of 0.001, the training batch size is 8 and the training epoch is 100 with early stopping [11] to avoid overfitting. During the validation phase, we choose the anomaly threshold θ based on the reconstruction error as in [26], but we use the average reconstruction error on the validation data instead of the training data since the validation data can better represent data which has not been used to train the model. Meanwhile we tune the model hyper-parameters to maximize the F1 score on the validation data. To summarize, we use the training set to train the autoencoder and the validation set to determine an appropriate θ and tune model hyper-parameters.

Table 2. F1 score for different autoencoders and datasets with training and validation set noise ratio $r = 0$.

	BPIC2012	BPIC2013	Loan	BPIC2017	Large	Huge
GAE	**0.95**	**0.67**	**0.98**	**0.72**	**0.93**	0.86
LSTMAE	0.64	0.37	0.86	0.63	0.90	**0.88**
AE	0.52	0.32	0.89	0.56	0.83	0.81
VAE	0.51	0.27	0.83	0.52	0.73	0.69

First we evaluate our proposed method and the other baselines on the six synthesized data sets mentioned above, with noise $r = 0$. Table 2 shows the results on the test sets. We observe that our GAE method performs better in 5 out of 6 cases than the other three baseline approaches in the non-noise settings. There are two main reasons for this improvement. Firstly, the GAE captures extra structural process information and relations among activity occurrences, which are key components in process data, in addition to process attribute features, and treats these activities as nodes (functional central components) within the neural network. The other three baseline approaches do not exploit that structure and treat the data as simple flat event series data. Secondly, for our case-level anomaly detection task, the objective function for the GAE, which is to recreate the edge label, becomes easier than for the other three autoencoders, which try to recreate the data itself with mixed features. Some data sets such as BPIC2012 and BPIC2017 contain long traces that result in large encoding feature vectors for AE, VAE and LSTMAE to recreate, and this can cause inefficient training and limiting their performance. The GAE however simplifies the task by recreating abstract structural information (i.e., binary edge labels) instead of data attributes themselves. Thus it is easier for the GAE training to converge.

In practice training and validation sets will have some degree of noise as mentioned above, and in order to test the effects of noise on the performance, assuming that in a normal system anomalous cases are rare [5,29], we set the noise parameter r to be $\{0.1, 0.2, 0.3, 0.4, 0.5\}$ for the six data sets. Figure 2 shows the F1 score under these different noise ratio settings, where we can observe that due to uncertainty and inconsistency introduced by noise in training and validation, model performance becomes generally worse. However the GAE approach still performs better in most situations (23 out of 30 experimental points) than the other baselines, suggesting that GAE is more robust to noisy data.

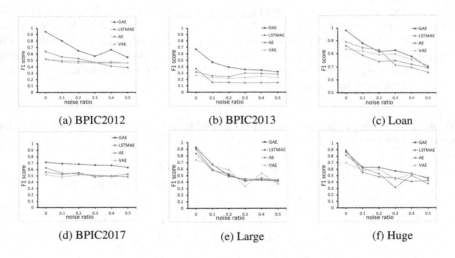

(a) BPIC2012   (b) BPIC2013   (c) Loan

(d) BPIC2017   (e) Large   (f) Huge

Fig. 2. F1 score for the six data sets with varying training/validation noise ratio r.

4.3   Anomaly Example and Diagnostic Information

In addition to identifying an anomaly, sometimes it is useful to explain or give insights on the nature of the anomaly. To that end, in this section, we provide an example that illustrates the information that our approach produces.

Figure 3a shows a BPMN model that was used by [23] to create the 'Loan' event log mentioned above. This model represents 'normal' process behaviour

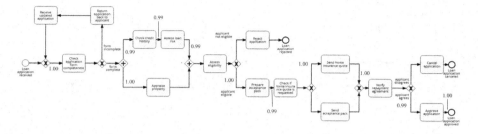

(a) A process model representing normal behavior annotated with edge anomaly scores from a normal trace.

CaseID	Activity	Timestamp	EventType
b1_101	Loan application received	2004-02-10T11:30:00.000+00:00	assign
b1_101	Loan application received	2004-02-10T11:30:00.000+00:00	complete
b1_101	Check application form completeness	2004-02-10T11:30:00.000+00:00	assign
b1_101	Check application form completeness	2004-02-10T12:11:43.834+00:00	complete
b1_101	Appraise property	2004-02-10T12:11:43.834+00:00	assign
b1_101	Check credit history	2004-02-10T12:11:43.834+00:00	assign
b1_101	Check credit history	2004-02-10T12:45:07.845+00:00	complete
b1_101	Assess loan risk	2004-02-10T12:45:07.845+00:00	assign
b1_101	Appraise property	2004-02-10T12:46:02.233+00:00	complete
b1_101	Assess loan risk	2004-02-10T13:05:47.283+00:00	complete
b1_101	Assess eligibility	2004-02-10T13:05:47.283+00:00	assign
b1_101	Assess eligibility	2004-02-10T13:07:04.188+00:00	complete
b1_101	Prepare acceptance pack	2004-02-10T13:07:04.188+00:00	assign
b1_101	Prepare acceptance pack	2004-02-10T13:52:51.236+00:00	complete
b1_101	Check if home insurance quote is requested	2004-02-10T13:52:51.236+00:00	assign
b1_101	Check if home insurance quote is requested	2004-02-10T14:10:44.533+00:00	complete
b1_101	Send home insurance quote	2004-02-10T14:10:44.533+00:00	assign
b1_101	Send home insurance quote	2004-02-10T14:19:59.779+00:00	complete
b1_101	Verify repayment agreement	2004-02-10T14:19:59.779+00:00	assign
b1_101	Verify repayment agreement	2004-02-10T14:41:08.538+00:00	complete
b1_101	Approve application	2004-02-10T14:41:08.538+00:00	assign
b1_101	Approve application	2004-02-10T14:52:57.812+00:00	complete
b1_101	Loan application approved	2004-02-10T14:52:57.812+00:00	assign
b1_101	Loan application approved	2004-02-10T14:52:57.812+00:00	complete

(b) Event log of normal trace b1_101, taken from the 'Loan' data set [23].

(c) GAE generated graph with edge anomaly scores for normal trace b1_101.

Fig. 3. An example of a normal case from the 'Loan' data set.

(ignore the blue numerical annotations for now). Figure 3b shows an example trace that is generated from this BPMN model and is included in one subset of the 'Loan' event log. The corresponding graph that is constructed by our GAE is shown in Fig. 3c. It is classified as a 'normal' trace with low reconstruction error.

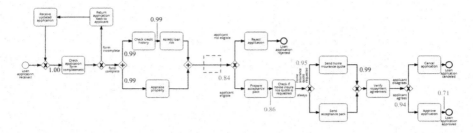

(a) A process model representing anomalous behavior annotated with edge anomaly scores from an anomalous trace.

CaseID	Activity	Timestamp	EventType
r1_10	Loan application received	2004-05-03T14:00:00.000+00:00	assign
r1_10	Loan application received	2004-05-03T14:00:00.000+00:00	complete
r1_10	Check application form completeness	2004-05-03T14:00:00.000+00:00	assign
r1_10	Check application form completeness	2004-05-03T14:09:02.570+00:00	complete
r1_10	Appraise property	2004-05-03T14:09:02.570+00:00	assign
r1_10	Check credit history	2004-05-03T14:09:02.570+00:00	assign
r1_10	Check credit history	2004-05-03T14:11:19.888+00:00	complete
r1_10	Assess loan risk	2004-05-03T14:11:19.888+00:00	assign
r1_10	Assess loan risk	2004-05-03T14:11:49.985+00:00	complete
r1_10	Appraise property	2004-05-03T14:52:26.357+00:00	complete
r1_10	Prepare acceptance pack	2004-05-03T14:52:26.357+00:00	assign
r1_10	Prepare acceptance pack	2004-05-03T15:20:39.245+00:00	assign
r1_10	Check if home insurance quote is requested	2004-05-03T15:20:39.245+00:00	assign
r1_10	Check if home insurance quote is requested	2004-05-03T15:20:56.809+00:00	complete
r1_10	Send home insurance quote	2004-05-03T15:20:56.809+00:00	assign
r1_10	Send home insurance quote	2004-05-03T15:29:23.537+00:00	complete
r1_10	Verify repayment agreement	2004-05-03T15:29:23.537+00:00	assign
r1_10	Verify repayment agreement	2004-05-03T15:43:44.163+00:00	complete
r1_10	Approve application	2004-05-03T15:43:44.163+00:00	assign
r1_10	Approve application	2004-05-04T10:26:41.331+00:00	complete
r1_10	Loan application approved	2004-05-04T10:26:41.331+00:00	assign
r1_10	Loan application approved	2004-05-04T10:26:41.331+00:00	complete

(b) Event logs of anomalous trace r1_10, taken from the 'Loan' data set

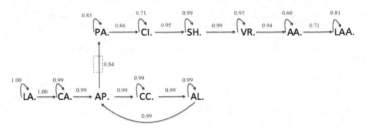

(c) GAE generated graph with edge anomaly scores for anomalous trace r1_10.

Fig. 4. An example of anomalous case.

The reconstruction error has been proposed in earlier work [26] as additional diagnostic information. However, note that the reconstruction error is unbounded and hence its interpretation is less intuitive than a probability. Since we use explicit graph edges in our model, we can obtain, for each edge of the trace, a prediction probability that can be used as an edge-specific anomaly score, based on Eqs. (7) and (8). These probabilities are shown in Fig. 3c adjacent to the edges. (Here, we use the first 2 letters to represent the activity name, e.g., "AE" stands for "Assess eligibility".) As expected, these probabilities are very high for a normal trace of our highly regular process. Figure 3b shows, for easier reference, the same probabilities played back in the original process model based on a matching of the graph edges.

Figure 4a shows a process model that can be seen as a concept drift with respect to the model in Fig. 3a: the activity 'Assess eligibility' has been removed. The traces generated from the process model in Fig. 4a can hence be considered as anomalies with respect to the normal behavior represented by Fig. 3a, Fig. 4b shows such an anomalous trace generated from the process model in Fig. 4a. The corresponding GAE graph and its edge anomaly scores are depicted in Fig. 4c. A drop in the anomaly score, marked in brown, now occurs on various edges, first between the activities "Access Loan Risk", "Appraise property" and "Prepare acceptance pack". This corresponds to the missing edges from the former two activities to the latter in the training set, where the flow has to go through the activity "Assess eligibility". Again, Fig. 4a shows, for easier reference, the same probabilities played back in the process model.

It is interesting to observe that some edges after this first anomalous point in the control flow are also affected with low scores, and the reason is that our objective function in the GAE is to predict a edge label m, which contains the absolute activity location information in a trace, based on positional vector p. Therefore, a case of delayed or early execution would also be punished with a low score. For example, "Approve application" happens earlier than usual (even if it correctly directly follows "Verify Repayment") and hence we observe a lower score on the edge toward it.

Also it should be mentioned that the GAE computes the embedding of each event type as a node embedding and makes predictions based on them. Neighboring events should have similar graph embeddings [16] in general since they are updated and synchronized closely with each other. Meanwhile edge predictions rely on events which are very close to each other, thus missing one event does not bring those scores sharply down to 0, and we can observe that edge anomaly scores are around 15% lower than the normal for respective edges.

In summary, our GAE setup detects anomalous process cases by taking into account both event ordering and the timestamps and activity durations in a trace. The edge prediction probability scores also reflect detected anomalies.

5   Conclusion

In this paper, we propose a new graph autoencoder approach for anomaly detection for business process event logs. As opposed to existing methods, we construct a graph for each log trace and apply a graph encoding in order to capture structural process information. Experimental results on six data sets with three types of anomaly settings demonstrates the advantages of our approach over other autoencoder based approaches, which do not use that structural process information. Also, experiments show our graph autoencoder is robust to a certain level of noise during training and validation, which we believe is beneficial for use in practice.

References

1. Aalst, W.V.: Process mining: data science in action (2016)
2. Aalst, W.V., Adriansyah, A., Medeiros, A.K.A.D., Arcieri, F., Baier, T.: Process mining manifesto. Business Process Management Workshops (2011)
3. Aalst, W.V., Medeiros, A.K.A.D.: Process mining and security: detecting anomalous process executions and checking process conformance. Electron. Notes Theor. Comput. Sci. **121**, 3–21 (2005)
4. Aalst, W.V., Weijters, A., Maruster, L.: Workflow mining: discovering process models from event logs. IEEE Trans. Knowl. Data Eng. **16**, 1128–1142 (2004)
5. Angiulli, F., Pizzuti, C.: Fast outlier detection in high dimensional spaces. In: PKDD (2002)
6. Bengio, Y.: Learning deep architectures for AI. Found. Trends Mach. Learn. **2**, 1–127 (2007)
7. Bezerra, F., Wainer, J.: Algorithms for anomaly detection of traces in logs of process aware information systems. Inf. Syst. **38**, 33–44 (2013)
8. Bezerra, F., Wainer, J., Aalst, W.V.: Anomaly detection using process mining. In: BMMDS/EMMSAD (2009)
9. Bose, R.P., Aalst, W.V., Žliobaitė, I., Pechenizkiy, M.: Dealing with concept drifts in process mining. IEEE Trans. Neural Networks Learn. Syst. **25**, 154–171 (2014)
10. Bruna, J., Zaremba, W., Szlam, A., LeCun, Y.: Spectral networks and locally connected networks on graphs. CoRR abs/1312.6203 (2014)
11. Caruana, R., Lawrence, S., Giles, C.L.: Overfitting in neural nets: Backpropagation, conjugate gradient, and early stopping. In: NIPS (2000)
12. Defferrard, M., Bresson, X., Vandergheynst, P.: Convolutional neural networks on graphs with fast localized spectral filtering. In: NIPS (2016)
13. Duvenaud, D., et al.: Convolutional networks on graphs for learning molecular fingerprints. In: NIPS (2015)
14. Gilmer, J., Schoenholz, S.S., Riley, P.F., Vinyals, O., Dahl, G.E.: Neural message passing for quantum chemistry. In: Precup, D., Teh, Y.W. (eds.) Proceedings of the 34th International Conference on Machine Learning. Proceedings of Machine Learning Research, vol. 70, pp. 1263–1272. PMLR, 06–11 August 2017
15. Gori, M., Monfardini, G., Scarselli, F.: A new model for learning in graph domains. In: Proceedings of the 2005 IEEE International Joint Conference on Neural Networks, 2005, vol. 2, pp. 729–734 (2005)
16. Hamilton, W.L., Ying, Z., Leskovec, J.: Inductive representation learning on large graphs. In: NIPS (2017)
17. Hinkka, M., Lehto, T., Heljanko, K., Jung, A.: Structural feature selection for event logs. ArXiv abs/1710.02823 (2017)
18. Jain, R., Abouzakhar, N.: Hidden Markov model based anomaly intrusion detection. Presented at the (2012)
19. Kingma, D.P., Ba, J.: Adam: a method for stochastic optimization. CoRR abs/1412.6980 (2015)
20. Kipf, T., Welling, M.: Variational graph auto-encoders. ArXiv abs/1611.07308 (2016)

21. Koninck, P.D., Broucke, S.V., Weerdt, J.: act2vec, trace2vec, log2vec, and model2vec: representation learning for business processes. In: BPM (2018)
22. Li, Y., Tarlow, D., Brockschmidt, M., Zemel, R.: Gated graph sequence neural networks. CoRR abs/1511.05493 (2016)
23. Maaradji, A., Dumas, M., Rosa, M., Ostovar, A.: Fast and accurate business process drift detection. In: BPM (2015)
24. Nguyen, H.C., Lee, S., Kim, J., Ko, J., Comuzzi, M.: Autoencoders for improving quality of process event logs. Expert Syst. Appl. **131**, 132–147 (2019)
25. Niepert, M., Ahmed, M., Kutzkov, K.: Learning convolutional neural networks for graphs. ArXiv abs/1605.05273 (2016)
26. Nolle, T., Luettgen, S., Seeliger, A., Mühlhäuser, M.: Analyzing business process anomalies using autoencoders. Mach. Learn. **107**(11), 1875–1893 (2018)
27. Nolle, T., Luettgen, S., Seeliger, A., Mühlhäuser, M.: Binet: multi-perspective business process anomaly classification. Information Systems, p. 101458, October 2019
28. Nolle, T., Seeliger, A., Mühlhäuser, M.: Unsupervised anomaly detection in noisy business process event logs using denoising autoencoders. In: DS (2016)
29. Ord, K.: Outliers in statistical data: V. barnett and t. lewis, 1994, 3rd edition, 584 pp., [uk pound]55.00, isbn 0-471-93094-6. International Journal of Forecasting 12, 175-176 (1996)
30. Pascanu, R., Mikolov, T., Bengio, Y.: On the difficulty of training recurrent neural networks. In: ICML (2013)
31. Paszke, A., et al.: Pytorch: an imperative style, high-performance deep learning library. ArXiv abs/1912.01703 (2019)
32. Pegoraro, M., Uysal, M.S., Aalst, W.V.: Discovering process models from uncertain event data. ArXiv abs/1909.11567 (2019)
33. Rogge-Solti, A., Kasneci, G.: Temporal anomaly detection in business processes. BPM (2014)
34. Rosa, M., Reijers, H., Aalst, W.V., Dijkman, R., Mendling, J., Dumas, M., García-Bañuelos, L.: Apromore: an advanced process model repository. Expert Syst. Appl. **38**, 7029–7040 (2011)
35. Rozinat, A., Aalst, W.V.: Conformance checking of processes based on monitoring real behavior. Inf. Syst. **33**, 64–95 (2008)
36. Sarno, R., Sari, P.L.I., Ginardi, H., Sunaryono, D., Mukhlash, I.: Decision mining for multi choice workflow patterns. Presented at the (2013)
37. Savickas, T., Vasilecas, O.: Business process event log transformation into bayesian belief network. In: ISD (2014)
38. Scarselli, F., Gori, M., Tsoi, A., Hagenbuchner, M., Monfardini, G.: The graph neural network model. IEEE Trans. Neural Networks **20**, 61–80 (2009)
39. Schölkopf, B., Williamson, R., Smola, A., Shawe-Taylor, J., Platt, J.C.: Support vector method for novelty detection. In: NIPS (1999)
40. Simonovsky, M., Komodakis, N.: Dynamic edge-conditioned filters in convolutional neural networks on graphs. Presented at the (2017)
41. Warrender, C., Forrest, S., Pearlmutter, B.A.: Detecting intrusions using system calls: alternative data models. In: Proceedings of the 1999 IEEE Symposium on Security and Privacy (Cat. No.99CB36344), pp. 133–145 (1999)
42. Zhou, C., Paffenroth, R.C.: Anomaly detection with robust deep autoencoders. Presented at the (2017)

Digital Innovation and Process Improvement

Drivers and Barriers of the Digital Innovation Process – Case Study Insights from a German Public University

Emil Kleider[1], Thomas Kreuzer[2], Benedict Lösser[1(✉)], Anna Maria Oberländer[1], and Torsten Eymann[1]

[1] FIM Research Center, Fraunhofer FIT Project Group Business & Information Systems Engineering, University of Bayreuth, Bayreuth, Germany
{emil.kleider,benedict.loesser,anna.oberlaender,
torsten.eymann}@fim-rc.de
[2] FIM Research Center, Fraunhofer FIT Project Group Business & Information Systems Engineering, University of Augsburg, Augsburg, Germany
thomas.kreuzer@fit.fraunhofer.de

Abstract. Due to growing digital opportunities, persistent legislative pressure, and recent challenges in the wake of the COVID-19 pandemic, public universities need to engage in digital innovation (DI). While society expects universities to lead DI efforts, the successful development and implementation of DIs, particularly in administration and management contexts, remains a challenge. In addition, research lacks knowledge on the DI process at public universities, while further understanding and guidance are needed. Against this backdrop, our study aims to enhance the understanding of the DI process at public universities by providing a structured overview of corresponding drivers and barriers through an exploratory single case study. We investigate the case of a German public university and draw from primary and secondary data of its DI process from the development of three specific digital process innovations. Building upon Business Process Management (BPM) as a theoretical lens to study the DI process, we present 13 drivers and 17 barriers structured along the DI actions and BPM core elements. We discuss corresponding findings and provide related practice recommendations for public universities that aim to engage in DI. In sum, our study contributes to the explanatory knowledge at the convergent interface between DI and BPM in the context of public universities.

Keywords: Digital innovation · Digital innovation process · Process innovation · Public university · Case study

1 Introduction

Public universities are in dire need to change. As a result of society's ongoing digitalization and related digitalization plans of legislators for higher education institutions [1], universities have been facing pressure to explore digital opportunities for several years

A. Polyvyanyy et al. (Eds.): BPM 2021, LNCS 12875, pp. 437–454, 2021.
https://doi.org/10.1007/978-3-030-85469-0_27

[2]. Hence, digital transformation is at the top of public universities' agendas [3]. The outbreak of the COVID-19 pandemic and related restrictions of physical contacts have even further accelerated the need to digitalize and innovate the education sector, creating a necessity for public universities to engage in digital innovation (DI), e.g., in digital lectures or digital student communication [4].

DI has traditionally been defined as the realization of new combinations of digital and physical components to produce novel products [5]. More recent research extended the understanding of DI by defining it as the "use of digital technology during the process of innovating" [6, p. 223] as a means or an end [7]. As such, DI is not just about digital technology per se, but also refers to the means to change and enable new paths of innovating [8]. While there is little research explicitly addressing DI at public universities, there is a mature body of knowledge on DI in the public sector in general, which universities in many countries belong to, including Germany and Austria [9]. Among the few studies that specifically address universities, mainly the role of technological change in innovation in higher education institutions has been studied [10], e.g., the impact of the technological transformation on university education and science [11]. Besides, recent research focuses on the switch to digital teaching in the course of the COVID-19 pandemic [12] and the establishment of hybrid campuses [4]. Despite the growing need for public universities to complement this digital progress in teaching with DI in administration and management, research on the process of DI in public universities' administration and management contexts remains scarce.

In sum, digital technologies and legislative pressure equally enable and require public universities to engage in DI – a dynamic that has been exacerbated by the COVID-19 pandemic. However, public universities struggle to meet the expectation to be at the forefront of DI in society and to act as DI pioneers in administration and management [10, 13]. Thus, it is crucial to understand how the DI process at public universities unfolds to better recognize and support its initiation, development, implementation, and exploitation. Against this backdrop, we ask the following research question: *How do public universities enact the DI process and what are related drivers and barriers?*

We address this twofold research question by an exploratory single case study [14] as DI at public universities is an emergent research field that has to be investigated with regards to its context. Specifically, we investigated the case of a German university (GU) to derive a structured overview of drivers and barriers from assessing the development of three digital process innovations in GU's administration and management. We took Business Process Management (BPM) as a theoretical lens on the DI process to structure our interviews and analysis approach. This way, we were able to draw from mature knowledge from both research fields to gain insights into our collected data. First, we relied on Kohli and Melville's [15] DI actions as a structuring element for the DI process. Second, we applied the core elements of BPM in the digital age following Kerpedzhiev et al. [16] to derive drivers and barriers of the DI process at public universities. Thereby, we locate our study at the intersection of two convergent research fields, i.e., DI and BPM, following recommendations from recent literature (e.g., [8, 17]). Our research contributes to the explanatory knowledge on DI at public universities, the convergent literature on DI and BPM, and fits into the management-related research avenue in BPM to study and improve the process of DI [18].

The remainder of our work is structured as follows: In the second section, we give an overview of the theoretical background of DI and BPM and elaborate on their convergence. Next, we describe our research method in section three before we illustrate the case at hand and units of analysis in section four. In section five, we present the results in terms of drivers and barriers and corresponding practice recommendations. We discuss our results in the sixth section and conclude with limitations and avenues for future research.

2 Background

2.1 Digital Innovation

An increasingly dynamic environment created by digital technologies affects not only companies but also public institutions [10]. Therefore, DI as a means to sense, seize, and transform opportunities and mitigate threats is crucial for public and non-public organizations to sustain future viability [19]. In this regard, digital technologies are used to extract, create, analyze, communicate, or exploit information in a specific context and are hence considered to be fundamental to DI [20]. DI can serve as a trigger for digital transformation as it leads to organizational changes – especially in incumbents-going beyond purely new organizing logics [21]. Thereby, DI shapes the environmental conditions that digital transformation, as a process, has to adapt to [21].

DI has been frequently discussed from an outcome-centric perspective related to novel processes, products, services, or business models [5, 22], but can also be understood as a process enabled or complemented by the use of digital technologies [6]. In their literature review, Kohli and Melville [15] broadly conceptualized the DI process along four actions (Fig. 1): *Initiate, Develop, Implement* and *Exploit. Initiate* includes triggers, opportunity identification, and initial decision making. *Develop* can be defined by the stages of designing, developing, and adopting new artifacts. *Implement* includes installing, maintaining, training, and incentives while *Exploit* aims to maximize returns and leverage the existing system and data for new purposes. External and internal factors influence these actions to ultimately create a DI outcome. Although the four actions are useful for structuring the DI process, in practice, they are not always fully present or sequential and can be difficult to disentangle.

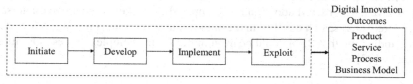

Fig. 1. DI process based on Kohli and Melville [15]

As already stated, higher education institutions often fail to fulfill the expectations by policy makers to serve as pioneers for DI [13]. In this regard, the relevance of digital technologies for teaching and also for its underlying administration and management has been recognized (e.g., [23]). However, although traditional innovation in public university contexts has received fundamental attention in recent literature (e.g., [13]), research on opportunities and challenges of DI in this context remains scarce. For our study, we understand DI at public universities as a process that unfolds along the four DI actions by Kohli and Melville [15].

2.2 Business Process Management

BPM is the practice and science of overseeing how work is performed to ensure consistent outcomes and to take advantage of improvement opportunities [24]. According to Dumas et al. [24], processes are defined as sets of activities in which humans and technology co-create value. In this regard, BPM strives for the continuous management of business processes as well as for the development of organizations' BPM capabilities [25]. BPM as a discipline provides methods, techniques, and tools to support the improvement, execution, management, and analysis of processes [24, 26]. It can be broadly conceptualized along six core elements: *Strategic Alignment, Governance, Methods, IT, People*, and *Culture* [26]. These core elements build one of the most frequently adopted frameworks for managing BPM in academia and practice [16]. Practitioners, for example, can use the core elements as structuring elements for project, program, and strategy management [26]. In the scientific BPM community, the core elements are well known, accepted, and used, e.g., for capability development [16] or as the structure of the well-known Handbook on BPM [25].

Strategic Alignment can be defined as the alignment of organizational goals and priorities with business processes. *Governance* refers to establishing relevant and transparent accountability and decision-making processes to align rewards and guide actions. *Methods* is targeted towards approaches and techniques that support and enable consistent process actions and outcomes. The *IT*-element refers to the software, hardware, and information management systems that enable and support process activities. *Culture* considers the collective values and beliefs that shape process-related attitudes and behaviors. Lastly, *People* includes the individuals and groups who continually enhance and apply their process-related expertise and knowledge [16, 26]. As digitalization places new demands on BPM, the core elements have been adjusted following a Delphi Study by Kerpedzhiev et al. [16] who suggested an integrated perspective on the core elements *Method* and *IT* due to their interrelatedness in the digital age.

BPM is often studied in a business context. In contrast, public sector organizations tend to have a lower BPM adoption rate compared to market-competitive organizations [17]. Moreover, research on BPM in the higher education context remains scarce despite studies indicating that BPM could be meaningful for the complex process structure of a university [27].

2.3 Convergence of DI and BPM

BPM traditionally focuses on incremental process improvement in terms of efficiency, effectiveness and customer experience rather than on disruptive process innovation [28]. Accordingly, recent research acknowledges that existing BPM methods are not able to capitalize on opportunities associated with DI, which is why the two have historically even been understood as opposing research streams [29]. However, as noted by Mendling et al. [8], BPM and DI still have a lot in common and could benefit from each other as they approach similar problems in completely different manners. Both BPM and DI are about processes, both are driven by emerging digital technologies and have an increasing importance of context [27, 30]. Recent research hence advocates that the two research streams could enrich each other with regard to methods, phenomena and assumptions [8]. While BPM could benefit from DI in terms of more innovative, faster and more efficient business processes [16, 18], DI could benefit from BPM in terms of a more systematic management of the inherent process transformation [8].

Accordingly, research just starts to investigate the interface of both disciplines. For instance, van Looy and Poels [18] call for an investigation of the DI process from a BPM perspective while formulating seven trends at the interface of DI and BPM, like ever changing customer experience and increasing need for business-IT alignment. Furthermore, Mendling et al. [8] proposed hypotheses that combine and resolve the apparently contradictory assumptions of the two disciplines in isolation. These are intended to create a balance over time between strong structure and complete unboundedness.

In conclusion, an analysis at the interface between DI and BPM in the context of public universities seems valuable as it poses unique challenges and specifically addresses the open and practice-relevant questions at the interface of both research disciplines. As already shown, recent literature established BPM as an eminently suitable theoretical lens for studying the DI process [8, 17], e.g., regarding its methods for process improvement [31]. Accordingly, we adopt the compilation of five BPM core elements suggested by Kerpedzhiev et al. [16] to analyze the DI process of public universities, as they were specifically built for the digital age, which fits our case and context.

3   Method

3.1   Research Design and Case Selection

To analyze how public universities enact the DI process and to identify related drivers and barriers, we conducted an exploratory single case study. A case study is capable of investigating emergent phenomena where the subject of investigation must be studied within its natural context [14, 32]. Exploratory case study research is used when the area is still in a state of understanding and description [14, 33]. As DI at public universities is an emergent topic that must be studied within its specific context [10], we considered an exploratory case study appropriate to address our research question.

We decided to conduct a single case study as it is appropriate for a representative or revelatory case [14], which applies to the special context of German public universities. As public service providers, they hardly compete with each other according to market principles [34]. Most German university students are enrolled at a public university [35], and many high-rated German universities are public ones. This is in contrast to other countries, e.g., the United States or Australia, where the top-rated universities are mostly private. Despite higher education legislation in Germany being primarily a matter of the federal states, there is one nationwide law defining admission requirements and responsibilities that apply to all universities. Hence, German public universities' organizational structure follows a similar and representative pattern, including university management responsible for strategic decisions and a university administration responsible for providing services for researchers, lecturers, and students [34, 35]. In addition, after the legal restrictions imposed due to the COVID-19 pandemic, German universities had to conduct their first completely digital semester in the summer of 2020, providing a unique opportunity to analyze the ad-hoc development of DI. Thus, the case of a German public university is not just representative but also of revelatory nature.

Following a purposive sampling approach, we chose the case of *GU* as a part of the previously mentioned representative group of German public universities [36]. A close link to its CIO provided us with access to a wide range of university management staff, internal and external (IT) experts, and process stakeholders. Following Benbunan-Fich et al.'s [37] advice to investigate more than one instance to derive insightful results, we adopted an embedded case study approach with multiple units of analysis [14], i.e., the DI process of three digital process innovations. We describe both *GU* and the three units of analysis in more detail in the case description section.

3.2 Data Collection and Analysis

We understand the DI process to unfold along four actions that are carried out to generate a DI outcome [15]. In the context of our case study, these DI outcomes refer to three digital process innovations in *GU*'s administration and management, i.e., digitally improved or re-engineered processes [15]. To derive drivers and barriers of *GU*'s DI process, we combined data collection methods from different sources of evidence to increase the internal validity, offset biases, and triangulate our results [32]. Specifically, we drew from primary and secondary data by combining semi-structured interviews with the screening of documents (Table 1).

Table 1. Overview of data sources

	Primary data: semi-structured interviews		Secondary data: documents
	1st interview round: 4 interviews	2nd interview round: 8 interviews	8 documents
Sources	• DI experts within the university • DI experts of the external service provider	• University management (UM) • IT experts (IT) • Process participants (PP) • Other involved employees (OE)	• Internal meeting protocols • Internal documents (process handbook) • Publicly available reports (e.g., recruiting guide, structure and development plan)

We collected data over a 10-week period between September and December 2020. Our primary data collection method comprised two rounds of semi-structured interviews [38]. Most interviews were conducted digitally, attended by at least two authors, and lasted one to two hours. We selected interviewees based on their role, expertise, and expected contribution. To gain a holistic understanding of *GU*'s DI process, we interviewed staff from different organizational units and ensured that at least one interview was in the IT department and the university administration for each unit of analysis.

In the first round, we conducted four interviews with DI experts of *GU* and the external IT service provider to gain an overview of the process landscape and to choose suitable units of analysis. In the second round, we aimed to gain a deeper understanding of the chosen units of analysis to identify drivers and barriers related to the DI process. Despite the frequent use of the terms drivers and barriers in innovation research (e.g. [39]), the understanding of these terms varies strongly since only a few studies explicitly address their meaning (e.g., [40]). To avoid ambiguity, we define drivers as factors that support (e.g., accelerating or facilitating) and barriers as factors that hinder (e.g., delaying or preventing) the DI process or individual DI actions. We followed this understanding of drivers and barriers accordingly when questioning the interviewees in the second round. Moreover, we defined two dimensions to structure our interviews, data, and findings. First, we drew from Kohli and Melville's [15] conceptualization of DI actions, i.e., *Initiate, Develop, Implement,* and *Exploit.* Second, we took a BPM-perspective on the DI process drawing from the five core elements of BPM, namely *Strategic Alignment, Governance, Methods/IT, Culture,* and *People* [16].

We analyzed the data iteratively during the process of data collection to reassess and adjust our approach after each interview, comparing it with previous findings to take advantage of the opportunity for collecting new or even better data [41]. Our analysis approach for primary data followed three steps: First, we analyzed the interview notes and compared them to the interview protocol to make sure all areas were addressed. Second, in line with [42], two authors independently analyzed the interviews and used open coding to assign a total of 329 statements related to the DI process. One statement consisted of at least one sentence addressing one DI action and one or more BPM core elements and was coded along the same two structuring dimensions. We then discussed the coded statements in the entire team of authors, compared them again with the interview notes where necessary and combined those with similar meaning to derive an initial set of 46 drivers and 34 barriers structured along the analysis dimensions. Third, by using axial coding techniques following Wolfswinkel et al. [42], the two authors involved in the open coding process identified interrelationships between the derived drivers and barriers of the initial set, e.g., by recognizing a mutual cause for different barriers related to communication that we aggregated into one overarching barrier. Hence, we were able to consolidate selected drivers and barriers to make them more meaningful. We thereby discussed interim results iteratively within the full author team to increase our understanding of the composed drivers and barriers.

In this regard, we observed five pairs of drivers and barriers that address the same topic but with contrasting manifestations in the real world. To include only the respective driver or barrier that had the strongest impact on the overall DI process, we compared both the number of mentions per manifestation as well as their influence implied by the interviewee's statements. After phrasing the resulting drivers and barriers to be as self-explanatory as possible, our final set comprises 13 drivers and 17 barriers (see results section). Based on our final set of drivers and barriers, we conducted two further workshops in the full author team to derive overall findings and corresponding practice recommendations. After the first workshop, we shared our findings, especially regarding the practice recommendations, with the CIO of *GU* to initially validate their usefulness and applicability. Accordingly, we discussed and incorporated resulting feedback in the second workshop.

4 Case Description

GU is a medium-sized German university with more than 2,300 active employees and more than 13,000 active students, almost half of whom study at the faculty of Law and Economics. In the early 2010s, *GU* initially presented an IT strategic plan, which was updated and partially implemented in the subsequent years pushing digitalization and DI. Hence, *GU* was comparably well prepared for the radical change of a COVID-19 driven digital semester in the summer term of 2020. It had multiple digital solutions in place prior to the pandemic, such as a system that allows lectures to be recorded and students to access recordings at any given time. Their digital infrastructure but also the acquired knowledge and experience with digital technologies facilitated the sudden introduction of new technical solutions like a live streaming software for fully virtual lectures. Additionally, *GU* provided remote access software to their students for accessing the university network and services necessary for digital teaching.

The university's administration and management also had to adjust to the fundamental changes in the teaching environment, e.g., by introducing a new communication platform to compensate for the lack of in-person communication. In this regard, *GU*'s DI activities aimed at digitally improving and adjusting their internal processes, i.e., digital process innovations. For our case study, we chose the DI process leading to three fully implemented digital process innovations at *GU* as units of analysis, i.e., *U1*, *U2*, and *U3*. Following our understanding of DI [15], we consider these three to be innovative as they are subjectively perceived as new by *GU*, regardless of whether they have been realized at other universities or private organizations before. Table 2 provides a short description of the DI outcomes of *U1*, *U2*, and *U3* together with an overview of the related DI actions and relevant actors performing them.

We used the first interview round to derive a consistent interpretation of the BPM core elements in the light of our study [16]. Thereby, *Strategic Alignment* particularly refers to decisions taken by *GU*'s management that affect all DI actions. The management staff also influences the core element *Governance* as it decides on university-wide rules and regulations, which makes this core element particularly context-dependent [43]. *Methods/IT* includes techniques, the IT infrastructure, and the resources within the IT department of *GU* that are available to manage the DI actions. *Culture* mainly evolves around the concept of acceptance and describes the attitude and behavior of the involved individuals towards *GU*'s DI process. Last, *People* focuses on the expertise and knowledge available to *GU* and necessary to successfully conduct the DI process.

Table 2. Units of analysis

	U1: Digital exam view	U2: Communication platform	U3: Application portal
DI outcome	• Digital inspection of graded exams by students • Available at any time via campus management software	• Communication platform for university staff • New communication channel to students integrated into campus management software	• Standardization of staff application process • New application portal instead of e-mail correspondence
Initiate	Activities targeted towards generating the initial idea, deciding for or against ideas, and determining basic funding of the DI. The initiation was mainly performed **by...**		
	...the university management (UM)	...the university management (UM)	... the department manager of human resources (PP)
Develop	Activities targeted towards the development of an initial artifact, such as a new process or digital solution. The development was mainly performed **by...**		
	... the IT-department (IT) supported by the external service provider (OE)	... the external service provider (OE) supported by the IT department (IT)	... the IT department (IT)
Implement	Activities targeted towards the go live of the initial artifact and the integration into the daily business. The implementation was mainly performed **by...**		
	... the IT department (IT) - step-by-step rollout	... the external service provider (OE) supported by the IT department (IT)	... the IT department (IT)
Exploit	Activities targeted towards the utilization of the DI outcome as well as leveraging existing systems with new DI initiatives. Exploitation was mainly conducted **in...**		
	... three faculties (PP)	... the entire university via the campus management system	... the human resource department (PP)

5   Results

5.1   Drivers and Barriers of the Digital Innovation Process

As the primary result of our study, we present 13 drivers (Table 3) and 17 barriers (Table 4) of the DI process at *GU*. We structure the drivers and barriers in each table following the two introduced dimensions for data collection and analysis. Thereby, we assign each driver and barrier to a DI action [15], titled *DIA*, and a BPM core element [16], titled *BCE*. As we found during the interviews that some drivers and barriers influence all four DI actions, we assign those to the category *Overarching* in *DIA*. We further provide related exemplary quotes, which are taken directly from the interviews, indicating the interviewee's role (see Table 1 for abbreviations).

Table 3. Drivers of the DI process at GU

DIA	BCE	Driver	Exemplary quote	ID
Initiate	St.	University structure and development plan that triggers initiatives for DI	"[...] the digitalization of the administration is an important part of the structure and development plan." (UM)	D1
	M./IT	Adoption of good practices from other universities and public administrations	"[...] the district office presented the application portal. It could be implemented with few changes." (IT)	D2
Develop	M./IT	Development and evaluation of minimum viable products	"[...] in the beginning it was about satisfying the requirements. Now we look at other features [...]" (IT)	D3
		Predefined solution space but open approach during develop phase	"[...] it was clearly specified what should be achieved [...] however we had freedom on how to implement it" (IT)	D4
Implement	M./IT	Short feedback cycles with clearly defined support/service interfaces	"[...] everybody [in this team] knows the appropriate contact person." (PP)	D5
	Cu.	Live demonstration of the need and benefit of the DI	"[...] it was smart to show the administration staff the potential of the technology, so they see what is possible." (IT)	D6
Exploit	M./IT	Consistently defined personal contact points for the technical support of users	"[...] the IT department was always available via telephone [...] with direct answer and help." (PP)	D7
	Cu.	User manuals and guidelines for handling the DI outcome	"[...] so she feels safer in its use[...] and also to increase the acceptance." (IT)	D8
	Pe.	Previous experience with IT applications and basic IT knowledge	"[...] within this [administration] team there are many people that are technically affine." (OE)	D9
Overarching	M./IT	Standardized and easily expandable IT infrastructure	"[...] one [campus management] system and settings for all faculties." (PP)	D10
	Cu.	Sufficient opportunities for feedback	"[...] call each other regularly to see how it goes." (PP)	D11
	Pe.	In-depth know-how and expert knowledge in the IT department	"[...] the know-how for such projects was available in the IT." (IT)	D12
		Motivated individuals in the IT department	"[...] individuals in the IT department move things forward [...]" (UM)	D13

Below, we provide further insights into our results by presenting overarching observations. It is worth noting that we derived these observations regarding the drivers and barriers from a single case which is why we do not claim that they are necessarily generalizable [14]. First, in the case under consideration, we identified more barriers than drivers which might indicate that the context of *GU* is challenging for DI. Further, we found barriers but no respective drivers related to *Governance*, which represents a BPM core element in particular shaped by the specific context due to expectations of transparency and performance of public institutions [43].

Second, drivers and barriers of the BPM core elements *Strategic Alignment* and *Governance* primarily influence the DI action *Initiate*. In contrast, *People* and *Culture* related drivers and barriers mostly influence *Implement* and *Exploit* actions. This particularly reflects the hierarchical structure of *GU* and the top-down driven nature of its DI process. Thereby, the first actions of the DI process mainly take place at the managerial levels of the university, whereas the latter actions (i.e., *Implement* and *Exploit*) involve more personnel from the operational levels, e.g., administration staff. The predominance of *Strategic Alignment* related barriers over corresponding drivers also indicates that the

Table 4. Barriers of the DI process at GU

DIA	BCE	Barrier	Exemplary quote	ID
Initiate	St.	High cost sensitivity of decision-makers given public spending restrictions	"[the management] hesitates if it costs money." (IT)	B1
		Limited triggering options for the initiation of DI, mainly due to legislative changes or organizational pain	"We are [legally] obligated to keep old files for five years, but we don't have any storage left. We had to do something." (PP)	B2
		Top-down initiation of the DI process with limited stakeholder involvement	"we were not involved, just informed at some point [about the new feature]." (PP)	B3
Develop				
Implement	Go.	Incomplete stakeholder participation in DI committees and teams	"[…] no one at the user level was involved [in the committee]." (PP)	B4
	Cu.	Lack of trust due to negative experiences with previous DI initiatives	"[…] it was difficult from the beginning because communication was an issue last time". (OE)	B5
Exploit	MIT	Lack of institutionalized feedback loops	"[…] we have brought the feedback, but there was no follow up on it." (PP)	B6
		Lack of structured evaluation of DI outcomes	"[…] there is hardly any evaluation [after the successful implementation of a new DI]." (UM)	B7
		Lack of homogenization of the DI outcome due to high individualization	"[…] no exchange of employees between different departments is possible due to differing processes." (PP)	B8
	Pe.	Time discrepancy between the implementation of DI solution and deployment of service and support	"[…] we would have needed the new feature, but no one knew it existed." (PP)	B9

(*continued*)

Table 4. (*continued*)

DIA	BCE	Barrier	Exemplary quote	ID
Overarching	St.	Lack of perceived support and guidance from university management	"[…] the initial solution could not be implemented due to a missing management decision". (PP)	B10
		Lack of perception and management of DI as a process	"[…] an evaluation, despite being a logical last step of it [the DI], is not done." (UM)	B11
	Go.	Lack of documentation of DI process and actions	"[…] the process documentation was developed externally." (IT)	B12
		Lack of predefined collaboration and cooperation model for DI	"[…] it was easier to contact them [the IT] although I am not supposed to." (PP)	B13
		Lack of a central management instance that aligns all DI phases	"[…] communication after a successful DI depends on the person in charge." (UM)	B14
	Cu.	Lack of innovation culture in the university's administration and faculties	"There are only a few people who generate ideas […], and sometimes DIs are even hindered." (IT)	B15
		Lack of predefined communication strategy regarding internal to internal and internal to external information exchange	"[…] useful DIs would be easier to implement if it would be clear what to communicate to whom, how and when." (OE)	B16
	Pe.	Lack of IT affinity in university administration	"[…] not open to new technologies […] and to protect non-affine team members [from IT overload]." (IT)	B17

top-down driven DI approach may bear downsides for DI process execution, e.g., limited triggering options for the initiation of DI (*B2*). Third, the BPM core element *Method/IT* takes a key role in the overall DI process.

Regarding Table 3, we identified *Method/IT*-related drivers within every DI action, which in most cases refer to activities and tasks of the IT department, e.g., by providing personal contact points for the technical support of users (*D7*). In addition, we observed the IT department to be a leading actor in other core elements than *Method/IT*. For example, the IT staff at *GU* is also responsible for handling the user manuals and guidelines for new technical systems (*D8*), which increases the acceptance of the users regarding the DI outcome. Further, the IT department promoted and conducted a live demonstration of the targeted DI outcome of *U1* for *GU*'s administration staff by organizing a visit to another university where the respective digital solution was already implemented and operational (*D6*). Accordingly, our data suggests that the IT department might be a major facilitator of the DI process. The university management in turn has a positive impact primarily during the initiation of the DI process as it anchors DI initiatives at the strategic level in *GU*'s structure and development plan (*D1*).

Regarding Table 4, we did not identify any barriers for the DI action *Develop* but many *Overarching* (*B10-B17*) barriers. This illustrates that *Develop*, which is dominated by the IT department at *GU*, hardly leads to directly assignable problems. On the contrary, we identified some *Overarching* aspects during the interviews to be particularly severe in hindering the entire DI process, e.g., the lack of perception and management of DI as a process (*B11*). Further, it is noteworthy that more than half of all identified barriers are characterized by the "lack of" activities or structures, e.g., a lack of documentation of the DI process (*B12*). There are fewer barriers referring to activities or structures of *GU* actively hindering or slowing down the DI process, e.g., the mainly top-down driven initiation (*B3*). Rather, the absence of certain activities or structures seem to have a negative impact on the DI process.

5.2 Overall Findings and Practice Recommendations

To further condense and structure the insights of our case study, we derived five overall findings drawing from the identified drivers and barriers together with practice recommendations (Table 5). Each finding relates to several drivers and barriers representing an overarching dynamic or pattern that significantly influences the DI process at GU. These findings aim at providing a starting point for developing actionable practices for public universities to overcome barriers and strengthen drivers for the successful development of DI. In this sense, we present two practice recommendations for each finding that we have developed in close collaboration with GU's CIO.

Table 5. Overall findings and practice recommendations

#	Overall findings	Practice recommendations
1	DI at *GU* follows the structure of a process but is neither perceived nor documented as such nor supported by BPM methods and practices *See also: B12, B13, B15, [...]*	• Develop a process understanding of the DI process across management levels • Institutionalize the DI process via targeted management roles and structures (e.g., DI office
2	The DI process at *GU* does not fully leverage the innovation potential of its stakeholders due to a decentralized but hierarchical organizational structure that hinders the DI culture *See also: B3, B5, B11, [...]*	• Define communication channels and interfaces to involve and encourage a broader stakeholder base in DI idea generation and conceptualization • Institutionalize feedback with a broad range of stakeholders to regularly evaluate whether the DI addresses their requirements

(continued)

Table 5. (*continued*)

#	Overall findings	Practice recommendations
3	The DI process at *GU* is mainly driven by pain points and legislative changes. It therefore focuses on addressing local problems rather than overarching opportunities *See also: B2, B9, D1, [...]*	• Explore opportunities for long-term value-adding and reusable solutions within legislative changes • Foster bottom-up generativity by giving employees opportunities to develop ideas besides day-to-day operations
4	The DI process at *GU* is strongly affected by culture- and people-related concerns regarding the use of digital technology *See also: B6, B17, D6, [...]*	• Reduce resistance and fear of change by demonstrating the need and benefit of DI via trainings • Ensure a consistent level of basic IT know-how among university administration staff
5	The DI process at *GU* benefits from a high performing IT-department that drives the DI in the *Develop*, *Implement*, and *Exploit* phase *See also: D3, D10, D12, [...]*	• Provide the IT department with the necessary resources and infrastructure to handle the increasing demand for DI • Establish long-term partnerships between external IT service providers and the IT department

6   Discussion, Limitations, and Conclusion

Public universities need to engage in Digital Innovation (DI), not only to tackle implications of COVID-19 related restrictions but also to benefit from novel digital opportunities and address expectations by society to serve as pioneers for DI. However, meeting these expectations is still a challenge, particularly in the administration and management context, where further understanding and guidance are needed. Thus, in this study, we investigated *how public universities enact the DI process and what related drivers and barriers are*. To address this question, we conducted an exploratory single case study at a German public university (*GU*) and examined the DI process of three digital process innovations. Building upon Business Process Management (BPM) as a theoretical lens, we presented drivers and barriers of the DI process at *GU* structured along four DI actions [15] and five BPM core elements [16] as our main contribution. In a second step, we enhanced the overview of drivers and barriers by deriving overall findings and practice recommendations for public universities.

Regarding theoretical implications, our findings contribute to existing research on innovation and DI (e.g., [10, 13]) in the public university context by providing a structured overview of drivers and barriers of the DI process. Thereby, we specifically contribute to the explanatory knowledge on DI at public universities by increasing our understanding of how their DI process unfolds in the real world. Further, we place our results at the converging interface of DI and BPM, which has been highlighted as a beneficial subject of investigation by recent research (e.g., [8, 18]). With our study, we demonstrate how to combine the two research streams by studying DI as a process while applying BPM as a theoretical lens. We draw from both disciplines and present a two-dimensional analysis approach based on the DI actions and the BPM core elements. As a result, our study contributes to the management-related research avenue in BPM, as identified by van Looy and Poels [18], to study and improve the DI process. Further, Mendling et al. [8] proposed that methods from DI and BPM could benefit each other. Our study shows that applying an empirical method (i.e., a case study), which is widely used in DI research but rarely in the BPM domain [8], facilitates research at the interface of both disciplines. Accordingly, we believe that the drivers and barriers, in combination with the overall findings, are a valuable starting point for future research on the DI process providing a basis for further theorizing and testing.

Regarding managerial implications, our work provides public universities with valuable insights into possible drivers and barriers of their DI process. For instance, public universities' decision-makers may want to screen the overview of drivers and barriers to prepare and accordingly refine their own DI process. Thereby, the practice recommendations explicitly offer a basis from which to defer practices for more effectively managing the DI process at public universities. In future research, one should refine and evaluate the practice recommendations in terms of their relationship to DI success.

As with every scientific work, our research is beset with limitations that stimulate future research. First, despite the single case of GU fulfilling the criteria for a representative and revelatory case that is worth analyzing in-depth, our results provide limited generalizability to a broader context [14]. Thereby, the identified drivers and barriers, but also the overall findings and practice recommendations, require further quantitative and qualitative examinations. For instance, future studies should conduct a multiple case study and investigate the DI process at other public universities to compare their findings to ours [32]. Further, our results should be evaluated regarding their transferability to the public sector in general or even the private sector. Second, while we intensively studied the data collected at GU, our overall period for data collection and the number of units of analysis were limited. Future research may delve deeper into the case at hand, include more units of analysis, and integrate other sources of data, for instance, by also considering the quality of the DI outcome. This way, one could adjust or complement our list of drivers and barriers and even aim to prioritize them regarding their impact on the success of the DI outcome. Third, as the convergence of DI and BPM is an emergent research topic, there were no existing field-tested methods or frameworks to structure and analyze our data. Although our chosen dimensions, i.e., the DI actions and BPM core elements, have initially proven their value and applicability, future research should address the need for tools specifically developed for studies at the intersection of both research streams, e.g., as proposed by Mendling et al. [8].

Overall, our study addresses the increasing relevance of DI for public universities. We derived valuable insights on drivers and barriers of the DI process at public universities and believe that our findings and practice recommendations are an appropriate starting point for the development of more generalizable theory and more fine-grained actionable practices in the future. In line with other fellow researchers, we see great value in bringing DI and BPM together and hope that our study shows the potential of their convergence in the context of public universities and the public sector in general.

References

1. European Commission: European Commission launches a public consultation on a new Digital Education Action Plan. https://ec.europa.eu/commission/presscorner/detail/en/ip_20_1066
2. Hedlund, H.: Architecting structural flexibility in design processes – a case study of public sector digital innovation. In: ECIS 2019 Proceedings (2019)
3. Faria, J.A., Nóvoa, H.: Digital transformation at the University of Porto. In: Za, S., Drăgoicea, M., Cavallari, M. (eds.) IESS 2017. LNBIP, vol. 279, pp. 295–308. Springer, Cham (2017). https://doi.org/10.1007/978-3-319-56925-3_24
4. Skulmowski, A., Rey, G.D.: COVID-19 as an accelerator for digitalization at a German university: establishing hybrid campuses in times of crisis. Hum. Behav. Emerg. Technol. **2**, 212–216 (2020)
5. Yoo, Y., Henfridsson, O., Lyytinen, K.: Research commentary—the new organizing logic of digital innovation: an agenda for information systems research. Inf. Syst. Res. **21**, 724–735 (2010)
6. Nambisan, S., Lyytinen, K., Majchrzak, A., Song, M.: Digital innovation management: reinventing innovation management research in a digital world. MIS Q. **41**, 223–238 (2017)
7. Vega, A., Chiasson, M.: A comprehensive framework to research digital innovation: the joint use of the systems of innovation and critical realism. J. Strateg. Inf. Syst. **28**, 242–256 (2019)
8. Mendling, J., Pentland, B.T., Recker, J.: Building a complementary agenda for business process management and digital innovation. Eur. J. Inf. Syst. **29**, 208–219 (2020)
9. Agasisti, T., Pohl, C.: Comparing German and Italian public universities: convergence or divergence in the higher education landscape? Manag. Decis. Econ. **33**, 71–85 (2012)
10. Vicente, P.N., Lucas, M., Carlos, V., Bem-Haja, P.: Higher education in a material world: constraints to digital innovation in Portuguese universities and polytechnic institutes. Educ. Inf. Technol. **25**(6), 5815–5833 (2020). https://doi.org/10.1007/s10639-020-10258-5
11. Smertenko, P., Dimitriev, O., Pochekailova, L., Cernyshov, L.: Technological transformations and their implications for higher education. In: Valsiner, J., Lutsenko, A., Antoniouk, A. (eds.) Sustainable Futures for Higher Education. CPE, vol. 7, pp. 67–75. Springer, Cham (2018). https://doi.org/10.1007/978-3-319-96035-7_8
12. Nuere, S., Miguel, L. de: The digital/technological connection with COVID-19: an unprecedented challenge in university teaching. Technol. Know. Learn., 1–13 (2020)
13. Lašáková, A., Bajzíková, Ľ, Dedze, I.: Barriers and drivers of innovation in higher education: case study-based evidence across ten European universities. Int. J. Educ. Dev. **55**, 69–79 (2017)
14. Yin, R.K.: Case Study Research: Design and Methods. Sage Publications (2009)
15. Kohli, R., Melville, N.P.: Digital innovation: a review and synthesis. Inf. Syst. J. **29**, 200–223 (2019)
16. Kerpedzhiev, G.D., König, U.M., Röglinger, M., Rosemann, M.: An exploration into future business process management capabilities in view of digitalization. Bus. Inf. Syst. Eng. **63**(2), 83–96 (2020)
17. van Looy, A.: A quantitative and qualitative study of the link between business process management and digital innovation. Inf. Manage. **58**, 103413 (2021)
18. van Looy, A., Poels, G.: A practitioners' point of view on how digital innovation will shape the future of business process management: towards a research agenda. In: Hawaii International Conference on System Sciences 2019 (2019)
19. Nambisan, S.: Digital entrepreneurship: toward a digital technology perspective of entrepreneurship. Entrep. Theory Pract. **41**, 1029–1055 (2017)

20. Berger, S., Denner, M.-S., Roeglinger, M.: The nature of digital technologies - development of a multi-layer taxonomy. In: ECIS 2018 Proceedings (2018)
21. Drechsler, K., Gregory, R., Wagner, H.-T., Tumbas, S.: At the crossroads between digital innovation and digital transformation. Commun. Assoc. Inf. Syst. **47**, 521–538 (2020)
22. Lee, J., Berente, N.: Digital innovation and the division of innovative labor: digital controls in the automotive industry. Organ. Sci. **23**, 1428–1447 (2012)
23. Välimaa, J., Hoffman, D.: Knowledge society discourse and higher education. High. Educ. **56**, 265–285 (2008)
24. Dumas, M., La Rosa, M., Mendling, J., Reijers, H.A.: Introduction to business process management. In: Dumas, M., La Rosa, M., Mendling, J., Reijers, H.A. (eds.) Fundamentals of Business Process Management, pp. 1–33. Springer Berlin Heidelberg, Berlin, Heidelberg (2018)
25. vom Brocke, J., Rosemann, M. (eds.): Handbook on business process management. Springer, Berlin, Heidelberg (2015)
26. Rosemann, M., vom Brocke, J.: The six core elements of business process management. In: vom Brocke, J., Rosemann, M. (eds.) Handbook on Business Process Management 1. IHIS, pp. 105–122. Springer, Heidelberg (2015). https://doi.org/10.1007/978-3-642-45100-3_5
27. Karabegovic, A., Buza, E., Omanovic, S., Kahrovic, A.: Adoption of BPM systems for process design in a higher education institution. In: 2018 41st International Convention on Information and Communication Technology, Electronics and Microelectronics (MIPRO), pp. 552–557. IEEE (2018)
28. Helbin, T., van Looy, A.: Is Business Process Management (BPM) ready for ambidexterity? Conceptualization Implementation Guidelines and Research Agenda. Sustainability **13**, 1906 (2021)
29. Grisold, T., vom Brocke, J., Gross, S., Mendling, J., Röglinger, M., Stelzl, K.: Digital innovation and business process management: opportunities and challenges as perceived by practitioners. Commun. Assoc. Inf. Syst. (2021)
30. Rosemann, M., et al.: Towards a business process management maturity model. In: ECIS 2005 Proceedings (2015)
31. Bruin, T. de, Rosemann, M.: Application of a Holistic Model for Determining BPM Maturity (2012)
32. Benbasat, I., Goldstein, D.K., Mead, M.: The case research strategy in studies of information systems. MIS Q. **11**(3), 369–386 (1987)
33. Bandara, W., Gable, G.G., Rosemann, M.: Factors and measures of business process modelling: model building through a multiple case study. Eur. J. Inf. Syst. **14**, 347–360 (2005)
34. Eskildsen, J.K., Kristensen, K., Juhl, H.J.: Private versus public sector excellence. The TQM magazine (2004)
35. Statistisches Bundesamt (Destatis): Bildung und Kultur. Private Hochschulen 2019 (2021)
36. Miles, M.B., Huberman, A.M.: Qualitative data analysis: An expanded sourcebook. Sage Publications (1994)
37. Benbunan-Fich, R., Desouza, K.C., Andersen, K.N.: IT-enabled innovation in the public sector: introduction to the special issue. Eur. J. Inf. Syst. **29**, 323–328 (2020)
38. Myers, M.D., Newman, M.: The qualitative interview in IS research: examining the craft. Inf. Organ. **17**, 2–26 (2007)
39. Agolla, J.E., van Lill, J.B.: An empirical investigation into innovation drivers and barriers in public sector organisations. Int. J. Innov. Sci. **8**(4), 404–422 (2016)
40. Wipulanusat, W., Panuwatwanich, K., Stewart, R.A., Sunkpho, J.: Drivers and barriers to innovation in the Australian public service: a qualitative thematic analysis. Eng. Manage. Prod. Serv. **11**, 7–22 (2019)

41. Dubé, L., Paré, G.: Rigor in information systems positivist case research: current practices, trends, and recommendations. MIS Q. **27**(4), 597–636 (2003)
42. Wolfswinkel, J.F., Furtmueller, E., Wilderom, C.P.M.: Using grounded theory as a method for rigorously reviewing literature. Eur. J. Inf. Syst. **22**, 45–55 (2013)
43. Santana, A.F.L., Alves, C.F., Santos, H.R.M., de Lima Cavalcanti Felix, A.: BPM governance: an exploratory study in public organizations. In: Halpin, T., et al. (eds.) BPMDS/EMMSAD -2011. LNBIP, vol. 81, pp. 46–60. Springer, Heidelberg (2011). https://doi.org/10.1007/978-3-642-21759-3_4

A Stakeholder Engagement Model for Process Improvement Initiatives

Charon Abbott[1], Wasana Bandara[1(✉)], Erica French[1], Mary Tate[2], and Paul Mathiesen[3]

[1] Queensland University of Technology, 2 George Street, Brisbane, Australia
Charon.abbott@hrd.qut.edu.au, {w.bandara,e.french}@qut.edu.au
[2] School of Information Management, Victoria University
of Wellington, Wellington, New Zealand
mary.tate@vuw.ac.nz
[3] Independent BPM and Business Innovation Practitioner, Brisbane, Australia
p.mathiesen@connect.qut.edu.au

Abstract. Despite cries from practice and academia, stakeholder engagement in Business Process Ma(BPM) is an under-explored area of research. Developing a comprehensive understanding of what factors influence stakeholder engagement is the first step towards addressing this. While diverse factors are briefly mentioned in prior literature, there has not been any holistic synthesis nor empirical investigation to this. This study presents the first empirically supported framework of stakeholder engagement factors for process improvement projects. The framework was built with a synthesis of literature applying Kassin's [1] social psychology framework as a theoretical lens, and empirical insights from a rich case study conducted at an Australian Financial service provider. The framework presents five levels namely; 'micro', 'meso', 'exo', 'macro', and 'chrono' which represents different 'systems' that host a range of factors that influence stakeholder engagement in process improvement projects. It provides an invaluable point of reference for BPM practitioners when designing stakeholder engagement and intervention programs, especially to develop sustainable strategies for change that enables successful outcomes. It also is a solid foundation and springboard for further academic research.

Keywords: Process improvement · Stakeholder engagement · Stakeholder theory · Case study · Robotic Process Automation · RPA · Organizational change

1 Introduction

Business Process Management (BPM) is rapidly growing, and its impact has exponentially increased in the digital age. As BPM initiatives involve rapid organisational changes [2] it is important that employees and other stakeholders are fully engaged and supportive of the proposed process changes, for them to succeed. Involving employees in the change and doing so early improves long term outcomes in three ways; through a psychological commitment to the end processes and systems; improved project requirements

© Springer Nature Switzerland AG 2021
A. Polyvyanyy et al. (Eds.): BPM 2021, LNCS 12875, pp. 455–472, 2021.
https://doi.org/10.1007/978-3-030-85469-0_28

identification; and success of the implementation [3]. Despite this, the factors influencing stakeholder engagement, even in broader stakeholder literature are under-explored [4]. Within BPM literature itself, the importance of effective stakeholder engagement is mentioned by many [e.g. 5, 6], and some directly and/or indirectly mention certain aspects that may contribute to the engagement of stakeholders [e.g. 7, 8], however, no research to date identifies a comprehensive set of factors which is vital to design impactful interventions.

This study aims to address this gap by exploring the question: "What factors influence the engagement of stakeholders when undertaking BPM projects?" In the context of this study the definition of the term 'stakeholder' is adopted from Freeman [9], and is defined as 'any group or individual who can affect or is affected by a business process management project'. The definition of 'engagement' was adapted from Kahn [10]. Employee engagement is 'when stakeholders are 'physically, cognitively and emotionally' involved in the BPM project'. This view of stakeholder engagement is supported by literature such as de Waal, Batenburg [3].

The remainder of the paper first presents the theoretical background, followed by the case study design. The case study findings are then presented, and the paper concludes with a summary discussion. A separate 'Ancillary Material' file is made available which contains information that supplements the main paper (see: https://tinyurl.com/nbmymjj3).

2 Background

A multi-phased hermeneutic literature review (following [11]) was conducted. The aim was to produce a *Theoretical* review Paré et al.'s [12] that would result in an a priori framework of process improvement engagement factors. This process was iterative. In the first iteration, literature specifically from the BPM field was reviewed. The study results of the first phase confirmed that there was limited research which had attempted to specifically address the issue of stakeholder engagement in a BPM context. While stakeholder engagement was recognized widely as an important facet for BPM success with some scholars mentioning potential contributing engagement factors, no research to date identified a comprehensive set. The search was next extended to broader domains recognized as relevant to BPM. Examples included searching within the domains of change management and employee engagement. Factors identified from the literature analysis were used to generate an initial set of codes. These codes were then used for a round of axial coding to identify key themes [30, 31]. Further details on the conduct of the literature review is presented in Sect. 1.1 of the Ancillary Material.

A series of potential stakeholder engagement factors emerged from this (see Column 2 of Table 1). These were initially grouped into five high level themes (Column 1 of Table 1), namely; 1) Individual, 2) Environmental, 3) Project-related, 4) Interpersonal, and 5) BPM lifecycle. Individual factors related specifically to particular stakeholders (e.g., prior history of change). Environmental factors pertained to factors that influence the stakeholder group from their surroundings and are outside their own control (e.g., location). Project-related factors related to the specific qualities of the Business Process Management (BPM) project. Interpersonal factors included communication from the project to the stakeholder group, and interpersonal relationships between stakeholder groups. Finally, the 'BPM lifecycle' theme captured the continuous cycle for managing processes across the phases of the project. This was central and cut through the other four themes. Part 1.2 of the Ancillary Material provides a rich overview of these themes and factors and they are also revisited below as the case study findings are presented.

Next, we sought for a meta-theoretical lens that could assist to: (i) better structure the emerging literature results, (ii) provide a theoretical base, and (iii) provide 'sense-making' support. A closer look at the extracted factors pointed to complex relationships between them. For example, the factors were operating at different levels, with complex interrelationships between different groups of factors, potentially influencing engagement in different directions (both positively and negatively) thus forming complex ecosystems. Within stakeholder literature, the complexity of stakeholder ecosystems has been acknowledged widely (e.g. [13, 14];) and is recognized to be underexplored [4]. The complex ecosystem of BPM engagement factors and layers we saw from the literature analysis, suggested a theory that captured a 'systems' perspective, as a potential meta-theoretical lens to further systematize and strengthen the conceptualization stemming from the literature review.

Given that BPM projects are social exercises that occur in the workplace, prior systems models that related to understanding engagement was looked at. We particularly tried to see if the literature-based themes and factors 'made sense' when applied to these theoretical views. The systems theory lenses of Bone [15] and Kassin et al. [1] were seeming fits. Both are based on similar theoretical foundations, provide a holistic overview of their topics, and are similarly structured. However, the various levels and

Table 1. Summary results: Literature review findings mapped to Kassin et al. [1]'s (2015) model

Literature review			Adapted definitions	Kassin et al. [1]'s model	
Themes	Resulting factors[#]	Supporting literature		Levels	Definitions (from p. xi)
Individual[i]	History of change[i]	[16, 17]	Personal factors affecting engagement of individuals or specific stakeholder groups	Micro	"The intra-individual level that considers the characteristics of the individual"
	Organisational role[i]	[18]			
	Personality[i]	[19]			
	Age[i]	[20]			
	Type of role[i]	[8]			
	Gender[i]	[7]			
	Length of service[i]	[17]			
Interpersonal<>	Office politics<>	[21]	Interpersonal interactions between stakeholder (s) or factors influencing those relationships, in which they play a direct role	Meso	"The interpersonal networks – the people that they share their lives with and those they interact with"
	Communication <>	[22]			
	Trust relationship between stakeholders<>	[16]			
	Supportive leadership<>	[23]			
	Principle of involvement <>	[6]			

(continued)

Table 1. (*continued*)

Literature review			Adapted definitions	Kassin et al. [1]'s model	
Themes	Resulting factors#	Supporting literature		Levels	Definitions (from p. xi)
(Organisational level) Environmental^ and project+	Staff workload ^	[21]	Environmental factors which influence stakeholder(s) at a project or organisational level	Exo	"The environments in which they live, work and interact"
	Location^	[17]			
	Project type +	[24]			
	Resourcing +	[25]			
	Cultural alignment +	[26]			
	Length of time project takes +	[23]			
	Number of projects in progress +	[21]			
	Project objectives +	[25]			
(Macro level) Environmental^	Culture ^	[27]	Environmental factors beyond the organisation	Macro	"The institutional patterns of culture (such as customary practices and beliefs) that help to define them and their behaviours"
	Economy ^	[21]			
BPM lifecycle	Lifecycle stages e.g., identification, discovery, analysis, redesign, implementation, monitoring and control##	[18]	The changing importance of different factors over the lifecycle of the project	Chrono	Kassin et al. [1] defines this as; "The socio-historical context in which they live". However, the original studies that Kassin adopts from [i.e. 28] defines this in terms of events and transitions over time which aligns with the BPM lifecycle changes

#The mapping of the factors to their themes is denoted by superscripts as follows: Individual $=^{I}$, Interpersonal $=^{<>}$, Environmental $=^{\wedge}$, Project $=^{+}$
##These lifecycle stages can change depending on which BPM lifecycle model adopted

their definitions presented by Kassin et al. [1] resonated more closely with our literature-based results, and was hence selected.

Table 1 presents a multi-level conceptual model of BPM stakeholder engagement factors, that maps the literature findings with the Kassin et al. [1] model. The original levels and definitions from Kassin et al. [1] are presented in Column 6 and the definitions as adapted in this study presented in Column 4. Taking a Systems view necessitated the original groupings to be reconfigured. Column 2 depicts the related factors (derived from the literature) pertaining to the revised groupings.

3   Case Study Design

A single in-depth case study approach was applied. Single case studies are known to provide rich insights and be well-suited for exploring novel and under-researched topics [29]. The unit of analyis was a single process improvement project. A suitable case candidate would; (i) be a clearly identifiable 'BPM project' - with clear objectives and an identifiable start and end; (ii) can be an internal or external process- but where the end-to-end process has been improved; (iii) multiple teams have been impacted or were involved with the improvement initiative; and (iv) the full project (or a recognizable phase) has been completed within the past six months of data collection.

The case study was undertaken in ABC Finance[1] an ASX listed, regional Australian Company. The Finance industry, in which the company operates, is constantly evolving and is challenged, with pressures from industry and regulatory changes. This drives the company's own ambitions to meet stakeholder needs and remain competitive. A Robotic Process Automation (RPA) optimization project was selected. This project sought to improve the performance of an RPA process which prepared new finance requests to be ready for a Credit Manager to assess; a process which involves many administrative activities and has varying impacts across different teams within the organization.

The predominant source of evidence was interview data. Other evidence from a demographic questionnaire and project related documentation were used to augment the interviews. Nine participants were recruited voluntarily across a broad spectrum of project and organisational[2] roles they held (see Table 2).

Table 2. Interviewee overview

	Project role	Organisational level
1	Project Manager	Team Leader
2	Project team member (business representative)	Senior Management
3	End user	Team Leader
4	Project team member	Individual Contributor
5	End user	Middle Manager
6	Project team member	Individual Contributor
7	End user	Individual Contributor
8	End user (external)	Individual Contributor
9	Project sponsor	Senior Management

---

[1] ABC Finance is a pseudonym to protect the anonymity of the organization and participants.

[2] The organisational level represents the reporting hierarchy within the case study. *Senior Management*, reports to an executive (a category not included in the sample respondents); a *Middle Manager*, has team leaders report to them; a *Team Leader* has individual contributors report to them and; an *Individual Contributor* have no direct reports.

Stakeholder engagement is a mature topic in many business domains, even though its investigation within the BPM project context has been limited. Therefore, it is likely that many factors affecting stakeholder engagement will have been investigated previously. In this study we used a hybrid approach between confirmatory and exploratory analysis to coding and theory development. This approach acknowledges that a *"fine line exists between interpreting data and imposing a pre-existing frame on it"* [30].

In the first round of coding, open codes were generated without reference to our a priori codes derived from literature [31]. After this initial round, we integrated our codes with the pre-existing codes and themes we had previously derived from research literature. Following this, we considered the remainder of the data that was not adequately explained by any existing theory. In this round we adopted a more grounded approach for the remainder of the data. Our emergent and unexplained findings were coded inductively and new codes were generated. Finally, theoretical coding [30, 32] was carried out on **both** the existing and emergent codes to identify relationships between categories and generate a new theoretical framework. The coding approach was governed by guidelines set by a pre-defined coding rules [38] and supported by the NVivo tool. The coding-quality was maintained - with a second coder reviewing the coding and regular corroboration sessions where the coding was discussed, challenged and improved.

4 Findings

The in-depth insights from the single case study were used to further re-specify and validate the literature-based synthesis (presented in Table 1). This resulted in a total of 36 engagement factors across five levels as visualized and summarized in Fig. 1 and Table 3. 21 factors identified in the literature were instantiated in the case data, 3 did not, and 12 new factors emerged from the case data. The bracketed numbers in Table 3 represent the number of interviewees who mentioned the factor and the number of times the factor was mentioned overall. Engagement factors newly identified from the case data, are displayed in bold and italics. An asterisk '*' denotes factors influencing a subset of a stakeholder group (remaining factors were found to influence all stakeholder groups). The greyed rows with the '^' symbol denotes engagement factors mentioned in literature but not instantiated in the case study data. Further supporting evidence is made available in Part 2 of the Ancillary Material.

Fig. 1. Multi-levels of BPM engagement factors

Table 3. Engagement factors evidenced through the case study

Levels		Engagement factor*	
Micro	Personal factors affecting engagement of individuals or specific stakeholder groups	History of change (7_28)	The impact of prior change experience on the individual
		Organisational role* (4_4)	Role played within the organisation
		Personality (9_41)	The character traits of the individual
		Age (3_4)	The chronological age of the individual
		Type of Role^ (-_-)	If the stakeholder role is for a specialist or generalist
		Gender^(-_-)	If the stakeholder is male, female or other
		Length of service (3_7)	How long the stakeholder has been in the role
		Impact on day-to-day role(7_54)*	How the project has changed daily responsibilities or impacted their responsibilities
		Impact on role status(8_22)*	How the project has impacted how the person perceives their role's security and standing in the organisation
		Prior role experience (6_15)	Experience from previous role(s)
		Experience with the domain (8_33)	If stakeholders have experience with the domain (RPA)
		Interest in the domain (7_10)	If stakeholders have an interest in domain (RPA)
Meso	Interpersonal interactions between stakeholder (s) or factors influencing those relationships, in which they play a direct role	Supportive Management (8_32)	Providing supportive actions and psychological support to subordinates

(continued)

Table 3. (*continued*)

Levels		Engagement factor*	
		Office politics* (2_3)	Actions which promoted a particular area/person's self interest
		Relationships between stakeholders (9_46)	Interpersonal business relationships between two or more individuals or groups
		Trust (7_19)	To be able to rely on the information provided or the behaviour of someone being correct and honest
		Communication (9_130)	Exchange of information either face to face or in writing, delivered to individuals or groups
		Principle of involvement* (4_4)	Stakeholder being involved with tasks within the project
		Respect (3_10)*	Perception of being treated with (or affording) people respect
		Sharing success (6_11)	Celebrating project successes
		Vested interest/KPI (7_27)	Motivation to succeed, driven by personal performance metrics
		Education/training (9_46)	Knowledge building and sharing about the project technology
Exo	Environmental factors which influence stakeholder(s) at a project or organisational level	Project type (9_165)	The category of project, including its characteristics
		Resourcing (8_40)	How many people are available to complete required tasks
		Location (3_15)	Where the stakeholder/s are physically located

(*continued*)

Table 3. (*continued*)

Levels		Engagement factor*	
		Cultural alignment (3_5)	If the project is aligned with the company's culture
		Length of time project takes (8_29)	Total time the project takes from commencement to completion
		Number of projects in progress (6_16)	How many other projects are being undertaken at the same time as the case study project
		Project goal (9_58)	Whether the project goal is incremental or transformational change
		Staff workload (1_1)	The amount of work required to be completed by stakeholders
		Organisational priorities (7_40)	The perception of what the organisation is focused upon
		Infrastructure (9_33)	The IT infrastructure, or organisational capability to deliver the project
Macro	Environmental factors beyond the organisation	Culture (9_46)	Team, Organisational or national culture, including shared values and assumptions
		Economy^ (-_-)	The country's production and consumption of goods & services
		Industry (7_15)	A group of companies with similar purposes
Chrono	The changing importance of different factors over the lifecycle of the project	BPM/Project lifecycle (9_84)	Stages of the BPM or project lifecycle

4.1 Micro Level Findings

There is strong support for the micro level of the engagement model, with five (5) of the seven (7) a priori factors instantiated (but two (2) did not), and five (5) new factors identified. Overall, micro level factors appear to be more important to stakeholders at the individual contributor level than to senior stakeholders (see Sect. 2.1 of Ancillary

Material). This suggests that the more senior your role, the less you are impacted by, or aware of, the micro level factors that influence engagement.

A priori factors supported by the case data: *History of change* Bordia et al. [16] and Chun, Davies [17] found the history of change to be highly influential on people's engagement. Seven (7) of the nine (9) interviewees also mentioned this factor. The investigated case was an optimisation project for a prior RPA implementation, with the aim of reducing the RPA exceptions. It is possible that the original project impacts the way people think about the subsequent one. Past experiences mentioned by interviewees were both positive and negative and could reasonably be expected to influence engagement similarly. *Organisational Role* also had support with four (4) interviewees mentioning this factor. Roles do play a crucial part in influencing other people's engagement; *"if I don't have an optimistic outlook then those people sitting underneath me definitely won't as well"* (interviewee #5). Herzig, Jimmieson [18] shared similar findings related to the middle managers' role. The *Personality* factor was very strongly supported, with all interviewees referring to some aspect of personality, specifically traits and characteristics. In particular, seventeen (17) quotes support the personality trait 'openness to experience', and nine (9) to 'conscientiousness'. This confirms the findings presented by Devaraj et al. [19]. Both **Age** and **Length of service** were supported. As expected, being younger was associated with greater engagement than being older. Cordery et al. [20], also found older persons were less open to change: *"Perhaps I do just like plodding along"* (an over 55 interviewee). 'Length of service' was similar, comparable with Chun, Davies [17] who identified stakeholders with a longer tenure (+10 years) appear less engaged.

A priori factors not instantiated by the case data: The lack of supporting evidence for 'type of role' and 'gender' may be due to the way in which this data was collected. Information regarding specialist roles and gender were collected in a demographic survey, with the intent that the analysis of any differences would be drawn out in the analysis, as it was deemed unlikely that interviewees would recognize the impact of the type of role they had or how their gender impacted their engagement. In addition, with only three female interviewees, if and how gender played a role was not mentioned nor probed to avoid raising potential gender bias.

New Factors: *Impact on day-to-day role* was well supported with fifty-four (54) references. The impacts of this factor are likely to be of particular importance in projects where the outputs are delivered iteratively. Earlier iterations change the impacted stakeholder's role and could potentially change their level of engagement. This is demonstrated in the quote "I've lost control over the process" Interviewee 7 *Impact on role status* was mentioned by a majority of interviewees, but with significantly different interpretations of the 'impact'. Middle and senior managers believed that the team were concerned about being made redundant as a result of robots being introduced; while the individuals themselves were not concerned, as they understood the project to be about assisting with growing the business. *Prior role experience* is similar to 'history of change', but refers to experience in previous positions, rather than to specific change projects. Experience gained from working in other roles, either within or externally to the organisation, could result in changes in engagement, either positively or negatively.

Two new engagement factors were more specifically related to the technology being implemented, in this case; RPA. Experience with the domain enabled people to know what was expected from the process improvement initiative, which can influence engagement, as can a lack of experience with RPA, both of which can be included within this factor. Eight (8) of the nine (9) interviews indicated that experience with RPA tended to increase engagement, whereas a lack of experience with RPA appeared to lower engagement. For example "we had a lot of knowledge of RPA..so, we had an expectation that we need to do it [optimize].. and the results showed that it was good that we had done it." Interviewee 1. Interest in the domain could have the potential to impact engagement as shown in the quote "I was very much excited about robotics". Interviewee 2. Where a technology influences people to be excited about it, they could be highly engaged with its deployment. If the technology does not live up to expectations there is also the possibility of disillusionment, which would have the opposite effect. This factor could interact with factors at other levels too, for example if there are many competitors with high profile cases of RPA this may increase stakeholders' interest in the technology.Meso level findings.

All six (6) engagement factors identified in the literature were identified within the case data, with four (4) additional factors recognized. The data also indicated that the majority of the meso level factors could impact people at all levels of the organization (see Sect. 2.2 of Ancillary Material). Exceptions were 'respect' and the 'principle of involvement' which appear to be more relevant to stakeholders at lower levels of the organisation. Also, these factors are tightly linked to each other.

A priori factors supported by the case data: **Supportive management** is an important factor in successful change [23] and was confirmed in eight (8) of the nine (9) interviews including both mentions of practical and emotional support. Conversely, a lack of support from a manager also was a factor, negatively impacting engagement. **Office Politics** was linked with this factor appearing in two (2) interviews, confirming the findings of Nicholds, Mo [21]. **Relationships between stakeholders** was a factor raised by every interviewee. Stakeholder relationships are important particularly across levels. Jones, Van de Ven [23] referred specifically to the relationships between employees and their managers. As expected, **trust** impacts engagement, with seven (7) interviewees, referring to trust. Bordia et al. [16] also found 'trust' an important factor for BPM success.

Communication, was strongly supported and mentioned on average fourteen (14) times in every interview. Finney [22], recognised different stakeholders require different types of 'communication' with different levels of detail. Kotter [33] suggests communication is a critical success factor when implementing any type of change. The **principle of involvement** [6] was also supported. Although this factor was only mentioned once in four (4) separate interviews the impact of the factor appeared to be substantial. For example, interviewee #7 said "I felt very excluded, and I would be in tears quite a bit [as.....] nobody came and sat with me to see how the [the process] worked" (Interviewee 7), whereas, interviewee #3 stated "I'm excited by it because I'm involved in it". Both of these examples demonstrate the power of this factor.

New Factors: Four (4) additional engagement factors were identified at this level, the first of which was **Respect**. The importance of respect was established in one third of the interviews. Moreover, the impact of this factor appeared high. Engagement was reduced where people felt they did not have the 'respect' of others, especially if they believed their voice was not being heard. For example, interviewee #3 said: *"I didn't quite feel respected for my skill set anyway, and then they wanted me to push changes, and communicate some of these robot back-end changes"*. This factor appears most relevant to individual contributors and team leaders as they are most likely not to feel excluded by a change process. Another important new engagement factor found in this case was *Sharing Success*, mentioned in two thirds the interviews. The Senior Managers instigated the sharing of the successes. These successes were designed to encourage sharing behaviours within the team, i.e., improved accuracy which assisted in improving the robot's completion rates, as demonstrated in this quote; *"having small wins and celebrating those small wins, and then also making sure that they're aware that we've got those small wins"* (Interviewee #2). However, dependent on the individual's micro factors the sharing of success may not always positively impact engagement and may be met with some cynicism.

Another factor with a substantial impact on engagement levels was *Vested Interest/key performance indicators (KPIs)*. This was mentioned in most of the interviews (7 out of 9). Examples such as: *"Well, I am frustrated [....] we are getting pressure from different areas to achieve different things, but they conflict each other"* (Interviewee #3), demonstrate how stakeholders can face challenges around this, often hidden, aspect of engagement. The engagement factor 'vested interest/KPIs' was mentioned by most interviewees across all levels of seniority and types of project role, demonstrating its widespread relevance. However, there is a stronger focus for more senior employees. As individual KPIs drive behaviour [34], this is something which should always be attended to as part of a BPM project and may impact stakeholders at any level of the organisation. The final additional factor was *Education/training*. This factor was discussed in every interview. Evidence indicates that not only is it important that stakeholders at all levels of the organisation be educated about the technology, but also, it is possible to see the consequences of stakeholders not being educated/trained. This was demonstrated by Interviewee #9 who said; *"I don't care that people feel aggrieved or whatever, but just feel aggrieved for the right reason.... It actually made me realise that people really don't understand"*.

4.2 Exo Level Findings

All eight (8) exo level engagement factors were identified with two (2) additional engagement factors confirmed. The engagement factors of this level were strongly supported in equal measure by people across all levels within the organisation with more senior employees having mentioned the exo engagement factors more often (see Sect. 2.4 of Ancillary Material).

A priori factors supported by the case data: *Project type* was the most strongly supported engagement factor across all 9 interviews. This is a broad category and includes the reason for the project. In this case the project was one aimed at growth so the project was viewed in a very positive way. This supports the findings of Bandara et al. [24]. *Resourcing* was also supported across eight (8) of the nine (9) interviews. This supports the finding of vom Brocke et al. [25], who explain how resources, including personnel, are important in

BPM practice as it impacts the ability to collaborate and innovate. *Location* was found to impact engagement with remote-based people expressing frustration being in a different location. This confirms the findings of Chun, Davies [17] who found remote employees had a more negative attitude towards change, in the case of a company merger. *Cultural Alignment*, was discussed in three (3) interviews., supporting Latta [26], who found both content and process need to be culturally aligned. Further, Jones, Van de Ven [23], found that the longer the change went on the more resistance to change was evident, confirming the *length of time the project took* was an important engagement factor. *Number of projects in progress* was also supported as an engagement factor in six (6) interviews. Nicholds, Mo [21] also note there is a limit to the amount of change that people can cope with.

Project goal was a factor identified in all interviews supporting the findings of vom Brocke et al. [25] who suggest that exploitation (i.e. incremental improvement) and exploration (i.e. radical change/innovation) change the context of BPM projects. *Staff workload* was found to be an engagement factor, although only supported in one interview, the impact on engagement noted was substantial. This supports the findings of Nicholds, Mo [21] who identified that workload, like the '*number of projects in progress*' impacted people's capacity for change.

New Factors: Two new factors were found including: *Organisational priorities* and *Infrastructure*. '*Organisational priorities*' was mentioned in seven (7) of the nine (9) interviews. This factor, which is related to the perception of organisational focus is linked to engagement. For example, if stakeholders believe the outcomes are important to the organisation they may be more engaged, as expectancy theory[3] supports. This may be explicitly communicated or a perception, as was the case in the following quote:

"As an organisation, I don't know whether we're really behind RPA... If I didn't know any better I'd say we were getting out of robotics as we were trying to get in as a business" (Interviewee #2).

The second new factor, '*Infrastructure*', was also well supported across all nine (9) interviews. This is another engagement factor which may be more relevant in projects which deliver iteratively. In sequential phase management of projects, where the product is delivered at the end of the project, infrastructure issues may not be evident throughout the project and unlikely to substantially influence engagement. This factor may potentially influence engagement for all stakeholders as they are likely to spend more time dealing with issues which arise from this factor, e.g. managing customer expectations, productivity impacts and time spent trying to resolve the issues. Within the case study this was expressed in the following quote: *"That's part of the issue that we're having now with network slowness; they [applications] go in [to the robot] and they don't go out"* (Interviewee #5).

---

[3] Expectancy theory posits that individuals will only make an effort if they believe that the amount of effort result in a particular performance and they will only exert a particular behaviour (performance) if they expect to achieve a certain outcome (McShane et al., 2010).

4.3 Macro Level Findings

The macro level findings supported in the case study appear to operate less explicitly than factors at other levels. Overall support for the a priori Macro level engagement factors was mixed, with one, namely *culture* instantiated with the case data; and the other, *economy* not. However, an additional factor was evident, which does have links to *economy* (hence are described together below).

A priori factors supported by the case data: Evidence of *'culture'* impacting engagement was found throughout the case study, from all interviewees. It was apparent from the interviews that the introduction of the RPA technology had impacted the team culture, as stakeholders openly discussed how the project had changed the norms of operation. This finding supports De Bruin, Rosemann [27] who found *'culture'* to be a critical component of BPM success.

A priori factors not instantiated by the case data, and new factors: Although there was no support in the case study for the factor of *economy* [21] a new factor - *industry* - was evident. We see this being related to the original factor *'economy'*– as a more concentrated aspect of it (i.e., Industry being a 'part of' economy) with seven (7) interviewees, recognising the factor. Respondents were not able to explicitly relate to or differentiate to these. However, it was evident that, whilst the interviewees were not conscious of the influence on them, that industry developments did impact people at all levels of the organisation. This is supported with comments such as: *"big [companies] are shedding people. They're going away from non-core activities, and they're all trying to automate, and all our competitors have robotics"* (Interviewee # 9).

4.4 Chrono Level Findings

At this level, the BPM lifecycle is not an engagement factor itself, but is important as to how this interacts with the factors at the other levels. Many of the comments made by interviewees were generalised but some were more specific: *"I think educating and getting people on board with the ideas of robotics is that it is not a perfect thing was probably more important to the start"* (Interviewee #1), which specifically mentions a period of time and the impact this had on the stakeholder. In a further example, one of the interviewees explained how their confidence grew over time, which is likely to have increased their engagement; *"I think I just got more confident with it, and I was like, 'oh yeah, I can do this"* (Interviewee #6). This quote demonstrates an interaction with *'experience of the domain'*, because as that grew over time, so did the confidence of the interviewee.

The importance of managing people's engagement at different points during the BPM project was understood by members of the project team and managers, with one interviewee stating: *"the other key is the people because you need their buy-in, but on top of that is what I include in the people, say it's taking them through the journey"* (Interviewee #2). This quote indicates the changing needs of stakeholders at different points in the project and the need to respond to them differently. In a further example the impact of the iterative nature of the project is revealed: *"So, as we've gone through that optimisation, we've changed the way things worked, and it makes perfect sense when you look at from a process perspective. ...... So, to say, 'look, this sounds great, but it's not one piece. You're impacting a lot of people.' It's very difficult to communicate"* (Interviewee 5). This quote not only shows how the project changed the process over time but also the importance of *'communication'* and the complexity of communicating the message repeatedly over time. It is critical that the communication strategy is carefully considered during planning and execution Kotter [33]. The chrono level is important, irrespective of the lifecycle model used (as situations and the engagement of stakeholders change over time irrespective of which model is used) and is applicable to all levels of the organisation.

5   Summary Discussions

Overall, we established that important BPM stakeholder engagement factors exist at many levels. Our model identifies five levels; namely; 'micro', 'meso', 'exo', 'macro', and 'chrono' which represents different 'systems' that host a range of factors (36 in total, 33 supported with case data) that influence stakeholder engagement in process improvement projects. There were a considerable number of individual differences of the influencing factors across the levels. While this is not surprising in itself, the degree to which these differences affect engagement was interesting. It seems that BPM projects of different types might generate different levels of stakeholder engagement, even within the same group of people. New technologies such as RPA generated interest, although they also have the potential to be disappointing and to reduce stakeholder engagement if they do not live up to expectations. Taking a slightly wider perspective, BPM projects do not occur in isolation, but take place within organizational and technical environments, that can have either a positive or negative effect on the project and the degree of engagement. The exo-level factors suggest that the program management approach in the organization, which encompasses things like number of projects and organizational priorities should be considered. Stakeholders may "zone out" if they are expected to give their attention to too many projects simultaneously, or if their workload is too high. Even more broadly, organizational culture and industry factors can affect the way stakeholders engage with a specific project.

5.1   Theoretical Implications

From a theoretical perspective, we offer a number of primary contributions. This includes: (i) confirmation and positioning of literature based and empirically derived stakeholder engagement factors in the context of business process improvement, (ii) harmonization and integration of these factors in a multi-layered system model, and (iii) identification of new factors at multiple levels.

Theoretical contribution to a domain can take a number of forms, including *"introducing new constructs"* and *"better conceptualizing of existing constructs"* [35]. Although many of our factors have been individually acknowledged in a range of studies, this is the first study, to our knowledge, to organize them into a conceptual framework. Therefore, the study aligns with the theory building concepts of discovery, description, mapping and relationship building [36]. The multi-level nature of our study is a first in

BPM stakeholder research. We demonstrate that it is not simply factors in the immediate environment of the BPM project that influence stakeholder engagement. BPM projects tend to have broad impacts in an organization, affecting multiple staff members and their work practices. The projects may be part of organizational programs of work, which may be managed with varying degrees of effectiveness. While our factors have been analyzed as engagement factors, it is not too much of a stretch to suggest that factors that might have an adverse impact on the *success* of the project, such as inadequate infrastructure or unclear organizational priorities would tend to have a negative impact on engagement. It would not be an exaggeration to say that our study suggests that ambitious BPM projects require sound management and a supportive organizational environment at multiple levels in order to sustain stakeholder engagement.

This study offers a number of avenues for further research, including investigating in more detail the interactions between factors, and developing instruments to evaluate levels of stakeholder engagement and the factors that contribute to them. Since it is well recognized that stakeholder involvement is essential to project success, our framework could also be used to develop an "early warning system" for identifying waning stakeholder engagement in a project and the factors that have contributed to it.

5.2 Practical Implications

Our study also has implications for practice. Better theorizing can help to bridge the perceived gap between industry and academia [37]. In consideration that project success is a desired outcome for any BPM initiative, the conceptual model presented in this study provides practitioners with a framework to analyze the factors which may influence stakeholder engagement at various levels. This is important as developing a better understanding of these factors allows a practitioner to more effectively design and manage interactions, perspectives and expectations of differing stakeholder groups. This enhanced process management capability (though not the only influence) should provide a practitioner with additional insight and ability to engage with and better meet the differing needs of stakeholders through the process improvement lifecycle. In the future, our framework can be deployed to develop a series of tools designed to assist practitioners in enhanced BPM stakeholder engagement. These could include stakeholder analysis questionnaires, summaries of the stakeholder groups to be considered during the BPM project, and practical methods to deal with the most common and impactful factors at the various stages of the project lifecycle. The model could also be used to provide analysis of the overall landscape of the organization and be used to aid the prioritization of BPM projects, targeting the ones which are most likely to succeed (with predicted higher engagement levels) in that particular organization.

6 Conclusion

Stakeholder engagement is critical to BPM project success, however research into what influences engagement has been limited. The case study confirmed (21 of 24) known engagement factors across different domains and discovered 12 additional factors. As discussed above, two of the factors ('type of role' and 'gender') seen in literature and not instantiated in the case study may be due to study design rather than the non-relevance of the factor. The third that was not completely instantiated ('economy') was linked to a new factor ('industry'), which was a more specialist 'part of' the original factor.

The holistic model presented in this paper provides a framework for further consideration of factors influencing stakeholder engagement in BPM projects. It provides a broad 'landscape' (i.e., a holistic view showing different layers of systems) of stakeholder engagement for BPM projects which could be consulted by the practitioner to ensure all relevant system levels have been considered. The model provides a basis upon which the important factors can be considered, understood by both academics and practitioners alike. This understanding of BPM stakeholder engagement will enable BPM projects to better address the human-centric challenges and progress towards BPM project success.

References

1. Kassin, S.M., Fein, S., Markus, H., McBain, K.A., Williams, L.: Social Psychology: Australian & New Zealand, 1st edn. Cengage Learning, South Melbourne, VIC (2015)
2. Nambisan, S., Lyytinen, K., Majchrzak, A., Song, M.: Digital innovation management: reinventing innovation management research in a digital world. Mis Q. 41(1), 223–238 (2017)
3. de Waal, B.M.E., Batenburg, R.: The process and structure of user participation: a BPM system implementation case study. Bus. Process. Manag. J. 20(1), 107–128 (2014)
4. Griffin, J.J.: Tracing stakeholder terminology then and now: convergence and new pathways. Bus. Ethics: Eur. Rev. 26(4), 326–346 (2017)
5. Thennakoon, D., Bandara, W., French, E., Mathiesen, P.: What do we know about business process management training? Current status of related research and a way forward. Bus. Process. Manag. J. 24(2), 478–500 (2018)
6. vom Brocke, J., Schmiedel, T., Recker, J., Trkman, P., Mertens, W., Viaene, S.: Ten principles of good business process management. Bus. Process. Manag. J. 20(4), 530–548 (2014)
7. Gorbacheva, E., Stein, A., Schmiedel, T., Müller, O.: The role of gender in business process management competence supply. Bus. Inf. Syst. Eng. 58(3), 213–231 (2016)
8. Trkman, P.: The critical success factors of business process management. Int. J. Inf. Manage. 30(2), 125–134 (2010)
9. Freeman, R.E.: Strategic management: a stakeholder approach. Vol. Book, Whole. Boston, MA, Pitman (1984)
10. Kahn, W.A.: Psychological conditions of personal engagement and disengagement at work. Acad. Manag. J. 33(4), 692–724 (1990). https://doi.org/10.2307/256287
11. Boell, S.K., Cecez-Kecmanovic, D.: A hermeneutic approach for conducting literature reviews and literature searches. Commun. Assoc. Inf. Syst. 34(1), 257–286 (2014)
12. Paré, G., Trudel, M.-C., Jaana, M., Kitsiou, S.: Synthesizing information systems knowledge: a typology of literature reviews. Inf. Manage. 52(2), 183–199 (2015)
13. Freeman, R.E.: Stakeholder theory: 25 years later. Philos. Manage. 8(3), 97–107 (2015). https://doi.org/10.5840/pom20098310
14. Mitchell, R.K., Agle, B.R., Wood, D.J.: Toward a theory of stakeholder identification and salience: defining the principle of who and what really counts. Acad. Manag. Rev. 22(4), 853–886 (1997)
15. Bone, K.D.: The bioecological model: applications in holistic workplace well-being management. Int. J. Workplace Health Manag. 8(4), 256–271 (2015)
16. Bordia, P., Restubog, S.L.D., Jimmieson, N.L., Irmer, B.E.: Haunted by the past: effects of poor change management history on employee attitudes and turnover. Group Org. Manag. 36(2), 191–222 (2011). https://doi.org/10.1177/1059601110392990

17. Chun, R., Davies, G.: The effect of merger on employee views of corporate reputation: time and space dependent theory. Ind. Mark. Manage. **39**(5), 721–727 (2010). https://doi.org/10.1016/j.indmarman.2010.02.010
18. Herzig, S.E., Jimmieson, N.L.: Middle managers' uncertainty management during organizational change. Leadersh. Org. Dev. J. **27**(8), 628–645 (2006)
19. Devaraj, U.S., Easley, R.F., Michael, C.J.: How does personality matter? Relating the five-factor model to technology acceptance and use. Inf. Syst. Res. **19**(1), 93–105 (2008). https://doi.org/10.1287/isre.1070.0153
20. Cordery, J., Sevastos, P., Mueller, W., Parker, S.: Correlates of employee attitudes toward functional flexibility. Hum. Relat. **46**(6), 705–723 (1993)
21. Nicholds, B.A., Mo, J.P.T.: Estimating performance from capabilities in business process improvement. Bus. Process. Manag. J. **22**(6), 1099–1117 (2016)
22. Finney, S.: Stakeholder perspective on internal marketing communication: an ERP implementation case study. Bus. Process. Manag. J. **17**(2), 311–331 (2011)
23. Jones, S.L., Van de Ven, A.H.: The changing nature of change resistance. J. Appl. Behav. Sci. **52**(4), 482 (2016). https://doi.org/10.1177/0021886316671409
24. Bandara, W., Indulska, M., Chong, S., Sadiq, S.: Major issues in business process management: an expert perspective. In: The 15th European Conference on Information Systems. St Gallen, Switzerland, University of St. Gallen (2007)
25. vom Brocke, J., Zelt, S., Schmiedel, T.: On the role of context in business process management. Int. J. Inf. Manage. **36**(3), 486–495 (2016)
26. Latta, G.F.: Modeling the cultural dynamics of resistance and facilitation interaction effects in the OC3 model of organizational change. J. Organ. Chang. Manag. **28**(6), 1013–1037 (2015). https://doi.org/10.1108/JOCM-07-2013-0123
27. De Bruin, T., Rosemann, M.: Towards a business process management maturity model. In: Bartmann, D., Rajola, F., Kallinikos, J., Avison, D., Winter, R., Ein-Dor, P., et al. (eds.) The Thirteenth European Conference on Information Systems. Verlag and the London School of Economics, Germany, Regensburg (2005)
28. Bronfenbrenner, U.: The ecology of human development experiments by nature and design. Harvard University Press, Cambridge, MA (1979)
29. Yin, R.K.: Case study research: design and methods. 5th ed., SAGE, Los Angeles (2014)
30. Charmaz, K.: Constructing Grounded Theory. Sage (2014)
31. Corbin, J., Strauss, A.: Basics of Qualitative Research: Techniques and Procedures for Developing Grounded Theory, 3rd ed., Sage Publications, Inc, Thousand Oaks, CA, US (2008)
32. Glaser, B.G.: Advances in the Methodology of Grounded Theory: Theoretical Sensitivity. University of California (1978)
33. Kotter, J.P.: Leading change: why transformation efforts fail. Harvard Bus. Rev. (2007)
34. Spitzer, D.R.: Transforming Performance Measurement Rethinking the Way We Measure and Drive Organizational Success. American Management Association, New York, (2007)
35. Barki, H.: Thar's gold in them thar constructs. ACM SIGMIS Database: DATABASE Adv. Inf. Syst. **39**(3), 9–20 (2008)
36. Handfield, R.B., Melnyk, S.A.: The scientific theory-building process: a primer using the case of TQM. J. Oper. Manag. **16**(4), 321–339 (1998)
37. Lynham, S.A.: Theory building in the human resource development profession. Hum. Resour. Dev. Q. **11**(2), 159–178 (2000)
38. Charmaz, K.: Constructing grounded theory: A practical guide through qualitative analysis. Sage, London (2006)

Author Index

Printed in the United States
by Baker & Taylor Publisher Services